MW00609588

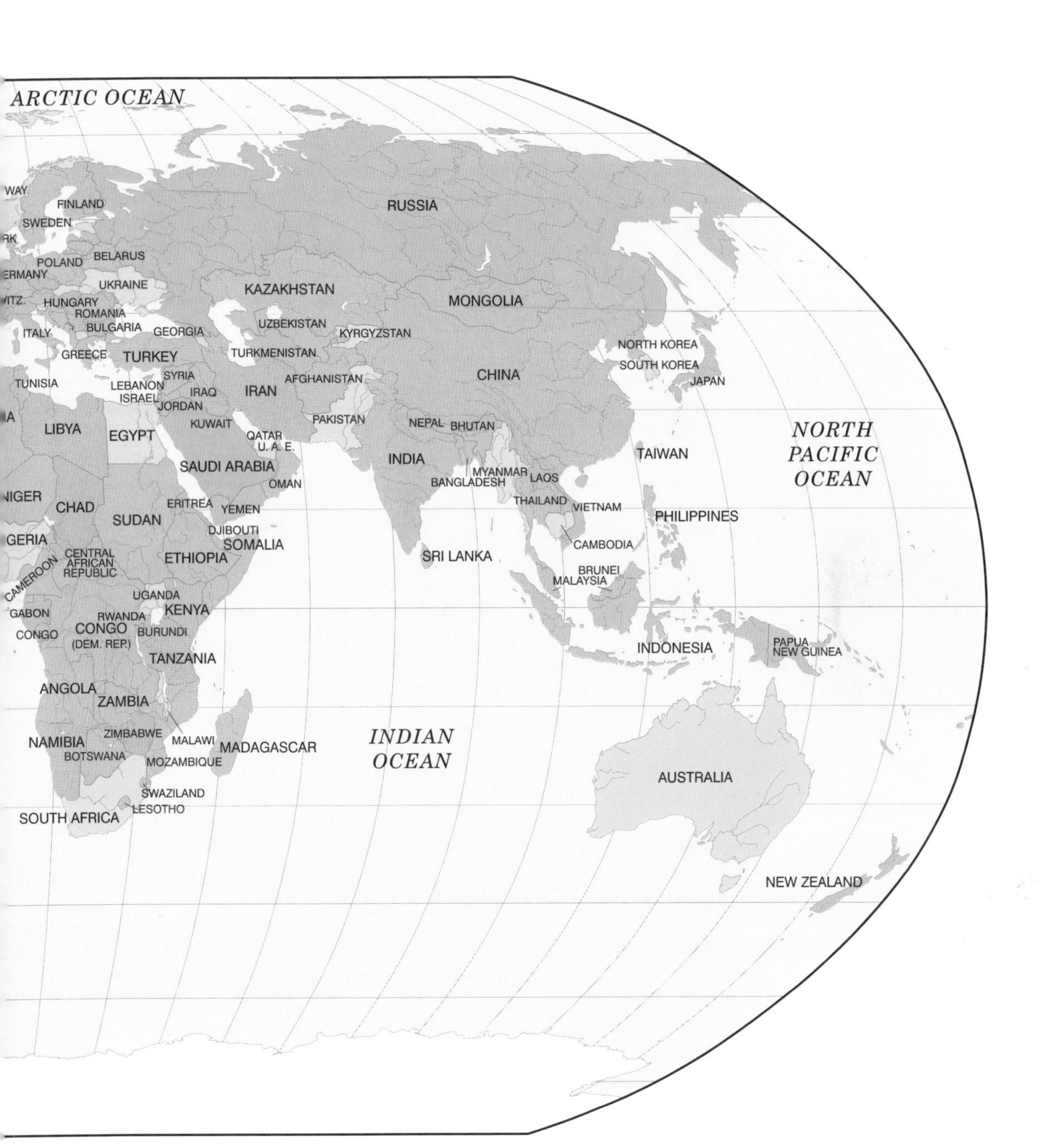
ARCTIC OCEAN
FINLAND
SWEDEN
RUSSIA
POLAND
BELARUS
UKRAINE
KAZAKHSTAN
MONGOLIA
HUNGARY
ROMANIA
BULGARIA
GEORGIA
UZBEKISTAN
KYRGYZSTAN
ITALY
GREECE
TURKEY
TURKMENISTAN
NORTH KOREA
SOUTH KOREA
JAPAN
TUNISIA
SYRIA
LEBANON
ISRAEL
IRAQ
JORDAN
IRAN
AFGHANISTAN
CHINA
KUWAIT
PAKISTAN
NEPAL
BHUTAN
LIBYA
EGYPT
QATAR
U. A. E.
NORTH PACIFIC OCEAN
SAUDI ARABIA
INDIA
TAIWAN
OMAN
MYANMAR
BANGLADESH
LAOS
CHAD
SUDAN
ERITREA
YEMEN
THAILAND
VIETNAM
PHILIPPINES
DJIBOUTI
SOMALIA
CAMBODIA
CENTRAL AFRICAN REPUBLIC
ETHIOPIA
SRI LANKA
CAMEROON
BRUNEI
MALAYSIA
UGANDA
GABON
RWANDA
KENYA
CONGO
CONGO (DEM. REP.)
BURUNDI
INDONESIA
PAPUA NEW GUINEA
TANZANIA
ANGOLA
ZAMBIA
NAMIBIA
ZIMBABWE
MALAWI
MADAGASCAR
INDIAN OCEAN
BOTSWANA
MOZAMBIQUE
AUSTRALIA
SWAZILAND
LESOTHO
SOUTH AFRICA
NEW ZEALAND

Understanding God's World Series

Understanding God's World Series

Understanding
NORTH AMERICAN HISTORY

—A Christian Perspective—

Grade 8

Rod and Staff Publishers, Inc.
P.O. Box 3, Hwy. 172
Crockett, Kentucky 41413-0003
Telephone: (606) 522-4348

Acknowledgments

We are indebted first of all to God who created the world and who upholds all things by the Word of His power. We are grateful that He has enabled the many who worked on this project. Kenneth Auker wrote the basic text; Marvin Eicher and Bennie Hostetler served as editors. The artwork (other than the old prints listed with the photograph credits) was drawn by John Mark Shenk. Others spent many hours writing some of the exercises, reviewing the material, giving helpful suggestions, and preparing the manuscript for publication.

We thank Digital Wisdom and Cartesia for the use of their maps. We are also grateful for the permissions that were granted for use of photographs. See pages 677 to 679 for credits.

—The Publishers

Printed in U.S.A.

ISBN 0-7399-0654-2

Catalog no. 19801

2 3 4 5 6 — 15 14 13 12 11 10 09 08 07 06

Table of Contents

These colonists are sleighing on the St. Lawrence River.

INTRODUCTION FOR THE STUDENT

Understanding North American History tells the story of North America—how Europeans discovered and explored this continent, what people lived here when Europeans came, and how the newcomers settled the land. It tells how the United States began and developed as a nation. In addition to United States history, this course includes an overview of Canadian history and of United States and Canadian geography. Though we seek a heavenly country (Hebrews 11:13–16), we live in a country of this world, and we should understand its history.

In this book, you will meet many people from the past—people who had an important influence in history. You will also discover many facts that will help you appreciate the historical heritage of America. You will learn how people lived in bygone days, how settlers pushed westward, and how economic and cultural changes took place.

You will also learn how God's people, the church, fared amid the changing scenes. You will learn lessons from history that you can apply to your own life. That is, you can learn from the mistakes of people who did wrong, and follow the example of those who did right. Above all, you will see that although man accomplishes many things, God overrules to bring about His purposes.

This book is divided into seven units. The first unit covers the geography of North America, and the other units each cover a segment of United States or Canadian history. Each unit includes several chapters (except Unit 1) that are divided into three sections each.

Each chapter begins with an introduction that raises questions to be answered in the chapter. Each section also has a brief introduction to its contents. Sections are further subdivided, with a centered heading identifying each subdivision. Main points under each heading are in bold italics. Here is an example.

Maryland

Lord Baltimore's Settlement. A number of colonies were founded by ***proprietors*** (pruh PRY ih turz) rather than companies. Proprietors were individuals, usually rich nobles, who received land and a charter from the king.

Note the term ***proprietors*** in the example above. This type style indicates that the term is a vocabulary word which you can find in the glossary at the back of the book. Names of important people are also in bold type where those people are introduced. By paying special attention to the headings, subheadings, and highlighted words, you can recognize the main ideas in a particular chapter or section. Each section is followed by exercises that check your understanding of the material, and each chapter is followed by a chapter review.

May God bless you as you study diligently for His glory and for your own benefit.

Cover Photograph: The Portland Head Light, near Portland, Maine. This lighthouse was the first to be commissioned by the new United States in 1790, and it was built in 1791 on George Washington's orders. The lighthouse symbolizes the new nation as a beacon of hope and freedom. It also symbolizes the light of God's truth shining in North America. The sea symbolizes the difficulties settlers had to overcome to establish homes in North America.

UNIT 1

NORTH AMERICAN GEOGRAPHY

Chapters in Unit 1

The United States includes a great variety of geographical features. This is Mount Shuksan in the state of Washington.

1 Geography of the United States and Canada

Alabama • Alaska • Arizona • Arkansas • California • Colorado • Connecticut • Delaware • Florida • Georgia • Hawaii • Idaho • Illinois • Indiana • Iowa • Kansas • Kentucky • Louisiana • Maine • Maryland • Massachusetts • Michigan • Minnesota • Mississippi • Missouri • Montana • Nebraska • Nevada • New Hampshire • New Jersey • New Mexico • New York • North Carolina • North Dakota • Ohio • Oklahoma • Oregon • Pennsylvania • Rhode Island • South Carolina • South Dakota • Tennessee • Texas • Utah • Vermont • Virginia • Washington • West Virginia • Wisconsin • Wyoming

United States

Canada

Alberta • British Columbia • Manitoba • New Brunswick • Newfoundland and Labrador • Northwest Territories • Nova Scotia • Nunavut • Ontario • Prince Edward Island • Quebec • Saskatchewan • Yukon Territory

GEOGRAPHY OF THE UNITED STATES AND CANADA

Focus for Reading

Why is it important to study geography? One reason is that geography teaches us about the greatness of God. It was God who decided what and where the various climates and geographical features (mountains, seas, resources, and so on) should be. The Lord is infinite; to Him the nations are as a drop of a bucket and as nothing and less than nothing (Isaiah 40:15, 17). Understanding this truth should cause us to fear God, worship Him, and give Him all glory for all things—rather than glorifying man and his achievements.

Further, the study of geography is necessary for understanding history. You must develop a sense of place: not only *what* happened and *when*, but also *where*. Dozens of major historical events have taken place in North America. In many cases, the land itself—along with the climate—has affected the way people lived and what they have done.

How are history and geography related? What kind of land does the United States include? How is Canada similar to the United States, and how is it different? Chapter 1 answers these questions in the following three sections.

1. History and Geography
2. United States Geography
3. Canadian Geography

1. HISTORY AND GEOGRAPHY

What is history? What is geography? How are these two subjects related? This first section will introduce these subjects and answer these questions.

History

An Account of Past Events. The word *history* comes from the Greek word *historia*, which means "a learning by inquiry; knowledge; a narrative." So history involves inquiring about the past and gaining knowledge about it. A narrative is a story, and history is the fascinating story of people in the past and their activities. Another way of looking at history is to see it as "His story"—God's story of His workings among men.

Answers to Important Questions. To understand history, you will need to learn the facts—*what* happened, *when* it happened, and *where* it happened. You will also study people—*who* did it—for it was men and women who did the things that happened in the past. And since they were real people just like us, your study of history can be filled with warmth and interest.

In addition, you should try to grasp the larger picture of *why* an event happened. Involved in this is an understanding of chronology—the order of historical events. Then, too, an understanding of causes and effects will help us to understand history. A major happening long ago is like a splash that sends ripples across a pond, affecting us today in ways that we may not even realize.

In summary, historians seek answers to questions like "What happened?" "When did it happen?" "Where did it happen?" "Who did it?" "Why did it happen?" and "What were the later effects of this incident?"

Geography

A Study of the Earth. The word *geography* comes from the Greek word *geographia*, which means "writing about the earth" (from *geo* "earth" and *graphein* "to write"). So geography is a study of the earth, especially the features of the earth's surface. Geographers ask questions such as "Where is a place located?" "What is that place like?" "What happened there?" "Why did it happen there rather than somewhere else?" Geography provides us with a sense of place.

A Subject Closely Related to History. In a study of history, we need to study geography too. The geography of America is the setting in which the events of American history took place. Furthermore, geography often had a direct bearing on the course of events.

For example, the coastal plain of New England is narrow, and the land is not very suitable for farming. Consequently, other occupations such as manufacturing and shipping goods, along with fishing, whaling, and shipbuilding, developed there. But the South has a broad coastal plain with plenty of excellent farmland. As a result, large farms called plantations developed there, and slavery flourished. These geographical differences between the North and the South eventually contributed to war between them.

Studying time lines and dates can help to give you a sense of history. In the same way, studying maps and pictures can give you a sense of geography. As you consider a major event, remember to ask, "Why did this event happen at this time and place?"

Focus for Thought

1. a. What is history?
   b. What questions does history answer?
2. a. What is geography?
   b. What questions does geography answer?
3. Summarize how history and geography are related.

New York City is the largest city in the United States. This view (looking north) shows part of Manhattan, one of the five boroughs of the city. The Empire State Building is in the center of the picture, the Hudson River and New Jersey are on the left, and the East River is on the right.

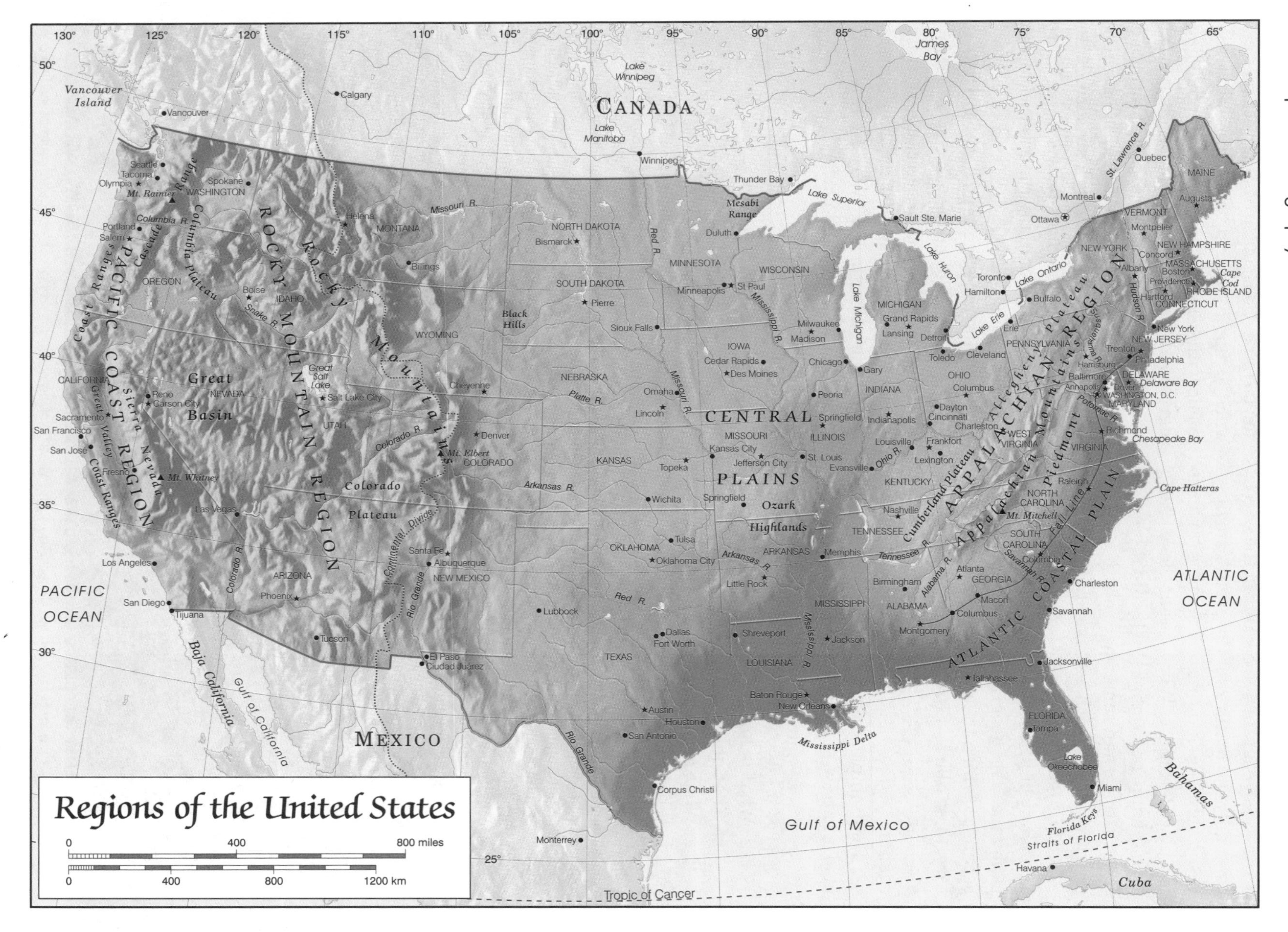
Regions of the United States
0 400 800 miles
0 400 800 1200 km
PACIFIC COAST REGION
ROCKY MOUNTAIN REGION
Rocky Mountains
CENTRAL PLAINS
APPALACHIAN REGION
ATLANTIC COASTAL PLAIN
Piedmont
Allegheny Plateau
Cumberland Plateau
Appalachian Mountains
Fall Line
Ozark Highlands
Great Basin
Colorado Plateau
Columbia Plateau
Great Valley
Sierra Nevada
Cascade Range
Coast Ranges
Black Hills
Mesabi Range
Continental Divide
CANADA
MEXICO
PACIFIC OCEAN
ATLANTIC OCEAN
Gulf of Mexico
Gulf of California
Baja California
Bahamas
Cuba
Straits of Florida
Florida Keys
Mississippi Delta
Tropic of Cancer
Cape Hatteras
Cape Cod
Chesapeake Bay
Delaware Bay
James Bay
Vancouver Island
Lake Superior
Lake Michigan
Lake Huron
Lake Erie
Lake Ontario
Lake Winnipeg
Lake Manitoba
Lake Okeechobee
Great Salt Lake
Mississippi R.
Missouri R.
Ohio R.
Tennessee R.
Arkansas R.
Red R.
Platte R.
Rio Grande
Colorado R.
Snake R.
Columbia R.
Hudson R.
Susquehanna R.
Potomac R.
Savannah R.
Alabama R.
St. Lawrence R.
Mt. Rainier
Mt. Whitney
Mt. Elbert
Mt. Mitchell
WASHINGTON
OREGON
CALIFORNIA
IDAHO
NEVADA
MONTANA
WYOMING
UTAH
COLORADO
ARIZONA
NEW MEXICO
NORTH DAKOTA
SOUTH DAKOTA
NEBRASKA
KANSAS
OKLAHOMA
TEXAS
MINNESOTA
IOWA
MISSOURI
ARKANSAS
LOUISIANA
WISCONSIN
ILLINOIS
MICHIGAN
INDIANA
OHIO
KENTUCKY
TENNESSEE
MISSISSIPPI
ALABAMA
GEORGIA
FLORIDA
SOUTH CAROLINA
NORTH CAROLINA
VIRGINIA
WEST VIRGINIA
PENNSYLVANIA
NEW YORK
NEW JERSEY
DELAWARE
MARYLAND
VERMONT
NEW HAMPSHIRE
MASSACHUSETTS
CONNECTICUT
RHODE ISLAND
MAINE
WASHINGTON, D.C.
Seattle
Tacoma
Olympia
Spokane
Portland
Salem
Boise
Helena
Billings
Sacramento
San Francisco
San Jose
Fresno
Los Angeles
San Diego
Tijuana
Reno
Carson City
Las Vegas
Salt Lake City
Phoenix
Tucson
Cheyenne
Denver
Santa Fe
Albuquerque
El Paso
Ciudad Juárez
Bismarck
Pierre
Lincoln
Omaha
Topeka
Wichita
Oklahoma City
Tulsa
Lubbock
Dallas
Fort Worth
Austin
San Antonio
Houston
Corpus Christi
Monterrey
Sioux Falls
Minneapolis
St Paul
Duluth
Des Moines
Cedar Rapids
Kansas City
Jefferson City
Springfield
St. Louis
Little Rock
Shreveport
Baton Rouge
New Orleans
Jackson
Memphis
Nashville
Madison
Milwaukee
Chicago
Peoria
Gary
Indianapolis
Evansville
Louisville
Lansing
Grand Rapids
Detroit
Toledo
Cleveland
Columbus
Dayton
Cincinnati
Charleston
Frankfort
Lexington
Birmingham
Montgomery
Atlanta
Macon
Tallahassee
Jacksonville
Tampa
Miami
Savannah
Columbia
Raleigh
Richmond
Baltimore
Annapolis
Dover
Philadelphia
Trenton
Harrisburg
Erie
Buffalo
Albany
New York
Hartford
Providence
Boston
Concord
Montpelier
Augusta
Vancouver
Calgary
Winnipeg
Thunder Bay
Sault Ste. Marie
Toronto
Hamilton
Ottawa
Montreal
Quebec
Havana
50°
45°
40°
35°
30°
25°
130°
125°
120°
115°
110°
105°
100°
95°
90°
85°
80°
75°
70°
65°

2. UNITED STATES GEOGRAPHY

The United States includes a diverse landscape from fertile plains and forested hills to barren deserts and trackless mountains. When the first Europeans arrived on Atlantic shores, wild forests stretched endlessly before them. Their descendants spread out until they occupied the land from the Atlantic to the Pacific and from the Far North to the Gulf of Mexico. Before we consider the details of that story, we will take a trip of our own across the land they settled.

On this tour, you will go very quickly to many different places. Concentrate especially on the names covered in the chapter exercises (many of which you know already), and try to learn as many more as you can. Finding place names on a map can help you to remember them better.

Location and Size

A Nation in North America. The United States is located on the continent of North America, with the Atlantic Ocean to the east, the Pacific Ocean to the west, Canada to the north, and Mexico to the south. Mexico is considered part of Latin America because its people have a Spanish heritage. But the United States and Canada, with their English heritage, are known as Anglo-America.

A Vast Country. The United States includes forty-eight ***contiguous*** (kuhn TIHG yoo uhs) states, as well as Alaska and Hawaii. The size of the United States is about 3,700,000 square miles (9,583,000 km^2), including Alaska and Hawaii. It is the fourth largest country in the world, stretching nearly 3,000 miles (4,828 km) from east to west and about 1,600 miles (2,575 km) from north to south.

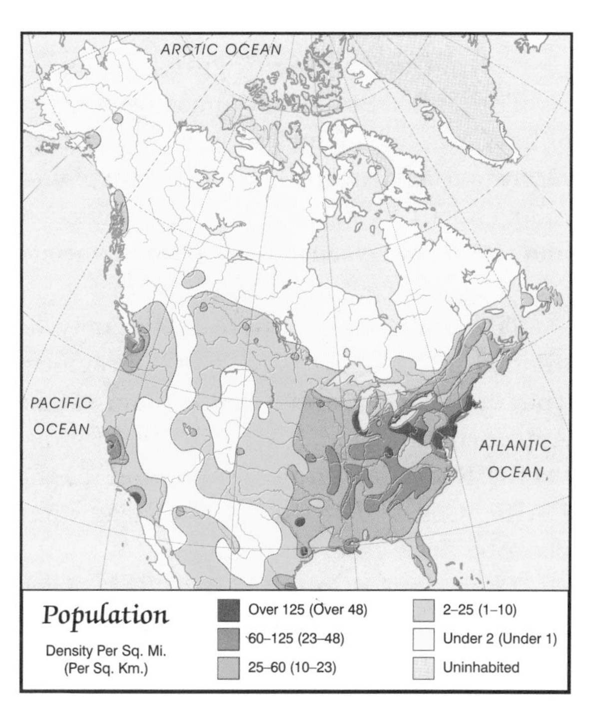

Population of North America

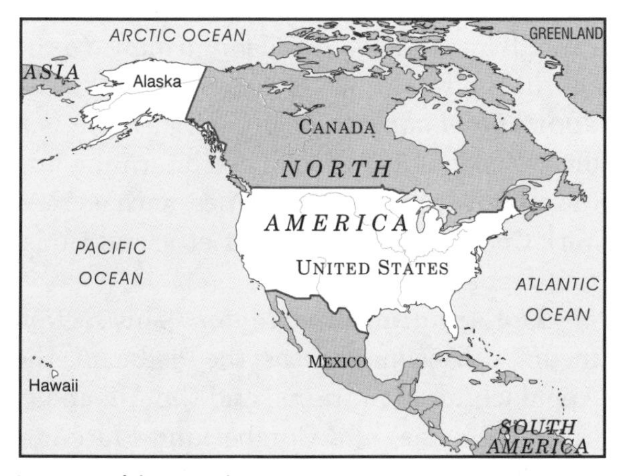

Location of the United States

Over 280 million people live in the United States, at an average of about 79 per square mile (31 per km^2). Of these people, about 75 percent live in ***urban*** areas and 25 percent live in ***rural*** areas.

The great size of the United States has influenced its development. Because land was abundant, almost everyone could own property—not just the rich as in many other nations. This contributed to a spirit of liberty and equality in the United States as the thousands of incoming settlers found new homes here.

Abundant natural resources also influenced development. God has blessed this country with great forests, vast stretches of fertile soil for farming, and minerals, such as iron ore, gold, copper, oil, and coal. These resources promoted the development of industry, which helped to make the United States a prosperous nation.

A ship on the Mississippi River at New Orleans, Louisiana. The Mississippi River drains an area of over 1,247,000 square miles (3,230,000 km²).

Geographic Regions

The United States has almost every type of landform to be found on earth. Its ***topography*** (surface features) includes level plains, rolling hills, lofty mountains, rugged plateaus, and fertile valleys. There is a broad variety of soil types, vegetation, and climate.

The contiguous United States may be divided into five main geographic regions. They are (1) the Atlantic Coastal Plain, (2) the Appalachian region, (3) the Central Plains, (4) the Rocky Mountain region, and (5) the Pacific Coast. The following paragraphs describe these geographic regions.

The Atlantic Coastal Plain. This region is a low, flat or rolling plain bordering the Atlantic Ocean and the Gulf of Mexico. The Atlantic Coastal Plain is only a few miles wide in the north, where it is indented by many bays. It broadens in the south until it extends all the way from the Atlantic Ocean into eastern Texas.

Mount Desert Island, Acadia National Park, Maine. The Atlantic Coastal Plain is very narrow in New England. Here it is almost nonexistent.

One major river that crosses the Coastal Plain is the Susquehanna River, which flows into a long ***estuary*** (EHS choo ehr ee), the Chesapeake Bay. Large rivers, such as the Savannah, Alabama, and Mississippi, flow through the broad plain in the south. The low region where the rivers rise and fall with the ocean tides is called the ***tidewater***. At the mouth of the Mississippi River is an enormous ***delta***, built from the tons of silt that the river carries downstream.

The Coastal Plain has a temperate climate, especially in the north, with adequate rainfall and with good soil for farming. In the south, the warm, moist region has a ***humid subtropical climate***. The Coastal Plain is a densely populated area of much farming and industry, with many large cities, such as New York City; Boston, Massachusetts; and Houston, Texas.

The Appalachian Region. This section includes three main areas: the Piedmont, the Appalachian Mountains, and the Allegheny (al ih GAY nee) and Cumberland Plateaus. The Piedmont begins where the Coastal Plain

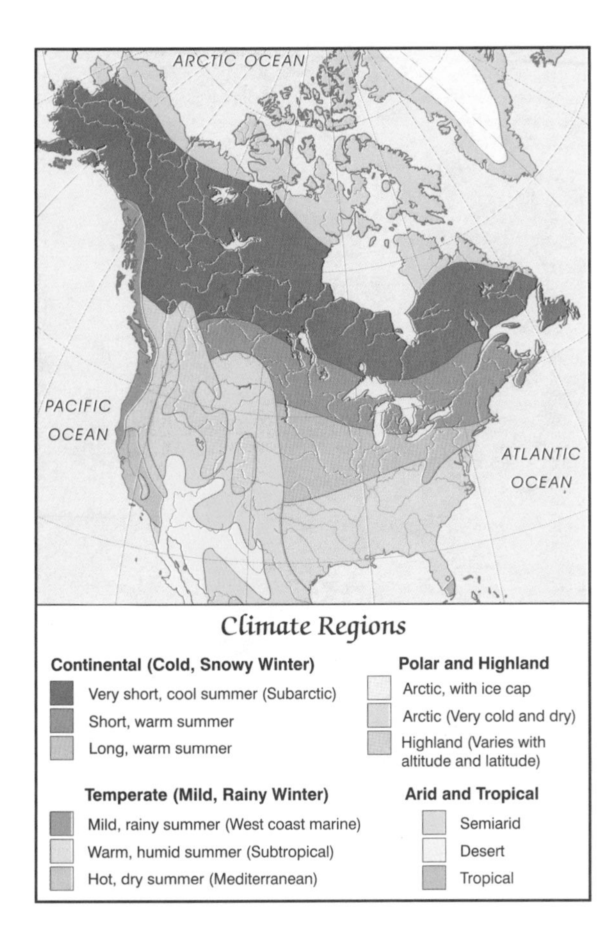

ends, at a slope called the ***Fall Line***. The slope has this name because of the many waterfalls there, which are useful in providing waterpower for industry. Many large cities have grown up along the Fall Line, including Philadelphia, Baltimore, and Richmond.

The Piedmont, from 300 to 1,000 feet (91 to 305 m) above sea level, is a lovely landscape of rolling hills and valleys. Like most of the Appalachian region, this area has a ***humid continental climate***, characterized by four distinct seasons. The natural vegetation is forests of ***deciduous hardwood*** (dih SIHJ oo uhs), with trees like maple and oak, or of ***coniferous softwood*** (koh NIHF ur uhs), with trees like pine and spruce.

Beyond the Piedmont are the Appalachian Mountains, a chain of rounded, forested mountains extending about 1,000 miles (1,609 km) from Maine to Alabama. The highest Appalachian peak is Mount Mitchell in North Carolina. This mountain rises to 6,684 feet (2,037 m) above sea level—the highest point in the United States east of the Mississippi.

A rugged ***plateau*** lies west of the Appalachian Mountains. Its northern part, the Allegheny Plateau, stretches westward from a range known as the Allegheny Mountains; and its southern part, the Cumberland Plateau, rolls westward from the Cumberland Mountains. Much of this plateau is forested and includes great quantities of coal, but it is not heavily populated. One of the largest cities of this area is Pittsburgh, Pennsylvania, which lies at the head of the Ohio River.

Numerous rivers flow out of the Appalachian Mountains. Among the largest ones are

Top: Appalachian Mountains in northern Pennsylvania. These are rounded mountains covered with deciduous hardwood forests. ***Bottom:*** Mount Mitchell, North Carolina. Located in the Blue Ridge Mountains, this is the highest peak in the Appalachians.

Left: Pittsburgh, the second largest city in Pennsylvania. Here the Allegheny and Monongahela Rivers join to form the Ohio River. The peninsula between the two rivers is called the Golden Triangle. ***Right:*** Ohio River, Ohio. This river flows 981 miles (1,579 km) from its beginning at Pittsburgh, Pennsylvania, to where it joins the Mississippi River at Cairo, Illinois. The Ohio is second only to the Mississippi in commercial importance.

the Ohio and Tennessee Rivers, flowing west into the Mississippi, and the Hudson, Susquehanna, and Potomac Rivers, flowing east into the Atlantic Ocean.

The Central Plains. This ***interior plain*** is the largest region of the United States. It stretches 1,200 miles (1,931 km) west from the Allegheny and Cumberland Plateaus to the edge of the Rocky Mountains, and extends from the Canadian border to the Gulf Coastal Plain. Several areas of higher elevation break up the monotony of the level land. They include the Ozark Highlands in Arkansas and Missouri, the Mesabi Range in Minnesota, and the Black Hills in South Dakota.

This land includes some of the most fertile soil on earth. Rainfall is sufficient for raising wheat in the eastern part, but the Central Plains become drier toward the west, until crop farming is impossible without irrigation. Cattle ranching is important in the dry areas. The continental climate of this region varies

Not all of the Central Plains region is flat. These knobby hills are in the Ozarks of northwestern Arkansas. The Ozarks rise as high as 2,300 feet (701 m) above sea level.

The Central Plains become drier toward the west. With irrigation, this region can produce bountiful crops in giant fields as shown here.

St. Louis, Missouri. Lying along the Mississippi River, this city served in the past as the gateway to the West. The domed building in the left foreground is the Old Courthouse, where the famous Dred Scott trial took place. (See Chapter 15.)

Chicago, Illinois. This is the third largest city in the United States. The Sears Tower, with a height of 1,454 feet (443 m), is one of the tallest buildings in the world.

greatly with the changing seasons, from blazing summers to freezing winters. Major cities include Chicago, Illinois, and St. Louis, Missouri. These are centers of transportation, commerce, and industry.

Several great rivers drain the Central Plains. One is the Mississippi River, the heart of the third longest river system in the world. With about 250 ***tributaries***, the Mississippi River system drains about 40 percent of the United States. In addition, the Great Lakes—especially Lake Superior and Lake Michigan—form a major part of the drainage system of the Central Plains.

Lake Superior is the largest of the Great Lakes. These five lakes together contain the largest concentration of fresh water in the world.

The Rocky Mountain Region. This region covers a large area of the western United States. It includes not only the Rocky Mountains themselves but also large plateaus and ***basins*** west of the Rockies. These scenic mountains extend 3,000 miles (4,828 km) from Canada into New Mexico. Their height ranges from 5,000 feet (1,524 m) to as high as 14,433 feet (4,399 m) at Mount Elbert in Colorado.

The ***Continental Divide*** runs along the Rocky Mountain peaks, separating the waters flowing into the Gulf of Mexico from those running into the Pacific Ocean. For example, the Missouri River begins in the Rocky Mountains

Going-to-the-Sun Mountain in Glacier National Park, Montana. This view is from St. Mary's Lake, one of the most beautiful lakes in the park. Notice the tree line and the steep cliffs of the peak that extend above the tree line.

Scenes From the Rocky Mountain Region:

Top: Denver, Colorado. The "Mile High City," with the Rocky Mountains looming behind, is the capital and largest city of Colorado. ***Middle:*** Snake River Gorge. The Snake River twists and turns like a snake as it flows 1,038 miles (1,670 km) from the Rockies into the Columbia River. ***Bottom:*** The rugged Grand Canyon is 277 miles long (446 km) and 1 mile deep (1.6 km). Its width varies from less than a mile to 18 miles (29 km). The Colorado River looks small in this picture, but it is a major river of the United States.

and flows east to the Mississippi, but the Snake River begins here and flows west to the Columbia. Denver, Colorado, is a leading city in the Rocky Mountain region.

In the western part of the Rocky Mountain region lies the Great Basin, a broad stretch of low land with ***internal drainage***. The rivers in this dry area flow into lakes and swamps that are very salty because they have no outlet. Sometimes a lake dries up completely, leaving a smooth, hard surface called a salt flat. The best example is the Great Salt Lake and the Great Salt Lake Desert in Utah. Salt Lake City is the largest city of the Great Basin, but it does not have a large population.

Death Valley, California, is the lowest, driest, and hottest place in the United States. Lowest point: 282 feet (86 m) below sea level. Annual rainfall: 2 inches (5 cm). Highest temperature: 134°F (57°C), recorded in 1913.

The Pacific Coast. This region includes several areas: the Pacific ranges, the Pacific valleys, and the Coast Ranges. The Pacific ranges consist of the Sierra Nevada in California and the Cascade Range in Oregon and Washington. Within the Sierra Nevada stands Mount Whitney, which soars to an altitude of 14,494 feet (4,418 m) and ranks as the highest mountain in the contiguous United States. The mighty Columbia River flows through a cut in the Pacific ranges.

West of the Pacific ranges lie the Pacific valleys, which have the mild, humid ***west coast marine climate***. Major cities here are Seattle in Washington and Portland in Oregon. In southern California, the Central Valley (Great Valley) provides excellent farmland for raising vegetables. Its warm, dry ***Mediterranean climate*** allows farmers to raise an abundance of oranges and olives, as well as grapes and many other crops.

The Coast Ranges run along the shores of the Pacific Ocean. There is little or no coastal plain here; rather, many of the mountains extend right out to the water. The Coast Ranges are broken by the San Francisco Bay, and then they continue into southern California. Large cities, such as Los Angeles and San Francisco, are located here. California is subject to many earthquakes because it lies in a region of ***faults***, or deep cracks in the earth's crust.

Scenes From the Pacific Coast Region:

First: Mountains of the Sierra Nevada. These granite mountains include Mt. Whitney, the highest point in the contiguous United States. ***Second:*** This orange grove is in the warm, sunny Mediterranean climate of southern California. ***Third:*** Mountains of the Coast Ranges in southern California. These dry mountains slope down to the Pacific Ocean. ***Fourth:*** San Francisco, California, is one of the largest cities on the west coast. It lies on a peninsula between the Pacific Ocean and San Francisco Bay. A mile-wide strait called the Golden Gate joins the bay and the ocean.

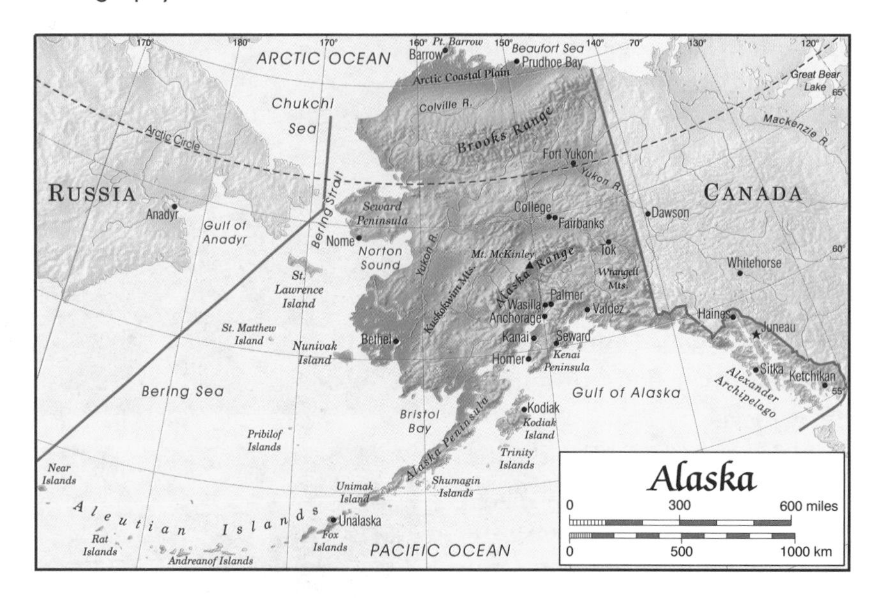

Alaska. This large state lies northwest of the other forty-eight states. Containing over 586,000 square miles (1,518,000 km^2), Alaska is more than twice the size of Texas. It has a coastal plain and a mountainous region in the north, and an area of highlands and lowlands in the central section. The Yukon River drains much of central Alaska.

In the south central part is the Alaska Range, curving from east to west. This range includes Mount McKinley, whose height of 20,320 feet (6,193 m) makes it the highest mountain in North America. In southeastern Alaska, a panhandle extends between Canada and the Pacific Ocean. To the southwest is the long Alaska Peninsula, with the Aleutian Islands stretching beyond it into the Pacific Ocean.

Much of Alaska is cold—especially the northern and central parts—but many valuable minerals have been found in this state. Alaska is not very densely populated. Among its major cities are Anchorage and Juneau (JOO noh), the capital.

Hawaii. Eight main islands and many smaller islands make up the state of Hawaii, which lies about 2,400 miles (3,862 km) southwest of the mainland United States. These islands are volcanic, and the island named Hawaii even boasts two active volcanoes: Mauna Kea and Mauna Loa. Hawaii is the largest island, but Oahu (oh AH hoo) has the most people.

The Hawaiian Islands have a pleasant climate year round, and the volcanic soil is fertile. Much rain falls on the windward slopes of the mountains; one location receives about 460 inches (1,168 cm) a year! Hawaii has great plantations that produce large crops of sugar cane and pineapples. The largest and most important city is Honolulu, the capital, located on Oahu.

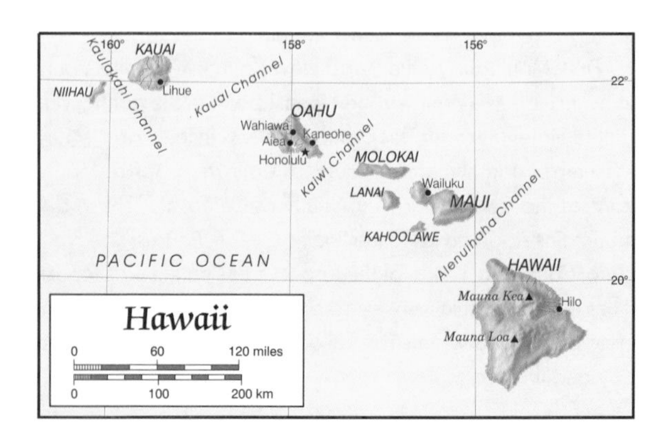

Diamond Head, on the southeast coast of Oahu, near Honolulu. Hawaii is known for the scenic beauty of its palms, sandy beaches, blue water, and volcanoes.

The United States holds several territories in addition to the fifty states. These include Puerto Rico and the Virgin Islands in the Caribbean Sea; and Guam, American Samoa, and a number of other islands in the Pacific Ocean. Truly God has provided a great variety of beautiful landforms and rich natural resources for the United States.

Focus for Thought

4. How has the development of the United States been affected
   a. by its large size?
   b. by its natural resources?
5. Copy and complete this chart of the seven geographic regions of the United States. You may want to turn an unlined page sideways and make each block about 1½ inches wide and 1 inch high. The first row is filled in for you. (One or two blocks may remain empty.)

Region	Geographic Features	Bodies of Water	Climate	Major Cities	Economic Activities
Atlantic Coastal Plain	low, flat, rolling narrow in north; wider in south	Atlantic Ocean Gulf of Mexico Chesapeake Bay Susquehanna R. Mississippi R.	temperate in north, humid sub-tropical in south	Boston New York Houston	farming industry
Appalachian Region					
Central Plains					
Rocky Mountain Region					
Pacific Coast					
Alaska					
Hawaii					

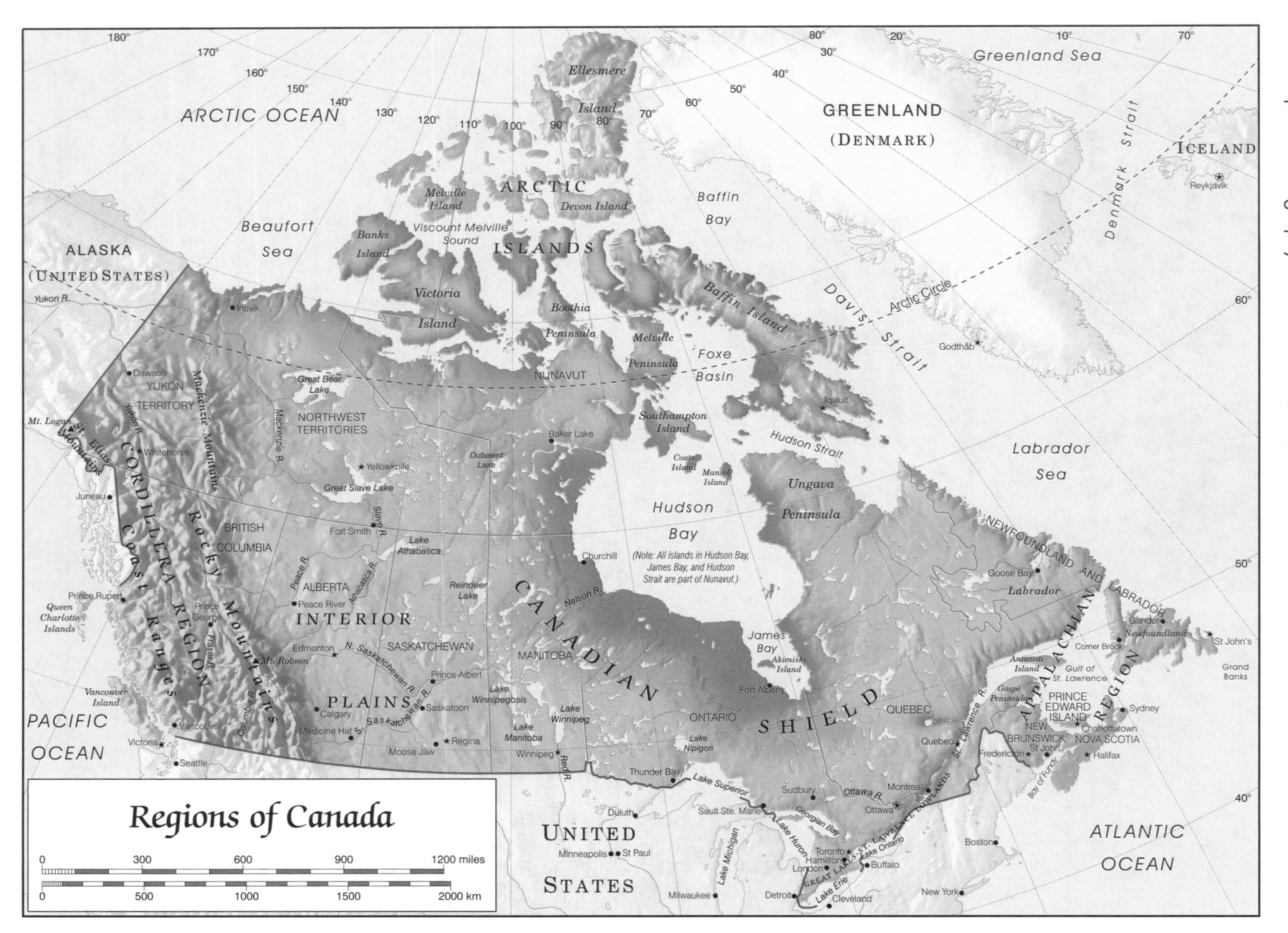
Regions of Canada
ARCTIC ISLANDS
CANADIAN SHIELD
INTERIOR PLAINS
CORDILLERA REGION
APPALACHIAN REGION
ST. LAWRENCE LOWLANDS
GREAT LAKES
ARCTIC OCEAN
PACIFIC OCEAN
ATLANTIC OCEAN
Beaufort Sea
Baffin Bay
Davis Strait
Labrador Sea
Greenland Sea
Denmark Strait
Hudson Bay
James Bay
Hudson Strait
Foxe Basin
(Note: All islands in Hudson Bay, James Bay, and Hudson Strait are part of Nunavut.)
GREENLAND (DENMARK)
ICELAND
Reykjavik
Godthåb
Arctic Circle
ALASKA (UNITED STATES)
UNITED STATES
YUKON TERRITORY
NORTHWEST TERRITORIES
NUNAVUT
BRITISH COLUMBIA
ALBERTA
SASKATCHEWAN
MANITOBA
ONTARIO
QUEBEC
NEWFOUNDLAND AND LABRADOR
NEW BRUNSWICK
NOVA SCOTIA
PRINCE EDWARD ISLAND
Ellesmere Island
Devon Island
Baffin Island
Victoria Island
Banks Island
Melville Island
Viscount Melville Sound
Boothia Peninsula
Melville Peninsula
Southampton Island
Coats Island
Mansel Island
Akimiski Island
Ungava Peninsula
Labrador
Newfoundland
Anticosti Island
Gaspé Peninsula
Gulf of St. Lawrence
Bay of Fundy
Vancouver Island
Queen Charlotte Islands
Mackenzie Mountains
Rocky Mountains
Coast Ranges
St. Elias Mountains
Mt. Logan
Mt. Robson
Great Bear Lake
Great Slave Lake
Lake Athabasca
Reindeer Lake
Dubawnt Lake
Lake Winnipegosis
Lake Manitoba
Lake Winnipeg
Lake Nipigon
Lake Superior
Lake Michigan
Lake Huron
Georgian Bay
Lake Erie
Lake Ontario
Mackenzie R.
Yukon R.
Slave R.
Athabasca R.
Peace R.
N. Saskatchewan R.
Saskatchewan R.
Fraser R.
Columbia R.
Nelson R.
Red R.
Ottawa R.
St. Lawrence R.
Inuvik
Dawson
Whitehorse
Juneau
Prince Rupert
Prince George
Vancouver
Victoria
Seattle
Yellowknife
Fort Smith
Peace River
Edmonton
Calgary
Medicine Hat
Saskatoon
Prince Albert
Regina
Moose Jaw
Winnipeg
Churchill
Baker Lake
Iqaluit
Thunder Bay
Fort Albany
Sault Ste. Marie
Sudbury
Toronto
Hamilton
London
Ottawa
Montreal
Quebec
Goose Bay
Fredericton
St. John
Halifax
Charlottetown
Sydney
Corner Brook
Gander
St. John's
Grand Banks
Duluth
Minneapolis
St Paul
Milwaukee
Detroit
Cleveland
Buffalo
New York
Boston
0 300 600 900 1200 miles
0 500 1000 1500 2000 km

3. CANADIAN GEOGRAPHY

Canada is also a spacious and beautiful land. It shares important features with the United States, yet has many distinctive features as well.

Location and Size

Northern Neighbor of the United States. Canada lies north of the United States in North America, between the forty-ninth parallel and the Arctic Ocean. Like the United States, Canada stretches from the Atlantic Ocean in the east to the Pacific Ocean in the west. It shares a border almost 4,000 miles long (6,437 km) with the United States.

Largest Nation in the Western Hemisphere. With an area of about 3,850,000 square miles (9,971,500 km^2), Canada is the largest nation in the Western Hemisphere and the second largest nation in the world. Its greatest distance—from Newfoundland in the east to the Alaskan border in the west—is about 3,400 miles (5,472 km). This country extends over 1,100 miles (1,770 km) north of the Arctic Circle, almost to the North Pole.

Since Canada extends so far north, much of it is cold. Climate is a major difference between the United States and Canada. The United States has climates that are mild and even tropical, but Canada has none of those. Its warmest summers are along the southern border and the Pacific coast. The rest of Canada generally has a frigid ***subarctic climate***, with an even colder ***arctic climate*** in the area inside the Arctic Circle. Most of the country has long, harsh winters with large amounts of snow and ice.

Because of the cold winters and short summers, farming is impossible in much of northern Canada. The majority of Canada's approximately 30 million people live within 200 miles (322 km) of the United States border, where it is warmer. In fact, most of the people live on only one-tenth of the land; the other nine-tenths is practically uninhabited! Canada is one of the least densely populated countries in the world, with an average of only 8 persons per square mile (3 persons per km^2).

Deciduous hardwood trees grow in the mild climate of southeastern Canada. The Far West, where the climate is wetter, is a region of tall trees such as the Douglas fir. North of these areas is a vast subarctic region covered by a great coniferous forest. As one continues north, however, the trees become smaller and

Ottawa, Ontario, the capital of Canada. The large building in the foreground is the Canadian Parliament building. The Ottawa River is the boundary between the provinces of Ontario and Quebec.

smaller until they disappear altogether. Here the subsoil is frozen permanently and is known as ***permafrost***.

Because of its abundant forests, Canada produces much timber and many lumber products. Also, God has blessed Canada with an abundance of mineral resources, such as gold, nickel, zinc, and copper. Canada is a naturally wealthy land.

Farm in the Great Lakes-St. Lawrence Lowlands of Ontario. The soil and climate of this region is excellent for farming.

Geographic Regions

Canada is a nation of ten provinces and three territories. It may be divided into five geographic regions: (1) the Appalachian region, (2) the Great Lakes-St. Lawrence Lowlands, (3) the Canadian Shield and Arctic Islands, (4) the Interior Plains, and (5) the Cordillera region (kawr duhl YAIR uh) in the west. The following paragraphs describe these five regions.

The Appalachian Region. This area includes the provinces along the Atlantic Ocean and Quebec's Gaspé Peninsula along the St. Lawrence River. It is an extension of the Appalachian region of the United States. The region has a humid continental climate similar to that of Maine, with long winters. The coast of Labrador is very cold because of the Labrador Current that brings cold water down from the north.

Peggy's Cove, Nova Scotia. This fishing village lies about 20 miles (32 km) southwest of Halifax.

The Appalachian region is important for dairying, potatoes, and fruits. Fishing is also important, particularly because of the Grand Banks, a rich fishing ground lying off the coast of Newfoundland.

The Great Lakes-St. Lawrence Lowlands. This region includes the low-lying land along the St. Lawrence River and the Ontario Peninsula that extends southwest between Lakes Ontario, Erie, and Huron. It is a level or rolling area, with only a small part of the nation's land but over half of its people. Large numbers live in Toronto, Canada's largest city, and in Montreal, its second largest city. Much of Canada's industry and commercial life is concentrated here.

The Niagara River thunders over the curved part of Niagara Falls (the Horseshoe Falls) at the rate of 50,000 to 100,000 cubic feet (1,400–2,800 m^3) per second. A treaty between the United States and Canada regulates the amount of water that may be diverted by hydroelectric plants; the intake for the Canadian plant is visible in the photograph. Maximum flow is maintained during the daylight hours of the tourist season.

Scenes From the Canadian Shield and Arctic Islands:
Top left: Pickle Lake in northern Ontario. Thousands of lakes dot the Canadian Shield, a vast area of hard rock that curves like a horseshoe around the Hudson Bay. ***Top right:*** Shore of Hudson Bay. Note the barren rocks of the Canadian Shield. ***Lower right:*** Iceberg off Baffin Island, Nunavut. This region is so cold that people need heavy coats most of the year.

This region is the heartland of Canada. The climate is humid continental, and the land is good for farming. In addition, transportation by land or water is easy here. The area has good highways, and ships can use the St. Lawrence Seaway to travel between the Great Lakes and the Atlantic Ocean. By using the Welland Ship Canal, ships can even bypass the great Niagara Falls between Lakes Ontario and Erie. Waterpower makes it possible to produce an abundance of hydroelectricity for the thousands of homes and factories.

The Canadian Shield and Arctic Islands. The Canadian Shield is a horseshoe-shaped area surrounding the Hudson Bay and covering about half of Canada. Near the Hudson Bay, much of the Shield is low and is dotted with lakes and marshes. The eastern part in Quebec is higher, climbing as high as 5,000 feet (1,524 m).

The rocky soil is not very good for farming, but mining is important because iron ore, nickel, silver, and gold are found here. Vast forests cover the land, so lumber and furs are also important.

The Arctic Islands, covered with snow and ice, lie north of the Hudson Bay. They include Ellesmere Island, reaching almost to the North Pole, and Baffin Island, one of the biggest islands in the world.

The Interior Plains. The Central Plains of the United States continue northward into Canada all the way to the Arctic Ocean. This region covers about one-fifth of Canada and includes Manitoba, Saskatchewan, Alberta, and the northeastern part of British Columbia.

As in the United States, the Interior Plains have fertile soil and are drier in the west than in the east. The southern part is important for raising wheat and other grains, but the northern part is too cold for much agriculture. Alberta has profited greatly from the discovery of oil and natural gas. Major cities

The Carrot River meanders through this level region to the east of Prince Albert in central Saskatchewan.

Edmonton, the capital of Alberta. This city is farther north than other major Canadian cities, most of which are near the southern border.

Mount Robson, sometimes called the "Monarch of the Canadian Rockies." Fur traders referred to this mountain as early as 1827, but climbers did not reach its summit until 1913. Mount Robson Provincial Park surrounds the mountain.

of the Plains region include Winnipeg in Manitoba, and Edmonton and Calgary in Alberta.

The Cordillera Region. This region is similar to the mountainous West in the United States (which is actually part of a chain stretching into South America). The Rocky Mountains extend on into Canada, the Coast Ranges continue along the coast, and a plateau region lies between them. The Rockies extend so far toward the northwest that they nearly meet the Coast Ranges.

In this region lies most of British Columbia and part of the Yukon Territory. The Rocky Mountains with their high peaks are very scenic. At 12,972 feet (3,954 m), Mount Robson is the highest peak of the Canadian Rockies.

The Coast Ranges rise abruptly from the Pacific Ocean. Narrow arms of the sea extend inland in deep cuts called ***fiords*** (FYAWRDZ). In the north, near the Alaskan border, the St. Elias Mountains raise their lofty peaks. The highest of these is Mount Logan, whose peak of 19,524 feet (5,951 m) is the highest point in Canada.

Because of the many large trees, lumbering is one of the main industries in British

River scene just north of Vancouver, British Columbia. The logs are a sample of the vast amounts of lumber that come from this province.

Columbia River at Revelstoke, British Columbia. This scenic spot is in the southeastern part of the province.

Columbia. Fishing is important along the Pacific coast. Rushing rivers are dammed to produce hydroelectric power, of which great amounts are used to smelt aluminum from bauxite. Vancouver is the largest city in British Columbia (and the third largest in Canada). The climate is mild and rainy here on the west coast.

River Systems of Canada. Canada may be divided into four drainage basins: the Atlantic basin, the Hudson Bay basin, the Arctic basin, and the Pacific basin. The Atlantic basin contains the most important system for trade; it includes the Great Lakes-St. Lawrence River system. The Hudson Bay basin includes the Red, Saskatchewan, and Nelson Rivers, as well as Lake Winnipeg.

The Arctic basin contains the Mackenzie River and its tributary, the Peace River, which empty into the Arctic Ocean. With a length of 2,635 miles (4,240 km), this is the longest river system in Canada. The Great Slave Lake and the Great Bear Lake are two large lakes also belonging to the Mackenzie system.

The Pacific basin includes three major rivers that empty into the Pacific. The Fraser River flows entirely within British Columbia. The Yukon River flows through the territory that bears its name, and also drains a large part of central Alaska. For more than half of its length, the Columbia River flows through the northwestern United States. Large tributaries like the Snake River help to make the Columbia the largest North American river (in volume) that flows into the Pacific Ocean.

As we learn about the way God has made the earth, we can say with the psalmist, "O LORD, how manifold are thy works! in wisdom hast thou made them all: the earth is full of thy riches" (Psalm 104:24).

Focus for Thought

6. a. What geographic regions of Canada are parts of similar regions in the United States?
   b. What regions does Canada have that the United States does not have?
7. How has the climate of Canada affected the settlement of the nation?

8. Copy and complete this chart of the five geographic regions of Canada. Follow the same pattern as for the chart of United States regions that you made in number 5.

Region	Geographic Features	Bodies of Water	Climate	Major Cities	Economic Activities
Appalachian Region					
Great Lakes-St. Lawrence Lowlands					
Canadian Shield, Arctic Islands					
Interior Plains					
Cordillera Region					

Geographical Highlights

A. Matching: Terms 1

1. Pertaining to the country, as opposed to the city.
2. Land formed by soil deposited at the mouth of some rivers.
3. Broad bay at the mouth of a river.
4. Low-lying region where rivers rise and fall with ocean tides.
5. Place at the edge of the Piedmont plateau, where waterfalls occur in rivers descending to the Coastal Plain.
6. Pertaining to the city, as opposed to the country.
7. Kind of trees that bear cones and usually have needles instead of broad leaves.
8. Flowing of water into inland lakes having no outlets to the ocean.
9. Low, bowl-shaped area surrounded by higher land; also, the area drained by a river system.
10. Kind of trees that lose their leaves for part of the year.
11. High ridge that separates water flowing into the Pacific Ocean from water flowing into the Gulf of Mexico.

a. basin
b. coniferous softwood
c. Continental Divide
d. deciduous hardwood
e. delta
f. estuary
g. Fall Line
h. internal drainage
i. rural
j. tidewater
k. urban

B. Matching: Terms 2

1. Subsoil that stays permanently frozen.
2. Surface features of a region.
3. In contact; adjoining.

a. contiguous
b. fault
c. fiord

4. Level land lying some distance inland from the ocean.
5. Crack or break in the crust of the earth, where earthquakes occur.
6. Account of happenings in the past.
7. Long, narrow bay extending inland in a steep-sided valley.
8. River flowing into a larger river.
9. Study of the earth, especially its surface features.
10. Large, elevated area of the same general height.

d. geography
e. history
f. interior plain
g. permafrost
h. plateau
i. topography
j. tributary

C. Matching: Bodies of Water

a. Arctic Ocean
b. Atlantic Ocean
c. Chesapeake Bay
d. Columbia River
e. Fraser River
f. Great Bear Lake
g. Great Lakes
h. Great Salt Lake
i. Great Slave Lake
j. Gulf of Mexico
k. Hudson Bay
l. Hudson River
m. Lake Winnipeg
n. Mackenzie River
o. Mississippi River
p. Missouri River
q. Niagara River
r. Ohio River
s. Pacific Ocean
t. Potomac River
u. Snake River
v. St. Lawrence River
w. Susquehanna River
x. Yukon River

1. United States rivers flowing east into the Atlantic Ocean (three answers).
2. Ocean to the north of North America.
3. Longest river in Canada.
4. Important river for shipping between the Great Lakes and the Atlantic.
5. Body of water in the Great Basin.
6. Lakes that are part of the Mackenzie River system (two answers).
7. River system draining about 40 percent of the United States.
8. River and its tributary draining the northwestern United States (two answers).
9. Ocean to the west of North America.
10. Lake Superior, Lake Michigan, Lake Huron, Lake Erie, Lake Ontario.
11. River flowing over a great waterfall between Lakes Erie and Ontario.
12. River of British Columbia that flows into the Pacific Ocean.
13. Body of water south of the United States.
14. Bay surrounded by the Canadian Shield.
15. Ocean to the east of North America.
16. River that drains central Alaska and flows into the Pacific Ocean.
17. Major tributary of the Mississippi that begins in the Rockies.
18. River that flows west out of the Appalachian Mountains.
19. Long, wide mouth of the Susquehanna River.
20. Canadian lake that drains into the Hudson Bay.

D. Matching: Geographic Features

a. Allegheny and Cumberland Plateaus
b. Appalachian Mountains
c. Coast Ranges
d. Great Basin
e. Central Plains
f. Mt. Logan
g. Mt. McKinley
h. Mt. Robson
i. Mt. Whitney
j. Ontario Peninsula
k. Pacific ranges
l. Pacific valleys
m. Piedmont
n. Rocky Mountains

1. Highest mountain in North America.
2. High western mountains stretching from Canada to New Mexico; part of a chain extending into South America.
3. Highest mountain in the Canadian Rockies.
4. Region of internal drainage where the Great Salt Lake is located.
5. Land stretching west from the Appalachian Mountains.
6. Vast, treeless, grassy land stretching from the Mississippi to the Rockies.
7. Region of rolling hills and valleys separating the Atlantic Coastal Plain from the Appalachian Mountains.
8. Highest mountain in the contiguous United States.
9. Rounded, forested mountains stretching from Alabama to Maine and extending into Canada.
10. Land in Canada extending southwest between the Great Lakes.
11. Highest mountain in Canada.
12. Valleys with a west-coast marine climate.
13. Mountains just west of the Great Basin.
14. Mountains along the western ocean.

E. Matching: Regions

a. Alaska
b. Appalachian region
c. Atlantic Coastal Plain
d. Canadian Shield
e. Central Plains
f. Cordillera region
g. Great Lakes-St. Lawrence Lowlands
h. Hawaii
i. Pacific Coast
j. Rocky Mountain region

1. Rocky region curving like a horseshoe around the Hudson Bay.
2. Low land bordering the Atlantic Ocean in the east and the Gulf of Mexico in the south.
3. Volcanic islands in the Pacific.
4. Mountains and valleys farthest west in the United States.
5. Canadian region including the Rocky Mountains and the Coast Ranges.
6. Heartland of Canada where most of the people live.
7. Broad region of fertile land drained by the Mississippi River system.
8. Largest state, which contains the highest mountain in North America.
9. Region including the Rocky Mountains and the Great Basin.
10. Piedmont, Appalachian Mountains, and Allegheny and Cumberland Plateaus.

F. Matching: Climates

a. arctic
b. humid continental
c. humid subtropical
d. Mediterranean
e. subarctic
f. west coast marine

1. Climate with four distinct seasons and a great contrast between summer and winter.
2. Very warm and moist climate.
3. Warm, dry climate suitable for raising oranges, grapes, and olives.
4. Mild, wet climate of the Pacific valleys.
5. Cold climate in Canada and Alaska where coniferous trees grow.
6. Very cold climate where no trees grow and deep soil layers are permanently frozen.

G. Matching: Cities

a. Anchorage
b. Boston
c. Calgary
d. Chicago
e. Denver
f. Edmonton
g. Honolulu
h. Houston
i. Juneau
j. Los Angeles
k. Montreal
l. New York
m. Pittsburgh
n. Portland
o. Salt Lake City
p. San Francisco
q. Seattle
r. St. Louis
s. Toronto
t. Vancouver
u. Winnipeg

1. Major Rocky Mountain city in the United States.
2. Three major cities of the Canadian Plains.
3. Major western port city of Canada.
4. Major Appalachian city in Pennsylvania.
5. Three cities of the Atlantic Coastal Plain.
6. Two great cities of the Central Plains in the United States.
7. Two largest cities of Canada.
8. Two large cities on the Pacific coast of California.
9. Two cities in Alaska.
10. Two major cities in the Pacific valleys.
11. Main city of Hawaii.
12. Major city of the Great Basin.

H. Deeper Discussion

1. Read Isaiah 40:12–17.
   a. What can a study of geography teach us about God?
   b. What should be our response as we observe the works of God in our world?
2. Explain how a knowledge of geography can improve your understanding of history.
3. What two factors encouraged the growth of cities along the Fall Line?

4. How do climate, soil, and topography affect the work that people do, the way they travel, and their general manner of life?
5. How have the United States and Canada benefited from their large size and abundant resources?

I. Chronology and Geography

1. Trace the outline of Map A in the Map Section, and label it "Geographic Regions of the United States." (You do not need to trace the state borders.)
   a. Draw the boundary lines of the five main geographic regions of the contiguous United States. Label the regions.
   b. Label the Piedmont, the Great Basin, Mt. Whitney, and Mt. McKinley.
   c. Using a blue colored pencil, trace the Hudson, Susquehanna, Potomac, Mississippi, Ohio, Missouri, Columbia, and Snake Rivers. Label them.
   d. Label the Atlantic Ocean, Pacific Ocean, Arctic Ocean (on the inset map of Alaska), Chesapeake Bay, Great Lakes, Great Salt Lake, and Gulf of Mexico.
   e. Label Boston, New York City, Pittsburgh, Chicago, St. Louis, Houston, Denver, Los Angeles, San Francisco, Seattle, Anchorage, and Honolulu.
2. Trace the outline of Map B in the Map Section, and label it "Geographic Regions of Canada." (You do not need to trace the province and territory borders.)
   a. Draw the boundary lines of the five main geographic regions of Canada. Label the regions.
   b. Label Mt. Logan, Mt. Robson, the Rocky Mountains, and the Coast Ranges.
   c. Using a blue colored pencil, trace the St. Lawrence, Mackenzie, Columbia, and Frazer Rivers. Label them.
   d. Label the Atlantic Ocean, Pacific Ocean, Arctic Ocean, Hudson Bay, Great Lakes, Lake Winnipeg, Great Slave Lake, and Great Bear Lake.
   e. Label Montreal, Toronto, Winnipeg, Calgary, Edmonton, and Vancouver.
3. Save your maps in a notebook or folder.

Mount McKinley, in Alaska, is the highest mountain in North America. Nugget Pond is in the foreground of this picture.

Unit 2
Times of Exploration and Settlement 1000–1750

Chapters in Unit 2

Columbus landed on the island of San Salvador, in the West Indies, on October 12, 1492.

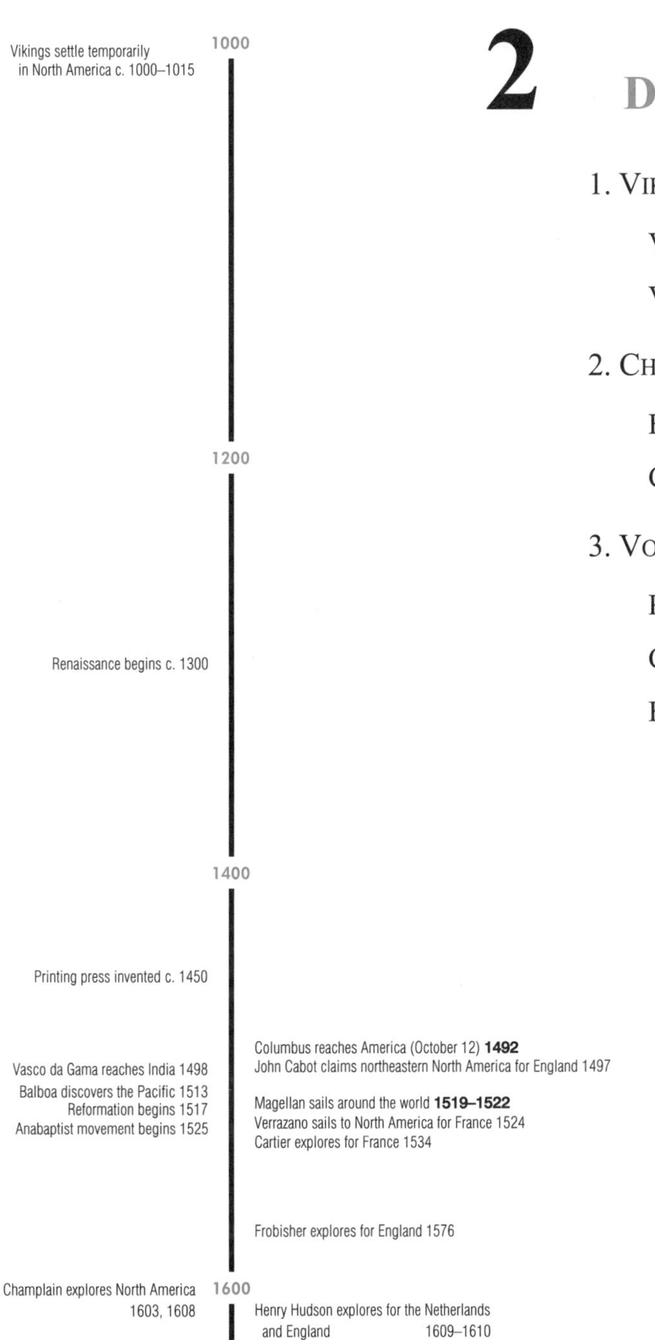

2 Discovery and Exploration

1. Vikings in North America
    - Vikings Come to America
    - Vikings Leave America
2. Changes in Europe
    - Europe in the Middle Ages
    - Changing Times in Europe
3. Voyages of Discovery
    - Portuguese Exploration
    - Columbus's Discovery
    - Exploration After Columbus

"The honour of kings is to search out a matter."
Proverbs 25:2

DISCOVERY AND EXPLORATION

Focus for Reading

God gave the following commission to the first man and woman: "Be fruitful, and multiply, and replenish [fill] the earth, and subdue it: and have dominion over the fish of the sea, and over the fowl of the air, and over every living thing that moveth upon the earth" (Genesis 1:28). After the Flood, the people built a large city and a tower in an effort to keep everyone together at one place. But God confounded their languages at Babel and "scattered them abroad from thence upon the face of all the earth" (Genesis 11:8). Clearly, God wanted people to spread out and subdue the whole world.

But five hundred years ago, most of North America was still wild and uncultivated. There were no roads; only a few scattered footpaths led through endless forests and across plains and deserts. A few Indians tilled small plots of ground or roamed the forests and prairies in search of wild game. These people lived in villages scattered here and there across the vast land. They had little knowledge of God, although they understood some things because His creation taught them. But they did not have God's Word to complete their understanding of Him.

One day this land would be home to hundreds of millions of people from all over the earth. How did this take place? What led to European exploration of North America? Three sections in this chapter help to answer these questions.

1. Vikings in North America
2. Changes in Europe
3. Voyages of Discovery

1. VIKINGS IN NORTH AMERICA

Though a few Vikings settled in North America around A.D. 1000, Europeans remained generally ignorant of the vast lands of the Western Hemisphere. Later the Viking settlements were abandoned and the discoveries forgotten. Almost five hundred years passed before Europeans again visited America.

Vikings Come to America

Discovery of Greenland. The Vikings (sometimes called Northmen or Norsemen) lived in the part of Europe known as Scandinavia, where Denmark, Norway, and Sweden are located. These fierce people crossed the stormy northern seas in swift, high-prowed ships, without benefit of compasses or modern navigation equipment. Their skill and daring on the ocean carried them to distant lands. They began to settle in places like Iceland and other northern islands of Europe.

The Vikings preserved the memory of their adventures in stories called ***sagas*** (SAH guhz). These stories tell how Eric the Red of Iceland sailed west and found a new land, which he

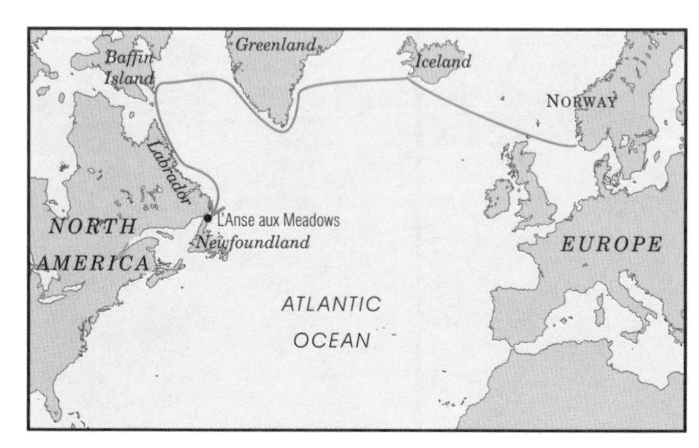

Viking Route to America

Vikings used sturdy, open boats called longships, which ranged in length from 45 to 75 feet (14 to 23 m) and were built with overlapping planks. A longship had one square sail, a high bow and stern with removable dragon heads, and a single starboard rudder. Shields and spears were stored along the sides of the ship.

Leif Ericson's discovery of America in A.D. 1000. Many historians believe this was in the area of Newfoundland, but some think it may have been as far south as Cape Cod.

explored. In 986 he planted a colony in this land. The land was cold and barren except for valleys near the sea. The sagas say Eric called it Greenland to attract settlers.

Discovery of North America. Eric the Red had a son named **Leif Ericson**, who heard about a new land even farther west. Leif decided to investigate. According to the sagas, he led a crew of thirty-five men to this new land, arriving about A.D. 1000. These were probably the first Europeans to arrive in North America.

Here on the North American coast, the men found wild wheat, wine berries, maple trees, and evergreens. Leif explored several places and gave them the following names: Helluland (land of flat rocks—probably Baffin Island), Markland (forest land—probably Labrador), and Vinland (wine land—probably Newfoundland).

Vikings Leave America

Failure of Viking Settlements. Leif lived in the area called Vinland for about a year, and Leif's brother Thorwald settled there around 1004. Other groups of Vikings lived at other places in Vinland for a time. But the settlements never prospered. Vinland was too far away from the Viking strongholds in Iceland and Norway. The settlements were also attacked by the native people, whom the Vikings called Skraelings (SKREHL ihngz)—literally, "screeching people" or war whoopers. The bitter cold climate may have been too harsh. By about 1015, all the Vikings had left.

For centuries, no one knew where Vinland had been. In the early 1960s, archaeologists uncovered eight homesteads at L'Anse aux Meadows (LANS oh MEH dohz) in northern Newfoundland. These homesteads were very similar to those uncovered on Iceland and Greenland. They also found a Viking blacksmith shop, complete with nails, rivets, and many iron tools. Other artifacts further confirmed that the Vikings had lived in North America, though the exact location of Vinland is still in question.

Credit for Discovering America. Why do people honor **Christopher Columbus** for discovering the New World when it is clear that he was not the first European to reach it? One answer is that the Viking settlements were not permanent. The Spanish and other Europeans following Columbus conquered and permanently settled the new lands. Another reason is that the Viking settlements held little importance to later people. Still another is that Europe in the eleventh century was not ready to settle America. The New World would have no more visitors from Europe for another five centuries.

Focus for Thought

1. Give the date of the Viking settlement in Greenland, and name the man who established it.
2. Who led the first group of Vikings to reach North America, and when did they arrive there?
3. Why did the settlements in Vinland eventually fail? Give at least two reasons.
4. Why does Christopher Columbus receive credit for discovering the New World when the Vikings had reached it earlier?

2. CHANGES IN EUROPE

Many changes took place in Europe during the period before Europeans came to North and South America. Under God's overruling hand, a series of events over many centuries led to Columbus's discovery of the New World.

Europe in the Middle Ages

The Manorial System. Historians divide history into three main periods: ancient history (4000 B.C.–A.D. 500), the Middle Ages (A.D. 500–1500), and modern times (A.D. 1500–present). European life in the Middle Ages was based on ***manorialism*** (muh NOR ee uhl ihz uhm), a system in which large estates called manors (MAN urz) were held by upper-class men called lords, or nobles. The manors included the castles of the lords and the huts of the serfs, who farmed the land in exchange for the lord's protection.

The serfs were required to work a certain number of days for the lord and to provide military service when necessary. They were not slaves to be bought or sold, but they could not easily leave the manor to seek a better life.

Each manor was self-sufficient. Instead of trading with others, the people supplied all their own needs. As a result, most Europeans lived very simply and knew little of what was happening in the rest of the world.

Ownership of the manors followed the principles of ***feudalism***. In this system, the king or queen granted large tracts of land to the highest nobles in the country. These nobles gave smaller pieces of land to lords of lower rank, who gave parcels to lords of still lower rank—all in exchange for loyalty and military service. When military service was needed, it was provided by knights who fought on horseback.

Spiritual and Intellectual Darkness. The Roman Catholic Church played an important role in people's lives. Everyone belonged to it, and few people dared to contradict the priest. The church leaders kept the Bible from the common people to keep them from finding out that some Catholic teachings were unscriptural. Literature and learning stayed with monks in Catholic monasteries. Because of these things, the first half of the Middle Ages is sometimes called the Dark Ages.

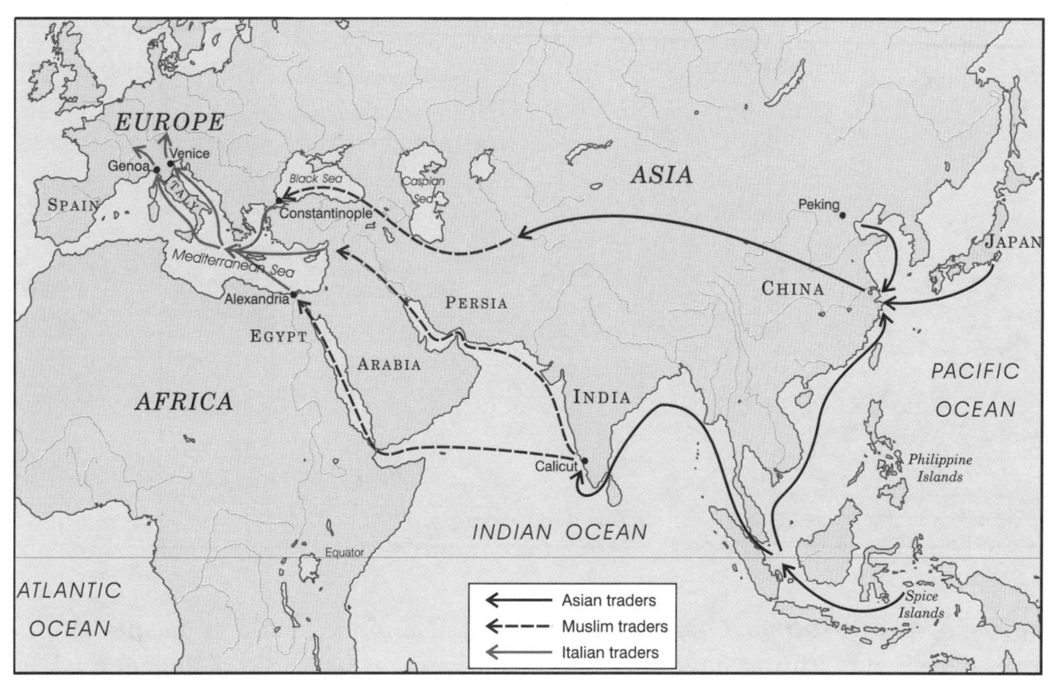

Trade Routes Before 1492

Changing Times in Europe

As long as Europeans lived on their manors and looked after their own affairs, they made little progress in learning or self-improvement. This is largely how things remained during the Dark Ages. But gradual changes did come, and they opened the way for discovery of the new lands in America. The following paragraphs describe some of these changes.

Trade With the Orient. A long series of changes began when Italian merchants established trade with the Orient (East). The Orient included the countries of India, China, Japan, and the East Indies. Around A.D. 1000, Italian traders began bringing oriental goods, such as silk and cotton cloth, sugar, spices, and perfumes, to Europe. They also dealt in jewels, dyes, medicines, and tropical foods, like figs and oranges. Many Europeans had never even heard of these luxuries.

Muslim traders brought these goods from the Orient to ports along the Mediterranean Sea, where Italian merchants loaded their ships with cargo for Europe. Other traders bought the goods from the Italians and sold them to lords in western and northern Europe. With so many middlemen, however, the goods were extremely expensive. This prompted Europeans to seek for trade routes to bypass the Muslims and Italians.

The Crusades. European trade with the Orient was increased by the Crusades. In these expeditions (1096–1291), numerous armies of Catholics fought the Muslims in Palestine, trying to win the so-called Holy Land for the Catholic Church. But the Crusaders did not succeed in driving the Muslims out of the Holy Land.

The lords who had gone on the Crusades developed a liking for the spices, foods, clothing, and other luxuries that the Muslims brought from the Orient. When these Crusaders returned to Europe, they still wanted these things. Italian traders sold even more oriental luxuries in Europe, with the result that they became quite wealthy. These ***capitalists*** began investing their money in many different businesses.

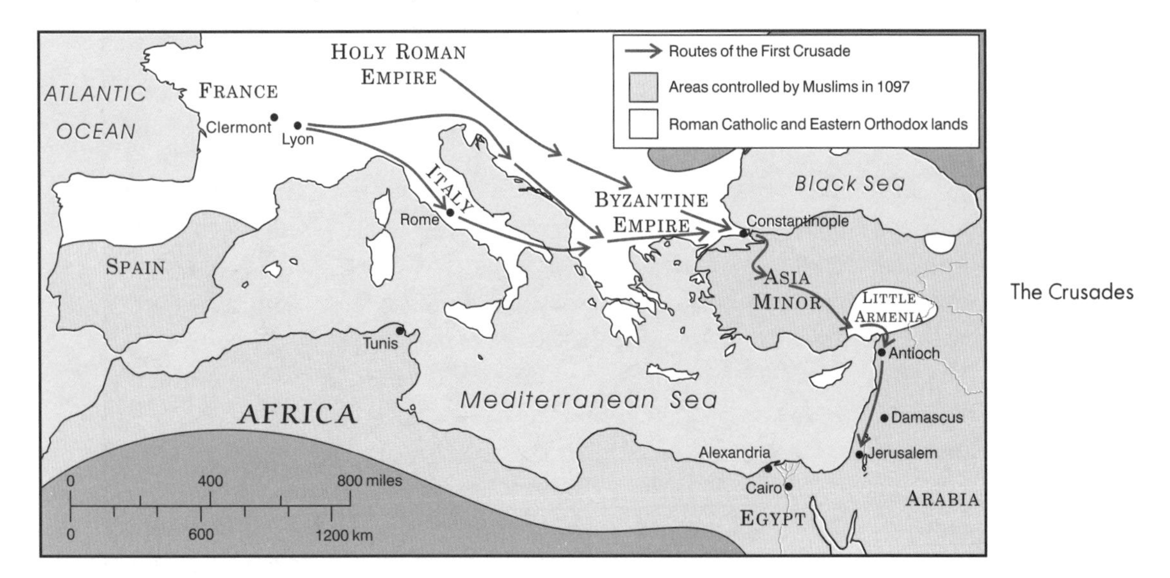

The Crusades

Decline of Manorialism. Gradually the agricultural system of Europe gave way to a more commercial system. Since the lords needed money or goods to exchange with the Italians, they began to manufacture goods for trade. As trade increased, people began living in towns, where most trading took place. The towns needed food, so farmers produced food to sell instead of raising only enough to feed their families. Lords began asking serfs to pay rent in money instead of service so that the lords could buy oriental luxuries. These changes weakened the manorial system.

With the growth of towns came another great change. Instead of only two classes of people (lords and serfs), a new ***middle class*** of people developed. This happened as serfs left the manors and became artisans and merchants. They were free to make and sell whatever products they wanted. All these developments helped to end manorialism in Europe.

Rise of Nationalism. As certain kings and lords became more powerful, they were able to establish strong governments that could protect the people. This helped the people to feel safer and more unified, and they began to take pride in belonging to the nation protected by their king. Such a feeling is called ***nationalism***. Because of nationalism, people of different nations were soon competing for trade so that their nations would become strong and wealthy. For example, Spanish and Portuguese explorers competed against each other to establish new trade routes for their nations.

A Spirit of Adventure. Some Europeans became so interested in Asia that they traveled there. The most famous of these travelers was Marco Polo, who visited China in the late 1200s and in 1298 published an account of his experiences. China was so different from Europe that most people thought Marco Polo just invented his strange stories. But the book helped to arouse a great interest in Asia.

The Renaissance. All these developments led to a new way of thinking in Europe. People began to think for themselves instead of simply accepting the ideas of Catholic church leaders and other authorities. They began devoting more time to art, music, literature, and science. The period of these changes lasted from about 1300 to 1500 and became known as the ***Renaissance*** (REHN ih sahns). This word means "rebirth."

The Renaissance began when Europeans started turning to ancient Greek and Roman writings instead of listening only to the church leaders. They had access to these old writings because when Constantinople fell to the Turks in 1453, many scholars fled from that city, bringing their books with them. These old books promoted new ideas and a new vision of man.

Revival of Humanism. As scholars of the Renaissance studied ancient Greek and Roman writings, they began thinking that religion is not necessary for guidance in life. Man is basically good, they said, and he simply needs cultivation to perfect his goodness. He should assert himself and prove his intelligence by producing great works of art, literature, and architecture. Many scholars concluded that since only the natural world can be perceived by the senses, the spiritual world might not even exist.

These new, man-centered ideas are called ***humanism***, and they fall far short of New Testament teaching. There *is* a spiritual world, and man must exercise faith in order to perceive it (Hebrews 11:1–6). Though the humanists' thinking had many errors, it did help to bring on the Reformation, which caused great changes in the churches of Europe.

Advances in Scientific Thought. Roger Bacon, who lived in the 1200s, declared that man should seek knowledge by experimentation. About four hundred years later, a man named Galileo Galilei (gal uh LEE oh gal uh LAY) disproved the age-old idea that heavy objects fell faster than light ones. Both men clashed with Catholic church leaders, who opposed this kind of experimentation. They forced Galileo to renounce his teaching that the earth moves around the sun.

In spite of opposition, a few men continued seeking the real truth about things in the natural world. By 1492, many people believed that the earth is a sphere. One of these was Christopher Columbus.

Improvements in Navigation. Through contact with the East, sailors were already using the compass to find their way across the seas. Better ship designs were another improvement, and so was the ***astrolabe***, an instrument for determining latitude by the stars. Just as important, sailors had access to a growing collection of fairly accurate maps. By 1492, the Azores, the Madeira Islands, the Canary Islands, and the entire west coast of Africa had been charted. These improvements in navigation made long voyages of exploration possible.

Improvement of Printing. One of the most important developments of the Renaissance was the improvement in printing. In the middle 1400s, a German named Johann Gutenberg invented a printing press with movable type. This consisted of small metal blocks with letters that could be arranged and rearranged easily to print any book quickly. Soon this invention replaced the time-consuming methods of copying text by hand and of engraving wooden blocks the size of whole pages.

Another development in printing was the use of paper, which the Arabs had made for centuries. Paper was brought to Europe during the Renaissance, and it soon replaced the old sheepskin parchment.

Johann Gutenberg (1395?–1468?) is credited with developing the first European printing press to use movable type.

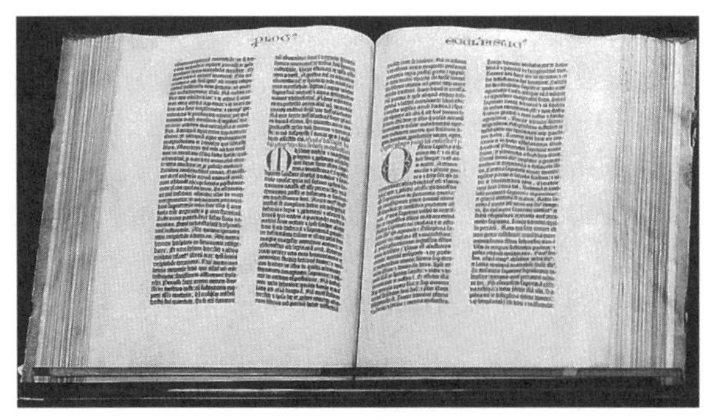
The Bible that Gutenberg printed was bound in three volumes. This is one of the three volumes, which are on display in the Library of Congress, Washington, D.C.

As a result of these developments, a large number of books suddenly became available to multitudes of Europeans. Within fifty years, almost 10 million books were printed. Some of these books spread humanistic ideas throughout Europe, but others spread the most important message of all—the Word of God. The first large book that Gutenberg printed was the Bible. When the Bible became available to the common people, it changed their lives as well as the course of history.

The Reformation. By studying the Bible, a number of men discovered that the Catholic Church was neither preaching nor practicing New Testament doctrines. This led to a movement called the ***Reformation***, which began in the 1500s. Its goal was to bring reform to the Roman Catholic Church.

Already in the 1300s, an English university teacher named John Wycliffe (WIHK lihf) had called for a return to the Word of God. Since the Bible was available only in Latin, he worked at producing an English translation. Wycliffe is sometimes called the "Morning Star of the Reformation."

Over one hundred years later, in 1517, Martin Luther caused a great stir in Germany when he published his "Ninety-five Theses" (THEE seez). This was a list of objections to certain Catholic practices. A few years later, Ulrich Zwingli and then John Calvin began working to establish new churches in Switzerland. These reform movements developed into powerful new Protestant denominations, so called because certain lords in the movement had *protested* against the Catholic Church. The new groups included the Lutheran Church in Germany, the Reformed Church in Switzerland, and the Anglican Church in England.

In 1525, a number of men in Switzerland began a movement that was neither Catholic nor Protestant. This was the Anabaptist movement, which later developed into the Mennonite faith. The first Anabaptist leaders had taken part in Zwingli's reform movement. But they believed that the church should be entirely separate from the civil government and that it should be guided only by the Word of God. Zwingli had taught the same thing earlier, but this doctrine seemed dangerous to many government leaders. Authorities were afraid they would lose power if they had no control of the people's religion, so they severely persecuted the Anabaptists.

The upheavals caused by the Reformation brought a century of wars to Europe. These wars caused untold suffering to multitudes of the common people. Many sought relief from the destruction and persecution in Europe by moving to the New World. Through the Renaissance and the Reformation, God arranged events at just the right time so that America would become a refuge for His persecuted people.

Focus for Thought

5. How did the following developments increase European interest in exploration?
    a. trade with the Orient
    b. the Crusades
    c. the rise of nationalism
    d. the spirit of adventure
    e. advances in scientific thought
    f. improvements in navigation

6. Why was Gutenberg's printing press such an important invention?
7. a. Give the names of four religious leaders who helped to bring about the Reformation. Place a star beside the one out of which Anabaptism eventually grew.
   b. What doctrine taught by the Anabaptists seemed threatening to governments in Europe?
8. How did the Reformation in Europe cause many people to move to the New World?

3. VOYAGES OF DISCOVERY

God's plan from the beginning was that man "replenish [fill] the earth, and subdue it." But this was not what motivated the exploration activity of Europeans in the 1400s. It was rather their desire to find new routes to the East, which offered luxuries such as spices, silks, jewels, and perfumes. For years the flow of these goods had been controlled by the Muslims and Italians, who sold them for high prices in Europe. These traders made handsome profits on the goods.

Merchants in Europe knew that if a direct sea route were found between Europe and the East, those profits would belong to them instead of to the Muslims and Italians. European monarchs also wanted to make their own nations rich and powerful by finding new trade routes.

Portuguese Exploration

Portugal was one of the first nations to seek an all-water route to the Orient. During the 1400s, a Portuguese prince named Henry the Navigator established a school for improved navigation. He sent out a number of expeditions along the west coast of Africa. Each expedition progressed farther south along the coast than the previous one, and then the men would return to report their discoveries.

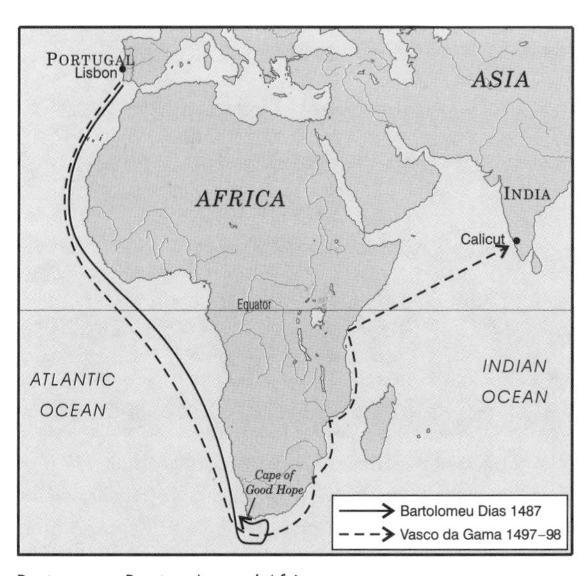

Portuguese Routes Around Africa

By 1487, Bartolomeu Dias had rounded the Cape of Good Hope, at the southern tip of Africa. **Vasco da Gama** sailed around this cape in 1497, and he reached India by 1498. Da Gama had discovered the long-sought water route to the East. Portugal became rich and powerful as silks, spices, and slaves poured in from the East and from African colonies.

Columbus's Discovery

A seasoned Italian sailor named Christopher Columbus had his own idea on how to get to the East—an idea that he called "The Enterprise of the Indies." He had read Marco Polo's account of the wealth in China and the surrounding lands. Columbus thought he could get to the rich lands in the East by sailing west across the Atlantic Ocean.

Appeal to Portugal. Columbus needed money, ships, and men to prove his ideas. When he appealed to King John II of Portugal, the royal advisers declared his ideas

Christopher Columbus (1451–1506)

unsound. Columbus believed China to be about 3,000 nautical miles (5,600 km) west of Portugal, but the advisers said it was double that distance. (The direct distance is actually about 11,000 nautical miles [20,400 km].) Besides, the Portuguese were busy with their own efforts to reach the East by sailing around Africa. Columbus was rejected in 1484.

Appeal to Spain. Columbus next approached **Ferdinand and Isabella**, king and queen of Spain. At first they refused to help because they were fighting the Muslims and because they thought the idea was unsound. After the Muslims surrendered, the monarchs again rejected Columbus, this time because of his exorbitant demands. He wanted the title "Admiral of the Ocean Sea," the authority to rule any new land he might discover, and one-tenth of any wealth he might find!

However, after the final rejection in January of 1492, the queen's treasurer convinced her that the expedition would not cost too much. Finally the queen agreed to sponsor him. A messenger hurried after Columbus, who was on the way to France with his proposal, and brought him back to the royal court. Columbus had waited six years for this approval.

Voyage to America. On the morning of August 3, 1492, Columbus set out with about ninety men in three ships: the *Niña,* the *Pinta,* and the *Santa María.* He had several goals: to gain wealth and fame for himself, to advance the interests of Spain, and to carry the Roman Catholic faith to new lands. He believed, as his name meant, that he was the "Christ-bearer."

Columbus started westward across the Atlantic Ocean. Determined, he kept his ships sailing even though the sailors threatened mutiny after sailing 3,000 miles (4,828 km) in thirty-three days without seeing land. The sailors were afraid they would never get home again. On October 9 or 10, Columbus promised his men they would continue sailing no more than three days before turning back.

In the early morning of October 12, 1492, the lookout shouted, "Land! Land!" That day Columbus and his men set foot on an island

A replica of the *Santa María*. Measuring about 117 feet (36 m) long, the *Santa María* was Columbus's flagship on his first voyage to the New World. It was later wrecked on a reef of present-day Haiti, and Columbus had to return home in the *Niña*.

that he named San Salvador ("Holy Saviour"). It was in the Bahamas, but Columbus believed that he had reached one of the islands in the East Indies.

Columbus returned to a hero's welcome in Spain. He made three more voyages to the New World in his lifetime. On these voyages, he claimed Hispaniola, Cuba, and a number of other islands for Spain. His third voyage brought him to the coasts of South America, and his fourth to Central America. As long as he lived, Columbus maintained that he had found a water route to the Orient. He died in 1506 at the age of fifty-five.

Columbus never found a new route to Asia, but he found something even better: a whole New World. Europe stood on the threshold of a great change. All of subsequent history would be affected by Columbus's discovery.

Exploration After Columbus

Line of Demarcation. Spain and Portugal disputed over Asia, since Columbus had claimed what he thought was Asia for Spain, and Portugal had already claimed Asia. To settle this dispute, the pope drew the Line of Demarcation in 1493 and granted Spain exclusive rights to all lands west of that line. Portugal contested the location of the line; and the next year, Spain agreed by the Treaty of Tordesillas (tawr day SEE yahs) to move the line farther west.

Unknown to the Spanish, this treaty allowed the Portuguese to claim a large section of South America. In 1500, Pedro Cabral left Portugal and headed for India, but he was blown off course and sailed to the east coast of South America. He claimed this land for Portugal, and it later became Brazil.

Naming of America. An Italian named **Amerigo Vespucci** (uh MEHR uh goh vehs POO chee) accompanied several voyages to South America in 1499 and 1501. Later he wrote about his experiences in what he called "the New World" rather than the Orient. In the early 1500s, one mapmaker wrote about Amerigo's land and labeled the great southern landmass on a map as *America*, from a Latin form of *Amerigo*. The name became popular, and people began calling the new lands America.

Further Spanish Explorations. Spanish explorers continued to broaden man's knowledge. In 1513, **Vasco de Balboa** crossed Panama and sighted the Pacific Ocean, the first European to view it from the east. He claimed for Spain all the land touched by this ocean.

In 1519, **Ferdinand Magellan** was sent to seek a passage to the Pacific, still in hopes of finding a way to the Orient. He sailed along the coast of South America until he reached its southern tip. There he passed through the stormy strait at Cape Horn, which today is called the Strait of Magellan. Then he sailed across the vast Pacific, enduring severe hardships on the way, only to lose his life in a battle with natives of the Philippines.

Discovery of the Pacific Ocean on September 29, 1513. Balboa named it the South Sea because he was facing south.

On October 21, 1520, Magellan and his men discovered the passage now known as the Strait of Magellan. They sailed through it and reached an ocean that he named Pacific (meaning "peaceful"), because it was more peaceful than the stormy strait he had just come through.

John Cabot describing his discovery of North America to King Henry VII. He claimed lands in northeastern North America for England in 1497.

Just one of Magellan's five ships returned to Spain in 1522. This ship was the first to circle the entire earth. With Magellan's voyage, Europeans realized the vastness of the Pacific Ocean and the true size of the earth. They learned that the Orient could indeed be reached by sailing west from Europe. However, the distance was so great that such a voyage was not practical.

Exploration of North America. The other European nations wanted a share in the discovery of riches. In 1497, England sent **John Cabot** to search for a way to the Orient. Cabot visited Labrador and Newfoundland, which he claimed for England. This claim was based on the European practice of giving possession of a new region to the country that discovered it. On that basis, England claimed all of northeastern North America.

After Magellan's voyage, explorers wanted to find a shortcut through North America as Magellan had found through South America. This they called the Northwest Passage. For about one hundred years, explorers searched in vain for this imaginary passage. One of these was **Giovanni da Verrazano** (joh VAH nee dah vehr uh ZAH noh), an Italian who sailed for France in 1524. He explored the North American coast from present-day North Carolina to Maine and Newfoundland, but he did not find the Northwest Passage.

Ten years later the French king sent **Jacques Cartier** (ZHAHK kahr TYAY) on a similar assignment. When he discovered the St. Lawrence River, he thought he had finally found a passage to China. But rapids soon halted his journey upstream, and he realized that the St. Lawrence was merely a river. However, Cartier's and Verrazano's voyages gave France a claim to the St. Lawrence River valley.

In spite of those failures, other explorers kept up the search. In 1576, Queen Elizabeth of England sent Martin Frobisher to seek the Northwest Passage by sailing farther north. When his way was blocked by ice, Frobisher had to turn back, having discovered Frobisher

Discovery of the Hudson River in 1609. Henry Hudson, sailing for the Dutch, discovered the river that now bears his name. The Dutch colony of New Netherland was founded on the basis of Hudson's exploration.

Bay. Also, Samuel de Champlain made several voyages for France from 1603 to 1608. He too was unsuccessful in finding the Northwest Passage, but he helped to establish the French more firmly in North America by exploring parts of what is now Canada.

Finally an Englishman named **Henry Hudson** made two more attempts. Sailing for the Dutch in 1609, he found the Hudson River and thought it could be the Northwest Passage. Like the others, he was disappointed when the Hudson turned out to be a river, but he claimed the Hudson River area for the Netherlands.

In 1610, Hudson went exploring for England and discovered the bay now called Hudson Bay. He sailed into it, hoping it would lead through North America. After camping during the harsh winter, his crew decided to go back to England. They set Hudson, his young son, and a few loyal crew members adrift in a boat. Hudson was never heard from again, but he established England's claim to the Hudson Bay region.

Though the goal of these explorers was to find a passage through America, they made important contributions to American history. First, they showed that these lands had riches of their own. Second, they increased the store of knowledge about North America. Finally, they established claims in the New World for nations of Europe.

Henry Hudson, his young son John, and seven of his men were set adrift by his crew.

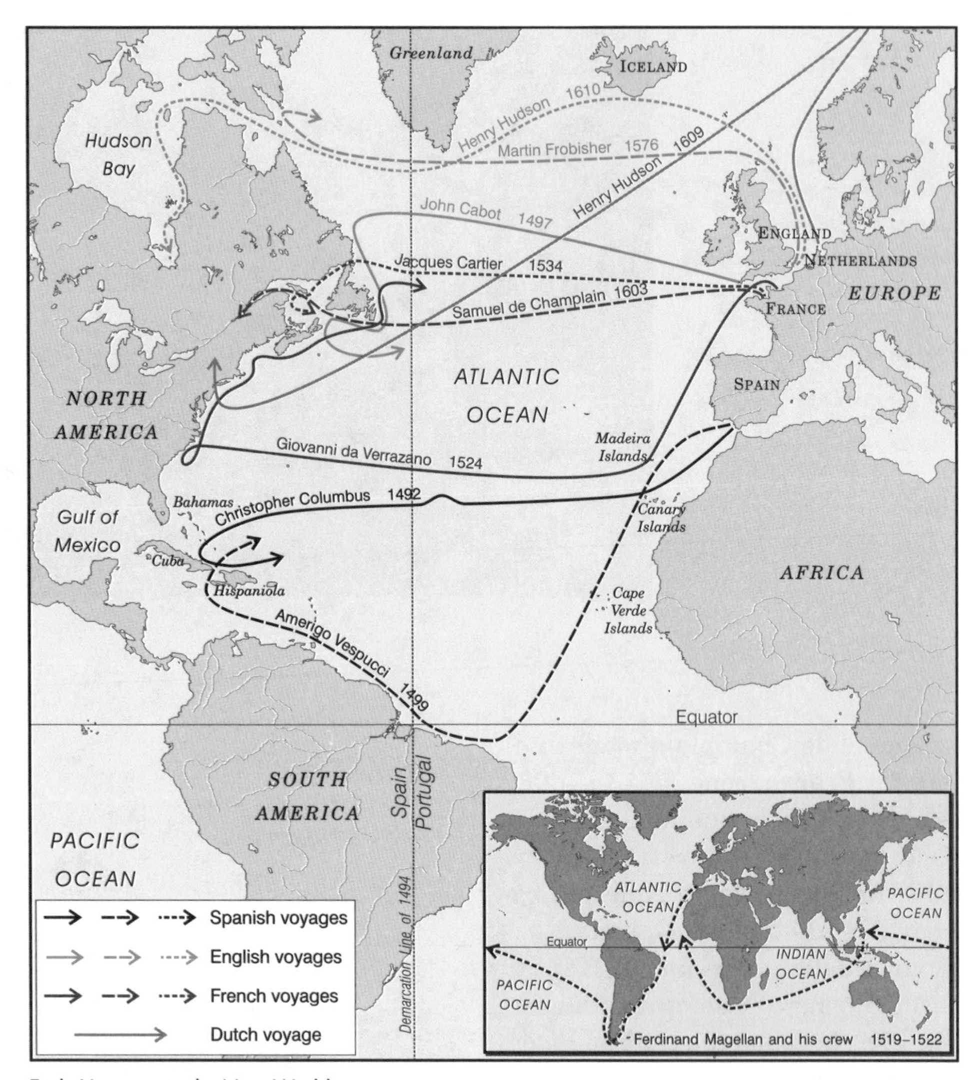

Early Voyages to the New World

Focus for Thought

9. Why is Amerigo Vespucci important in American history?
10. How was it decided which lands in the New World belonged to which European nations?
11. For each of the following nations, name the men who explored the New World and the areas each nation claimed as a result of that exploration. In one case the same explorer's name will be used for two different nations.
    a. Portugal (not including Amerigo Vespucci)
    b. Spain (two men, not including Vespucci or Magellan)
    c. England (two men, not including Martin Frobisher)
    d. France (three men)
    e. Netherlands

Historical Highlights

A. Matching: People

a. Amerigo Vespucci
b. Christopher Columbus
c. Ferdinand and Isabella
d. Ferdinand Magellan
e. Giovanni da Verrazano
f. Henry Hudson
g. Jacques Cartier
h. John Cabot
i. Leif Ericson
j. Vasco da Gama
k. Vasco de Balboa
l. Vikings

1. Explorer who claimed northeastern North America for England in 1497.
2. "Admiral of the Ocean Sea" who discovered the New World in 1492.
3. Man who described the new lands as being a new world rather than part of the Orient.
4. Viking who explored the northeastern coast of North America around A.D. 1000.
5. Captain of five ships, one of which became the first to sail around the world (1519–1522).
6. Scandinavian people who settled Iceland, Greenland, and Vinland around A.D. 1000.
7. Explorer of the North American coast for France in 1524.
8. Explorer who claimed part of America for the Netherlands in 1609.
9. Explorer who discovered in 1513 that a great ocean lay west of America.
10. Explorer of the St. Lawrence River area for France in 1534.
11. Explorer who reached the Orient by sailing around Africa.
12. King and queen of Spain when Columbus went on his voyage of discovery.

B. Matching: Names and Terms

a. astrolabe
b. capitalist
c. feudalism
d. Line of Demarcation
e. manorialism
f. middle class
g. nationalism
h. Orient
i. Reformation
j. Renaissance
k. saga
l. San Salvador
m. *Santa María*
n. Vinland

1. Rebirth of learning and culture in Europe.
2. Ship commanded by Columbus when he discovered the New World.
3. Boundary drawn by the pope to give Spain rights to the New World.
4. The East.
5. Instrument used by medieval sailors to determine the latitude of their ship.
6. System in which a lord owned the land and serfs farmed it for him.
7. Temporary Viking settlement in North America, probably in present-day Newfoundland.
8. Person who invests money in a project in order to make a profit.
9. Island where Columbus landed in the New World.
10. People who were neither lords nor serfs.
11. A story of Viking adventures, first handed down orally and later put into writing.
12. Great change in the religious system of Europe.
13. System of loyalty in Europe during the Middle Ages, by which noblemen of lower rank received land from noblemen of higher rank.
14. Pride in belonging to one's nation; patriotism.

C. Multiple Choice

Write the letter of the best answer.

1. The Renaissance
   a. led to a revival of Roman Catholic thought.
   b. encouraged people to reject all their old ideas.
   c. brought a renewed interest in art, music, literature, and science.
   d. brought an age of mental and spiritual darkness.
2. Why did the Reformation take place?
   a. Materialism moved men to seek the truth.
   b. Martin Luther was upset because of errors in the Roman Catholic Church.
   c. Certain kings left the Roman Catholic Church and established Protestant churches.
   d. Various men saw errors in the Roman Catholic Church and determined to correct them.
3. The Anabaptist movement
   a. grew out of Calvin's teaching.
   b. emphasized thrift and hard work.
   c. promoted the idea that the church and state should be separate.
   d. reformed the Roman Catholic Church from within.
4. How did the Reformation affect American history?
   a. Many people sought relief from troubles in Europe by moving to America.
   b. It broke the power of the Roman Catholic Church.
   c. It resulted in several new Protestant denominations.
   d. Calvin, Zwingli, and Luther sent many of their followers to the New World.
5. The Italians
   a. sought ways to reduce the price of goods from the East.
   b. tried to improve the overland trade routes to the East.
   c. were the first Europeans to reach the East by sailing around Africa.
   d. were the first Europeans to control the trade routes to the East.
6. Christopher Columbus
   a. was a capitalist who financed his own voyages.
   b. was right in thinking that the East could be reached by sailing west, but was wrong in estimating the distance.
   c. was honored all his life for having discovered the New World.
   d. was eager to establish Protestantism in new lands.

D. Deeper Discussion

1. Make an application of Job 12:22 in terms of European discovery and exploration. Remember that the Atlantic Ocean was known as the Sea of Darkness at this time.
2. Would the explorations in the 1400s have taken place without the Renaissance? Explain.
3. Compare the timing of the Reformation and the exploration of the New World. What does this timing suggest?
4. What kind of personality and character did Columbus have?
5. Why can it be said that Columbus's discovery of the New World is one of the most important happenings in history?
6. How do the discoveries and explorations of about five hundred years ago affect you today?

E. Chronology and Geography

1. Make a time line of some of the important events that changed Europe, using the list below. First, choose a scale that fits the span of years to be covered. For this time line, use 1 centimeter = 50 years. The illustration at the right shows you how to begin. (Metric units work well because they are based on tens. In later chapters, a more practical scale will be 1 centimeter = 10 years.) Draw a line and mark it off in centimeters. Then label the marks.

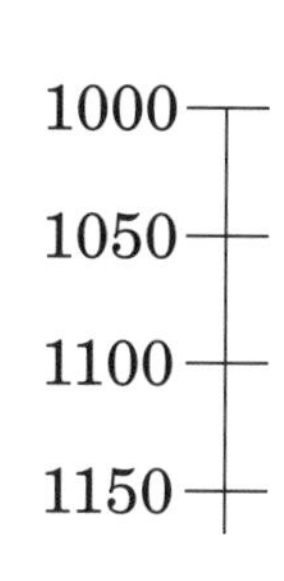

   Write in each event for your time line at the appropriate place. If you write the years directly on the line instead of to the left, you can place events on both sides of the time line. (See the time line on page 37.) A brace (}) may be used to indicate a span of years.

   Printing press invented
   Reformation begins
   Trade with the Orient begins
   Marco Polo publishes his book
   Renaissance
   Crusades

2. Match the numbers on the map to the names below.

   ___ a. Cabot
   ___ b. Cartier
   ___ c. Champlain
   ___ d. Columbus
   ___ e. Frobisher
   ___ f. Hudson (1609)
   ___ g. Hudson (1610)
   ___ h. Verrazano
   ___ i. Vespucci

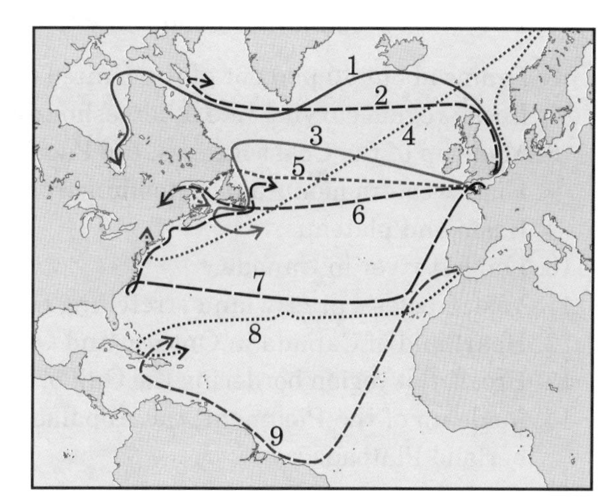

3. Copy and complete this chart of early explorers in the New World.

Explorer	Exploration Dates	Sponsoring Country	Areas Explored
Cabot			
Cabral			
Balboa			
Magellan			
Verrazano			
Cartier			
Frobisher			
Champlain			
Hudson			

So Far This Year

These exercises review what you have learned so far this year. Try to do as many as you can without looking back for the answers.

A. Matching: Climates

1. Sunny and mild; good for oranges and olives.
2. Very warm and moist.
3. Wet and mild; found in Pacific valleys.
4. Cold climate in Canada and Alaska.
5. Climate of four seasons.

a. humid continental
b. humid subtropical
c. Mediterranean
d. subarctic
e. west coast marine

B. Matching: Physical Features

a. Appalachian region
b. Atlantic Coastal Plain
c. Pacific Coast
d. Central Plains
e. Rocky Mountain region
f. Canadian Shield
g. Great Lakes-St. Lawrence Lowlands
h. Mississippi River
i. Mackenzie River

6. Drains about 40 percent of the United States.
7. Rocky region curving like a horseshoe around Hudson Bay.
8. Made up of the Coast Ranges, the Pacific ranges, and the Pacific valleys.
9. High, western mountains extending from Canada to New Mexico; region includes Great Basin and plateaus.
10. Longest river in Canada.
11. Vast, treeless, grassy land stretching from the Mississippi to the Rockies.
12. Heartland of Canada in Ontario and Quebec.
13. Broad, flat region bordering the Gulf of Mexico and the ocean east of the United States.
14. Made up of the Piedmont, the Appalachian Mountains, and the Allegheny and Cumberland Plateaus.

C. Matching: Explorers

a. Amerigo Vespucci
b. Christopher Columbus
c. Vasco de Balboa
d. Ferdinand Magellan
e. Giovanni da Verrazano
f. Henry Hudson
g. Jacques Cartier
h. John Cabot
i. Leif Ericson
j. Vasco da Gama

15. Explorer of the northeastern coast of North America for England in 1497.
16. "Admiral of the Ocean Sea" who discovered the New World in 1492.
17. Explorer who discovered in 1513 that a great ocean lay west of America.
18. Viking who explored the northeastern coast of North America around A.D. 1000.
19. Explorer who reached the Orient by sailing around Africa.
20. Explorer of the North American coast for France in 1524.
21. Explorer who claimed part of America for the Netherlands in 1609.
22. Man who described the new lands as being a new world rather than part of the Orient.
23. Explorer of the St. Lawrence River area for France in 1534.
24. Captain of five ships, one of which became the first to sail around the world (1519–1522).

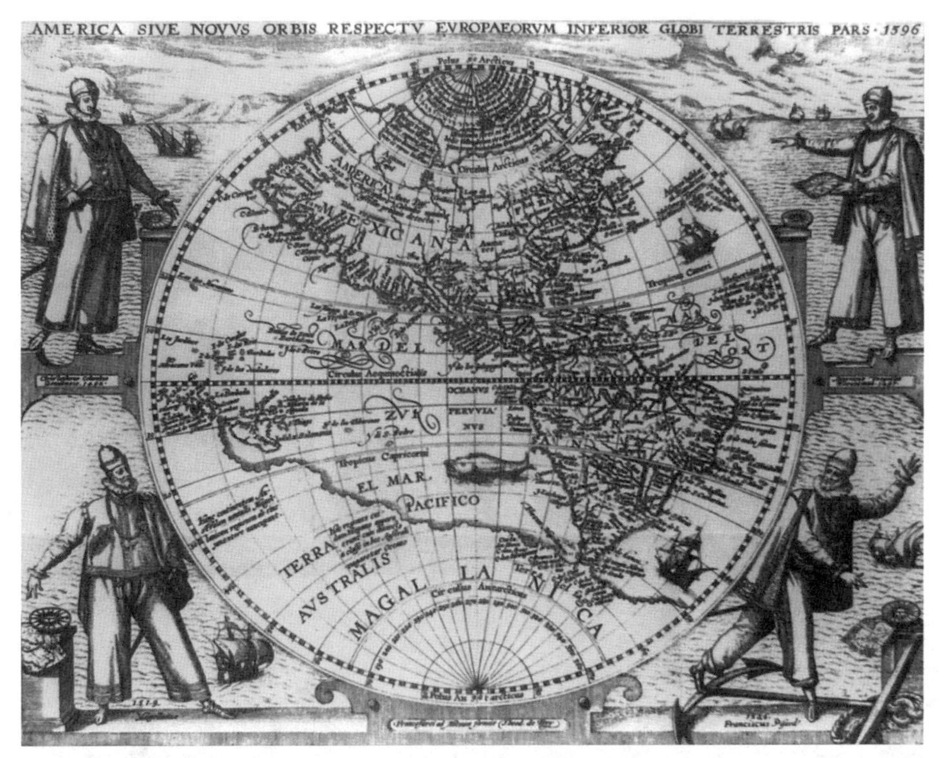

Early map of the Americas, first published about 1600. It is ringed with portraits of Christopher Columbus, Amerigo Vespucci, Francisco Pizarro, and Ferdinand Magellan (clockwise from top left).

An Indian family moving from one place to another. Note the travois that the horses are pulling.

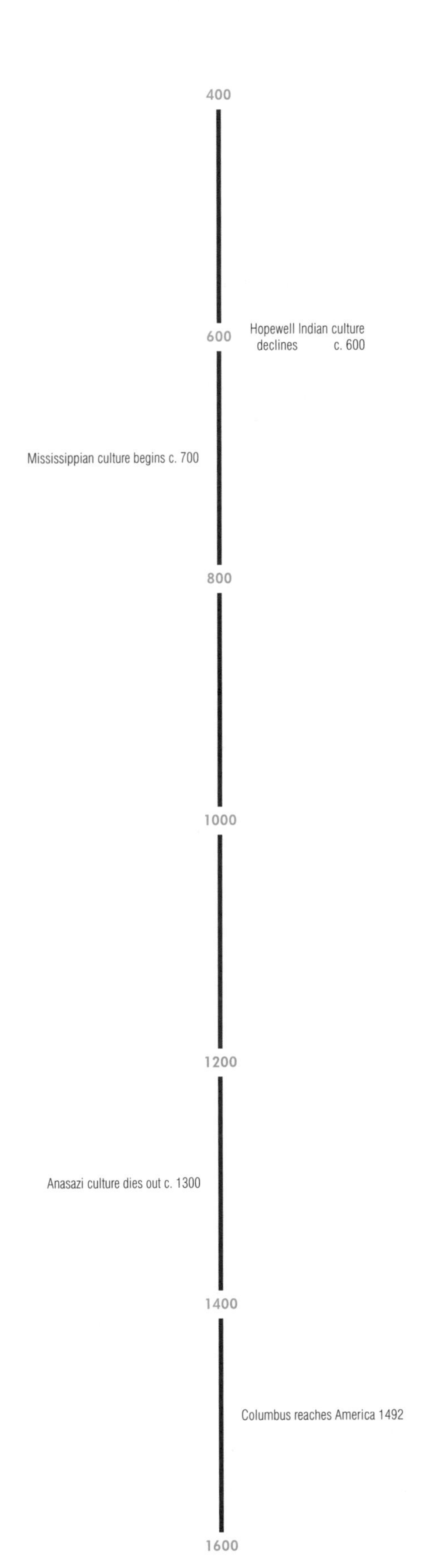

3 American Indians

1. Indians Before Columbus
    - Indian Origin and Culture
    - Early Indian Civilizations
2. Indians at the Time of Columbus
    - Indians of the Northeast
    - Indians of the Southeast
    - Indians of the Plains
    - Indians of the Southwest
    - Indians of the Far West
3. Indian Contributions
    - The Columbian Exchange
    - The Collision of Cultures

"In [God's] hand is the soul of every living thing, and the breath of all mankind."

Job 12:10

American Indians

Focus for Reading

When Columbus arrived in America, he mistakenly named the native people Indians because he believed that he had reached the East Indies. They were not Indians, however, but people who had lived in America long before the Europeans came. Their ways of life differed from that of the newcomers. When the Europeans arrived, their civilization collided with the beliefs and practices of the natives.

What were the Indians like? Where and how did they live? In this chapter, you will read three sections that explain Indian cultures and how they mixed and clashed with the European culture.

1. Indians Before Columbus
2. Indians at the Time of Columbus
3. Indian Contributions

1. INDIANS BEFORE COLUMBUS

Indians had many different ways of life when Columbus visited America. In addition, their ways of living had changed over the centuries before 1492, just as European life had changed. But many of the Indians' lives changed drastically after Columbus came. You will first study the Indians as they were long before these great changes took place.

Indian Origin and Culture

Arrival in America. How did the native peoples get to America? Scholars have proposed various answers to this question. Many believe the ancestors of the Indians crossed from Asia into North America by a narrow strip of land called the Bering Strait land bridge. Some believe people could have sailed across the ocean.

Although the Bible does not give all the details, it does provide a foundation for answering this question. First, the Indians descended from Adam through Noah as everyone else did. Many Indians even had their own story of a supernatural Creation. When the people at Babel tried to build a great tower, the ancestors of the Indians must have been among them. But God confused the languages, and Genesis 11:9 says, "From thence did the LORD scatter them abroad upon the face of all the earth."

American Indians had many unrelated languages—as many as three hundred in North America and one thousand in the whole New World. This fact indicates a connection with the confusion at the Tower of Babel. Also, Genesis 10:25 speaks of the earth being divided. These verses from Genesis suggest that people spread all over the world after the Flood.

Many evidences of old Indian civilizations are gone because of the destruction of the Indian peoples and because most Indians kept no written records. However, archaeologists have studied extensively about Indians by examining ancient Indian villages, campsites, and ***artifacts*** (manmade things such as tools and ornaments).

A Variety of Cultures. Some Indians lived in the woods. Others roamed the flat, treeless plains. Still others lived in barren desert regions. In these varied environments, Indians developed different ways of living.

Culture refers to the customs and values of people. It includes such things as the language, the clothing, the art and music, and the beliefs of a people. Culture also involves technology (the kinds of tools people use) and the established ways of doing things. As many as two thousand different Indian cultures existed in the New World in 1492. Estimates of the number of Indians at that time vary from 8.4 million to 112 million.

Early Indian Civilizations

The Mound Builders. Several major Indian civilizations had come and gone before Columbus arrived. In eastern North America, a culture called the Mound Builders existed apparently before the time of Christ. The Adena people lived in the Ohio River valley and built huge mounds of earth to bury their dead. One serpent-shaped mound in Ohio is ¼ mile long (0.4 km).

It appears that the Adena group was succeeded by the Hopewell people, also centered in Ohio. They traded far and wide for things such as copper from the Great Lakes, grizzly bear teeth from the Rockies, and shells from the seacoast. They too built burial mounds. Eventually their culture spread into the area from the Gulf of Mexico to the Great Lakes. By about A.D. 600, they had declined.

The Mississippian culture, another group of Mound Builders, began in the Mississippi River valley around A.D. 700. These people built large settlements and mounds. The mounds served either as burial places or as foundations for temples. Cahokia, east of St. Louis, Missouri, was such a large community that at one time nearly forty thousand people lived there. It had a temple mound that covered about 15 acres (6 ha).

Southwestern Farming Communities. The Hohokam (huh HOH kuhm) and Anasazi (ahn uh SAHZ ee) cultures grew up in the Southwest. These were similar in that the people grew corn, squash, and beans by using irrigation and other techniques for farming dry land. The Hohokam in particular developed irrigation canals.

The Anasazi lived in villages called ***pueblos*** (PWEHB lohs). (The Hohokam later adopted the practice of living in pueblos too.) A pueblo was usually constructed with stone or adobe (bricks made of sun-dried clay). It generally had several stories and was built on

The Mound Builders made huge burial and ceremonial mounds like this one, called Monk's Mound. About 100 feet high (30 m) and covering 16 acres (6.5 ha), this is the largest of over 100 mounds near Cahokia, Illinois.

Indian ruins at Canyon de Chelly National Monument in Arizona. Long ago, cliff dwellers made their homes here.

Five-story Indian pueblo at Taos, New Mexico. Notice the dome-shaped clay ovens at the right, used for baking pottery and bread.

a cliff under a rock canyon wall or in the mouth of a cave. Later the Anasazi built adobe pueblos on mesas, which are flat-topped elevations with steep, rocky sides. Pueblo Bonito in New Mexico had hundreds of rooms for as many as one thousand people.

Another ancient Indian culture, the Mogollon, produced spectacular pottery with pictures of animals, insects, and people. These civilizations ended by about A.D. 1300, but their influence lived on in the American Southwest.

Focus for Thought

1. a. What is meant by the term *culture*?
   b. What are some specific things that are part of your culture?
2. What was similar about the Hopewell and Mississippian cultures?
3. What was similar about the two Southwestern farming cultures?
4. Which group of Southwestern farming cultures
   a. especially used irrigation?
   b. were cliff dwellers?
   c. made spectacular pottery?

2. INDIANS AT THE TIME OF COLUMBUS

For convenient study, Indians are often divided into ***culture areas***. Within a culture area, various tribes lived similarly because they faced similar problems. Geography and climate helped determine culture areas because these factors affect the way people live. The Indians of a given area used related languages and obtained their food in similar ways. Even their beliefs were alike in many ways.

Historians usually divide North America into about ten different Indian culture areas. This section describes five of the culture areas in what is now the United States.

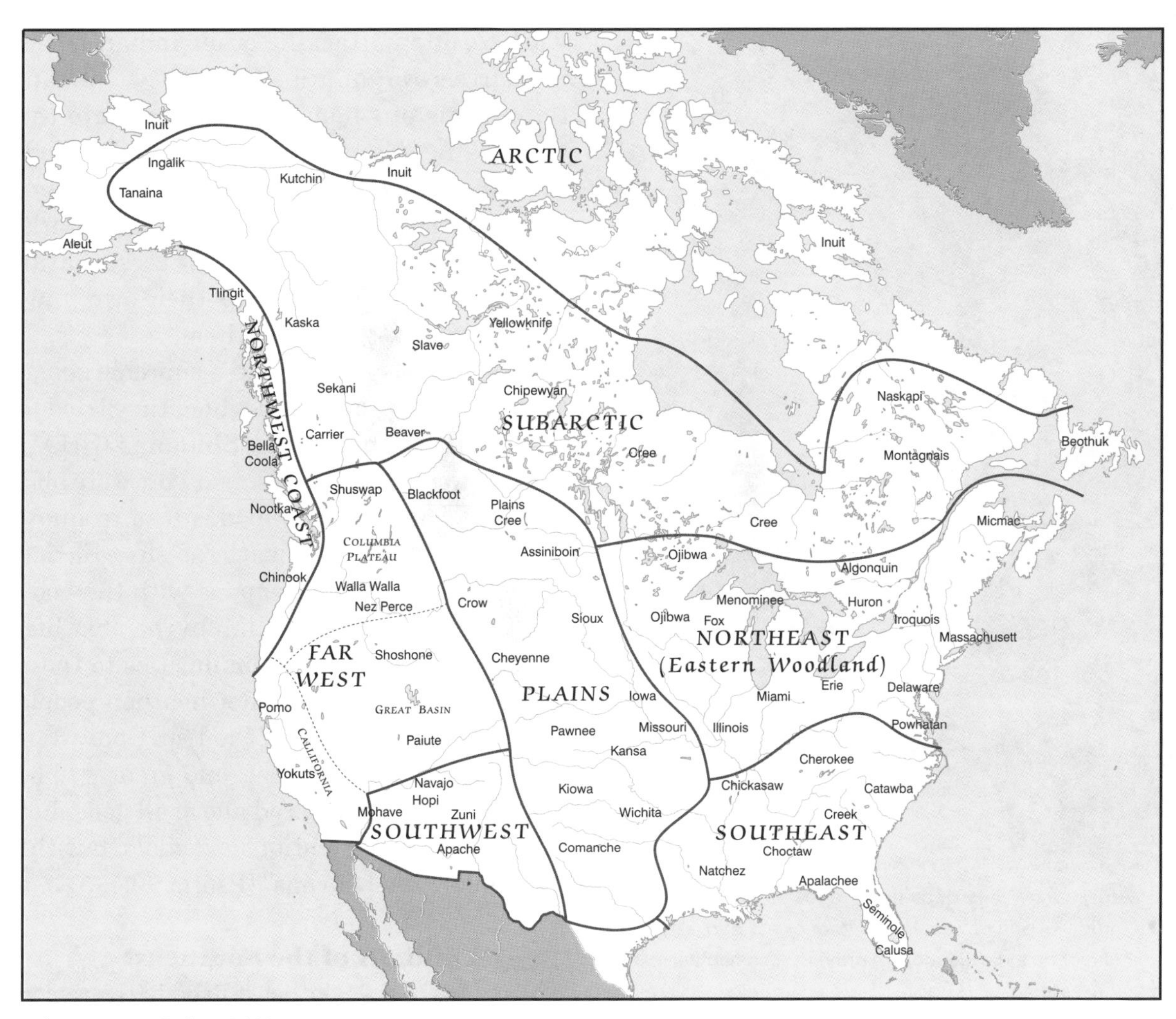

Indian Regions Before 1492

Indians of the Northeast

The Northeast area is bounded by the Great Lakes in the north, North Carolina in the south, the Atlantic Ocean in the east, and the Mississippi River in the west. Tribes living in this region were of two main classes. One included the Huron, the Iroquois (IHR uh kwoy), and others who spoke Iroquoian languages. The other was the Algonquian (al GAHNG kwee uhn) speaking peoples, such as the Delaware. These tribes are called Woodland Indians because many lived in the eastern forests.

The Iroquois are typical of the Woodland Indians. For protection in war, five Iroquois tribes formed the Iroquois League, or Five Nations. They were the Seneca (SEHN ih kuh), Cayuga (kay YOO guh), Onondaga (ahn uhn DAW guh), Oneida (oh NY duh), and Mohawk (MOH hawk). In 1722, the Tuscarora (tuhs kuh RAWR uh) joined them, and the confederacy was called the Six Nations. These tribes were centered in what is now New York.

The Iroquois built villages of longhouses made of poles bent in an inverted **U** and covered with bark. The longhouse, divided by a hallway down the middle, had rooms for as many as ten families, as well as rooms for meetings and ceremonies. A ***palisade*** made of vertical poles protected the village.

Around the village, the Iroquois grew corn,

Artist John White depicted various scenes of 1585 in the Indian village of Secotan on Roanoke Island, Virginia: (*a*) tomb of an Indian leader, (*b*) praying, (*c*) a heathen ceremony, (*d*) eating, (*e*) tobacco, (*f*) ripe cornfield, with a man on a platform to scare the birds away, (*g*) young corn, (*h*) newly sprouted corn, (*i*) pumpkins, (*k*) cooking.

beans, and squash. Women did much of the work. The men hunted game, such as deer and bear, from which they obtained skins and furs as well as meat. Fish, nuts, and wild berries added to their diet.

The Iroquois organized as clans (groups of families of common descent), which were divided into longhouse families. Each longhouse family might have several individual families. The oldest woman in the longhouse was head of the family. A council of old men called sachems (SAY chuhmz) governed the village, but the women family heads could appoint the sachems or remove them.

The Iroquois League was powerful and warlike, often attacking other Indian tribes in quarrels over hunting land. They took captives, some of whom they adopted into the tribe, while others they tortured and killed. The religion of the Iroquois included animism, the idea that every object in the natural world has a spirit. Since they thought these spirits deserved as much respect as their own, they were careful not to offend them.

Iroquois also believed in a supreme being, to whom they prayed and whom they tried to contact through dreams. Shamans (SHAH muhns) were people who supposedly were able to contact the spirit world. Most Iroquois believed in life after death, so they buried things like tools and weapons with the body of a dead person to help him in the next life. These beliefs had many similarities to those of the Canaanites and other heathen people who lacked knowledge of the true God.

"For the LORD is great, and greatly to be praised: he is to be feared above all gods. For all the gods of the nations are idols: but the LORD made the heavens" (Psalm 96:4, 5).

Indians of the Southeast

Indians of the Southeast lived in the region from present-day North Carolina south to the Gulf of Mexico and from the Atlantic Ocean west to the Mississippi River. These tribes included the Cherokee, Creek, Seminole,

Village of grass huts in the region of Kansas (Wichita Indians).

Choctaw, and Natchez. The Southeastern Indians lived in villages with one hundred or more houses made of poles covered with grass and mud. A village usually had a palisade for protection, and it included a mound where their temple was located.

The Southeast tribes were farmers, growing corn, squash, beans, melons, pumpkins, and tobacco in the rich soil. Men and women farmed and provided the food. Hunting also supplied food, especially deer and turkey. Women wove baskets and mats, made pottery, and tanned skins.

The village had a chief and a council. Some powerful chiefs ruled over numerous villages. The council consisted of warriors who decided important matters. Smoking tobacco was special to them and was done in connection with funerals, healing, and making peace.

Indians disguised in wolf skins, hunting buffalo.

Blackfoot Indians with a horse and a travois.

Indians of the Plains

The plains extended from Canada to the Gulf of Mexico and from the Mississippi River to the Rocky Mountains. Here lived tribes such as the Blackfoot, Cheyenne (shy AN), Comanche (kuh MAN chee), Crow, and Sioux (SOO). Many tribes moved through and into the plains from other areas.

Before the coming of white men, Plains Indians lived in villages near rivers and streams. They lived in earth lodges made of sod and brush supported by logs. In spring, the women would plant crops such as corn and beans near the villages.

In summer and again after the fall harvest, hunting parties went in search of bison (buffalo). The hunters lived in tepees, movable cone-shaped lodges of skins mounted on poles. Tepees were simple to set up and dismantle so that the hunters could easily move them about. They transported their belongings by using a ***travois*** (truh VOY), two poles joined together in a **V** shape and pulled by a dog while the other end dragged on the ground. The Indians did not have wheels or even horses.

Decorated tepees of the Plains Indians (Blackfoot tribe).

Buffalo hunting was a major part of life for the Plains Indians. They hunted buffalo on foot before they had horses. They killed them by using knives, spears, and bows and arrows, or by stampeding them over a cliff. The buffalo supplied them with meat, bones for tools, and hides for clothing, tepees, and containers. The women preserved buffalo meat by drying it. They made ***pemmican*** (PEHM ih kuhn) by crumbling the dried meat and mixing it with melted buffalo tallow; then they stored the pemmican in bags of bull's hide.

With the introduction of horses (brought by Spanish explorers), Plains Indians could hunt buffalo much more easily. Their way of life changed to living in tepees and hunting buffalo all the time. And since hunting was now easier, these Indians had more time for fighting.

Plains Indians fought over territory and horses, and they measured their greatness by counting coups (KOOZ). This was a system of honor received for heroic acts such as killing or touching an enemy, or for capturing a horse, weapon, or some other item in battle. The Comanche were especially known as fierce fighters.

Plains Indians believed in the powers of nature. They thought that certain animals, such as wolves, beavers, and bears, had special powers. They held an annual sun dance in which they danced, sang, and prayed to obtain help in farming, hunting, and fighting. Often this ceremony included rituals for seeking visions from the "Great Spirit," along with self-torture to fulfill a vow or receive pity from their gods.

Indians of the Southwest

The Southwest region included present-day Arizona, New Mexico, and parts of Texas. This area was inhabited by Hopi (HOH pee) and Zuni (ZOO nee) Indians, who were descendants of the Hohokam and Anasazi. These tribes and others are sometimes called Pueblo Indians. Later, the warlike Apache (uh PACH

Masked Hopi dancers of Arizona. The dancing was intended to bring visits from kachinas (spirits), who supposedly caused rain to fall and corn to grow.

ee) and Navajo (NAV uh hoh) invaded the Southwest region.

The Hopi illustrate the culture of the farming Indians that lived in this area. Hopi villages were pueblos made of sun-dried bricks (adobe). These houses were built one on top of another like apartment buildings, with one family's roof serving as another family's porch. The pueblos were divided into rooms for numerous families. People entered their houses by ladders that were set in holes in the roof. The ladders could then be pulled inside for protection.

The Hopi farmed in the desert. They carefully conserved any rainwater. They dug canals to irrigate their crops with water from a nearby river, and they planted their corn in trenches as deep as 12 inches (30 cm). By these means they were able to grow corn, squash, beans, and tobacco. The Hopi also raised turkeys for meat and feathers. They had great skill in weaving cloth and making pottery and baskets.

The Hopi were deeply religious. An important part of a pueblo was the kiva (KEE vuh), an underground room used for religious ceremonies. This room was symbolic of the spirit

Hogan of Navajo Indians in Arizona.

underworld, where the Hopi believed human souls went after death. They thought that the underworld spirits, called kachinas (kuh CHEE nuhz), could send rain and bring good harvests. They did not realize that all good things come from God and that they were actually serving evil spirits.

The Hopi did believe in a universal spirit. They engaged in snake dances and other elaborate ceremonies to please the spirits. The Hopi were generally peaceful people who emphasized the good of the entire community rather than the benefit of individuals.

The Navajo Indians lived in hogans made of logs and mud. They were a warlike, hunting tribe at one time, but later they raised sheep. Their descendants still herd sheep in the vast deserts of Arizona, near their Hopi neighbors.

Indians of the Far West

The Far West region included California, the Great Basin, and the Columbia Plateau in the American West. Tribes of this area included the Pomo (POH moh), Shoshone (shoh SHOH nee), Paiute (py YOOT), and Nez Perce (NEHS PURS).

Crude shelters of Great Basin Indians in northwestern California. Look carefully to see the children sitting beside the huts.

Most California Indians lived in villages with men as leaders. Shamans and supernatural spirits were part of their religion. Some of the people ate foods made from acorn flour. Others supported themselves by fishing along the Pacific coast. Most were roaming foragers rather than settled farmers.

Great Basin Indians lived on poor land. Whites called them "diggers" because they had to dig for roots to eat. These Indians also ate nuts and berries, as well as small animals like snakes and rodents. They hunted rabbits for food and skins, and they even ate insects. Small bands often lived in simple shelters as they moved about, searching for food. They believed in powerful animal spirits, and women shamans served as healers.

Plateau Indians lived in communities along riverbanks. During winter, they lived in houses of logs and earth that were partially underground. They fished, mostly for salmon, and gathered wild plants such as carrots and berries. Deer, elk, and rabbits added meat to their diets. After white men arrived, the fur trade and horses changed their lifestyle in various ways.

Other Indian culture areas included the Northwest Coast Indians, the Subarctic Indians, and the Arctic Indians. Most of these areas were located in what is now Canada. The Arctic peoples were the Inuit (IHN yoo iht), better known as Eskimos.

Focus for Thought

5. What is an Indian culture area?
6. List the five main Indian culture areas, and give their locations and boundaries in terms of the present-day United States.
7. Copy and complete the following chart. The spaces for Indians in the Northeast are filled in for you. (You may leave a blank space if the text gives no information for that category.)

	Living Quarters	Economic Activities	Tribal Government	Religion
Northeast	Longhouse villages	farming, hunting	Sachems (appointed by women), five-nation confederacy	animism, shamans, a supreme being, life after death
Southeast				
Plains				
Southwest				
Far West				

3. INDIAN CONTRIBUTIONS

The coming of the white man had drastic effects on the Indians. But the Indians likewise influenced the white men in many ways. The collision of two different cultures often resulted in violence and other tragic results.

The Columbian Exchange

With the coming of the Europeans came a great intermingling of new ideas, words, foods, and cultures. This is called the "Columbian exchange" (because of Columbus). From the Europeans, Indians received horses and sheep. The Europeans also brought the Bible and Christianity, even though many did not live as the Bible teaches.

Europeans introduced new crops, such as wheat, sugar cane, and bananas. They also brought kettles, traps, guns, and liquor. Many Indians caught diseases such as smallpox and measles, against which they had no defense. Thousands of Indians died in the resulting epidemics.

From the Indians, the Europeans received help for surviving in the new land. They learned how to hunt and fish and how to grow new crops. These included tomatoes, corn, potatoes, peanuts, and pumpkins. White men also adopted a number of Indian inventions, such as the canoe, the hammock, and snowshoes.

Another important Indian contribution is names and words. *Raccoon, skunk, moose, pecan, kayak, toboggan,* and *moccasin* are all words of Indian origin. The most common Indian words are place names. These include the names of states (Alaska, Kentucky, Utah), cities (Chicago, Omaha, Seattle), and rivers (Mississippi, Susquehanna).

Indians engaged in more fighting after the Europeans came. When the Indians had

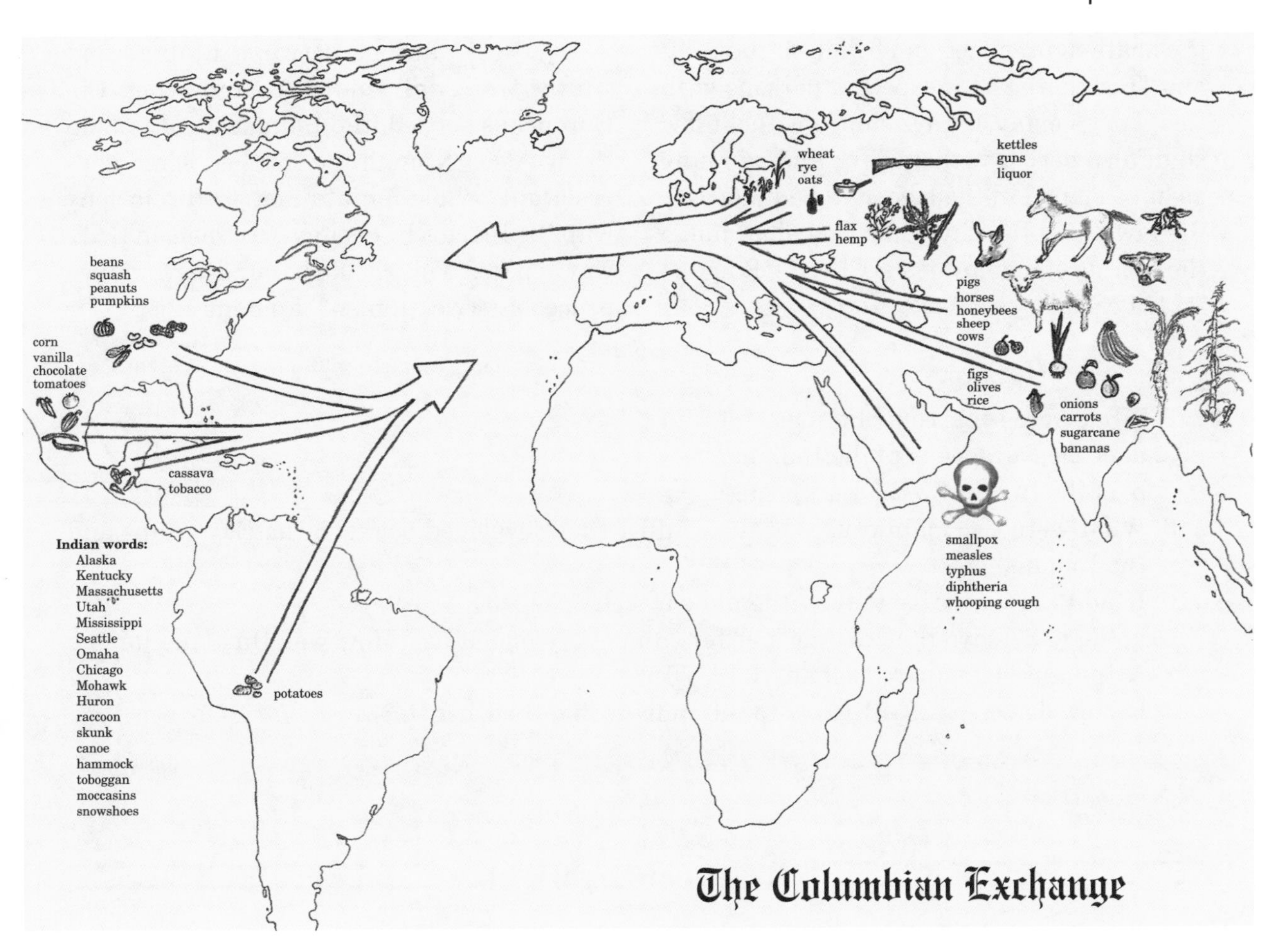

The Columbian Exchange

horses and guns, hunting took less time and they had more time for war. Tribes such as the Comanche and Apache roamed the Central Plains, raiding and terrorizing other Indian tribes and stealing horses from them.

The Collision of Cultures

When the Europeans came, their culture clashed with the cultures of native Americans. This brought on a long struggle between the Indians and the Europeans, in which the Indians fought to maintain their ways of life and the Europeans fought to establish farms and towns.

One cause of conflict was the economic difference. Indians had no concept of private land ownership as Europeans did. They considered the land as belonging to everyone, in the same way as the sea or the air. Also, Indians believed the earth was sacred, and they tried not to offend their nature gods. Most Europeans believed that man should "subdue" the earth according to God's command in Genesis—though many were merely seeking their own selfish advantage, instead of being good stewards of God's creation.

Another cause of conflict was the religious difference. The white men saw the Indians as savages to be converted. When most Indians refused to accept the newcomers' religion, the whites fought against them in the same spirit as the Catholics had fought the Muslims in Europe.

In the conflict that raged for more than three centuries, both Indians and white men did wrong, and each side misunderstood the other. Europeans had the Bible, so they were more accountable. But that did not excuse the heathen practices and beliefs of the Indians. "For there is no respect of persons with God. For as many as have sinned without law shall also perish without law: and as many as have sinned in the law shall be judged by the law . . . in the day when God shall judge the secrets of men by Jesus Christ" (Romans 2:11, 12, 16).

Not all relations between Indians and whites were unfriendly. At first when the Europeans settled, the Indians tried to help them. Also, through the conflict, some nonresistant people maintained good relations with the Indians by dealing with them in God's way of peace. This should be our desire, to "live peaceably with all men" (Romans 12:18).

Focus for Thought

8. What were some contributions
   a. of the Europeans to the Indians?
   b. of the Indians to the Europeans?
9. What were two main causes of the conflict that developed between the Europeans and the Indians?
10. Read Paul's message to the Athenians in Acts 17:22–31.
    a. Verse 27 says that God is "not far from every one of us." How was this true for the Indians? (Compare Romans 1:19, 20.)
    b. How do verses 29–31 apply to the Indians and their beliefs?

Historical Highlights

A. Matching: Culture Areas

Match the culture areas to the descriptions. Letters may be used more than once.

1. Area from North Carolina to the Gulf of Mexico and from the Atlantic Ocean to the Mississippi River.
2. Area from the Mississippi River to the Rocky Mountains.
3. Area where Indians lived in longhouses.
4. Area where Indians had houses of poles covered with grass and mud.
5. Area where Indians grew corn, beans, melons, and pumpkins on good farmland.
6. Area in present-day Arizona and New Mexico.
7. Area where warriors counted coups.
8. Area where Indians prepared pemmican.
9. Area where Indians used acorn flour.
10. Area where Indians herded sheep.
11. Area of sun dance tradition.
12. Area between the Great Lakes and North Carolina.
13. Area in California, the Great Basin, and the Columbia Plateau.
14. Area where Indians used travois.

a. Northeast
b. Southeast
c. Plains
d. Southwest
e. Far West

B. Matching: Tribes and Groups

Match the tribes or groups to the statements below. Letters may be used more than once.

1. Indians that were divided into clans.
2. Culture that made large piles of earth for ceremonies and burial.
3. Tribe that lived in hogans.
4. Tribe that lived in pueblos.
5. Tribe that lived on the Central Plains.
6. Group that adopted some captives and killed others.
7. Tribe that used kivas.
8. Indians who lived along riverbanks and fished for salmon.
9. Eskimos who lived in the Arctic.
10. Indians governed by sachems.
11. Indians who made foods from acorn flour or went fishing.
12. Plains tribe of fierce fighters.
13. Indians called "diggers" who lived on poor land.
14. Tribes called the Five Nations.
15. Tribe that farmed with irrigation.

a. California Indians
b. Comanche
c. Great Basin Indians
d. Hopi
e. Inuit
f. Iroquois
g. Mound Builders
h. Navajo
i. Plateau Indians

C. Matching: Terms

1. Customs and values associated with a certain group of people.
2. Indian village of multilevel apartment houses made of stone or adobe.
3. Underground room used for religious ceremonies.
4. One of the old men who governed the Iroquois.
5. Pair of poles drawn by a dog or horse, used by Plains Indians to carry their belongings.
6. Manmade object, such as a tool or weapon, that is of interest in archaeology.
7. Region where a number of Indian tribes had basically the same culture.
8. Fence made of vertical poles.
9. Bricks made of sun-dried clay.
10. Dwelling made of poles bent in a **U** shape and covered with bark.
11. Dry, crumbled meat mixed with buffalo tallow.

a. adobe
b. artifact
c. culture
d. culture area
e. kiva
f. longhouse
g. palisade
h. pemmican
i. pueblo
j. sachem
k. travois

D. Matching: Lifestyles

1. Areas where Indians obtained food mainly by hunting (two answers).
2. Area where Indians obtained food mainly by farming.
3. Areas where Indians obtained food by both hunting and farming (two answers).
4. Area where Indians lived the most peaceably.
5. Areas where Indians wandered about as nomads (two answers).

a. Northeast
b. Southeast
c. Plains
d. Southwest
e. Far West

E. Deeper Discussion

1. Give a Biblical explanation of Indian origins.
2. How did different Indian cultures develop?
3. Many primitive peoples have practiced animism. What is animism?
4. a. Why did the Columbian exchange take place?
   b. What were some results?
5. In the 1800s, white men almost wiped out the great buffalo herds in the West. Why did this cause severe hardship for the Plains Indians?
6. When the Europeans brought guns and horses to the American plains, the Plains Indians quickly recognized the value of these things. How did guns and horses affect the lifestyle of the Plains Indians?
7. How were some people able to get along well with the Indians?

F. Chronology and Geography

1. Give the approximate number of *centuries* between each of the following things and the arrival of Columbus.
   a. The decline of the Hopewell people.
   b. The rise of the Mississippian Mound Builders.
   c. The end of the early southwestern farming societies.
2. Trace the outline of Map C in the Map Section, and label it "Indians of North America." (You do not need to trace the rivers or the outlines of Greenland and Iceland.)
   a. Draw boundary lines to show the five main Indian culture areas discussed in the second section of this chapter. Also draw boundary lines to show the Northwest Coast, the Subarctic, and the Arctic areas. Label these areas using all capital letters.
   b. Label the following groups or tribes: Iroquois, Huron, Algonquin, Delaware, Cherokee, Creek, Seminole, Choctaw, Natchez, Blackfoot, Cheyenne, Comanche, Crow, Sioux, Hopi, Zuni, Apache, Navajo, Pomo, Shoshone, Paiute, and Nez Perce.

This Inuit hunter has killed a seal.

Many old Spanish missions can still be seen in California. This one at San Juan Capistrano is famous for the swallows that depart in October and return about March 19 each year.

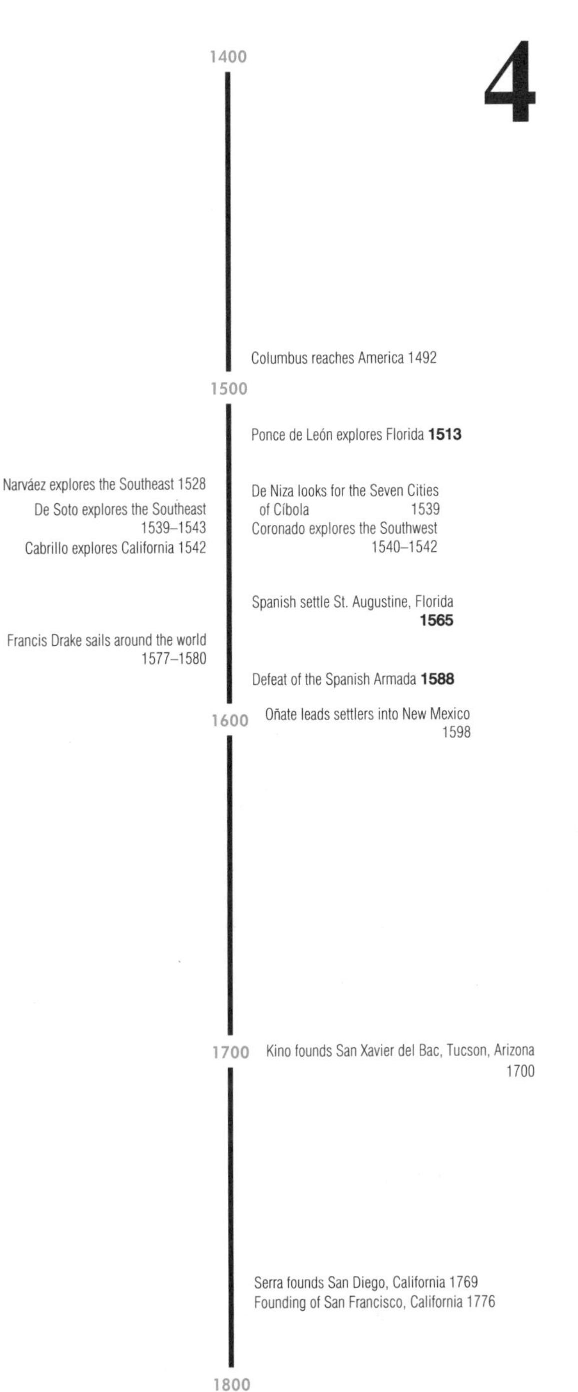

4 Spanish Exploration and Settlement

1. Spanish Exploration of North America
    - Spanish Exploration of Florida and the Southeast
    - Spanish Exploration of the Southwest
2. Spanish Settlement of North America
    - The Spanish Mission System
    - Spanish Settlement in Florida
    - Spanish Settlements in the Southwest
3. Spanish Decline
    - Other Countries Weaken Spain
    - The Spanish Armada
    - Spanish Influences

"He that is greedy of gain troubleth his own house."
Proverbs 15:27

Spanish Exploration and Settlement

Focus for Reading

After Columbus's discovery, the Spanish explored and settled a large part of southern and southwestern North America. These Spaniards had two chief motives: to find gold and other riches, and to convert the Indians to Catholicism. Because of these motives, they clashed many times with the native peoples in the New World. Spanish power declined later, which allowed other nations—particularly England—to colonize most of North America. Yet the Spanish left a lasting influence on the land and its people. Three sections in this chapter describe the activities of the Spanish in North America.

1. Spanish Exploration of North America
2. Spanish Settlement of North America
3. Spanish Decline

1. SPANISH EXPLORATION OF NORTH AMERICA

Beginning in the 1500s, Spain built a huge empire in the New World. In 1521, Hernando Cortés (kor TEHZ) conquered the Aztecs in Mexico and established the colony of New Spain. About ten years later (1532), Francisco Pizarro (pih ZAHR oh) overthrew the Incas in Peru. Spanish conquistadors (kahn KWIHS tuh dawrs) greedily sought gold as well as adventure and fame, and Spanish rulers tried to make Spain the richest and strongest nation in Europe. The Spanish also wanted to spread the Roman Catholic faith to the natives. These goals led them to colonize the Americas—first Central America, then South America, and finally parts of North America.

Spanish Exploration of Florida and the Southeast

Ponce de León in Florida. Among the first Spanish explorers in North America was **Ponce de León** (PAWN say day lay AWN). While governor of Puerto Rico, which he had conquered in 1509, this man heard stories about a "Fountain of Youth" in a northern country. The stories said that if a person drank water from this spring or bathed in it, he would become young again. Ponce de León set out on an expedition toward the north in 1513. According to legend, his goal was to find the Fountain of Youth.

Ponce de León never found such a spring, but he did find a long peninsula that he named Florida ("full of flowers"). He may have given it that name because he saw many flowers along the coast or because it was Easter week, called *Pascua Florida* in Spanish.

After doing some exploring, Ponce de León left Florida and obtained permission from the

Ponce de León seeking for the Fountain of Youth in 1513. According to legend, the Spanish explorer was searching for the mythical fountain when he discovered Florida. The fountain was supposed to be on an island called Bimini, now part of the Bahamas.

After discovering the Mississippi River in May 1541, Hernando de Soto and his men built boats and crossed it, exploring land west of the river. De Soto was later buried in the Mississippi.

Spanish king to settle the new land. He did not return until 1521; and when he did, he was wounded in a battle with the Indians and died soon afterward. Even though his settlement was never established, Ponce de León did claim Florida for Spain. Other Spaniards settled there later and made Florida a foothold for further exploration.

Narváez in Florida. Soon **Pánfilo de Narváez** (PAHN fee loh day nahr VAH ays) gained permission to move into Florida. He landed at what is now Tampa Bay, on Florida's west coast, in April 1528. There he divided his men into two groups and sent the ships on to seek a good port along the Gulf coast while he and the rest marched inland to seek riches.

But Narváez never found the rich cities he looked for, and many of his men died from sickness and Indian attacks. Then he could not make contact with his ships in the Gulf—for they had sailed back to Spain! Desperate, he and his men built flimsy boats and tried to sail to Mexico. But storms on the Gulf of Mexico separated the boats, and Narváez perished at sea. The survivors wrecked on the shores of Texas in November 1528.

Among the survivors were about eighty men, including **Cabeza de Vaca** (kah BAY sah day VAH kah). Less than twenty remained alive until the next spring, and they were soon captured by the Indians. Finally in 1534, de Vaca, a black slave named Estevanico (ehs tay vahn EE koh), and two others ran away and headed by land for Mexico. They wandered in the harsh desert for eighteen months, surviving among the Indians by pretending to be medicine men. In 1536, they finally met some Spaniards in northern Mexico, from where they traveled to Mexico City. They had not found riches, but they had learned much about the land.

Hernando de Soto in the Southeast. **Hernando de Soto** (ur NAHN doh day SOH toh) was appointed to seek the rich Indian civilization that Narváez had failed to find. De Soto led an expedition that landed at Tampa Bay in May 1539. He explored north through what is now Georgia and the Carolinas. Then he traveled west through Alabama, reaching the Mississippi River by 1541. De Soto and his party were the first white men to cross the Mississippi.

Continuing west from the great river, de Soto explored present-day Arkansas and Oklahoma. Then he caught a fever and died in May 1542. To keep vengeful Indians from learning of his death, de Soto's men weighted his body and sank it in the Mississippi River. But they were not able to reach Mexico by land. So they built makeshift boats and floated down the Mississippi and across the Gulf to Mexico in 1543.

The expedition seemed a total failure. It had stirred up Indian hostilities and had failed to find gold. However, it did greatly increase geographical knowledge of the southeast region. But the first permanent Spanish settlement in Florida would not be founded until 1565.

Spanish Exploration of the Southwest

From Mexico, the Spanish moved northward until they had settled the American Southwest. Their motivation at first was to find riches, as it was elsewhere. Later, the Spanish moved north to gain land and to establish a ring of forts to protect Mexico from other nations. They also wanted to convert the Indians to Catholicism. Few of these Spaniards understood the meaning of true spiritual conversion.

Marcos de Niza in New Mexico. When Cabeza de Vaca and Estevanico arrived in Mexico City, the stories of their wanderings aroused great interest. Though the country through which they had passed was not rich, they had heard rumors of a rich land to the north. The ruler of New Spain thought this rich land could be the fabled Seven Cities of Cíbola (SEE boh lah), which according to legend were made entirely of gold. To search this out, a group led by Friar **Marcos de Niza** (day NEE zuh) and guided by Estevanico went north in 1539, the same year de Soto began exploring the Southeast. They were to survey the country and report back to New Spain.

De Niza sent Estevanico ahead as a guide, along with some Indians. Estevanico was to send back messengers with crosses when he discovered settlements—the larger the cross, the bigger the city. Soon a messenger came with a man-sized cross, and de Niza was excited indeed. Estevanico had found Zuni pueblos, which glistened like gold in the sun, and he thought they must be Cíbola.

Then disaster struck. The Zuni killed Estevanico and the Indians, but two escaped and reported to de Niza. He pressed on to "Cíbola" but only viewed the place from a distance. Then he returned to Mexico City and gave a fantastic report about the riches he had seen.

Francisco de Coronado in the Southwest. **Francisco de Coronado** (koh roh NAH doh) prepared a large force to look for the golden cities. In 1540, he set out from Mexico, accompanied by Friar Marcos de Niza and hundreds of soldiers and Indians. When they reached the first of the "Seven Cities" in July, they were shocked. De Niza had been lying! Cíbola was nothing more than a Zuni pueblo of about eight hundred people, described by the Spanish chronicler as "a little, crowded village, looking as if it had been crumpled all up together." The rest of the Seven Cities were also small pueblo villages. De Niza was sent back to Mexico City.

Coronado did not find the golden cities, but he did find trouble with the Indians. The Zuni Indians fought a vicious battle against the Spaniards but were subdued. The rest of

Coronado and his men looked vainly for the legendary Seven Cities of Cíbola. One group of searchers became the first Europeans to see the Grand Canyon.

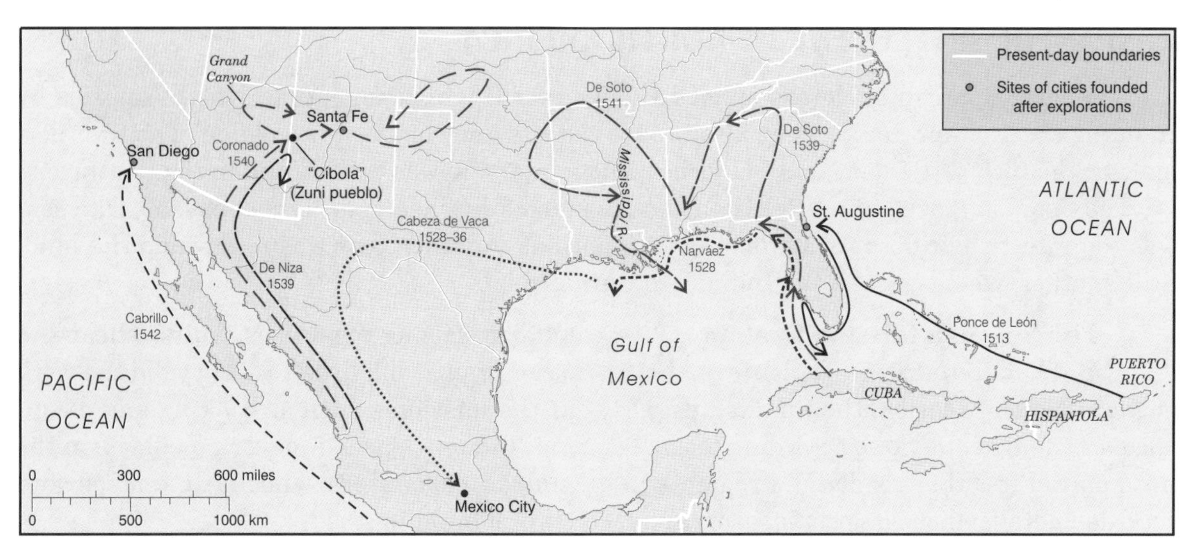

Spanish Explorations in North America

the Seven Cities pueblos soon surrendered also. From the Indians, Coronado heard more tales of rich lands to the northwest, so he continued his exploration. One party went in search of a great river that was reported to be west of them. They discovered the Grand Canyon but found no gold.

Coronado's expedition then moved northeast in pursuit of another supposedly rich land named Quivira (kee VEER ah). On this journey he engaged in more fighting with the Indians and even burned some at the stake. Clever Indians kept leading him on with tales of Quivira riches, and Coronado continued exploring through what is now New Mexico, Oklahoma, and Kansas. He found much dry, barren country as well as vast, fertile plains and hordes of bison—but no gold. Finally realizing that they had been deceived, Coronado and his men straggled back to Mexico City in 1542, a dejected band of fewer than one hundred soldiers. Coronado lost his fortune and his reputation, and he died in obscurity twelve years later at the age of forty-four.

Cabrillo in California. In 1542, **Juan Rodríguez Cabrillo** (hwahn roh DREE gays kah BREE yoh) sailed along the Pacific coast of North America. He discovered San Diego Bay and claimed it for Spain. After Cabrillo died in 1543, his crew continued northward as far as modern Oregon, claiming the Pacific coast of North America for Spain.

These explorations failed to establish Spanish settlements in North America. Because of Coronado's failure to find gold, the Spanish concentrated more on developing Mexico. Not until fifty years later did the Spanish try to colonize the Southwest.

Focus for Thought

1. Name the Spanish explorer who discovered Florida, and tell when he discovered it.
2. a. What two Spaniards explored southeastern North America while searching for wealth?
   b. What major river did one of them discover?
3. Which Spaniard went out in 1540 and explored the southwestern part of what is now the United States?
4. What man claimed California for Spain?
5. What were the results of the Spanish explorations in the Southeast and the Southwest?

2. SPANISH SETTLEMENT OF NORTH AMERICA

The early Spanish explorers opened the way for Spanish settlers in North America by claiming the land for Spain. They also broadened the knowledge of the region. The first permanent Spanish settlement was in Florida, and a later one was established in the Southwest.

The Spanish moved into these areas not so much for riches as for other reasons. One goal was to protect their borders against foreign nations. Another goal was to develop the land. Still another was to convert the Indians to Catholicism.

The Spanish Mission System

A Methodical Plan. To achieve their goals in North America, the Spanish developed a system of ***missions*** according to a definite plan. First they explored a region and recorded details about its people, geography, plants, and animals. Then Catholic missionaries moved in and settled the Indians in tightly controlled villages. A village usually included a church building, some houses, some farmland, and a fort called a ***presidio*** (prih SEE dee oh) to keep order and protect the mission.

Civilizing the Indians. When the Indians were settled, the missionaries worked at teaching them Roman Catholic doctrines and practices. They also tried to civilize the Indians by teaching them Spanish customs and the Spanish language. The Indians learned to farm, raising vegetables, fruits, wheat and other grains, and livestock. They did the work at the missions, such as cooking and cleaning. Indians learned to work as blacksmiths and as carpenters who built houses and church buildings.

The Indian missions were strictly controlled because the Spanish believed in ***absolutism***. This is a system in which one person (usually a king) has complete authority over everyone under him, and no one may question the decrees of a person higher in rank. The mission Indians were not free, but had to obey the orders of their superiors and submit to the discipline of the mission routine. They could not leave the mission once they were baptized. Any surplus they produced went to the mission.

The Spanish missions were successful

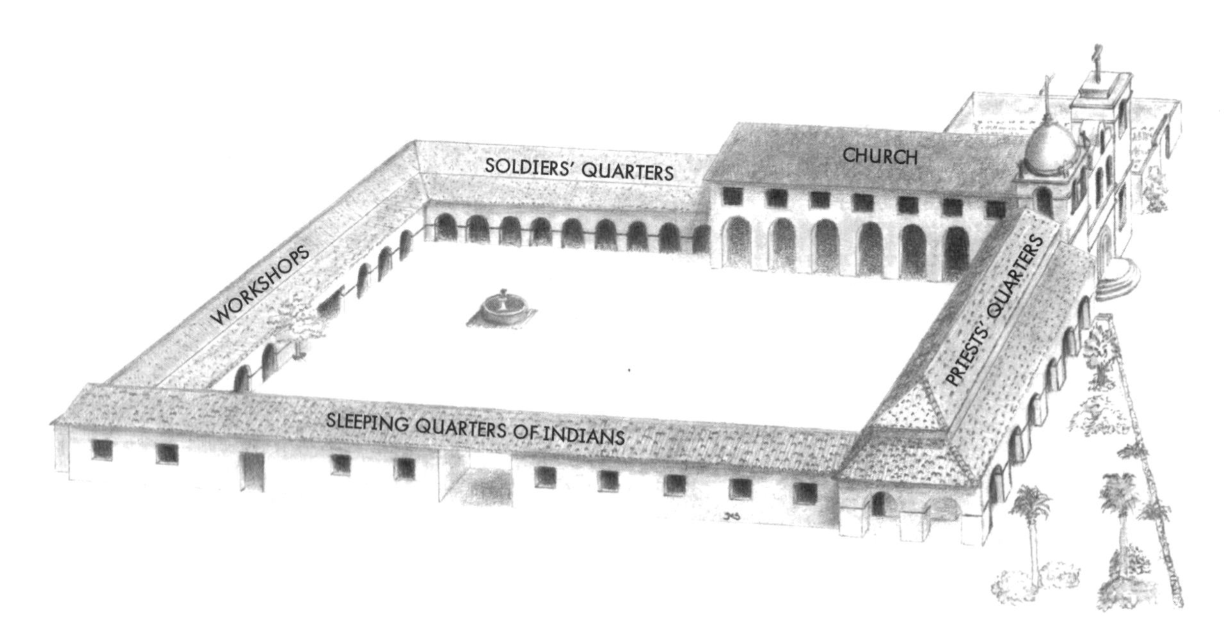

A Spanish Mission

only in part. Many Indians returned to their former religion and lifestyle at the first opportunity. Others, such as the roving Apaches, were never civilized or converted to Catholicism.

The Spanish mission called the Alamo. A religious procession emerges from the chapel, bearing a cross and lighted tapers. The Indians at the right show respect, but others go on with their work.

Spanish Settlement in Florida

The first Spanish settlement in North America was established to drive out Huguenots (French Protestants) who had trespassed on Spanish territory. These Protestants settled near present-day Jacksonville, Florida, in 1564. One year later, the Spanish determined to drive the Huguenot "heretics" and trespassers from their Catholic land.

The Spanish built a fort called St. Augustine about 35 miles (56 km) south of the French. From St. Augustine, they attacked the French and destroyed their settlement, killing about nine hundred men, women, and children. The town of St. Augustine, planted in 1565, became the first permanent town built by Europeans on land that later became part of the United States.

From St. Augustine, the Spanish built missions in western Florida and in Georgia. This later led to conflict with the English and the Indians. Florida remained in Spanish hands for most of the years until 1821.

Spanish Settlements in the Southwest

England was gaining strength in the late 1500s. The Spanish became concerned that the English might establish colonies to their north from which to invade Mexico. So the Spanish began building settlements to defend their northern ***frontier***. This movement began in the 1590s, about fifty years after Coronado's expedition.

The Spanish in New Mexico. In 1598, **Juan de Oñate** (HWAHN day oh NYAH tay) led a group of soldiers, settlers, friars, and livestock to start the first colony in New Mexico. Oñate chose an Indian pueblo for his capital and ordered the Indians to leave. This town was renamed San Juan (san WAHN). The Spanish proceeded to take the region on both sides of the Rio Grande from the Indians. But the outposts were abandoned in 1601 by all but a few Spaniards. Oñate continued to explore throughout the region.

Laying out of St. Augustine, Florida, in 1565. This Spanish city became the oldest permanent European settlement in what is now the United States.

The Spanish tried again in 1609, partly because they wanted to convert the Indians. This time they laid out a new town on the banks of the Rio Grande to be the capital of New Mexico. They called it Santa Fe (san tuh FAY), which means "holy faith"; this is the oldest capital city in the United States. Santa Fe established the Spanish firmly in the region. By 1680, about twenty-five hundred whites lived in the region of New Mexico and western Texas.

Indian Rebellion. Even though many missions had been planted and the Indians seemed to be accepting Catholicism, Indian bitterness was increasing. The Indians in the province of New Mexico suffered mistreatment from both church and state. The church made the Indians work long hours in the fields, vineyards, and gardens. The greedy and cruel civil leaders forced the Indians to work for them. The Indians became bondmen in their own land.

In 1680, an Indian named Popé (poh PAY) united the Pueblo Indians against the Spanish. They intended to destroy every Spaniard and rid their land of every trace of Spanish culture. The furious Indians killed four hundred Spaniards and destroyed their homes, farms, and churches. Within eleven days, almost two thousand Spanish settlers fled south to El Paso.

After Popé died in 1688, the Spanish returned to Santa Fe to reconquer the Pueblos in 1692. The Indians were given the choice to surrender or be destroyed. They chose to surrender, and the Spanish again ruled the land of the Pueblo Indians. The valleys and mountains surrounding Santa Fe became populated with settlers from the south.

The Spanish in Texas. When La Salle

Following is part of a report on a Spanish mission, written by a friar fourteen years after the San Antonio missions were established.

In the mission pueblo there were living at this time three hundred and eleven Indians of both sexes and all ages. Of these, two hundred and seventy-five were baptized [converts] and thirty-six were being instructed in the doctrines. . . .

The Indian pueblo, where the [converts] lived, consisted of two rows of small huts built on either side of a [water ditch]. These were built of adobe bricks and were generally roofed with straw. Along each row of houses there was a sort of street. . . .

The mission was well supplied with lands for the raising of crops and the pasturing of stock. . . . All the land under cultivation was irrigated by a large ditch which brought an abundant supply of water from the river. All the products raised by the [converts] were used for their maintenance.

To cultivate the fields and carry on the other work about the mission, [this particular mission] had twenty-three yoke of oxen, . . . a blacksmith shop, . . . a carpenter shop, . . . and all the necessary chisels and hammers for stone carving and masonry.

In the room where the women and such men as were not capable of working in the fields were employed, there were three looms, six pairs of cards [for carding wool], eight combs, six shuttles, and twenty spinning wheels. To weave the various kinds of cloth, the [converts] used wool from the mission sheep and the cotton raised on the mission farms.

claimed the Mississippi River valley for France in 1682, the Spanish became alarmed at this new enemy on their frontier. They sent an expedition to destroy the new French settlement as soon as they heard of it. But the French fort had already been destroyed by Indians.

The Spanish founded a few missions by 1693, but these were abandoned because of disease, crop failures, and opposition from the Indians. When the French settled New Orleans along the Mississippi in 1718, the Spanish once more set out to plant missions in Texas. One of these was San Antonio, founded in 1718. Its first chapel was called the Alamo. The growth of Texas was slow, partly because of raids by the fierce Comanche Indians.

Missions in Arizona and California. A Jesuit priest named **Eusebio Kino** (ay oo SAY bee oh KEE noh) first built missions among the Pima Indians in Mexico. Then he moved north into Arizona, and in 1700 he established San Xavier del Bac (sahn ZAY vih ur dehl BAHK) near modern Tucson, Arizona. Later he planted six more missions in present-day Arizona.

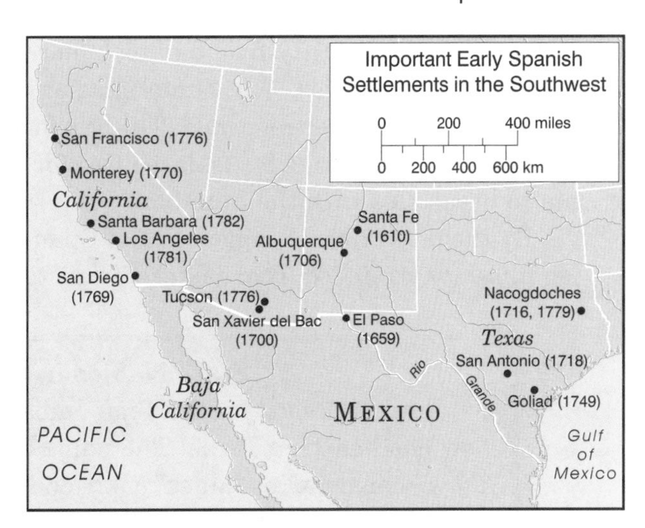

Spanish mission of San Xavier del Bac near Tucson, Arizona. This is the famous mission founded by Eusebio Kino in 1700. It is still in use as a Roman Catholic church.

Kino's work led to the colonizing of Baja (BAH hah) California; that is, Lower California. The Spanish did not begin settling Alta (Upper) California until the 1760s, when English and Russian explorers arrived in that region. A Franciscan friar named **Junípero Serra** (hoo NEE peh roh SEHR rah) built San Diego in 1769, the first of twenty-one Franciscan missions in California. (The Franciscans were an order of Catholic monks.)

Serra then directed the building of nine more missions. By 1776, at the same time the Americans on the east coast were declaring independence from Britain, the Spanish founded San Francisco. Los Angeles was founded in 1781, and the last Franciscan mission was built in 1823.

In the 1770s, a group of Spaniards exploring the Arizona-California border met some Yuma Indians who aided them and asked for Spanish missionaries to come. Two missions were set up among the Yuma by 1780. However, the missionaries allowed their cattle to graze in the Indians' cornfields and took the best farmland for themselves. The vengeful Indians turned on the Spanish settlers, massacred fifty-five, and took more than seventy captives. The Yuma missions closed down and never reopened. This crushing defeat set the stage for isolated California to break ties with the Spanish.

By the late 1700s, a ragged line of Spanish missions stretched from eastern Texas to central California. These served as the northern outposts of Spanish power in America, and formed a barrier against Spain's enemies. Nevertheless, American traders and settlers would soon overwhelm the few Spaniards in the region, and the Southwest would become part of Anglo-America instead of Latin America.

State Names in the Spanish Southwest

Texas is named for the Tejas Indians, a group of tribes that lived in what is now northeastern Texas. The name comes from the Spanish pronunciation of *Tejas,* which means "allies" or "friends."

Arizona is derived from the Indian word *arizonac,* which is thought to mean "few (or little) springs."

California is supposed to be named for a mythical island of that name, which was said to be in the region. A Spanish author wrote that the island was "very close to the Earthly Paradise" and that the weapons of its inhabitants were "all of gold, as well as the harness of the wild beasts which they ride after taming, for there is no other metal on the whole island." Queen Califia was said to rule the mythical island.

Focus for Thought

6. a. What were the goals of the Spanish missions?
   b. What was the purpose of the presidios?
7. How successful were the Spanish in converting the Indians?
8. Why did the Spanish try to settle New Mexico in the 1590s and again in the early 1600s? Give two reasons.
9. Why did the Spanish begin settlements in eastern Texas in the late 1600s and early 1700s?
10. What two men brought Spanish settlers to California in the 1700s?
11. a. In what year was St. Augustine founded? San Francisco?
    b. How much time passed between these years?
12. In what part of the present United States were the Spanish missions located?

3. SPANISH DECLINE

For a whole century, Spain faced almost no competition in the New World. But as other European nations saw Spain grow rich and powerful, they too wanted a share of America's riches. Also, by the 1500s, some nations had broken away from the Roman Catholic Church and had become Protestant. As the defender of Catholicism, Spain wanted to force those other nations back into the Catholic Church.

However, "the most High ruleth in the kingdom of men." Instead of continuing to rise in power, Spain began to decline and eventually lost her possessions in North America.

Other Countries Weaken Spain

European Trade Warfare. The Spanish colonies were allowed to trade only with Spain. In spite of this, ships from other nations traded secretly with those colonies. Many Spanish colonists were glad for this secret trade because the foreign goods were cheaper and arrived more often. But the secret trade reduced the profits that Spain made from her colonies.

Another form of trade warfare was piracy. Pirate ships from the Netherlands, France, and England attacked Spanish ships and stole their treasures. They also raided Spanish colonies along the seacoast. The rulers of these nations did not officially approve of piracy, but they looked the other way as long as the pirates attacked only the Spanish.

Rivalry With England. In the late 1500s, England became strong enough to challenge the Spanish domination of the sea. English raiders were daring sea captains whom the Spanish called pirates but the English called ***sea dogs***.

One English captain was **Francis Drake**, who went on a raiding trip in 1577. He rounded the southern tip of South America and sailed north along the west coast, making one raid after another on the unsuspecting Spanish. Loaded with treasure, Drake did not want to run the risk of returning by the way he had come. So he started for home by heading west across the Pacific! He sailed to the East Indies, from there southwest to round the tip of Africa, and then north to England by 1580. Drake had circled the earth, the first man to do so since the time of Magellan.

The Spanish Armada

The English were delighted with Drake, but the Spanish were furious. When **King Philip II** demanded that Drake be beheaded, **Elizabeth I**, queen of England, made him a knight instead. Enraged, Philip decided to punish the English for their robberies. He strengthened the Spanish navy for a number of years, and in 1588 he launched the Invincible Armada (ar MAH duh), a fleet of 130 ships, to attack England. These ships were to carry the Spanish army from the Netherlands to invade England.

As a devout Roman Catholic, King Philip felt sure that God would grant victory to the Spanish. Was it not their duty to punish England for leaving the Holy Mother Church and becoming a Protestant nation? But the mission ended in disaster for the Spanish. The English attacked them in the narrow English Channel, where the small, light English ships outmaneuvered the huge, clumsy Spanish ships. English sailors sent burning fire ships adrift, which blew into the Spanish fleet and scattered them. The Armada never reached the Spanish army in the Netherlands, which was to attack England.

Queen Elizabeth knighting Francis Drake in 1581. Drake had raided Spanish settlements along the west coast of South America and then sailed around the world. In 1588, Drake led one squadron of English ships in the battle against the Spanish Armada.

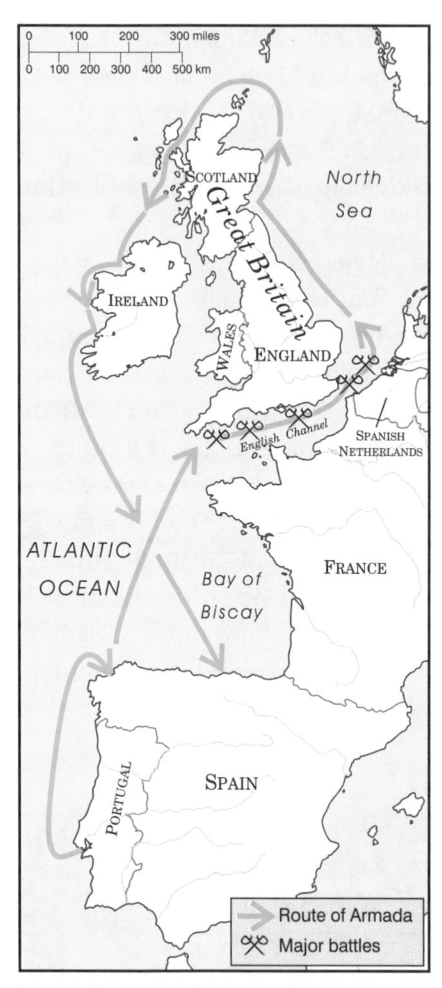

Route of the Armada

The remaining Spanish ships tried to reach home by sailing north around Great Britain. Off the northern end of the island, they ran into severe storms that wrecked more of the ships. Only half of them returned to Spain. The English said, "God blew with His winds, and they were scattered."

The defeat of the Spanish Armada marked a major turning point in history. Although it is not correct to say that God was on the side of England, He does accomplish some of His purposes by the "stormy wind fulfilling his word" (Psalm 148:8). From that time on, Spain was no longer the "Mistress of the Sea." She continued to collect treasures and plant colonies in the New World, but her power was waning. This allowed other nations to establish colonies in America.

England strengthened her influence in the New World and gained a foothold on the east coast of North America. This land did not yield gold and silver, but the settlements established there would eventually become the most powerful and wealthy nations in the New World. The language, customs, and freedoms of England were transplanted there, and its colonies were Protestant rather than Catholic.

Spanish Influences

Though Spanish power declined, the Spanish influence on Anglo-America continued. That influence is still evident today in a number of ways.

New Animals and Crops. The Spanish brought horses to America. These spread from Mexico throughout the West over about two hundred years, drastically changing Indian ways of life. The Spanish also brought cattle. When settlers in Texas crossed their stock with wild cattle escaped from the Spanish, the result was the Texas longhorn. These tall, gaunt, narrow-hipped cattle had enormous horns measuring up to 8 or 9 feet (2 to 3 m) from tip to tip. The Spanish brought sheep too, which flourished in the dry Southwest and became an important part of Indian life. In addition, Spanish settlers introduced wheat and other crops, such as oranges and olives.

Navajo Indian herding sheep. The Spanish in the Southwest brought sheep, which became important to the Navajos.

Spanish Names and Customs. Many people living in the United States today are of Spanish descent. Spanish words like *corral* and *tornado* have become part of the English language. American place names such as *San Antonio, Santa Fe,* and *Los Angeles* are Spanish. And old buildings of Spanish architecture can still be seen. Thus the Spanish legacy in America lives on.

Focus for Thought

13. In what two ways did other European nations weaken Spain through trade?
14. a. For what two things was King Philip trying to punish the English when he sent the Spanish Armada against them?
    b. Why was he confident of success?
15. In what way was the defeat of the Spanish Armada a turning point in history?
16. What effects did the Spanish have on southwestern North America?

Historical Highlights

A. Matching: People

a. Cabeza de Vaca
b. Elizabeth I
c. Eusebio Kino
d. Francis Drake
e. Francisco de Coronado
f. Hernando de Soto
g. Juan de Oñate
h. Juan Rodríguez Cabrillo
i. Junípero Serra
j. Marcos de Niza
k. Pánfilo de Narváez
l. Philip II
m. Ponce de León

1. Man who sought the Fountain of Youth.
2. Explorer who discovered the Mississippi River.
3. Man who made an overland journey on foot after being shipwrecked on the Narváez expedition.
4. Ruler of the country attacked by the Spanish Armada.
5. Spaniard who led settlers to Pueblo country and established San Juan.
6. Man who explored California and claimed San Diego Bay in 1542.
7. Explorer who lost his life at sea after exploring the Southeast.
8. Captain who plundered Spanish ships.
9. Explorer who sought the Seven Cities of Cíbola in 1540.
10. Franciscan friar who founded San Diego, California, in 1769.
11. Ruler who sent the Invincible Armada against England.
12. Jesuit priest who planted missions in Arizona.
13. Friar who told fantastic stories about "golden cities."

B. Matching: Terms

a. absolutism
b. civilize
c. frontier
d. mission
e. presidio
f. sea dog

1. To bring out of a primitive state by education and discipline.
2. System in which one person has complete authority in all matters.
3. Fort built to keep order and protect a Spanish mission.
4. Spanish outpost established to convert and civilize Indians.
5. Pirate supported by the English government in the 1500s.
6. Edge of a settled area.

C. Matching: Dates

1. De Soto's expedition
2. St. Augustine founded
3. Florida discovered
4. Coronado's expedition
5. First mission in California
6. Spanish Armada defeated
7. Pueblo revolt

a. 1513
b. 1539–1543
c. 1540–1542
d. 1565
e. 1588
f. 1680
g. 1769

D. Matching: Places

a. Arizona
b. California
c. Florida
d. Georgia and the Carolinas
e. Mississippi River
f. New Mexico
g. New Spain
h. Santa Fe
i. Seven Cities of Cíbola
j. St. Augustine

1. Legendary places that turned out to be Indian pueblos.
2. Region settled in the 1700s to oppose English and Russian claims.
3. Region explored by de Soto.
4. Spanish colony also called Mexico.
5. Major feature first crossed by white men as de Soto searched for wealth.
6. Land discovered by Ponce de León in his search for the Fountain of Youth.
7. Pueblos' land that was settled by Spanish colonists led by Oñate.
8. Area where Eusebio Kino set up missions.
9. First town built by Europeans in what is now the United States.
10. Capital of New Mexico.

E. Multiple Choice

Write the letter of the best answer.

1. How did the Spanish deal with the Indians they found?
   a. They overpowered the uncooperative Indians.
   b. They respected the Indians' wishes.
   c. They settled in uninhabited areas.
   d. They bought supplies from the Indians.

2. Why were de Soto and Coronado disappointed when they explored the southern part of what is now the United States?
   a. The natives were uncivilized, heathen people.
   b. The natives were hostile.
   c. The explorers failed to find productive soil.
   d. The explorers failed to find gold and jewels.
3. How were the Pueblo Indians bondmen in their own land?
   a. They were held in large prison compounds.
   b. They were not allowed to raise food on their own soil.
   c. They were forced to serve the religious and civil leaders who occupied their land.
   d. Their land was the scene of feuding between Spanish leaders.
4. Why did the Pueblo Indians revolt in 1680?
   a. They did not like to work in fields, vineyards, and gardens.
   b. They had suffered mistreatment under the Spanish.
   c. They found the Roman Catholic doctrines offensive.
   d. They resented the strange new customs of the Spanish.
5. The Spanish destroyed the Huguenot settlement in Florida for all the following reasons *except* that
   a. the Huguenots were trespassing on land claimed by Spain.
   b. the Huguenots were Protestants.
   c. the Huguenots had killed Spanish settlers in Florida.
   d. the Spanish did not want French people living on their land.
6. What was the purpose of the Spanish missions among the Indians?
   a. to protect and police the Indians
   b. to civilize and convert the Indians
   c. to obtain workers for mission projects
   d. to protect the settlers who had moved into the area
7. Which one of these was *not* associated with a Spanish mission?
   a. missionaries
   b. fort
   c. gardens and fields
   d. livestock raising
   e. carpenter and blacksmith skills
   f. gold mines
   g. Spanish manners and customs
8. Why was the arrival of horses in the West so important?
   a. Longhorn cattle came with them.
   b. Buffalo began to disappear.
   c. Horses had never been seen in the West before.
   d. Horses changed the Indians' lifestyle.
9. What was the outcome after the Spanish Armada was defeated?
   a. Spanish power increased and English power decreased.
   b. Spanish power decreased and English power increased.
   c. Both Spanish and English power decreased.
   d. Both Spanish and English power increased.

F. Deeper Discussion

1. How did absolutism affect the way that the Spanish dealt with hostile Indians?
2. Why were some Indian groups open to the Spanish culture and religion, but others were not?
3. What were some merits of the Spanish mission efforts?
4. When the defeated Spanish Armada returned to Spain, Philip II said to the commander, "I sent you to fight against men, not with the winds." According to Job 37:12, why did the winds act as they did?
5. Why were the Spanish ultimately unable to maintain the American Southwest as part of their territory?

G. Chronology and Geography

1. Make a time line of Spanish activities that affected America, using the information in Part C. Follow the instructions in Chapter 2 for making a time line.
2. Using an enlarged copy of Map C, label it "Exploration of North America." (You will use your "Exploration of North America" map in Chapters 5, 11, and 18.)
   a. Draw green lines to show the explorations of Ponce de León, Narváez, Cabeza de Vaca, de Soto, de Niza, Coronado, and Cabrillo.
   b. Label each route with the explorer's name and the date(s) of his exploration.
   c. Make a legend to show that green lines represent Spanish explorations, blue lines represent French explorations, brown lines represent American explorations, and red lines represent British explorations.
   d. On your map, label the following important Spanish missions: San Antonio, San Xavier del Bac, San Diego, San Francisco, and Los Angeles.

So Far This Year

A. Matching: Indian Tribes

1. Plains tribe of fierce fighters.
2. Culture that made large heaps of earth for ceremonies and burial.
3. Southwest Indians who lived in hogans.
4. Indians governed by sachems and called the Five Nations.
5. Tribe that had pueblos with kivas.
6. Another name for Eskimos.
7. Indians who went fishing or made foods from acorn flour.
8. Indians who lived along riverbanks and fished for salmon.
9. Indians called "diggers" who lived on poor land.

a. California Indians
b. Comanche
c. Great Basin Indians
d. Hopi
e. Inuit
f. Iroquois
g. Mound Builders
h. Navajo
i. Plateau Indians

B. Completion

Write the correct name, term, or date for each description.

10. A climate of four seasons.
11. The heartland of Canada in Ontario and Quebec.
12. Explorer of the northeastern coast of North America for England in 1497.
13. Explorer of the St. Lawrence River area for France in 1534.
14. Year the Spanish Armada was defeated.
15. Man who sought the Fountain of Youth.
16. Explorer who discovered the Mississippi River.
17. Explorer who sought the Seven Cities of Cíbola, 1540–1542.
18. Spanish system used to convert and civilize the Indians, and to fortify their frontiers.

Reconstruction of the original French fort at Port Royal, Nova Scotia.

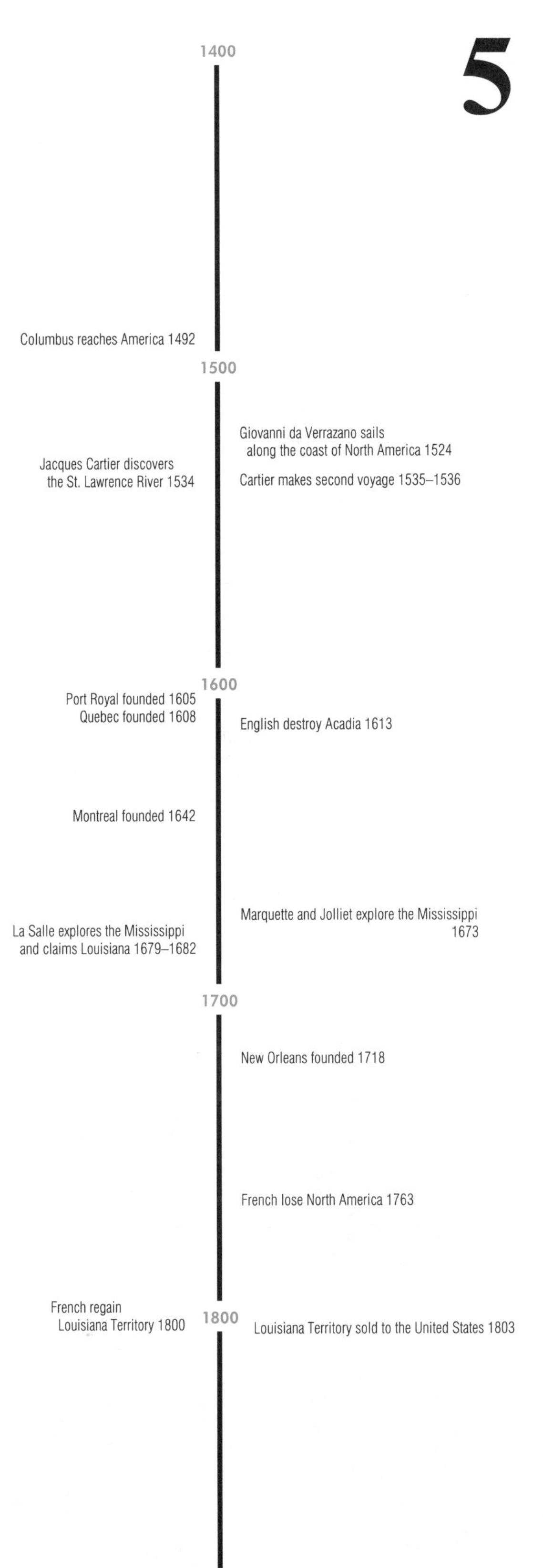

5 New France

1. Settlement of New France
    - Early French Exploration
    - The Colony of Acadia
    - Champlain, the "Father of New France"
2. Institutions in New France
    - Religion in New France
    - Government in New France
    - The Economic System of New France
3. Expansion of New France
    - French Expansion Into the Mississippi Valley
    - French Influence in North America

"In the multitude of people is the king's honour: but in the want of people is the destruction of the prince."
Proverbs 14:28

New France

Focus for Reading

Like other European nations, France was eager to claim her share of the New World. French explorers set out in the first half of the 1500s to stake a claim to North America—or if possible, to find a passage through the New World to the East Indies and China. These early attempts failed, however, and France paid little further attention to North America until about 1600. New France was planted in the next hundred years, and the colony grew until it covered a large part of North America.

How did the French establish New France in North America? How did people live in New France? How did New France expand to occupy much of the continent? These questions are answered in three sections of this chapter.

1. Settlement of New France
2. Institutions in New France
3. Expansion of New France

1. SETTLEMENT OF NEW FRANCE

Beginning in 1524, French sailors explored parts of North America as they sought a "Northwest Passage" to China. France then tried to establish a colony in North America, but the first attempt was not successful.

Early French Exploration

The first two French expeditions to North America were led by Giovanni da Verrazano and Jacques Cartier. You have already met these men in Chapter 2.

Exploration by Verrazano. Giovanni da Verrazano, an Italian, reached North America in 1524. He explored the east coast all the way from present-day North Carolina to Newfoundland. No further French efforts were made in that decade.

Exploration by Cartier. In 1534, Jacques Cartier discovered and named the St. Lawrence River as he sought the Northwest Passage for King Francis I. Then Cartier returned to France, believing that he had found a water route to China.

The next year he returned and sailed up the St. Lawrence, taking two Indian youths with him. As the expedition moved along, Cartier asked the youths for the names of the Indian villages they passed. Their answer each time was *Canada*, which is simply an Indian word for village; but Cartier thought the geographic area had that name. Eventually the name was applied to the

Early French explorers of North America: Top: Verrazano and Cartier; ***Bottom:*** Champlain and de Monts.

Cartier with Indians of Hochelaga in 1535. The Indian village was not the rich Asian city that he had hoped to find. Today the city of Montreal stands at the site of Hochelaga.

great northern land that we think of today.

When Cartier reached Stadacona, near the site of modern Quebec, he was disappointed to find that it was only a primitive village. Cartier also visited Hochelaga (hahsh uh LAG uh), a larger village located at the place where Montreal now stands. But Hochelaga was no rich oriental city, and by then Cartier saw that the St. Lawrence River did not lead to Asia. He returned to his base near Stadacona.

Cartier's men built a fort and stayed for the winter, but soon they were dying of scurvy. A helpful Indian told him about an evergreen tree whose leaves or bark could be boiled to make a healing tea. Cartier tried it with amazing results—his men were soon on their feet and in good health. In six days they used the leaves and bark of a whole tree!

First Attempt at Colonization. The explorations of Verrazano and Cartier gave France a claim to the St. Lawrence region. Cartier returned home in 1536, and a few years later, a group of about two hundred men prepared to sail for Canada. This expedition was headed by a man named Roberval (raw behr VAL), with Cartier serving as his chief of navigation. Their purpose was to establish a colony in North America and convert the Indians to Catholicism. The prospective settlers were French gentlemen, along with a number of criminals who were to do the heavy labor.

Cartier sailed before Roberval in 1541 and built a new settlement beyond his previous fort. He was unable to find a great Indian kingdom, but he did find what looked like diamonds and gold. So the next year, he and his men set sail for France, loaded with what they thought was gold-bearing rock. At Newfoundland they met Roberval, who had just arrived and who now ordered them to return to the colony. But Cartier sailed away at night and returned to France.

Roberval went on to Cartier's settlement and spent the winter of 1542–1543 there. Many of his men died of scurvy. In 1543, he explored the region further. Unwilling to face another Canadian winter, he left by September 1543.

Thus the first French colony ended in failure. Canada seemed to lack gold and other immediate riches, and disease and harsh winters made settlement difficult. A strong attraction was needed before the French would make another effort to settle in Canada.

The Colony of Acadia

By 1600, the new land did offer a strong attraction: the fur trade. Since beaver hats

This map of New France was drawn by Samuel de Champlain.

were fashionable in Europe, beaver furs from North America came into great demand. Several traders gained a ***monopoly*** on furs—the right to be the only ones dealing in that market. One of these was a Huguenot named **Pierre du Gua, Sieur de Monts** (MAWN).

Founding of Acadia. In 1603, de Monts received permission to establish a colony in Canada where the Huguenots would have religious freedom and the Indians would be taught Roman Catholicism. A friend named **Samuel de Champlain** (sham PLAYN) would go with de Monts as mapmaker. Champlain had experience in Canada, having explored the St. Lawrence River earlier.

The new colony was called Acadia (uh KAY dee uh), and it included the land around the Bay of Fundy, near present-day Nova Scotia and New Brunswick. When the colonists arrived in 1604, they chose to settle on an island near the mouth of the St. Croix River (KROI), today the border between Maine and New Brunswick. But the unsheltered island suffered the full blast of the cold northwest winds, and almost half of the settlers died of scurvy that first winter. They did not know about the evergreen tea that had saved Cartier's men.

The next spring they moved the settlement from the island to a better location across the Bay of Fundy in what is now Nova Scotia. De Monts returned to France; and Champlain stayed at the new settlement, which was called Port Royal. That spring the settlers in Acadia planted vegetables and grain, and the fall harvest was so good that the storehouse was full for the winter of 1606–1607.

Fall of Acadia. Then events took a turn for the worse. In 1607, de Monts received a message that he could no longer have monopoly trading privileges and official support. All the colonists in Acadia had to return to France. However, an upper-class settler named **Poutrincourt** (poo tran KOOR) did not want to see the project abandoned, so he returned to Acadia in 1610 with his own group of settlers. Finding the buildings in fairly good condition, Poutrincourt and his men set about to restore things.

But in 1613, an English ship captain discovered the French in Acadia—territory that England had claimed. He captured most of the men and took them to Jamestown, Virginia, where the enraged English governor threatened to hang them all. The governor sent three ships north to destroy the Port Royal settlement—buildings, crops, and livestock. This was one of the first incidents in the quarrel between France and England over land in America—a quarrel that would last for years to come.

Importance of Acadia. The Port Royal settlement was significant for several reasons. For one thing, it was the first sincere attempt by French colonists to support themselves by agriculture. Second, the settlement enjoyed a good relationship with the Indians. Third, since de Monts was a Huguenot, the Roman Catholic faith was not compulsory. Even though de Monts had promised that Catholicism would be taught to the Indians, no one in Acadia was forced to accept any certain religion.

Champlain, the "Father of New France"

Quebec—First Permanent French Settlement. Champlain returned to the St. Lawrence region in 1608 to explore further and establish another colony. More than sixty years had passed since Cartier had been in the area. During that time an epidemic had wiped out the Indians whom Cartier had visited, and now only the ruins of their villages remained.

Samuel de Champlain is known as the "father of New France" for his work in exploring and settling New France.

Near one of the ruined villages, Champlain began his settlement in July 1608. It was located on a level strip of ground overlooked by cliffs, at a place where the St. Lawrence narrowed. He named it Quebec, from an Indian word for "place where the river narrows." Champlain had about thirty men; but the first winter, all except eight of them died of scurvy. The settlers had heard of the tea made from evergreen trees that had cured Cartier's men, but they were unable to make use of it.

Alliance With the Huron Indians. Champlain soon discovered that his settlement lay between warring Indians. When he had explored the St. Lawrence in 1603, Champlain promised the French king's support to the Huron and Algonquin tribes. These Indians feared the Iroquois, a league of five tribes who lived southeast of them. Now they expected the French to help them fight the Iroquois.

In the spring of 1609, Champlain accompanied the Huron and their allies when they fought the Iroquois near the southern tip of Lake Champlain. By the power of the white men's deadly guns, the Huron gained a swift victory over their enemies. But the French gained the long-standing enmity of the powerful Iroquois. After that humiliating defeat, all five tribes of the Iroquois League vowed undying hatred toward France and all Frenchmen.

Champlain and the French did not realize the far-reaching effects of their choice to support the Huron against the Iroquois. The results were bitter hatred and ceaseless warfare for generations to come as the Iroquois allied themselves with the English against the French and their Indian comrades. This illustrates the Bible teaching

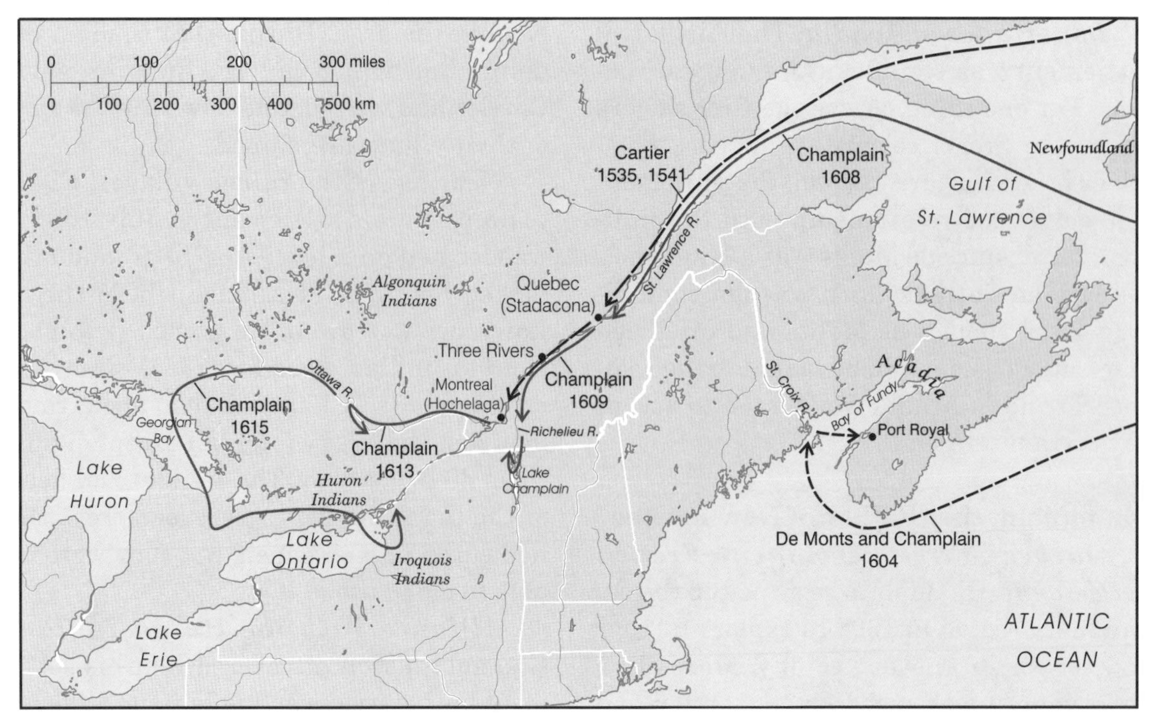

Early French Explorations and Settlements

that "whatsoever a man soweth, that shall he also reap" (Galatians 6:7).

Further Efforts for New France. For the rest of his life, Champlain worked to maintain and expand New France. One thing he helped to do was establish the fur trade. He also helped to begin mission work among the Indians by several groups of Catholics. In addition, Champlain promoted settlement in New France by making several trips to France and bringing new settlers to Canada.

By 1635, when Champlain died, a firm footing had been established for New France. The number of settlers was small, but the fur trade was well established and Catholic missionaries were working among the Indians. Three Rivers was settled in 1634, and Montreal was founded in 1642. Champlain had helped to begin a vast North American empire for France.

Miramichi, a French settlement on the Gulf of St. Lawrence. The French settled along the St. Lawrence River in settlements such as this one.

Focus for Thought

1. Give the meaning of the Indian word from which the name *Canada* is derived.
2. a. When did the French establish their first colony in America?
   b. Why did the French abandon their early attempts at settlement?
3. The Port Royal settlement was important for what three reasons?

4. a. The French based their claim to the St. Lawrence region on the work of two explorers. Name these explorers, and give the dates of their explorations.
   b. England also claimed the region of Acadia. Give the name of the English explorer and the date of his exploration. (See Chapter 2.)
   c. Which of these two nations had the earlier claim to Acadia?
5. Name the founder of Quebec, and give the date of the founding.
6. Who were the Indian allies
   a. of the French?
   b. of the English?
7. In what ways was Samuel de Champlain the "father of New France"?

2. INSTITUTIONS IN NEW FRANCE

As the French settled in North America, they brought with them their religion, language, and customs. The way people lived in New France still affects some parts of Canada and the United States today. In this section, you will learn about important aspects of life in New France.

Religion in New France

A Roman Catholic Colony. The religion of any people is the foundation on which its other policies are built. While the Huguenots of the earliest days had some religious liberty, the French Catholic monarchy soon took that liberty away and allowed only Catholics in New France. Many French Huguenots then moved to the English colonies farther south.

The Roman Catholic Church influenced the settlers in many ways. Each village had a priest and a church. The priest served as the schoolteacher and many times as the doctor also. The schools existed more to make priests and loyal Catholics than to teach the people how to read and write.

Indeed, the Catholic Church discouraged secular reading (there were no newspapers), and the only approved Bible was the Latin Vulgate. Only a small circle of clergy, officials, and a few others had any education. Most of the common people lived in ignorance.

Jesuits Among the Huron. In 1625, a new group of missionaries came to Canada. They were members of a Catholic order called Jesuits, who were known for their discipline, commitment, and courage. Their goal was threefold: (1) to convert the Indians to Catholicism, (2) to civilize the Indians, and (3) to bring the Indians under French authority.

The Jesuits entered the mission fields of New France with great enthusiasm, but they found the work difficult and discouraging. Requirements for baptism were simple. The Indians merely had to state that they

French cathedral in Quebec City. This building illustrates the central role of the Catholic Church in New France.

Paul Le Jeune (1591–1664), leader of the Quebec Jesuits from 1632 to 1639. He wrote the first eleven annual reports known as the "Jesuit Relations," which informed Europeans of happenings in Canada.

accepted the Roman Catholic faith and give evidence of a civilized lifestyle. But the Indians did not easily give up their gambling, fighting, drinking, polygamy, and Sunday hunting. Besides, not all the white men lived up to the standards that the missionaries demanded of the converts.

The Indians showed hostility in numerous ways. They threw stones at chapels and burned mission buildings, and in one case they dragged a priest through a campfire. Yet the Jesuits persisted, baptizing children and the dying. By 1640, they had baptized as many as twelve hundred Indians.

But while the Jesuits worked among the Huron and Algonquin, trouble was brewing among the Iroquois. Each year they became bolder in their attacks. Finally in 1648, the Iroquois started a full-scale war against the Huron. They destroyed several villages and murdered the missionaries with horrible torture. In just three years they wiped out all the Huron except a few survivors. Thus ended the mission efforts among the Huron.

Jesuits Among the Iroquois. Refusing to be defeated, the Jesuits now tried to work among the Iroquois. A treaty in 1653 allowed them to set up a mission on Iroquois territory. But the Iroquois were so hostile that the missionaries soon lived in constant fear for their lives. When the Jesuits finally left, war broke out between the French and the Iroquois.

After a French victory over the Iroquois, the missionaries followed the soldiers back to the Iroquois villages. But the Iroquois were even more bitter now. They treated the Jesuits as hostages and any converted Indians as traitors. In 1687, the Jesuits abandoned their efforts among the Iroquois.

The French had largely failed in their threefold aim of converting the Indians, civilizing them, and establishing French authority over them. Although Jesuits did serve with great zeal, they failed to teach the Indians the true Gospel of Jesus Christ and salvation from sin. "For the grace of God that bringeth salvation hath appeared to all men, teaching us that, denying ungodliness and worldly lusts, we should live soberly, righteously, and godly, in this present world" (Titus 2:11, 12).

Government in New France

An Absolutist Policy. When **Louis XIV** became the French king in 1654, he adopted a policy of absolutism. Some writers have said that he boasted, "I am the state." He ruled as if he believed it. In New France, political power was in the hands of a few men who answered only to Louis XIV.

Three main figures controlled the government of New France. One was the governor, who reported to the king. Another was the bishop, who handled church matters. A third was the intendant, who controlled the budget and took care of judicial matters. There was also a council appointed by the king, whose members carried out the business of governing the colony. But since the common people had no voice in the government, political freedom was nonexistent in New France.

The king received many appeals for things such as ships, money, skilled workers, and help for the needy. But since nothing could travel any faster than a sailing ship, communications were exasperatingly slow. Often it took a year or more to receive official word on a matter. Eighteen years after the founding of Quebec, the population was only one hundred people. Only two self-supporting families were found among these; the rest were supported by the government.

The Economic System of New France

The Seigneurial System. Landholding in New France operated by the ***seigneurial system*** (sayn YUR ee uhl), which was a form of the old manorial system in Europe. Noblemen known as ***seigneurs*** (sayn YURZ) received large tracts of land containing several thousand acres. The seigneurs paid nothing for their land—not even rent—but they did need to promise loyalty to the French king.

A seigneur's most important obligation was to get settlers established on his land to clear it. He also needed to build a manor house for himself, along with a wine press and buildings such as a mill and a bakery to serve the settlers. In addition, the seigneur had to find a priest to serve his community.

Each tenant, or ***habitant*** (ah bee TAHN), obtained a title deed from the seigneur for his own parcel of ground. The tenant was to work the soil and pay a rental fee for the privilege. The habitants also needed to work for the seigneur several days each year: one day at plowing, one at seeding, and one at harvesting.

In the early years, each parcel included some river frontage and extended in a long,

Jean Talon, a French official from 1665 to 1672, visits some of the 2,000 colonists he helped to settle in New France. He encouraged manufacturing, shipbuilding, mining, and trade with the West Indies.

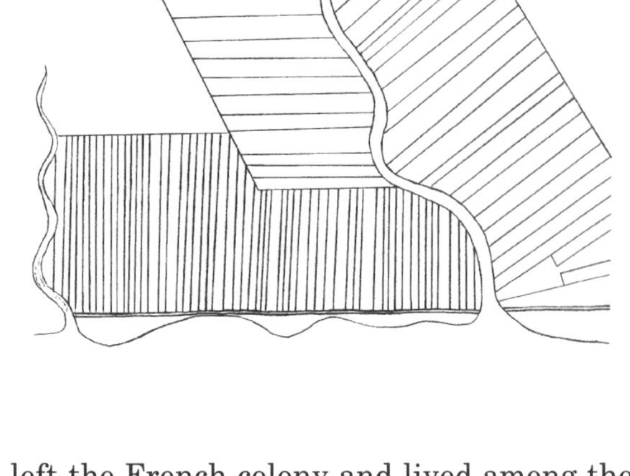

This aerial photograph shows strip farms on Ile E'Orleans, an island in the St. Lawrence River. To the right is a map of New France, showing narrow parcels of land extending inland from the St. Lawrence River and one of its tributaries.

narrow strip away from the river. The habitant's house, barn, and outbuildings were built beside a road that ran along the river. Thus a string of dwellings lined the banks of the lower St. Lawrence and Richelieu Rivers.

Every year on St. Martin's Day (November 11), the habitants gathered at the seigneur's house to make their rental payments. Each habitant paid a small amount of money, along with six chickens and a bushel of grain for each 50 to 60 acres (20–24 ha) of his land.

The seigneurial system placed no great burden on the habitants, yet it hindered the growth of the colony. People will usually work much harder if they can own property themselves than if all the land belongs to someone else. Population and agriculture grew slowly, and New France needed much support from the mother country.

The Fur Trade. The financial welfare of New France depended not on farming but on furs. When the fur trade prospered, New France prospered; and when it suffered, the colony suffered. Up to one-third of the people depended in some way on the fur trade.

Many of the furs came from Indians on the rich fur grounds near the Great Lakes and other regions far to the west. To maintain contact with these regions, some white men left the French colony and lived among the Indians. These men became known as ***coureurs de bois*** (koo RURZ duh BWAH); that is, "forest runners"; and they lived wild, reckless lives in the woods.

Literally hundreds of young men deserted civilization to become coureurs de bois. One governor wrote that their lives consisted of "doing nothing, caring for nothing, following

Fur traders seeking trade with the Indians. The French offered knives, kettles, trinkets, and other items in exchange for the Indians' beaver pelts, which were in demand in Europe for making hats.

Coureurs de bois braved many hardships to bring furs from the Indians to French settlements.

every inclination, and getting out of the way of all correction." Once they had a taste of this wild, loose living, few ever returned to civilization. Romans 1:21–32 describes the life of people who follow such a willful and lawless course. "And even as they did not like to retain God in their knowledge, God gave them over to a reprobate mind, to do those things which are not convenient" (Romans 1:28).

Laws were passed in an effort to keep the young men in the colony—but it was actually through French policy that the coureurs de bois existed. For instead of having trading posts among the Indians, the French required that the Indians' furs be brought to settlements along the St. Lawrence River. Therefore, every spring a great fleet of canoes came eastward down the waterways—a fleet that grew larger and larger as more canoes joined it. The fur ***flotilla*** (floh TIHL uh) that arrived in Montreal in 1693 contained four hundred canoes, two hundred coureurs de bois, and twelve hundred Indians.

The Montreal merchants would prepare for the flotilla by having all kinds of merchandise available for trade. They offered things such as muskets, gunpowder, blankets, knives, hatchets, kettles, various trinkets, and—worst of all—liquor. The trading would go on for two weeks, and during this time all Montreal was in an uproar because of the drunken visitors. They clearly illustrated the truth of Proverbs 20:1: "Wine is a mocker, strong drink is raging: and whosoever is deceived thereby is not wise."

Everyone knew that liquor was not good for the Indians. The Catholic leaders tried to stop the trade; but the dealers insisted that if they did not sell it, the Indians would get it from the English. Then the Indians would deal more and more with the English (who paid better prices for furs), and the French trade and Roman Catholicism would be lost. The governor sided with the traders, and the liquor trade continued.

In summary, the fur trade was a hindrance rather than a help to New France. One historian states that it caused the colony to "put its economic energies into what was at best a . . . transitory source of national wealth, and to neglect the solid foundations of agriculture and industry, which in the long run would have profited its people much more." A similar thought is found in Ecclesiastes 5:9, which says that "the king himself is served by the field."

Focus for Thought

8. a. What was the required religion in New France?
   b. What kind of government did the French have?
   c. What was the French system of land ownership?
   d. What were some weaknesses of the colony at New France?
9. What did the French missionaries hope to accomplish among the Indians?
10. What were the responsibilities
    a. of a seigneur?
    b. of an habitant?
11. a. What was one aspect of the seigneurial system that favored the habitants?
    b. What was one aspect that did not favor them?
12. a. What part did the coureurs de bois have in the fur trade?
    b. What part did liquor have in the fur trade?
    c. Describe the consequences of departing from God and from God-ordained authority, as the coureurs de bois did. (See Romans 1:28–32.)

3. EXPANSION OF NEW FRANCE

During the late 1600s, the French became interested in expanding New France for several reasons. One was to build up the fur trade. Another was to prevent other nations from moving west and taking away the fur trade. A third was to find the mouth of the Mississippi, which would provide them with an ice-free port the year around. To meet these goals, several men explored the Mississippi region and claimed it for France.

French Expansion Into the Mississippi Valley

Exploration by Marquette and Jolliet. An explorer named **Louis Jolliet** (JOH lee eht) heard Indian stories of a "great water" that he thought could be a route to Asia. When he went to search for it, he took with him a Jesuit priest named **Jacques Marquette** (ZHAHK mahr KEHT), whose goal was to found missions among the Indians along the Mississippi.

Marquette and Jolliet traveled down the Mississippi River, hoping the river would lead to the Pacific Ocean.

In 1673, Marquette and Jolliet, along with five companions, paddled their canoes up the Fox River from Lake Michigan. After they carried their canoes overland to the

Wisconsin River, they floated down to the Mississippi and proceeded south. They pressed on until they reached the place where the Arkansas River flows into the Mississippi from the west. By that time they realized that the river was not a passage to Asia, but flowed into the Gulf of Mexico. So they turned around and came back to Lake Michigan by way of the Illinois River. Jolliet returned to Quebec in 1674.

La Salle's Claim of Louisiana. A French noble and fur trader named **Robert de La Salle** (luh SAL) was determined to find a way through North America to Asia. In dealing with the Indians, he heard about a great river that flowed south to the sea. Thinking this might be the long-sought water route to the Orient, La Salle began planning for exploration.

Before he went, La Salle heard how Marquette and Jolliet had found the great river, so he decided to find the mouth of the Mississippi. He also wanted to secure the fur trade of the region for the French, and claim the land for the king.

In 1682, La Salle canoed down the Mississippi River. When he reached the Gulf of Mexico, he claimed for France all the land drained by the river. (*Inset:* A portrait of La Salle.)

La Salle and his men started down the Mississippi River in February 1682, and that April they reached its mouth. In a formal ceremony, La Salle claimed for France all the area drained by the Mississippi from the Great Lakes to the Gulf of Mexico. He named this territory Louisiana after Louis XIV, the king of France.

The Settling of Louisiana. La Salle returned to Quebec and then sailed to France, where he convinced the king to set up a colony in the lower Mississippi River valley. Four ships with settlers and supplies were dispatched to the Gulf of Mexico in 1684. But the voyage was beset with one problem after another—disease, quarreling, and other difficulties. Once the sailors had to fight off an attack by the Spanish.

The greatest problem was that La Salle missed the mouth of the Mississippi and sailed about 400 miles (644 km) too far west. Here he searched in vain for the river along the coast of what is now Texas. Then he lost his four ships. Finally he left a few survivors at a fort near present-day Port Lavaca, and with several companions he started north toward the Great Lakes to seek help for the stranded expedition. The party suffered severe hardships on the way, and La Salle was killed by one of his own men in 1687. The few settlers who stayed in Texas were soon killed or captured by the Indians.

Because of La Salle's work, France laid claim to the entire Mississippi River valley. Forts were built at various places throughout the region to hold the territory for France. The forts were used as trading posts, missions, and defense outposts. By 1700, New France stretched all the way from the St. Lawrence in the north to the mouth of the Mississippi in the south.

Louisiana was first settled in 1699; and in 1718, New Orleans was founded and later

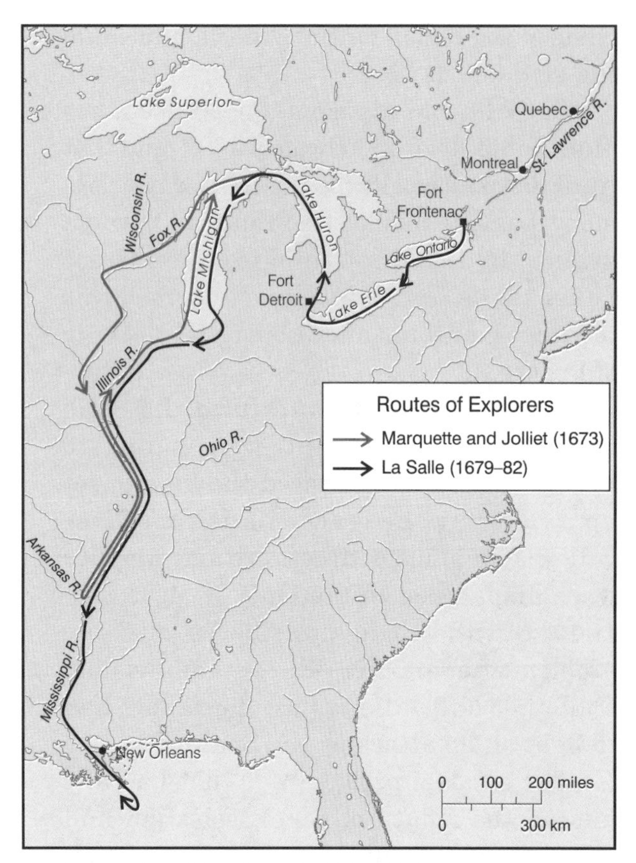

Exploration of the Mississippi River Valley

became the capital of Louisiana. The West was all open Indian territory, and in the East the Appalachian Mountains separated New France from the English settlements along the Atlantic coast. The area west of the Mississippi stayed under French control for most of the years until 1803, when the young United States obtained it through the Louisiana Purchase. In all, French power in North America lasted about 250 years after Cartier explored the St. Lawrence.

French Influence in North America

The French left their mark on North America in several ways. In Canada, both English and French are official languages. Many people in modern Quebec speak French, and most are Catholics. The French Canadians follow French customs and laws. Some of them even want Quebec to be independent because of differences between them and Canadians of English descent.

In the United States, the state of Louisiana shows the effects of French colonization in that it has parishes instead of counties. Many of the people in southern Louisiana are Catholics. Also, place names like Louisiana, New Orleans, and St. Louis are French.

Differences Between French Colonies and English Colonies. New France was large in area, while the English colonies were considerably smaller. Yet New France never grew very large in terms of population. By 1750, the whole area had less than sixty thousand people, whereas the English colonies had well over a million. This slow growth occurred for several reasons.

One reason was that farming was not as profitable in New France because of the climate. Also, with land ownership restricted in New France, men turned to the fur trade to make profits. This trade brought great wealth but hindered development. The fur

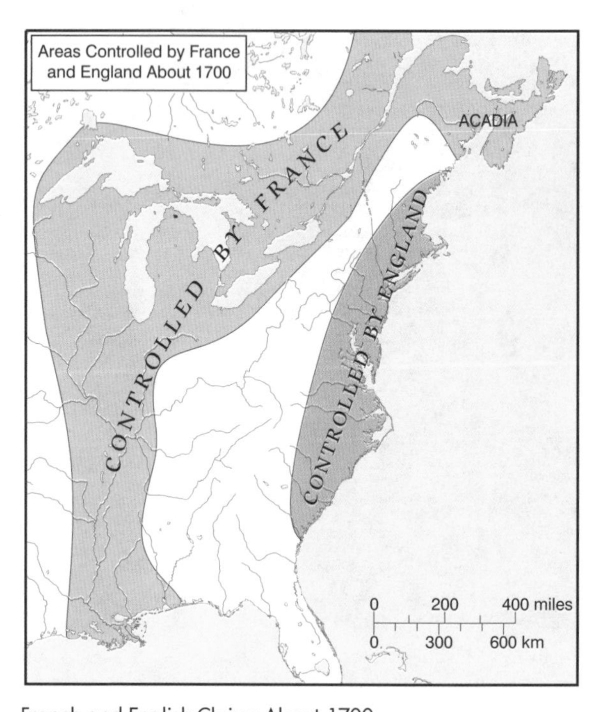

French and English Claims About 1700

traders did not want settlers to clear the forest and drive away the fur-bearing animals. By contrast, many of the English colonists came for the express purpose of farming because land was freely available.

Another reason was that New France did not offer the freedoms that the English colonies did. While everyone in New France had to be a Catholic, most English colonies had more freedom of religion. In addition, the French settlers had no self-government, whereas the English colonists were allowed to make many decisions themselves. And in France, the absolutist government prevented the rise of a middle class like the one that developed under the freedoms granted in England. It was from this middle class that thousands of settlers came to America.

For these and other reasons, large numbers of people moved to the English colonies on the coast of North America while smaller numbers moved to New France. But the expansion of both empires in North America was bound to bring a clash. The same territory could not be ruled by two conflicting powers.

Focus for Thought

13. What did Marquette and Jolliet discover about the Mississippi River?
14. What did La Salle's exploration do for New France?
15. Why did the French build forts in the Mississippi River valley?
16. Describe some present-day effects of the French colonies in America.
17. Give several contrasts between New France and the English colonies.

Historical Highlights

A. Matching: People

a. De Monts
b. Giovanni da Verrazano
c. Jacques Cartier
d. Jacques Marquette
e. Louis XIV
f. Louis Jolliet
g. Poutrincourt
h. Robert de La Salle
i. Samuel de Champlain

1. "Father of New France."
2. Men who explored the Mississippi to the Arkansas River in 1673 and 1674 (two answers).
3. Explorer who claimed for France the area drained by the Mississippi.
4. Early explorer who made three trips to the St. Lawrence region.
5. French king who ruled by the principle of absolutism.
6. First explorer sent by France.
7. Huguenot businessman who headed the Port Royal colony.
8. Upper-class settler who tried to hold on to the Port Royal colony.

B. Matching: Groups

1. Strongly dedicated Roman Catholic workers.	a. Algonquin
2. Indians who were baptized in large numbers (two tribes).	b. coureurs de bois
3. Indians who sided with the English.	c. habitants
4. French Protestants.	d. Huguenots
5. Noblemen who owned land in New France.	e. Huron
6. "Forest runners" who gathered furs from the Indians and brought them to trading centers.	f. Iroquois
	g. Jesuits
7. Settlers who worked a seigneur's land in New France.	h. seigneurs

C. Matching: Places and Terms

1. River along the Quebec and Montreal settlements.	a. absolutism
2. Town where annual fur-trading fair was held.	b. Acadia
3. Town founded by Champlain.	c. Canada
4. Unsatisfactory site for the settlement in Acadia.	d. flotilla
5. Name derived from Indian word for *village*.	e. monopoly
6. Poutrincourt's beloved settlement, destroyed by the English.	f. Montreal
7. French name for the area around the Bay of Fundy.	g. Port Royal
8. Strict principle by which New France was ruled.	h. Quebec
9. Form of manorialism transplanted to New France.	i. seigneurial system
10. Group of canoes traveling together.	j. St. Croix
11. Exclusive control over the market of a certain product.	k. St. Lawrence

D. Deeper Discussion

1. The Indians that the French found were primitive and warlike tribes. How do people get into such a condition? Read Romans 3:10–18.
2. How did the French alliance with the Huron and Algonquin against the Iroquois affect the subsequent history of North America?
3. The French policy of absolutism kept New France from developing into a successful, flourishing colony. Give several factors that hindered its development.
4. a. To what extent did the Jesuits succeed among the Indians?
   b. To what extent did they fail?
5. How did the fur trade
   a. lower the morals of people in New France?
   b. affect the Indians?
   c. hinder the development of New France?
6. In what way did La Salle's claim complete a bridge across the North American continent?
7. Why did French expansion into the Mississippi River valley lead to conflict?

E. Chronology and Geography

1. Match the numbers on the map to the place names below.

___ a. St. Lawrence River
___ b. Richelieu River
___ c. Ottawa River
___ d. Lake Champlain
___ e. Georgian Bay
___ f. Algonquin Indians
___ g. Quebec
___ h. Montreal
___ i. Newfoundland
___ j. Acadia
___ k. Iroquois Indians
___ l. Huron Indians

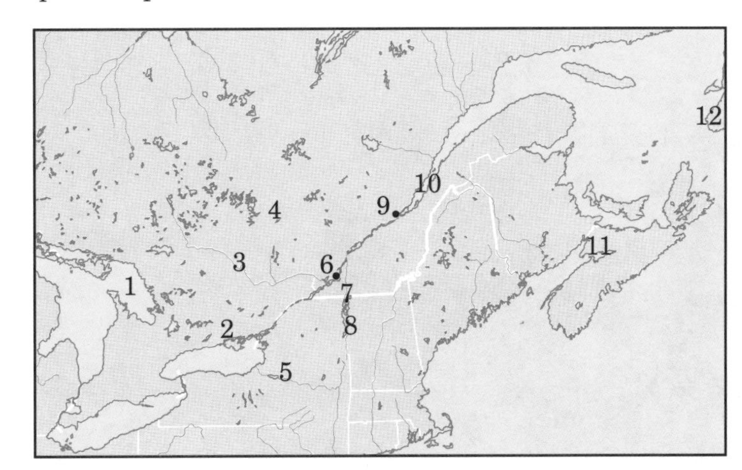

2. On your map entitled "Exploration of North America," draw blue lines to show the explorations of Cartier, Champlain, Marquette and Jolliet, and La Salle. Label the lines.
3. Write the dates for the following events.
   a. First exploration by Jacques Cartier.
   b. Founding of St. Augustine.
   c. Defeat of the Spanish Armada.
   d. Founding of Quebec.
   e. Exploration of Marquette and Jolliet.
   f. La Salle's claim of Louisiana.

The Pilgrims landed at Plymouth on December 26, 1620. They faced many hardships as they established a settlement in the forbidding New England wilderness.

6 English Colonies

1550

Settlers arrive at Roanoke Island 1587

1600

Founding of Jamestown, Virginia **1607**

King James Bible authorized 1611

Pilgrims found Plymouth, Massachusetts **1620**

Dutch purchase Manhattan Island 1626

First Puritans arrive in the area of Massachusetts Bay Colony 1628

Boston in Massachusetts Bay Colony founded 1630

First colonists land in Maryland 1634

Hartford and the Connecticut colony founded 1636

Roger Williams founds Providence, Rhode Island 1636

1650

Charter for Carolina granted to eight proprietors 1663

New York and New Jersey established as English colonies 1664

Founding of Charles Town, South Carolina 1670

New Hampshire separates from Massachusetts Bay Colony 1680

Charter for Pennsylvania granted to William Penn **1681**

Founding of Philadelphia, Pennsylvania 1682

First Mennonites arrive at Germantown **1683**

1700

Founding of Delaware 1704

Carolina officially separates into North and South Carolina 1712

James Oglethorpe founds Savannah, Georgia **1733**

1750

"And they found fat pasture and good, and the land was wide, and quiet, and peaceable."
1 Chronicles 4:40

English Colonies

Focus for Reading

By 1600, Spain had subdued vast territories in the Americas, and France had also gained a foothold in the New World. But England did not yet have even one successful colony. The only region open for the English was the east coast of North America, forested and forbidding. Yet from the first permanent settlement in 1607 at Jamestown, Virginia, to the last colony of Georgia in 1733, England managed to plant a thin line of thirteen colonies that stretched from New England to Florida. From that late beginning, English power grew until it dominated North America.

Why did England establish colonies in North America? How were the thirteen colonies founded? In this chapter, three sections answer these questions.

1. The First English Settlements
2. New England, Maryland, and the Carolinas
3. The Middle Colonies and Georgia

1. The First English Settlements

As you saw in Chapter 2, John Cabot explored the northeastern coast of North America for England in 1497. On that basis, England claimed all of northeastern North America. But England showed little interest in further exploration or colonization for over fifty years. By the latter half of the 1500s, England was growing in power during the reign of Queen Elizabeth I. Englishmen began exploring again, and their efforts laid the foundations for successful settlements.

Unsuccessful Attempts

The Lost Colony. In 1587, an English nobleman named **Sir Walter Raleigh** (RAW lee) wanted to start a settlement along the east coast of North America. That year he sent off more than one hundred colonists under the leadership of John White, and in July they arrived at Roanoke Island near present-day Cape Hatteras, North Carolina. There, on August 18, John White's daughter and her husband became the parents of the first English child to be born in North America. They named her **Virginia Dare**, after the name of the Virginia colony.

Governor White returned to England for supplies soon afterward. But because his country was at war with Spain, he could not go back to America until the Spanish Armada was defeated. The governor finally returned to Roanoke Island in 1590, only to find the settlement deserted. The letters *CRO* were carved on one tree, and on another was the word *Croatoan* (the name of a local Indian tribe); but those were the only clues left by the settlers. No one ever found out for sure what became of the settlers of the lost colony.

The Plymouth Company Settlement. Queen Elizabeth died in 1603 and was succeeded by **King James I**, who authorized the King James Bible in 1611. Two groups of businessmen appealed to the king in 1606, seeking permission to start a colony in America. They were called the London Company and the Plymouth Company, and they hoped to make profits by investing in America.

King James divided the territory lying between 34 and 45 degrees north latitude, giving a ***charter*** to each of the companies. This was a legal document that granted the right to settle a certain region and set up a government there. The Plymouth Company received the northern portion, and the London Company received the southern portion, which included the present state of Virginia.

In 1607, the Plymouth Company landed 120 settlers at the mouth of the Kennebec River in present-day Maine. The newcomers hoped to establish a fishing colony, but things did not go well for them. The winter was severe, and the colony's president died. After about a year, the project was abandoned and everyone went home to England.

The Founding of Jamestown

In spite of these failures, English people still wanted to come to America. Some came mainly for excitement and adventure. Many came to make a better living for themselves or to find easy riches. Poor people in England saw America as a place of opportunity. Others came for more political freedom from oppressive kings. Many more came for greater religious freedom. From 1607 to 1733, thousands of Englishmen settled the thirteen colonies that later became the United States.

Settlement of Jamestown. In May 1607, three ships with 105 Englishmen sponsored by the London Company entered the Chesapeake Bay. These men sailed up a broad river, which they named the James River in honor of the king. They built a village and fort on a low-lying peninsula and named it Jamestown.

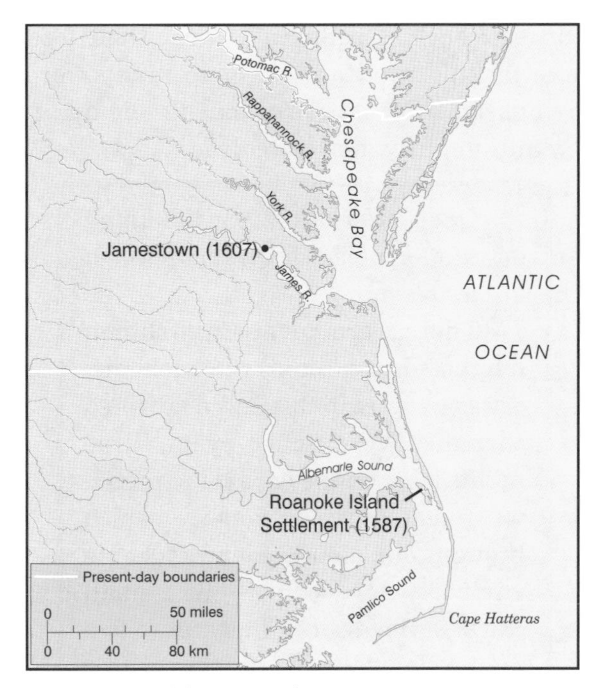

Jamestown and the Surrounding Area

Troubles in the Colony. The Jamestown settlers quickly faced problems. They had been warned not to build their houses on low ground, but they did not heed this advice. Many became sick with malaria transmitted by mosquitoes from nearby marshes. The water was bad, and the colonists suffered

The first permanent English settlers arrived in the New World in May 1607. These settlers came in the *Susan Constant*, the *Godspeed*, and the *Discovery*, and they founded Jamestown about 60 miles (97 km) up the James River.

illnesses such as pellagra because their food was lacking in vitamins. Soon many were dying, sometimes three or four in one night. By autumn fifty men were dead.

> *One settler wrote the following description about the first months at Jamestown.*
>
> There were never Englishmen left in a foreign country in such misery as we were in this new discovered Virginia. We watched every three nights lying on the bare cold ground, what weather soever came; . . . which brought our men to be most feeble wretches. Our food was but a small can of barley, sodden in water to five men a day. Our drink, cold water taken out of the river; which was at flood very salt, at low tide full of slime and filth; which was the destruction of many of our men. Thus we lived for the space of five months in this miserable distress, not having five able men to man our bulwarks upon any occasion.

Another problem was the settlers' poor attitude toward work. Over one-third of them were gentlemen who thought hard work was for people of lower rank. They did not recognize that work is honorable and laziness is sin. The Bible says that we should be "working with [our] hands the thing which is good" (Ephesians 4:28).

Perhaps the greatest problem was the colonists' zeal for quick wealth. The main reason many of them had come was to find gold and other treasures; and when 120 more immigrants arrived in 1608, the newcomers soon thought they had discovered gold in the soil. **John Smith**, principal founder of Jamestown, reported as follows: "There was now no talk, no hope, no work, but dig gold, wash gold, refine gold, load gold." In England the shiploads of "gold" proved to be worthless dirt.

Jamestown had so few good workers that John Smith wrote to England, "I entreat you rather to send but thirty carpenters, husbandmen, gardeners, fishermen, blacksmiths, masons, diggers up of trees' roots, well provided, than a thousand of such as we have." Three presidents in succession tried to rule Jamestown, but none of them was able to improve matters in the colony.

Contribution of John Smith. Finally in September 1608, John Smith became the president. He established a policy of "no work, no food," similar to the Biblical principle in 2 Thessalonians 3:10. Every man was required to work six hours each day toward filling the common storehouse with food. After two Indians taught the colonists how to plant corn, they planted 30 or 40 acres (12 or 16 ha). With his firm leadership, Smith

Captain John Smith (1580?–1631), president of Jamestown in 1608 and 1609, saved the colony in its early years by his firm leadership.

Within one year after arriving at Jamestown, John Smith was captured by the Indians. The following account is a part of Smith's story of his experience among the Indians.

[Smith] demanding for their captain, they showed him Opechancanough . . . to whom he gave a round, ivory double compass dial. Much they marveled at the playing of the fly and needle, which they could see so plainly and yet not touch it because of the glass that covered them. . . .

Notwithstanding, within an hour after they tied him to a tree, and as many as could stand about him prepared to shoot him; but the king, holding up the compass in his hand, they all laid down their bows and arrows, and in a triumphant manner led him to [the town of] Orapaks, where he was after their manner kindly feasted and well used. . . .

[Afterward] a long consultation was held, but the conclusion was this: two great stones were brought before Powhatan. Then as many as could laid hands on him, dragged him to them, and thereon laid his head; and being ready with their clubs to beat out his brains, Pocahontas the king's dearest daughter, when no entreaty could prevail, got his head in her arms, and laid her own upon his to save him from death.

Whereat the emperor was contented he should live to make him hatchets, and her bells, beads, and copper; for they thought him as well of all occupations as themselves.

finally got the colony to run smoothly.

Then Smith was severely burned in a gunpowder explosion and had to return to Europe. Without his leadership, the Jamestown colony lapsed into what later colonists called "the starving time," during the winter of 1609–1610. In six months, the population dropped from five hundred men to sixty.

The survivors planned to return to England in the spring of 1610. Just as they reached the mouth of the James River, they met ships from England bringing a new governor, more colonists, and fresh supplies. The Jamestown colony was saved.

Success of the Virginia Colony

After its new beginning, Jamestown and the Virginia settlement developed into a successful colony. Several factors contributed to this. One was a time of peace with the Indians. In 1611, the English kidnapped Pocahontas, the beloved daughter of the powerful Indian chief **Powhatan**, and they held her for a ransom of food and supplies from the Indians. While the English held Pocahontas in captivity, **John Rolfe** decided to marry her. This marriage brought the return of peace with the Indians.

A second factor was the cultivation of tobacco. In 1612, John Rolfe successfully introduced a mild tobacco to the Virginia colony. This crop sold well in England, and it helped Virginia to become financially successful. But tobacco also caused a demand for slaves to help grow it—and the tobacco habit became a "lust of the flesh" that has enslaved thousands of people ever since.

As a third factor, in 1616, the London Company decided to grant each settler a plot of ground. In this way, he could support himself rather than depending on a common storehouse. With this incentive, soon three

This reconstruction shows how the original buildings at Jamestown might have looked.

Some Highlights of Jamestown

Pocahontas (1595?–1617). She adopted the English name Rebecca and married John Rolfe.

The wedding of Pocahontas and John Rolfe.

First meeting of the Jamestown House of Burgesses, on July 30, 1619. This was an important step toward self-government because it was the first representative legislative body in the American colonies.

A Dutch ship brought the first 20 blacks to sell at Jamestown in 1619, which was the beginning of slavery in the colonies.

Wives for the settlers at Jamestown. This was a major development because the establishing of homes and families helped to make Jamestown a permanent settlement.

or four men were producing as much as two dozen men had produced formerly! This system of ***private enterprise*** worked because the settlers put forth more effort when they received personal benefits from their labors (Proverbs 16:26).

A fourth factor was families, which added stability to the colony. The first colonists were men with no permanent interest in Virginia; they expected to return to England someday. By 1619, young women were persuaded to go there. Because of the resulting marriages and families, the settlers began to think of Virginia as their home.

A final factor occurred in 1619. The colonists were allowed to elect men called ***burgesses*** (BUR jihs ihz) to represent them in government. As free Englishmen, they now had a voice in managing their own affairs. This local participation gave added efficiency to the governing of Virginia. Eventually it led to representative government in the United States.

Virginia became a ***royal colony*** in 1624, governed directly by the king rather than the London Company. The colony offered peace and security, just and fair laws, a staple crop of tobacco, and an abundance of land. Before 1658, the Church of England was the official church of Virginia; but in later years, everyone except Quakers had freedom of religion.

Focus for Thought

1. For each country below, give the name of the first permanent settlement founded in North America, when it was founded, and where it was located.
   a. England b. Spain (Chapter 4) c. France (Chapter 5)
2. Who directed the planting of the colony at Roanoke? (Note that the capital of North Carolina is named in his honor.)
3. Briefly describe what happened to the Roanoke colony.
4. Describe three of the problems faced by the Jamestown colonists.
5. Explain how each of the following things contributed to the success of the Virginia colony.
   a. tobacco
   b. plots of land
   c. families
   d. burgesses

2. NEW ENGLAND, MARYLAND, AND THE CAROLINAS

The second successful English colony in America was founded by the Pilgrims in 1620. The Massachusetts Bay settlement was established soon afterward, and the two became the colony of Massachusetts. More colonies developed later as other parts of the English territory were settled.

The Plymouth Colony

Puritans and Separatists. The Church of England broke away from the Catholic Church during the Reformation, but its richly robed clergymen and elaborate ceremonies still resembled those of the Catholics. People known as Puritans insisted that the church be purified of these things and return to a simple form of worship. Many Puritans stayed in the Church of England and worked for reform from within. Others, called Separatists, withdrew from the official church and established illegal congregations of their own.

Soon persecution arose, and by 1609, one Separatist group had left England to seek refuge in the Netherlands. These people became known as Pilgrims. But in the Netherlands, the Pilgrims became concerned about the effects of the surrounding society on their children. They wanted their children to learn English ways rather than Dutch ways. The Pilgrims decided to move to America so that they could live and worship in freedom.

Pilgrims' Arrival in America. The Pilgrims obtained a charter from the London Company to settle at the mouth of the Hudson River, which was then part of the Virginia colony. They set out in a ship called the *Mayflower*, and after sixty-six days they anchored near the North American coast on November 21, 1620. However, they soon realized that they were not in Virginia, but at Cape Cod in what is now Massachusetts—some distance northeast of the land they were authorized to settle. The Pilgrims decided to settle here anyway. Some of the men explored the area to find the best location for their new settlement.

Mayflower in Plymouth Harbor in 1620. The *Mayflower* was 90 feet long (27 m) and carried 102 passengers to America. The rough voyage lasted 66 days.

But only about one-third of the passengers were Pilgrims. Many of the rest (whom the Pilgrims called Strangers) were members of the Church of England. Some of these Strangers threatened to start their own settlement, since they thought they were outside the control of any government. The Pilgrim leaders wanted the assurance that the settlers would work together for the common welfare of the group; so while they were still aboard the *Mayflower,* they prepared a document that guaranteed fair treatment for everyone. This document, known as the Mayflower Compact, was signed by forty-one of the forty-four men on the ship. The signers pledged to work together in establishing a settlement and to govern it with "just and equal laws."

Founding of the Plymouth Colony. The settlers landed at Plymouth on December 26, 1620. They built a few rude houses for shelter; but that winter, so many died of the "General Sickness" that by spring only half of the original number remained. Then in March an Indian suddenly appeared among them. To the astonished settlers, he announced in English, "Welcome, Englishmen."

The Mayflower Compact was signed in the cabin of the *Mayflower.* The Mayflower Compact was the first agreement for self-government enacted in America.

The Pilgrims held their first public worship service in North America on Sunday, January 31, 1621. They were very glad for the privilege to meet openly without fear of persecution.

Top left: Pilgrims walking to church. Since they did not practice nonresistance, the men carried weapons even on Sunday for defense against Indian attacks. ***Top right:*** First Thanksgiving at Plymouth, in 1621. Sometime in the fall, the Pilgrims invited the Indians to share in a feast of gratitude for the bountiful harvest. ***Bottom right:*** Plimoth Plantation is a re-creation of the settlement at Plymouth, Massachusetts. Visitors can see what the settlement was like in 1627, seven years after its founding.

Samoset had learned English from sea captains with whom he had sailed. He promised to bring other Indians to trade with the Pilgrims; and one day he showed up with **Squanto**, who spoke better English and whose story was even stranger than that of Samoset. Two times Squanto had been kidnapped from his native land and taken to Europe. In 1618, when he returned to the area the second time, he had found his tribe completely gone.

The Pilgrims considered Squanto a special gift from God. They found him very useful as an interpreter, and by his help they made a peace treaty with Chief Massasoit, whose tribe had adopted him. Squanto taught the Pilgrims how to raise corn by placing four kernels and a fish (for fertilizer) in each hillock of soil. He also showed them how to tap maple trees to make maple syrup, where to find eels, and many other valuable things.

The Plymouth Colony thrived in the summer of 1621, and that fall the settlers brought in such a bountiful harvest that Governor **William Bradford** set aside a special time of thanksgiving. The settlers prepared a large feast and invited the Indians to share it with them: wild ducks and turkeys, fish, clams, lobsters, berries, corn bread, and other foods.

The Indians brought five deer, and they enjoyed the occasion so much that they stayed for three days.

The Pilgrims made a significant contribution to the United States. The Mayflower Compact was an important step toward self-government. The Pilgrims also allowed religious freedom in their settlement, and they practiced separation of church and state. These practices helped to form a basis for the principles on which the United States was founded.

The Massachusetts Bay Colony

In 1628, a group of Puritans from England settled at present-day Salem, along the coast north of the Plymouth Colony. Almost a thousand colonists arrived in June 1630, and later that year they founded Boston. Unlike the impoverished Pilgrims, these were well-to-do businessmen fully equipped with tools, goods, and weapons. The settlement, called the Massachusetts Bay Colony, flourished under the able leadership of **John Winthrop**, its first governor. It grew until it had about ten thousand settlers by 1640. It absorbed the smaller Plymouth Colony in 1691, when the whole settlement received a new charter.

A Union of Church and State. A primary purpose of the Massachusetts Bay Colony, called New England, was to be the new "Israel of God." The Puritan leaders intended to show the world that it was possible to have a truly godly society. John Winthrop said, "We shall be like a City upon a Hill; the eyes of all people are upon us." The state was responsible to punish civil crimes like theft and murder as well as religious crimes like heresy and blasphemy. By having the church and state work together, they planned to enforce right living in the colony.

John Winthrop (1588–1649) was governor of the Massachusetts Bay Colony. He brought about 1,000 colonists to Massachusetts Bay in 1630.

As with any attempt to unite the church and state, the Puritan attempt failed. It is not possible to live by New Testament principles and also take part in civil government. The only Scriptural approach is to separate the church from the state. As someone has said, the Christian's duty to the state is to "pray, pay, and obey."

Puritan Effects on the United States. The Puritans passed laws requiring that all children be taught to read and write, and thus they established the principle of formal education for children. Because of their diligent training, they succeeded well in producing men and women of character and ability. The Puritans believed in supplying one's own needs by hard work, and they provided good models of upright living.

Many New Englanders were among the settlers who moved west in later years. The Puritans multiplied to such an extent that two centuries later they were ancestors of one-third of the entire white population in the United States.

Rhode Island

The church–state system of the Puritans was soon challenged by **Roger Williams**, the pastor of an independent church at Salem, Massachusetts. Williams declared that the king of England had no right to grant land to colonies without paying the Indians for it. He also maintained that government leaders have authority only in civil matters, not religious ones. Forcing religion on a person was out of harmony with the New Testament, he said, because "forced religion stinks in God's nostrils."

The Puritans brought Williams to trial in 1635 and found him guilty of holding dangerous opinions. He was banished from the

Left: Roger Williams among the Narragansett Indians in 1636. From them he purchased land to establish Providence, a colony with complete religious freedom. ***Right:*** In 1636, Thomas Hooker and members of his church moved from Massachusetts to Connecticut for political and religious freedom.

colony and sentenced to be deported to England. But he and his wife fled in the cold of winter to some of his Indian friends.

In 1636, Williams and a number of other exiles from Massachusetts founded a settlement called Providence in the area that is now Rhode Island. More people came, and eventually four settlements in Rhode Island were authorized to operate under one government. A charter granted in 1663 established religious freedom and the separation of church and state in Rhode Island.

Since Roger Williams believed in religious freedom, no one in his colony was persecuted for holding any kind of belief, even atheism. Eventually many Quakers found refuge in the Providence colony. Today Roger Williams is remembered as the first to establish a government that granted freedom of conscience to all citizens.

Connecticut

The fertile Connecticut River valley attracted settlers from Massachusetts in the mid-1630s. One group was led by the eloquent preacher **Thomas Hooker**, who founded the town of Hartford in 1636. Soon other towns were founded, one by a separate group of Puritans at New Haven.

Hooker and others desired more political freedom than Massachusetts allowed. In 1639, Connecticut became the first English colony to establish a government with a written constitution, called the Fundamental Orders of Connecticut. This government was like that of Massachusetts in that the church and state were joined; however, government officials in Connecticut were elected by the people. The colony received its charter in 1662, and the New Haven settlement was joined to it in 1665.

Occupations in Colonial Times

Distributed throughout this book is a series of articles on major occupations in the early days of the United States. For various reasons, most of these occupations no longer have a significant place in the life of the average American in the 2000s. One reason is the Industrial Revolution with its mass production and the shift from animal power to machine power. Closely related are improvements in the production and transportation of raw materials and finished products. Also related are new inventions, crops, and products that have changed the way people provide food, clothing, and shelter for themselves. For example, plastic made from petroleum is used today for many things that were formerly made of wood or metal.

Rope making

"A threefold cord is not quickly broken" (Ecclesiastes 4:12).

Rope making was a common occupation in colonial times, especially near seaports. Most new rope was used in the rigging of new sailing ships, and older ships needed much replacement rope because their ropes wore out from hard use, weathering, and salt spray. Ropes were made by hand in long spaces or buildings called ropewalks; the length of rope that could be made depended on the length of the ropewalk.

The first ropewalks were set up in Salem, Massachusetts, in 1635. Many of the early ropewalks were in the open air. They consisted of a level space about a quarter mile (400 m) long, which was marked off by a series of pegged posts to hold the finished rope as it was made. To avoid interference from bad weather, later rope makers worked in long, narrow sheds that were often more than 1,000 feet (305 m) long and about 30 feet (9 m) wide. Open windows along the sides gave light for the three or four rope makers that worked side by side in the tunnel-like buildings.

Hemp was a common fiber used to make ropes. Hemp fiber was first beaten to soften it; then it was pulled by hand across a board with metal prongs extending from it. This combing removed snarls and short fibers, and prepared the hemp for spinning.

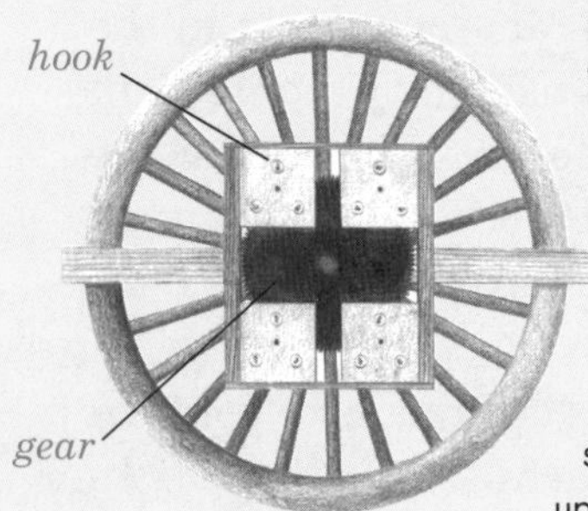

At one end of a ropewalk stood a wheel connected by gears to twelve or more metal hooks. When a boy turned the wheel, the hooks spun around. In this way, one boy could produce the power needed to keep several spinners busy at the same time. A spinner would take a bunch of prepared hemp, wind it many times around his waist, and hook a loop of fibers around a roller hook. Then the spinner would act like a human spider, slowly backing away from the spinning wheel and feeding fiber into the spinning yarn. His expert fingers fed the fiber in smoothly, compressing it to an even size as it twisted. The spinner made gestures or rang an overhead bell to let the boy know how fast he should turn the wheel. To keep the finished yarn from touching the ground, the spinner tossed it up to overhead hooks as he passed under them.

A rope maker spun the hemp in a series of opposite twists, generally three. (See Ecclesiastes 4:12.) He took advantage of the tendency of yarns to untwist; the reverse twisting helped to bind a cord together. A spinner would first spin the fibers from left to right to make yarn. After two hundred to three hundred yarns were spun, rope makers twisted them together loosely and dipped them in hot tar. They pressed the tar into the yarns by pulling them through a metal disk, which removed excess tar but left enough to protect the fibers from the weather. The tarred yarns were then separated, and several were looped onto the roller hooks. Then he spun several of these yarns together, twisting from right to left to make a strand. Finally, he wound together several strands (usually three) with a left-to-right twist to make the rope. This same method is still used to make rope today, except that machines do the work that people formerly did, and synthetic fibers have largely replaced natural fibers.

The quality of the rope varied according to the skill and strength of the spinner. Temperature also played a role. Most ropewalks were closed during the winter months because the tarred yarns became too stiff to work into rope. Spinners commonly worked in the unheated sheds until their fingers became too numb to do a good job.

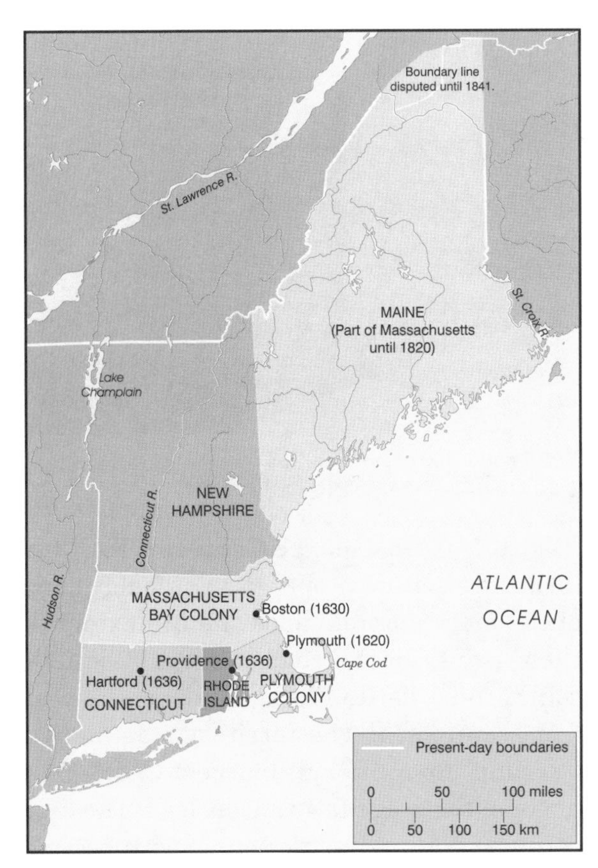

The New England Colonies

The New Hampshire Colony

New Hampshire and Maine also grew out of the Massachusetts colony. This territory was granted to Sir Ferdinando Gorges and John Mason in 1622, who divided the land between them in 1629. Gorges took the section called Maine, and Mason took the region of New Hampshire. But neither man had much success in getting his colony settled, and gradually settlers from Massachusetts Bay Colony began to move there.

Eventually Massachusetts took over the whole area, but in 1680 New Hampshire received a charter as a separate colony. Maine continued to be part of Massachusetts until 1820, when it became a state of the United States.

Maryland

Lord Baltimore's Settlement. A number of colonies were founded by ***proprietors*** (pruh PRY ih turz) rather than companies. Proprietors were individuals, usually rich nobles, who received land and a charter from the king. Some of them expected to establish manorial systems and rent their land to people of lower rank.

In 1632, a gentleman entitled **Lord Baltimore** became proprietor of all the land north of the Potomac River and south of the fortieth parallel. The new colony was named Maryland after Queen Henrietta Maria, the wife of King Charles I. But before the charter was issued, Lord Baltimore died and the land passed to his son, also called Lord Baltimore.

The first colonists landed in Maryland in 1634 and founded St. Marys City north of the Potomac River. They obtained the place by peaceable negotiation with the local Indians, who were in the process of moving out anyway. The settlers made immediate use of the Indians' houses, fields, and gardens, which helped them to prosper from the beginning. Tobacco became important, and rich people used many workers to plant large estates.

Religious Freedom in Maryland. Since Lord Baltimore was a Roman Catholic, he wanted his colony to be a refuge for fellow Catholics—who now were a persecuted

Cecilius Calvert, also known as the second Lord Baltimore, was the founder of Maryland. He never visited Maryland, but made his brother Leonard Calvert its governor.

Baltimore in 1752. It had a population of about 300 at that time.

minority in England. But other people who professed the Christian religion were also welcome in his colony.

The majority of settlers in Maryland were Protestant, but the Catholic minority held the reins of government. This fact created various problems for the young colony. Religious matters were calmed in 1649 when the colonial government issued the Act of Toleration, which read as follows:

> Whereas the enforcing the conscience on matters of religion hath frequently fallen out to be of dangerous consequence in those commonwealths where it hath been practiced, . . . no person within this province, professing to believe in Jesus Christ, shall be in any ways troubled, molested, or discountenanced, for his or her religion, or in the free exercise thereof.

The government of Maryland faithfully upheld the Act of Toleration, and it also granted political freedom and the privilege of private enterprise. These broad freedoms attracted hundreds of people, and by 1660 Maryland had a population of eight thousand settlers.

The Carolinas

In 1663, King Charles II granted land south of Virginia to **Lord John Berkeley** (BURK lee), **Sir George Carteret** (KAR tur iht), and six other proprietors. Probably none of the men comprehended the full extent of their grant, for it stretched from Virginia's southern border to Florida and east to west from sea to sea! The territory was named Carolina (from the Latin form of *Charles*) in honor of the king's father, Charles I. The first permanent English settlement in what became South Carolina was founded at Charles Town (near modern Charleston) in 1670.

The proprietors of Carolina expected to rent out their land by a manorial system, but their plan failed because land was so plentiful. What farmer wanted to pay rent when he could easily get land of his own? Actually, Carolina developed in much the same way as Virginia and Maryland, and most white men possessed their own land.

The eight proprietors wanted to produce specialty items such as silk and raisins in their territory. They tried many different crops, but they were successful only with ***naval stores*** (pine products such as tar and pitch, used to seal cracks in wooden ships). Pine and cypress trees flourished in the Carolina region, and they produced resins that yielded pitch, tar, and turpentine. A steady supply of black slaves was imported to do the hard work of cutting trees and boiling tar. Later, rice and indigo (for dyes) were grown for profit in South Carolina.

Cooperage (Barrel Making)

"And the barrel of meal wasted not, neither did the cruse of oil fail, according to the word of the Lord, which he spake by Elijah" (1 Kings 17:16).

Coopers have skillfully made wooden barrels by hand for hundreds of years. Millions of barrels were needed in colonial days, because many products were stored and shipped in barrels, especially in the South. Some were "dry" barrels for products such as flour, rice, tobacco, indigo, salt, sugar, and nails. Others were "wet" barrels for liquid items such as molasses, tar, resin, and wine. Besides his work with storage barrels, a cooper was kept busy making and mending kegs, buckets, and tubs.

Each barrel was a large cylinder-shaped container that bulged outward in the middle. The sides were made of strips of wood (staves) bound together by wooden or metal hoops. Each stave was cut wider in the middle to allow for the bulge, which added strength to the barrel but wasted space when the barrels were shipped. The top and bottom of each barrel were flat wooden circles (heads) shaped from pieces of plank and held together with dowels. The heads fit into grooves made for them at the end of the staves. Marsh reeds were used to seal the grooves of "wet" barrels. Iron hoops were riveted around the barrel to hold it together. If wooden hoops were used instead, three of them were needed to equal the strength of each iron hoop.

Oak was the main wood used. Oak logs were cut into rough planks that were stacked and covered with leaves to dry slowly. A cooper made barrel staves by using an axe and drawknife to cut the planks to the proper length and width. He shaped and hollowed the inside of each stave. All the staves had to be planed exactly right in order to fit tightly together in the finished barrel. For the next step, a cooper had to know whether he was making a "stout cask" (a heavy one) or a "slight cask." He boiled the staves for a stout cask and soaked them for a slight cask.

To put a barrel together, a cooper would assemble the staves with their top ends touching and the bottom ends splayed. He put a rope or a hoop of ash around the top, close to where the first hoop would be. He placed the top head in the groove and hammered the top iron hoop into position to hold the staves. Then he forced the rope or ash hoop farther down the staves to squeeze them close together. With the staves thus held securely, the cooper suspended the barrel over a fire so that the wet staves would become soft and pliable. Then he hammered the next two hoops in their places, flipped the barrel over, and repeated the process at the other end. A cooper could make ten barrels per day by this method.

A new wooden barrel had to be "pickled" for three days by filling it with a concentrated brine mixture that neutralized the tannic acid in the wood. Then the barrel was rinsed thoroughly and was ready for use. If it was to hold liquids, a bunghole was drilled and a wooden bung (stopper) was inserted.

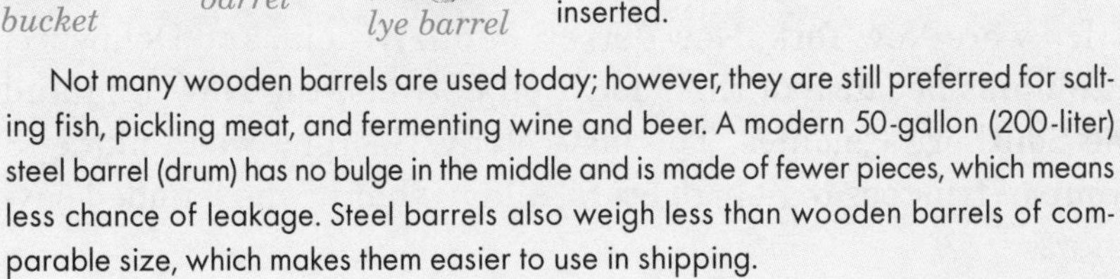

bucket *barrel* *lye barrel*

Not many wooden barrels are used today; however, they are still preferred for salting fish, pickling meat, and fermenting wine and beer. A modern 50-gallon (200-liter) steel barrel (drum) has no bulge in the middle and is made of fewer pieces, which means less chance of leakage. Steel barrels also weigh less than wooden barrels of comparable size, which makes them easier to use in shipping.

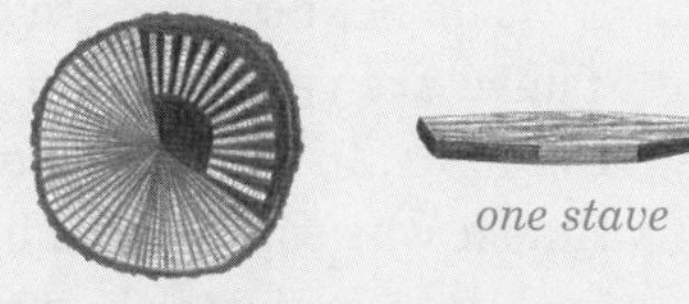

one stave

Many staves could be cut from a log.

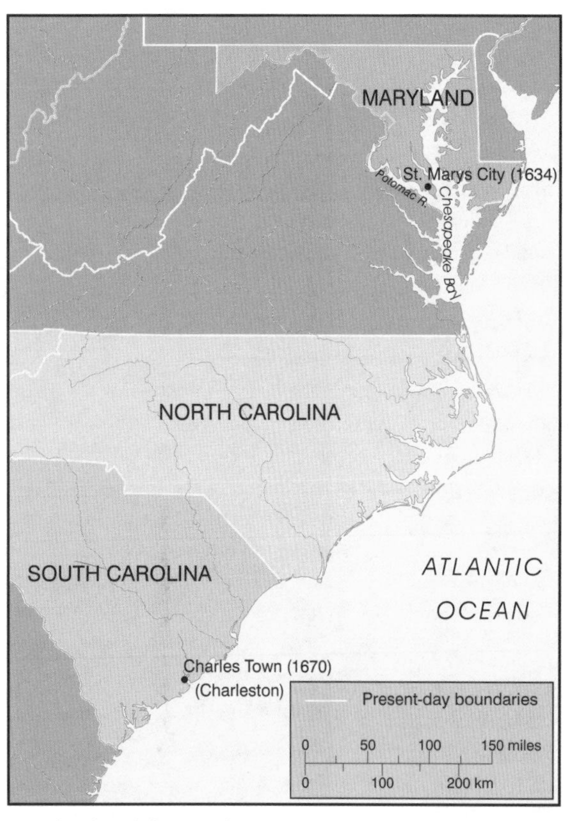

Maryland and the Carolinas

Formation of North Carolina and South Carolina. As the years passed, northern and southern Carolina became different in character. Most settlers in northern Carolina produced naval stores and tobacco on a small scale. In southern Carolina, the upper-class settlers developed large plantations and used slave labor.

The people themselves were different. Northern Carolina had many Moravians and Quakers, along with numerous immigrants from Virginia. Southern Carolina was the home of immigrants from various parts of Europe, including many Huguenots from France. In 1712, Carolina was officially divided into North Carolina and South Carolina. Each part became a royal colony of England in 1729.

Focus for Thought

6. a. In what year did the Pilgrims arrive in America?
   b. Why did they draw up the Mayflower Compact?
7. Explain how the goal of the Puritans in New England was different from the goal of the settlers at Jamestown.
8. For what is Roger Williams remembered today?
9. Name the founder of Connecticut, and give the year of its founding.
10. How did New Hampshire become a colony?
11. What important freedom was granted by the Act of Toleration?
12. a. What was the aim of the proprietors who established the Carolina territory?
    b. What were two major differences between the northern and southern parts of Carolina?

3. THE MIDDLE COLONIES AND GEORGIA

The next colonies to be settled were New York, New Jersey, Pennsylvania, and Delaware. These are called the Middle Colonies because of their location between the New England Colonies, in the north, and the Southern Colonies. The last colony, Georgia, was unique in that it was established by a group of trustees to help debtors, and in that it was founded several decades later than the others.

New York

Founding of New Netherland. **Henry Hudson**, an Englishman sailing for the Netherlands, sought the Northwest Passage in 1609. Sailing up the river that now bears his name, Hudson claimed the surrounding area for the Dutch and called it New Netherland. In 1624, the Dutch built Fort Orange near present-day Albany and began trading with the Iroquois.

Soon a Dutch settlement grew up between the Delaware and Hudson Rivers. Its governor, Peter Minuit (MIHN yoo iht), bought Manhattan Island from the Indians in 1626 for merchandise valued at twenty-four dollars. The town of New Amsterdam developed on the southern end of Manhattan Island.

But the New Netherland settlement was not very successful. The Dutch used a plan known as the patroon (puh TROON) system, which was a form of manorialism. In this system, if a man brought fifty rent-paying settlers to New Netherland, he received a large tract of land and was honored as a patroon. But with so much land available at little or no cost, few settlers wanted to pay rent. Only five patroonships were actually granted, and eventually the patroon system lost out to the private ownership of land.

New Netherland Becomes New York. The English did not want a Dutch colony separating New England from their southern colonies. Also, they wanted control of the harbor at New Amsterdam. So in March 1664, King Charles II of England gave all the region between Connecticut and Maryland to his brother James, the Duke of York.

In August 1664, a fleet of English warships sailed into the harbor of New Amsterdam and the English demanded that the Dutch governor surrender to England. Governor **Peter Stuyvesant** (STY vih suhnt) fussed and fumed and stamped his wooden leg, but he found that his Dutch countrymen were tired of his harsh rule. They refused to help him fight, and thus the Dutch colony of New Netherland passed peaceably to the English.

In 1626, Peter Minuit bought Manhattan Island from the Indians for trinkets worth $24 at the time.

The Dutch colony was renamed New York in honor of its new proprietor, the **Duke of York**. New Amsterdam became New York City. When James, the Duke of York, became King James II, New York became a royal colony. By then it included all the land in present-day New York, New Jersey, and Delaware.

New Jersey

Soon after New York came into the possession of James, the Duke of York, he gave the land between the Hudson and Delaware Rivers to two of his friends, Lord John Berkeley and Sir George Carteret. They received this grant only a year after both had become proprietors of Carolina. Since Carteret had served well on the English island of Jersey, the Duke of York named the area New Jersey.

In 1674, Berkeley sold his share of New Jersey to several Quakers who wanted to establish a haven for their group. Eight years later, the Quakers were able to purchase the rest of New Jersey. In 1738, New Jersey became a royal colony, governed directly by the king of England.

Pennsylvania

A Colony for Quakers. During the mid-1600s, the Society of Friends (Quakers) was established in England by George Fox. He taught that there was "that of God in every man," and that people should follow this "Inner Light" for spiritual guidance. The Quakers emphasized a quiet, peaceable life so that the "Inner Light" could readily guide them. They dressed in simple clothing and refused to swear oaths, to take part in war, and to give special titles of honor to anyone.

The Quakers correctly understood that the Sermon on the Mount is to be lived and not held only as an ideal. But they spiritualized other parts of the New Testament; for example, they refused the literal observance of baptism and Communion. By emphasizing the "Inner Light" more than the Bible, they opened themselves to deception.

The Quakers suffered much contempt and persecution because of their beliefs. Then in 1667 they were joined by **William Penn**, the youthful son of Admiral William Penn of the English navy. Admiral Penn died three years later, with King Charles II owing him a large sum of money. In 1680, William Penn asked the king to repay the debt with a tract of land in America. Penn hoped to establish a colony where Quakers would be free to live and worship as they chose.

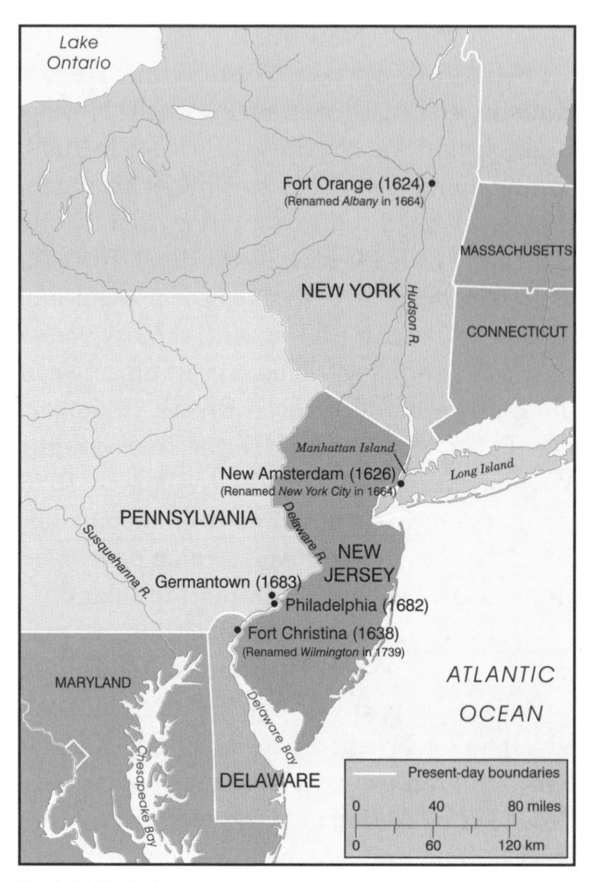

The Middle Colonies

William Penn (1644–1718) founded Philadelphia, the City of Brotherly Love. His colony offered religious freedom for many persecuted people in Europe, including Mennonites, Amish, and Quakers.

Founding of Pennsylvania. The only English territory available was the land between New York and Maryland. In 1681, King Charles II issued a charter that gave William Penn almost unlimited control over this territory. It was called Pennsylvania (Latin for "Penn's Woods"), in honor of Admiral William Penn.

Penn started advertising to attract settlers. He promised cheap land and new opportunities for farmers and laborers, as well as religious freedom to anyone who professed to believe in God. Philadelphia, the "greene countrie towne," was established in 1682; and by the end of the next year, the colony had

William Penn made a treaty with the Indians in 1682. Penn and the chief of the Delaware Indians are said to have exchanged wampum belts under the Shackamaxon elm near present-day Philadelphia. Penn's fair treatment of the Indians spared his colony from Indian attacks for many years.

four thousand people and Philadelphia had swelled to 150 houses.

In 1683, the first Mennonites arrived, thirty-four of them, and they settled north of Philadelphia at Germantown. Many other Germans, as well as Irish, Dutch, and Scottish people, came to Pennsylvania.

Even though Charles II had deeded Pennsylvania to him, William Penn paid the Indians for the land in his colony. As the colony grew and more land was needed, he made additional purchases. This fair treatment won the respect and friendship of the Indians, with the result that Pennsylvania never had a major Indian uprising like the colonies in New England and Virginia had.

Penn's "Holy Experiment." William Penn wanted to try a "Holy Experiment" in his colony. He planned that it would be settled by virtuous people and governed by godly men acting on Christian principles. Unlike the Puritan colony, Pennsylvania would have both religious and political freedoms, all maintained in the spirit of ***pacifism*** (PAS uh fihz uhm)—that is, a policy of settling disputes by nonviolent means. Pacifists avoid fighting but may still use other kinds of force, such as lawsuits. By contrast, truly nonresistant people follow Jesus' command to "resist not evil." They do not use force of any kind.

William Penn drew up a constitution called a Frame of Government for Pennsylvania. It guaranteed the freedom of worship and the right to trial by jury. All free inhabitants had the right to vote, and all who believed in God and in Jesus Christ could hold government offices. A number of ideals expressed in this document later became part of the United States Constitution.

The "Holy Experiment" suffered after Penn returned to England in 1684. The men appointed to manage the colony refused to follow Penn's constitution and instructions. Reluctantly Penn realized that outward force was necessary to compel obedience to the laws. His "Holy Experiment" was not working.

Penn found that he could not operate his colony by New Testament principles established for the church. The government has been ordained of God to keep order in an unruly society, whereas the church has been established as a holy people "zealous of good works."

Penn lost his colony in 1692, but he regained it two years later when he promised to provide money and men for its military defense. He felt justified in doing this because necessity required it. Penn had received little return from the settlers for all the money

Philadelphia in 1756. The city flourished as the capital of Pennsylvania and was the leading city of the colonies in wealth and population.

he had invested in Pennsylvania, and he wanted his colony back if at all possible.

Prosperity in Pennsylvania. William Penn finally returned to America in 1699. By that time Philadelphia, the City of Brotherly Love, was a thriving town of five thousand people, one of the largest in the English colonies. Its citizens wore fine clothing; prosperous farms covered the surrounding land; and shipbuilding had sprung up along the river. Pennsylvania had become one of the most successful colonies in America.

Delaware

Delaware was first settled by the Swedes as New Sweden. Later the Dutch took over the area, but they in turn were conquered by the English. Delaware was then part of New

The Liberty Bell. In 1751, a bell was cast to commemorate the liberties Penn had granted in his colony. On the bell was inscribed, "Proclaim liberty throughout all the land unto all the inhabitants thereof" (Leviticus 25:10). This 2,080-pound (943-kg) bell became known as the Liberty Bell. Rung in 1776 to announce the adoption of the Declaration of Independence, the Liberty Bell became a symbol of American freedoms and was rung on July 4 of every year until 1835. That year the bell developed a crack while tolling for the funeral of John Marshall. In 1846, it cracked irreparably while being rung for George Washington's birthday. Today it hangs in a special pavilion in Philadelphia.

Netherland, which was given to the Duke of York and renamed New York.

When William Penn acquired Pennsylvania, he wanted a harbor for his colony, so he persuaded the Duke of York to grant him the region of Delaware. However, in 1704, Delaware was set up as a separate colony.

Georgia

The last English colony on the Atlantic coast was established in a manner different from that of any other. In 1732, twenty-one ***trustees*** obtained a charter from King George II to establish a colony for honest debtors in England—prisoners guilty of no greater crime than being unable to pay their debts. The colony was also to serve as a ***buffer*** between English South Carolina and Spanish Florida. General **James Oglethorpe** (OH guhl thawrp), a member of the British Parliament, was the leader of this ***humanitarian*** effort.

The entire project was planned in England. The colony would be called Georgia, after the king, and it would have no slaves, no rum, and no self-government. Land would be obtained peaceably from the Indians by treaty. Each settler would receive 50 acres (20 ha) and be outfitted for the first year by Oglethorpe himself, and those with more means could buy as much as 500 acres (202 ha). The project was praised from the pulpit and lauded by the press.

Oglethorpe brought the first colonists to Georgia and founded Savannah in 1733. But only a few debtors went there; instead, most of the settlers were people who sought freedom and opportunity. Industries in Georgia could not compete with those in the

James Oglethorpe (1696–1785) governed Georgia for nine years and returned to England in 1743.

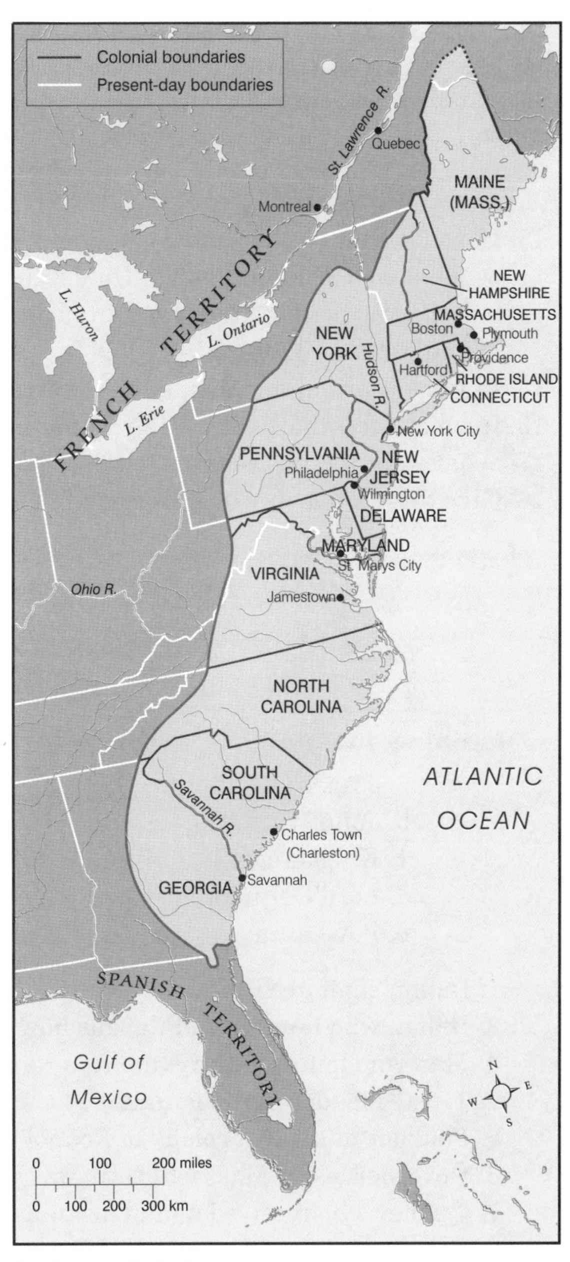

The Thirteen Colonies

Savannah, Georgia, in 1734. It is called the "Mother City of Georgia" because it was the first white settlement in the colony. Savannah was one of the first planned cities in America.

nearby slave-holding colonies. Rum and other illegal products were smuggled in. And the colonists did not like the laws made by the trustees.

Since Georgia did not work out as planned, the trustees gave up their charter in 1752 and Georgia became a royal colony. Later the rule against slavery was dropped, and Georgia developed an economy like that of South Carolina.

Focus for Thought

13. How did New Netherland come under English control?
14. a. What was William Penn's "Holy Experiment"?
    b. Is it ever possible to create an ideal society on earth? Explain. (See Genesis 3:16–19 and Romans 3:20–23.)
15. In what year did the Mennonites first arrive in Pennsylvania, and where did they settle?
16. In what ways did Penn's "Holy Experiment" fail?
17. What were the two reasons for Georgia's founding?
18. Give three ways in which Georgia fell short of its idealistic goals.

Historical Highlights

A. Matching: People 1

a. James Oglethorpe
b. John Winthrop
c. King James I
d. Lord Baltimore
e. Powhatan
f. Sir Walter Raleigh
g. Squanto
h. William Bradford
i. William Penn

1. Indian chief in Virginia.
2. Indian who taught the Pilgrims how to live in the wilderness.
3. Man who founded Maryland as a haven for Catholics.
4. Trustee leader in the founding of Georgia.
5. Founder of the lost colony of Roanoke.
6. Governor of the Massachusetts Bay Colony.
7. Quaker who received a land grant as payment for a debt.
8. Governor of the Plymouth Colony.
9. Authorized Jamestown settlement and a new version of the Bible.

B. Matching: People 2

a. Duke of York
b. Henry Hudson
c. John Cabot
d. John Rolfe
e. John Smith
f. Lord Berkeley
g. Peter Stuyvesant
h. Roger Williams
i. Sir George Carteret
j. Thomas Hooker
k. Virginia Dare

1. Man who established a settlement in the Connecticut River valley.
2. Nobleman who received the Dutch territory of New Netherland.
3. First explorer to claim North American land for England.
4. Dutch governor who surrendered New Netherland to the English.
5. First English child born in America.
6. Man who married Pocahontas and introduced a new kind of tobacco.
7. Proprietors who sold their land to Quakers (two answers).
8. Jamestown leader.
9. Explorer for whom a river and a bay are named.
10. Founder of Rhode Island, who insisted on freedom of conscience and fled from the Puritans.

C. Matching: Terms 1

a. burgesses
b. Huguenots
c. London Company
d. naval stores
e. Pilgrims
f. private enterprise
g. proprietors
h. Puritans
i. Quakers
j. royal colony
k. Separatists
l. slaves
m. trustees

1. Persons who care for property entrusted to them.
2. People who withdrew from the Church of England and formed congregations of their own (two answers).
3. People guided by the "Inner Light."
4. Colony owned and managed by the king.
5. French Protestants who settled in South Carolina.
6. Noblemen who received land from the king and who sometimes expected to rent it to men of lower rank.
7. Representatives who took part in colonial government.
8. Group of investors who sponsored Jamestown.
9. Persons who are considered the property of a master.
10. People who wanted to purify the Church of England from within.
11. Pine products such as tar and pitch, used to seal cracks in wooden ships.
12. System in which individuals have their own property and receive the benefits of their own labor.

D. Matching: Terms 2

a. buffer
b. charter
c. gold
d. humanitarian
e. pacifism
f. tobacco
g. Act of Toleration
h. Frame of Government
i. Fundamental Orders
j. "Holy Experiment"
k. *Mayflower*
l. Mayflower Compact

1. Ship that carried Pilgrims and Strangers to America.
2. Serving to promote human welfare.
3. First written constitution for an English colony.
4. Policy of settling disputes by nonviolent means rather than by fighting.
5. Item sought earnestly by early explorers and colonists.
6. William Penn's constitution for Pennsylvania.
7. Territory between two enemy nations that helps to reduce the likelihood of conflict.
8. Product that brought economic success to Jamestown.
9. Maryland law granting religious freedom.
10. William Penn's attempt to have a colony based on Quaker idealism.
11. Agreement signed by Pilgrims and Strangers to make "just and equal laws."
12. Legal document granting the right to settle and govern a certain region.

E. Matching: Places

a. Carolina
b. Connecticut
c. Delaware
d. Georgia
e. Massachusetts Bay Colony
f. New Amsterdam
g. New England
h. New Netherland
i. Northwest Passage
j. Philadelphia
k. Plymouth
l. Providence

1. Location of Thomas Hooker's settlement.
2. Name of the Pilgrims' settlement.
3. Dutch territory in America.
4. Land first settled by the Swedes and the Dutch.
5. Town that was renamed New York City.
6. Shortcut to the Orient sought by Hudson and others.
7. Name of the Puritans' settlement.
8. Name derived from the Latin form of *Charles*.
9. Region including Plymouth, Massachusetts, Rhode Island, Connecticut, and New Hampshire.
10. City of Brotherly Love.
11. Name of Roger Williams' settlement.
12. Colony established as a haven for debtors.

F. Place Names

Explain how each of the following received its name.

1. Jamestown
2. Maryland
3. New York
4. New Jersey
5. Carolina
6. Pennsylvania
7. Georgia

G. Deeper Discussion

1. What was involved in starting a colony? Consider such items as obtaining legal rights, transportation, planning, and establishing the actual settlement.
2. Why was the communal system of Jamestown replaced by a system of private enterprise?
3. a. What did the Pilgrims, Puritans, and Quakers gain by emigrating to America?
   b. Why were these things important to them?
4. Explain why systems based on European manorialism did not work in America.
5. Pennsylvania and Georgia were founded with idealistic goals. Why did the idealism fail?
6. Why did the Pennsylvania settlers prosper from the beginning while those in Virginia had great difficulties?
7. What character qualities did the Puritans and Quakers have that made them excellent colonists?

H. Chronology and Geography

1. The following chart shows the thirteen colonies in the order of their founding *by the English*. Copy and complete the chart, noting these specific directions.
   a. Use dates from the chapter time line.
   b. Fill in two lines for Massachusetts, as indicated.
   c. For New Hampshire and Delaware, write "Separated from ___" in the last column (indicating the colonies that they were separated from).
   d. For Carolina, write the dates of the original charter and of the separation of North Carolina and South Carolina under "Year Founded." Fill in the other two columns with just one line for Carolina as a whole.

Colony	Year Founded	Founder	Reason for Founding
Virginia			
Massachusetts: Plymouth Massachusetts Bay			
Maryland			
Rhode Island			
Connecticut			
Carolina: Chartered Separated			
New York			
New Jersey			
New Hampshire			
Pennsylvania			
Delaware			
Georgia			

2. Trace Map D in the Map Section, and label it "The Thirteen Colonies."
   a. Label the thirteen colonies.
   b. Label the following early settlements with their names and founding dates: Jamestown—1607, Plymouth—1620, Fort Orange (Albany)—1624, New Amsterdam (New York)—1626, Boston—1630, St. Marys City—1634, Providence—1636, Hartford—1636, Fort Christina (Wilmington)—1638, Charles Town—1670, Philadelphia—1682, and Savannah—1733. (Parentheses indicate the later name of a place.)
   c. Use three different colors to show the New England Colonies, the Middle Colonies, and the Southern Colonies. Include a legend to show what the colors represent.

So Far This Year

Write the letter of the correct answer.

1. A wet, mild climate found in the Pacific valleys is a _____ climate.
   a. humid continental
   b. Mediterranean
   c. humid subtropical
   d. west coast marine
2. The _____ is a rocky region in Canada that curves like a horseshoe around Hudson Bay.
   a. Cordillera region
   b. Canadian Shield
   c. Great Lakes-St. Lawrence Lowlands
   d. Appalachian Region
3. _____ explored the northeastern coast of North America for England in 1497.
   a. Henry Hudson
   b. Giovanni da Verrazano
   c. John Cabot
   d. Jacques Cartier
4. The New World was named after _____.
   a. Amerigo Vespucci
   b. Christopher Columbus
5. _____ claimed part of North America for the Netherlands in 1609.
   a. Ferdinand Magellan
   b. Vasco de Balboa
   c. Vasco da Gama
   d. Henry Hudson
6. In the system called _____, a lord owned the land and serfs farmed it for him.
   a. feudalism
   b. capitalism
   c. manorialism
   d. democracy
7. The _____ was a form of manorialism transplanted to New France.
   a. seigneur
   b. seigneurial system
   c. culture area
   d. coureurs de bois
8. _____ is called the "father of New France."
   a. Jacques Cartier
   b. Robert de La Salle
   c. Giovanni da Verrazano
   d. Samuel de Champlain
9. _____ claimed the area drained by the Mississippi River for France.
   a. Robert de La Salle
   b. Louis Jolliet
   c. Jacques Marquette
   d. Samuel de Champlain
10. The Spanish Armada was defeated in the year _____.
    a. 1565
    b. 1588
    c. 1513
    d. 1539
11. The _____ were the Indian tribes who sided with the French.
    a. Iroquois
    b. Huron and Algonquin
12. _____ was the leader at Jamestown who helped the colony to survive.
    a. John Smith
    b. Thomas Hooker
    c. Roger Williams
    d. Lord Berkeley

A Puritan girl of colonial times.

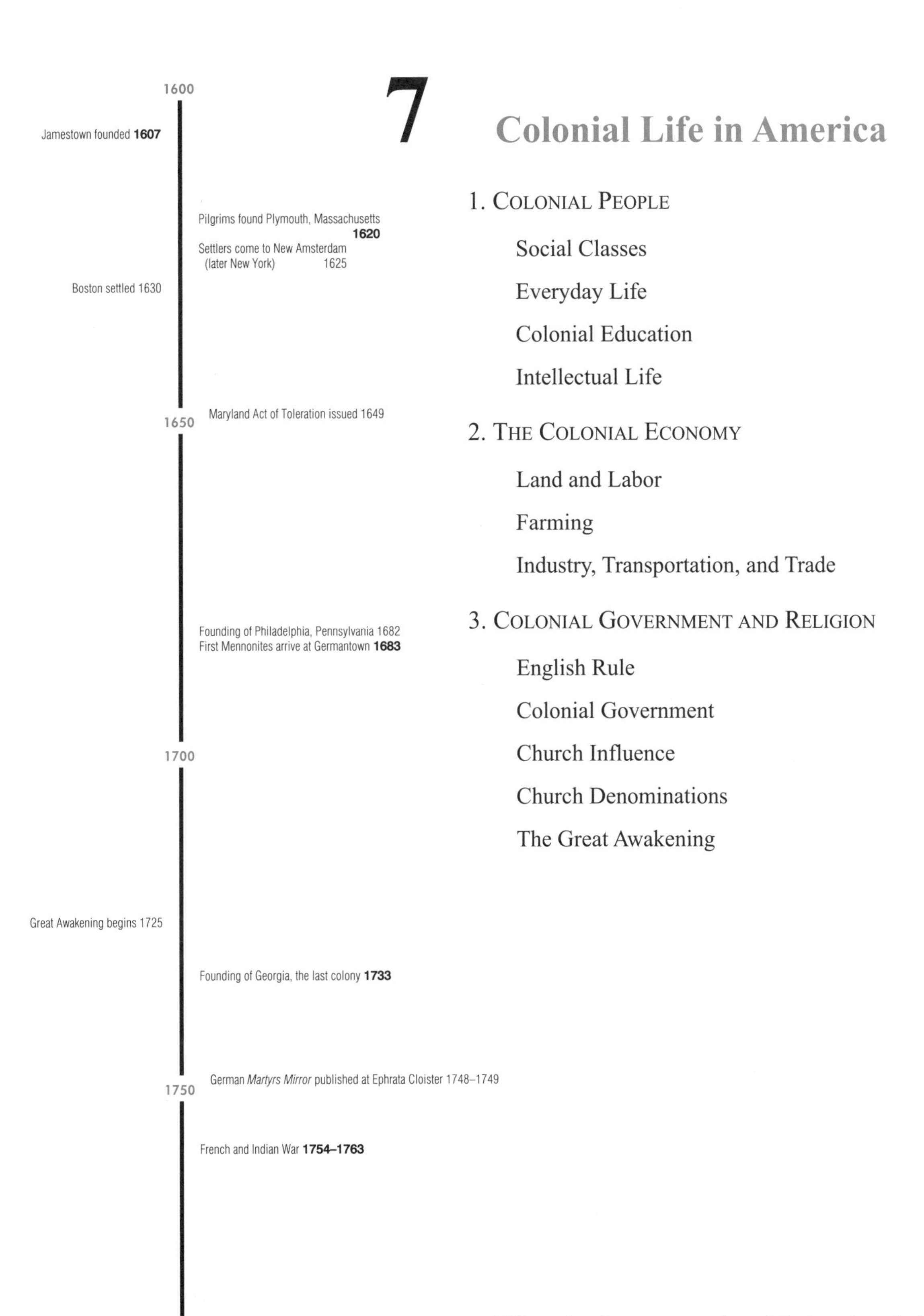

7 Colonial Life in America

1. COLONIAL PEOPLE
   - Social Classes
   - Everyday Life
   - Colonial Education
   - Intellectual Life
2. THE COLONIAL ECONOMY
   - Land and Labor
   - Farming
   - Industry, Transportation, and Trade
3. COLONIAL GOVERNMENT AND RELIGION
   - English Rule
   - Colonial Government
   - Church Influence
   - Church Denominations
   - The Great Awakening

"When thou hast eaten and art full, then thou shalt bless the LORD thy God for the good land which he hath given thee."

Deuteronomy 8:10

Colonial Life in America

Focus for Reading

People came to America from many different European countries. But most of the white people in eastern America were English, so the language, customs, and laws of England prevailed in the colonies of that region. For convenient study, those colonies may be placed in three groups: the New England Colonies (Massachusetts, Rhode Island, New Hampshire, Connecticut); the Middle Colonies (Pennsylvania, New York, New Jersey, Delaware); and the Southern Colonies (Maryland, Virginia, the Carolinas, and Georgia).

Since conditions in colonial America were much different from what they are now, colonial life was also much different from what life is today. In this chapter, you will learn how people lived in colonial America by studying the following aspects of colonial life.

1. Colonial People
2. The Colonial Economy
3. Colonial Government and Religion

1. COLONIAL PEOPLE

When people lived in colonial America over two hundred years ago, their lives were as ordinary as ours are today. They went to school, to work, and to church. But their houses, schools, work, and church life differed from ours in many ways.

Social Classes

There was little class distinction among the first settlers because everyone was struggling to survive in the wilderness. But as the colonies progressed, several social classes emerged. The ***better class***, or aristocracy, was the smallest class and included government officials, plantation owners, and church leaders. A man in this class might have the title "Gentleman," "Esquire," or "Master."

The ***middling class*** included the owners of small farms and businesses. They might be called "Goodman," "Goodwife," or "farmer." The ***meaner sort***, or lower classes, included unskilled workers who owned little or no land and could not vote. People of this group had no titles but were referred to by their last names.

For some poor people, the only means of getting to America was by becoming ***indentured servants***. By this arrangement, a ship captain agreed to bring a person to America, and then he sold the person for a higher price than the cost of the voyage. When someone in the New World bought him, the person was required to work for his master for a period of four to seven years. Then he received his freedom.

The rank of indentured servants was below that of the meaner sort. Even lower were the black slaves, who remained in bondage for life.

There was an important difference between classes in Europe and classes in America. European classes were based on birth, but American classes were based on wealth. Except for slaves, anyone in America who prospered in his business could rise to a higher social class. This is why America became known as a land of opportunity.

However, we must remember that "God is no respecter of persons" (Acts 10:34) and that He forbids respect of persons among men (James 2:9). For Christians, there are no class distinctions.

Colonial kitchen in New England. Note the various tasks that the family members are doing.

Everyday Life

Family Life. Families of twelve or more children were common in colonial times, but many children died before adulthood. A large family was an advantage because of all the work that needed to be done. The men provided a living, and the women and children helped at home.

Children received much religious training at home, especially in New England. Thus the family served as the most important unit of colonial society. This was in line with God's plan, in which a husband and wife are to leave their parents and establish their own home (Mark 10:6–9).

Houses and Furniture. The first settlers lived in crude houses made of sticks or in log cabins, first built by the Swedes in the 1600s. Wood frame houses were common through most of the colonial period, especially in New England, and many had either a single story or a story and a half.

Families of poor farmers often had crude wooden furniture that included a table, a bench, and some stools. They slept on simple mattresses called ticks, filled with straw or leaves, and they used skins or quilts for covers. Dishes were made of wood or pewter, and utensils (if used) were made of wood, bone, or iron.

Houses of rich people were more luxurious, having fine imported furniture, such as four-poster beds with feather ticks. Their children often slept in trundle beds that could be kept under a big bed during the day and pulled out at night. Many rich people also used eating utensils of silver, and tended their fireplaces with brass tools.

Food and Clothing. Food was plentiful in the colonies after the first several years. The settlers ate much meat from cattle and hogs as well as from game and fish. Vegetables and fruits were available in season, and pickling or drying preserved them for later use.

Wealthy people followed European fashions and dressed in fine clothes made of expensive fabrics. Men wore long coats, knee-length breeches, silk stockings, and shoes with buckles of gold or silver. Women wore dresses with thin waists and hoop skirts. They often adorned themselves with jewelry and fancy hats, and carried a fan.

The middling class and the meaner sort had to settle for simpler clothes, often made of homespun wool or linsey-woolsey (linen and wool). Some wore leather breeches, and the deerskin coat and coonskin cap were common, especially on the frontier.

Everyday items from the 1600s. The center picture shows the inside of an old-time New England farmhouse.

Cloth making

"She layeth her hands to the spindle, and her hands hold the distaff" (Proverbs 31:19).

Most colonial pioneers made their own clothing, and they did all the work by hand. They began by growing flax for linen, and raising sheep for wool. Then they spun the linen and wool fibers into thread and yarn. Next they wove the thread or yarn into cloth on a loom, and then they sewed the cloth into garments. (There were no sewing machines until Elias Howe patented the first one in 1846.)

Linen was made from the strong stem fibers of flax, which can be from 6 to 40 inches (15 to 102 cm) long. At harvesttime, flax stalks were pulled and then dried in the sun; later the seeds were removed. The stems were allowed to rot for several weeks by soaking them in a bog or slow-moving stream, or by spreading them on the grass and keeping them wet. This process was called retting, and it loosened the fibers from the woody stem. The stems were again dried, and the woody parts were removed by beating them (scutching). Then the fibers were combed (hackled), which separated the long fibers called *line* from the short fibers called *tow*. Line was put onto a distaff to be spun; it did not need to be carded. Tow could be spun to make a coarse yarn, but it had to be carded first.

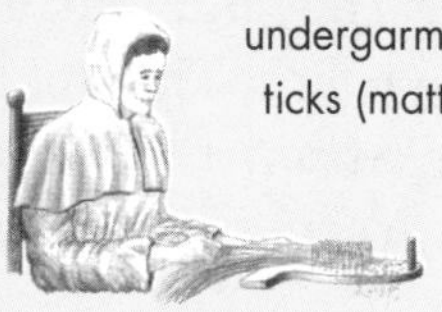

Linen (line) was used for shirts, dresses, undergarments, head coverings, bedding, and ticks (mattresses that were stuffed with straw or cornhusks). Scraps of the cloth were stitched together to make bed quilts. Almost all American households raised flax to make linen until Eli Whitney invented the cotton gin in 1793; then cotton became more popular than linen.

Wool was used to make coats, scarves, stockings, men's knee-length breeches, and other garments. Sheep were sheared once a year, usually in the late spring when they could do without their heavy fleece. A fleece needed to be washed to remove dirt and debris. Wool did not spoil; it could be stored for later use or shipped easily. Besides using the wool to make clothes, fleeces could be bartered, sold, or used instead of money to pay bills.

Clean wool or tow was carded between two rectangular wooden paddles each covered with short wire spikes on one side. Carding aligned the fibers in one direction; the fibers stuck together in rolls about a foot long. Spinning came next.

Spinning consisted of stretching and twisting the straight fibers to make thread or yarn ready for weaving or knitting. A young girl was taught the basics of spinning by using a simple spindle (a weighted stick). Later she learned to use a spinning wheel, which was one of two sizes. The smaller wheel was about 3 feet (1 m) high, and a person sat down and used a foot treadle to operate it. A distaff held the flax or wool fibers to be spun. The larger wheel, used only for wool, was about 5 feet (1.5 m) high, and a person stood to operate it. Both the wheel and the wool needed to be kept warm to make the best yarn, so wool was usually spun in a chimney corner.

A wooden device called a reel stood near the spinning wheel to measure the spun yarn into skeins. Often the skeins were dyed before weaving by using available plant materials or a rich blue dye called indigo, which was raised on Southern plantations. The dyed yarn was used to thread a loom with vertical (warp) threads, which were interwoven with horizontal (weft or woof) threads. Finished cloth was fulled by beating it in hot, soapy water to make it stronger and denser by shrinking. Then it was stretched and dried on a frame, and finally it was combed with dried teasel blooms to raise the nap.

Many garments were made of linsey-woolsey, a rough cloth produced by weaving linen and wool together. On a loom, the warp threads were linen and the weft threads were wool. Linsey-woolsey often had more linen than wool in it.

A quilting bee of colonial times.

God's people recognize the vanity of worldly fashions and are content with plain, simple clothing. Jesus said, "After all these things [food and clothes] do the Gentiles seek. . . . But seek ye first the kingdom of God" (Matthew 6:32, 33).

Recreation. Most colonists were so busy with their work that they had little time for leisure. So they sometimes mixed work and play by coming together for a quilting bee, a corn-husking bee, or a barn-raising bee. They did play a few games, such as shuffleboard. The wealthy had more time for recreation; they engaged in sports like horse racing and fox hunting.

A dame school of colonial times.

Colonial Education

Schools in New England. The Puritans of Massachusetts wanted everyone to be able to read the Bible. In 1647, they passed the first colonial law requiring all children to attend school. It became known as the Ole Deluder Satan Act because it began with these words: "It being one chief project of the old deluder, Satan, to keep men from the knowledge of the Scriptures . . ." Many children attended "dame schools," in which a housewife taught them to read and write.

In most New England schools, children began learning with the ***hornbook***. This was a flat board with a handle, on which was a paper covered by a thin sheet of transparent horn. The hornbook included things like the alphabet and the Lord's Prayer. After mastering the hornbook, a student moved to the *New England Primer* (PRIHM ur), a book including rhymes such as "A — In *Adam's* Fall / We sin-ned all." First published in 1690, the *Primer* was the first and perhaps most popular textbook published in colonial America.

After going through the *Primer*, children

A In *Adam's* Fall
We ſinned all.

B Thy Life to mend,
This *Book* attend.

C The *Cat* doth play,
And after ſlay.

D A *Dog* will bite
A Thief at Night.

E An *Eagle's* Flight
Is out of Sight.

F The idle *Fool*
Is whipt at School.

As runs the *Glaſs*,
Man's Life doth paſs.

My *Book* and *Heart*
Shall never part.

Job feels the Rod,
Yet bleſſes God.

Proud *Korah's* Troop
Was ſwallowed up.

The *Lion* bold
The Lamb doth hold.

The *Moon* gives Light
In Time of Night.

Top left: Hornbooks. A ribbon was often attached so the hornbook could be worn about the neck. Some hornbooks of the 1700s were made of gingerbread. When the student had learned a letter, he could eat that letter! ***Top right:*** A colonial schoolroom. The children standing before the teacher will recite the lesson they have memorized. ***Bottom right:*** Pages from an early *Primer*. Note the Bible lessons and moral teachings associated with each letter. Also note that the letter *s* was written as ſ within a word and as *s* at the end of a word.

studied the Psalms, the New Testament, and other parts of the Bible. New England schools emphasized the basics and the memorization of facts. They were strictly disciplined, following the adage "Spare the rod and spoil the child."

Some colonial people of New England pursued higher education. The first college in America was Harvard College, established near Boston by the Puritans in 1636. Its primary purpose was to prepare men for the ministry, as the Puritans believed in well-trained church leaders.

Schools in the Middle Colonies. People of the Middle Colonies did not consider education as important as did those of New England. In New Jersey, laws required children to attend school, but they were not always enforced. In Pennsylvania, the Quakers did not think higher education was necessary, but they believed in a practical education. One law said that all parents must see that their children learn to read and write.

Mennonites and other denominations in Pennsylvania usually had schools associated with their churches. **Christopher Dock** was a well-known teacher of the 1700s. He taught until he was an old man, and it is said that he died on his knees at school while praying for his students.

Schools in the South. Most education in the South was private and was limited to the children of wealthy plantation owners. One reason was that the plantations were large and the people scattered. Many planters hired tutors to teach their children at home. Others established private schools called ***old-field schools*** because they were often built on fields that were worn out from growing tobacco.

Some wealthy parents sent their sons to college in England or to the College of William and Mary at Williamsburg, Virginia. Founded in 1693, this was the second college established in the English colonies.

Benjamin Franklin flying a kite in a thunderstorm in 1752. This experiment proved that lightning is electricity. However, it was dangerous because Franklin could have been killed.

Intellectual Life

Colonial Publications. Little printing was done at first, for the early settlers did not have much time for reading. The first printing press was set up in 1638 at Cambridge, Massachusetts. Most of the first books published were religious or historical. Among them were the *Bay Psalm Book*, a hymnal; *History of Plymouth Plantation*, by William Bradford; and *Poor Richard's Almanac*, a collection of sayings published by Benjamin Franklin.

A noteworthy book produced at the request of the Mennonites was the *Martyrs Mirror*, translated into German and published at the Ephrata Cloister during 1748 and 1749. This was the largest book published in the colonies up to that time. The first regularly published newspaper was begun in 1704 at Boston.

Science in the Colonies. In the 1700s, a movement called the ***Enlightenment***, or Age of Reason, swept over Europe and spread to the American colonies. Philosophers and scientists began to be "enlightened" by human reasoning rather than by looking to the Bible and religious leaders. A popular idea of the time was that God did not sovereignly overrule the world, but that He had set the universe in motion and then withdrawn from it. This false belief is called ***deism*** (DEE ihz uhm).

Another development of the Enlightenment was an increase in scientific pursuits. Various people performed numerous experiments to discover things for themselves. Among these was Benjamin Franklin, who became famous for his experiments with electricity. Important botanists (men who study plants) were John Bartram of Philadelphia and Alexander Garden, for whom the gardenia is named.

But medical science was still primitive, and most ailments were treated with various household remedies. Doctors prepared "elixirs and potions," which might include chemicals such as sulfur and drugs such as opium. The common medical treatment for many ills was to "bleed, purge, and sweat" and then "bleed, purge, and sweat" some more.

Focus for Thought

1. List the three classes of people in colonial society. Then write each of the following after the class in which it would fit: bishop, craftsman, governor, plantation owner, small farmer, unskilled laborer.

2. How did the clothing of rich people compare with that of poor people?
3. Describe colonial education in New England, in the Middle Colonies, and in the South.
4. Why was education emphasized more strongly in New England than in the other regions?
5. How did the Enlightenment affect colonial America?

2. THE COLONIAL ECONOMY

The colonists made their living in different ways, just as people do today. The kinds of work they did and the number of available workers varied from region to region, and so did the lifestyles of the workers. This section discusses the production of goods and services by colonial Americans.

Land and Labor

One of the chief goals of many immigrants was to obtain land. The abundance of land in America was a great contrast to Europe, where countries were crowded and only a few people owned land. The methods of obtaining land varied from New England to the Southern Colonies.

The Township System of New England. In New England, colonial governments granted parcels of land to groups of people. Each parcel was a ***township***, called simply a town by New Englanders. The town was planned and built by settlers called town proprietors. In the center was the town common where the school, market, town hall, and

Layout of a New England town. (1) gristmill (2) pen for stray animals (3) minister's home (4) meetinghouse (5) village well (6) blacksmith shop (7) general store (8) village common (9) village cow pasture (10) schoolhouse

church were located. Around that were the lots for houses, and beyond those were the farmers' fields, on the outer borders of the township.

The township also had reserved lands, owned by the community and open for anyone to use. These lands could be distributed to later inhabitants as the town grew. The township system resulted in numerous small farms as well as the tendency of New Englanders to live in towns.

The Headright System of the South. In Virginia and other southern colonies, land was parceled out by the ***headright*** system to individual settlers rather than groups. Under this system, 50 acres (20 ha) was given to every settler ("head") or to whoever paid for the settler's transportation. For example, if a rich man paid for a poor person's passage to America, the rich man would receive 50 acres. In this way, some rich men in the South established great plantations.

To receive a title to his land, an owner had to get the boundaries marked, have a crop planted, and have a dwelling built on his land. Also, an annual fee called a ***quitrent*** usually had to be paid. This fee was not rent but a carryover from feudalism. By paying this money, the landowner was "quit," or released, from any other feudal obligations. The quitrent was paid chiefly in colonies owned by proprietors, such as the Carolinas.

The Mixed System of the Middle Colonies. In the Middle Colonies, land was granted to individuals (as in the South), but often it was organized into townships (as in New England). The parcels were usually larger than the ones in New England but smaller than the plantations of the South. A notable exception was New York, where Dutch patroons had received plantation-sized farms of up to 24 square miles (62 km^2).

The Labor Force. The colonies were in constant need of workers to clear forests, build houses and barns, plant and harvest crops, and much more—especially on southern plantations. There were many more acres of land than people to work the land. This led to higher wages in America than in England.

If a boy wanted to learn a trade, he usually became an ***apprentice*** (uh PREHN tihs). His parents would make a contract with a craftsman, agreeing that their son would work for him without pay for perhaps seven years. When the apprenticeship was over, the young man was free and became a ***journeyman***. Then he could work for wages under the same craftsman or others.

Farming

Nine out of ten settlers were full-time farmers, and even those who had other work did some farming as a sideline activity. This was true partly because everyone needed food but mostly because of the abundance of fertile land.

Small Farms in New England. The land in New England was rugged, the soil was thin and stony, the winters were cold, and the growing season was short. But farming was still important there. The people worked their own small farms, which were clustered around the towns.

Because wheat did not grow well in New England, corn became the most important crop. Barley, oats, and rye were also produced, as well as vegetables from gardens and fruits from orchards. Livestock included an ox team to provide power, hogs to provide pork, sheep to give wool, and cows to give milk for butter and cheese.

Plantations in the South. Great plantations grew up on the broad coastal plain of the South. These were owned by rich men of the better class, who controlled most of the affairs in the South.

One of the main crops was tobacco, especially in Maryland, Virginia, and North Carolina. Southern farmers also raised grains such as wheat and corn, and fruits such as oranges where the climate permitted. Many of the crops in the South were raised for sale to European countries, mainly England.

As the plantations grew, they needed more and more people to work them. But the Indians did not make good plantation workers, and few white people wanted to do such hard work. So thousands of black slaves were brought to America, and thus slavery became firmly established in the South.

Not nearly all the farms in the South were plantations. There were also many small farms, often located farther west in the more hilly backcountry. Here the farmers cleared small areas and raised grains and fruit. They did their own work or had only a few slaves.

Pioneer farm in New York in 1801. Farmers had to work very hard to cut down trees, uproot stumps, build cabins and barns, and plant crops.

Slave advertisement from the 1780s. As shown on this poster, black slaves were advertised and sold like livestock.

The Middle "Breadbasket" Colonies. The soil and climate of the Middle Colonies were well suited for farming. Farms were larger than the ones in New England but smaller than the southern plantations. Families usually worked their own farms, but many had indentured servants. Some had slaves, especially in New York.

Wheat became the main cash crop, but other grains—such as barley, oats, and rye—were also grown. The Middle Colonies raised so much extra grain for export that they became known as the "breadbasket colonies." Beef and dairy cattle were also important, as well as horses, hogs, sheep, and chickens.

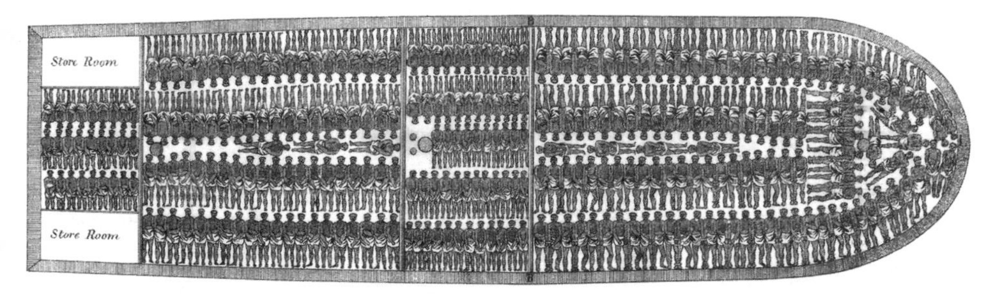

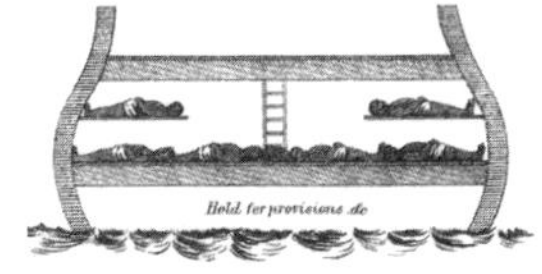

Slaves were transported on the slave ship *Brookes.* This British ship carried about 450 slaves: 292 crammed into the lower deck, 130 stowed in shelves along the sides (see the cross section at the right), and about 29 in a small upper section near the stern. One can hardly imagine the suffering of the slaves on the voyage to America.

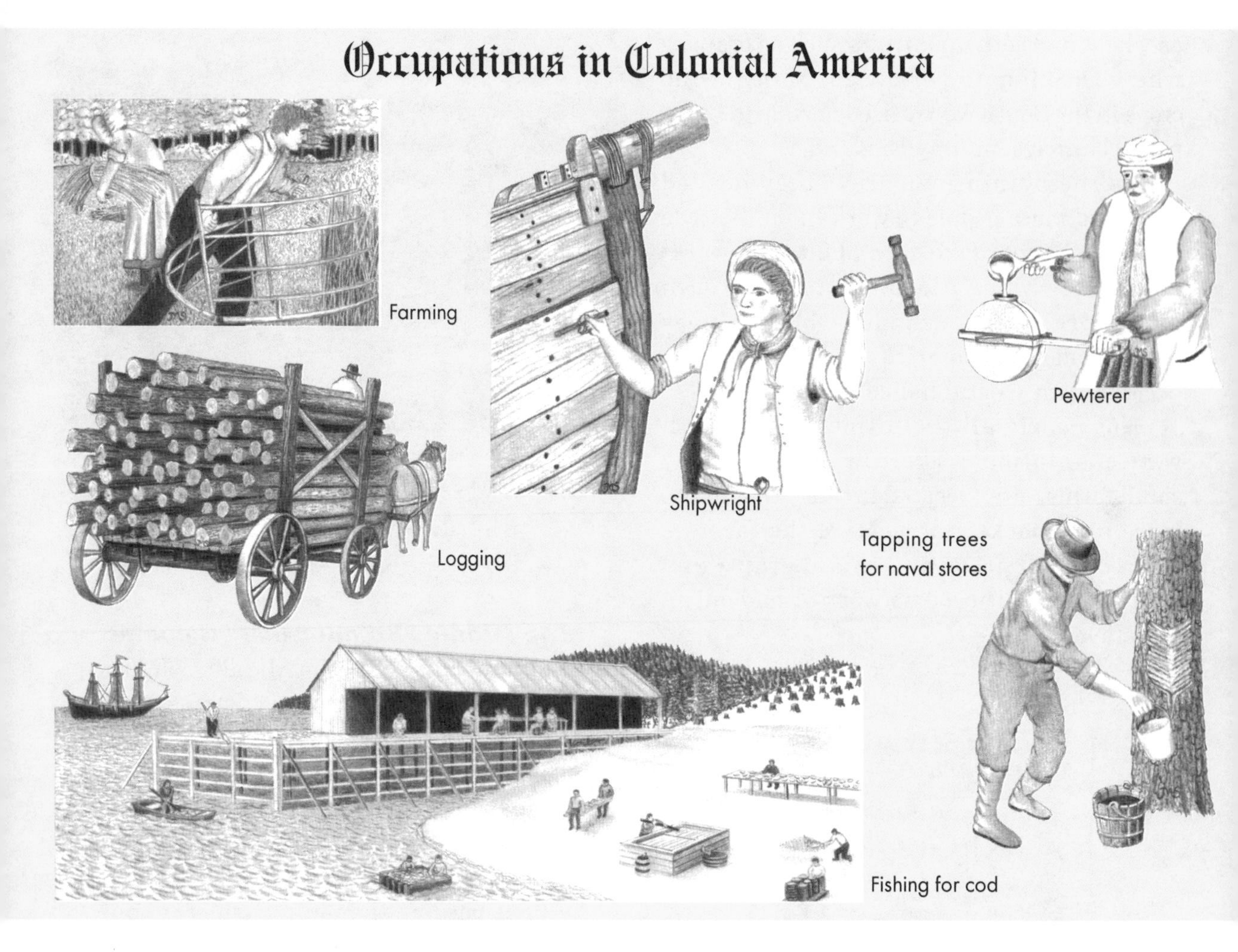

Industry, Transportation, and Trade

Growth of Industry. Businesses developed slowly in colonial America because most people were farmers. Other reasons were the lack of good transportation, the lack of money to start businesses, and the scarcity of workers. When a large industry did develop, it often began as a household industry designed to supply the family's needs.

For example, a man might have become skilled at making a certain product for his family, such as shoes. Gradually he began making shoes for other people, and thus a shoemaking business developed. Cloth making and leather working were some other important household industries. But there was little industry in the South, for the planters bought the things they needed from England.

Forest Products. Since trees were plentiful, lumbering was an important colonial business. Colonists used lumber for many things, including houses, furniture, tools, and barrels. Trees also provided naval stores for use in shipbuilding. New England exported much lumber, and both New England and North Carolina produced naval stores.

A related industry was shipbuilding. Because of the abundant timber, the colonists, especially those in New England, could build fine ships for sale to Europeans.

Shipping, Fishing, and Whaling. Farming was not very profitable in New England, and there were many natural harbors. Therefore, seafaring soon became important in that region. A number of large cities grew up along the coast, and many merchants became rich through buying, selling, and shipping goods.

Many New Englanders caught fish on rich fishing grounds such as the Grand Banks near Newfoundland, and they sold the fish to other colonies and to Europe. A more dangerous occupation was whaling, which brought in whale oil for use in lamps. Another major occupation—a detrimental one—was the production of rum, a strong drink made from molasses shipped from the West Indies.

TANNING

"Unto Adam also and to his wife did the LORD God make coats of skins, and clothed them" (Genesis 3:21).

Leather, often made from deerskins, was used to make simple shoes, boots or moccasins, and leather leggings and vests to keep men warm in winter. A good tanner (a man who made leather from hides) was an asset to any community. He did most of his work outdoors before cold weather came because he needed a good supply of water and tannin to do his work. Tannin is a chemical found in the bark and roots of trees such as oak, hemlock, spruce, and larch. The bark was removed from the trees in the early spring, soon after the sap had risen. About half a ton of oak bark had enough tannin to cure two fresh hides weighing about 110 pounds (50 kg) each.

A hide was cleaned by soaking it in a large stone basin for three or four days. It was then taken out and the hair scraped off; the removed hair could be spun into yarn. Next, the scraped hides were soaked for two or three weeks in a pit filled with a solution of water and lime. The solution was renewed daily. Sometimes the hides were placed in a smokehouse, where the heat and moisture would loosen the hair more quickly and make the hides more pliable.

beam

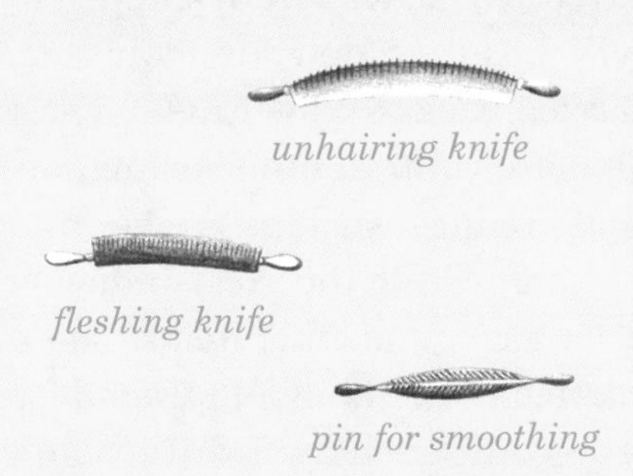
unhairing knife

fleshing knife

pin for smoothing

Tanners used varied methods, depending on the quality of the hide and the intended purpose of the leather. To produce high-quality leather for making pliable breeches or other clothing, a tanner started by spreading a soaked hide on his beam (a curved "table"). He scraped and shaved off the remaining hair, skin, and anything else that would not respond to tanning. His curved knife fit the curve of the beam—this made the job easier. Then he soaked the hide for two days in sulfuric acid, which opened the pores so that the tannin would penetrate readily. Next the tanner placed the hide in a succession of pits that contained solutions of tannin ooze. This process took from three months to a year, depending on the weight of the hide.

Every month the tanner renewed and strengthened the tannin solutions, and every day he waded into the pits in heavy wooden shoes that the tannin did not penetrate. He used long-handled hooks to stir the hides and see if they were sufficiently tanned. When they were finished, the tanner hauled the hides out and hung them up to dry. He passed a high-quality hide between wooden rollers until it was soft and pliant. If it was a coarser hide, he used a metal instrument to beat it smooth. The leather was then ready for use.

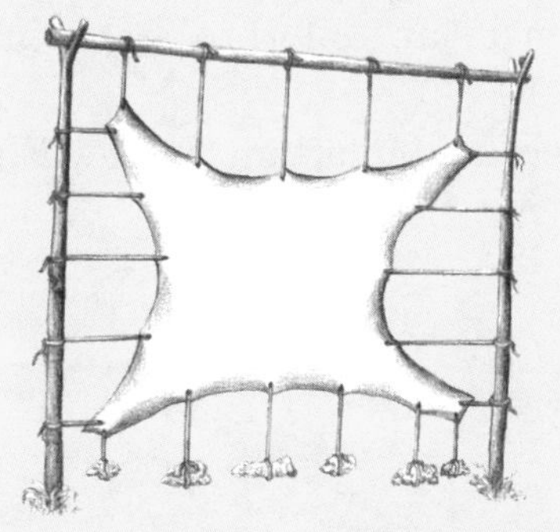

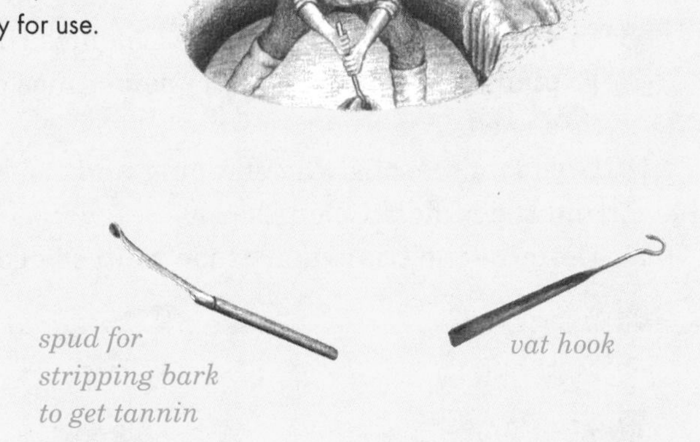
spud for stripping bark to get tannin

vat hook

Stagecoach on the Pennsylvania Turnpike in 1792.

Manufacturing. Furnaces for smelting iron ore were first established in New England. Later most iron was produced in the Middle Colonies, especially Pennsylvania, because coal and other raw materials were readily available there. Crude iron called ***pig iron*** was in strong demand for nails, kitchen utensils, and tools. The Middle Colonies also became known for making watches, guns, and other mechanical items. In both New England and the Middle Colonies, hat making for export became profitable.

Colonial Transportation. Many roads in colonial times were nothing more than widened Indian trails. They were often dusty or muddy and were plagued by washouts, mud holes, and stumps. Besides traveling on horseback, people rode in carts or carriages (in the cities), and later they traveled in stagecoaches—so called because they went from city to city in stages.

Travel by water was the simplest and cheapest form of transportation. Many people lived near rivers, which were the colonial highways for travel and trade. In the South, most plantations were located along a river and had their own dock. But water travel was slow; it took four or five days to travel from New York to Carolina, and three to eight weeks to cross the Atlantic.

Colonial Trade. Much trade in colonial days was done directly with England, but several systems called the ***triangular trade*** also developed. Such a system involved shipping one kind of merchandise to one place, picking up another kind and taking it to a second location, and then loading a third cargo to be carried back home.

In one triangular trade route, rum was shipped from New England to Africa and was traded for slaves. The slaves were shipped to the West Indies and traded for molasses, which was carried back to New England and used to make more rum. In other triangular routes, colonial products such as lumber and grain would be shipped to the West Indies to be exchanged for sugar and other items. These items were carried to England and traded for manufactured goods, such as furniture and cloth, to be sold in the colonies.

Focus for Thought

6. a. Because of the township system, how did people tend to settle in New England?
   b. How did the headright system affect the settlement of the South?
7. What was the difference between an apprentice and a journeyman?
8. In what way were the Middle Colonies the "breadbasket colonies"?
9. Explain how a large industry sometimes developed from a man's effort to supply his family's needs.
10. Give two reasons why shipping and manufacturing became important in New England and the Middle Colonies.
11. Describe the triangular trade routes of colonial days.

BLACKSMITHING

"The smith with the tongs both worketh in the coals, and fashioneth it with hammers, and worketh it with the strength of his arms" (Isaiah 44:12).

Many people today think of a blacksmith only as a person who shoes horses. In colonial times, any man who worked with iron was a blacksmith; one who shod horses was known as a farrier. The word *blacksmith* is derived from "black metal," a former name for iron. Generally, a colonial blacksmith supplied all the iron objects needed at neighboring houses and farms: kettles, frying pans, grates, hinges, locks, and tools of various kinds, along with plows, wagon axles, machinery parts, shoes for horses and oxen, and many other items. A blacksmith also did repairs on damaged metal items.

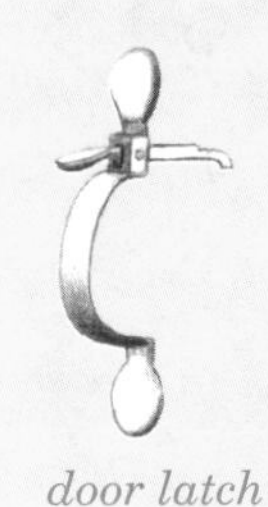

door latch

A blacksmith's shop, called a smithy or a forge, was an important part of a colonial settlement. Men often gathered there and discussed items of current interest. Children also enjoyed visiting a village smithy. They were fascinated by the puffing bellows, clanging noises, fiery sparks, red-hot metal, and neighing horses that were there to be shod.

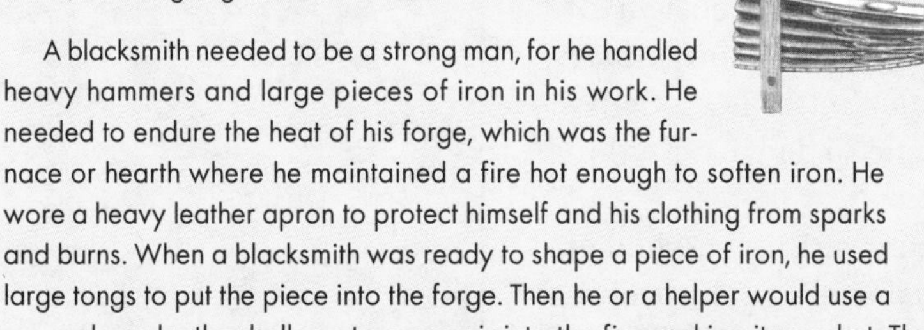

flatiron

hacksaw

A blacksmith needed to be a strong man, for he handled heavy hammers and large pieces of iron in his work. He needed to endure the heat of his forge, which was the furnace or hearth where he maintained a fire hot enough to soften iron. He wore a heavy leather apron to protect himself and his clothing from sparks and burns. When a blacksmith was ready to shape a piece of iron, he used large tongs to put the piece into the forge. Then he or a helper would use a huge leather bellows to pump air into the fire, making it very hot. The blacksmith left the piece of iron in the fire until it was red-hot. Using tongs, he removed the hot iron and set it on his anvil, where he hammered the iron into the right shape. He usually repeated the heating and hammering process several times to get the desired result. To cool a finished piece, the blacksmith plunged it into a barrel of water.

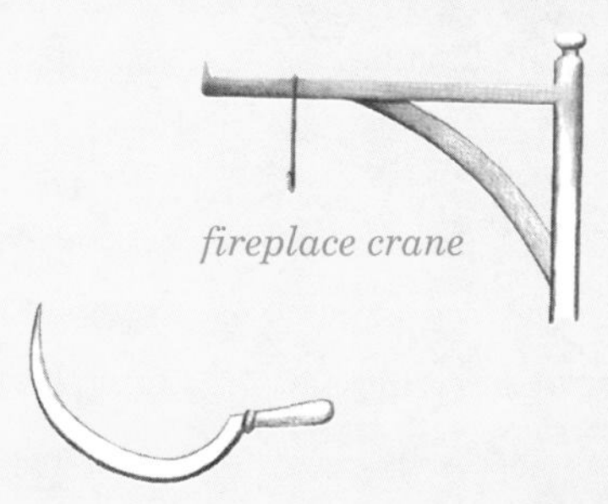

fireplace crane

sickle

Blacksmiths worked with cast iron as well as wrought iron, which are both made from pig iron (blocks of crude iron as it first comes from iron ore). Cast iron is pig iron with some other materials added. It cannot be shaped, no matter how hot it is heated; so it is poured into molds and allowed to harden into objects like frying pans. Wrought iron is almost pure iron mixed with a glasslike material. It can be hammered into various shapes when hot, and it resists rust better than cast iron does.

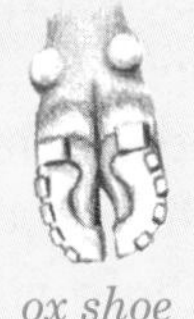

ox shoe

Supplying shoes for horses and oxen was a very common job for a blacksmith (farrier). He often made enough shoes to have a good supply ready to meet the demand. An ox shoe was in two pieces (oxen have cloven hoofs), each with cleats to help the animal pull heavy loads. To shoe a horse, the farrier used knives and coarse files to clean and shape the sole and rim of the horse's hoof. He selected a horseshoe of the proper size and noted what changes were needed to make it fit the hoof. Then he heated the shoe red-hot, hammered it into the right shape, cooled it in water, and nailed it to the horse's hoof. The nails caused the horse no pain, for they were driven into the tough part of his hoof that contained no nerves.

3. COLONIAL GOVERNMENT AND RELIGION

Since the colonies belonged to England, the English government had final authority over them. But each colony also had its own government, for the English allowed the colonies many freedoms. With freedom of religion in most places, a variety of churches flourished in the colonies. Many of these churches still exist today.

English Rule

Though holding final authority over the colonies, England seldom enforced its laws strictly, especially the trade laws. This policy, called ***salutary neglect*** (SAL yuh tair ee), gave the colonies considerable freedom to develop their own trade. For example, a number of laws required the Americans to trade only with England. But many Americans traded with other nations anyway—something fairly simple to do with England so far away.

Actually, the citizens of England had enjoyed exceptional freedoms for centuries. As far back as 1215, English nobles had forced King John to recognize a document called the Magna Carta (Great Charter), which gave them various rights and freedoms. By 1689, the English Bill of Rights granted privileges such as the right to trial by jury, the right to bear arms, and protection against cruel and unusual punishments. The English people cherished these rights and freedoms.

The English colonists wanted their freedoms to continue in America. Each colony had a written charter that spelled out how the government was to operate. These charters granted to colonists the same privileges as Englishmen. The American colonists viewed these freedoms as their rights, and they thought the government was obligated to respect those rights.

The Bible says, "Let every soul be subject unto the higher powers"—whether or not the government respects the "rights" of citizens.

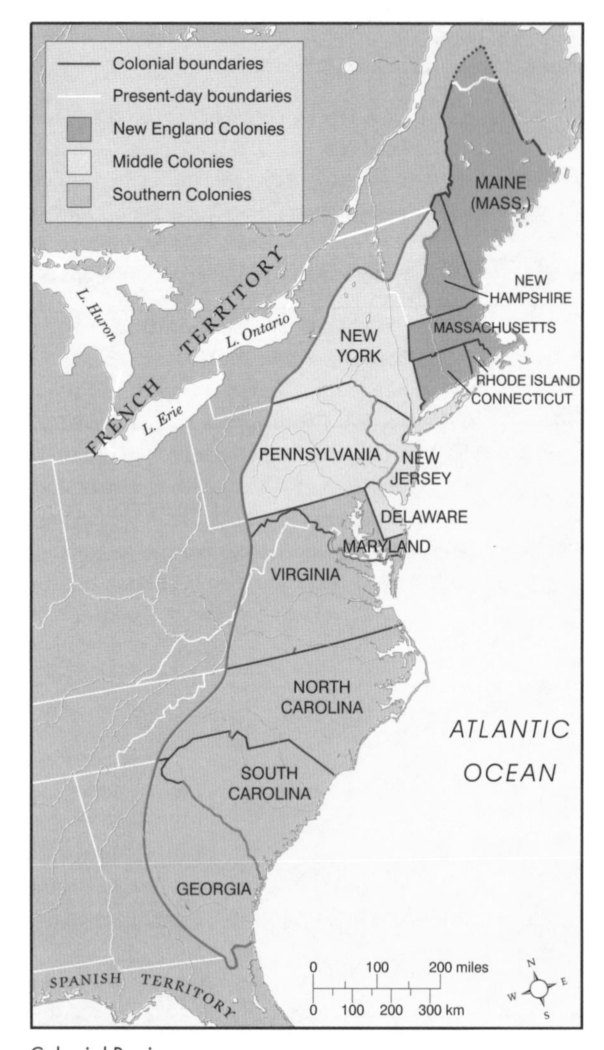

Colonial Regions

Colonial Government

There were three kinds of English colonies: the royal colony, under the direct control of the king; the proprietary colony, governed by a proprietor; and the charter colony, governed on the basis of its charter. Rhode Island and Connecticut were charter colonies; Pennsylvania, Maryland, and Delaware were proprietary colonies; and the other eight were royal colonies.

In a royal colony, the king appointed the governor and members of the upper house of the legislature. In a proprietary colony, these officials were appointed by the proprietors;

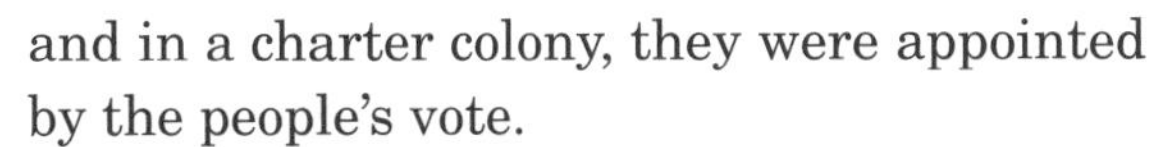

Restoration of the capitol in Williamsburg, Virginia. The Virginia Assembly and the General Court met in the original building, which was constructed from 1701 to 1705.

These Pilgrims are at a New England town meeting. Voting was done by casting ballots into a hat.

and in a charter colony, they were appointed by the people's vote.

The Governor. A colonial governor had many powers. He was head of the militia, he called and dismissed the ***legislature***, and he could veto laws.

The Legislature. All the colonies except Pennsylvania had a two-house legislature. The ***upper house*** had twelve to eighteen members from the better class. It advised the governor and proposed laws, but it had little real power.

The ***lower house*** had more members and greater power. Its members were representatives elected by voters and coming from each town or county. The lower house made laws, controlled taxes and government spending, and controlled the governor's salary. For this reason the governor was obliged mainly to the lower house.

Town Meetings and County Governments. In New England, a local government developed in each town because most people lived in towns. The people held ***town meetings***, open to everyone, where they discussed matters and made decisions by voting. This system is still in use today.

Town meetings were not practical in the South, for people lived farther apart and few towns existed. Instead, the local governing unit was the county. Local government was administered by a sheriff and a ***justice of the peace***, who acted as judge and tax collector. These men were usually planters appointed by the governor.

Penalties for Crime. Colonial punishments were swift and sure, and often they were matched to the offense. For example, if a person was guilty of blasphemy, his tongue might be pierced; and someone guilty of theft might be branded with the letter *T*. The death penalty, usually hanging, was meted out for serious crimes like murder and treason. Some crimes were punished by whipping, often the Biblical "forty stripes save one."

Milder punishments were given for lesser crimes. A woman who scolded too much might be placed on a ducking stool and dunked underwater. If someone was guilty of lying or of missing Sunday services without a good reason, he might have to sit with his hands and feet fastened in the stocks for several hours. Another device for punishment was the ***pillory***, a post with a wooden framework in which the offender's head and hands were fastened. The punishments would be meted out in public, and people would often jeer and throw eggs and rotten fruit at the offender.

These penalties were common in all the colonies, although punishment was more strict and severe in early New England. The Bible says of the government, "He beareth not the sword in vain: for he is the minister of God, a revenger to execute wrath upon him that doeth evil" (Romans 13:4).

Colonial punishments in Boston in 1657. They included the ducking stool, the pillory, and the stocks.

Church Influence

Colonial churches had strong influence in places where the government supported an official church. One example is New England, where the Puritans mixed church and state. Another is the South, where the Anglican Church (Church of England) was the official church and everyone had to pay taxes to support it. In colonies such as Pennsylvania, where many different nationalities lived, no one church held such influence.

Many colonial governments made laws based on Bible principles. For instance, Sunday observance was enforced by regulations known as ***blue laws*** (so called because they were bound in blue paper). These laws made church attendance compulsory and prohibited activities like playing games and hunting or fishing on Sunday. Such laws did not make the people or the government Christian, but they did make people mindful of right and wrong.

A tithing-man is about to wake up a sleeper.

Colonial church building. Religion was an important part of colonial life, especially in the early days.

Church Denominations

The Congregational Church in New England. The Congregational Church of the Puritans was the official church in all of New England except Rhode Island. In the church services, men sat on one side, women on the other, and boys in the balcony. If someone slept or caused a disturbance, the tithingman would use his long pole. On one end were some feathers or a rabbit's tail to tickle the women and girls, and on the other end was a hard knob or rabbit's foot to rap the men and boys.

Services were usually held in the morning and afternoon, each lasting over two hours. One Puritan preacher wrote that he prayed for an hour and a quarter and preached for an hour and three quarters. Puritan influence in New England was strong during the colonial period, but it waned in the 1700s.

The Anglican Church in the South. The Anglican Church was the official church of England; therefore, England wanted it to be the main church in the colonies. This came to pass in Maryland, Virginia, and the other southern colonies. The Anglican Church was also found in other colonies, but its influence in the South was stronger than elsewhere.

The Anglican Church was similar to the Roman Catholic Church, and it was less strict than the Congregational Church in New England. People in the South lived more as they pleased, and religion had less influence on their lives. Their services were not nearly as long as those of the Puritans, with a short sermon that "did not greatly perturb the consciences of the hearers."

Other Churches. Major colonial churches also included Presbyterians, Baptists, Quakers, and Catholics. Besides these were the Anabaptist groups, including the Mennonites and Amish. After the first group of Mennonites came in 1683, many more followed in the 1700s to escape persecution. The area of Lancaster, Pennsylvania, especially attracted many Mennonites.

The Great Awakening

Religious devotion in colonial America had largely cooled down by the beginning of the 1700s. Because of the Enlightenment, many people were ignoring God and looking to man's ideas for guidance. People became wealthier and lost interest in spiritual things while the churches became more worldly. Because the church and state were not separate in some colonies, the official churches became cold and formal.

A Great Revival Movement. Between 1725 and 1750, a religious movement known as the Great Awakening swept through the colonies. This was a revival campaign that emphasized personal salvation and dramatic religious experiences. The Great Awakening was led by men such as **Jonathan Edwards** of Massachusetts and **George Whitefield** (HWIHT feeld) from England.

Edwards preached powerful sermons that stirred people's emotions, including one entitled "Sinners in the Hands of an Angry

George Whitefield (1714–1770) was a leader in the colonial Great Awakening.

Jonathan Edwards (1703–1758) was another leader in the colonial Great Awakening. Edwards also wrote numerous books on religious topics.

God." George Whitefield preached to thousands of people, often outdoors, with such fervor that many began crying for mercy. These men proclaimed the importance of being converted but neglected to emphasize correct doctrine. The Bible says, "Ye must be born again" (John 3:7); but it also says, "Take heed unto thyself, and unto the doctrine" (1 Timothy 4:16).

Effects of the Great Awakening. The Great Awakening had important results in the colonies. First, it was one of the first influences that united the colonies, since George Whitefield preached in most of them. Second, it divided several of the established churches, including the Congregationalists and the Presbyterians, into those who supported the Awakening and those who opposed it. Third, it favored the common people and the more popular churches, such as Baptists and Methodists, over the established churches. This also brought about greater separation of church and state, and thus it helped lay the groundwork for the American Revolution.

As a fourth result, the Great Awakening led to more outreach work, including missionary endeavors to the Indians and the founding of numerous colleges. Fifth, it set a pattern for later revival movements in America. In a general sense, however, the Great Awakening produced only a limited degree of spiritual improvement; for many of the "conversions" were little more than emotional upheavals.

The Great Awakening also affected the Mennonites. Some of them enjoyed the emotional preaching and emphasis of the revival preachers. One such man was a Mennonite bishop named Martin Boehm, who left the church about 1775. He later helped to found the United Brethren Church, which today is part of the Methodist Church. This was one of the first schisms in the Mennonite Church in America.

The Mennonite Church of that day did need revival; but because of imbalances in the Great Awakening, that movement failed to meet the need. To counter its influence on Mennonite young people, the bishop Christian Burkholder published a book called *Addresses to Youth* in 1804.

Focus for Thought

12. a. What are some rights that the English had because of the Magna Carta and the Bill of Rights of 1689?
    b. What written document did each English colony have, which granted the colonists the same privileges that Englishmen had?
    c. What did the colonists consider as the duty of the government in relation to these rights?
    d. What command does the Bible give on this point?
13. Name the three kinds of colonies, and tell how each kind was governed.

14. How would the prompt and severe punishments of colonial times have deterred criminals? (See Ecclesiastes 8:11.)
15. Why did many people's religious devotion cool down in the 1700s?
16. Name six effects that the Great Awakening had on colonial America.

Historical Highlights

A. Matching: Terms 1

a. apprentice
b. bee
c. deism
d. headright
e. hornbook
f. journeyman
g. plantation
h. quitrent
i. township
j. better class
k. breadbasket colonies
l. indentured servant
m. meaner sort
n. middling class
o. naval stores
p. old-field school
q. pig iron
r. triangular trade

1. Money paid yearly to be free from feudal obligations.
2. Materials used to seal cracks in wooden ships.
3. Social group of highest rank.
4. Unskilled persons who did not own land.
5. Person working to repay the cost of his voyage to America.
6. Small farmers and craftsmen.
7. Crude metal as it first comes from a blast furnace.
8. System in which each person entering a colony received 50 acres (20 ha).
9. Boy working without pay under a master for a certain time, in order to learn a craft.
10. One who worked for wages after completing an apprenticeship.
11. Flat board used for basic teaching in New England schools.
12. Social occasion where a group worked together at a certain job.
13. Middle colonies that exported grain.
14. Land granted to a group of people in New England.
15. Huge farm in the South.
16. System of commerce that involves taking one cargo to a certain place, taking a second cargo from there to another place, and taking a third cargo from there back to the starting point.
17. False idea that God created the world and then withdrew from it.
18. Institution located on soil worn out by tobacco growing.

B. Matching: Terms 2

a. backcountry
b. blue laws
c. charter colony
d. justice of the peace
e. legislature
f. lower house
g. pillory
h. proprietary colony
i. royal colony
j. salutary neglect
k. stocks
l. tithing-man
m. town meeting
n. upper house

1. New England assembly for discussions and voting.
2. Person who kept people awake in church.
3. Colony that operated on the basis of its charter.
4. Part of legislature representing the better class but having little power.
5. Part of legislature elected by voters and having greater power.
6. Lax enforcement of laws, which allowed colonial trade to develop.
7. Official who was a judge and tax collector.
8. Hilly region of small farms in the South.
9. Group of people appointed to make laws.
10. Colony that was supervised by its upper-class owner.
11. Device used to fasten the head and hands of lawbreakers.
12. Regulations on Sunday activities.
13. Colony owned by the king.
14. Device used to fasten the hands and feet of lawbreakers.

C. Matching: Names

1. First colonial law requiring all children to attend school.
2. Puritan church, dominant in New England.
3. First college in the United States, in New England.
4. Second college in the United States, in Virginia.
5. Religious revival in the 1700s.
6. Noted schoolteacher in colonial Pennsylvania.
7. Leaders of the Great Awakening (two answers).
8. Age of Reason.
9. Church of England, dominant in the South.

a. Anglican Church
b. Christopher Dock
c. College of William and Mary
d. Congregational Church
e. Enlightenment
f. George Whitefield
g. Great Awakening
h. Harvard College
i. Jonathan Edwards
j. Ole Deluder Satan Act

D. Deeper Discussion

1. Modern conditions are quite different from those in colonial days. Yet the Bible says that "there is no new thing under the sun" (Ecclesiastes 1:9). How can these facts be reconciled?
2. a. Why are class distinctions common among men?
   b. How should the Christian view class distinctions?
3. How did the Enlightenment lead to scientific inquiry?
4. What is erroneous about deism?
5. How did the Bible affect colonial living?
6. How did the Great Awakening fall short of a true revival?

E. Chronology and Geography

1. Find the number of years between each of the following events, using the time line at the beginning of the chapter.
   a. The founding of Jamestown, the first successful English colony, and the Mennonites' arrival in Pennsylvania.
   b. The Mennonites' arrival in Pennsylvania and the founding of Georgia.
   c. The Mennonites' arrival in Pennsylvania and the beginning of the Great Awakening.
   d. The Mennonites' arrival in Pennsylvania and the publishing of the *Martyrs Mirror*.
   e. The printing of the *Martyrs Mirror* and the beginning of the French and Indian War.
2. Explain how geography contributed to different ways of making a living in colonial America.

Unit 3

Times of Founding, 1650–1790

Chapters in Unit 3

8. British North America
9. The American Revolution
10. American Government

The city of Quebec in 1759.

8 British North America

1. British and French Rivalry
   - The Basis for Rivalry
   - The Colonial Wars
2. The French and Indian War
   - Conflict in the Ohio River Valley
   - British Defeats, French Victories
   - British Victories, French Defeats
3. Nonresistant People During the Colonial Period
   - Mennonite Immigration
   - The Quakers and the Mennonites
   - War Experiences of Nonresistant People

1680

First Mennonites arrive in America **1683**

King William's War begins 1689

Treaty of Ryswick ends King William's War 1697

1700

Queen Anne's War begins 1702

Treaty of Utrecht ends Queen Anne's War 1713

1720

1740

King George's War begins 1744

Treaty of Aix-la-Chapelle ends King George's War 1748

German *Martyrs Mirror* published at Ephrata Cloister 1749

Washington defeated at Fort Duquesne; French and Indian War begins **1754**

Braddock defeated at Fort Duquesne 1755

Jacob Hochstetler massacre 1757

Fort Louisbourg and Fort Duquesne fall to the British 1758

Quebec falls to the British 1759

1760

New France surrendered to the British 1760

Treaty of Paris ends the French and Indian War **1763**

1780

"Yea, the Lord *shall give that which is good; and our land shall yield her increase."*

Psalm 85:12

BRITISH NORTH AMERICA

Focus for Reading

By the middle 1600s, England, France, and Spain had all established colonies in America. This led to rivalry among these nations for mastery of the continent. The result was a series of wars spanning seventy-five years, in which the British gained power over most of North America.

Many Mennonites and other nonresistant people migrated to America during this time. These people found their beliefs severely tested through the many fights and raids by white men as well as Indians. How did the British take over much of North America? How did peaceable Christians fare during those times? Three sections in this chapter answer these questions.

1. British and French Rivalry
2. The French and Indian War
3. Nonresistant People During the Colonial Period

1. BRITISH AND FRENCH RIVALRY

England may properly be called Great Britain after 1707, when England, Wales, and Scotland united into one kingdom. Both Great Britain and France were trying to expand their power at that time. In their efforts, these nations clashed in North America and in other places around the world. Their struggle in North America led to the French and Indian War, by which most of Anglo-America came under British control.

Daniel 7 portrays several empires as ravenous beasts. To God, the European nations must have appeared like beasts as they fought over territory in America.

The Basis for Rivalry

Conflicting Claims. Before 1763, Spain, France, and Great Britain controlled different parts of North America. However, Spain's power declined by the middle 1700s, so the French and the British were left to compete for control of North America.

The French claimed all the land drained by the Mississippi River while the British claimed all the land westward from their colonies along the Atlantic coast. These conflicting claims led to fighting over the land, especially in the Mississippi and Ohio River valleys.

About 1660, Radisson and Groseilliers explored the Lake Superior area. They were probably the first white men to explore north and west of the Great Lakes.

The Fur Trade. Beaver furs were in great demand during the 1600s. Their soft, silky undercoat of fine hair, called "beaver wool," was highly prized for making beaver hats worn by the fashionable men in Europe. The French controlled most of the fur trade in Canada, where beavers had the thickest, most luxurious fur. The English, confined to the regions farther south, looked for ways to increase their share of the prosperous trade. In the 1660s they had their opportunity.

Two French brothers-in-law, **Radisson** (ra dee SAWN) and **Groseilliers** (groh zeh YAY), wanted to establish the fur trade in the Hudson Bay region. They brought a great quantity of furs to Quebec, but the governor of New France accused them of illegal trading and confiscated their furs. So in 1665 the two Frenchmen took their story to England, where it caught the interest of **Prince Rupert**, a nephew of King Charles II. Prince Rupert saw that England had a chance to build on her claim to the Hudson Bay region (discovered by Henry Hudson) and to make a great profit at the same time. He organized an expedition to be sent to Canada.

In 1668, Radisson and Groseilliers went along to America with Prince Rupert's expedition. That winter they gathered a large supply of deep, silky furs, and the next spring they sold the furs in England at a tremendous profit. Prince Rupert immediately sought a charter to establish a trading company in the Hudson Bay region. This area is sometimes called Rupert's Land.

The king granted a charter to the Hudson's Bay Company in 1670. By 1685, the company had built five forts along the bay, and more were built in the following years. These trading centers collected many furs from Indians who did not want to make the long trip to the St. Lawrence. The English paid higher prices and traded better goods for the Indians' furs than the French did. Thus the English became established on the Hudson Bay.

The jealous French sent men to attack the English forts. Sometimes one side won and sometimes the other, with several forts changing hands a number of times. This conflict did not end until the conclusion of Queen Anne's War in 1713, when the British regained all their forts on the Hudson Bay.

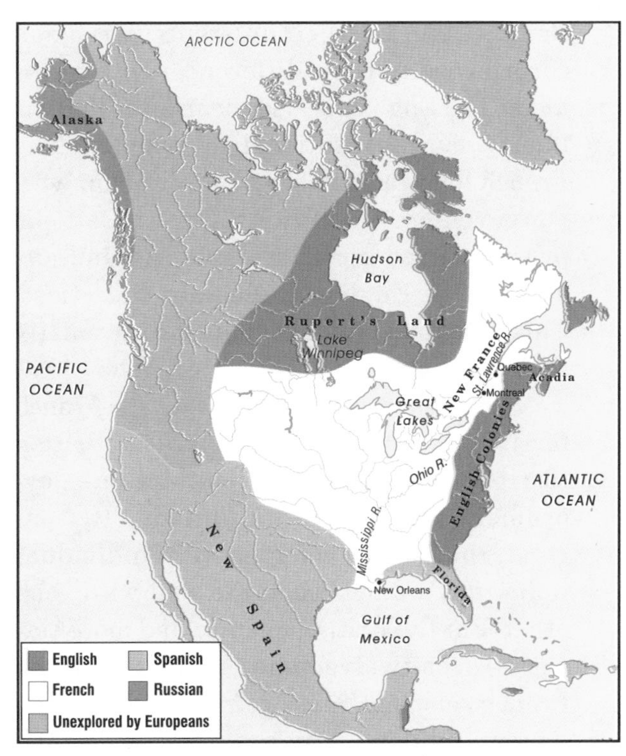

European Claims in North America About 1755

Later the French built forts in the areas of Rainy Lake and Lake Winnipeg to trade with the Indians farther west. The British also tried to develop trade in that area. In 1754, the Hudson's Bay Company sent Anthony Henday to persuade the Indians of the West to deal with them instead of with the French. Henday did not succeed; but on his journey west, he became probably the first European to see the Rocky Mountains.

Alliances With the Indians. You saw in Chapter 5 that the French first traded with the Huron and Algonquin Indians for furs. This brought the French into conflict with the Iroquois tribes, who were enemies of the Huron and Algonquin. The Iroquois then traded with the British and sided with them. These alliances with Indian tribes became important to the Europeans throughout the colonial wars.

Religious and Political Differences. England was Protestant, but France was

Roman Catholic. Their difference in religion contributed to their differences in government. The English prided themselves in their liberty and constitutional government. The French followed a policy of absolutism, with power centered in the king. French Catholic priests stirred up the Catholicized Indians against the English Protestant "heretics." This religious element helped to intensify their fighting zeal.

Strengths and Weaknesses. The French territory was much larger than the British territory. The people were under one government and could work unitedly. By contrast, the British colonies were individual units that did not cooperate well with each other. But the British colonies had more settlers—over twelve times as many as the French colonies. These settlers would make a greater difference in establishing English claims to America than the wars did.

However, "the race is not to the swift, nor the battle to the strong" (Ecclesiastes 9:11). It was God's overruling hand that determined the outcome of the rivalry in North America.

The Colonial Wars

Within seventy-five years—from 1689 to 1763—Great Britain and France engaged in four wars between themselves. The wars were fought mainly in Europe, but they also spilled over into North America.

King William's War. The first war, known in America as King William's War, began in 1689. That summer a great party of Iroquois descended on a town near Montreal and killed men, women, and children. In return, French and Indian war parties from New France attacked a number of settlements in New England and New York, and again many people were killed.

This set a pattern for Indian ***frontier raids*** in later wars. An army of New Englanders attacked Port Royal and Quebec in 1690 but had to withdraw. The French also conquered some of England's forts around Hudson Bay. By 1697, both sides in Europe were tired of fighting and signed the Treaty of Ryswick, which returned all the American lands to their original owners. King William's War had caused much bloodshed, but it solved none of the original problems.

Puritans fortifying their house against an Indian attack. How can you tell that they did not practice nonresistance?

Queen Anne's War. The second war began in 1702 and was known in America as Queen Anne's War. Again the French and the Indians made repeated attacks on New England settlements. In one of them, 200 Indians and 50 Canadians raided Deerfield, Massachusetts. They killed 53 settlers on a

Indian raid at Deerfield, Massachusetts, in 1704. Such raids were common in the French and Indian wars.

cold winter night and took 111 captives to New France. In retaliation, the British captured the Acadian town of Port Royal and changed its name to Annapolis Royal in honor of Queen Anne.

Peace was restored in 1713 by the Treaty of Utrecht (YOO trehkt). In this treaty, the British received Newfoundland, Acadia (Nova Scotia), much of present-day New Brunswick, and the territories taken from the Hudson's Bay Company. France retained the present-day Cape Breton Island and Prince Edward Island, as well as the St. Lawrence and Mississippi valleys. This gave more American territory to France than Britain, but France was greatly weakened.

Great Britain enjoyed a time of peace and prosperity after the Treaty of Utrecht. Her growing merchant fleet, protected by the powerful British navy, was able to trade freely with the colonies. Also, Georgia was established during this time to guard the southern boundary of the colonies. In this way Great Britain became a strong, wealthy European power.

King George's War. A third war, which Americans called King George's War, broke out between England and France in 1744. In America, New England colonists and the British navy managed to capture Fort Louisbourg, a French stronghold on Cape Breton Island. But after four years, both nations grew weary of fighting. All possessions were returned to their former owners in 1748 by the Treaty of Aix-la-Chapelle (ayks lah shah PEHL).

Restoration of Fort Louisbourg on Cape Breton Island, Nova Scotia. The British captured this strategic French fortress in 1745 but returned it to the French at the end of King George's War. In 1758, the British took it again in their conquest of Canada.

Removal of the French Acadians. When Queen Anne's War ended with the Treaty of Utrecht, the French Acadians of Nova Scotia found themselves in a predicament. They were now living on British territory, but they were still loyal Frenchmen. They did not want to give up their French language or their Roman Catholic religion. They hoped that the French might reconquer the region and that they would not need to help the British fight the French.

As English colonists moved into Acadia, the British government decided that the Acadians must promise to support the British in time of war. If they did so, they could retain their property, customs, language, and religion. But the Acadians would not promise allegiance to the British king. Therefore, in 1755 the British authorities decided that the Acadians must be moved out by force.

Soon British soldiers arrived to round up the Acadians. Some gave themselves up, some were removed from their homes by force, and some fled to the woods and escaped to other parts of New France. About six thousand Acadians were resettled in English colonies along the Atlantic coast. One British officer said, "This affair is more grievous to me than any service I was ever employed in."

The Acadians were unhappy with the strange land, strange people, strange customs, and Protestant religion of their new surroundings. Many of them eventually made their way south to New Orleans or back north to New France.

Focus for Thought

1. Name and describe three things that caused conflict between the British and the French in North America.
2. How did Great Britain develop the fur trade around the Hudson Bay?
3. Write *Great Britain* or *France* to answer each question.
   a. Which had more American territory under her control?
   b. Which had more people in America?
   c. Which one's colonies were better united?
4. What was the general result of the colonial wars from 1689 to 1748, especially the first and last ones?
5. How did the Treaty of Utrecht benefit the British and help them to prosper?
6. Why were the French Acadians forcibly moved to other locations?

2. THE FRENCH AND INDIAN WAR

The French and Indian War (1754–1763) was the fourth war between the British and the French. The British gave the war this name because they fought both the French and their Indian allies. This last war between the British and French in North America resulted in British control over most of the continent.

In studying any war, we do well to remember that fighting comes from the "lusts that war" within people (James 4:1). There is no such thing as a good war or a just war.

Conflict in the Ohio River Valley

Rival Claims in the Ohio River Valley. The Ohio River valley, extending from the Allegheny Mountains to the Mississippi River, became a major scene of conflict. The French had asserted their claim to this land under La Salle, but English fur traders began moving into the region. Some even built trading posts there. To clinch the French claim to the area, the governor of New France sent Céleron de Bienville (sayl ur AHN duh byan VEEL) to formally take possession of the land for France in 1749.

Céleron buried lead plates along the Ohio River, which declared that the land belonged to the king of France. But in the late 1740s a group of Virginia gentlemen formed the Ohio Company to settle the region. They received a grant of 200,000 acres (81,000 ha) with a promise of more if they could settle it. In 1750, they sent Christopher Gist to survey the land.

To counter this English threat, Governor Duquesne (doo KAYN) of New France sent almost fifteen hundred men to build a line of forts in what is now northwestern Pennsylvania (from Erie to Franklin). In 1753, Governor Dinwiddie of Virginia sent **George Washington**, a young officer from Virginia, to warn the French to leave these forts because they were on British territory. But the French commander refused.

Beginning of the French and Indian War. The English then decided to establish a fort where the Allegheny and the Monongahela (muh nahng guh HEE luh) Rivers join to form the Ohio River, at the site of present-day Pittsburgh. A few men began building a fort there, but a large French army forced them to stop. The French then built a strong fort on the site and named it Fort Duquesne.

To drive out the French, Governor Dinwiddie sent a group of soldiers under George Washington to Fort Duquesne in the spring of 1754. Washington built Fort Necessity in preparation for battle; but when a strong

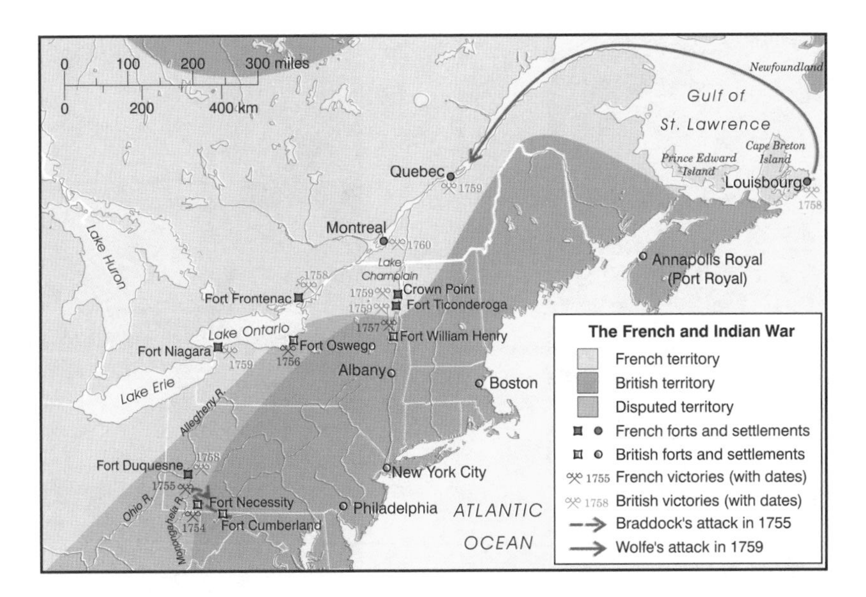

force of French and Indians attacked in July, Washington was defeated and returned to Virginia. This engagement in 1754 is considered the beginning of the French and Indian War, even though Britain did not officially declare war on France until 1756.

British Defeats, French Victories

Defeat of General Braddock. The British sent an army in 1755 under General **Edward Braddock** to destroy Fort Duquesne. The general—accustomed to fighting in Europe—planned an open attack on the fort. The colonists who accompanied him warned that the French and Indians would attack from hidden positions, but Braddock scorned their advice.

When the British neared the fort, the French and Indians began firing on them from behind the surrounding trees. The redcoated British troops were easy targets, and the French quickly killed or wounded two-thirds of them—including General Braddock himself. George Washington, his aide, suffered only bullet holes through his clothing and was able to help the army retreat. The British had received a humiliating defeat at the hands of the French.

Braddock's defeat marked the last attempt to take Fort Duquesne for several years. It also left western Pennsylvania and Virginia open to attacks by the Indians, who made repeated raids on British frontier settlements. Scores of pioneers were killed, and survivors straggled back to civilization.

Other British Losses. For the next two years, the French defeated the British in battle after battle. The British failed in their effort to take the French Fort Niagara and to advance toward Canada by way of Lake Champlain. The British Fort Oswego on Lake Ontario was destroyed in 1756, and Fort William Henry in New York was destroyed in 1757. By all appearances, the French were set to win the war.

Burial of General Braddock in 1755. He was killed in the battle against Fort Duquesne.

British statesman William Pitt (1708–1778) helped the British to become strong enough to win the wars against the French from 1756 to 1763.

General Montcalm (1712–1759) commanded the French armies during the Battle of Quebec.

British Victories, French Defeats

A New Secretary of State. **William Pitt** became the British secretary of state in 1756. Pitt was determined to raise a military force strong enough to crush the French. He borrowed great sums of money, chose better generals, and persuaded the colonists to volunteer more soldiers. On both sides of the Atlantic, the English people enthusiastically supported William Pitt in his vision.

The British captured Fort Duquesne in 1758. They renamed it Fort Pitt, and it later became the city of Pittsburgh.

While Pitt was strengthening Great Britain, New France was becoming weaker through strife and ***corruption***. The French governor disagreed with General **Montcalm** over how the war should be conducted. The governor and the treasurer were giving stolen presents to their Indian allies to keep them loyal. General Montcalm wrote, "What a country, where rascals grow rich and honest men are ruined."

By 1758, the course of the war was changing. That year Louisbourg, Fort Frontenac, and Fort Duquesne fell to the British; and in 1759 they took Fort Niagara, Fort Ticonderoga, and Crown Point. Their final objective that year was Quebec itself.

British Mastery of North America. The city of Quebec was a natural fortress, protected by a cliff with a height of 300 feet (91 m) along the St. Lawrence River. British forces arrived in the summer of 1759, and they managed to scale the heights outside Quebec. When the French army attacked, the British defeated them and took Quebec on September 13, 1759. Both the French general Montcalm and the British general **James Wolfe** were mortally wounded, and that day

French power in Canada was broken.

The British general Amherst captured Montreal the next year. After that defeat, the French surrendered New France to the British on September 8, 1760. But peace between Britain and France was not restored until the Treaty of Paris was signed in 1763. This treaty ended the widespread conflict between the two nations.

Now Britain was victorious over France as well as Spain in North America and other parts of the world. The end of this conflict marked the beginning of the British Empire. Following are the main terms agreed upon at the Treaty of Paris in 1763.

1. France ceded to Great Britain all lands east of the Mississippi River except New Orleans, which went to Spain.
2. France regained two small islands south of Newfoundland to serve as shelters for French fishermen. These two islands were all that remained of New France.
3. Spain, which had sided with France in the war, ceded Florida to Great Britain in order to regain Cuba and the Philippines.
4. Canadians were allowed to return to France within eighteen months, and Roman Catholics were allowed freedom of religion within British possessions.

Changes Brought by the French and Indian War. After the French and Indian War, North America was never again the same. The British now controlled all the territory from the Hudson Bay south to Florida and west to the Mississippi (except New Orleans). But the British thought the colonies should help repay the great sum of money that Britain had borrowed to win the war. So they tried to govern this territory in a way that would bring the most profits to England. This caused the colonists to resent the British, for they felt that they too had done much to win the victory over France.

Also, to keep peace with the Indians in the newly acquired Ohio River valley, the British passed a law forbidding the colonists to settle west of the Appalachian Mountains. This caused even more resentment among the colonists. They began talking of governing themselves without English involvement, and this led eventually to the American Revolution.

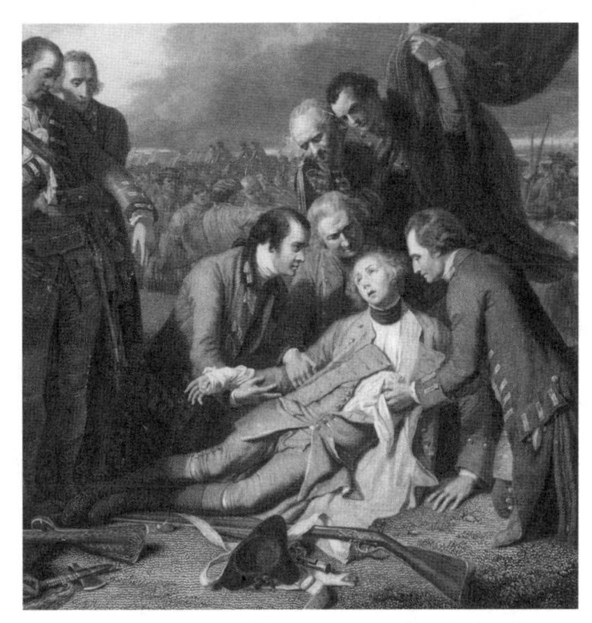

General James Wolfe died in the Battle of Quebec. The British won the battle even though their general was killed.

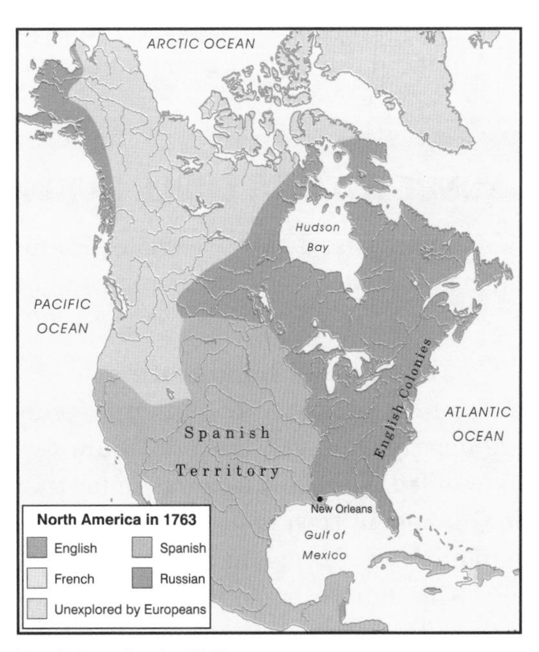

North America in 1763

British soldiers drilling at Quebec, about 1760. Note the damaged buildings in the background.

In governing French Canada, the British tried to establish the laws and customs of England. They sought to replace French absolutism with constitutional self-government. New France was renamed Quebec, the Quebec territory was reduced in size, and British colonists were encouraged to move into Quebec. In spite of such efforts, the French Canadians never really became British. They were French Catholics at heart, and they wanted to stay that way.

Focus for Thought

7. What was the result of General Braddock's defeat at Fort Duquesne?
8. How did William Pitt transform the British war effort?
9. What troubles were weakening New France at this time?
10. a. Give the location and date of the decisive battle in the French and Indian War.
    b. Give the name and date of the treaty that officially ended the French and Indian War.
11. What did the British gain as a result of the French and Indian War?

3. NONRESISTANT PEOPLE DURING THE COLONIAL PERIOD

Mennonites and other religious groups came to America to escape persecution. Through diligence and hard work, they prospered in America. Yet even here their faith was tried, especially during the colonial wars of the 1700s.

Mennonite Immigration

The first immigrants to Pennsylvania were mostly Quakers, since William Penn had founded the colony as a haven for them. The Quakers in turn invited the persecuted Mennonites in Europe to come to Pennsylvania. The Dutch Mennonites were tolerated in the Netherlands by the end of the 1500s, but the Anabaptists in Switzerland were still persecuted even in the 1700s. Many of the Swiss Brethren had moved to an area of Germany called the Palatinate, where they had a measure of religious freedom. But they were barely tolerated even there, and they also suffered because of wars.

William Penn sent agents to Europe to promote his colony and encourage settlers to move there. One Quaker agent, Jacob Telner,

Mennonite meetinghouse at Germantown, built in 1770. This is the oldest Mennonite meetinghouse in use in North America.

Hans Herr House. The Mennonite minister Christian Herr, son of Hans Herr, built this house in 1719. It also served as the place of worship in the first Mennonite settlement in Lancaster County.

was a former Dutch Mennonite. He and five other men bought 18,000 acres (7,290 ha) of land north of Philadelphia. Then in 1683, Telner arranged for a group from Krefeld, Germany, to move to Pennsylvania. This group included a number of Mennonites, the first ones to immigrate into Pennsylvania. They settled at Germantown, and later more Quakers and Mennonites moved to that area.

When Mennonites moved to America, their purpose was not to establish a religious ***utopia*** (yoo TOH pee uh) as the Quakers and Puritans wanted. Having suffered much oppression in Europe, the Mennonites simply wanted to live in peace as "the quiet in the land," and to enjoy the fruits of their labors.

The real flood of Mennonite immigration did not begin until after 1700. About 1702, the Germantown settlement expanded into the Skippack-Franconia area in Bucks, Chester, and surrounding counties. And from 1707 through 1754, several thousand Mennonites and hundreds of Amish settled in Pennsylvania.

Settlers from the Palatinate, including the bishop Hans Herr, moved directly into the Lancaster area around 1710. From the settlements at Franconia and Lancaster, Mennonites moved out into other counties in Pennsylvania, as well as to Maryland, Virginia, Ohio, and Ontario.

The Amish began coming in 1736. They tended to settle in communities separate from the Mennonites, such as at Northkill in Berks County. Jacob Hertzler, the first

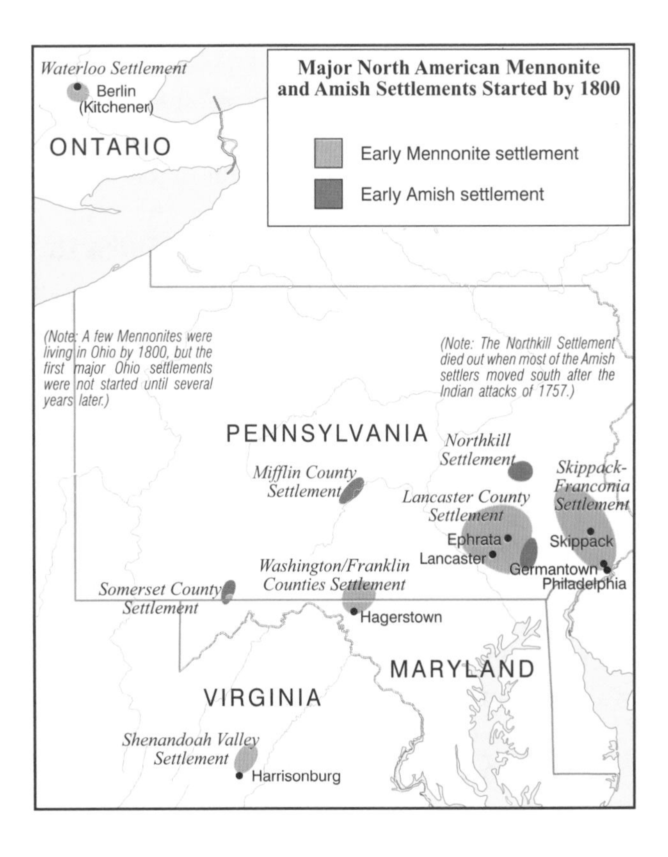

Amish bishop to move to America, settled there in 1749.

Most of the Mennonite immigrants were too poor to pay for their own passage, but God provided for them. Mennonites in the Netherlands established the Commission for Foreign Needs in 1710, which paid the way for many Mennonite immigrants. Others received help from individual congregations in Europe and America. For this reason, few Mennonites and Amish had to become indentured servants. They repaid their debt as they were able, by contributing to the fund for the poor or by helping to pay the passage of others.

The Quakers and the Mennonites

Quaker Control of Pennsylvania. At first the Quakers controlled the government of Pennsylvania, for most of the settlers were Quakers. As the years went by and Quakers became a minority, they used various means to maintain their control, such as by giving the eastern areas greater representation than the western areas.

Quakers and Mennonites shared several beliefs, such as freedom of conscience, simplicity in dress and lifestyle, refusal to swear oaths, and refusal to take part in war. But there were numerous differences too. Quakers said they were guided by the "Inner Light," whereas Mennonites accepted the Bible as their guide for life. Quakers were usually merchants and artisans who settled in cities, but most Mennonites were farmers. Quakers held government offices in Pennsylvania, but Mennonites usually did not take part in government.

In spite of these differences, the Mennonites and other Germans supported the Quakers in government and even voted for them. This helped the Quakers to stay in control. The Mennonites felt that the Quakers would promote peace and continue to grant freedom to them. Since the Mennonites had experienced persecution in Europe, they had never before had opportunity to vote. However, later events convinced the Mennonites that voting violates Scriptural principles.

Loss of Quaker Control. The Scotch-Irish were another group of people moving into Pennsylvania. These were Presbyterian Scots who had been settled in Ireland by King James I. When the Anglican rulers again oppressed them, they began migrating to America in great numbers. These people moved farther west and settled on the frontier.

The Scotch-Irish settlers caused trouble by claiming land without legal title to it and by killing Indians. When the Indians retaliated, these settlers requested that the Quaker government punish the Indians by military force. But the Quakers refused, for they did not believe that the Indians were the root of the problem. They thought that if the white settlers treated the Indians fairly, as Penn had done, they would be peaceful. So the Quakers did not send a military force to protect the frontier.

A decisive election was held in 1756. The governor was already a non-Quaker, and it appeared that the Quakers might lose control of the Assembly as well. Fearing a loss of their freedoms, the Mennonites voted for Quaker candidates. But the Quakers lost control of the Assembly anyway, and some resigned rather than support the war effort. After this, most Mennonites no longer took part in voting.

War Experiences of Nonresistant People

Preparations by the Mennonites. As signs of war increased, the Mennonites fortified themselves in several ways. One way was by publishing the first American edition of the old martyrs' hymnal, the *Ausbund* (OWS buhnt), in 1742. Another way was to publish the Dutch *Martyrs Mirror* in German. For help with this great task, they appealed to the

Ausbund,
Das ist:
Etliche schöne
Christliche
Lieder,
Wie sie in dem Gefängnüß zu Bassau in dem Schloß von den Schweitzer-Brüdern, und von anderen rechtgläubigen Christen hin und her gedichtet worden.
Allen und jeden Christen welcher Religion sie seyen, unpartheyisch fast nützlich.
Germantown:
Gedruckt bey Christoph Saur / 1742.

Title page of the 1742 *Ausbund,* which was printed in Germantown, Pennsylvania, by Christopher Sauer.

Dutch Mennonites in 1745 by writing a letter that began with these words: "Since . . . the flames of war are mounting higher, and it cannot be known whether the cross and tribulation may not all the sooner fall to the lot of the defenseless Christians, it becomes us to strengthen ourselves for such circumstances . . . and to make every preparation for the steadfast constancy in our faith."

But the Dutch were slow in responding to this request. So the Mennonites in Pennsylvania appealed to **Peter Miller**, a Seventh-day German Baptist at the Ephrata Cloister, who translated the *Martyrs Mirror* into German and published it in 1748. At 1,512 pages, this was the largest book produced in America up to that time.

Sufferings of Nonresistant People. Some nonresistant people were spared during the colonial wars, as described in the poem "The Unbarred Door." (See Lesson 94 of Rod and Staff's English 9 and 10, Book One, for an abridged version of this poem.) But the Indians did not usually stop to ask whether the inhabitants were peaceable. Therefore, nonresistant people on the frontier suffered along with other settlers.

One example is the family of **Jacob Hochstetler**, an Amish man who lived in the Northkill settlement in Berks County. The Indians attacked one night in 1757, but Jacob refused to let his sons shoot at them. When the Hochstetlers tried to escape from their burning home, the Indians killed several of the family and took Jacob and two sons into captivity. (See "One Dark Night" in Rod and Staff's Eighth Reader.)

In 1764, the Indians killed a minister named John Roads (Rhodes) and most of his family, including one son who climbed a tree

Der
Blutige Schau-Platz
oder
Martyrer
Spiegel der Tauffs-Gesinten
oder
Wehrlosen-Christen,
Die um des Zeugnuß JEsu ihres Seligmachers willen gelitten haben, und seynd getödtet worden, von Christi Zeit an bis auf das Jahr 1660.
Vormals aus unterschiedlichen glaubwürdigen Chronicken, Nachrichten und Zeugnüssen gesammlet und in Holländischer Sprach heraus gegeben
von T. J. V. BRAGHT.
Nun aber sorgfältigst ins Hochteutsche übersetzt und zum erstenmal ans Licht gebracht.
Arbeite und hoffe
EPHRATA in Pensylvanien,
Drucks und Verlags der Brüderschafft. Anno MDCCXLVIII.

Title page of the 1748 *Martyrs Mirror,* which was printed at the Ephrata Cloister.

Indians returning English captives in 1764. After the British won the French and Indian War, Colonel Boquet required the Indians to give up all the white people that they had captured.

and one who tried to escape by swimming across a river. The Indians took four children captive but killed three of them; the other returned after three years. One daughter fled into the barn with her eighteen-month-old sister; when an Indian tried to burn the barn, the older girl carried the baby 12 miles (19 km) to her brother's home and so escaped.

Nonresistant men were not forced to serve in the army during the French and Indian War. However, Mennonites did provide wagons, teams, and drivers to carry food and provisions for Braddock's expedition in 1755. This represented a compromise of their nonresistant position. Also, nonresistant people sent wagonloads of flour, meat, and clothing to aid refugees fleeing because of the frontier raids. One such group included six hundred people who fled to eastern Pennsylvania, having lost houses, barns, and cattle, and escaping with only their lives.

After the end of the war, Colonel Henry Boquet (boh KAY) brought four hundred captives from among the Indians to Carlisle, Pennsylvania. There, families whose members had been taken captive by the Indians went to seek their loved ones. Among the captives was Regina of Buffalo Valley, who identified her mother only when the mother sang a German hymn that Regina remembered from her childhood. (See "Regina, the German Captive" in Rod and Staff's Seventh Reader.) Thus the horror of the French and Indian War came to a close.

Focus for Thought

12. How were the motives of the Mennonites different from the motives of the Puritans and Quakers for coming to America?
13. Though most Mennonites and Amish were very poor, few of them had to become indentured servants in America. How did God provide for them?
14. Compare the Mennonites with the Quakers
    a. in their beliefs.
    b. in their preferred place of settlement.
    c. in their involvement with government.
15. How did it come about that the Quakers lost control of the Pennsylvania Assembly?
16. Before the French and Indian War, what two things did the Mennonites do to help maintain their belief in nonresistance?
17. How did nonresistant people put their beliefs to practice during the French and Indian War?

Historical Highlights

A. Matching: People

a. Dutch Mennonites
b. General Braddock
c. George Washington
d. Jacob Hochstetler
e. James Wolfe
f. Montcalm
g. Peter Miller
h. Prince Rupert
i. Radisson and Groseilliers
j. Scotch-Irish
k. William Penn
l. William Pitt

1. American officer who was sent to Fort Duquesne.
2. Prime minister of Great Britain during the French and Indian War.
3. French traders who helped to start British fur trading in the Hudson Bay region.
4. People who helped Mennonites come to America.
5. French general in the French and Indian War.
6. Man who founded Pennsylvania.
7. Nobleman who established British fur trading in the Hudson Bay region.
8. British general who defeated the French at Quebec.
9. Amish man who would not kill Indians.
10. Man in charge of translating and publishing the German *Martyrs Mirror*.
11. People who settled in the frontier regions and made trouble with the Indians.
12. British general defeated at Fort Duquesne.

B. Matching: Places

a. Acadia
b. British Empire
c. Ephrata Cloister
d. Fort Duquesne
e. Fort Louisbourg
f. Germantown
g. Hudson Bay
h. Northkill
i. Ohio River valley
j. Palatinate
k. Quebec
l. Rupert's Land

1. Area over which conflicting claims led to the French and Indian War.
2. French fort built where Pittsburgh now stands.
3. Site of the decisive battle of the French and Indian War.
4. Area in Nova Scotia from which the British removed French Canadians.
5. Body of water around which the British developed their fur trade.
6. All the territory ruled by Great Britain.
7. French fortress on Cape Breton Island.
8. Place where the *Martyrs Mirror* was translated and printed.
9. Another name for the Hudson Bay region.
10. German region to which the Swiss Anabaptists moved before coming to America.
11. Town in Pennsylvania where Mennonites first settled.
12. Amish settlement in Pennsylvania.

C. Matching: Dates

1. Treaty of Paris.	a. 1668
2. Beginning of French and Indian War.	b. 1683
3. Four wars between France and England.	c. 1689–1763
4. Battle of Quebec.	d. 1697
5. Braddock's attack on Fort Duquesne; Acadians forced to move.	e. 1713
6. Treaty of Utrecht ends Queen Anne's War.	f. 1748
7. Arrival of British expedition in the Hudson Bay.	g. 1754
8. Treaty of Aix-la-Chapelle ends King George's War.	h. 1755
9. Hochstetler family massacred; William Pitt becomes prime minister.	i. 1756
	j. 1757
10. Treaty of Ryswick ends King William's War.	k. 1759
11. Quakers lose control of Pennsylvania Assembly.	l. 1763
12. First Mennonites arrive in Pennsylvania.	

D. Matching: Names and Terms

a. Commission for Foreign Needs	g. *Martyrs Mirror*
b. corruption	h. Queen Anne's War
c. frontier raid	i. "quiet in the land"
d. Hudson's Bay Company	j. Treaty of Paris
e. King George's War	k. Treaty of Utrecht
f. King William's War	l. utopia

1. Company established to develop the fur trade in Rupert's Land.
2. Agreement in 1763 that officially ended England's conflict with France.
3. Book published by Pennsylvania Mennonites to encourage nonresistance.
4. Third colonial war, 1744–1748.
5. Sudden attack on an English settlement by French and Indians.
6. Treaty that ended Queen Anne's War.
7. Misuse of a public office for the sake of illegal gain.
8. Ideal society desired by the Puritans and Quakers.
9. Dutch Mennonite organization that aided emigrating Swiss Mennonites.
10. First colonial war, 1689–1697.
11. Status desired by Mennonites and Amish in America.
12. Second colonial war, 1702–1713.

E. Multiple Choice

Write the letter of the best answer.

1. How did Great Britain receive the opportunity to establish its influence in Canada?
   a. Two angered French traders told the British about the opportunities there.
   b. France failed to develop the fur trade in northern Canada.
   c. Henry Hudson had explored the St. Lawrence region for Great Britain.
   d. The Indians around Lake Superior preferred to trade with the British.
2. Why was beaver fur in such demand?
   a. There was an abundance of fur.
   b. Women's styles had recently changed.

c. The Indians made most of their clothing from beaver fur.
d. Beaver hats were fashionable in Europe.

3. Which one of the following statements best explains why the Acadians were forced to move?
   a. Many British colonists began moving into Nova Scotia.
   b. The Acadians rebelled against the British.
   c. The Acadians were not willing to become British subjects.
   d. The Acadians refused to give up their customs, language, and property.
4. What makes the French and Indian War so important in the history of North America?
   a. The Indians were finally subdued by the British.
   b. The British were finally subdued by the French.
   c. The French were removed as a power in North America.
   d. All of Canada became Protestant.
5. Why was it almost certain that war would break out between the British and the French in North America?
   a. Both wanted the Indians to support them.
   b. Both were determined to control North America.
   c. The British and the French were traditional enemies.
   d. The English were Protestant but the French were Catholic.
6. What was the strongest factor that determined the outcome of the wars between Britain and France?
   a. the Indian allies
   b. the strength of the armies
   c. the number of people
   d. God's overruling hand
7. How did the French Canadians respond to their new English rulers?
   a. They obeyed English laws but remained French at heart.
   b. They returned to France within a year after the Treaty of Paris was signed.
   c. They did away with all government corruption.
   d. They welcomed the English as liberators.
8. Why did the British authorities forbid settlers to cross the Appalachian Mountains?
   a. They wanted to prove their authority over the colonists.
   b. They were afraid the colonies would stir up more trouble with the French.
   c. They wanted to keep peace with the Indians.
   d. They thought the land west of the Appalachians should belong to the Indians.
9. Which of the following was *not* a reason for Quaker immigration to Pennsylvania?
   a. to have religious freedom
   b. to have economic opportunity
   c. to participate in the "Holy Experiment"
   d. to provide a haven for destitute Mennonites
10. Which religious body was most directly involved in the emigration of the Palatinate Mennonites?
    a. French Catholics
    b. English Quakers
    c. Dutch Mennonites
    d. Scotch-Irish Presbyterians
11. Which of the following was *not* a reason for Mennonite immigration?
    a. to establish an ideal government
    b. for religious freedom
    c. for economic opportunity
    d. to live in peace and quietness

12. For what *two* reasons were the Scotch-Irish displeased with the Quaker government?
    a. The Quakers sent them to the frontier.
    b. The Quakers showed equal respect to Indians and white men.
    c. The Quakers refused to protect them by armed force.
    d. The Quakers refused to let them settle where they wished.
13. How were the Quakers able to maintain control of the Pennsylvania Assembly until 1756?
    a. by outnumbering the other settlers
    b. by the support of Scotch-Irish voters
    c. by order of King Charles II
    d. by the support of German voters, including Mennonites
14. Which one of the following was *not* an effect of the French and Indian War on the nonresistant people?
    a. printing the *Martyrs Mirror*
    b. suffering for refusal to help General Braddock
    c. helping refugees from the frontier
    d. massacre by the Indians

F. Mennonites and Quakers

Write whether each item is associated with the Mennonites (M), *with the Quakers* (Q), *with both groups* (B), *or with neither group* (N).

1. persecuted in Europe
2. freedom of conscience
3. farmers
4. artisans
5. found economic opportunity
6. "Inner Light"
7. merchants
8. "the quiet in the land"
9. Philadelphia
10. German
11. Lancaster
12. held government offices
13. Skippack-Franconia
14. nonparticipation in war
15. Indian fighters
16. English
17. Scotch-Irish
18. "Holy Experiment"; attempted utopia
19. refusal of oaths
20. simplicity

G. Deeper Discussion

1. Is there any connection between the French defeat and the corruption in the French Canadian government? Explain your answer.
2. Compare the reasons for the immigration of the Quakers, Mennonites, and Scotch-Irish by answering the following questions.
    a. What did all three groups have in common?
    b. What were the major differences?
3. a. Why did the Mennonites vote in the 1700s?
    b. In what way did they succeed by voting?
    c. In what way did they fail?
4. Read Matthew 5:38–48 and Romans 12:14–21. From these verses, explain why it is wrong for Christians to take part in warfare.

5. Read Romans 13:1–7 and 1 Timothy 2:1, 2. Observe that although Christians should not take part in government, they still have certain duties to the government. Name at least two of these duties.

H. Chronology and Geography

1. Trace Map C again, and label it "European Claims in North America About 1755."
   a. Use different colors to show British, French, Spanish, and Russian claims at this time. Add a legend to the map.
   b. Label the following early settlements: St. Augustine, Santa Fe, San Diego, San Francisco, Quebec, Montreal, New Orleans, Jamestown, Boston, New York City, and Philadelphia.
2. a. Why was the location of Fort Duquesne so important to both the British and the French?
   b. In what way did geography affect this importance?
3. a. What two major North American waterways did the French control?
   b. How did this give them an advantage over the British?
4. How did the geography of Quebec help to protect the city against attack?

So Far This Year

A. Matching: Terms

1. Aristocracy; upper-class people.
2. Person working to repay the cost of coming to America.
3. Colony governed by the king.
4. Colony owners hoping to rent land to people of lower rank.
5. Colony governed by a proprietor.
6. Small farmers and craftsmen.
7. Colony operating on the basis of its charter.
8. Legal document from the king, granting the right to settle a certain region and establish a government there.
9. People who withdrew from the Church of England and moved to America.
10. People who wanted to purify the Church of England from within.
11. Maryland law granting religious freedom.
12. Unskilled laborers who did not own land.
13. Agreement signed by Pilgrims and Strangers to make "just and equal laws."
14. Branch of government that makes laws.

a. Act of Toleration
b. better class
c. charter
d. charter colony
e. indentured servant
f. legislature
g. Mayflower Compact
h. meaner sort
i. middling class
j. Pilgrims
k. proprietary colony
l. proprietors
m. Puritans
n. royal colony

B. Names

Write the names of the persons or things described.

15. Leader of Jamestown who established a policy of "no work, no food."
16. Founder of Rhode Island, who insisted on freedom of conscience.
17. Founder of Maryland.
18. Quaker who received a land grant as payment for a debt.
19. Trustee leader in the founding of Georgia.
20. Leaders of the colonial religious revival (two men).
21. Religious revival in the 1700s.
22. Age of Reason.
23. Church of England; official church in the South.
24. Puritans; official church in New England.

C. Dates

Write the date of each event.

25. Pennsylvania received a charter.
26. Plymouth was founded.
27. Georgia was founded.
28. Jamestown was founded.

A Canadian trapper.

Approval of the Declaration of Independence in Congress, at Independence Hall.

9 The American Revolution

1. American and British Disagreements
   - Developments Leading to Disagreement
2. Independence Declared and Won
   - The First Continental Congress
   - The Outbreak of War
   - The Second Continental Congress
   - The Declaration of Independence
   - The Course of the American Revolution
3. Nonresistant People During the Revolution
   - Nonresistant Groups
   - Issues of Nonresistance
   - Nonresistant Experiences

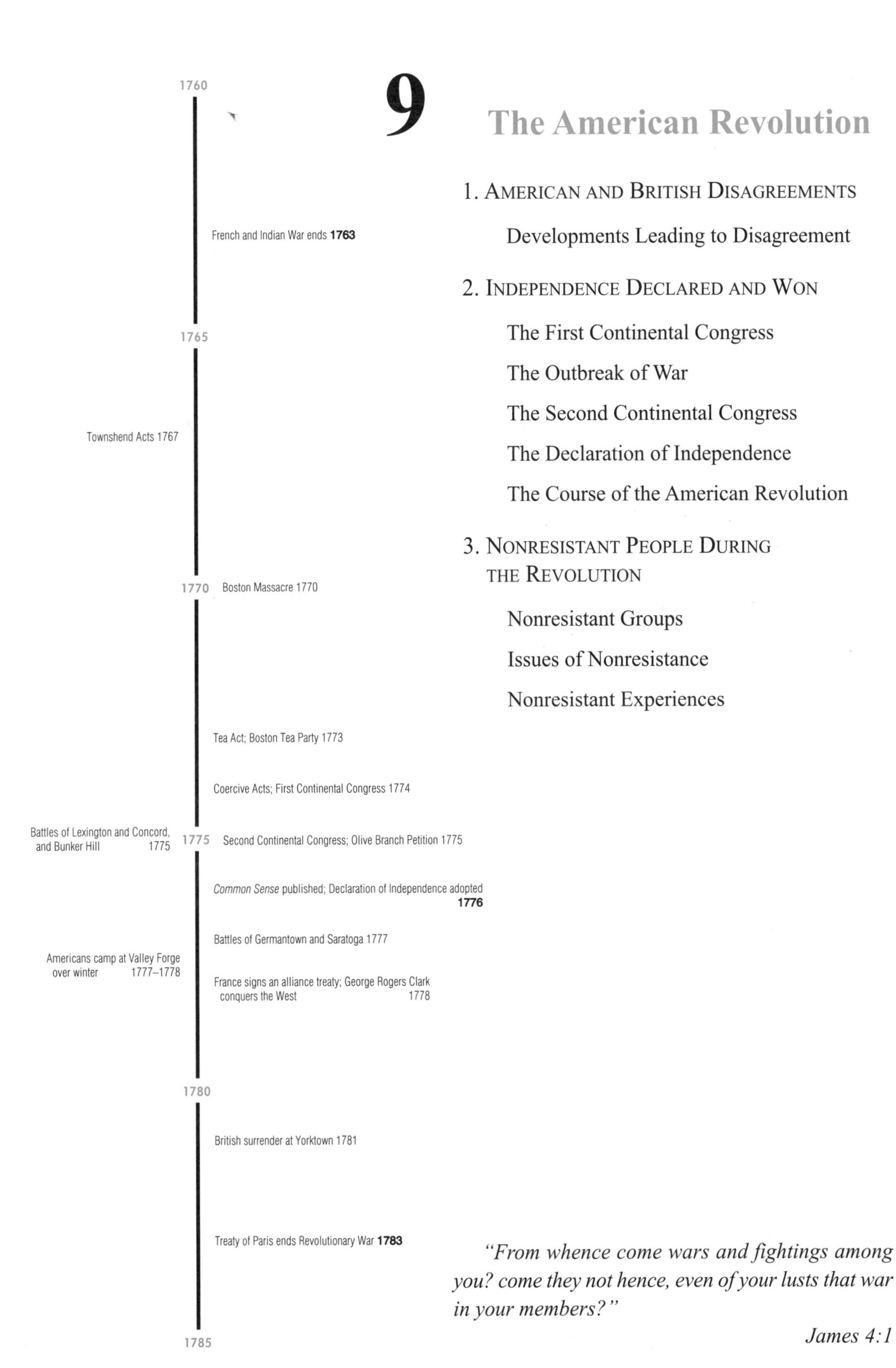

"From whence come wars and fightings among you? come they not hence, even of your lusts that war in your members?"

James 4:1

THE AMERICAN REVOLUTION

Focus for Reading

After the French and Indian War ended in 1763, a series of disagreements arose between the British government and its colonies in America. The disagreements became so strong that the colonies declared themselves independent in 1776. This was followed by the American Revolution, through which the colonies gained independence from Great Britain and established the United States of America. What was involved in the American Revolution? This chapter includes the following sections.

1. American and British Disagreements
2. Independence Declared and Won
3. Nonresistant People During the Revolution

1. AMERICAN AND BRITISH DISAGREEMENTS

As you saw in Chapter 7, the British government granted the American colonists a great deal of liberty to govern themselves. This self-government, combined with their self-sufficient lifestyle, produced a group of self-reliant people with an independent spirit. As long as American interests did not clash with British interests, there was little trouble. But when the British tried to control the colonies more strictly, conflicts arose.

"Only by pride cometh contention: but with the well advised is wisdom" (Proverbs 13:10).

Developments Leading to Disagreement

British Economic Control. Britain operated its colonies on the principle of ***mercantilism*** (MUR kuhn tee lihz uhm), the idea that colonies should bring financial gain to the mother country. The American colonies would provide raw materials such as wood, iron, and cotton for the factories in England; the colonies in turn would buy manufactured goods such as kettles, hats, and clothing from England. This was very profitable for England because manufactured goods were worth more than the raw materials needed to make them.

To keep the system working, the British passed laws regulating trade. Some laws said that certain products of the colonies, such as sugar, tobacco, and indigo, could be sold only to Britain. Other laws stated that foreign goods destined for America had to be shipped through Britain first. Still other laws restricted manufacturing in the colonies so that British manufacturing would be more profitable. For example, the Hat Act of 1732 said that colonial hat manufacturers could not sell their hats to other colonies or to Britain. Such laws tended to make the colonists feel resentful toward the mother country.

Laws and Taxes. Great Britain was deeply in debt when the French and Indian War ended in 1763. Since the large territory gained by the British would be costly to govern, Great Britain needed to raise more money. The British thought it only reasonable that this money should come from the colonies.

That same year, an Ottawa Indian chief named **Pontiac** masterminded a plan to expel the British from Indian lands in Ohio. Various tribes were to each destroy the fort nearest them and then to raid the defenseless frontier settlements. The British managed to subdue what they called Pontiac's Conspiracy. But to avoid further conflict with the Indians, Britain issued the Proclamation of 1763. This law stated that the lands

Pontiac, an Ottawa chief, meeting British Major Robert Rogers. Pontiac later led a great alliance of Indian tribes to oppose white settlements west of the Appalachians.

west of the Appalachians were closed to settlement, and that all the settlers already there would have to move out.

A new prime minister, **George Grenville**, took office in 1763. He developed a program to raise more ***revenue*** from the colonies and to control them more firmly. First, he determined to end salutary neglect and strictly enforce the trade laws. Second, he proposed new laws to raise money. The British legislature (Parliament) passed the Sugar Act in 1764, which actually reduced the tax on sugar and molasses but was to be strictly enforced. Parliament also passed the Currency Act, which restricted colonies from issuing paper money and said that all debts must be paid in gold or silver coins.

The next year Parliament passed the Stamp Act to produce even more revenue. The Stamp Act stated that the colonists must buy stamps and put them on all printed matter, which included newspapers, almanacs, and legal documents, such as wills, deeds, and licenses.

Tax stamp of 1765. The Stamp Act required that stamps such as this be put on legal papers, playing cards, newspapers, and other items.

In 1765, Parliament passed the Quartering Act, which required the colonists to lodge British soldiers in barns or vacant buildings. Supplies for the soldiers were to be provided by the colony where they were stationed. This law would save money for the British government; and besides, it seemed only logical that colonists should pay for their own defense.

Colonial Objections. The colonists who wanted to move west were upset by the Proclamation of 1763, and some settled beyond the Appalachians regardless of the law. Merchants and ship owners opposed stricter enforcement of trade laws because they made large profits by smuggling. Many people had little gold or silver and therefore could not pay their debts under the Currency Act. And the Americans viewed the British soldiers as oppressors rather than defenders. They felt that the Quartering Act was actually a kind of tax.

The Stamp Act caused the strongest opposition. The colonists were accustomed to voting for their own taxes, and they objected to paying taxes that they had not approved. When the stamps arrived in America, people refused to buy them. Publishers defiantly circulated newspapers without stamps. Angry

Riot in Boston against the Stamp Act. The sign reads, "The Folly of England and the Ruin of America."

Propaganda poster of colonial days. Benjamin Franklin used it in 1754 to urge unity against the French and Indians, and Paul Revere used it in the 1770s to urge unity against the British. It was based on the idea that a snake cut in pieces would live if the pieces were rejoined.

colonists formed associations called the Sons of Liberty, declaring that they would fight if necessary to protect their freedoms. A popular slogan was "Taxation without representation is tyranny"—for the colonies had no representatives in Parliament.

In 1765, representatives from nine colonies met in New York City to protest the Stamp Act. This assembly, called the Stamp Act Congress, drew up a protest to send to Great Britain. The representatives stated their allegiance to the king, but they spelled out their belief that only their own legislatures—not Parliament—could levy taxes on them.

Finally colonists began to ***boycott*** (refuse to buy) British goods, and trade with Britain dropped. Then the British merchants joined the cry to ***repeal*** the Stamp Act. The act was withdrawn in 1766. But on the same day, Parliament issued a Declaratory Act, stating its dominion over the colonies "in all cases whatsoever," including taxation. The colonists applauded the repeal, but they resented Parliament's declaration of authority over them.

The Townshend Acts. **Charles Townshend** (TOWN zuhnd), the British treasurer, proposed other laws to raise money from the colonies. In 1767, Parliament passed the Townshend Acts, which levied taxes on imports such as glass, lead, paper, paint, and tea. A board of customs was established in Boston to supervise collection of the taxes.

The Townshend Acts also provided ***writs of assistance***, which allowed British officials to search any building for smuggled goods. If illegal goods were found, the accused person would be tried without a jury in one of the new courts established for this purpose. Another Townshend provision was that the salaries of the governor and other British officials were to be paid out of money raised by the Townshend Acts. Also, the Assembly of New York was forbidden to meet because that colony had not complied with the Quartering Act.

Again the colonists' anger was roused. The writs of assistance seemed like an invasion of their privacy and security. Since the legislature could no longer control the governor's salary, they had less control over the governor. And if the New York legislature could be forbidden to meet, other assemblies likewise might be dissolved.

Once more the colonists boycotted British goods. Parliament, they declared, had no right whatsoever to tax them. Violence broke out, and tax collectors were tarred and feathered. The British tax commissioners in Boston were harassed until they withdrew to the safety of a fortress in the harbor.

Tarring and feathering of John Malcolm at Boston in 1774. This action shows how strongly the Americans resented British tax collectors.

The Boston Massacre. Because of violence in Boston, British troops stayed there to keep order. But on March 5, 1770, a group of rowdy men and boys from the town began throwing snowballs and sticks at the soldiers guarding the customs house. More soldiers arrived, a crowd gathered, and a scuffle broke out. British guns were fired, and soon five Bostonians were dead and six more were wounded. This incident became known as the Boston Massacre, and it stirred heated passions against the British as the story spread through the colonies.

In April 1770, Parliament repealed all the Townshend taxes except the one on tea. Protest died down, trade improved, and peaceable relations returned for several years.

To sustain the spirit of resistance, **Samuel Adams** and other Bostonians organized a Committee of Correspondence. This committee would inform other towns about past, present, and future violations of colonial rights. By 1773, similar committees had sprung up throughout the other colonies, uniting them against British acts that the colonists did not approve.

The Tea Act. In 1773, the British government passed the Tea Act, which allowed the East India Company to bypass middlemen and sell tea in the American colonies at a very low price. The only tax on the tea would be the Townshend duty established in 1767. The British government thought the Americans would not mind paying this tax, since the tea was so cheap. But the colonists were enraged by the Tea Act. Colonial merchants felt that the British government was trying to put them out of business. Many Americans interpreted the Tea Act as a way of bribing them into paying the tax on tea.

The Committees of Correspondence spread word that the colonists should reject the tea. When the first tea ships arrived, they were greeted by mobs that kept them from being unloaded. Some tea ships returned to Britain with their cargo still aboard. But in Boston, the governor insisted that the ships must unload their cargo whether the colonists wanted it or not.

In response, on the night of December 16, 1773, a group of men and boys disguised themselves as Indians and staged the Boston Tea Party. They boarded the tea ships in the Boston harbor and dumped 342 large cases of tea, worth thousands of dollars, into the water. Many Americans cheered the Tea Party, but others were shocked at this reckless destruction of property.

The Coercive Acts. Parliament could not allow the Boston Tea Party to go unpunished. In 1774, it passed the Coercive (koh UR sihv) Acts, which the Americans called Intolerable Acts. These acts declared that the port of Boston would be closed until the destroyed tea was paid for. They forbade town meetings, annulled the Massachusetts Charter,

Boston Tea Party of December 16, 1773. This action led to the Coercive Acts and the First Continental Congress.

and again declared that the Bostonians must quarter British soldiers. General **Thomas Gage** was sent from Great Britain to enforce the Coercive Acts.

The same year, Parliament passed the Quebec Act, which extended the old Quebec borders as far south as the Ohio River. This was in conflict with the claims of Virginia, Connecticut, and Massachusetts on those western lands. The colonists also noted that Quebec had no representative assembly, something they saw as a threat to their liberties. They added the Quebec Act to their list of Intolerable Acts. If neither side gave in, war was almost certain.

Focus for Thought

1. Name the law that each description refers to.
   a. It stated that lands west of the Appalachians were closed to settlement.
   b. It said that the tax on sugar must be strictly enforced.
   c. It restricted colonies from issuing paper money and said that all debts must be paid in gold or silver coins.
   d. It required the colonists to buy stamps for all printed matter, including legal documents.
   e. It required the colonists to provide lodging and supplies for British soldiers.
2. Why did the colonists especially oppose laws such as the Stamp Act?
3. What did the colonists do to keep from paying the taxes levied on certain goods?
4. a. Who started the events on March 5, 1770, which led to the Boston Massacre?
   b. Who received the blame for it?
5. Why were the Committees of Correspondence formed?
6. a. Why were the Coercive Acts passed?
   b. What did the colonists call them?

2. INDEPENDENCE DECLARED AND WON

After Parliament passed the Coercive Acts, the colonists became more and more united in their opposition to Great Britain. Finally they took the drastic step of breaking ties with Great Britain and then fighting to secure their independence. God sovereignly overruled so that the United States was established as a new nation.

The First Continental Congress

Soon after the Coercive Acts were passed, the Committees of Correspondence spread the word that there would be a meeting of colonial leaders to decide what should be done. That meeting, held at Philadelphia in September 1774, became known as the First Continental Congress. It was attended by fifty-six men from all the colonies except Georgia.

But the delegates found it hard to agree on what to do. One group, called ***Tories***, wanted to pay for the tea and avoid future confrontations. Another group, known as ***Whigs***, favored a major boycott of Great Britain to force recognition of the colonies' rights. Some began talking of complete independence, reasoning that since Parliament did not have the right to tax the colonies, it had no authority over them at all.

On October 14, 1774, the delegates adopted a Declaration and Resolves, which asserted that only colonial legislatures could make laws for the colonies. They called for

Prominent men before and during the American Revolution:
Left: King George III (1738–1820) ruled Great Britain at the time of the American Revolution. ***Middle:*** Patrick Henry addressing the Virginia Assembly. He delivered his best-known speech in 1775, calling for Virginia to arm against Great Britain and saying, "Give me liberty, or give me death!" ***Top right:*** Samuel Adams (1722–1803) was a patriot of Massachusetts who helped to organize the Committee of Correspondence. ***Bottom right:*** Thomas Paine (1737–1809) wrote *Common Sense*, a pamphlet that persuaded many Americans to support the cause of independence.

repeal of the Coercive Acts, and they set up a boycott of British goods. Finally, the delegates set a date for meeting again the next spring if their demands were not recognized.

The Outbreak of War

Instead of backing down as the Americans hoped, Parliament passed more laws against them. Soon many of the ***patriots***, who favored independence, began conducting military drills and storing ammunition at Concord, Massachusetts. When this was reported to General Gage, the British commander in Boston, he determined to destroy the war supplies. He also planned to capture John Hancock and Samuel Adams, two of the main patriot leaders. Hancock and Adams fled from Boston to avoid arrest.

In April 1775, Gage ordered British troops to pass through Lexington, Massachusetts, and destroy the powder and guns stored at Concord. Through the efforts of **Paul Revere** and others, the patriots were warned of the British move. John Hancock and Samuel Adams escaped, and ***minutemen*** (men ready to fight on a minute's notice) prepared to meet the British at Lexington.

When the troops arrived at Lexington, fighting broke out between them and the colonial minutemen. The British passed through Lexington, marched to Concord, destroyed what military supplies they could find, and then returned to Boston. Along the way, patriot soldiers attacked the British from behind trees and buildings. The shots at Lexington and Concord have been called

Paul Revere's ride on April 18, 1775. He and other men warned the patriots of the British plan to march to Concord, Massachusetts, the next day.

Retreat of the British from Concord. The patriots fired at the soldiers from behind trees and stone fences, and the British burned buildings along the way.

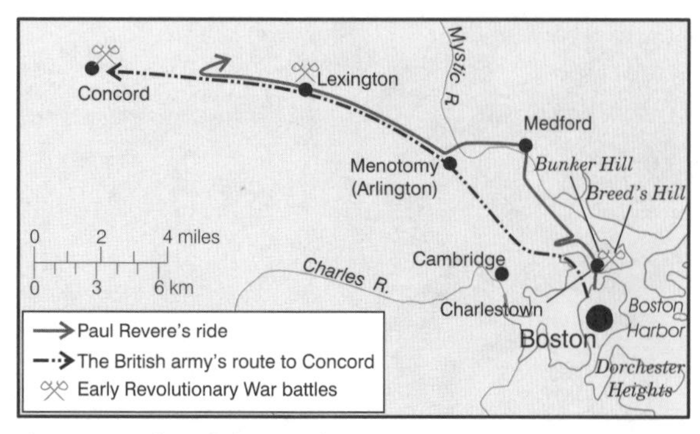

The First Battles of the Revolutionary War

"shots heard around the world" because they started the American Revolution, or Revolutionary War.

The Second Continental Congress

In May 1775, the colonial leaders assembled in Philadelphia for the Second Continental Congress. The leaders voted in June to raise a regular army with George Washington of Virginia as its commander. In July they sent the Olive Branch Petition to **King George III** as a final plea to avert war. Soon afterward they drew up a statement entitled "Declaration of the Causes and Necessity of Taking Up Arms."

While the Congress met in Philadelphia, more fighting broke out elsewhere. In May 1775, a patriot expedition led by Ethan Allen conquered the British forts of Ticonderoga and Crown Point in New York. But the Americans were defeated in June when they fought the bloody Battle of Bunker Hill against the British in Boston. However, the British withdrew from Boston in March 1776 after the patriots used cannons to fortify the heights around the city.

George Washington taking command of the American army at Cambridge, Massachusetts.

In August 1775, King George issued the Proclamation of Rebellion. This statement declared that the thirteen American colonies were in rebellion against Great Britain. The king also hired Hessian soldiers—an act that outraged the colonists because they regarded the Hessians as cruel and ruthless.

The Declaration of Independence

Early in 1776, a patriot named **Thomas Paine** published a pamphlet entitled *Common Sense*. His main point was that it was only common sense for the American colonies to be independent from Great Britain. This powerful piece of ***propaganda*** (prahp uh GAN duh) blamed King George III and Parliament for the colonies' troubles. Over one hundred thousand copies of the booklet were sold in six months, and it convinced many people to support the cause of independence.

Finally in June 1776, the Second Continental Congress appointed a committee of five men to write a statement declaring that the colonies were independent from Great Britain. **Thomas Jefferson**, a member of the committee, did most of the writing. The

Benjamin Franklin reading a draft of the Declaration of Independence. Thomas Jefferson (standing) did the writing, and John Adams (seated) helped to produce the final draft.

resulting Declaration of Independence was adopted on July 4, 1776.

The Declaration of Independence asserted that the American colonies were separate from Great Britain and that the United States was a new nation. It gave reasons for the separation as well as a brief statement of the principles on which the new nation would be founded. These principles were later included in the Constitution of the United States.

The 3 million American people were divided on the issue of independence. As many as one-third of them were ***Loyalists*** (people who wanted to remain subject to Britain). Loyalists supported the British, and some even joined the British forces. The patriots tarred and feathered Loyalists, ran them out of town, and seized or destroyed their property. Because of this, many Loyalists fled to Canada.

The Americans Versus the British, 1763–1776	
British Actions	**American Reactions**
Proclamation of 1763	Continuing settlement of the West
1765—Stamp Act 1766—Repeal of Stamp Act	Refusal to buy stamps; protest by the Stamp Act Congress; boycott of British goods
1767—Townshend Acts 1770—Repeal of Townshend Acts	Boycott of British goods; harassment of tax collectors
1770—Boston Massacre	Committees of Correspondence organized
1773—Tea Act	Boston Tea Party
1774—Coercive Acts (Intolerable Acts)	First Continental Congress; boycott of British goods
1775—British raid on Lexington and Concord	Resistance by minutemen; American Revolution begins
1775—Proclamation of Rebellion	*Common Sense* published; Declaration of Independence adopted (1776)

Washington crossing the Delaware River on the night of December 25, 1776. His victories at Trenton and Princeton bolstered American confidence.

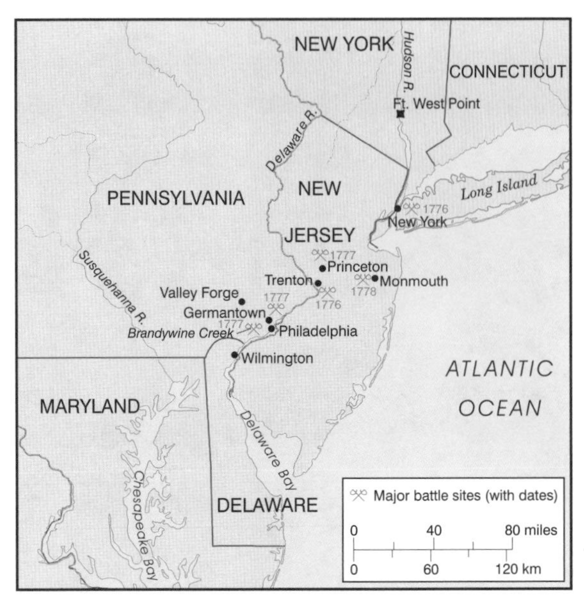

Battles of the Revolutionary War in the Middle Colonies

The Course of the American Revolution

Early Defeats and Victories. At first the war went badly for the Americans. Washington tried to defend New York City against a British attack in 1776, but he was defeated and forced to withdraw. New York City was a prize for the British, since it had a good harbor and was well situated for a base from which to attack the Americans.

After Washington's defeat, he and his troops fled through New Jersey, crossed the Delaware River, and entered Pennsylvania. But on Christmas night of 1776, Washington and his army took boats back across the Delaware River and attacked the Hessian soldiers at Trenton. After taking about one thousand prisoners, Washington next defeated the British general **Charles Cornwallis** at Princeton. These victories greatly encouraged the Americans.

British surrender at Saratoga, New York, on October 17, 1777. This American victory was a major turning point in the Revolution.

In 1777, the British general Howe sailed into the Chesapeake Bay, defeated Washington's army, and took over Philadelphia (the American capital at the time). The Continental Congress fled and began meeting in York, Pennsylvania. American forces attacked the British in the Battle of Germantown on October 4, 1777, but they were again defeated.

A Decisive Victory at Saratoga. The British wanted to cut off the New England Colonies from the Middle Colonies. To do this, they planned to have armies march from three directions and converge at Albany, New York. But only one of the armies came close to its goal, and that one was surrounded by American soldiers at Saratoga, just north of Albany. With no hope of escape, the British general Burgoyne and nearly six thousand soldiers surrendered to the American general Horatio Gates on October 17, 1777.

This victory at Saratoga was a turning point for several reasons. First, the defeat of a large British army made it appear that the

Winter scene at Valley Forge during the winter of 1777–78. Nearly one-fourth of Washington's 10,000 men died that winter due to hunger, exposure, and smallpox.

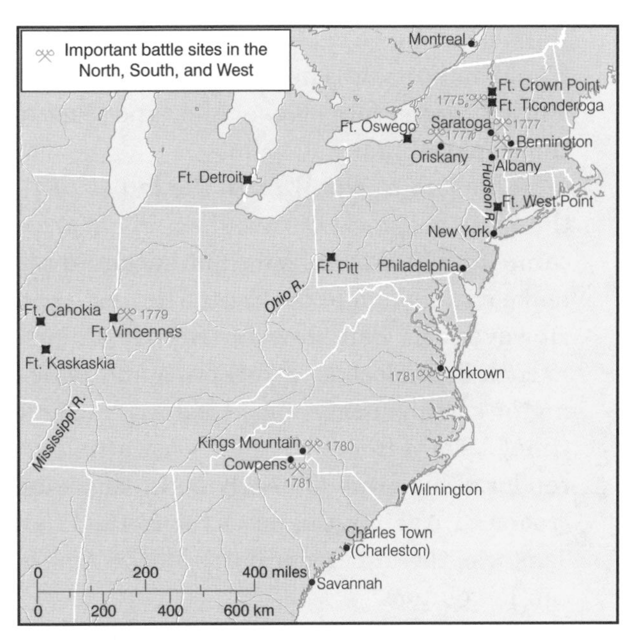

Other Battle Sites of the Revolutionary War

Americans could actually win the war. Second, the victory gave hope that the French might be persuaded to help the Americans fight the British.

In February 1778, the French signed an alliance treaty in which they agreed to support the Americans. This aided the patriots tremendously, for now France sent them money, soldiers, and supplies. It was such a great change of events that the British actually offered peace if the Americans would forsake their drive for independence. But the American Congress rejected the offer.

Later Developments. The American army retreated to Valley Forge in December 1777, and there they suffered through a miserable winter. Many soldiers did not have shoes or proper clothing, many became sick, and a large number deserted the army. But more soldiers joined the encampment the next spring. Among them was a Prussian named Baron von Steuben (STOO buhn), who was sympathetic to the American cause. He began a program of military drill to strengthen the army.

During the war, Indians raided frontier settlements as they had done in the French and Indian War. A man named **George Rogers Clark** decided to stop this. In 1778 he marched into present-day Indiana and

Cornwallis surrendered at Yorktown on October 19, 1781. The battle at Yorktown was the last major conflict in the war, but the Revolution did not officially end until the Treaty of Paris was signed in 1783.

Illinois, where he captured a number of forts from the British. These victories gave the United States control over the land west of the Appalachians.

The End of the War. In the fall of 1781, the British general Cornwallis and his army camped at Yorktown, Virginia, intending to make a campaign in the South the next year. However, the British were trapped when a French fleet blockaded Yorktown and Washington's army attacked by land at the same time. After a fierce battle, Cornwallis surrendered his army of nearly eight thousand troops to Washington on October 19, 1781. This was the last major battle of the American Revolution.

On September 3, 1783, the British signed the Treaty of Paris, in which they recognized the former thirteen colonies as "free, sovereign, and independent states." Their territory included all the land south of Canada (except Florida) and east of the Mississippi River. The Americans had finally achieved their goal of becoming an independent nation.

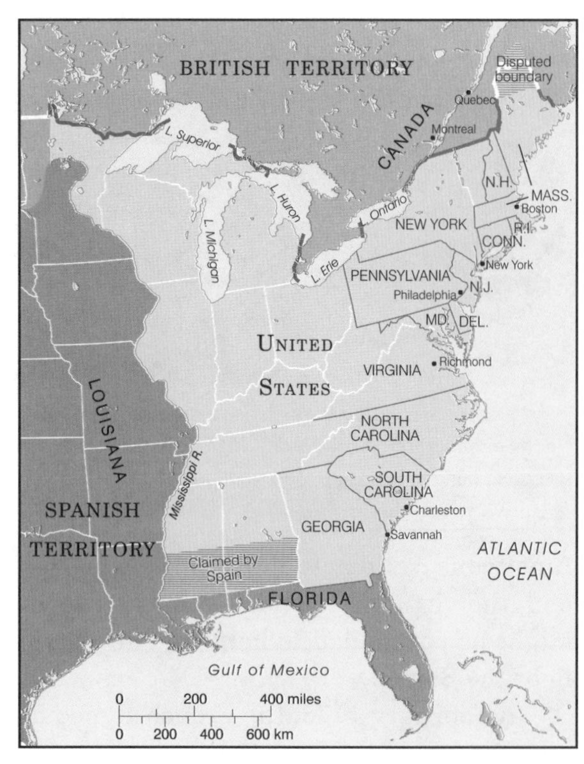

The United States in 1783

Focus for Thought

7. a. At the First Continental Congress, how did some delegates reason that Parliament had no authority over the colonies?
   b. What was wrong with their reasoning? (See Romans 13:1, 6, 7.)
8. Name the document that officially declared American independence, and give the date when it was adopted.
9. What things made the war discouraging for the Americans in 1776 and 1777?
10. In what two ways was the victory at Saratoga a turning point in the war?
11. What events led to Cornwallis's surrender?
12. a. What did the British acknowledge in the Treaty of Paris?
    b. What territory did the United States include at that time?

3. NONRESISTANT PEOPLE DURING THE REVOLUTION

The events surrounding the Revolution once more tested the faith of those who believed that Christians should not take up arms. This section discusses the issues that faced the nonresistant people during that time.

The First Continental Congress recognized the position of the nonresistant people. In July 1775, it stated, "As there are some people who from religious principles can not bear arms in any case, this Congress intends no violence to their consciences, but earnestly recommends . . . them . . . to contribute as liberally . . . [as] they can consistently with their religious principles." A few months later, the Mennonites and Dunkers wrote to the Pennsylvania Assembly as follows:

We find ourselves indebted to be thankful to our worthy Assembly for . . . allowing those, who, by the doctrine of our Saviour Jesus Christ, are persuaded in their consciences to love their enemies, and not to resist evil, to enjoy the liberty of their conscience. . . . It being our principle to feed the hungry and give the thirsty drink, we have dedicated ourselves to serve all men in every thing that can be helpful to the preservation of men's lives, but we find not freedom in giving, or doing, or assisting in anything by which men's lives are destroyed or hurt. We beg the patience of all those who believe we err in this point.

Nonresistant Groups

At the time of the American Revolution, the three main religious groups opposed to war were the Mennonites, the Amish, and the Quakers. Three others were the Dunkers (also known as German Baptists or Brethren), the Schwenkfelders, and the Moravians.

The Dunkers were much like their Mennonite neighbors, but their practice of baptism by immersion earned them their distinctive name. The Schwenkfelders were named for their leader, Caspar Schwenkfeld. They were the persecuted remnant of a Quaker-like group in Silesia (present-day southwestern Poland). The Moravians had come from Moravia, and they engaged in mission efforts to reach blacks, Indians, and Germans.

These nonresistant people in Pennsylvania cared little about the protests over taxes in far-off Massachusetts. They considered it wrong to revolt against the British government, for that was the legitimate authority established by God. They also were afraid that a patriot government might take away their freedoms. Finally, they feared war and wanted to avoid it as much as possible.

The nonresistant people were not Loyalists helping the British; neither were they patriots. They were mindful that the Bible says, "The powers that be are ordained of God. Whosoever therefore resisteth the power, resisteth the ordinance of God: and they that resist shall receive to themselves damnation" (Romans 13:1, 2). These people believed that they owed loyalty to Great Britain, the "power" ordained at that time. So they tried to obey that government. Patriots sometimes misunderstood this position and viewed them as Loyalists. After the war, some Mennonites also fled to Canada.

Issues of Nonresistance

Fines. After the Revolutionary War started, many of the colonists began to muster (assemble) for military drills. Resentment flared against those who refused to muster, for it did not seem fair that only a few people should risk their lives to gain independence for everyone. In November 1775, the Pennsylvania Assembly voted that every able-bodied man between the ages of fifteen and sixty-three had to muster, or he would pay a fine of two pounds ten shillings (British units of money). According to one Quaker, this meant paying out more money in one year than his total taxes in the previous twenty years!

Many Quakers refused to pay the fine, for they understood that it would be aiding the war effort against the British king. The Schwenkfelders paid it because they considered it their responsibility to pay any tax levied by the government. The Mennonites and Amish varied in their response, but most did not pay the fine.

War Taxes. In 1777, a war tax of three pounds ten shillings was enacted. This tax brought a new dilemma to the nonresistant groups. Though Christians should pay taxes to the government, does that include an illegitimate, rebellious government? A few Mennonites paid the tax, but others refused because they believed it was imposed by a wrongful government.

The Oath of Allegiance. In June 1777, the Pennsylvania Assembly passed a law requiring the Oath of Allegiance to be taken by all white males above eighteen years. The purpose of the oath was to compel each one to declare his loyalty to the patriot cause. It stated, "I [name] do swear, or affirm, that I renounce and refuse all allegiance to George the Third, King of Great Britain . . . and that I will be faithful and bear true allegiance to the Commonwealth of Pennsylvania as a free and independent state."

The law said that if a man refused to take the oath, he would not be allowed to vote, possess arms, or travel outside his local town or county. By 1778, the penalties forbade any legal action by a person refusing the oath; he could not even make a will or receive an inheritance or deed. The guilty person would also have to pay double tax and a fine of ten pounds. If he still refused to cooperate, he would be exiled from the state and his land given to the next of kin who would take the oath.

These laws were a great hardship for the nonresistant people. They had promised loyalty to the king of Great Britain when they became naturalized citizens not many years before. If they took the new oath, they would be breaking their former promise. Besides, they did not believe it right to support an effort to overthrow the British government. So the nonresistant people refused to take the Oath of Allegiance.

Most American officials were lenient with the nonresistant groups, for they understood that these people were not trying to aid the British cause. But in some localities, the officials carried out the penalties prescribed in the law.

Nonresistant Experiences

Persecution for Refusing the Oath. Besides the fines for not joining the militia, fines and jail sentences were imposed on some who refused to take the Oath of Allegiance. In one case, twelve men of Saucon, Pennsylvania, were jailed for not taking the oath. Then all their movable property was inventoried and sold at an auction. Other Mennonites bought some of the goods, but the owners lost almost everything they had except their houses and farms.

Plundering by Armies. When an army came into a community, the local people often suffered great hardship and loss. Those who lived near Philadelphia had to host part of Washington's army for nine months over the winter of 1777–78 when it camped near Valley Forge. Soldiers gathered up chickens, milk, meat, produce—whatever they could find to feed the army. They carried off thousands of fence rails for firewood and gathered up blankets, shoes, and cloth. By the time the army left, the countryside was stripped.

The British soldiers did similar plundering in the vicinity of Philadelphia. They destroyed Matthias Pannebecker's milling equipment and took his grain and flour. The army also took horses to use in the war, and sometimes young men went along with the team pulling a wagon of supplies for the army.

Ironies of Nonresistance

- Two wagons arrived at the Ephrata Cloister one day, sent by the Continental Army to obtain musket wadding. The Cloister surrendered several hundred unsold volumes of the huge *Martyrs Mirror*. On its title pages were the words "The Bloody Drama of the Defenseless Christians."
- Martin Meylin, a Mennonite, is credited with the earliest design of the Kentucky rifle (also known as the Pennsylvania rifle). This gun was called "the most fatal widow-and-orphan maker in the world." Of course, Meylin did not intend that it be used against humans, but he lived to see the day when it was.
- General Francis Nash (whose namesake is Nashville, Tennessee) was mortally wounded in the Battle of Germantown and was carried to the house of a Mennonite farmer, where he died. Because there was no other suitable burying place, this American general was buried with full military honors in the cemetery at the Towamencin Mennonite Meetinghouse.

Other Financial Hardships. Nonresistant people had little faith in the paper money of the colonies. They preferred to do business with the British, who offered hard cash and high prices. General Washington became infuriated with those who made their way into Philadelphia to sell their market produce to the British for cash while the American army suffered from hunger. To stop this, guards were placed along the roads leading into Philadelphia.

Abraham Hunsberger managed to slip into Philadelphia with his produce, but the British thought he was a spy and put him in prison. There he sang songs during the night and was soon released. Another, Mathias Tyson, was caught heading to Philadelphia with eggs. For his offense, American soldiers tied him to a tree, pelted him with the eggs, and threatened to kill him if he did the same thing again.

Assistance for Needy People. The nonresistant people willingly cared for sick and wounded soldiers who came to them. In Pennsylvania, religious communities as well as private homes served as hospitals at Ephrata, Bethlehem, and Lititz. When a Mennonite minister named John Bear and his wife helped care for wounded soldiers at the Ephrata Cloister, both contracted typhoid fever and died in 1778. The nonresistant people also gave food and other aid to soldiers who came to their doors, regardless of which side they were on.

But it was risky to help soldiers in those days. In one case, three Mennonite men in Lancaster were arrested for giving food and shelter to British prisoners who had escaped. In another, an elderly woman served a meal to an American posing as a British prison escapee. She was sentenced to a heavy fine or severe whipping, for her action showed that she was willing to help the British.

Ephrata Cloister at Ephrata, Pennsylvania. Here John Bear and his wife cared for soldiers wounded in the Battle of Germantown.

The Revolution had a refining effect on the members of the nonresistant churches. The war constrained them to be either totally committed to their church or to give up their church membership. As a result, these nonresistant people withdrew completely from politics and became the "quiet in the land." Rather than trying to make changes by political means, they contributed to society by godly and peaceable living.

Focus for Thought

13. Name six religious groups opposed to war at the time of the American Revolution.
14. Give two reasons why the nonresistant people did not sympathize with the patriots.
15. a. What three main issues faced the nonresistant people during the Revolution?
    b. How did they respond to these issues?
16. How did the nonresistant people practice the Bible principle of showing love to all men?
17. How did the Revolution serve to refine the nonresistant churches?

Historical Highlights

A. Matching: People

a. Charles Townshend
b. General Cornwallis
c. General Gage
d. George III
e. George Grenville
f. George Rogers Clark
g. George Washington
h. Paul Revere
i. Pontiac
j. Samuel Adams
k. Thomas Jefferson
l. Thomas Paine

1. British officer who surrendered at Yorktown.
2. Patriot general in command of the entire American army.
3. Leader of an Indian uprising in the Ohio region.
4. King of Great Britain.
5. Writer of the Declaration of Independence.
6. Patriot leader who helped organize Committees of Correspondence.
7. British treasurer who proposed laws taxing imports into the colonies.
8. Patriot leader who gained control of land west of the Appalachians for the United States.
9. Writer of *Common Sense.*
10. Patriot who warned the minutemen that the British were coming.
11. British prime minister who developed a program to raise revenue in the colonies.
12. British officer who sent troops from Boston to Concord.

B. Matching: Terms

a. boycott
b. Loyalists
c. mercantilism
d. minutemen
e. patriots
f. propaganda
g. repeal
h. revenue
i. Tories
j. Whigs
k. writs of assistance

1. Government income, usually obtained by taxation.
2. Refusing to buy certain goods as a way to gain what one demands.
3. Men ready to fight on a minute's notice.
4. Persons who favored remaining subject to Great Britain (two answers).
5. Persons who favored opposition to Great Britain (two answers).
6. Search warrants allowing officials to search any building for smuggled goods.
7. To withdraw something, especially a law.
8. Material publicized to spread certain ideas, usually with a strong, one-sided emphasis.
9. Idea that colonies should serve for the profit of the mother country.

C. Matching: Names

a. Boston Massacre
b. Boston Tea Party
c. *Common Sense*
d. Oath of Allegiance
e. Parliament
f. Pontiac's Conspiracy
g. Treaty of Paris
h. Committees of Correspondence
i. Declaration of Independence
j. First Continental Congress
k. Olive Branch Petition
l. Proclamation of Rebellion
m. Second Continental Congress
n. Stamp Act Congress

1. Meeting at which delegates voted to raise an army and declare independence.
2. Formal statement that the American colonies were an independent nation.
3. Legislative body in Great Britain.
4. Meeting in which delegates reasoned that Parliament had no authority over them.
5. Pamphlet promoting independence from Great Britain.
6. Incident when British soldiers killed five Bostonians.
7. Organizations that spread word of British acts that displeased the patriots.
8. Uprising by a group of Indian tribes in 1763.
9. Agreement that ended the Revolution in 1783.
10. Incident when cargo was destroyed to protest tax levied on it.
11. Meeting held in New York to protest the Stamp Act.
12. Plea to avert war sent by colonial leaders to King George III.
13. Declaration from King George III that the colonies were in rebellion.
14. Promise to support the new patriot government.

D. Matching: Acts

In this set, the letters may be used more than once.

a. act(s) mainly for producing revenue
b. act(s) mainly intended to assert British authority over the colonies
c. act(s) not directly intended for the colonies but affecting them

1. Sugar Act
2. Stamp Act
3. Declaratory Act
4. Townshend Acts
5. Proclamation of 1763
6. Coercive Acts (Intolerable Acts)
7. Quebec Act
8. Currency Act
9. Quartering Act
10. Tea Act

E. Matching: Places

a. Boston
b. Lexington and Concord
c. New York City
d. Philadelphia
e. Saratoga
f. Valley Forge
g. Yorktown

1. Turning point of the Revolutionary War.
2. Place of "shots heard around the world," which started the American Revolution in 1775.
3. Place where Washington's army camped during the winter of 1777–78.
4. Location of final British surrender.
5. Meeting place for First and Second Continental Congresses.
6. City over which the Battle of Bunker Hill was fought.
7. Excellent base for military operations, captured by the British in 1776.

F. Deeper Discussion

1. Explain the reasoning behind the slogan "Taxation without representation is tyranny."
2. Suggest a good reason why the tax on tea was retained while the rest of the Townshend Acts were repealed.
3. Did England have a right to raise revenue in the colonies for her own benefit? Explain.
4. How did Great Britain fail in her management of the rebellious colonies?
5. a. Could the colonies have won the war without French aid? Explain.
   b. Could they have won without the overruling providence of God? Explain.
6. Explain why the nonresistant people were misunderstood and resented by the patriots.
7. Read Romans 13:1–7. According to these verses, could Christians have participated in the colonial rebellion? Why or why not?

G. Chronology and Geography

1. Find the dates for the following events; then make a time line of events from 1763 to 1776 that led up to the Revolution. Follow the instructions in Chapter 2 for making a time line.

   Declaration of Independence made public
   Townshend Acts passed
   Sugar Act and Currency Act passed
   Coercive Acts passed
   Stamp Act repealed; Declaratory Act passed
   Fighting breaks out at Lexington and Concord
   Publishing of *Common Sense*
   Boston Massacre; Townshend Acts repealed
   Proclamation of 1763
   Tea Act passed; Boston Tea Party
   Proclamation of Rebellion
   Stamp Act passed

2. Consider General Cornwallis's encampment at Yorktown, Virginia. How did geography contribute to his being trapped there?

IN CONGRESS, JULY 4, 1776.

The unanimous Declaration of the thirteen united States of America,

When in the Course of human events, it becomes necessary for one people to dissolve the political bands which have connected them with another, and to assume among the powers of the earth, the separate and equal station to which the Laws of Nature and of Nature's God entitle them, a decent respect to the opinions of mankind requires that they should declare the causes which impel them to the separation. —— We hold these truths to be self-evident, that all men are created equal, that they are endowed by their Creator with certain unalienable Rights, that among these are Life, Liberty and the pursuit of Happiness. — That to secure these rights, Governments are instituted among Men, deriving their just powers from the consent of the governed, — That whenever any Form of Government becomes destructive of these ends, it is the Right of the People to alter or to abolish it, and to institute new Government, laying its foundation on such principles and organizing its powers in such form, as to them shall seem most likely to effect their Safety and Happiness. Prudence, indeed, will dictate that Governments long established should not be changed for light and transient causes; and accordingly all experience hath shewn, that mankind are more disposed to suffer, while evils are sufferable, than to right themselves by abolishing the forms to which they are accustomed. But when a long train of abuses and usurpations, pursuing invariably the same Object evinces a design to reduce them under absolute Despotism, it is their right, it is their duty, to throw off such Government, and to provide new Guards for their future security. — Such has been the patient sufferance of these Colonies; and such is now the necessity which constrains them to alter their former Systems of Government. The history of the present King of Great Britain is a history of repeated injuries and usurpations, all having in direct object the establishment of an absolute Tyranny over these States. To prove this, let Facts be submitted to a candid world. —— He has refused his Assent to Laws, the most wholesome and necessary for the public good. —— He has forbidden his Governors to pass Laws of immediate and pressing importance, unless suspended in their operation till his Assent should be obtained; and when so suspended, he has utterly neglected to attend to them. —— He has refused to pass other Laws for the accommodation of large districts of people, unless those people would relinquish the right of Representation in the Legislature, a right inestimable to them and formidable to tyrants only. —— He has called together legislative bodies at places unusual, uncomfortable, and distant from the depository of their Public Records, for the sole purpose of fatiguing them into compliance with his measures. —— He has dissolved Representative Houses repeatedly, for opposing with manly firmness his invasions on the rights of the people. —— He has refused for a long time, after such dissolutions, to cause others to be elected; whereby the Legislative powers, incapable of Annihilation, have returned to the People at large for their exercise; the State remaining in the mean time exposed to all the dangers of invasion from without, and convulsions within. —— He has endeavoured to prevent the population of these States; for that purpose obstructing the Laws for Naturalization of Foreigners; refusing to pass others to encourage their migrations hither, and raising the conditions of new Appropriations of Lands. —— He has obstructed the Administration of Justice, by refusing his Assent to Laws for establishing Judiciary powers. —— He has made Judges dependent on his Will alone, for the tenure of their offices, and the amount and payment of their salaries. —— He has erected a multitude of New Offices, and sent hither swarms of Officers to harrass our people, and eat out their substance. —— He has kept among us, in times of peace, Standing Armies without the Consent of our legislatures. —— He has affected to render the Military independent of and superior to the Civil power. —— He has combined with others to subject us to a jurisdiction foreign to our constitution, and unacknowledged by our laws; giving his Assent to their Acts of pretended Legislation: — For Quartering large bodies of armed troops among us: — For protecting them, by a mock Trial, from punishment for any Murders which they should commit on the Inhabitants of these States: — For cutting off our Trade with all parts of the world: — For imposing Taxes on us without our Consent: — For depriving us in many cases, of the benefits of Trial by Jury: — For transporting us beyond Seas to be tried for pretended offences: — For abolishing the free System of English Laws in a neighbouring Province, establishing therein an Arbitrary government, and enlarging its Boundaries so as to render it at once an example and fit instrument for introducing the same absolute rule into these Colonies: — For taking away our Charters, abolishing our most valuable Laws, and altering fundamentally the Forms of our Governments: — For suspending our own Legislatures, and declaring themselves invested with power to legislate for us in all cases whatsoever. — He has abdicated Government here, by declaring us out of his Protection and waging War against us. —— He has plundered our seas, ravaged our Coasts, burnt our towns, and destroyed the lives of our people. —— He is at this time transporting large Armies of foreign Mercenaries to compleat the works of death, desolation and tyranny, already begun with circumstances of Cruelty & perfidy scarcely paralleled in the most barbarous ages, and totally unworthy the Head of a civilized nation. —— He has constrained our fellow Citizens taken Captive on the high Seas to bear Arms against their Country, to become the executioners of their friends and Brethren, or to fall themselves by their Hands. —— He has excited domestic insurrections amongst us, and has endeavoured to bring on the inhabitants of our frontiers, the merciless Indian Savages, whose known rule of warfare, is an undistinguished destruction of all ages, sexes and conditions. In every stage of these Oppressions We have Petitioned for Redress in the most humble terms: Our repeated Petitions have been answered by repeated injury. A Prince, whose character is thus marked by every act which may define a Tyrant, is unfit to be the ruler of a free people. Nor have We been wanting in attentions to our Brittish brethren. We have warned them from time to time of attempts by their legislature to extend an unwarrantable jurisdiction over us. We have reminded them of the circumstances of our emigration and settlement here. We have appealed to their native justice and magnanimity, and we have conjured them by the ties of our common kindred to disavow these usurpations, which, would inevitably interrupt our connections and correspondence. They too have been deaf to the voice of justice and of consanguinity. We must, therefore, acquiesce in the necessity, which denounces our Separation, and hold them, as we hold the rest of mankind, Enemies in War, in Peace Friends.

We, therefore, the Representatives of the united States of America, in General Congress, Assembled, appealing to the Supreme Judge of the world for the rectitude of our intentions, do, in the Name, and by Authority of the good People of these Colonies, solemnly publish and declare, That these United Colonies are, and of Right ought to be Free and Independent States; that they are Absolved from all Allegiance to the British Crown, and that all political connection between them and the State of Great Britain, is and ought to be totally dissolved; and that as Free and Independent States, they have full Power to levy War, conclude Peace, contract Alliances, establish Commerce, and to do all other Acts and Things which Independent States may of right do. —— And for the support of this Declaration, with a firm reliance on the protection of divine Providence, we mutually pledge to each other our Lives, our Fortunes and our sacred Honor.

John Hancock

Button Gwinnett, Lyman Hall, Geo Walton.

Wm Hooper, Joseph Hewes, John Penn

Edward Rutledge, Thos Heyward Junr., Thomas Lynch Junr., Arthur Middleton

Samuel Chase, Wm Paca, Thos Stone, Charles Carroll of Carrollton

George Wythe, Richard Henry Lee, Th Jefferson, Benja Harrison, Thos Nelson jr., Francis Lightfoot Lee, Carter Braxton

Robt Morris, Benjamin Rush, Benja Franklin, John Morton, Geo Clymer, Jas Smith, Geo Taylor, James Wilson, Geo Ross

Caesar Rodney, Geo Read, Tho M:Kean

Wm Floyd, Phil Livingston, Frans Lewis, Lewis Morris

Richd Stockton, Jno Witherspoon, Fras Hopkinson, John Hart, Abra Clark

Josiah Bartlett, Wm Whipple, Saml Adams, John Adams, Robt Treat Paine, Elbridge Gerry, Step Hopkins, William Ellery, Roger Sherman, Samel Huntington, Wm Williams, Oliver Wolcott, Matthew Thornton

The Declaration of Independence was signed by 56 members of the Continental Congress. John Hancock's signature is large so that "George the Third might read it without his spectacles."

Signing of the Constitution of the United States.

10 American Government

1. THE ARTICLES OF CONFEDERATION
   - Framing and Ratification of the Articles
   - Achievements of the Confederation
   - Problems of the Confederation
2. THE CONSTITUTIONAL CONVENTION
   - Prelude to the Constitutional Convention
   - The Work of the Constitutional Convention
   - Ratification of the Constitution
3. THE CONSTITUTION
   - Principles of the Constitution
   - The Constitutional Government
   - The Bill of Rights

1775

Declaration of Independence adopted **1776**

1780

Articles of Confederation ratified **1781**

Treaty of Paris ends Revolutionary War **1783**

1785 Land Ordinance of 1785 instituted

Constitutional Convention held from May to September; Northwest Ordinance of 1787 instituted **1787**

Government under Constitution begins **1789**

1790

Bill of Rights added to Constitution **1791**

1795

"Honour all men. Love the brotherhood. Fear God. Honour the king."

1 Peter 2:17

American Government

Focus for Reading

When the thirteen American colonies gained independence from Britain, the new nation became one of the "powers that be [which] are ordained of God" (Romans 13:1). To establish a new system of government, the colonies began by each forming an individual state government. Then the states joined together in a "firm league of friendship" under the Articles of Confederation. But this arrangement soon proved to be weak, so they sought to improve the national government. The result was the Constitution of the United States. The government established under the Constitution has continued to operate for over two hundred years.

Why did the Articles of Confederation need to be improved? How was the new Constitution developed? What kind of government did it provide for? These questions are answered in three sections of this chapter.

1. The Articles of Confederation
2. The Constitutional Convention
3. The Constitution

1. THE ARTICLES OF CONFEDERATION

Even before the American Revolution was over, the thirteen colonies established their own governments as individual states. The Second Continental Congress also prepared a plan for a government over all the states. This plan was called the Articles of Confederation.

Framing and Ratification of the Articles

State Governments. During 1776 and 1777, each of the thirteen colonies drew up a written plan of government called a ***constitution***. The governments under these constitutions had three branches: a ***legislative branch***, an ***executive branch***, and a ***judicial branch***. The legislative branch made laws, the executive branch had a governor to enact and enforce the laws, and a court system decided how the laws applied to specific cases.

Because the people distrusted governors with too much power, they made the legislatures the strongest part of the state governments. Most of the state constitutions also included a bill of rights, which specifically protected important rights such as religious freedom and freedom of the press. This shows how important it was to Americans that their governments be limited by written documents.

The Articles of Confederation. Being independent from Great Britain meant that the only government over the states was the Second Continental Congress. But this Congress was only a temporary institution, so it set about to provide a permanent national government over all the states.

In June 1776, just before the Declaration of Independence was approved, the Second Continental Congress appointed a committee to write a constitution for the new nation. This committee presented a plan in July, but Congress discussed and modified it for over a year before adopting it. The final plan, called the Articles of Confederation, was adopted in November 1777.

The Articles were then submitted to the states for ***ratification***. A disagreement over land claims west of the Appalachians prevented unanimous ratification for several years. Finally all thirteen states ratified the Articles by March 1, 1781. Government under

Western Land Claims

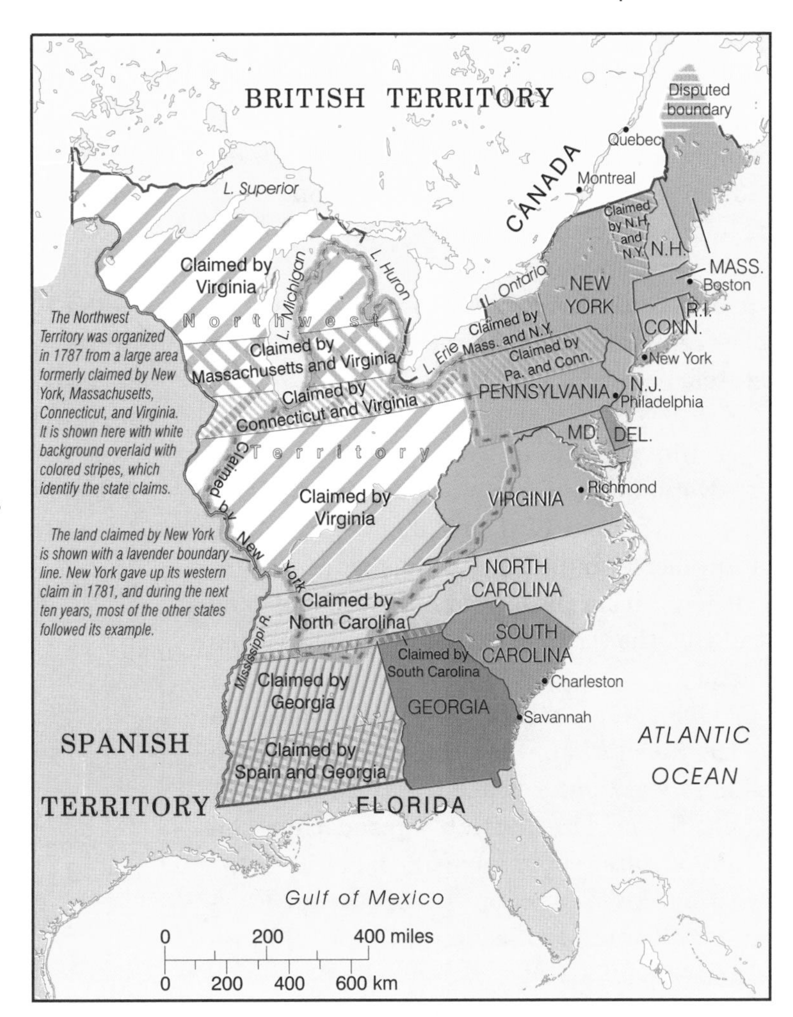

the Articles of Confederation began the same day, with the Revolution still in progress.

National Government Under the Articles. The Articles provided for a type of government called a ***confederation***. This was a union in which the states had more power than the national government, and the national government had only the powers granted to it by the states. The resulting national government was very weak, but that was what the framers of the Articles wanted. They were afraid that a strong national government would be a threat to freedom.

Under the Articles, the national government consisted of a single legislative body called Congress. This Congress was in charge of matters that affected the whole nation, but the states retained authority over local

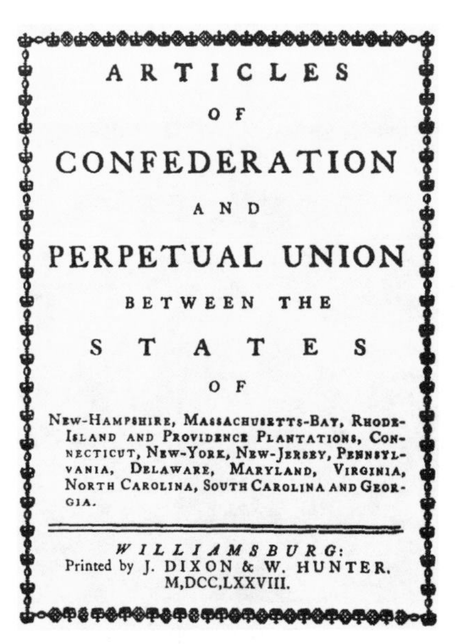
ARTICLES
OF
CONFEDERATION
AND
PERPETUAL UNION
BETWEEN THE
STATES
OF
NEW-HAMPSHIRE, MASSACHUSETTS-BAY, RHODE-ISLAND AND PROVIDENCE PLANTATIONS, CONNECTICUT, NEW-YORK, NEW-JERSEY, PENNSYLVANIA, DELAWARE, MARYLAND, VIRGINIA, NORTH CAROLINA, SOUTH CAROLINA AND GEORGIA.

WILLIAMSBURG:
Printed by J. DIXON & W. HUNTER.
M,DCC,LXXVIII.

Title of the Articles of Confederation. Though this plan provided for a "perpetual" union of the states, the union was too weak to produce a strong nation.

matters. Congress had the power to wage war and make peace, deal with foreign nations, carry the mail, borrow and coin money, and settle quarrels between states. Congress could ask the states for money, but it had no authority to enforce its requests. The states retained the authority to raise taxes and to enforce laws. To modify the Articles required unanimous approval by the states.

Achievements of the Confederation

National government under the Articles lasted only from 1781 to 1789. Nevertheless, a number of important things were accomplished during those years. Some historians call this the "critical period of United States history."

One accomplishment was the conclusion of the Revolution, when the Americans were able to work out a peace treaty that was in their favor. The British agreed that the United States could have all the land as far west as the Mississippi River (except Florida). This was specified in the Treaty of Paris signed in 1783.

A second accomplishment of the Confederation was a plan for managing the lands west of the Appalachian Mountains. Part of the plan was the Land Ordinance of 1785, which provided for the sale of lands bounded by the Ohio River, the Mississippi River, and the Great Lakes. This was called the Northwest Territory and later the Old Northwest. The land in this region was divided into townships of 6 miles (9.7 km) square, with every township divided into thirty-six sections each containing 1 square mile (2.6 km^2).

Signing of the preliminary Treaty of Paris, which became effective in 1783. Standing at the left are John Jay and Benjamin Franklin.

Division of Public Lands According to the Ordinance of 1785

Township (6 mi. square)

6	5	4	3	2	1
7	8	9	10	11	12
18	17	16	15	14	13
19	20	21	22	23	24
30	29	28	27	26	25
31	32	33	34	35	36

HALF SECTION (320 Acres)	
Quarter Section (160 acres)	Half Quarter (80 acres)

A third accomplishment was the Northwest Ordinance of 1787, which provided a plan of government and statehood for new territories. According to this plan, a territory was first ruled by a governor, secretary, and three judges, all chosen by Congress. When the population reached five thousand free men, the territory could choose a representative assembly. As soon as a territory reached a population of sixty thousand free citizens, it could become a state.

The Northwest Ordinance provided for self-government, freedom of religion, fair representation in the legislatures, and no slavery in each territory that became a state. Each new state was to be equal with the older states. This plan provided an orderly, three-stage pattern for adding new states to the nation.

Problems of the Confederation

Government under the Articles was unsatisfactory in many ways. The main problem was that the Articles made the national government so weak that it could not govern the nation effectively. It had this weakness because the framers were afraid that a strong national government would be a threat to freedom.

Problems of Unity. National unity was lacking because each state was more concerned about its own interests than about the welfare of the nation. The states taxed each other on interstate commerce, and they considered fighting each other when disputes arose. For example, Pennsylvania and Connecticut nearly went to war over Connecticut's claim in northern Pennsylvania.

The new nation was heading toward lawless confusion because the national government grew weaker while the state governments grew stronger. By placing too many restrictions on the national government, the Americans had made their nation unstable.

Problems With Foreign Nations. The United States was weak in relating to other nations. Europeans in particular looked upon the new nation with contempt. The British closed the West Indies to American trade. They refused to withdraw from some forts in the Northwest Territory, in violation of the terms of the Treaty of Paris. The British pointed out that the United States had also violated the treaty by failing to return property taken from Loyalists.

In addition, Spain disputed with the United States about the boundary of Florida and about trade on the Mississippi River. Pirates in the Mediterranean Sea preyed freely on United States trading ships. The government under the Articles could do little about these matters.

First currency and coins of the United States. The paper money quickly became almost worthless because it could not be redeemed in gold or silver. Named "continental currency," it gave rise to the phrase "not worth a continental."

Problems in Finances. Because Congress had no power to levy taxes, the Confederation was plagued with money woes from the beginning. Congress could raise money only by asking the states for contributions, printing paper money, selling land west of the Appalachian Mountains, and borrowing from foreign countries. But the United States already owed huge debts for the Revolution, and so did the states.

To finance the war, Congress had printed much paper money. This money quickly lost value because the people had little confidence in it and because it could not be redeemed in gold or silver. By 1781, a bushel of corn was priced at $40.00 and a barrel of flour at $1,575.00. Wage earners such as soldiers and day laborers were especially discontented, for their pay was almost worthless.

The United States suffered a severe financial depression after the war. One reason was that the West Indies were closed to United States trade. Another was that Britain sold many products to the United States while the Americans sold much less to the British. This meant that much of the gold and silver in America flowed to Britain to pay for merchandise and debts.

One way to solve trade problems was to regulate trade by law. But Congress could not do that, and the states would not grant Congress the power to tax imports. Only the individual states could regulate trade. Some states printed paper money, but it also became worthless.

A few states tried to raise money by heavy taxation. But some people, especially small farmers in New England, could not pay their debts or their taxes. When creditors took their farms from them, they were furious. In Massachusetts, **Daniel Shays** led a revolt known as Shays's Rebellion in 1787 to keep courts from foreclosing on the unfortunate farmers. When Congress proved too weak to curb the rebellion, the armed forces of Massachusetts had to take the responsibility.

In addition to these problems, men who had fought in the Revolution had not received their pay. Foreign nations that had loaned money to the United States were not being repaid. The reason was that Congress could only ask the states for funds; the national government had no power to deal with states that did not respond.

Many people began to see that the Articles must be changed to provide a stronger national government. This movement led to a meeting in Philadelphia to modify the Articles of Confederation in 1787.

Focus for Thought

1. Which had more power under the Articles of Confederation—the states or the national government?
2. What major accomplishment was achieved in 1783 by the government under the Articles of Confederation?
3. a. What plan provided for the dividing and selling of lands bounded by the Ohio River, the Mississippi River, and the Great Lakes?
   b. What plan provided an orderly pattern for adding more states to the original thirteen?
4. a. What was the main problem with the Articles of Confederation?
   b. What was the reason for this problem?
5. Due to the weakness of the Confederation, what problems did the United States experience in the following areas?
   a. in unity   b. with foreign nations   c. in finances

2. THE CONSTITUTIONAL CONVENTION

Because of the many problems in the national government, an important convention was held in 1787 to revise the Articles of Confederation. This convention resulted in the Constitution of the United States, a completely new plan of government for the nation.

Prelude to the Constitutional Convention

By 1786, many people were keenly aware of the problems in the national government. Congress finally addressed the problem by planning a meeting "for the sole and express purpose of revising the Articles of Confederation." This meeting, called the Constitutional Convention, was to be held in Philadelphia in 1787.

Fifty-five delegates attended the Convention, arriving from all the states except Rhode Island. George Washington agreed to serve as presiding officer, and he stabilized the Convention with his dignity and prestige. **James Madison**, later called "father of the Constitution," dedicated himself tirelessly to writing the document. Madison sat up front, where he could easily participate and take extensive notes. Aged **Benjamin Franklin** added his insights to the discussions.

May 25, 1787, was the first day of the Constitutional Convention. The delegates met in the Pennsylvania State House, called Independence Hall today. They decided to maintain complete secrecy in their proceedings, with the windows shut and dirt shoveled onto the streets so that noise would not disturb them. This was done so that public opinion would not influence the work before it was finished, and so that the delegates could freely express their opinions and change their minds.

The Work of the Constitutional Convention

A Completely New Plan. Early in the Convention, the delegates decided that it would not be enough just to modify the Articles of Confederation. Since the Confederation was so weak, they wanted a constitution for a national government that was stronger than the states.

No one person masterminded the United States Constitution. It was rather developed as the delegates offered ideas, discussed

James Madison as he appeared during his last year at the Continental Congress. As a delegate to the Constitutional Convention, he exercised such influence that he became known as the "father of the Constitution."

Pennsylvania State House, Philadelphia, in 1776 (later called Independence Hall). The Second Continental Congress declared independence here in 1776, and the Constitutional Convention was held here in 1787.

them, and compromised until they reached agreements that satisfied most of them.

The ***Founding Fathers*** realized that the new government would need a number of broad powers. Among these were the power to raise taxes, to issue money, to organize a court system, and to regulate trade between the states and with foreign countries. Also, the government would need authority to take the actions necessary for exercising its powers. The states would surrender much power to the national government, which would be supreme over the state governments.

The delegates recognized the danger of letting the national government grow too strong. Therefore, the Constitution placed limits on it by clearly stating what powers it had and did not have. On the other hand, the delegates also understood the selfish nature of man, and they saw that the government had to be strong enough to keep order in society. So they tried to devise a government with enough power to do its work, yet limited enough to preserve the freedom of the people.

The Issue of Representation. Heated debates racked the Constitutional Convention. One of the most serious differences was on how the states should be represented in Congress. One proposal, the Virginia Plan, was presented by Edmund Randolph of Virginia. It called for a strong national government with three branches like those of state governments. The legislature would be Congress, the executive branch would be headed by a president, and the judicial branch would be a system of courts. The states would be represented in Congress according to their population. This plan favored the large states, since the ones with more people would have the more representatives in Congress.

States with small populations objected to the Virginia Plan. They felt that their states would have little voice in the new government because of their lower populations. Other delegates thought the Virginia Plan made the national government too strong.

William Paterson of New Jersey had a slightly different proposal. His New Jersey Plan also provided for a three-branch government and a legislature that was ***unicameral*** (yoo nih KAM ur uhl)—with only one house; but each state would be represented equally. But delegates from larger states objected to the New Jersey Plan. They thought their states would not be represented fairly, since they would have only as much power in Congress as the smaller states. With each side determined not to give in, the issue of representation threatened to end the Convention in failure.

Finally in July, **Roger Sherman** of Connecticut proposed the Great Compromise, also known as the Connecticut Compromise. He suggested that Congress be ***bicameral*** (by KAM ur uhl)—having two houses. One house would be the Senate, in which every state would be represented equally by two senators. The other house would be the House of Representatives, in which the states would be represented according to their populations. The larger states would have more representatives. The Great Compromise became the solution to the issue of representation.

Other Issues and Compromises. On the slavery issue, the Convention reached a strange compromise. Delegates from southern states, which had many slaves, thought slaves should be included in the population counted for representation in Congress. Delegates from northern states, which had few slaves, thought this would give the southern states an unfair advantage. The issue was settled by the Three-Fifths Compromise, which said that for purposes of Congressional representation, only three-fifths of the slaves would be counted. Black slaves were generally considered as mere property; but when it was an advantage to count them as persons, white people readily did so.

During the debates, Benjamin Franklin proposed that each session be opened with prayer because "the small progress we have made after four or five weeks . . . [and] our different [ideas] on almost every question . . . is . . . a melancholy proof of the imperfection of the human understanding. We indeed seem to feel our own [lack] of political wisdom, since we have been running around in search of it. . . . How has it happened . . . that we have not hitherto once thought of humbly applying to the Father of lights to illuminate our understanding . . . ? I have lived . . . a long time; and the longer I live, the more convincing proofs I see . . . that God governs in the affairs of men. And if a sparrow cannot fall to the ground without His notice, is it probable that an empire can rise without His aid?" The proposal was debated for a time, but then it was dropped without a vote.

The Commerce and Slave Trade Compromise settled the issue of Congressional control over commerce and the slave trade. This compromise stated that Congress could control foreign trade, but it could not tax exports and would not end the slave trade before 1808. Slavery was contrary to the spirit of the Declaration of Independence; but if it had been forbidden at this point, the Convention would have been hopelessly divided. As it was, the slavery issue remained unsolved until seventy-four years later, when it was settled by a terrible civil war.

Another issue was the election of presidents. Some thought Congress should choose the president, but others pointed out that this would give Congress control of the presidency. Should the common people choose the president? The delegates thought they might not be qualified to elect the president directly. They reached a compromise saying that each state would choose as many electors as it had representatives in Congress. These electors, called the Electoral College, would then elect the president.

When the Convention ended on September 17, 1787, thirty-nine delegates signed the new Constitution. Other delegates refused to sign because they did not agree with it. The document was then sent to the existing Congress, and Congress submitted the Constitution to the states for ratification.

James Madison recorded the following incident at the close of the Constitutional Convention.

Whilst the last members were signing it, Doctor Franklin, looking toward the President's Chair, at the back of which a . . . sun happened to be painted, observed to a few members near him, that painters have often found it difficult to distinguish in their art a rising from a setting sun. "I have," said he, "often and often in the course of the session, and the [changes] of my hopes and fears as to its issue, looked at that behind the President without being able to tell whether it was rising or setting. But now at length I have the happiness to know that it is a rising and not a setting sun."

Ratification of the Constitution

Nine of the thirteen states needed to ratify the Constitution before it would go into effect. As the Constitution was published and people read it, they responded in various ways. Some, called Federalists, approved of the Constitution because it seemed to be the answer to the problems of the Confederation government. Others, called Anti-Federalists, believed that the Constitution gave the national government too much power. And since the Constitution included no bill of rights, they feared that nothing would keep the national government from taking away their freedoms.

On December 7, 1787, Delaware became the first state to ratify the Constitution. Pennsylvania was next, and by June 1788 nine states had done the same. However, the Constitution was still not accepted by two important states: Virginia and New York. Virginia finally ratified on June 25, 1788, with a proposal for a bill of rights to be included in the Constitution.

In New York the struggle was intense. To persuade New Yorkers to accept the document, James Madison, **Alexander Hamilton**, and **John Jay** published a series of eighty-five articles called the *Federalist Papers*, which explained the plan of the Constitution. New York finally ratified the Constitution in July 1788. North Carolina did not ratify until 1789, and Rhode Island not until 1790. The Constitutional government began in 1789.

The Constitution of the United States outlines a form of government that has proved stable for over two centuries. Many nations founded after the United States have used it as a model for their own constitutions. For Christians, the Constitution has served as one answer to their prayer that they may live "a quiet and peaceable life in all godliness and honesty" (1 Timothy 2:2).

Focus for Thought

6. Why was the Constitutional Convention held in secret?
7. The delegates wanted a new government that would not be plagued by the weaknesses of the Confederation. What kind of government would that be?
8. a. How would states be represented in Congress under the Virginia Plan? under the New Jersey Plan?
   b. What was the main objection to each plan?
9. How did the Great Compromise settle the issue of representation?
10. Explain how two other issues were settled with compromises.
11. a. What was the position of the Federalists regarding the Constitution?
    b. What was the position of the Anti-Federalists?

3. THE CONSTITUTION

The Bible does not give a pattern for civil government, because it was written to direct the people of God rather than the state. But God did say, "Them that honour me I will honour" (1 Samuel 2:30). Since the framers of the Constitution honored Bible teachings such as fairness and respect, God allowed their efforts to succeed even though they were worldly-minded men.

The Constitution contains principles that have helped to produce a stable, free society in the United States. It also outlines how the national government is to operate. After the Constitution went into effect, a Bill of Rights was added to guarantee certain freedoms to the people.

Principles of the Constitution

The Preamble (introduction) of the Constitution states some of the important principles embodied in the Constitution. It reads as follows:

> "We the People of the United States, in Order to form a more perfect Union, establish Justice, insure domestic Tranquility, provide for the common defense, promote the general Welfare, and secure the Blessings of Liberty to ourselves and our Posterity, do ordain and establish this Constitution for the United States of America."

"We the People of the United States." The Founding Fathers believed in government by the consent of the people. They saw themselves as representatives of the people, and they intended to submit the Constitution to the voting public to be ratified.

"In Order to form a more perfect Union." The Constitution was written to produce a better and stronger union of states than that under the Articles of Confederation.

"Establish Justice." The new government would have authority to administer justice in the nation, between individuals as well as between the government and the people.

"Insure domestic Tranquility." Domestic tranquility is civil peace, which is enforced by policemen and other officers of the law. Citizens do not need to rise in armed rebellion to avenge their wrongs.

"Provide for the common defense." The "common defense" of a nation is provided by its military forces. God has ordained that the civil government defend its people; but as citizens of the heavenly kingdom, Christians have no part in that defense.

"Promote the general Welfare." The government is responsible not only to protect individual citizens but also to promote the general well-being of the public. Its laws and actions should benefit all the people (general) rather than only special groups. The government does this by maintaining conditions that allow the people security and freedom, and by providing things such as highways, inspectors, postal service, law enforcement, and the coining of money.

"Secure the Blessings of Liberty to ourselves and our Posterity." The Founding Fathers were concerned that the liberties they enjoyed would continue for many generations. They wrote the Constitution to help accomplish that.

The Constitutional Government

A Federal System. The United States has a ***federal*** system of government. This means that powers are divided between the national government and the state governments. The national government has authority over national matters, and state governments have authority over local matters. The term *federal* is also used in referring to the national government. For example, a federal law is a law established by the federal (national) government.

Since the Constitution is the "supreme law of the land," if a state law conflicts with a federal law, the federal law prevails. Also, the federal government must operate according to the Constitution.

A Republican Government. As a ***republic***, the United States has no king or queen but is controlled by the people. A republic is a representative democracy rather than a pure democracy. In a pure democracy, all the people participate directly in government, as in the New England town meetings. In a representative democracy, the people elect officers to represent them, and these men actually manage the affairs of government.

Although the Constitution provides for a government with various officers, it does not grant sovereignty (final authority) to any government. Sovereignty belongs to the people.

Separation of Powers. The Founding Fathers understood that selfish human

Distribution of Powers in the Federal System

The Constitution divides powers between the federal government and the state governments. Delegated powers are held only by the federal government, concurrent powers are held by both federal and state governments, and reserved powers are reserved for the states alone.

Delegated Powers	*Concurrent Powers*	*Reserved Powers*
Establish standard weights and measures. Maintain armed forces and declare war. Operate a postal system. Regulate copyrights and patents. Regulate interstate and international trade.	Borrow money. Charter banks. Collect taxes. Establish courts. Establish criminal laws.	Make marriage laws and traffic laws. Establish schools. Regulate trade within the state. Establish local government. Regulate voting laws and procedures.

nature would be a great threat to successful government. To keep any one person or group from becoming too powerful, they divided the federal government into legislative, executive, and judicial branches. This division is based on a principle called the ***separation of powers***.

The legislative branch is the part of government that proposes new laws. It is composed of the Senate and the House of Representatives, together known as Congress. The House represents the voice of the people in the government. Members of the House are elected every two years, and the number of representatives for each state is determined by the population of the state. The House now has 435 representatives, a limit established in 1913.

The Senate represents the voice of the states in the national government. Members of the Senate are elected every six years. Each state has two senators, which makes a total

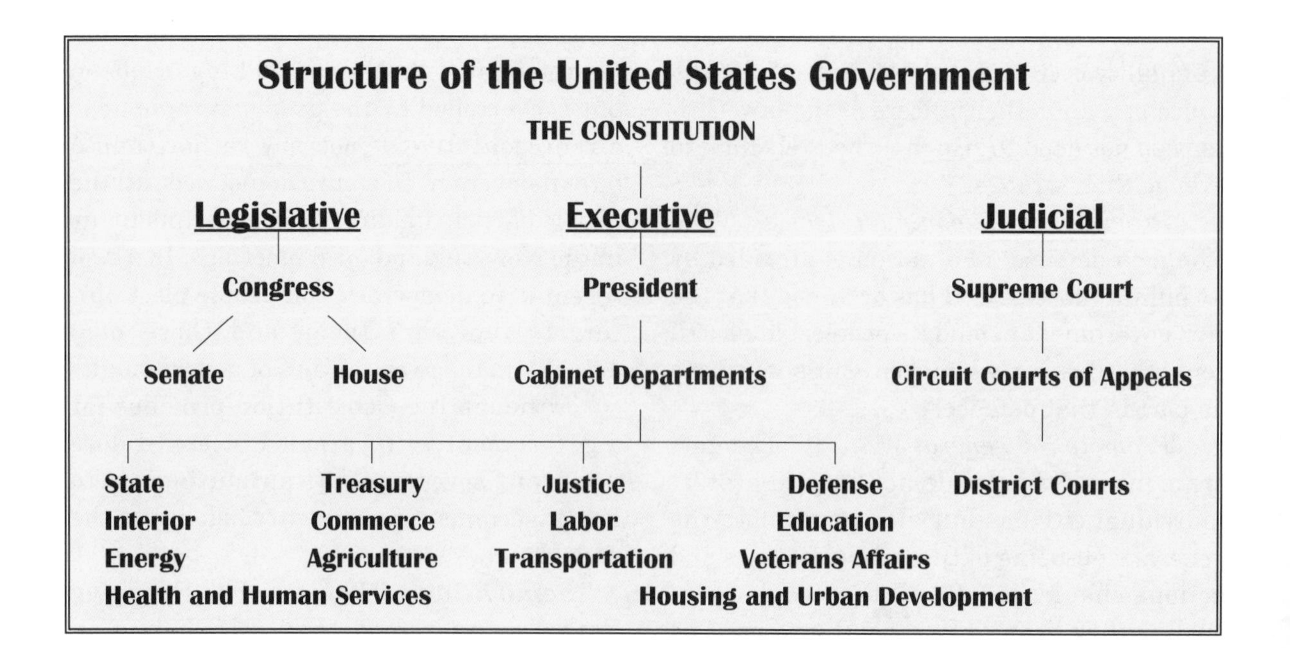

Left: The United States Capitol in the 1840s. This is the earliest-known photograph (daguerreotype) of the Capitol. ***Right:*** The Capitol as it looks today. The Senate meets in the north (left) wing, and the House of Representatives meets in the south (right) wing. In this photo, the Supreme Court building is partially hidden by the north wing of the Capitol, and the original Library of Congress building stands somewhat behind the south wing of the Capitol.

of one hundred senators in Congress.

The executive branch administrates the government and enacts the laws proposed by the legislature. That is, the president signs a proposed law to put it into effect; or if not, he ***vetoes*** (rejects) the law. This branch also enforces the established laws through the Federal Bureau of Investigation (FBI) and other agencies. The executive branch is headed by the president and the vice president, who are elected to four-year terms.

The executive branch includes a number of departments, such as the Department of Defense (which supervises the armed forces) and the Department of the Treasury (which issues money). Each department is headed by a secretary, and all the secretaries together are known as the president's ***Cabinet***. They serve as advisers to the president.

The judicial branch decides how federal laws apply in specific cases, and whether federal and state laws are constitutional. The judicial system consists of district courts, courts of appeals, and the Supreme Court—which is the final court of appeal with regard to any law. The Supreme Court is a panel of nine judges called justices, of which the leading one is called the chief justice.

Checks and Balances. The Constitution provides for a number of ***checks and balances*** in the federal government. This means that each branch has certain ways of limiting the powers of the other branches. One example is the president's power to veto laws passed by Congress. Another is his power to appoint federal judges—but they must be approved by the Senate.

As another check, a two-thirds majority of Congress can override a presidential veto. Congress may also ***impeach*** the president (bring him to trial for misconduct) and remove him from office if he is found guilty. And the Supreme Court may declare that a law passed by Congress is unconstitutional and therefore not valid. This is called the power of ***judicial review***.

Flexibility. The Constitution is flexible enough so that the federal government can deal with situations that did not even exist when it was written. It contains an ***elastic clause***, which states that Congress may "make all laws which shall be necessary and proper." This clause has been understood to mean that Congress may assume powers that the Constitution does not specifically mention.

The Founding Fathers also made provisions for the Constitution to be amended (changed). Congress or any state may suggest an amendment, but it becomes part of the Constitution only if it is approved by the legislatures of three-fourths of the states. Only 27 amendments were added to the Constitution in its first 220 years.

The Bill of Rights

Government under the Constitution began in 1789 with the first session of the new Congress. Twelve amendments to the Constitution were proposed in this session, of which ten were ratified by 1791. These amendments are also known as the Bill of Rights because they guarantee certain rights to the citizens of the United States. Five of the amendments are quoted and discussed here.

The First Amendment guarantees freedom of religion, speech, and the press. This means that religious groups may practice their faith without interference from the government. Ministers may preach sermons without fear of being arrested, and Christians may publish Gospel literature without fearing government restrictions.

Amendment 1

Congress shall make no law respecting an establishment of religion, or prohibiting the free exercise thereof; or abridging the freedom of speech, or of the press; or the right of the people peaceably to assemble, and to petition the Government for a redress of grievances.

Amendment 4

The right of the people to be secure in their persons, houses, papers, and effects, against unreasonable searches and seizures, shall not be violated, and no Warrants shall issue, but upon probable cause, supported by Oath or affirmation, and particularly describing the place to be searched, and the persons or things to be seized.

Amendment 5

No person shall be held to answer for a capital, or otherwise infamous crime, unless on a presentment or indictment of a Grand Jury, except in cases arising in the land or naval forces, or in the Militia, when in actual service in time of War or public danger; nor shall any person be subject for the same offense to be twice put in jeopardy of life or limb; nor shall be compelled in any criminal case to be a witness against himself, nor be deprived of life, liberty, or property, without due process of law; nor shall private property be taken for public use, without just compensation.

Amendment 6

In all criminal prosecutions, the accused shall enjoy the right to a speedy and public trial, by an impartial jury of the State and district wherein the crime shall have been committed, which district shall have been previously ascertained by law, and to be informed of the nature and cause of the accusation; to be confronted with the witnesses against him; to have compulsory process for obtaining Witnesses in his favor, and to have the assistance of counsel for his defense.

Amendment 8

Excessive bail shall not be required, nor excessive fines imposed, nor cruel and unusual punishments inflicted.

The Fourth Amendment guarantees the security of private property. An officer of the law must have a search warrant for a specific place in order to search it. Further, he can obtain a search warrant only if he has a good reason to suspect a person of a crime.

The other three amendments protect the rights of persons accused of a crime. No one may be punished without a fair and prompt trial. No one found innocent by a jury may be tried again for the same offense (which is called "double jeopardy"). No one may be forced to testify against himself.

In addition, the government may not take private property without paying its fair value. And the government may not inflict "cruel and unusual punishments." This restriction outlaws torture and other unjust measures like those used against the Anabaptists.

The Bill of Rights is founded on the principle of respect for all people and their property, and as such it is an application of the Bible command to "love thy neighbour as thyself." We should not think that we deserve the freedoms it guarantees, but we should praise the Lord that our "lines are fallen . . . in pleasant places" (Psalm 16:6). We should live upright lives as responsible people before God so that these freedoms may truly be a blessing to us.

Focus for Thought

12. Explain what is meant by a federal system of government.
13. a. What are two characteristics of a republic?
    b. How is a republic different from a pure democracy?
14. What is the reason for separation of powers?
15. Name the branch of federal government described by each sentence.
    a. It makes laws.
    b. It is headed by a president and a vice president.
    c. It consists of district courts, circuit courts of appeals, and the Supreme Court.
    d. It enacts and enforces laws.
    e. It decides how laws apply to specific cases.
    f. It consists of the House of Representatives and the Senate.
16. Describe two ways that government branches can check each other's powers.
17. a. What is the purpose of the Bill of Rights?
    b. When was it added to the Constitution?
18. Answer with the number of an amendment shown in the text. Which amendment
    a. would prohibit punishment by crucifixion?
    b. prevents a person from being retried for an offense after he has once been tried and found innocent?
    c. grants Christian publishers the right to freely publish and distribute literature?
    d. prohibits an officer of the law from entering someone's house without having specific authority?
    e. grants the right to a trial by jury?
    f. prohibits the government from taking a person's property without paying for it?
    g. grants freedom of conscience?
    h. permits an accused person to gather witnesses in his defense?
    i. requires that a trial be held in the same local area where the offense was committed?
    j. freely permits orderly religious gatherings?

Historical Highlights

A. Matching: Names

One answer in this set will be used twice.

a. Alexander Hamilton
b. Benjamin Franklin
c. Constitutional Convention
d. George Washington
e. James Madison
f. John Jay
g. Old Northwest
h. Roger Sherman
i. Shays's Rebellion

1. Proposed the Great Compromise during the Constitutional Convention.
2. Suggested prayer during the Constitutional Convention.
3. Authors of the *Federalist Papers* (three answers).
4. Chairman who stabilized the Constitutional Convention.
5. "Father of the Constitution."
6. Uprising against high taxes and foreclosure on farms in Massachusetts.
7. Meeting that produced the Constitution.
8. Region bounded by the Ohio River, the Mississippi River, and the Great Lakes.

B. Matching: Terms 1

a. Cabinet
b. checks and balances
c. chief justice
d. confederation
e. Congress
f. constitution
g. Electoral College
h. executive branch
i. federal
j. Founding Fathers
k. House of Representatives
l. judicial branch
m. legislative branch
n. president
o. republic
p. Senate
q. separation of powers
r. Supreme Court

1. Dividing of government into three branches.
2. Division of government that proposes new laws.
3. Head judge of the Supreme Court.
4. Weak union in which states have more power than the national government.
5. Kind of government system with powers divided between the states and the national government.
6. Head of the executive branch.
7. Written plan of government.
8. Group appointed as advisers to the president.
9. Division of government that enacts and enforces laws.
10. Methods by which branches of government limit each other's powers.
11. Government managed by elected representatives.
12. Division of government that decides whether laws have been broken or whether laws are constitutional.
13. Federal lawmaking body that includes the Senate and the House of Representatives.

14. Highest judicial body in the nation.
15. Group of men who elect the president.
16. Part of Congress with states represented proportionately.
17. Part of Congress with states represented equally.
18. Men who framed the Constitution of the United States.

C. Matching: Terms 2

a. Anti-Federalists
b. bicameral
c. elastic clause
d. Federalists
e. impeach
f. judicial review
g. Preamble
h. ratification
i. unicameral
j. veto
k. Articles of Confederation
l. Bill of Rights
m. Commerce and Slave Trade Compromise
n. *Federalist Papers*
o. Great Compromise
p. New Jersey Plan
q. Northwest Ordinance of 1787
r. Three-fifths Compromise
s. Virginia Plan

1. Proposal that settled the issue of representation.
2. People who supported the new Constitution.
3. Having a legislature with two houses.
4. Introduction to the Constitution.
5. Proposal that settled the issue of counting slaves for representation.
6. Unsatisfactory plan for governing the United States.
7. To reject a proposed law.
8. To bring to trial for misconduct in office.
9. Proposal calling for states to have proportionate representation in Congress.
10. Proposal calling for states to have equal representation in Congress.
11. Proposal about control of trade and slavery.
12. People who opposed the new Constitution.
13. Law that provided a plan of government and statehood for new territories.
14. Having a legislature with only one house.
15. Series of articles defending the Constitution.
16. The act of giving formal agreement to.
17. Action in which a court examines a law to determine whether it is constitutional.
18. Statement in the Constitution saying that Congress may assume powers not specifically mentioned in the Constitution.
19. First ten amendments to the Constitution, which guarantee certain freedoms.

D. Principles From the Preamble to the Constitution

Match the letters of the phrases from the Preamble to the sentences on the next page.

a. "We the People of the United States"
b. "In Order to form a more perfect Union"
c. "Establish Justice"
d. "Insure domestic Tranquility"

e. "Provide for the common defense"
f. "Promote the general Welfare"
g. "Secure the Blessings of Liberty to ourselves and our Posterity"

1. The court will decide who is at fault.
2. Paper money is a convenient way to pay for purchases.
3. The citizens, not a king, are the final authority.
4. The army, navy, and air force are responsible to protect the nation.
5. People are arrested for starting a riot.
6. The freedoms enjoyed in the United States have continued for many years.
7. The Articles of Confederation did not provide for a strong national government.

E. The Bill of Rights

To which amendment shown in this chapter could a citizen of the United States appeal if he were to face the following situations? Answer with the number of that amendment.

1. A search warrant that does not describe the objects to be found in the search.
2. A $10,000 fine for the first offense of driving without a license.
3. Conviction of a crime without a public trial by jury.
4. Denial of military exemption because of religious beliefs.
5. Using force and threats against a person accused of robbery, to make him tell where he hid the stolen goods.

F. Deeper Discussion

1. The framing of the Constitution involved much compromise (two disagreeing parties each yielding so that agreement can be reached). When is compromise right, and when is it wrong?
2. Why did God allow the work of the Founding Fathers to succeed even though they were worldly-minded men?
3. Read Ecclesiastes 8:11. What else in addition to law is necessary for man to live in an orderly society?

G. Chronology and Geography

1. Explain why each date is important.
   a. 1781
   b. 1787
   c. 1789
   d. 1791
2. Consider the large size of the United States.
   a. How would the size contribute to the difficulty of governing the nation under a weak national government?
   b. Why would the size make a pure democracy impractical?
3. Trace the outline of Map A again, and label it "The States of the United States."
   a. Trace the borders of the original thirteen states. (Draw their present borders, even though some states originally included more area.)
   b. Label the original thirteen states. (Write the names of small states outside the United States border and draw arrows to their locations.)
   c. Color the original thirteen states (present areas only) all the same color. In Chapters 12, 16, 19, and 26, you will use other colors for states admitted in later periods.
   d. Memorize the names and locations of these states.

So Far This Year

Write whether each statement is true (T) *or false* (F).

1. The French and Indian War began in 1754 and ended in 1763.
2. Mennonites first arrived in America in 1607.
3. The Constitution was adopted on July 4, 1776.
4. The Second Continental Congress declared independence from Great Britain.
5. Americans who supported Great Britain in the Revolution were called Loyalists.
6. Conflicting claims over the Hudson Bay led to the French and Indian War.
7. The battle at Fort Duquesne was the decisive battle of the French and Indian War.
8. Thomas Jefferson wrote a stirring pamphlet called *Common Sense* that promoted American independence.
9. The French and Indian War is important in the history of North America because the French were removed as a North American power.
10. The Americans and British disagreed about Parliament's authority over the colonies.
11. The Battle of Lexington was the turning point in the Revolution.
12. The Battle of Saratoga was the last major battle of the Revolution.
13. General Cornwallis was the British general whose defeat ended the Revolution.
14. The nonresistant groups were Tories.
15. At the end of the American Revolution, the British gained all the land from the Atlantic to the Mississippi and from Canada to Florida.
16. Nonresistant people prepared for the French and Indian War by having the *Martyrs Mirror* published in German.
17. An issue that nonresistant people faced in the French and Indian War was the Oath of Allegiance.
18. The Treaty of Paris ended the Revolutionary War in 1763.
19. John Cabot explored the northeastern coast of North America for England in 1497.
20. Jacques Cartier explored the St. Lawrence River area for France in 1524.

UNIT 4

TIMES OF GROWTH, 1790–1850

Chapters in Unit 4

11. National Beginnings
12. National Progress
13. National Development
14. National Expansion

George Washington at Christ Church on Easter Sunday, 1795.

11 National Beginnings

1780

George Washington becomes president; French Revolution begins 1789

1790

Bill of Rights added to Constitution; Vermont becomes a state; first Bank of the United States 1791

Washington re-elected; Kentucky becomes a state 1792

Neutrality Proclamation 1793

Jay Treaty with Britain 1794

Whiskey Rebellion 1794

Pinckney Treaty with Spain 1795

Tennessee becomes a state; John Adams elected president 1796

XYZ Affair 1797–1798

Alien and Sedition Acts 1798

1800

Capital moved to Washington, D.C.; Thomas Jefferson elected president 1800

Louisiana Purchase; Ohio becomes a state **1803**

Jefferson re-elected; *Addresses to Youth* published by Christian Burkholder 1804

Lewis and Clark expedition 1804–1806

Embargo Act; *Leopard-Chesapeake* incident 1807

James Madison elected president 1808

1810

War of 1812 begins; Madison re-elected **1812**

Oliver Hazard Perry wins Battle of Lake Erie 1813

Washington, D.C. burned; Treaty of Ghent signed **1814**

Battle of New Orleans 1815

1820

"How say ye, We are mighty and strong men for the war?"

Jeremiah 48:14

National Beginnings

Focus for Reading

Government under the Constitution began in 1789 with George Washington as president. One of the challenges of the early years was to establish the government on a sound footing. Another challenge was to manage the rapidly growing nation. A more troublesome task was to deal with foreign nations, particularly Britain and France. Difficulties intensified until war broke out in 1812 between the United States and Great Britain. In this chapter, three sections discuss these issues.

1. The Federalists
2. The Jeffersonians
3. The War of 1812

1. THE FEDERALISTS

When George Washington became president in 1789, he took on the great task of carrying out a new and untried plan of government. Numerous problems loomed within and without the United States, and they all had to be faced in the first years of the Constitutional government. It would be a major accomplishment to establish the new nation on a solid foundation.

"Righteousness exalteth a nation: but sin is a reproach to any people" (Proverbs 14:34).

Organizing the Government

The Executive Branch. In 1789, the Electoral College unanimously chose George Washington as president, and **John Adams** became the vice president. The new Congress then created three departments in the executive branch. They were the Department of State, in charge of dealing with foreign nations; the Department of War, in charge of defending the nation; and the Department of the Treasury, in charge of revenue and spending. Congress also established the offices of attorney general to manage the government's legal affairs and of postmaster general to supervise the mail service.

Inauguration of George Washington in 1789 at Federal Hall, New York. This marked the beginning of the United States government under the Constitution.

President Washington chose a man to serve as the head of each department. He appointed Thomas Jefferson as secretary for the Department of State, Henry Knox for the Department of War, and Alexander Hamilton for the Department of the Treasury. Edmund Randolph became the first attorney general. These men began meeting with President Washington to help him make decisions, and they became known as his Cabinet.

The Judicial Branch. Congress passed the Judiciary Act of 1789, which set up the Supreme Court with a chief justice and five

Washington and his Cabinet. From left to right: George Washington; Henry Knox, secretary of war; Alexander Hamilton, secretary of the treasury; Thomas Jefferson, secretary of state; Edmund Randolph, attorney general.

John Jay (1745–1829) was the first chief justice of the United States Supreme Court. He also negotiated the Jay Treaty with Great Britain in 1794.

associate justices. This law also provided for federal courts lower than the Supreme Court. For the chief justice, President Washington chose **John Jay**.

Dealing With Economic Problems

Alexander Hamilton's Program. When Hamilton became the secretary of the treasury, the United States was in deep financial trouble. So Hamilton devised a program to put the United States on a sound financial footing. First, Hamilton wanted to pay the debt of over $40 million from the Confederation period, which the United States still owed to foreign nations and American citizens. He also thought the federal government should take on all the debts of the states, since most of them were from the Revolution. He planned to pay these debts by selling ***bonds*** that the government would repay with interest over fifteen to twenty years.

Hamilton's ideas met opposition in Congress. Some states (mostly in the South) did not think the state and national debts should be combined, for they had already paid their debts. To gain support from the Southern states, Hamilton promised that he would try to have the national capital located in the South. Congress then approved Hamilton's proposal and also decided that the new capital should be located on land obtained from Maryland and Virginia. This land was called the District of Columbia, and the capital city of Washington, D.C., was established there in 1800.

View of Washington, D.C., in 1880, showing Pennsylvania Avenue from the western part of the Capitol grounds.

The Capitol when first occupied by Congress in 1800. It was used by the Senate, the House of Representatives, and the Supreme Court.

The south side of the White House in 1846. John Adams was the first president to live in this building, which was called the President's House at first.

The north side of the White House as it appears today.

The White House. President John Adams and his wife were the first to occupy the President's House (called the White House after the War of 1812). They lived there less than four months before his term expired. Soon after moving to the President's House, Mrs. Adams wrote to her daughter as follows: "The house is made habitable, but there is not a single apartment finished [inside], except the plastering has been done. . . . We have not the least fence, yard, or other convenience [outside], and the great audience room I make a drying-room of, to hang up the clothes in."

Hamilton next proposed a national bank where the government and private citizens could deposit money, and where the government could borrow money as needed. Hamilton believed such a bank would help to stabilize the economy, but opponents thought it was unconstitutional. However, in 1791 Congress granted a charter for the first Bank of the United States, to be located in Philadelphia.

Hamilton also wanted to raise more revenue for the federal government. Congress had already approved a ***tariff*** (TAR ihf) on certain imports in 1789. Hamilton further proposed an ***excise tax*** (EHK syz) on domestic products, and Congress approved such a tax on whiskey in 1791.

The Whiskey Rebellion. Farmers west of the Appalachians made much whiskey from corn, since whiskey could more easily be transported to markets across the mountains than corn could. Whiskey even became a kind of money in the West. These farmers opposed the whiskey tax, for they thought it hurt them more than other people. In 1794, a group in western Pennsylvania took up arms and drove off the tax collectors.

To put down this Whiskey Rebellion, Washington and Hamilton sent an army of over twelve thousand men against the rebels. They arrested several of the leaders and dispersed the angry farmers. The whiskey tax would be paid. This affair demonstrated that the federal government intended to enforce its laws and would command respect.

Political Parties

Men in the government tended to either support or oppose Secretary Hamilton's program, and they grouped together in their support or opposition. After a time, these groups became organized as political parties.

The Federalists. Those who supported Hamilton became known as Federalists. Many of these were businessmen, bankers, and manufacturers from New England and the

Middle Atlantic States. This party promoted a strong federal government operating on a ***loose interpretation*** of the Constitution.

In other words, the Federalists believed that the government should be able to make "all laws necessary and proper." They thought it had considerable freedom to assume powers not specifically spelled out in the Constitution. They tended to view Great Britain as their model.

The Democratic-Republicans. Thomas Jefferson was the main leader of the group opposing Hamilton's program. He and James Madison founded the Democratic-Republican Party, which was the forerunner of the modern Democratic Party. This group favored a weak federal government that operated on a ***strict interpretation*** of the Constitution—exercising only the powers specifically spelled out in the Constitution. Most of its supporters were farmers or skilled craftsmen. They tended to favor France more than Britain.

George Washington did not officially join either party, but he tended to favor the Federalist view. For this reason, the terms of George Washington and of John Adams, his successor, are known as the Federalist Era.

Political parties are part of the system of this world. The people of God are "in the world" but not "of the world" (John 17:11, 14); therefore, they do not associate with political parties.

Left: George Washington (1732–1799) was the first president of the United States. He served from 1789 to 1797 and favored the Federalist Party. ***Right:*** John Adams (1735–1826) was the second president of the United States. He served from 1797 to 1801 and was a Federalist.

Dealing With Foreign Nations

France. In 1789, France was rocked by an upheaval known as the French Revolution. The French people rose up against their king and the nobles. They turned against the church and tried to rid the nation of Christianity. The French king was beheaded in 1793, and violence prevailed until **Napoleon Bonaparte** (nuh POH lee uhn BOH nuh pahrt) made himself dictator in 1799.

To prevent the spread of French revolutionary ideas, Britain and other nations declared war on France. That meant the United States should help France, according to the treaty made in 1778 during the American Revolution. But President Washington decided not to help either side in the conflict. So he issued a Neutrality Proclamation in 1793, which said the United States would be "friendly and impartial" to the warring nations.

Great Britain. The British were not pleased with the Neutrality Proclamation. They decided to use their powerful navy to prevent the United States from trading with France. British ships began stopping American ships and searching them for British sailors, who sometimes left their navy to sail with Americans. If any sailor on an American ship was suspected of having left the British navy, he was ***impressed*** into the British navy (forced to serve in it). But the British impressed many sailors who were American citizens and not British at all.

Americans were upset not only for that reason but also because Britain had not complied with the terms of the Treaty of Paris. The British still held some forts around the Great Lakes that they had promised to give up. Also, the British restricted American trade with the British West Indies. Because of these issues, some Americans wanted to go to war against Britain.

But President Washington sent John Jay to negotiate with the British, and in 1794 they signed an agreement known as the Jay Treaty.

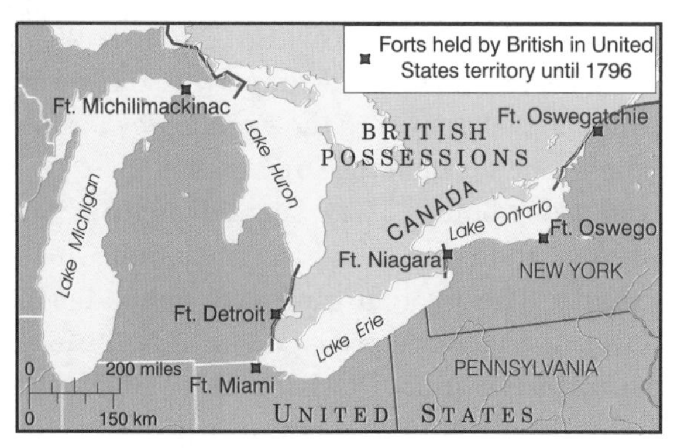

British Forts in American Territory

Under this treaty, the British agreed to give up their forts around the Great Lakes by 1796 and to pay for ships they had seized in the West Indies. The Americans agreed to pay debts that their citizens owed to British merchants before the American Revolution, and to leave the Mississippi River open to both countries. The Jay Treaty did little to stop British interference with American shipping, but it did help the United States to avoid war.

Spain. The Spanish occupied the lands across the Mississippi River. After the Jay Treaty was established with Britain, the Spanish also decided to settle with the United States. Thomas Pinckney negotiated the Pinckney Treaty with Spain in 1795. This treaty allowed American merchants to trade on the Mississippi and to use New Orleans as a port of deposit (storage place for cargo). Spain also recognized the American claims to lands east of the Mississippi. One by one, the United States was surmounting its problems.

End of the Federalist Era

Election of John Adams. In the election of 1796, John Adams received the highest number of electoral votes, so he became president. Thomas Jefferson received the next highest number and became vice president. This meant that the president was a Federalist and the vice president was a Democratic-Republican!

The Alien and Sedition Acts. The French were displeased with the Jay Treaty. They believed the United States was siding with Britain against them in violation of the 1778 alliance treaty made during the American Revolution. When the French seized a number of American merchant ships in 1796 and 1797, many Americans became angry. They grew angrier still when they found out in 1798 that three French officials had demanded a bribe and a loan of over $10 million before they would discuss the problems. This episode was called the XYZ Affair because the three Frenchmen were identified as X, Y, and Z. Numerous battles broke out between French and American ships even though neither nation officially declared war.

The Federalists now saw an opportunity to gain a political victory over the Democratic-Republicans, who favored France. The Federalists claimed that the United States needed protection against supporters of France, so they persuaded Congress to pass the Alien and Sedition Acts in 1798.

These acts said that a person had to live in the United States fourteen years before he could become a citizen. (The previous requirement was five years.) The president could remove from the country any aliens that he considered dangerous. And it was illegal to criticize the government in any false or malicious way. Under the new laws, at least twenty-five people, mostly newspaper editors, were tried for sedition. Many people were outraged because this seemed like a gross violation of the freedoms of speech and of the press.

The Alien and Sedition Acts were a failure for the Federalists. Instead of helping them, these acts caused many Americans to think that the Federalist Party was becoming too strong and was threatening their freedoms. The result was greater popularity for Thomas Jefferson and the Democratic-Republicans, who favored a weaker federal government. By 1800, the Federalists were voted out of power and never regained control of the government.

Meanwhile, President Adams sent a delegation to negotiate with France, and they worked out the Convention of 1800. This agreement ended the alliance treaty of 1778 and provided for unhampered trade between the two nations.

These events show that elected officials tend to do what seems most expedient so that they can remain in power. But this is a poor principle to live by, for what is expedient is not always right. Yet God overruled so that the environment of the United States remained favorable for His children.

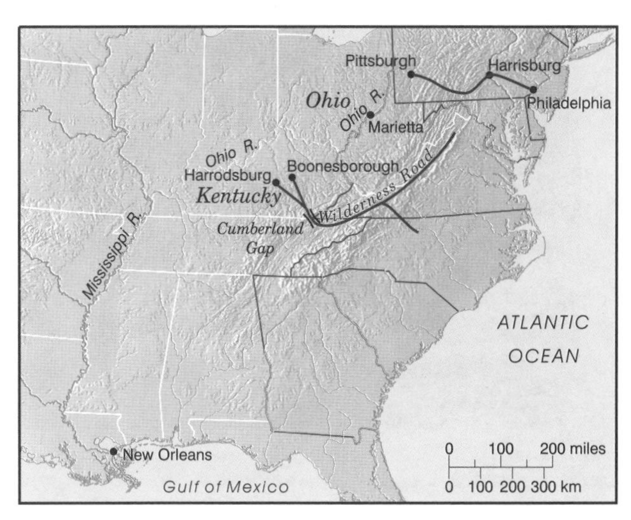

Early Routes to the West

Westward Movement

In 1767, **Daniel Boone** found fertile soil near present-day Lexington, Kentucky. When the land was opened for white settlement, Boone led frontier families to Kentucky over the Wilderness Road he had blazed. The Wilderness Road, passing through the Cumberland Gap, was the southern route to the West.

The main northern route to the West followed the Ohio River from Pittsburgh, the first permanent English settlement west of the Appalachians. Since Pittsburgh was located where the Ohio River began, it became a natural "gateway to the West." Pioneers could float west on the Ohio River in flatboats, and they could send produce and other goods down the Ohio to the Mississippi and on to New Orleans.

The opening of routes to the West allowed a flood of settlers to pour across the Appalachians. Kentucky became the fifteenth state in 1792, and in 1796 Tennessee entered the Union as the sixteenth state. (Vermont had become the fourteenth state in 1791.) Ohio also grew rapidly, and in 1803 it became the seventeenth state.

Daniel Boone (1734–1820) escorting pioneers. Boone (leading the horse) cleared the Wilderness Road; and by 1800, about 200,000 pioneers had used it to move west.

Old Fort Harrod, Harrodsburg, Kentucky. Daniel Boone and others began the settlement of Kentucky by building forts like this one. The higher building at the end of the row is the block house, located on the outer wall to protect the fort.

Flatboat on the Tennessee River. Many pioneer families moved to the West by putting their goods and livestock on a flatboat and floating down a river. Note the long steering oars.

Focus for Thought

1. Name the first three departments in the executive branch, along with their functions and their secretaries.
2. Copy and complete the following table to compare the first two political parties.

Party	Things Favored by Party	Leaders

3. a. How did President Washington avoid going to war to help France?
   b. How was war avoided with Great Britain?
4. What benefits did the Pinckney Treaty give the United States?
5. Why did the Alien and Sedition Acts make the Federalists unpopular?
6. Name in order the four states added to the Union between 1790 and 1805, and the year of admission for each.

2. THE JEFFERSONIANS

In 1801, Thomas Jefferson became the third president of the United States. This was the first transfer of power from one political party to another. Jefferson and other leaders who followed his course became known as Jeffersonians, and they made many changes in the government. But on the whole, the system established by George Washington and the Federalists still functioned smoothly under Jeffersonian leaders. God was allowing peace and stability to continue in the new nation.

Jeffersonian Democracy

A Close Election. In the election of 1800, Thomas Jefferson and Aaron Burr received the same number of electoral votes. Which man was to be president, and which one vice president? In such a situation, the House of Representatives needed to decide. But the House had to vote thirty-six times before an agreement was reached! It was finally decided that Thomas Jefferson would be president and Aaron Burr vice president.

To address this problem, the Twelfth Amendment was added to the Constitution. This amendment provided for separate ballots

Thomas Jefferson (1743–1826) was the third president of the United States. He served from 1801 to 1809 and was a Democratic-Republican.

Monticello, Thomas Jefferson's home near Charlottesville, Virginia. Jefferson himself designed this magnificent residence. He was also a gardener, inventor, scientist, writer, and politician.

for president and vice president.

Changes in the Federal Government. President Jefferson made some significant changes in the federal government. One of these was in government laws and taxes. The Alien and Sedition Acts were allowed to expire, and the years of residence required for citizenship was restored to five. Excise taxes were repealed, including the tax on whiskey. But the Bank of the United States and Hamilton's financial system were allowed to continue.

President Jefferson also wanted to lower the government debt and reduce spending. To save money, he reduced the number of men working for the government and decreased the size of the military. By lowering expenses, President Jefferson reduced the government debt from $83 million when he took office to $57 million when he left office.

Strengthening of the Supreme Court. Just before John Adams left office, he had appointed a Federalist named William Marbury as a justice of the peace. Jefferson opposed this appointment; so he ordered James Madison, the secretary of state, to withhold the official papers that would make Marbury a judge. Marbury then brought suit for an order from the Supreme Court to force Madison to issue the papers. He based his suit on a law passed in 1789, which said the Supreme Court could issue a "writ of mandamus" (man DAY muhs) to order a government worker to do his job.

Much tension surrounded the case of *Marbury v. Madison*. If the Court ruled in favor of Marbury, the judicial branch could find itself in a struggle with the executive branch. If the Court ruled against Marbury, it would appear that the Court was afraid to challenge the president.

The Court did neither. Chief Justice John Marshall agreed that Marbury was wrongfully deprived of his commission. However, Marshall declared that the Supreme Court could not issue the mandamus, because the 1789 law giving the Court this power was

John Marshall (1755–1835) became chief justice of the United States in 1801. He was so influential that he became known as the "Great Chief Justice."

unconstitutional. So the case was dismissed.

This was the first time the Supreme Court declared a Congressional law unconstitutional. The ruling strengthened the Supreme Court because it established the power of judicial review, by which the Court can declare laws unconstitutional. This decision also demonstrated that the Constitution was the supreme law of the land.

The Louisiana Purchase

Negotiation of the Louisiana Purchase. In 1800, Spain and France made a treaty in which Louisiana became a French territory. President Jefferson was concerned when he heard about it. What about American trade on the Mississippi River? What if the French closed the port of New Orleans? Jefferson decided he would try to buy New Orleans, and he sent two delegates to France in an effort to make the purchase. But when they met with Napoleon in April 1803, he offered to sell all of Louisiana to the United States!

The Americans were astounded. They discussed the terms of the offer with Napoleon and settled on a price of about $15 million for more than 800,000 square miles (2,072,000 km^2) of land. This was just over 2.5 cents per acre—one of the greatest bargains in history! The Americans had not been authorized to buy all of Louisiana, but they signed the agreement on May 2, 1803.

This transaction put President Jefferson into a predicament. He had believed in a strict interpretation of the Constitution, but it did not specifically say that the government could buy territory. Taking advantage of Napoleon's offer would require a loose interpretation as favored by the Federalists.

Jefferson decided that the president must do what was best for the nation. The Constitution did provide for the making of treaties, and he would interpret that principle loosely in this case. The Senate debated the matter and ratified the treaty, and in December 1803 the French officially turned Louisiana over to the United States.

The Louisiana Territory was transferred from France to the United States in New Orleans on December 20, 1803. Elaborate ceremonies marked the occasion as the French flag came down and the American flag went up.

The Louisiana Purchase doubled the size of the United States. All or parts of thirteen states would be made from it, including Louisiana, Arkansas, Missouri, Iowa, the Dakotas, Nebraska, and Oklahoma. In addition, the new territory gave the United States a basis from which to expand even further across North America.

The Lewis and Clark Expedition. Jefferson commissioned **Meriwether Lewis** and **William Clark** to explore the Louisiana Territory. These men set out from St. Louis with a group of forty men in the spring of 1804. By November they arrived in present-day North Dakota, and there they employed an Indian woman named **Sacajawea** (sak uh juh WEE uh), along with her husband, to be their guide and interpreter. Lewis and Clark reached the Pacific Ocean in November 1805, eighteen months after they had started.

The explorers turned eastward again the next spring, but this time Lewis and Clark

Left: Lewis and Clark with Sacajawea (1787?–1812), their Shoshone guide and interpreter. Her brother was a Shoshone chief from whom the explorers obtained horses for the journey across the Rocky Mountains. ***Right:*** Lewis and Clark at the mouth of the Columbia River in 1805. Having spent two years in exploring the western wilderness, they claimed the land for the United States.

headed two groups following different routes. They reunited along the Missouri River, and by September 1806, they were back in St. Louis. The party had traveled 8,000 miles (12,874 km), enduring sicknesses, injuries, rough terrain, rushing rivers, and attacks by Indians and grizzly bears—with the loss of only one man.

The Lewis and Clark expedition provided a wealth of valuable information about the Louisiana region. The explorers had found several passes through the Rockies and made friends with various Indian tribes. They had shown that there is no direct water route to the Pacific Ocean. Their detailed maps and scientific reports of the journey were highly valuable in establishing a claim to the territory. Soon a large stream of settlers was flowing into the lands of the Louisiana Purchase.

Pike's Exploration of the West. In 1805, an army officer named **Zebulon Pike** went northward to explore the headwaters of the Mississippi River. During 1806 and 1807, he followed the Arkansas River into present-day Colorado to explore its headwaters, and there he tried to climb the high mountain that today bears his name (Pikes Peak). But he lost his way, wandered south, and was arrested in Spanish territory. When the Spanish released him, Pike returned home in 1808.

Problems in Trade

After the American Revolution, United States trade with other nations increased greatly. But trade with nations around the Mediterranean Sea was dangerous because of pirates that infested the Barbary Coast of northern Africa. These Barbary pirates attacked and seized ships in the Mediterranean.

Spaniards escorting Zebulon Pike and his men into Santa Fe. Pike, an officer of the United States army, was exploring the West when he was captured by the Spanish. He discovered and named Pikes Peak.

The United States After 1803

Present-day boundaries
Lewis and Clark's route west
Lewis and Clark's return journeys
Pike's exploration of the Southwest

(Numbers in parentheses indicate when new states were admitted to the Union.)

To keep their ships from being attacked, the United States and other nations paid money to the pirates.

But in 1801 the ruler of Tripoli (now in Libya) demanded more protection money. Instead of paying more, President Jefferson sent warships to guard American merchant ships. The United States battled the pirates over the next four years. In one episode, Stephen Decatur burned the American ship *Philadelphia* in the Tripoli harbor after the pirates had captured it. Finally in 1805, an agreement was reached that was favorable to the United States.

Trade issues also brought problems with Britain and France. In 1803, another war broke out between Britain and France. President Jefferson determined that the United States would stay neutral in this conflict and so should be able to trade with both sides. But in 1805, the British defeated the French fleet in the Battle of Trafalgar (truh FAL gur), and

Burning of the *Philadelphia* in the harbor of Tripoli in 1804. The American ship had been captured by the Barbary pirates.

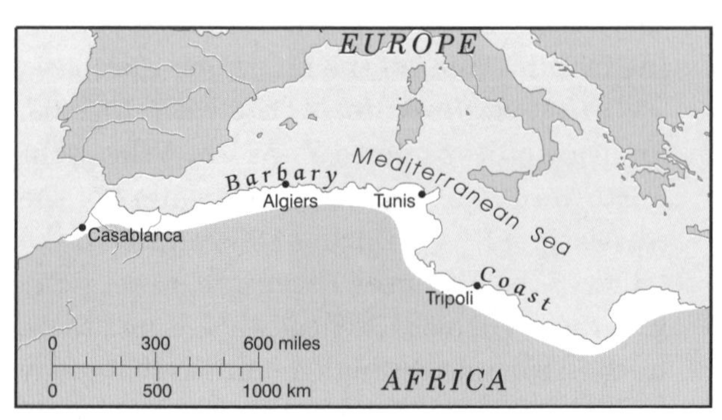

The Barbary Coast

Great Britain again dominated the seas.

The British placed a blockade around France to cut off that nation's sea trade. In turn, the French seized ships that were heading for British ports. Both Britain and France captured a large number of American ships, and the British impressed thousands of American sailors into their navy.

In 1807, the British warship *Leopard* stopped the American warship *Chesapeake* near Virginia. When the American captain refused to let his ship be searched for British sailors, the *Leopard* fired on the *Chesapeake*. Three sailors were killed and eighteen wounded. The British then boarded the *Chesapeake* and impressed four sailors, of which three were Americans. People in the United States were angered and began clamoring for war.

President Jefferson did not want to go to war, for his navy was much too weak to challenge the British. So he got Congress to pass the Embargo Act, which cut off all American trade with foreign nations. He hoped that the embargo would deprive the warring nations of sorely needed American goods so that they would stop seizing American ships.

The Embargo Act was a complete failure. It had little effect on Britain and France, but it was disastrous to America. Farmers could not sell their products, merchants went bankrupt, and sailors and dock workers lost their jobs. Some ship captains ignored the embargo and sailed anyway, and the British and French continued seizing their ships.

The Embargo Act was repealed in 1809, just before Jefferson left office. It was replaced by an act that allowed Americans to trade with all nations except Britain and France, but that law too was of little avail. In spite of all that Jefferson had done, war broke out just three years after he left the presidency.

Focus for Thought

7. What were some important changes that President Jefferson made in the federal government?
8. a. How did President Jefferson compromise his principles to buy Louisiana?
   b. How was the Louisiana Purchase valuable to the United States?
9. What were some fruits of the Lewis and Clark expedition?
10. a. What was the purpose of the Embargo Act?
    b. Why was this act a failure?

3. THE WAR OF 1812

The War of 1812 is sometimes called "the second war for American independence." Though the United States had won political independence in the Revolution, the young nation was still hampered by interference from Great Britain, especially in trade; so fighting broke out again. But the War of 1812 would become one of the best examples of the folly of war. The peace treaty did not deal with the issues contributing to the war, and the greatest battle was fought after the war had officially ended.

Events Leading to War

Trade Issues. As stated in the previous section, the British and French had been seizing American merchant ships and restricting United States trade. Jefferson tried in several ways to establish America's right to free international trade, but all his efforts failed. Finally it appeared that war was the only way to assert American independence from European affairs.

Problems With the Indians. Growing troubles with the Indians in the West (land west of the Appalachians) were another factor leading to war. The Indians became increasingly hostile as westward settlement continued and white men took more and more of their territory. An Indian leader named **Tecumseh** (tih KUHM suh) and his brother, known as the "Prophet," tried to unite the tribes east of the Mississippi to resist the white man's advance. In 1811, **William Henry Harrison** led an army to fight the Indians at their headquarters on the Tippecanoe River in Indiana.

While Tecumseh was away trying to rally more Indians to his cause, the "Prophet" suddenly attacked Harrison's forces. After fierce fighting, Harrison's men defeated the Indians in the Battle of Tippecanoe on November 7, 1811. Harrison's victory ended the Indians' plans for unity. But settlers in the West blamed Britain for the conflict, believing the British had stirred up the Indians and provided them with weapons.

The Demand for War. People in the West and South clamored for war. They

Shawnee chief Tecumseh (1768–1813) tried to unite Indian tribes to oppose white settlers on their lands and was later killed in fighting for the British in the War of 1812.

James Madison (1751–1836) was the fourth president of the United States. He served from 1809 to 1817 and was a Democratic-Republican.

blamed the British for the problems they had with the Indians and for the low prices they received for their products. They also believed that by going to war, the United States could take Canada from the British and Florida from the Spanish. Then, they reasoned, their troubles with the Indians would cease because the Indians would no longer have European support.

These people elected representatives to Congress who held the same ideas. Most of these representatives were young and bold, and they were nicknamed ***war hawks*** because they strongly promoted war with Britain. The war hawks included **Henry Clay** of Kentucky and **John C. Calhoun** (kal HOON) of South Carolina. Both men were elected in 1811 to the House of Representatives.

Finally on June 1, 1812, President Madison asked Congress to declare war on Britain. Congress passed the declaration, and the president signed it on June 18. The War of 1812 had begun.

"He loveth transgression that loveth strife: and he that exalteth his gate seeketh destruction" (Proverbs 17:19).

The War of 1812

The Campaign Into Canada. Since the British navy was much stronger than the American navy, it seemed logical to attack the British by land in Canada. The Americans

Oliver Hazard Perry in the Battle of Lake Erie, September 1813. After his flagship, the *Lawrence,* was severely damaged, Perry's men rowed him to the *Niagara,* from which he continued to command the battle. Perry is famous for his words, "We have met the enemy, and they are ours."

U.S.S. *Constitution*, built by 1797. It was called *Old Ironsides* because of the way British shot bounced off its wooden sides during a fierce battle in the War of 1812.

planned a threefold attack in 1812, but none of their plans succeeded. In the end, instead of taking Canada, the Americans found themselves defending their Northwest Territory against the British!

But in September 1813, Oliver Hazard Perry won a fierce battle with the British on Lake Erie. This naval battle gave the Americans control of Lake Erie, from which they could threaten Detroit. The British soon retreated from Detroit; and at the Battle of the Thames, William Henry Harrison defeated them in October. The Indian leader Tecumseh was killed while helping the British in this battle.

The Campaign of the British. By 1814, Napoleon was defeated in Europe and the British could concentrate on the war against the United States. That August they marched into Washington, D.C., and burned the government buildings—including the president's mansion and the Capitol. President Madison fled with his wife Dolley just before the British arrived. Mrs. Madison saved important documents and a picture of George Washington, but the presidential mansion was ruined. After the war, it was painted white to cover the fire damage; so it became known as the White House.

The next British attack was on Fort McHenry, which guarded the approach to Baltimore by sea. The bombardment of the fort lasted over twenty-four hours on September 13 and 14; but the fort did not surrender, and finally the British left.

A young American lawyer named Francis Scott Key had been on a British ship during the bombardment. As the battle raged, he watched the large flag that flew over the fort, fervently hoping that it would not be lowered in surrender. When morning came

In August 1814, the British captured Washington, D.C. They set fire to the President's House, the Capitol, and other buildings.

Francis Scott Key in the Baltimore harbor. Inspired at the sight of the flag still flying over the fort, he wrote "The Star-Spangled Banner" on the back of a letter. The poem was set to music, and in 1931 it was adopted as the national anthem of the United States.

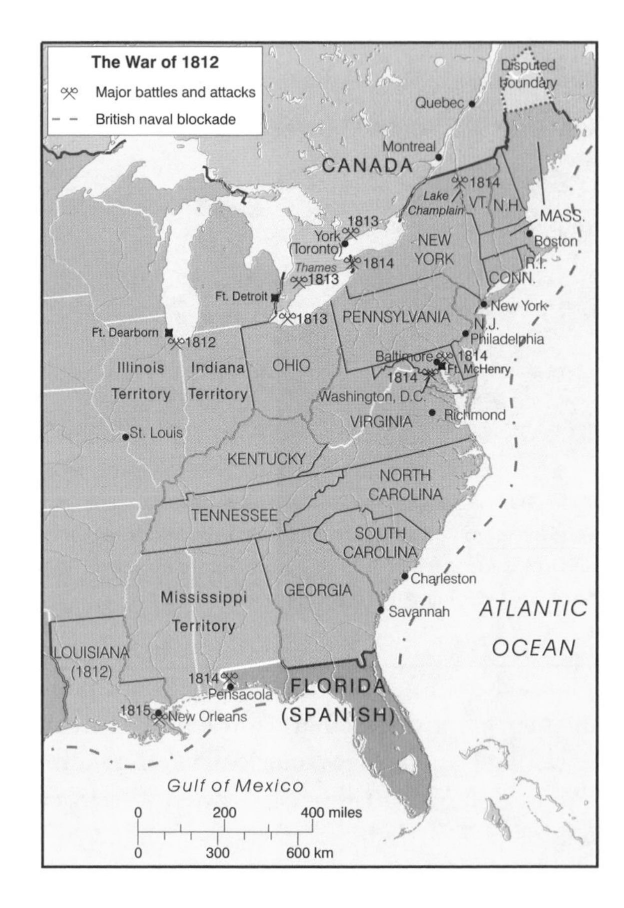

on September 14, he rejoiced to see that the flag was still flying. Francis Scott Key expressed his feelings in a poem called "The Star-Spangled Banner," which later became the national anthem of the United States.

Also in 1814, a large British army advanced from Canada to attack New York. Only a small American force stood between the British and New York City. But that September, Captain Thomas Macdonough (muhk DAHN uh) destroyed a British fleet in the Battle of Lake Champlain. The British general and his army then retreated into Canada.

The Peace Treaty and the Battle of New Orleans. Even as fighting continued, British and American statesmen were negotiating to end the war. When they heard of the American victory on Lake Champlain, the British were ready to compromise. The Treaty of Ghent (GEHNT), signed on December 24, 1814, restored things as they had been before the war. It was basically an agreement to stop fighting, for it did not deal with impressment, trade, or other issues that had started the war. Those issues were no longer important, however, since Napoleon had been defeated.

But because of slow communications, the most important battle was fought after the war had officially ended! On December 24, 1814—the same day the peace treaty was signed—British soldiers began landing near New Orleans. General Andrew Jackson attacked the British at once; then he retired to defend the city. He built defenses along the Mississippi River to protect his army.

The British charged on January 8, 1815, but Jackson's men successfully opposed them and saved New Orleans. News of this battle arrived in Washington about the same time as news of the Treaty of Ghent. Since people associated the victory at New Orleans with the peace treaty, Jackson became a hero.

Effects of the War of 1812

Relations Abroad. Even though the Treaty of Ghent restored matters to their former state, the War of 1812 had important results. Canadians felt bitter against the United States because of the attacks during the war. European nations gained respect for the United States because it had not been defeated by powerful Britain. Relations between the two nations improved afterward, and no more wars were fought between them.

Results at Home. The War of 1812 helped to increase nationalism in the United States. People became more patriotic and took more pride in their country. Manufacturing grew because during the war, Americans had to make for themselves what they formerly had purchased from abroad. Westward expansion also increased, since Indian power east of the Mississippi had been broken by the war.

But the War of 1812 is a sad commentary on the foolishness of war. If only the United States had waited a little longer, war might have been prevented altogether. (The original issues faded away after Britain defeated France.) If news of the Treaty of Ghent had only arrived sooner, how many lives might have been spared! Matters at the end of the war were much the same as at the beginning. But many young men had lost their life in the war and had passed unprepared into eternity.

Mennonites of the Early 1800s. The Mennonites and other nonresistant groups faced little testing during the War of 1812 because it was fought by volunteer soldiers. But the Mennonites faced other threats. One was pietism, a movement closely connected to the Great Awakening. Pietism emphasized emotions and personal experience rather than doctrine and form. Because of spiritual coldness in the Mennonite Church of that time, some young people and others were lured away by pietistic teachings and church groups.

To deal with this threat, the bishop Christian Burkholder published a book in 1804. This book, *Addresses to Youth,* was used especially as an instruction book for young people. It was an effort to reinforce the Biblical teachings about conversion, obedience, and a sound Christian walk of life.

Two new hymnals were also produced in southeastern Pennsylvania about this time. In 1803, the Franconia Mennonites published *Die Kleine Geistliche Harfe (Zion's Harp)* in Germantown. It was followed in 1804 by the *Unpartheyisches Gesang-buch*, published by Lancaster Mennonites. This second hymnal included martyrs' hymns from the old German *Ausbund* and was printed in Lancaster. It is still in use today. Mennonite communities also operated a number of schools for their children during this period.

Ein
Unpartheyisches
Gesang-Buch
enthaltend
Geistreiche Lieder und Psalmen,
zum
Allgemeinen Gebrauch
des
Wahren Gottesdienstes.
Auf Begehren der
Brüderschaft der Menonisten Gemeinen
aus vielen Liederbüchern gesammelt.
Mit einem dreyfachen Register.
Zum Erstenmal ans Licht gestellt.
Lancaster:
Gedruckt bey Johann Albrecht, 1804.

The title page of the German hymnal used by the Mennonites of Lancaster, Pennsylvania. The title means "Nondenominational Songbook." The book contains 62 psalms and 390 hymns, of which 60 hymns are from the German *Ausbund*. This book is still used by some Mennonite denominations today.

Focus for Thought

11. Explain how each of the following contributed to war with Britain.
    a. trade b. problems with the Indians c. war hawks
12. a. Why did the Americans attack Canada?
    b. What were the results?
13. a. What major battle was fought after the War of 1812 officially ended?
    b. What American general became famous because of this battle?
14. What two provisions were included in the Treaty of Ghent?
15. Give four effects of the War of 1812.

Historical Highlights

A. Matching: People

a. Alexander Hamilton
b. Daniel Boone
c. George Washington
d. Henry Clay
e. James Madison
f. John Adams
g. John C. Calhoun
h. John Jay
i. John Marshall
j. Meriwether Lewis and William Clark
k. Napoleon Bonaparte
l. Sacajawea
m. Tecumseh
n. Thomas Jefferson
o. William Henry Harrison
p. Zebulon Pike

1. Opened the Wilderness Road to Kentucky.
2. Chief Justice who strengthened the Supreme Court by establishing judicial review.
3. Tried to create an Indian confederacy.
4. Federalist leader and first secretary of the treasury.
5. Defeated Indians at Tippecanoe.
6. First president; served from 1789 to 1797.
7. Leader of Democratic-Republican Party; third president; served from 1801 to 1809.
8. Explored the Louisiana Purchase from 1804 to 1806.
9. Tried to climb a mountain in Colorado, now named after him.
10. War hawks (two answers).
11. French leader who sold Louisiana to the United States.
12. President during the War of 1812; served from 1809 to 1817.
13. First chief justice of the Supreme Court.
14. Second president; a Federalist; served from 1797 to 1801.
15. Indian woman who helped to guide the Lewis and Clark expedition.

B. Matching: Terms

a. bond
b. chief justice
c. excise tax
d. impress
e. judicial review
f. loose interpretation
g. strict interpretation
h. tariff
i. war hawks
j. Democratic-Republicans
k. Department of State
l. Department of the Treasury
m. Department of War
n. Federalists
o. Whiskey Rebellion

1. Part of government in charge of revenue and spending.
2. Resistance to paying taxes in western Pennsylvania in 1794.
3. Idea that the government should be free to assume powers not specifically described in the Constitution.
4. Bold young congressmen who promoted war.
5. To force into military service.
6. Part of government responsible for defending the nation.
7. Head judge of the Supreme Court.
8. Idea that the government should exercise only the powers specifically described in the Constitution.
9. Power of the Supreme Court to declare a Congressional law unconstitutional.
10. Party in favor of strict interpretation of the Constitution.
11. Party in favor of loose interpretation of the Constitution.
12. Tax levied on certain domestic products.
13. Part of government dealing with foreign nations.
14. Certificate of debt to be paid back with interest.
15. Tax levied on certain imports, often to protect domestic industries.

C. Matching: Names

a. Alien and Sedition Acts
b. Bank of the United States
c. Embargo Act
d. Federalist Era
e. Jay Treaty
f. *Marbury v. Madison*
g. Pinckney Treaty
h. Treaty of Ghent

1. Period when George Washington and John Adams were in office.
2. Treaty that settled issues with Spain in 1795.
3. Case that established the power of the Supreme Court to declare laws unconstitutional.
4. Treaty that settled issues with Britain in 1794.
5. Law that stopped all exports.
6. Laws that limited rights of foreigners and forbade criticism of the government.
7. Treaty that ended the War of 1812.
8. Institution for depositing and borrowing government funds.

D. Deeper Discussion

1. What are some contrasts between the French Revolution and the American Revolution?
2. How did the Alien and Sedition Acts violate the Bill of Rights?
3. Were the Americans justified in their claim that the British stirred up the Indians? Explain.
4. What lessons can be learned from the following facts about the War of 1812?
   a. The main issues faded soon after the war started.
   b. The Battle of New Orleans was fought after the Treaty of Ghent had been signed.
5. Contrast pietism with a proper emphasis on obedience in the Christian walk of life.
6. Read John 18:36 and 2 Corinthians 5:20. If God's children apply the truths of these Scriptures, can they be nationalistic? Explain.

E. Chronology and Geography

1. Trace the outline of Map A again, and label it "Territorial Growth of the United States." (You will use this map again in Chapters 12 and 14.)
   a. Draw boundary lines to show the area included in the Louisiana Purchase. Label this area, but do not color it yet.
   b. Draw the border as it was between Florida and the Spanish territory at the time of the Louisiana Purchase. Also draw a line from the northern end of the Mississippi River straight north to the present border between the United States and Canada. Label the area north of Florida and east of the Louisiana Purchase "The United States in 1783." Color this area.
2. On your map entitled "Exploration of North America," draw brown lines to trace the route of Lewis and Clark. Label the route.
3. Using the map "Regions of the United States" in Chapter 1, describe the regions that Lewis and Clark explored.
4. Name the states of which all or part were formed from the Louisiana Purchase.
5. From memory, list the presidents of this chapter in order, along with the dates for their terms of office. Give two sets of dates if a president served two terms. (Note that election years are divisible by 4, such as 1800, 1804, and so on. Also remember that an elected president's term begins in the year after the election.)

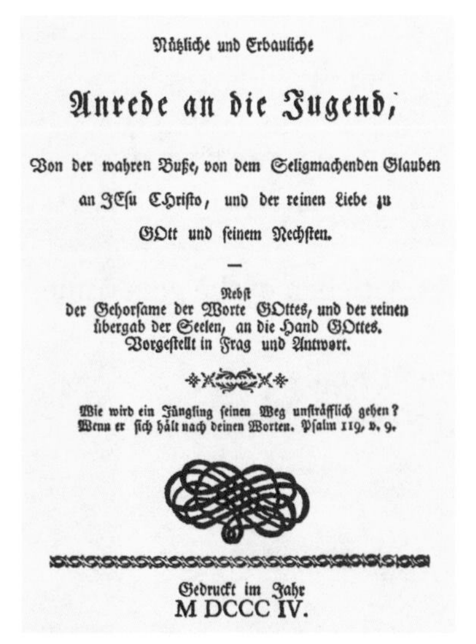
Nützliche und Erbauliche

Anrede an die Jugend,

Von der wahren Buße, von dem Seligmachenden Glauben
an JEsu CHristo, und der reinen Liebe zu
GOtt und seinem Nechsten.

—

Nebst
der Gehorsame der Worte GOttes, und der reinen
übergab der Seelen, an die Hand GOttes.
Vorgestellt in Frag und Antwort.

Wie wird ein Jüngling seinen Weg unsträfflich gehen?
Wenn er sich hält nach deinen Worten. Psalm 119, v. 9.

Gedruckt im Jahr
M DCCC IV.

Title page of Christian Burkholder's *Addresses to Youth*, 1804 edition. The first two lines on this page say, "Useful and Edifying Addresses to the Youth."

So Far This Year

A. Completion (1)

Write the correct name or term for each description.

1. Man who discovered Florida in 1513 while seeking the Fountain of Youth.
2. Explorer who sought the Seven Cities of Cíbola, 1540–1542.
3. Explorer who discovered the Mississippi River, 1539–1543.
4. Leader of Jamestown who established a policy of "no work, no food."
5. Founder of Rhode Island who insisted on freedom of conscience.
6. Founder of Maryland.
7. Quaker who received a land grant as payment for a debt.
8. Trustee leader in the founding of Georgia.
9. Two leaders of the colonial Great Awakening.
10. Branch of government that makes laws.
11. Branch of government that decides cases about laws.
12. Branch of government that enacts and enforces laws.
13. Part of legislative branch with states represented proportionately.
14. Part of legislative branch with states represented equally.
15. Group of men who elect the president.

B. Completion (2)

Write the correct term or date that belongs on each blank.

16. Under the Constitution, the American government is divided into three branches. This is according to the principle of ___.
17. The president may reject, or ___, a proposed law that Congress has passed.
18. Congress may ___ a president, or bring him to trial for misconduct in office.
19. The Constitution provides ways for government branches to limit each other's power. These limits are called ___.
20. In a ___ system, government powers are divided between the states and the national government.
21. A written plan of government is called a ___.
22. The Constitutional Convention was held in the year ___.
23. The United States government under the Constitution began in the year ___.
24. The first ten amendments to the Constitution, added in 1791, are called the ___.
25. Since the United States government has no king, it is called a ___.
26. The man called "father of the Constitution" was ___.
27. A form of manorialism, transplanted to New France, was the ___.
28. The Spanish used a ___ system to convert and civilize the Indians, and to fortify their frontiers against enemies.

C. Matching: Dates

Write the letter of the correct date for each description.

29. Year when Georgia was founded.	a. 1607
30. Year when Plymouth was founded.	b. 1620
31. Year when Jamestown was founded.	c. 1681
32. Year when Pennsylvania received a charter.	d. 1733

Andrew Jackson traveling to Washington, D.C., to be inaugurated in 1829. He was acclaimed as the representative of the common people.

12 National Progress

1. THE ERA OF GOOD FEELINGS
   - Growth of Nationalism
   - Treaties With Other Nations
   - The Monroe Doctrine
   - Sectionalism and the Missouri Compromise
   - A Troubled Presidency
2. THE AGE OF JACKSON
   - Jacksonian Democracy
   - The Nullification Crisis
   - Indian Removal
   - Economic Developments
3. THE RISE OF THE WHIGS
   - The Whig Party
   - The Van Buren Administration
   - The Whigs in Power

1810

Treaty of Ghent signed **1814**

James Monroe elected president; Clay's American System proposed 1816

Panic of 1819; Adams-Onís Treaty (Transcontinental Treaty) 1819

1820

Missouri Compromise passed; Monroe re-elected 1820

Monroe Doctrine proclaimed **1823**

John Quincy Adams elected president 1824

Andrew Jackson elected president 1828

1830

Nullification crisis; Jackson re-elected 1832

Seminole War 1835–1842

Martin Van Buren elected president 1836

Panic of 1837

1840

William Henry Harrison elected president 1840

William Henry Harrison dies; John Tyler takes office 1841

Webster-Ashburton Treaty negotiated 1842

James K. Polk elected president 1844

1850

"And it shall come to pass, if thou shalt hearken diligently unto the voice of the LORD thy God, . . . that the LORD thy God will set thee on high above all nations of the earth."

Deuteronomy 28:1

National Progress

Focus for Reading

The years after the War of 1812 brought rapid growth and change to the United States. New states joined the Union as western migration continued and new territories were settled. Nationalism increased, and economic growth brought prosperity during this period. Such major changes took place during Andrew Jackson's administration as president that those years are called the Age of Jackson or the Jacksonian Era.

Although the beginning of this time was called the Era of Good Feelings, all these changes produced stresses that brought disharmony. Many of the issues discussed in this chapter arose out of competing interests in the nation. This chapter focuses on the political affairs of the period, while the next chapter discusses the economic and cultural trends. The following sections deal with the political issues from 1815 to 1845.

1. The Era of Good Feelings
2. The Age of Jackson
3. The Rise of the Whigs

1. THE ERA OF GOOD FEELINGS

With the close of the War of 1812, a new spirit of nationalism and unity prevailed in the United States. A newspaper first called this period the Era of Good Feelings when it described the way former political foes united to support President James Monroe in 1817. But this era gave way to ill feelings and dissension in the election of 1824 and the administration of John Quincy Adams.

Growth of Nationalism

In the presidential election of 1816, **James Monroe** defeated the last Federalist to seek the presidency, and the Federalists ceased to exist as a political party. Only one political party remained—the Democratic-Republicans—and this provided a setting for political harmony. There continued to be one political party with little opposition throughout President Monroe's two terms (1817–1825).

James Monroe (1758–1831) was the fifth president of the United States. He served from 1817 to 1825 and was a Democratic-Republican.

Henry Clay and His American System. In 1816 Henry Clay, a leading representative, introduced a protective tariff for the benefit of new industries that had begun during the War of 1812. Such a tariff would be higher than a tariff merely for revenue, and it would make foreign goods, particularly from Britain, too expensive to compete with American goods.

Henry Clay believed that American manufacturers would flourish under this plan. Also, the government could use money from the tariff to finance internal improvements—projects such as roads and canals—that would encourage trade between the states and build up the home market. As part of his plan, Clay favored a second Bank of the United States, since the first bank's charter had expired in 1811. These proposals later became known as the American System.

Left: Henry Clay (1777–1852) was a war hawk leader who advocated war with Great Britain in 1812. He also promoted his plan, called the American System, to boost American manufacturing. ***Right:*** The National Bank in Philadelphia.

Clay's plan gained wide support, and in 1816 a protective tariff was enacted. Congress also approved a new Bank of the United States and issued a charter lasting twenty years.

Conflict Over the Bank of the United States. In 1819, the United States suffered a period of financial hardship known as the Panic of 1819. To restrict unsound lending, the new Bank of the United States had made loans harder to get. Especially in the West, where many settlers borrowed money to buy land, people blamed the bank for the hard times.

Many people in the South and West thought the bank made the federal government too strong. But when the state of Maryland challenged the bank before the Supreme Court, Chief Justice John Marshall ruled that the bank was constitutional. This ruling was based on a loose interpretation of the Constitution, and it strengthened the powers of the federal government over the states.

Treaties With Other Nations

Agreements With Great Britain. Boundary disputes between the United States and Canada were settled during the Era of Good Feelings. By treaties in 1817 and 1818, the border was established along the forty-ninth parallel between the Lake of the Woods and the Rockies. Also in the 1818 treaty, the United States and Britain agreed on joint occupation of the Oregon Country in the Northwest. This meant that the two nations would share that territory.

The Adams-Onís Treaty. The United States was eager to have the Spanish territory of Florida, which consisted at the time of East Florida (the main peninsula) and West Florida (the panhandle extending to New Orleans). Indians from East Florida made frequent raids on American settlements in Georgia, but Spain was not strong enough to enforce order. So in 1818, President Monroe commissioned **Andrew Jackson** to put an end to the Indian raids. Jackson invaded Florida and conquered two Spanish forts, including one at Pensacola. The Spanish protested Jackson's operations, but they realized that they were too weak to retain Florida.

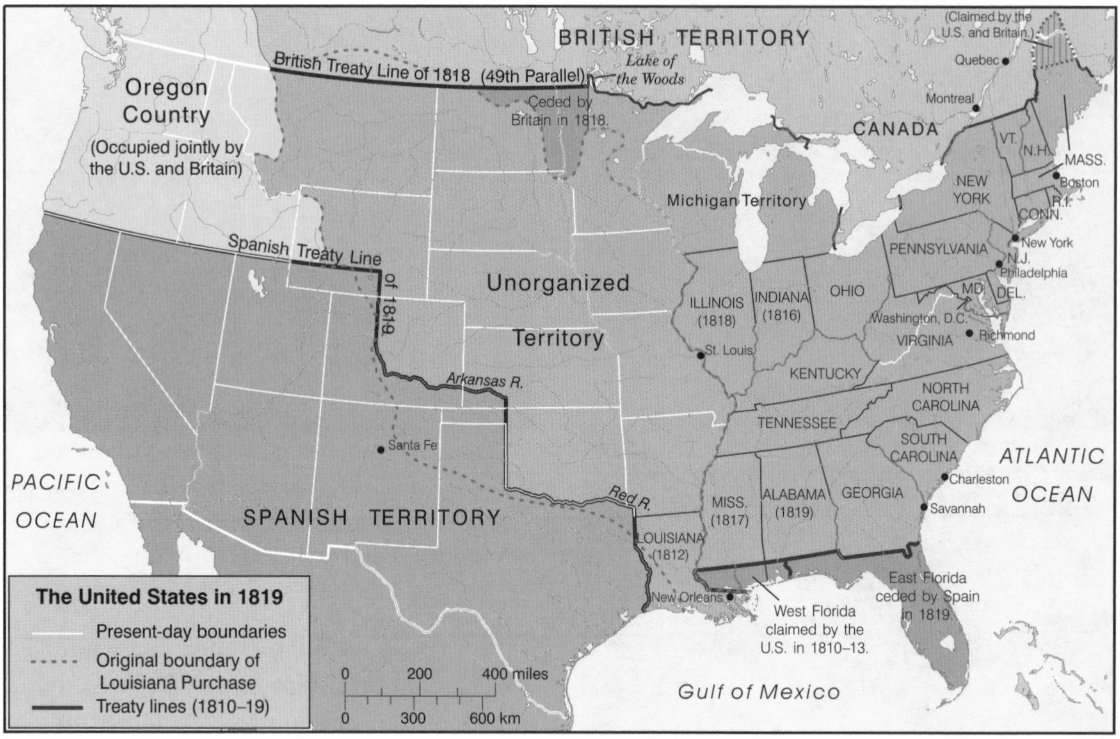

In 1819, Secretary of State **John Quincy Adams** negotiated the Adams-Onís Treaty with Luis de Onís, the Spanish ambassador to the United States. With this treaty, the United States received all of Florida for payment of $5 million. This money was not given to Spain but to Americans who had claims for property damage against Spain. The Spanish renounced claims to the Oregon Country, and the United States gave up claims to Texas. This Transcontinental Treaty, as it is also called, foreshadowed the nation's expansion to the Pacific Ocean.

The Monroe Doctrine

Threats From Foreign Nations. In 1821, the Russians declared that they owned the land that is now the state of Alaska and all the land as far south as the fifty-first parallel. They ordered foreign ships to stay away from the North American coast between Alaska and Oregon. But American trading ships visited this area regularly, and the United States and Britain had claimed some of the same land as part of the Oregon Country. Therefore, the United States viewed this situation with concern.

At the same time, Spain's vast empire in America was breaking apart. The American and French revolutions had spread ideas of independence, and the Napoleonic Wars in Europe gave Spain's colonies in America an opportunity to revolt. From 1810 to 1822, Spain's Latin American colonies won their independence.

In 1815, several European nations made an alliance, partly to help Spain regain her colonies in America. It was rumored that France planned to send an army to America to reconquer the Spanish colonies. President Monroe was concerned about this, for he did not want a new Spanish or French empire in America.

Issuance of the Monroe Doctrine. The president took several steps to deal with these problems. First, the United States officially recognized the new Latin American governments in 1822. Second, a warning letter was sent to Russia, which later gave up its claims to land south of Alaska. Finally, President Monroe presented to Congress a new statement of American policy toward European nations. This statement, which became known as the ***Monroe Doctrine***, contained the following three points.

1. "The American continents . . . are henceforth not to be considered as subjects for future colonization by any European powers."

2. If any European nation interfered in the affairs of nations in the Western Hemisphere, the United States would view it as "the manifestation of an unfriendly disposition toward the United States."

3. "Our policy, in regard to Europe . . . , is not to interfere in the internal concerns of any of its powers."

In short, the Monroe Doctrine stated that European nations were to stay out of American affairs, and the United States in turn would stay out of European affairs.

At the time, the United States was too weak to enforce the Monroe Doctrine. But the British favored the policy, and Americans knew they would help to enforce it. The Monroe Doctrine became the basis of American ***foreign policy*** for nearly a century.

Sectionalism and the Missouri Compromise

Growth of Sectional Differences. In the early 1800s, the United States consisted of three main sections: the North, the South, and the West. The North and the South were divided by the boundary between Pennsylvania and Maryland, and the West was the land beyond the Appalachian Mountains.

Seeds of ***sectionalism*** began to sprout during the Era of Good Feelings. Four main issues contributed to the discord: cheap land, the national bank, protective tariffs, and slavery.

Westerners thought the federal government should sell land cheaply to settlers and make it easy for people to develop the West. They favored internal improvements, which were government-paid projects such as roads and canals, to improve transportation. Many Westerners opposed the Bank of the United States, believing it made the federal government too strong and hindered development. Some Westerners supported tariffs and slavery, but others opposed them.

Northerners opposed cheap land, considering land a national treasure that should bring in considerable revenue. Most of them favored a national bank as well as high tariffs to protect their manufacturing. Many opposed internal improvements because they benefited the West more than the North. Finally, most Northerners were firmly opposed to slavery.

People in the South opposed cheap land and internal improvements, and they tended to oppose a national bank. They especially opposed high tariffs because these raised the prices of manufactured goods, which the South imported. Also, Southerners felt that slavery was necessary, and this feeling grew stronger as cotton production soared. Slavery became the most divisive issue of all.

Most or all of these issues grew out of the love of money, which the Bible calls "the root of all evil" (1 Timothy 6:10). What a terrible crop of evil would come forth in the succeeding years!

State	Year Admitted	Slave or Free
Louisiana	1812	Slave
Indiana	1816	Free
Mississippi	1817	Slave
Illinois	1818	Free
Alabama	1819	Slave

The Missouri Compromise. A number of new states were formed in the early 1800s. Each one entered the Union as a slave state or a free state (see the chart). For a time the number of free states and slave states remained equal, so the slave and free states had equal representation in the Senate.

Then in 1819, Missouri applied for admission as a new state. This caused great contention in Congress, for Missouri would doubtless become a slave state—thus upsetting the balance in the Senate. No solution could be found until later in 1819, when Maine applied for admission to the Union. Then the Missouri Compromise was introduced, proposing that Maine be admitted as a free state and Missouri as a slave state. Moreover, in the rest of the Louisiana Territory, slavery would be forbidden north of a line drawn at 36°30' N, but it would be permitted south of that line.

The Missouri Compromise passed in 1820. But the heated debate over slavery foreshadowed a far more violent conflict in the years to come.

John Quincy Adams (1767–1848) was the sixth president of the United States. He served from 1825 to 1829 and was a Democratic-Republican.

A Troubled Presidency

When John Quincy Adams (son of former president John Adams) took office in 1825, he faced problems at once. Andrew Jackson, his opponent, felt that Adams had been elected unfairly. Since no candidate in 1824 had received a majority of electoral votes, the

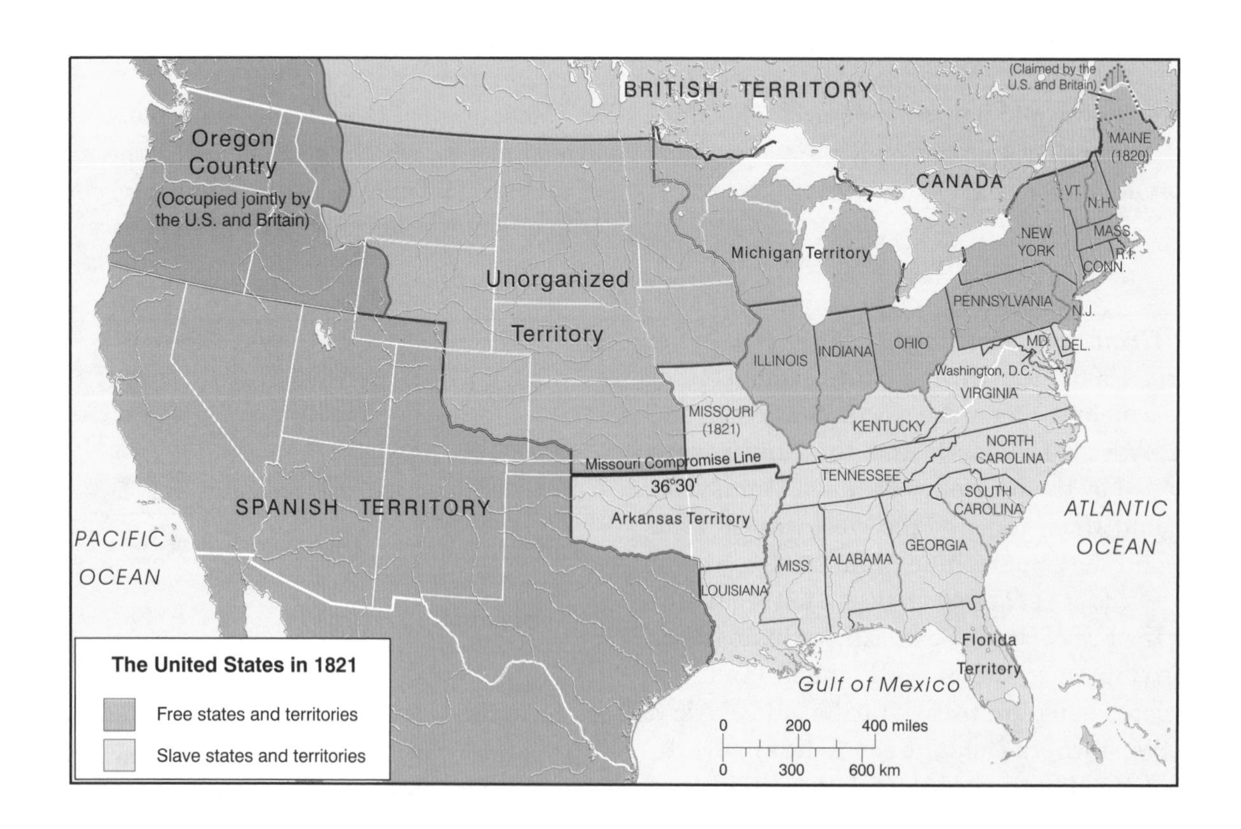

House had chosen John Quincy Adams—even though Jackson had received a larger number of popular votes. Jackson determined to defeat Adams in the next election. This led to a split in the Democratic-Republican Party. Those who supported Andrew Jackson were known as Democrats. Supporters of John Quincy Adams and Henry Clay called themselves National Republicans.

Adams never became popular with the people. He proposed a program of many internal improvements, which seemed to show that he wanted to increase the federal government's power too much. One of his main accomplishments was the passage of a high protective tariff in 1828. But President Adams would be defeated by Andrew Jackson, a common man with a new style of leadership.

Focus for Thought

1. Why were the first years of James Monroe's presidency called the Era of Good Feelings?
2. Why did conflict arise over the Bank of the United States?
3. Why was the Transcontinental Treaty (alternate name for the Adams-Onís Treaty) especially significant?
4. Explain in your own words each of the three points of the Monroe Doctrine.
5. The following table shows four main issues that contributed to sectionalism. Copy the table and fill it in by writing whether each section favored (*F*) or opposed (*O*) that issue. If support in a section was mixed, write *M*.

	North	South	West
Cheap land			
National bank			
Protective tariffs			
Slavery			

6. How did the Missouri Compromise settle the issue of slavery in Missouri and in the rest of the Louisiana Territory?

2. THE AGE OF JACKSON

President Andrew Jackson was a common man, and he put common people in many government positions during his two terms as president (1829–1837). This brought changes in American society and politics. Jackson's two administrations were also occupied by battles between sectional interests, and between supporters and opponents of Jackson.

Jacksonian Democracy

A Common Man. Andrew Jackson was the first president to be born in a log cabin. (All the former presidents were from wealthy, aristocratic families.) As one of the common people, Jackson provides an example of the truth that "the most High ruleth in the kingdom of men, and giveth it to whomsoever he will, and setteth up over it the basest [lowest] of men" (Daniel 4:17). Jackson believed that common people could participate in government and that the government should consider

Andrew Jackson (1767–1845) was the seventh president of the United States. He served from 1829 to 1837 and was a Democrat.

all citizens to be equal. His "common man ideal" made America more democratic as the common people gained a stronger voice in government.

Jackson's ideal, called Jacksonian democracy, soon spread across the nation. One reason was the influence of the western frontier, where people saw everyone as equal because everyone faced similar struggles. Numerous states revised their constitutions to give common people more rights, and elections became more democratic. For example, states began to abolish the requirement that voters must own property, and this allowed more people to vote.

Andrew Jackson favored a strict interpretation of the Constitution. He believed in a limited government that gave individual citizens plenty of freedom to succeed in business or other endeavors. The motto of his administration was "That government governs best which governs least."

The Spoils System. President Jackson dismissed many officeholders from the previous administration and replaced them with his supporters. This practice became known as the ***spoils system*** because "to the victor belong the spoils." In this case, the spoils were government jobs that went to friends, relatives, and other supporters. President Jackson did not begin this practice, but he used it on a wider scale than previous presidents had done.

The Nullification Crisis

The Issue of Protective Tariffs. When the Adams administration had passed a high tariff bill in 1828, people in the South strongly opposed it. They called it the "tariff of abominations" because they believed it benefited the North at the expense of the other states. The protective tariff raised the prices of goods because it limited foreign competition. Consequently, northern factories made higher profits because they could charge more for their products.

In the South, people bought many goods instead of manufacturing them. They had to either pay higher prices for imports because of the tariff, or pay higher prices to northern factories. Southerners greatly resented this; for they reasoned that if the North could force the tariff upon them, the North could also force them to abolish slavery.

The Issue of States' Rights. South Carolina led the opposition to protective tariffs. Especially outspoken was Vice President John C. Calhoun, who wrote a strong protest against them. Calhoun also wrote articles promoting ***states' rights***. This concept was based on the idea that the Union held only those powers that the states had agreed to give it. Since the states had granted those powers, Calhoun reasoned, the individual states were supreme over the federal government.

John Calhoun (1782–1850), of South Carolina, was a war hawk leader who promoted war with Great Britain in 1812. He also strongly promoted states' rights.

Daniel Webster speaking in reply to Hayne. This speech ended with Webster's famous "liberty and union" statement.

In 1830, a famous debate about states' rights took place between Senator Robert Hayne of South Carolina, who supported states' rights, and Senator Daniel Webster of Massachusetts, who argued that the Union was supreme over the states. Webster closed his oration with these words: "Liberty and union, now and forever, one and inseparable." The Webster-Hayne debates focused on a major issue that would not be settled until the Civil War.

The Issue of Nullification. In 1832, Congress passed a new tariff law that again was opposed by South Carolina. That year South Carolina decided to ***nullify*** the 1828 and 1832 tariff laws. That is, it would declare those laws null and void within the borders of that state. Leaders in South Carolina threatened to ***secede*** (sih SEED) from the Union if the federal government tried to force them to accept the tariffs. (Both nullification and secession are extreme applications of states' rights.)

Andrew Jackson opposed states' rights. When he heard of South Carolina's plans for nullification, he became furious and made plans to use military measures to enforce the laws. It is said that he threatened to "hang Calhoun as high as Haman" if South Carolina seceded.

State nullification of federal laws would have led to chaos and breakup of national unity. The crisis was resolved before military force was needed when Henry Clay helped to work out a compromise tariff bill. This bill, passed in 1833, called for a gradual reduction in tariffs over ten years. South Carolina accepted the compromise tariff, but it did not give up the idea of states' rights and nullification. That issue would also be settled by the Civil War.

Indian Removal

Indians were not considered United States citizens until 1924. Each tribe was considered a foreign nation to be dealt with by treaties and armies. In the early 1800s, many Americans believed that all Indians should be moved west of the Mississippi. Some people said that moving the Indians was necessary for them to be preserved as a people. But the main reason for wanting to move them was that many Indians lived on good cotton-growing land, whereas the land west of the Mississippi was considered barren. (Another reason was that gold had been discovered on Indian land in Georgia.)

Jackson had fought many battles against Indians, as in the War of 1812 and on his Florida campaign in 1818. As president, Jackson removed over forty thousand Indians, made over ninety treaties for removal of the Indians, and gained millions of acres of Indian land in the East in exchange for lands in the West.

Removal of the Five Civilized Tribes. The Creek, Cherokee, Chickasaw, Choctaw, and Seminole Indians lived in the area of Tennessee, Alabama, Georgia, and Florida. These tribes were called civilized because they had adopted many practices of the white men. The Cherokee especially had learned to operate farms, sawmills, gristmills, and blacksmith shops. Christian missionaries worked among these Indians. A Cherokee leader

Sequoyah (1770?–1843), a Cherokee Indian leader, devised an alphabet for writing the Cherokee language.

Indian Removal to Western Reservations

Eastern homelands
Indian reservations established 1820–1840
Removal routes
Boundaries in 1830
Present-day boundaries

named Sequoyah (for whom sequoia trees are named) had even developed an alphabet for writing his native language.

In 1830, Congress passed the Indian Removal Act, which provided that the Indians be removed with their consent. The Chickasaw and Choctaw consented, but most of the Cherokee did not. Therefore, the federal government sent soldiers to force the Cherokee from their homes and start them moving west. Their journey of 1,200 miles (1,931 km) to Oklahoma in 1838 and 1839 became known as the Trail of Tears. About a fourth of the Cherokee nation perished on the way.

> *One observer gave the following description of the Trail of Tears as the Cherokee passed through Kentucky.*
>
> The forward part of the train was just pitching their tents for the night, and though some thirty or forty wagons were already stationed, we found the road literally filled with the procession for about 3 miles (4.8 km) in length. A great many ride on horseback and multitudes go on foot. Even aged females, apparently ready to drop into the grave, were traveling with heavy burdens attached to the back on sometimes frozen ground and sometimes muddy streets, with no covering for the feet except what nature had given them. We learned from inhabitants on the road where the Indians had passed that they buried fourteen or fifteen at every stopping place and that they will not travel on the Sabbath. Then they must not merely stop; they must worship. As a whole, they carry in their countenances everything but the appearance of happiness. Some have a downcast, dejected look; others a wild, frantic expression. Most of them seemed intelligent and refined. Several missionaries were accompanying them to their destination.

Cherokee on the Trail of Tears. About 4,000 Cherokee died because of cold weather and insufficient food, and because the escorting soldiers refused to stop so that sick and exhausted people could recover.

"Woe to them that devise iniquity, and . . . practise it, because it is in the power of their hand. And they covet fields, and take them by violence; and houses, and take them away: so they oppress a man and his house, even a man and his heritage" (Micah 2:1, 2).

Wars With the Indians. The Seminole Indians refused to move. Some escaped to the Everglades in Florida; and there, led by Chief Osceola, they fought the seven-year Seminole War against the United States. (This is sometimes called the second Seminole War because of an earlier war fought from 1816 to 1818.) By 1842, the Seminole Indians were defeated and forced to move west.

The Sauk and Fox Indians of Wisconsin and Illinois had been forced to move west in 1831. Chief Black Hawk of the Sauk Indians led them back to Illinois in 1832, but these Indians were defeated later that year in the Black Hawk War. In general, these injustices were committed by white men who considered themselves Christians.

Left: Seminole chief Osceola (1804?–1838) led the Indians in the Seminole War. He was successful in battle but was captured by treachery. ***Right:*** Black Hawk (1767–1838) was a chief of the Sauk Indians. His effort to regain their lands east of the Mississippi led to the Black Hawk War.

Economic Developments

The Bank Controversy. Like many people from the West, Andrew Jackson distrusted the second Bank of the United States. He believed that it had too much power, that it gave special privileges to the wealthy, and that it was not even constitutional. Jackson vehemently opposed the bank, saying, "The bank is trying to kill me, but I will kill it!"

Jackson worked against the Bank of the United States in both of his terms as president. First he vetoed a bill to recharter the bank. Finally he decided to destroy the bank by removing the government deposits and transferring them to numerous state banks that became known as wildcat banks. (Jackson's enemies called them "pet banks.") In 1836, the Bank of the United States ceased to exist as a national bank.

Prosperity and Hardship. The economy boomed in the 1830s for several reasons. The wildcat banks and others loaned money freely, especially for land purchases. The federal government sold so much western land that it paid off the national debt and accumulated a surplus! Land values rose sharply, and it seemed as if prosperity had come to stay.

But the prosperity rested on shaky foundations. Banks made loans too freely, and they issued much paper money without assets to back it up. In his second administration, President Jackson became alarmed about the reckless borrowing and spending. He feared that the government was selling land to speculators for worthless paper money. So in 1836, Jackson issued the Specie Circular, which said that government land could be sold only for specie (gold and silver coins).

This proclamation helped to bring on the Panic of 1837—after Jackson left office—because people rushed to the banks to exchange their paper money for gold and silver coins. When the banks had too little specie for all the paper money they had issued, they were forced to close, leaving many people with worthless paper money. Land values fell so much that land became worth less than people had paid for it, and often less than they had borrowed for it!

The Panic of 1837 led to the first major depression that the United States had known. "Wilt thou set thine eyes upon that which is not? for riches certainly make themselves wings; they fly away as an eagle toward heaven" (Proverbs 23:5).

End of Jackson's Administration. Jackson had been a strong, vibrant president. He had made many enemies because of his strong views and forceful attacks. But he also had many friends and supporters, and his influence was so strong that several presidents after him followed his ideas and policies.

Focus for Thought

7. What were the two main ideas of Jacksonian democracy?
8. Why did the South oppose protective tariffs?
9. a. On what basis did South Carolina say that a federal law could be nullified?
   b. How would nullification have affected the United States?
10. a. Around 1830, why did many white people want to move the Indians to lands across the Mississippi?
    b. What was the Trail of Tears?
11. Why did President Jackson oppose the Bank of the United States?
12. Explain what brought on the Panic of 1837.

3. THE RISE OF THE WHIGS

Opposition to Jackson and the Democrats became organized in the mid-1830s as the Whig Party. Nevertheless, Jackson's designated successor, **Martin Van Buren,** was easily elected in 1836. But four years later the opposing party won the election, and a troubled Whig administration began.

Opposing Political Parties, 1796–1840	
Federalists	Democratic-Republicans
(Federalists disappear)	Democratic-Republicans
National Republicans replace Federalists	Democratic-Republicans (Democrats)
Whigs replace National Republicans	Democrats (same as today's Democrats)

The Whig Party

Around 1832, a new political party began forming to oppose President Jackson. This party included bankers, businessmen, and others who favored a national bank, high tariffs, and a strong federal government. They were called Whigs because they opposed "King Andrew" just as Whigs had opposed King George III in the American Revolution.

Andrew Jackson let it be known that he favored Martin Van Buren, the vice president during his second term, as his successor. To oppose Van Buren, the Whigs chose three candidates, one from each section. The Whigs hoped that no candidate would receive a majority of electoral votes, and then the House would need to choose the new president. However, Van Buren defeated the Whigs by a clear majority of votes.

Martin Van Buren (1782–1862) was the eighth president of the United States. He served from 1837 to 1841 and was a Democrat.

The Van Buren Administration

A Financial Crisis. The Panic of 1837 struck the nation almost as soon as Van Buren took office. With banks closing, businesses closed too; thousands of people lost their jobs and suffered severe hardships. According to one newspaper of that time, 90 percent of the factories in the East closed. This depression lasted until 1843.

President Van Buren did little to fight the depression, for he thought it should be relieved by the people and the states. This was in keeping with his belief in little government interference in business affairs and strict interpretation of the Constitution. Whigs and others blamed Van Buren for the depression, even though its causes had more to do with Jackson's policies than Van Buren's.

The Independent Treasury Act. Since Jackson had taken the United States Treasury deposits out of the national bank, government money had been deposited in state banks. Van Buren wanted to completely separate the government's money from banks because he believed the Treasury deposits had encouraged the state banks to lend too much. To prevent another panic from occurring, he proposed an independent treasury with the government's money stored at Washington, D.C., and in subtreasuries around the country. Congress passed the Independent Treasury Act in 1840.

Poster used in Harrison's "log cabin campaign" of 1840. The log cabin symbolized Harrison's humble origin as opposed to the aristocratic Martin Van Buren.

William Henry Harrison (1773–1841) was the ninth president of the United States. He served in 1841 and was a Whig.

The Whigs in Power

The Brief Term of William Henry Harrison. By 1840, the Whigs organized a strong campaign to defeat Van Buren and the Democrats. The Whig candidate, **William Henry Harrison**, became popular through tactics that included speeches, parades, and songs. His slogan was "Tippecanoe and Tyler too!"—referring to Harrison, the victor in the Battle of Tippecanoe, and **John Tyler**, the candidate for vice president. The campaign succeeded, and Harrison became the first Whig to be elected president.

The new administration got off to a rough start. Harrison delivered an inaugural address of record length—over an hour and a half—without wearing hat or overcoat on a cold, drizzly March 4. He caught a severe cold that later developed into pneumonia. At the same time, many Whigs were seeking their share in the "spoils" of governmental offices to be granted by the president. The pressure was too much for the 68-year-old Harrison; and on April 4, 1841, he became the first president to die in office. Harrison's administration had lasted only one month.

Difficulties in the Tyler Administration. When Vice President John Tyler succeeded to the office of president, he faced a difficult situation. No vice president had ever taken the office of a deceased president before. Was Tyler really the president, or was he merely acting as president? Tyler believed that he was president as fully as Harrison had been. He and others succeeded to the presidential office on that basis, but the question was not officially answered until the Twenty-fifth Amendment was added to the Constitution in 1967.

President Tyler's opponents made the most of the uncertainty surrounding "his accidency," as they called him. Henry Clay, his rival in the Whig Party, determined to have his proposals enacted regardless of Tyler. He introduced two bills for a national bank, and Congress passed them. But the president

John Tyler (1790–1862) was the tenth president of the United States. He served from 1841 to 1845 and was a Whig.

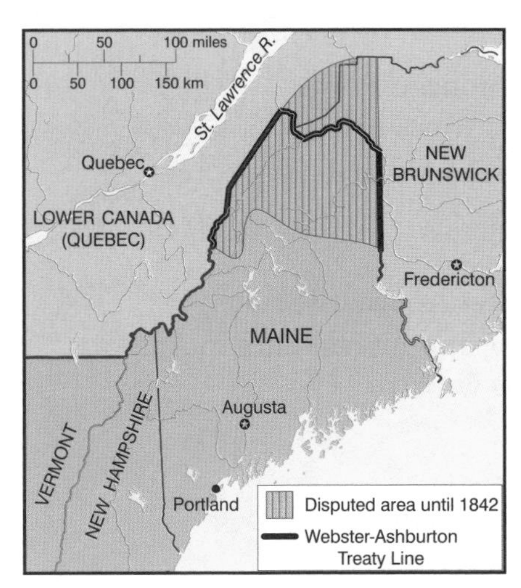

The Webster-Ashburton Treaty Line

vetoed both bills—with the result that his entire Cabinet resigned except for Daniel Webster. Finally the Whigs expelled President Tyler from their party. Some even made an unsuccessful attempt to impeach the president.

Disputes at Home and Abroad. Differences between the United States and Great Britain had almost led to war during Van Buren's term. One point of disagreement was the boundary between Maine and Canada. In 1842, Secretary of State Daniel Webster resolved this issue by negotiating the Webster-Ashburton Treaty. It stated that the disputed area would be divided between Canada and Maine, and it also established the United States–Canadian border between Lake Superior and the Lake of the Woods.

A major issue later in Tyler's term was whether or not Texas should be admitted to the Union as a state. This dispute led to sectional conflict that opened further wounds in the Union. The story of Texas is told in Chapter 14.

The troubled Whig administration came to an end after 1844 when James Polk, a Democrat, was elected president. In Polk's administration, the influence of Andrew Jackson would live on.

Focus for Thought

13. a. How did the Whigs receive their name?
    b. What things did they favor?
14. Why did President Van Buren do little to relieve the depression after the Panic of 1837?
15. What things did the Whigs do to help William Henry Harrison win election as president?
16. Why did William Henry Harrison serve such a brief term as president?
17. a. What uncertainty surrounded Tyler's administration?
    b. Why did Tyler's own party (the Whigs) turn against him?
18. What borders were established by the Webster-Ashburton Treaty?

Historical Highlights

A. Matching: Presidents

You will use each answer twice.

a. James Monroe
b. John Quincy Adams
c. Andrew Jackson
d. Martin Van Buren
e. William Henry Harrison
f. John Tyler

1. First president to die in office.
2. Son of a former president.
3. President when Webster-Ashburton Treaty was negotiated.

4. President who represented the common man.
5. President during a split in the Democratic-Republican Party.
6. President during the Panic of 1837.
7. First vice president to fill the position of a president who died in office.
8. President during the Era of Good Feelings.
9. First Whig president.
10. President who had served as vice president under Andrew Jackson.
11. President who issued a statement against European interference in America.
12. President who had thousands of Indians moved west.

B. Matching: Terms

a. Adams-Onís Treaty
b. American System
c. Era of Good Feelings
d. foreign policy
e. Independent Treasury Act
f. Missouri Compromise
g. Monroe Doctrine
h. nullify
i. protective tariff
j. secede
k. sectionalism
l. Seminole War
m. Specie Circular
n. spoils system
o. states' rights
p. Trail of Tears
q. Transcontinental Treaty
r. Webster-Ashburton Treaty
s. Whigs

1. To withdraw formally from an organization.
2. Agreement about slavery in the Louisiana Territory.
3. Treaty that settled disagreements over boundaries with Canada.
4. Proclamation stating (1) that America was no longer to be colonized by European nations, (2) that European nations were not to interfere in the affairs of American nations, and (3) that the United States would not interfere in the affairs of European nations.
5. Henry Clay's plan for a tariff to protect manufacturers, finance internal improvements, and establish a national bank.
6. Struggle between the United States and Osceola and his tribe over Indian removal to lands in the West.
7. Political party that opposed Andrew Jackson.
8. Time of national unity and harmony, with only one political party.
9. Journey of Cherokee Indians who were forced to move west.
10. Treaty with Spain that gained Florida and established borders (two answers).
11. To set aside; declare void.
12. Idea that states have more power than the federal government.
13. Law by which government money was separated from private banks.
14. Statement that only gold and silver would be accepted for government lands.
15. The manner of a nation or national leader in relating to other nations.
16. Practice in which the winner of an election rewards his supporters with government positions.
17. High tax on imports, designed to limit competition from foreign merchants.
18. Devotion to the interests of a local region rather than the whole nation.

C. True or False

Write whether each statement is true (T) *or false* (F).

1. Andrew Jackson promoted many of the same ideas as the Federalist Party had.
2. Andrew Jackson was honored by the common people because he identified with them.
3. Jackson vigorously exercised the powers of the presidency.
4. Jackson closed the Bank of the United States because it interfered with the economic stability of the nation.
5. Jackson supported states' rights and sided with South Carolina on the issue of nullification.
6. The Whig Party was more like the Federalists than like the Democratic-Republicans.
7. Martin Van Buren thought the federal government should make strong efforts toward economic improvement after the Panic of 1837.

D. Deeper Discussion

1. Could the young United States have enforced the Monroe Doctrine at the time it was proclaimed? Explain.
2. a. In what ways might protective tariffs be helpful?
   b. How might they be harmful?
3. What would happen if any state could declare a national law null and void?
4. a. What were the underlying causes of sectionalism?
   b. In what ways could the sections actually have helped each other?
5. How might Jackson's economic policies have contributed to the Panic of 1837?
6. The Bible says that people are not to "trust in uncertain riches" or to lay up treasures on earth, "where moth and rust doth corrupt, and where thieves break through and steal."
   a. How do the economic events of the Jacksonian Era, especially the panics of 1819 and 1837, demonstrate the truth of these verses?
   b. How should Christians respond? (See 1 Timothy 6:17–19 and Matthew 6:19, 20, 33.)

E. Chronology and Geography

1. On your map entitled "The States of the United States," draw the borders of the eleven states admitted between 1791 and 1821. The admission dates for these new states are given on maps on pages 234, 248, and 250.
   a. Label the states with their names and dates of admission.
   b. Color these eleven states a different color from the original thirteen states.
   c. Start a legend showing what each color represents.
   d. Memorize the names and locations of these states.
2. Do the following on your map entitled "Territorial Growth of the United States." (See maps on pages 248 and 259 for the location of the treaty lines.)
   a. Draw and label the British Treaty Line of 1818.
   b. Draw and label the Spanish Treaty Line of 1819.
   c. Label the area south of the British Treaty Line that was ceded by Britain in 1818. Color it a different color from the one you used for the United States in 1783.
   d. Label East Florida and West Florida. Use a third color to color them.
   e. Use a different color to color the remainder of the Louisiana Purchase after the treaties of 1818 and 1819.
   f. Draw and label the Webster-Ashburton Line, and color the area Britain ceded in 1842.
3. Memorize the names of the first ten presidents in order.

Race between steamboats *Robert E. Lee* and *Natchez*. The use of steam engines on water and rail transformed America in the first half of the 1800s.

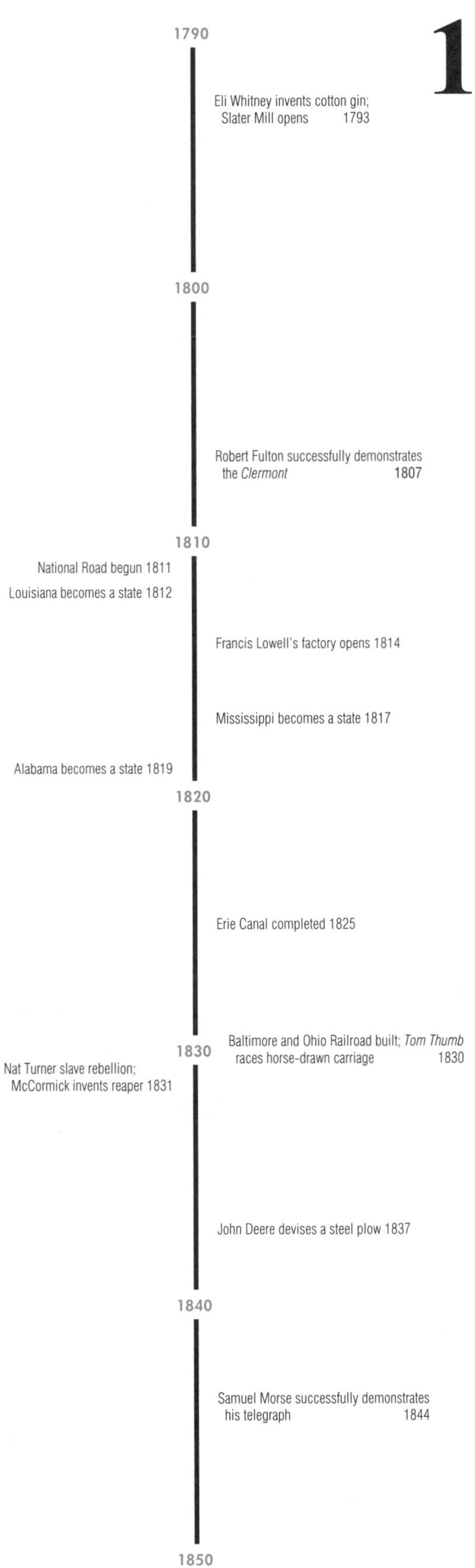

13 National Development

1. The Industrial North
   - The Industrial Revolution
   - Advances in Transportation and Communication
   - Social Changes

2. The "Cotton Kingdom" South and the Growing West
   - King Cotton
   - Southern Agriculture and Society
   - Westward Movement
   - Western Agriculture and Commerce

3. The Reform Spirit
   - Social Movements
   - Religious Movements
   - Developments Among the Mennonites

"[God] changeth the times and the seasons: he removeth kings, and setteth up kings: he giveth wisdom unto the wise, and knowledge to them that know understanding."

Daniel 2:21

National Development

Focus for Reading

In 1825, a hymn writer penned the following words: "Chance and change are busy ever; / Worlds decay, and ages move." These lines are surely true of the period in which they were written. You saw in Chapter 12 that the first half of the 1800s was a time of rapid political change. This chapter continues the theme of change, but focuses on the economic and social changes of that period. What changes occurred in farming, industry, and society? What caused these changes? In this chapter, three sections discuss the economic and social changes of the years 1815 to 1850.

1. The Industrial North
2. The "Cotton Kingdom" South and the Growing West
3. The Reform Spirit

1. THE INDUSTRIAL NORTH

In 1815, the Northeast (including the Middle Atlantic States and New England) was primarily a region of trade, seafaring, small farming, and manufacturing things by hand. But it rapidly developed into a region of factories until, by 1850, most of the manufactured products in the United States came from the Northeast. Steam locomotives puffed across miles of steel rails, and steamboats churned on all the navigable rivers in the land. Numerous large cities had appeared, and the United States was well on its way to becoming an industrialized nation.

The Industrial Revolution

Advent of the Industrial Revolution. The ***Industrial Revolution*** was the change from producing handmade goods at home to producing machine-made goods in factories. This change began in England in the late 1700s when weavers first began making cloth in textile factories. They did this by using new machines that could spin thread and weave cloth much faster than was possible by hand. The English carefully guarded their weaving technology. They passed laws saying that no textile workers, machines, or plans for such machines could leave the country.

But in 1789, 21-year-old **Samuel Slater** disguised himself as a farm worker and came to the United States. Having memorized the design of the machines, Slater built the equipment for a new cotton-textile mill, located at Pawtucket, Rhode Island. This was the first successful spinning mill in the United States.

Restoration of Slater Mill in Pawtucket, Rhode Island. In the foreground is the Blackstone River, which powered the mill.

It began production in 1793; and by 1815, Slater was operating a weaving factory. Thus the Industrial Revolution came to America.

This revolution caused some great changes. Formerly, households either made their own things such as clothes and shoes, or craftsmen made things by hand one item at a time. When the Industrial Revolution

Weaving with power looms. The machinery was driven by large pulleys and belts that were turned by water wheels.

came, workers began going to factories and operating machines that made things. The factories produced large numbers of goods in a short time, with the result that manufactured products became much cheaper. People began buying goods in stores rather than making them at home.

Further Developments in Industry. The use of ***interchangeable parts*** also contributed to the Industrial Revolution. In 1798, **Eli Whitney** contracted to make ten thousand guns for the United States Army. He began by making machines that could produce barrels, triggers, stocks, and other parts that were exactly the same. Then he put the parts together, thus producing guns much more rapidly than in the old way of making complete guns one at a time. And if a part broke or wore out, it could easily be replaced with a new part.

Several other developments contributed to the early growth of industry. In 1814, **Francis Lowell** built a factory that had spinning machines to make thread as well as power looms to weave cloth. This was the first factory to do all the steps of manufacturing at one place. The idea worked well, and other American factories soon applied the same principle in making many other products.

Growth of Industry in the North. Industry grew much faster in the North than in other sections of the United States. The land was not as profitable for agriculture, and New England and the Middle Atlantic States had iron ore and other raw materials needed for manufacturing. The North also had an abundance of energy to power its factories: water in swift streams, and lumber and coal for steam power. Finally, the many natural harbors along the coast made it easy for ships to bring raw materials for the factories and to carry finished products away to markets around the world.

Advances in Transportation and Communication

Ocean Travel. American merchants, many from New England, sent their ships throughout the world for trade. In 1790, Captain Robert Gray became the first American to sail around the world. Whaling also became important in New England. Whalers hunted sperm whales for their oil and whalebone, and they made great profits in this hazardous occupation.

New types of shipping increased trade. One advance was the use of larger vessels to carry more cargo. Another was the advent of ships called packets, which made regular trips between New York and London. Americans

The clipper ship *Great Republic,* which had a length of 325 feet (99 m). Clipper ships got their name from the way they "clipped" off the miles. One traveled 465 miles (748 km) in a 24-hour period, a record not matched by a steamship until 25 years later.

Whaling

"They that go down to the sea in ships, that do business in great waters; these see the works of the LORD, and his wonders in the deep" (Psalm 107:23, 24).

Colonial whalers sailed the oceans in search of their huge prey. Besides learning about the habits of whales, these men also gained geographical knowledge that improved the accuracy of maps. Whalers visited many foreign ports, which increased American interest in places such as the Hawaiian Islands.

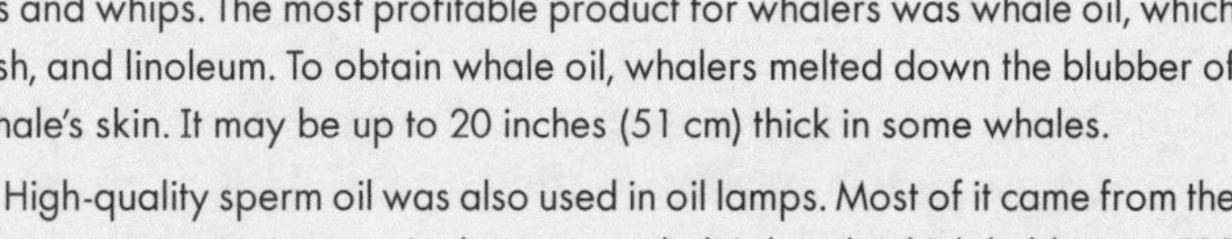

There are two types of whales—baleen and toothed. Of the baleen whales, American whalers hunted mostly the right whale and the bowhead whale. Baleen whales have whalebone (baleen) instead of teeth in their mouths to strain plankton out of seawater. Whalers also sought the sperm whale, which is the largest of the toothed whales.

Whalers risked their lives to obtain valuable products from whales. One product was whalebone, which has hundreds of thin plates of material similar to fingernails. Whalebone was used to make such things as brushes and whips. The most profitable product for whalers was whale oil, which was used in oil lamps and in lubricants, soaps, varnish, and linoleum. To obtain whale oil, whalers melted down the blubber of baleen whales. Blubber is the layer of fat under a whale's skin. It may be up to 20 inches (51 cm) thick in some whales.

High-quality sperm oil was also used in oil lamps. Most of it came from the large spermaceti organ in the sperm whale's head, which held up to 500 gallons (1,893 *l*) of sperm oil. Whalers cooked the spermaceti organ together with the blubber to obtain crude sperm oil. Then they chilled the oil, which caused a white wax (spermaceti) to solidify and separate from the pale yellow oil. Spermaceti was used to make ointments, cosmetic creams, and fine wax candles.

Whalers also searched for ambergris, which they sometimes found in the intestines of sperm whales. Fresh ambergris is a soft, dark substance with a foul smell. After exposure to sun, air, and salt water, it hardens and develops a pleasant scent. Ambergris served as a spice in Eastern countries and was used to fix the scent of perfumes in Europe and America. Some has been found floating in clumps on the sea or washed up on beaches. Because of its rarity, ambergris was worth more than its weight in gold.

Whales are mammals, so they must come to the surface to breathe. When a lookout on a colonial whaling ship saw a whale spouting (breathing through its blowhole), he pointed toward the whale and shouted, "There she blows!" Three or four open boats about 28 feet long (9 m) quickly set out, each equipped with barbed harpoons attached to long ropes and carrying a crew of six men. When a boat was as close to the whale as possible, the harpooner hurled one or two harpoons into the whale. Sometimes harpooners from several boats struck the whale at the same time.

The crew had to be ready for the panicked reaction of the wounded whale. If he dived deep into the sea, the rope had to be cut before the boat was pulled under. Sometimes the angry whale attacked a whaleboat, destroying it and making the men swim for their lives. Worse yet, a whale might ram the whaling ship itself and possibly cause it to sink. If that happened, the survivors floated in small boats on the open sea until they perished or were rescued.

Usually the wounded whale went for a high-speed race (called a "Nantucket sleigh ride") across the water, pulling the whaleboat behind. The crew held on and hauled in slack line as they could, until the whale grew weak and slowed down. More line was hauled in and the boat drew near its prey. Finally, a whaler stabbed the whale with a long lance, trying to hit a vital spot. If he was successful, the whale would thrash around in circles until it died.

"Nantucket sleigh ride"

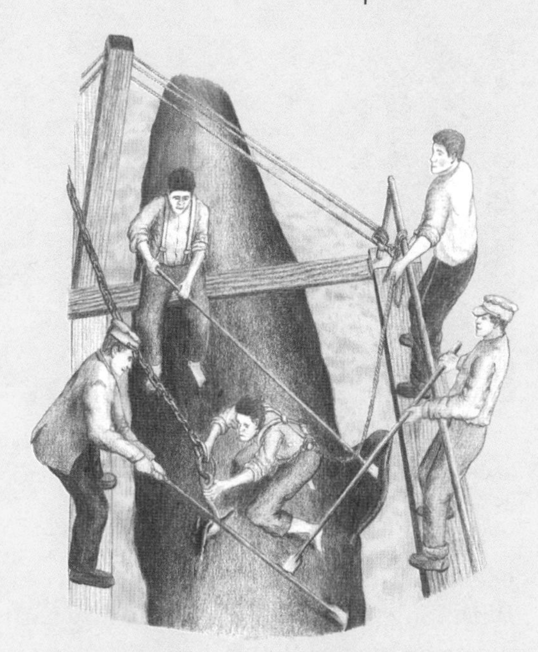

The dead whale was towed back to the ship, where it was strapped to the side and a platform placed over it. A man (secured by a lifeline) dropped onto the slippery whale and embedded a blubber hook in its side. He cut the flesh, and the hook was hoisted up with a piece of blubber perhaps 15 feet (5 m) long. The blubber was dropped on the deck. Then the hook was placed again, and the next piece of blubber was peeled off. The whale's body rolled around in the water until all the blubber was removed. If it was a sperm whale, the whalers cut into the stripped body to obtain the spermaceti organ and seek ambergris. Then the whale's body was abandoned for the sharks to eat.

On deck, the whalers cut the blubber into small pieces, boiled it down into oil, and stored the oil in barrels. They kept very busy when a whale was being caught and processed, but most days were dull and boring. Some men used their idle time to do scrimshaw, the art of carving intricate designs on the bones or teeth of whales. Whalers also made tools and toys of bone.

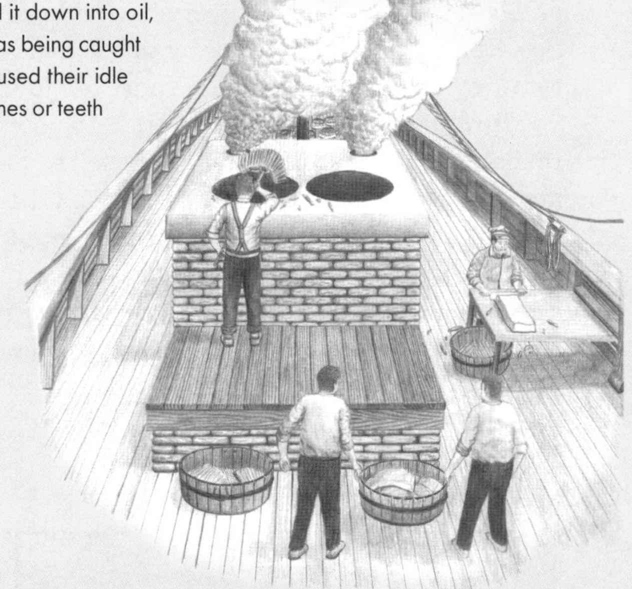

When a whaling ship arrived at a port city, the oil was tested by inspectors for quality and the barrels were marked for distribution. Some oil was purchased by peddlers who sold it door-to-door to housewives and machinists, and the rest went for commercial uses. Whalebone and ambergris were sold to industries. The whalers received a percentage of the profits from these sales. Some men eagerly signed up to go whaling again, but many went only once. A typical whaling crew consisted of different nationalities and races, and each man lived on the ship for months or years with only a wooden bunk and a sea chest to call his own.

American whaling was at its peak from 1820 to 1850, when more than 730 ships were sailing from ports mostly in Massachusetts and California. The industry declined over the next twenty years, especially after Edwin Drake drilled the first oil well in 1859. Petroleum soon replaced whale oil as the main source of lighting and lubricating products.

Stagecoach on Lancaster Pike in 1795. The milestone in the lower right corner is inscribed, "14 M[iles] to P[hiladelphia], 49 [miles] to L[ancaster]."

Fairview Inn along the National Road.

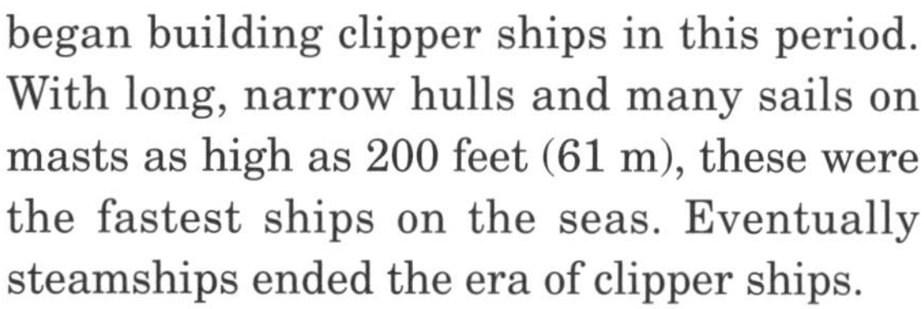

began building clipper ships in this period. With long, narrow hulls and many sails on masts as high as 200 feet (61 m), these were the fastest ships on the seas. Eventually steamships ended the era of clipper ships.

Roads. In general, early American roads were rough, rutted, and dusty or muddy. Rivers and streams usually had to be forded or ferried because there were no bridges. Sometimes logs were laid side by side to make corduroy roads, but these were quite bumpy.

Turnpikes provided one solution to poor roads. Private companies built these roads and charged tolls for using them. Among the first ones was the Lancaster Turnpike, built from 1792 to 1794 between Philadelphia and Lancaster, Pennsylvania. Some turnpikes had a stone foundation and a surface of crushed stone, making them fairly smooth and well drained. Others were surfaced by covering them with planks laid side by side.

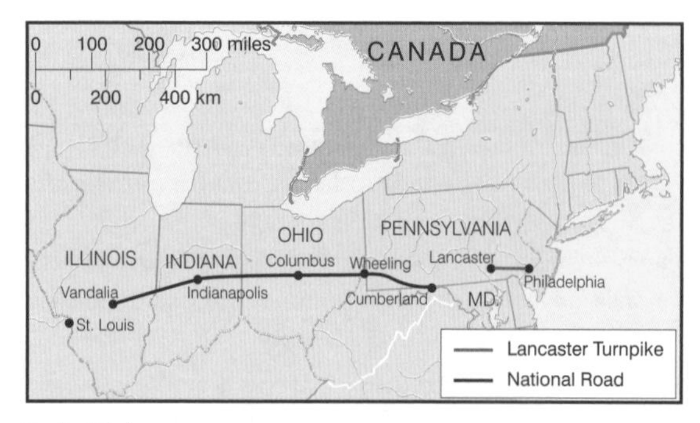

Early Highways

Beginning in 1811, the federal government built the National Road for improved transportation to the West. At first this road ran from Cumberland, Maryland, to Wheeling, Virginia (now West Virginia), on the Ohio River. Later it was extended to Vandalia, Illinois, and it eventually became known as U.S. Route 40. The National Road became a major highway traveled by stagecoaches, freight wagons, horseback riders, and droves of cattle and pigs. Today Interstate 70 follows much the same course.

Rivers and Canals. West of the Appalachians, the best means of transportation was by water, particularly the Mississippi River system. People used flatboats to float their products down the Mississippi to New Orleans, steering the boats with oars as the current carried them along. Upon reaching their destination, they tore the flatboats apart and used the lumber for building because it was not practical to take the boats back upstream.

Businessmen in New York wanted a share of the profitable trade on the Mississippi River. They envisioned a canal between Lake Erie and the Hudson River, by which western settlers could send their products down the Hudson River to New York City instead of to New Orleans. Led by Governor DeWitt Clinton, New York constructed the 363-mile (584-km) canal by 1825 at a cost of $7 million. But the

This view of the Erie Canal shows the five double locks at the village of Lockport. These locks raised and lowered boats 66 feet (20 m) to overcome the difference between the water levels of Lake Erie and the Genesee River.

Canal boat on the Erie Canal. Notice the passengers on the roof and the towline extending to the horses on shore.

Erie Canal soon paid for itself and generated profits of $3 million per year.

Canal boats were pulled by horses and mules walking on a towpath at 2 to 4 miles (3 to 6 km) per hour. They could transport much larger loads in much less time than wagons could carry. The price of shipping between Buffalo and New York dropped from $100 per ton by land to $15 per ton by canal, and the shipping time dropped from twenty days to eight. Soon other states developed canal systems too, and farmers in the West were able to ship their products to markets throughout the nation.

Steamboats. **James Watt** of Scotland built the first practical steam engine in 1769. Soon inventors were trying to use the steam engine to power ships. One of these inventors was **Robert Fulton**, who built a steamboat in 1807 that became known as the *Clermont*.

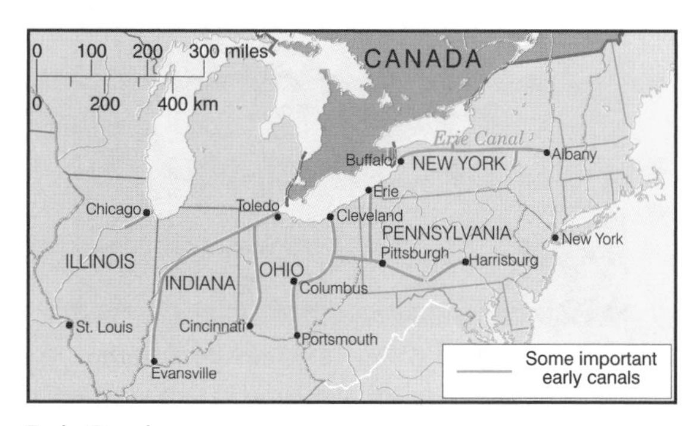

Early Canals

People called it "Fulton's Folly," but Fulton soon showed that his steamboat could travel the 300 miles (483 km) from New York City to Albany and back in only sixty-two hours. Steamboats quickly came into widespread use because of their speed and because they could travel upstream as well as downstream. By 1830, as many as two hundred of them were steaming up and down the Mississippi River.

Railroads. England built the first public railroad in the 1820s, but Americans were not far behind. The Baltimore and Ohio Railroad, built in 1830, extended 13 miles (21 km) from Baltimore. Upon this brief stretch, an engine named *Tom Thumb* raced a horse-drawn

The *Clermont,* built by Robert Fulton. Its 20-horsepower steam engine propelled the boat at an average of 5 miles per hour (8 km/h).

The *Tom Thumb,* one of the earliest railroad locomotives.

"Lightning express" trains of the middle 1800s.

carriage and lost the race when its engine broke down! In spite of this, the railroad age had dawned.

Rail travel was often troublesome and uncomfortable. Smoke and soot blew into passengers' faces, and sparks sometimes damaged their clothing. Accidents occurred frequently. Varying track gauges (widths) caused many difficulties in the early days. But gradually the problems were overcome and rail transportation improved. By 1850, the United States had almost 9,000 miles (14,484 km) of railroad tracks. Railroads put most canals out of business because trains could travel faster and go to more places than canal boats could.

The Telegraph. In the 1830s, **Samuel F. B. Morse** developed the telegraph to send messages over electric wires. Congress agreed that the federal government would finance a line between Baltimore and Washington, D.C.; and in 1844, Morse sent his first message over the line: "What hath God wrought!" (Numbers 23:23). From this beginning, telegraph wires extended across the country until they reached the Pacific coast by 1861.

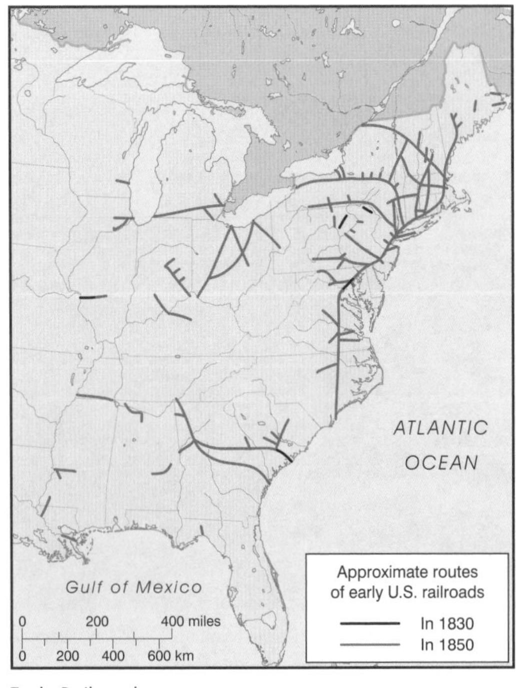

Early Railroads

Samuel F. B. Morse (1791–1872) and his telegraph. This invention speeded the communication of news and increased safety in transportation.

Left: Seamstress at a sewing machine in 1853. After the Industrial Revolution, workers such as this woman used machines to make thousands of products. ***Right:*** Chestnut Street, Philadelphia, in 1844. Cities grew rapidly in the 1800s as thousands of immigrants moved in.

The telegraph contributed to better communications and thus to safer rail travel. It allowed news to be spread over the country in a matter of minutes. God had allowed man to discover one of His marvelous principles and put it to practical use.

Social Changes

The industrial changes in the North were accompanied by changes in society itself. Among these were a new type of worker, the growth of cities, and increased immigration.

A New Type of Worker. The advent of factories caused great changes in the kind of work that people did. Instead of making items from start to finish, each worker now concentrated on just one step in the manufacturing process (such as spinning thread). He worked for perhaps fourteen or fifteen hours each day, and he repeated the same routine over and over, day after day.

Working conditions, as in Francis Lowell's factories, were not unpleasant at first, though in some places they were definitely worse by the 1840s. In spite of this, the factory system brought a general increase in the living standards of Americans.

Growth of Cities. Factories were a direct cause for the growth of cities. As workers moved near them, houses, stores, banks, and churches grew up; and soon canals and railroads linked one growing town to others. New York became the largest city of the early 1800s, and Philadelphia the second largest. Western towns like St. Louis, Cincinnati, and Chicago also grew rapidly.

The large cities often had vast areas of slums, where poor people lived in rundown houses along garbage-covered streets. Many of the tenements (apartment houses) lacked running water and were poorly heated and ventilated. But because of immigrants and rural people moving in, cities continued to grow with the factories.

Increased Immigration. Beginning in the 1820s, the number of immigrants coming to the United States increased greatly. In the 1830s, six hundred thousand came; in the 1840s, 1.7 million came. Most of these people were Irish or German, and all were looking for new opportunities. The Irish came especially in the late 1840s because their home country suffered from the Irish Potato Famine, which was caused by a blight. Wealthy immigrants usually moved west, but the poorer ones tended to settle in cities in the North and work in factories.

Some Americans despised the immigrants for various reasons, and sometimes fights and disturbances resulted. The newcomers were willing to work hard for little pay, which kept wages low for everyone. Many immigrants were Roman Catholic at a time when most Americans were Protestant. We need to remember that Christians must not despise anyone, but should follow the Bible teaching to "love thy neighbour as thyself."

Focus for Thought

1. What was the Industrial Revolution?
2. What contributions did Eli Whitney and Francis Lowell make to the growth of industry?
3. What were two reasons for the rapid growth of industry in the North?
4. Why did railroads put canals out of business?
5. What were two great improvements that resulted from use of the telegraph?
6. Name and describe three social changes that accompanied the industrial changes in the North.
7. For what reasons were immigrants despised by some Americans?

2. THE "COTTON KINGDOM" SOUTH AND THE GROWING WEST

Before 1860, the South had little industry and remained primarily agricultural. Because of slavery and the plantation system, a "planter aristocracy" controlled the South. Cotton was "king" because it dominated Southern commerce.

The West in the 1830s meant the area beyond the settled communities, sometimes termed the frontier. It extended from west of the Appalachians to the Mississippi River. As this area was settled, the West came to have a growing influence and importance in the United States.

King Cotton

Invention of the Cotton Gin. Southern farmers raised little cotton in colonial times. Removing seeds from cotton bolls was such slow work that a slave could clean only 1 pound (0.45 kg) of cotton per day. But in 1793, Eli Whitney invented the cotton gin to clean cotton mechanically. This machine increased a slave's daily production to 50 pounds (23 kg),

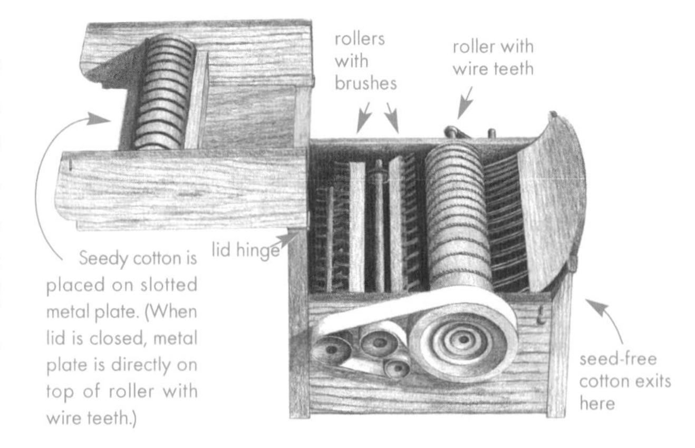

This diagram shows a small working model of Whitney's cotton gin with its lid open to expose the working parts. To operate it, the lid is closed, and seedy cotton is placed on the curved metal plate that has narrow slots in it. The cotton is drawn into the gin by turning the roller studded with many short wire teeth. These teeth pass through the slots in the metal plate and catch the cotton fibers. The fiber is pulled from the seeds because the seeds can not pass through the narrow slots. The seeds remain on the metal plate until disposed of. The fiber passes through the slots and is removed from the teeth by brushes mounted on a roller that revolves in the opposite direction. Other rollers with brushes direct the seedless cotton to the place where it is removed from the gin.

Eli Whitney (1765–1825) invented the cotton gin in 1793.

The cotton gin contributed to a great increase in cotton production and in the demand for slaves.

Many bales of cotton were shipped to textile mills in New England and in Europe. This heavily loaded riverboat is docked at Baton Rouge, Louisiana.

and soon large gins were built that could clean 1,000 pounds (454 kg) of cotton per day.

Because of the cotton gin, cotton became the most profitable crop in the South. At the same time, more and more cotton was needed for the factories in the North and in England. Cotton growing spread rapidly, and slaves became highly valuable because slave labor seemed to provide the only way to make cotton raising profitable. Whereas slavery had been on the verge of dying out, it now became firmly established in the South.

Development of the "Cotton Kingdom." Planters in the Southeast began raising cotton so intensively that the soil soon wore out. Seeking more fertile land, many planters then moved west and established great plantations in Alabama, Mississippi, and Louisiana. These areas grew so rapidly that Louisiana became a state in 1812, Mississippi in 1817, and Alabama in 1819. Together with Georgia, this region became known as the "Cotton Kingdom."

Cotton became one of the most important products of the United States. Whereas the total output was only ten thousand bales of cotton in 1793, production soared to over one hundred thousand bales in 1801 and over 2 million bales by 1850. Southerners believed that their own wealth as well as the nation's depended on cotton. So they said, "Cotton is king."

Southern Agriculture and Society

The Plantation System of the South. A plantation in the South had three characteristics: vast fields and large-scale production, a staple crop that provided the main income, and slave labor. The owner, called a planter, generally lived with his family in a mansion called the "big house." Around the big house were a kitchen, a smokehouse, and other outbuildings, as well as a barn and a grist mill. Nearby stood the overseer's house and the slave cabins.

Many planters lived in ease and luxury, with frequent parties and other kinds of entertainment. Only about 3 percent of Southerners were large plantation owners with more than fifty slaves, but this "planter aristocracy"

An overseer supervises slaves during cotton harvest.

Slave cabins at Savannah, Georgia, in 1903. The cabins originally housed slaves who were raised for market.

Stanton Hall in Natchez, Mississippi. Wealthy southern planters lived in elaborate mansions such as this one.

controlled the South. They held local government offices and served as congressmen.

Slaves did the work on a plantation. They might be field hands, household servants, or artisans like blacksmiths and carpenters. Most slaves were field hands who worked from dawn to dusk at plowing, planting, hoeing, and picking cotton. Household servants did housework, such as cooking meals, washing clothes, and caring for children. Artisans were in charge of maintaining the buildings and equipment.

The plantation system would not have worked without slaves, yet slavery hindered the industrial development of the South. Planters invested their money in land and slaves rather than in factories and stores. As a result, industry in the South lagged far behind that of the North. Even Southern farming remained backward. While fertilizers, new implements, and improved farming methods boosted crop yields in the North, most Southerners followed the same inefficient practices year after year.

Life of the Slaves. The slaves lived in rude one-room huts that had a fireplace but no windows. They slept on wooden planks for beds. In addition to doing the field work, slaves also had to get firewood and cook for themselves. The planter gave them their food (cornmeal, bacon, and molasses) and their clothing.

Treatment of slaves varied greatly. Some masters gave them plenty to eat and allowed

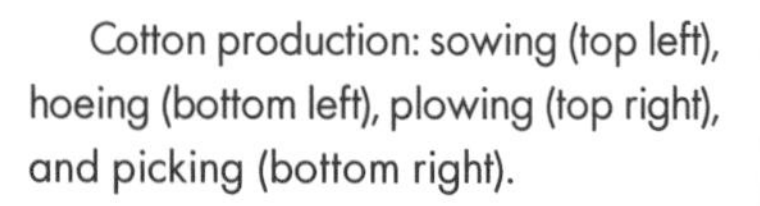

Cotton production: sowing (top left), hoeing (bottom left), plowing (top right), and picking (bottom right).

Slaves working in a rice field. Some plantations raised crops other than cotton, such as rice, indigo, sugar cane, and tobacco.

Slave auction at Richmond, Virginia. These auctions separated parents from children and even husbands from wives.

time off for recreation. Other masters provided slaves with barely enough food and made them work long hours every day. The whip was commonly used to keep slaves working.

Slavery was demeaning no matter how the slaves were treated. They had to work for a master rather than for themselves, and they lacked freedom and opportunities to develop their education and abilities. Many masters had little respect for family ties among blacks. They sold slave children to other masters, and they even sold husbands and wives separately if it was profitable to do so.

Slaves rebelled against their masters in various ways. Some simply worked slowly or even destroyed the master's property. Others ran away, hiding in swamps or trying to escape to a free state or Canada. A number took part in slave rebellions. One of these was Nat Turner, who led a rebellion in Virginia because he believed that God had chosen him to free the slaves. In 1831, he and about seventy followers killed fifty-seven white people before Turner was captured and hanged.

Southern whites punished slave uprisings severely. In the case of the Turner rebellion, whites retaliated by killing over one hundred blacks, guilty or innocent. States also passed ***slave codes*** saying that slaves could not buy their freedom or even be freed by their owners. These codes prohibited blacks from learning to read or write. They called for the death penalty for slaves taking part in revolts.

Many slaves found solace in religion. Heaven seemed real to them, since earth was a place of hardship and toil. Slaves often attended the Methodist and Baptist churches of the white people, but they had to sit in the balcony. Some slaves formed churches just for blacks. They sang songs known as spirituals, which emphasized heaven and deliverance.

The Bible does not directly condemn slavery, but it does give some basic principles relating to it. To the Colossians, Paul wrote, "Servants [slaves], obey in all things your masters according to the flesh" (3:22); and "Masters, give unto your servants that which is just and equal; knowing that ye also have a Master in heaven" (4:1). But since slavery itself is not "just and equal," the very practice of owning slaves is contrary to New Testament principle. It also violates the ideal of loving one's neighbor as himself.

Small Farms in the South. While a minority of planters controlled the South, most Southern whites lived on small farms rather than on plantations. For their own use, they raised food crops, such as corn, and they produced a few bales of cotton for a cash crop. Some of these farmers owned a slave or two, but in general they worked their own land with the help of their families. Actually, three-fourths of the Southern white population owned no slaves at all.

Cities in the South. The South was generally a section of rural communities. Of the ten largest cities in the nation, Baltimore and New Orleans were the only ones in the South. People living in cities included artisans, merchants, and professionals, such as doctors and lawyers. Numerous free blacks also lived in cities. Although better off than in slavery, they too lived with many restrictions, and they were in constant danger of being forced into slavery.

The following selections are the testimonies of former slaves. They show what life was like for a slave in the South. Each selection is taken from a longer writing and was someone's actual experience.

If at any time of my life more than another, I was made to drink the bitterest dregs of slavery, that time was during the first six months of my stay with Mr. Covey. We were worked in all weathers. It was never too hot or too cold; it could never rain, blow, hail, or snow too hard for us to work in the field. Work, work, work was scarcely more the order of the day than of the night. The longest days were too short for him, and the shortest nights were too long for him. I was somewhat unmanageable when I first went there, but a few months of this discipline tamed me. Mr. Covey succeeded in breaking me. I was broken in body, soul, and spirit. My natural elasticity was crushed, my intellect languished, the disposition to read departed, the cheerful spark that lingered about my eye died; the dark night of slavery closed in upon me; and behold, a man transformed into a brute!

Sunday was my only leisure time. I spent this in a sort of beast-like stupor, between sleep and wake, under some large tree. At times I would rise up, a flash of energetic freedom would dart through my soul, accompanied with a faint gleam of hope, that flickered for a moment, and then vanished. I sank down again, mourning over my wretched condition. I was sometimes prompted to take my life, and that of Covey, but was prevented by a combination of hope and fear. My suffering on this plantation seems now like a dream rather than stern reality.

Our house stood within a few rods of the Chesapeake Bay, whose broad bosom was ever white with sails from every quarter of the habitable globe. Those beautiful vessels robed in purest white, so delightful to the eye of freemen, were to me so many shrouded ghosts, to terrify and torment me with the thought of my wretched condition. I have often, in the deep stillness of a summer's Sabbath, stood all alone upon the lofty banks of that noble bay, and traced, with saddened heart and tearful eye, the countless number of sails moving off to the mighty ocean. The sight of these always affected me powerfully. My thoughts would compel utterance; and there, with no audience but the Almighty, I would pour out my soul's complaint, in my rude way, with an apostrophe to the moving multitude of ships: "You are loosed from your moorings, and are free; I am fast in my chains, and am a slave! You move merrily before the gentle gale, and I sadly before the bloody whip! You are freedom's swift-winged angels, that fly round the world; I am confined in bands of iron! O that I were free! O that I were on one of your gallant decks, and under your protecting wing! Alas! betwixt me and you the turbid waters roll. Go on, go on. O that I could also go! Could I but swim!

If I could fly! O, why was I born a man, of whom to make a brute! The glad ship is gone; she hides in the dim distance. I am left in . . . unending slavery. O God, save me! God, deliver me! Let me be free! Is there any God? Why am I a slave? I will run away. I will not stand it. Get caught or get clear, I'll try it. . . . Only think of it; one hundred miles straight north, and I am free! Try it? Yes! . . . Let but the first opportunity offer, and come what will, I am off. Meanwhile I will try to bear up under the yoke. I am not the only slave in the world. . . . It may be that my misery in slavery will only increase my happiness when I get free.

—Written by Frederick Douglass

I am convinced that in nine cases in ten, the hardships and sufferings of the coloured population of lower Virginia, are attributable to the poverty and distress of its owners. In many instances, an estate scarcely yields enough to feed and clothe the slaves in a comfortable manner, without allowing any thing for the support of the master and family; but it is obvious that the family must be first supported, and the slaves must be content with the surplus—and this, on a poor, worn-out tobacco plantation, is often very small, and wholly inadequate to the comfortable sustenance of the [slaves]. There, in many places, nothing is allowed to the poor Negro, but his peck of corn per week, without the sauce of a salt herring, or even a little salt itself.

Wretched as may be the state of the Negroes in their quarters, that of the master and his wife and daughters, is, in many instances, not much more enviable in the old apartments of the Great House. The sons and daughters of the family are gentlemen and ladies by birthright—and were the former to be seen at the plow, or the latter at the churn or the wash tub, the honor of the family would be stained, and the dignity of the house degraded. People must and will be employed about something; and if they cannot be usefully occupied, they will most surely engage in some pursuit wholly unprofitable. So it happens in Virginia—the young men spend their time in riding about the country, whilst they ought to be plowing or harrowing in the cornfield; and the young women are engaged in reading silly books, or visiting their neighboring houses, instead of attending to the dairy, or manufacturing cloth for themselves and their brothers.

During all this, the father is too often defending himself against attorneys, or making such terms as he can with the sheriff, for debts in which he has been involved by the vicious idleness of his children, and his own [lack] of virtue and courage to break through the evil tyranny of old customs, and to compel his offspring to learn in early life to procure their subsistence by honest and honorable industry. Pride forbids the sale of the slaves, as long as it is possible to avoid it, . . . [lest] it shall be said, "The master was obliged to sell them." . . . In this conflict of pride and folly against industry and wisdom, the slave holders have been unhappily engaged for more than fifty years.

—Written by Charles Ball

Sunday was a great day on the plantation. Everybody got biscuits, Sundays. The slave women went down to Marster's [Master's] for their Sunday allowance of flour. All the children ate breakfast at the Great House [Master's house] and Marster and Missus gave out fruit to all. The slaves looked forward to Sunday as they labored through the week. It was a great day. Slaves received good treatment from Marster and all his family.

The slave children all carried a mussel shell in their hands to eat with up to the Great House. The food was put on large trays; and the children all gathered around and ate, dipping up their food with their mussel shells, which they used for spoons. Those who refused to eat or those who were ailing in any way had to come back to the Great House for their meals and medicine until they were well.

Marster had a large apple orchard in the Tar River low grounds and up on higher ground; and nearer the plantation house, there was on one side of the road a large plum orchard and on the other side was an orchard of peaches, cherries, quinces, and grapes. We picked the quinces in August and used them for preserving. Marster and Missus believed in giving the slaves plenty of fruit, especially the children.

Marster had three children, one boy named Dallas, and two girls, Bettie and Carrie. He would never allow slave children to call his children "Marster" and "Missus" unless the slave said "Little Marster" or "Little Missus." He had four white overseers, but they were not allowed to whip a slave. If there was any whipping to be done, he always said he would do it. He didn't believe in whipping, so when a slave got so bad he could not manage him, he sold him.

Marster didn't quarrel with anybody; Missus would not speak short to a slave, but both Marster and Missus taught slaves to be obedient in a nice quiet way. The slaves were taught to take their hats and bonnets off before going into the house, and to bow and say, "Good mornin' Marster Sam and Missus Evaline." . . . When Marster or Missus walked in the grove, the little Negroes would follow along after them like a gang of kiddies. Some of the slave children wanted to stay with them at the Great House all the time. They knew no better, of course, and seemed to love Marster and Missus as much as they did their own father and mother. Marster and Missus always used gentle means to get the children out of their way when they bothered them, and the way the children loved and trusted them was a beautiful sight to see. . . .

We were allowed to have prayer meetings in our homes, and we also went to the white folks' church. But they would not teach any of us to read and write. Books and papers were forbidden. Marster's children and the slave children played together. I went around with the baby girl Carrie to other plantations visiting. She taught me how to talk low and how to act in company. My association with white folks and my training while I was a slave is why I talk like white folks.

—Spoken by Mary Anderson

Left: Cincinnati in 1802. ***Right:*** Cincinnati in 1841. The city grew rapidly in just forty years.

Westward Movement

In the early 1800s, thousands of Americans left their homes in the East and moved to fertile lands in the West. Hundreds of immigrants joined the westward migration. Many of these pioneers traveled in canvas-topped ***Conestoga wagons*** (kahn ih STOH guh). When they reached the Ohio River, they loaded their possessions and cattle on flatboats or steamboats and floated downstream to their destination.

When a pioneer found a suitable location, he first marked the boundaries of his claim by notching trees with an ax. Then he cut down trees and built a lean-to or open shed, in which his family lived until he built a log cabin. The next job was to clear the land by cutting down the trees or ***girdling*** them (removing a strip of bark all around to kill them). Then he planted corn amid the stumps and dead trees. The pioneer would split some logs to make rails for fences around his fields.

A log cabin was rude and small, with a dirt floor and with split logs for a door and for furniture. Gourds served as cups and deer antlers as clothing pegs. The family ate the food they raised, supplemented by game and fish. If other pioneers lived nearby, they often worked together on large and difficult jobs. At a "raising," neighbors helped to build a cabin, or at a "log rolling," they rolled logs together for burning.

As time passed and more settlers moved in, the pioneer farmer developed a more settled life. He built a frame house, developed the clearing into a proper farm, and eventually sold his surplus crops. Soon would come other advances like sawmills, stores, banks, and churches. If favorably located, the settlement might grow into a town and then a city, as did Chicago and numerous other places.

Western Agriculture and Commerce

New inventions in agriculture. By 1830, the pioneers had moved beyond the eastern

A pioneer farmer's cabin in the West.

A pioneer farmer plowing with oxen.

forests and were learning to farm the open prairies. But it was almost as difficult to break the prairie sod as to clear a forest for planting. The thick, tough mat of grass roots had to be turned over with a ***breaking plow***. This was a large wooden plow with a moldboard weighing 125 pounds (57 kg) and a beam 15 feet (4.5 m) long. Later plows had a wrought iron plowshare (lower cutting edge) and a moldboard covered with wrought iron.

The prairie breaker turned the sod completely over by cutting only 3 inches (7.62 cm) deep. Four yoke of oxen were needed to pull the plow, and it could turn over 3 acres (1.2 ha) in one day. Plowing could be done only when the ground was softened by spring rains. But the sticky soil clung to the rough moldboard instead of sliding off. Also, the wrought iron share was soon dulled by the soil, and it had to be sharpened repeatedly.

In 1837, an Illinois blacksmith named **John Deere** devised a plow with a polished iron moldboard and a steel share. This plow stayed sharp longer, and the soil fell cleanly away from the moldboard. It worked so well that it became known as the "singing plow"; and within twenty years, Deere was producing ten thousand plows every year. Breaking the sod was so much easier that many more new settlers were attracted to the prairie, and the population of the West swelled by thousands every year.

The mechanical reaper was another device that improved farm production. This horse-drawn machine was invented by **Cyrus McCormick** in 1831, and it cut grain much faster than a man could do with a scythe. Since the harvesting of grain took much less time and labor, farmers were able to plant more grain than ever before.

Other factors also increased farm production in the West and elsewhere. New farming implements included rakes, mowers, and seed drills. Canals and railroads provided transportation for shipping grain and livestock greater distances at lower costs.

Farmers harvesting grain with a reaper. As machinery was improved, farmers could produce more and more grain and other crops.

Development of Western Commerce. The West became important as a source of food. For example, Cincinnati became known as "Porkopolis" because of all the pork that was packed there. Droves of hogs and cattle moved across the mountains into Baltimore and the South, and corn and wheat became major exports. Much of this western commerce traveled down the Mississippi to New Orleans.

But with the coming of canals, especially the Erie Canal, some of the western trade was diverted to the East. Some manufacturing centers developed in the West. Pittsburgh, Pennsylvania, became a large producer of iron, and products made from iron, such as steam engines. Louisville, Kentucky, produced much rope from hemp that was grown locally. Railroads especially helped to develop the West, which grew in wealth, population, and importance as time passed.

Focus for Thought

8. a. When was the cotton gin invented, and by whom?
   b. What effects did it have?

9. What were the three characteristics of a Southern plantation?
10. a. How was slavery a hindrance to the South?
    b. Why was it demeaning to the slaves?
11. What are two ways that small farmers in the South were different from planters?
12. By what two means did many pioneers move west in the early 1800s?
13. What two inventions boosted agricultural production, and who invented them?

3. THE REFORM SPIRIT

From 1820 to 1860, many Americans believed that people could accomplish almost anything they tried to do. If they could settle the West and invent new machines, they could also solve social problems, such as drunkenness and crime. This belief led to an age of various reform movements.

Social Movements

Reformers started various movements in the 1800s to attack specific problems in society. Three of the main ones were the ***temperance movement***, the drive for educational reform, and the drive for ***abolition*** (ab uh LIHSH uhn).

The Temperance Movement. One group of reformers launched a campaign against strong drink. They organized local temperance societies that later banded together as the American Temperance Union. These groups published many books and pamphlets denouncing strong drink and its evils. Some promoted moderation in drinking, but others emphasized total abstinence.

The temperance movement included a drive to have alcoholic beverages outlawed altogether. Maine passed the first "dry law" in 1846, and thirteen other states soon did the same. Proverbs 23:29–35 gives strong warnings against strong drink. For the Christian, abstinence is the only way to avoid being caught in this snare.

The Educational Reform Movement. Most schools of the early 1800s were operated by churches or local communities, but many poor people could not afford to send their children to school. Reformers thought society would be improved if everyone knew how to read and write, for then people could better provide for themselves and participate in elections and government. They believed education would help to reduce crime.

Horace Mann became a leader in the movement to reform education. He promoted "free" (tax-supported) public schools available to all children, and he called for compulsory attendance laws and "normal schools" for training teachers. Most states had some kind of public schools by 1860.

The early public schools used textbooks based on Biblical principles and emphasizing high moral values. One of these was the McGuffey reader series, and another was a spelling book published by **Noah Webster** and known as the "blue-backed speller." But

Noah Webster (1758–1843) produced the "blue-backed speller" in 1783 and *An American Dictionary of the English Language* in 1828.

eventually the public schools became completely secularized, or separated from religious teaching.

With the coming of public schools, the education of children shifted from being a responsibility of parents and churches to being a responsibility of the state. The Bible says, "Ye fathers, . . . bring them up" (Ephesians 6:4). Unfortunately, the Mennonites accepted public schooling over time, and one by one the church schools closed. Not until the middle 1900s would there again be a strong movement among the Mennonites to operate their own schools.

The Abolitionist Movement. The drive to abolish slavery was probably the strongest and most controversial reform movement. In one early effort, the American Colonization Society, formed in 1817, bought land in Africa and sent numerous freed slaves there. But since few blacks in America wanted to go to Africa, this movement was not very successful, even though the African territory later became the independent nation of Liberia.

In 1833, an extreme abolitionist named **William Lloyd Garrison** organized the American Anti-Slavery Society. Garrison boldly declared in the first issue of his paper, *The Liberator*: "I do not wish to think, or speak, or write with moderation. No! no! . . . I am in earnest—I will not equivocate—I will not excuse—I will not retreat a single inch—AND I WILL BE HEARD."

Abolitionists used pamphlets, pulpits, newspapers, magazines, and novels to arouse public indignation against the South. Some helped slaves to escape from their masters. Evangelist **Charles G. Finney** and poet **John Greenleaf Whittier** stirred up antislavery feelings. Former slaves such as **Frederick Douglass** and Sojourner Truth spoke out against slavery.

Southerners defended slavery on the basis that they actually helped the blacks by taking them from Africa and teaching them Christianity. They claimed that slaves were better off than workers in the North, asserting that slaveholders cared for their slaves and loved them. They even quoted Scriptures in support of slavery.

Abolitionists and anti-abolitionists attacked each other with many harsh words and sometimes with acts of violence. Nonresistant Christians agreed that slavery was not right, but they considered it wrong to use force in opposing slavery. The slavery issue grew more complex until it became entangled with other issues and helped to bring on the Civil War.

Left: William Lloyd Garrison (1805–1879) was an outspoken abolitionist leader. His newspaper, *The Liberator,* stirred up strong feelings against slavery. ***Middle:*** Frederick Douglass (1817?–1895) was a former slave who campaigned against slavery. He published an abolitionist newspaper called the *North Star*. ***Right:*** Charles G. Finney (1792–1875). His revivals in the 1820s and 1830s affected thousands of people and influenced the temperance and abolitionist movements.

Religious Movements

The American pioneers had little time for religion amid all their work of clearing land and making a living. Besides, almost no churches existed on the frontier. This contributed to a lawless, immoral way of life for many pioneers. One Virginia preacher complained, "I found the principles of the Gospel . . . as little known and thought of as if the people had never [attended] a church or heard a sermon in their lives."

To reach the rural people, preachers known as ***circuit riders*** began traveling on circuits of 200 to 500 miles (322 to 805 km), preaching at various points along the way. One of these was Peter Cartwright, who rode thousands of miles and preached in scores of different places. Circuit riders faced all kinds of weather and many dangers as they carried the Gospel to unchurched people in the West.

Revivalism. A religious revival called the Second Great Awakening began in the late 1790s and continued into the early decades of the 1800s. This revival served as the motivation for many reforms, especially the temperance movement and abolition.

Many ***camp meetings*** were held in the West during the Second Great Awakening. These were meetings under the open sky, with felled trees serving as benches. Families would come from great distances to hear the Gospel preached, bringing tents and other provisions with them. Preachers spoke in different parts of the camp so that the thousands gathered could all hear the message.

These preachers delivered thundering sermons in which they warned the people to flee the wrath of God and be saved. Sometimes emotions veered out of control as the listeners went into a religious hysteria. They would scream, whirl in circles, roll on the ground, or hop like frogs until they collapsed. But time would prove that many of the "conversions" in these meetings were not genuine, for they did not change people's lives. Also, the Bible says that all things in a worship service should be done "decently and in order" (1 Corinthians 14:40).

Noted evangelists such as Charles G. Finney carried the methods of the camp meetings to New York, Boston, and other cities of the East. Finney used new tactics such as inviting sinners to come forward to the "anxious bench," and he held meetings daily instead of weekly. His greatest work was in Rochester, New York, where he labored half a year and wrought a great change in that city.

Religious revival affected the nation in numerous ways. Interest grew in foreign mission work, and the Board of Commissioners for Foreign Missions was founded in 1810. Under

A camp meeting scene. People responded to the passionate sermons by weeping, waving their arms about, and crying to God for mercy.

Adoniram Judson (1788–1850) helped to found the Congregationalist and Baptist foreign missionary societies. He was a pioneer American missionary to Burma (now called Myanmar).

this board, **Adoniram Judson**, the "father of American missions," went to Burma and translated the Bible into Burmese. (See "Adoniram Judson, Missionary to Burma," in Rod and Staff's Seventh Reader.) The American Tract Society was founded in 1812, and the American Bible Society in 1816, to make tracts and Bibles available to the people. The Sunday school movement also began in this period.

New Cults. A number of false religions began during this time of revivalism. In 1831, a preacher named William Miller began saying that Jesus would come back in 1843 or 1844. Thousands of Millerites sold their property, dressed in white robes, and gathered at the appointed time to await Jesus' return. When Miller's prophecies failed, many followers forsook him; but the largest group reorganized as the Seventh-day Adventist Church. Jesus clearly said of His return, "Of that day and hour knoweth no man, no, not the angels of heaven, but my Father only" (Matthew 24:36).

Another false religious group was the Church of Jesus Christ of Latter-day Saints, or Mormons. Their leader was **Joseph Smith**, whose Book of Mormon was accepted by the group as an addition to the Bible. Revelation 22:18 clearly says, "If any man shall add unto these things, God shall add unto him the plagues that are written in this book." And Galatians 1:8 says, "Though we, or an angel from heaven, preach any other gospel unto you than that which we have preached unto you, let him be accursed." (Joseph Smith claimed to have received special revelations from God and an angel.)

Smith gained a following in New York and later moved west to Ohio and then to Illinois. There he was arrested because he approved polygamy (having more than one marriage partner), and a mob attacked and killed him while he was in jail. Brigham Young then led the Mormons to Utah in 1847.

Social Experiments. A few reformers tried to establish utopias in an effort to reach human perfection. These people thought that if they tried hard enough and worked together, they could develop an ideal society. Some of them were religious groups and some were social organizations, but all failed because sinful man can never attain perfection in this world. Among the social experiments were Brook Farm in New England and New Harmony in Indiana. Religious communities included the Shakers, the Oneida Community in New York, and the Amana Community in Iowa.

Developments Among the Mennonites

Westward Movement. In the late 1700s, Mennonites began moving west and north from their population centers in eastern Pennsylvania and in Virginia. In the 1790s, some moved to the area near Pittsburgh and the Jacob's Creek settlement near what is now Scottdale. From there the Mennonites expanded into Ohio, beginning in 1799 and increasing after the War of 1812.

Many Anabaptists in Switzerland migrated directly to Ohio in the 1820s and 1830s. Mennonites began moving to Indiana around 1840, with the Yellow Creek settlement in Elkhart County being the most important. From 1830 to 1860, Mennonites and Amish moved westward to Illinois, Iowa, and Missouri.

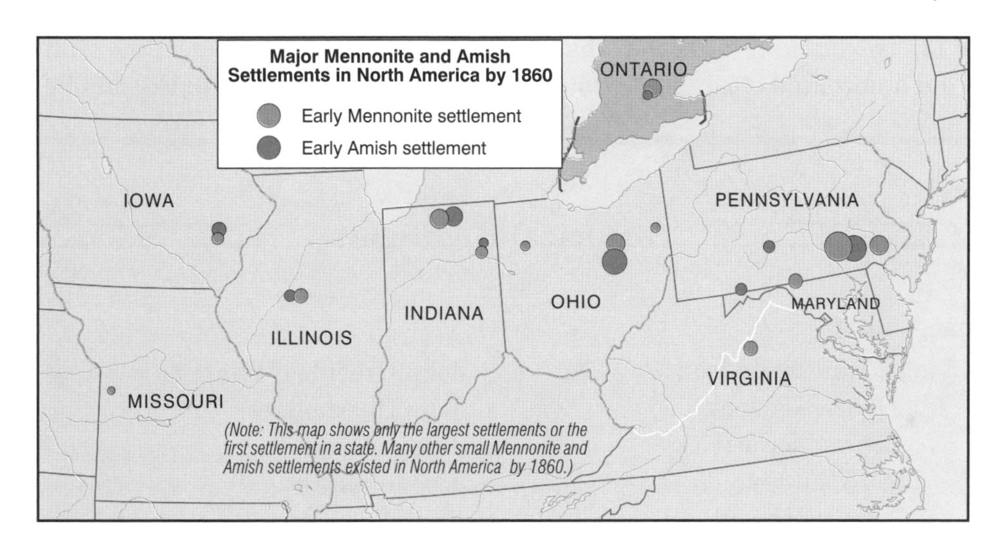

Mennonites in Changing Times. The Mennonites also had to deal with the rapid changes in society and religion, though they were generally slow to change their practices. Mennonites at first retained German as their language, and for many years they refused Sunday schools, evangelistic meetings, and prayer meetings. They wanted to live a quiet and peaceable life of separation from the world.

But not all Mennonites were satisfied with the old traditions. One such was **John Oberholtzer** of eastern Pennsylvania, who favored greater leniency in matters of dress and lifestyle. In 1847, he and his supporters withdrew from the Franconia District and formed the new Eastern Conference. By about 1860, Oberholtzer's group joined with Mennonites of the West to form the General Conference Mennonites. This group accommodated rapidly to worldly trends.

Jacob Stauffer in Lancaster County believed that the Mennonite Church was becoming too lenient in discipline. He too withdrew, and in 1845 he started the Stauffer (Pike) Mennonite Church. The Stauffer Mennonites then enforced a stricter discipline.

Mennonites accepted a new kind of singing in this period. The main leader was **Joseph Funk** of Virginia, who introduced the use of seven shaped notes to correspond with the seven tones of the scale. He also promoted singing in harmony rather than in unison, as was the former practice. To teach music, Funk held many singing schools and published a book later known as the *Harmonia Sacra*. This book taught harmony and was used at singing schools in many states.

Jesus said, "I will build my church; and the gates of hell shall not prevail against it" (Matthew 16:18). In the midst of change and deception, Jesus was still building His church.

Focus for Thought

14. Describe two things that supporters of the temperance movement did to promote their cause.
15. Some reformers worked to make education available to everyone.
    a. In what ways did these reformers think this would improve society?
    b. What shift in the education of children did public schools help to bring about?
16. a. What are two ways in which abolitionists worked against slavery?
    b. How did nonresistant Christians view the actions of the abolitionists?
17. How did circuit riders and camp meetings bring the Gospel to settlers in the West?

18. What are two lasting effects that the Second Great Awakening had on the United States?
19. How did a new kind of singing come into the Mennonite Church in the middle 1800s?

Historical Highlights

A. Matching: People

a. Adoniram Judson
b. Charles Finney
c. Cyrus McCormick
d. Eli Whitney
e. Francis Lowell
f. Frederick Douglass
g. Horace Mann
h. James Watt
i. John Deere
j. John Greenleaf Whittier
k. John Oberholtzer
l. Joseph Funk
m. Joseph Smith
n. Noah Webster
o. Robert Fulton
p. Samuel F. B. Morse
q. Samuel Slater
r. William Lloyd Garrison

1. Inventor of the mechanical reaper.
2. Promoter of educational reform.
3. Inventor of the telegraph.
4. "Father of American missions."
5. Built first practical steam engine.
6. Inventor of the cotton gin; used interchangeable parts.
7. Founder of the Mormons.
8. Abolitionist poet.
9. Brought Industrial Revolution to America by building textile machines from memory.
10. Published the "blue-backed speller."
11. Invented a steel plow for use on the prairie.
12. Built the *Clermont*, the first successful steamboat.
13. Evangelist who used new methods to win converts.
14. Extreme abolitionist who published *The Liberator*.
15. Mennonite leader who favored greater leniency.
16. Former slave who spoke out against slavery.
17. Virginia Mennonite who devised shaped notes and held singing schools.
18. Built the first factory to make raw cotton into cloth at one place.

B. Matching: Terms 1

a. abolition
b. breaking plow
c. camp meeting
d. circuit rider
e. cotton gin
f. girdling
g. interchangeable parts
h. plantation
i. "planter aristocracy"
j. slave code
k. temperance movement
l. turnpike

1. Small group of rich men who controlled the South.
2. Elimination of slavery.

3. Removing a strip of bark around a tree to kill it.
4. Large, heavy implement used to turn over prairie sod.
5. Effort to stop the use of strong drink.
6. Minister who traveled about, preaching to pioneers.
7. Evangelistic gathering held outdoors or in a tent.
8. Road for which users pay toll.
9. Large farm that produced one main crop and used slave labor.
10. Parts that can be interchanged because they are made exactly alike.
11. Set of laws placing restrictions on slaves.
12. Device for removing seeds from cotton.

C. Matching: Terms 2

a. American Colonization Society
b. Conestoga wagon
c. Cotton Kingdom
d. Erie Canal
e. Industrial Revolution
f. McGuffey reader
g. National Road
h. Second Great Awakening

1. Religious revival that began in the late 1790s.
2. Change from producing handmade goods at home to producing machine-made goods in factories.
3. Name given to the South because it depended on cotton.
4. Route extending from Cumberland to Vandalia.
5. Canvas-topped vehicle used by pioneers moving west.
6. Association with the goal of moving freed blacks to Africa.
7. Reading text used in schools of the 1800s.
8. Waterway that joined Lake Erie to the Hudson River and diverted western trade to New York City.

D. Deeper Discussion

1. a. What were some benefits of the Industrial Revolution?
   b. What were some detriments?
2. a. How did slavery degrade the blacks?
   b. How was it degrading to the slaveholders?
   c. How did slavery hinder the South?
3. Why can man not solve spiritual and social problems by using his own intellect and abilities?
4. Can national evils be overcome by making laws against them? Explain.
5. How have time and experience shown that the expectations of Horace Mann and the educational reformers were wrong?
6. a. Give evidence from this chapter of the religious confusion in the United States during the first half of the 1800s.
   b. Why did Mennonites reject many of the religious innovations of this time?
7. How did the camp meetings in the West deviate from Scriptural principles for worship as given in 1 Corinthians 14:23–33, 40?

E. Chronology and Geography

Describe how the frontier moved westward from the mid-1700s to the mid-1800s.

So Far This Year

A. Matching: Terms 1

1. Time of national unity and harmony.
2. Agreement that ended the War of 1812.
3. Agreement that settled differences with Spain in 1795.
4. Agreement that settled a slavery problem.
5. Agreement that gained Florida in 1819.
6. Agreement that settled differences with Britain.
7. Declaration about involvement of European and American nations in each other's affairs.
8. Assembly that declared independence.
9. Agreement that ended the American Revolution.

a. Adams-Onís Treaty
b. Era of Good Feelings
c. Jay Treaty
d. Missouri Compromise
e. Monroe Doctrine
f. Pinckney Treaty
g. Second Continental Congress
h. Treaty of Ghent
i. Treaty of Paris

B. Matching: Terms 2

10. Practice in which the winner of an election rewards his supporters with government positions.
11. Political party that opposed Andrew Jackson.
12. Idea that states are supreme over the federal government.
13. Political party that favored loose interpretation and strong government.
14. Devotion to the interests of a local region rather than the whole nation.
15. Supreme Court's power to declare a law unconstitutional.
16. System in which lords owned land and serfs farmed it for them.
17. Political party that favored strict interpretation and limited government.
18. Supporters of Great Britain.
19. Persons favoring independence.

a. Democratic-Republicans
b. Federalists
c. judicial review
d. Loyalists
e. manorialism
f. patriots
g. sectionalism
h. spoils system
i. states' rights
j. Whigs

C. Completion: People and Places

Write the correct name for each description.

20. Federalist leader and first secretary of the treasury.
21. Man who opened the Wilderness Road to Kentucky.
22. Two men who explored the Louisiana Purchase from 1804 to 1806.
23. Chief justice who strengthened the Supreme Court.
24. British general whose defeat ended the Revolution.
25. Patriot general in command of the entire American army.
26. Battle that was the turning point in the Revolution.
27. Location of the beginning battle of the Revolution.
28. Location of the last major battle of the Revolution.
29. Place where conflicting claims led to the French and Indian War.
30. Site of the decisive battle in the French and Indian War.

In 1848, the manufacturing city of Lowell, Massachusetts, had 50 factories that employed 8,635 women and 3,995 men. The textile mills had 301,297 spindles and 8,749 looms, and produced 1,920,900 yards (1,756,480 m) of cotton cloth per week.

Hundreds of pioneers moved westward as the nation continued to expand.

14 National Expansion

1. TEXAS AND THE MEXICAN WAR
   - The Story of Texas
   - Expansionist Fever
   - The Mexican War
   - Events After the War
2. THE OREGON TERRITORY
   - Oregon Fever
   - The Oregon Trail
   - Progress Toward Statehood
3. CALIFORNIA AND THE GOLD RUSH
   - Discovery of Gold
   - The Gold Rush
   - Statehood of California

"Wait on the LORD, and keep his way, and he shall exalt thee to inherit the land."

Psalm 37:34

NATIONAL EXPANSION

Focus for Reading

After two hundred years of pioneering, Americans were still moving westward in the 1840s. By treaty, by war, and by sheer force of numbers, they conquered deserts, mountains, and valleys until they reached the Far West. Three sections in this chapter tell the story of westward expansion to the Pacific Ocean.

1. Texas and the Mexican War
2. The Oregon Territory
3. California and the Gold Rush

1. TEXAS AND THE MEXICAN WAR

Though Texas belonged to Mexico, Americans began colonizing the region in the 1820s. Texans gained independence from Mexico by the 1830s, and within another decade they sought to join the United States. To many Americans, this was simply another step toward gaining the land all the way to the Pacific.

President Polk determined to accomplish that goal even if it meant war. In 1846, the Mexican War did expand the United States by thousands of square miles. But the war also added to the conflict that led eventually to the Civil War.

The Story of Texas

American Settlers in Texas. Spain had originally explored and settled eastern Texas, and in 1819 the United States relinquished its claims to Texas in the Transcontinental Treaty (Adams-Onís Treaty). When Mexico became an independent nation in 1821, it inherited Texas from Spain. But its control over Texas was weak, and few Mexicans lived there. However, many Americans greatly desired the vast, rich land in Texas.

In 1821, a Missourian named **Stephen Austin** received a grant of land in Texas from the Mexican government, which wanted more settlers in Texas. Austin had little difficulty attracting Americans to this land. He could offer families over 4,000 acres (1,600 ha) of land at prices much lower than the $1.25 per acre charged for United States public land. Soon many farmers in the United States wrote *G.T.T.* (for "Gone to Texas") on their farmhouse doors, and by 1835 the American population in Texas reached thirty thousand.

Stephen Austin (1793–1836), the "father of Texas." Thousands of Americans moved to Texas while he was the head of the colony.

Independence for Texas. By the early 1830s, some Texans began to resent Mexican control. The settlers were required to become Mexican citizens, join the Catholic Church, and free their slaves. They agreed to these conditions but found ways to get around them. For example, the settlers would free their slaves but then sign them to a lifetime contract as indentured servants. Differences in language and way of life also caused tension between Americans and Mexicans.

The Alamo was the chapel of a Catholic mission founded in the early 1700s. The building had been in ruins for some time before the famous battle for Texan independence was fought there. It has been restored as a historical site.

Fearing that Texas might slip from its grasp, Mexico restricted further immigration from the United States in 1830. From then on, relations between Texas and Mexico deteriorated, especially when a harsh ruler named **Santa Anna** came to power in Mexico. By 1835, many Texans wanted independence. Revolution broke out, and Santa Anna marched an army against the rebels. Texas declared independence from Mexico on March 2, 1836.

Santa Anna had already arrived in San Antonio, Texas, in February 1836. He was opposed by a force of 187 Texans, who found refuge in an old mission called the Alamo. After besieging the Texans for thirteen days, Santa Anna's troops finally forced their way into the Alamo and killed all the defenders. Among the slain were **David (Davy) Crockett**, a well-known frontiersman, and **James (Jim) Bowie**, inventor of the bowie knife.

Santa Anna then pursued **Samuel (Sam) Houston** and his small army as they retreated through Texas. Finally the Texans attacked Santa Anna's army at San Jacinto (san juh SIHN toh) on April 21, 1836. The Texans routed the entire Mexican army and even

Left: Sam Houston (1793–1863) became the first president of Texas after its independence from Mexico. When Texas became part of the United States, Houston served as a senator and later as a governor of Texas. ***Right:*** Santa Anna's surrender to Sam Houston. General Houston lies under a tree, resting his broken right leg after the Battle of San Jacinto. He holds out his right hand to Santa Anna (standing).

captured Santa Anna. They refused to release him until he met their demands, and in this way they forced Santa Anna to sign a treaty granting independence to Texas.

The Texans organized their independent territory as the Lone Star Republic, with Sam Houston as its first president. But most Texans wanted to be part of the United States, so in 1836 they requested admission into the Union.

Many Americans wanted Texas to be admitted. Southerners coveted the good land for cotton growing, and they also saw in Texas an opportunity to expand slavery to balance the growing North and West. But Northerners opposed this expansion of slavery and Southern power. Besides, admitting Texas might lead to war with Mexico. So for ten years Texas remained an independent nation known as the Lone Star Republic.

Expansionist Fever

By the 1840s, a new spirit of expansionism swept the nation. It was based on an idea described by a journalist in 1845 as "our ***manifest destiny*** to overspread the continent allotted by Providence for the free development of our yearly multiplying millions." In other words, Americans believed that the United States was clearly destined by God to spread over the whole North American continent. They considered the nation as the "great center from which civilization, religion, and liberty should radiate and radiate until the whole continent shall bask in their blessing."

The Lord did bless the United States to the extent that the nation upheld basic principles of justice and right. And because of people's belief in manifest destiny, the nation expanded significantly by gaining various new territories, as you will see in the rest of this chapter. But the people were wrong in thinking that God had a spiritual mission for their country. Such a mission belongs to the church, not to an earthly nation.

In 1844, **James K. Polk** was elected to the presidency. He and the Democratic Party stood for expansion of the United States, particularly the annexation (adding) of Texas and Oregon. Congress passed a resolution annexing Texas in February 1845; and in December of that year, Texas became the twenty-eighth state of the United States.

The Lone Star Republic (1836–1845)
Important battles
UNITED STATES
Santa Fe
Boundary line according to Texas and the U.S.
Disputed Territory
Boundary line according to Mexico
TEXAS
Battle of San Jacinto
Austin
The Alamo
San Antonio
Goliad
MEXICO
Chihuahua
Rio Grande
Nueces R.
Monterrey
0 100 200 300 miles
0 200 400 km

The Mexican War

Disputes With Mexico. The Mexican government had never recognized the treaty signed by Santa Anna (or the independence

James K. Polk (1795–1849) was the eleventh president of the United States. He served from 1845 to 1849 and was a Democrat.

of Texas). When Texas was admitted to the Union, Mexico ended diplomatic relations with the United States. A further dispute involved the boundary of Texas. Mexico asserted that it was the Nueces River, but the United States said it was the Rio Grande, 150 miles (241 km) farther south. Besides, Mexico had not paid a large debt that it owed to some citizens of the United States.

Americans were also eager to gain the Mexican territories of New Mexico and California. Merchants had developed a profitable trade with Santa Fe, the capital of New Mexico; and California had become important for trade in the Pacific. If settling the disputes and gaining these lands meant war, so be it, thought many Americans. They felt confident that the United States could defeat Mexico.

Outbreak of War. President Polk sent General **Zachary Taylor** to protect the border of Texas in 1845. He also sent a man named John Slidell (sly DEHL) to negotiate with the Mexicans. Slidell was to offer up to $30 million for New Mexico and California, and to cancel Mexico's debt of several million dollars—if the Mexicans would recognize Texas as part of the United States and accept the Rio Grande border. But the Mexican government was in too much chaos to make any treaty. Slidell returned to Washington and urged that the Mexicans be "chastised."

In January 1846, President Polk ordered General Taylor to advance to the Rio Grande. In April, Mexican troops crossed the Rio Grande and attacked the Americans, killing several of them. The Mexicans viewed the Americans as invaders of their territory, but President Polk proclaimed that Mexico had invaded the United States. Congress declared war on Mexico on May 13, 1846.

Campaigns of Taylor and Kearny. General Taylor invaded Mexico by crossing the Rio Grande. He fought several battles in which he won victories over Mexican armies larger than his own. Taylor finally defeated

Zachary Taylor at Monterrey in northern Mexico. Monterrey fell to American forces on September 24, 1846.

Santa Anna's army at Buena Vista (BWAY nuh VEES tuh) in February 1847. But the Mexican government still would not give in.

General **Stephen Kearny** marched an army to Santa Fe, New Mexico, and conquered it without a fight in August 1846. The hardest part had been the long march from Kansas! From there, part of the army advanced into Mexico and won victories near El Paso and near Chihuahua. Kearny and the remaining troops proceeded to California.

Americans eagerly read the latest news about the Mexican War.

Winfield Scott's entrance into Mexico City on September 14, 1847. The United States flag flew above the National Palace (the Halls of Montezuma) to welcome the American troops.

In California, American settlers led by Captain **John Frémont** had already revolted and established the Bear Flag Republic in June 1846. Then in July, two officers proclaimed American control and took over several Californian cities. By the time General Kearny arrived in December, the Mexicans in California had revolted against their new American masters. With Kearny's aid the Americans defeated the Mexicans and took over California.

Sonoma
San Francisco
Monterey
California
Los Angeles
San Diego
Mexican Cession
New Mexico
Santa Fe
Fort Leavenworth
Gadsden Purchase
El Paso
Disputed Territory
TEXAS
Austin
Houston
San Antonio
Nueces R.
Rio Grande
Chihuahua
PACIFIC OCEAN
Monterrey
Buena Vista
MEXICO
Gulf of Mexico
Mexico City
Veracruz
0 200 400 miles
0 200 400 600 km
The Mexican War (1846–1847)
Important battles

The Mexican War and United States Acquisitions in the Southwest

The Mexican Cession. When Mexico still refused to give in, President Polk ordered General **Winfield Scott** to invade the heart of the country and capture Mexico City. General Scott landed at Veracruz and fought his way inland, and at last his men raised the United States flag over Mexico City in September 1847. This was the first time the American flag fluttered in victory over a foreign capital.

Finally in February 1848, the Mexican government was ready to make peace. In the Treaty of Guadalupe Hidalgo (GWAHD uh loop hih DAHL goh), Mexico recognized the border of Texas at the Rio Grande and also gave about 525,000 square miles (1,360,000 km^2) of land to the United States. This Mexican Cession included land in the present states of California, Arizona, New Mexico, Utah, Nevada, Colorado, and Wyoming. In return, the United States agreed to pay Mexico $15 million and to reimburse American citizens the $3.25 million that Mexico owed them.

Effects of the Mexican War. The Americans gained a vast stretch of land through the Mexican War, but they also gained the ill feelings of the Mexicans. In addition, the war reopened the old slavery question: should it be allowed or forbidden in new territories? Because of this issue and several others, the Mexican War contributed to the Civil War.

All the American soldiers who fought in the Mexican War were volunteers. So military service was not an issue for nonresistant people.

Zachary Taylor (1784–1850) was the twelfth president of the United States. He served in 1849 and 1850, and was a Whig.

Events After the War

Election of Zachary Taylor. Three political parties competed for the presidency in the election of 1848. They were the Democrats, the Whigs, and the Free-Soil Party (which opposed slavery in new territories). Zachary Taylor of Mexican War fame won the election as a Whig. So the Whigs regained power, but for the last time.

The Gadsden Purchase. Several years after the war, Americans found a favorable route for a southern railway to California; but it was south of the border designated in the treaty. So the United States sent James Gadsden to Mexico, and he bought a strip of land south of New Mexico and Arizona for $10 million. This Gadsden Purchase was concluded in 1853.

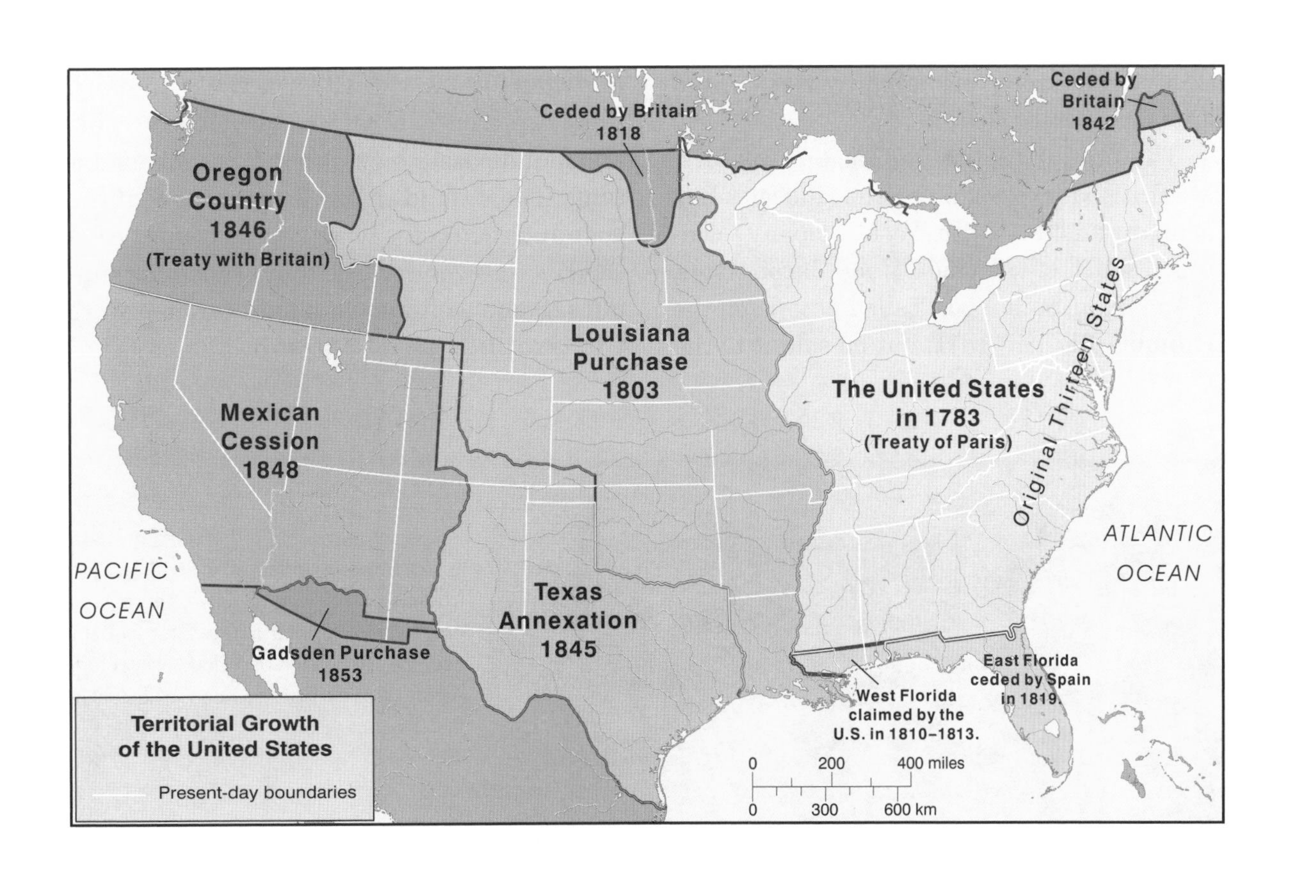

Focus for Thought

1. Give several answers to each question.
   a. Why were Americans eager to settle Texas?
   b. Why did American settlers in Texas want to be independent?
2. a. What happened at the Alamo?
   b. How did Texas gain independence soon after the incident there?
3. What did the Texans name their new nation, and how long was it an independent republic?
4. a. What was meant by *manifest destiny*?
   b. How was this idea expressed in the 1800s?
5. What were three disputes that contributed to the Mexican War?
6. List the provisions of the Treaty of Guadalupe Hidalgo.
7. What were three effects of the Mexican War?

2. THE OREGON TERRITORY

The fertile valleys of Oregon held a special attraction for many Americans. At first only fur traders lived there; but by the 1840s, thousands of Americans moved there to farm the rich soil. Through this process of moving in and settling, Oregon became part of the United States.

Oregon Fever

Exploration of the Far West. Oregon Country included the present states of Washington, Oregon, and Idaho, as well as the province of British Columbia. It also included parts of Montana and Wyoming. Since 1818, it had been jointly occupied by the United States and Great Britain.

The first attraction in Oregon was furs. Two British fur companies—the Hudson's Bay Company and the North West Company—controlled much of the trade. John Jacob Astor, an American, built a post called Astoria on the Columbia River in 1811; but he sold it to the North West Company during the War of 1812. The Hudson's Bay Company built Fort Vancouver at the junction of the Columbia and Willamette (wuh LAM iht) Rivers.

The fur traders contributed much to the opening of the Far West. These hardy ***mountain men*** lived in the wilderness like Indians. They explored new regions, developed trails, and found passes by which to cross the mountains. They would gather furs throughout the year and then come to an annual ***rendezvous*** (RAHN duh voo), where they traded for supplies. Some well-known mountain men were **Christopher (Kit) Carson**, James (Jim)

Astoria as it appeared in 1813. This fur-trading post in what is now Oregon was established by John Jacob Astor in 1811 near the site of Lewis and Clark's winter fort. Astoria was the first American settlement in the Oregon region.

Left: A mountain man with his ponies. ***Right:*** A summer rendezvous. Fur traders, mountain men, and Indians gathered at these annual festivals to trade furs and obtain supplies for the next year. It was a time of feasting, drinking, and merrymaking.

Bridger, and Thomas Fitzpatrick.

Jedediah Smith was a noted explorer of the West. He discovered the South Pass through the Rocky Mountains, and in 1826 he became the first American known to enter California by land. A Canadian named Peter Ogden followed the Snake River and gained much information about the Northwest for the Hudson's Bay Company. Ogden was probably the first white man to see the Great Salt Lake in present-day Utah.

Later, John Frémont explored the West and wrote a book that became a guide for people traveling west. The explorations of Frémont and others allowed the blank maps of the West to be filled in with landmarks and useful directions. Mountain men often guided groups of pioneers moving west.

The mountain men endured great hardships for furs and fame. We can learn from their courage, for Christians also need to "endure hardness" in this world. But the Christian cause is much higher than that served by the mountain men. And since these men often lived rough, ungodly lives, they are not worthy models for us.

Growth of Interest in Oregon. Mission work helped to raise interest in Oregon. A story circulated that Nez Perce Indians had visited St. Louis and requested the "white man's book from heaven." To help these Indians, a group sponsored by the American Board of Commissioners for Foreign Missions and led by **Marcus Whitman** traveled to Oregon and established the Whitman Mission in 1836. (See "Two Brave Messengers" in Rod and Staff's Seventh Reader.) Dr. Whitman wrote glowing letters that enthusiastically promoted the bounties of Oregon. Emigration societies held meetings at which speakers described the region in terms such as "a land flowing with milk and honey." These reports, coming after the Panic of 1837, encouraged many to make the move to Oregon. The first wagon train of settlers started for Oregon in 1841.

Dr. Whitman made a difficult journey to the East in the winter of 1842–43 to save his mission from closing. Continued support of the mission was granted, and he also informed officials in Washington about conditions and possibilities for settling Oregon. By that time, "Oregon fever" was raging in Missouri, Ohio, and many eastern states. When Whitman headed west in 1843, he guided a caravan of some 1,000 Oregon-bound pioneers that later

WAGON MAKING (WHEELWRIGHT AND WAINWRIGHT)

"And under the borders were four wheels; and the axletrees of the wheels were joined to the base: and the height of a wheel was a cubit and half a cubit. And the work of the wheels was like the work of a chariot wheel: their axletrees, and their naves, and their felloes, and their spokes, were all molten" (1 Kings 7:32, 33).

Wagons of colonial days did not have "molten" wheels like the ones described above, but the art of making wheels was important. Even though people traveled by boat as much as possible because of the few good roads, they often used carts and wagons to haul produce, supplies, and farm equipment. A wheelwright made and repaired wheels, and a wainwright made and repaired wagons.

To make a wheel, the wheelwright used his tools to saw and shape the various wooden parts—the spokes, the fellies (formerly called felloes), and the wooden parts of the hub. He shaped the ends of each spoke into sturdy pegs that fit into the hub at the end closest to the center, and into the fellies at the outer end. Fellies were curved pieces of wood that formed the wooden rim of a wheel. Each felly had two spokes pounded tightly into holes made for them, and a peg on one end to fit into a hole in the next felly.

The wheelwright forced the spokes into the fellies and then forced all the fellies together. He used an auger to shape the center hole where the axle would fit through. (Iron was used for strength in hubs and axles, especially for heavy wagons, but some early wagons had mostly wooden parts.) An iron or steel rim was heated and then welded and fastened tightly around the fellies of the new wheel. Water was poured over the hot metal rim to make it shrink onto the wheel and bind the wooden parts tightly together. The iron or steel rim also helped the wheel to withstand the rigors of traveling over the rough roads of those times.

A wainwright fashioned wagons and coaches out of wood such as swamp oak, white oak, and hickory. In colonial days, these vehicles did not have the luxury of springs or other features to cushion the ride for the traveler. The seats were hard planks, and some stagecoach riders complained of bruises, aching arms, and blistered hands from hanging on to avoid being thrown about. Coaches floundered through mudholes and bumped terribly over corduroy roads. Travel was more pleasant in winter, when sleighs could be used.

The famous Conestoga wagon was named for the Conestoga Valley in Lancaster County, Pennsylvania, where it was first built by German farmers in the early 1770s. Conestoga wagons carried most of the people and freight traveling westward over the Allegheny Mountains from the 1770s to about 1850. This large wagon was designed to carry about 5 tons (4,500 kg) of freight over rough ground, being pulled by six or eight horses. When the team of horses was hitched to the wagon, the unit stretched about 60 feet (18 m)!

The Conestoga wagon had several features that helped pioneers and their possessions to reach their destinations safely. Broad-rimmed wheels helped to prevent bogging down on muddy roads. If a waterway had to be forded, the wheels could be taken off and the wagon body used as a boat. The wagon had a deep bed that was about 13 feet (4 m) long and a little over 3 feet (1 m) wide. The ends were built higher than the middle to help keep cargo from falling out when the wagon went over a steep hill. The wagon had a cover of white homespun canvas about 24 feet (7 m) long, which was fitted over hoops to make a high, rounded shape. This canvas cover protected the contents and occupants from sun and rain, and the front and back ends could be closed in stormy weather. The harnesses of the horses often had bells that rang cheerily as the wagon moved along.

After 1850, a covered wagon called the prairie schooner was used by pioneer families moving to the western prairies and beyond. Though smaller than the Conestoga, this wagon was still large; it measured about 10 feet long, 4 feet wide, and 8 feet (3 m by 1.2 m by 2.4 m) high. A typical prairie schooner carried about 2,000 pounds (907 kg) of cargo. Part of this weight consisted of items that the pioneers would need at their new homes, and the rest was supplies needed to sustain the travelers and animals on the journey.

became known as the first "Great Migration." Angry Indians murdered Dr. Whitman in 1847; but from 1843 to 1866, almost 350,000 pioneers traveled the Oregon Trail.

The Oregon Trail

The Course of the Trail. For much of the way, the Oregon Trail ran along rivers. Pioneers would start from Independence or Westport, Missouri, which were then on the western border of the United States. They followed the Santa Fe Trail west into Kansas, and then they headed northwest to the Platte River in present-day Nebraska. The travelers followed this river and its fork, the North Platte, for 600 miles (966 km).

In Wyoming, Fort Laramie served as a place for rest, repairs, and replenishment of supplies—and then the pioneers pressed on toward Oregon. Having crossed the Rockies by the South Pass, they now entered Oregon Country. Most travelers stopped at Fort Bridger in Wyoming and then at Fort Hall (modern Pocatello) in Idaho. After following the Snake River and its gorge across Idaho, they finally entered what is Oregon today.

But the greatest obstacle still remained—crossing the Blue Mountains just east of the Columbia Plateau. After they accomplished this, the pioneers arrived at Fort Walla Walla, near the Whitman mission. Then they either floated down the Columbia River or traveled overland to their destination, the Willamette River valley. They had journeyed over 2,000 miles (3,219 km) in all.

Life on the Trail. Each family had a covered wagon (prairie schooner) that contained their belongings and supplies. Horses or oxen pulled the wagons; oxen were stronger and more reliable. The people had to travel as light as possible because of the steep mountains on the journey; so most furniture had to be left behind. Many families took along a cow for milk, perhaps a horse, and supplies purchased at the place where they started their journey.

Top: Starting point of the Oregon Trail at Independence, Missouri. Wagon trains of 30 to 200 wagons would form here and leave in May for the six-month journey to Oregon. The wagons weighed up to 7,000 pounds (3,175 kg) and were pulled by teams of up to 12 horses or oxen.

Middle: South Pass through the Wind River Mountains. This broad pass made it possible for wagons to cross the continental divide. It rose so gradually that "the traveler would scarcely perceive that he was ascending," even though it rose to 7,412 feet (2,259 m). South Pass marked the halfway point on the journey.

Bottom: Camp at Fort Bridger in Utah Territory. Wagon trains often reached Fort Bridger in August and stopped there for food, supplies, and refreshment. Fort Bridger, established by mountain man Jim Bridger, was located in the Green River valley in what is now western Wyoming.

Large groups of wagons traveled together, led by a captain and directed by a guide. All who were able would walk beside the wagons as the oxen strained westward. The wagons averaged 1 mile (1.61 km) per hour and traveled 16 miles (26 km) on a good day! At nightfall, the travelers selected a suitable place with firewood, grass, and water. They formed a tight circle with their wagons to afford protection against Indians and wild animals, and to make a corral for their livestock. Almost everyone slept in tents or in bedrolls under the wagons.

Life on the Oregon Trail was harsh. Travelers had to endure blazing sunshine and choking dust as well as wind, rain, and mud. Sickness and accidents brought death to many; one source says there was an average of one grave for every 500 feet (152 m) of trail. The pioneers had to ford rivers or float their wagons across. Climbing steep grades required the use of additional oxen, and going down required unhitching the oxen, locking the brakes, and hanging on to ropes as the wagons slowly descended.

Settlers crossing the rugged mountains of the Sierra Nevada. Their motto was "Keep moving," for they had to cross this range before snowstorms came.

Many oxen died of thirst or fatigue, and furniture and other heavy items often had to be discarded along the trail. Supplies of food and drinkable water sometimes ran dangerously low. Wagons creaked and groaned; wheel rims came off as the wood dried and shrank. Indians were mostly a nuisance at first, merely stealing and begging from the travelers. But after 1850, more and more settlers made their homes on the plains instead of passing through. Then the Indians began attacking any white people who came upon their land.

One of the most important rules of the trail was "Keep moving." Pioneers left in May as soon as the prairie grass came up; and with reasonable success in traveling, they reached their destination five or six months later. They had to cross the high western ranges before the mountain passes were closed by winter snow. In one case, a party led by George and Jacob Donner started along the Oregon Trail in 1846 and then followed a branch of the trail that led to California. They were trapped by snow in the Sierra Nevada of eastern California, and many in the group perished.

Progress Toward Statehood

As thousands of Americans poured into Oregon Country, the British realized that the days of joint occupation were numbered. President Polk had campaigned for election by using the slogan "Fifty-four forty or fight." That is, he and his supporters were ready to fight if necessary to gain all of Oregon up to 54°40' N. In 1846, President Polk notified Britain that the United States would terminate joint occupation within a year. Would war break out over Oregon?

Neither Britain nor the United States wanted war. When the British proposed that

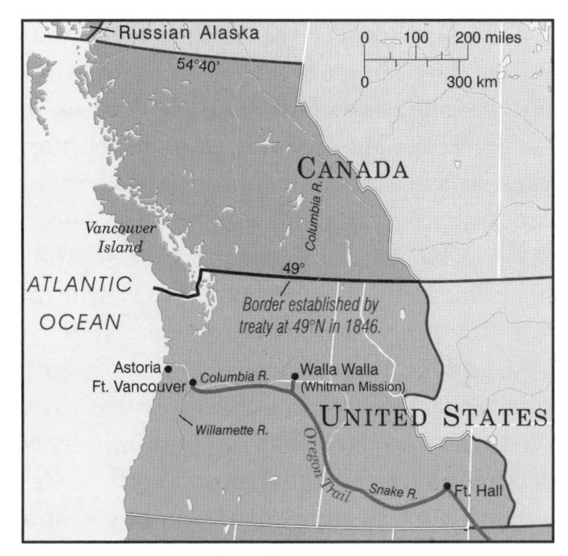

The Division of Oregon Country

Oregon Country be divided at 49° N, the United States accepted. Now the border with Canada extended along the forty-ninth parallel all the way to the Pacific. However, the British retained all of Vancouver Island even though it extends south of 49° N.

The United States organized its share of Oregon Country into the Oregon Territory in 1848. This territory included land in the present states of Washington, Oregon, and Idaho. In 1853, Oregon's present boundaries were drawn when the Washington Territory was created. In 1859, Oregon became a state.

Focus for Thought

8. How did the mountain men contribute to interest in the Far West?
9. a. Why did missionaries go to Oregon?
   b. How did Marcus Whitman influence settlers to move there?
10. On the Oregon Trail, why did pioneers need to
    a. travel light?
    b. work together?
    c. keep moving?
11. a. How was the Oregon Country divided between the United States and Great Britain?
    b. What modern states contain land that was part of this territory?

3. CALIFORNIA AND THE GOLD RUSH

In January 1848, shortly before the Mexican War ended, gold was discovered in California. A great gold rush started as soon as news of the discovery spread to the East. The "golden shore" of California developed rapidly, and about two years later the territory became a state.

Discovery of Gold

John Sutter operated a large ranch at the site of present-day Sacramento, California. In January 1848, a man named James Marshall was building a sawmill for Sutter on the American River, about 50 miles (80 km) from Sutter's Fort. While inspecting the millrace one day, Marshall noticed some particles that looked like gold. He collected some of them and dashed back to Sutter's Fort, where he and Sutter tested his find. The particles were gold!

Sutter's Mill in the area of Sacramento, California. Here James Marshall discovered gold on January 24, 1848.

After General Kearny conquered California, the region officially became a territory of the United States by the Treaty of Guadalupe Hidalgo. The discovery of gold occurred just nine days before this treaty ended the Mexican War on February 2, 1848.

The Gold Rush

The Race to California. At first only some local people went digging for gold. Many did not even believe that gold had been found. But the word spread in newspapers, and soon people were leaving their jobs to head for the gold-bearing hills. Reports of rich gold strikes reached the East by the end of 1848. When President Polk reported the discovery to Congress in December, the great gold rush was on.

The men heading for California were dubbed "forty-niners" because thousands of them made the journey in 1849. Most of the miners were single men, but some families and even women set out. In addition, people from South America, Australia, and even China came to look for gold. Almost one hundred thousand newcomers arrived in California in 1849.

The forty-niners traveled by three main routes. The shortest way was by overland routes such as the Old Spanish Trail or the Oregon Trail. These routes were difficult and dangerous because of mountains, deserts, and attacks by Indians and robbers. The second way was by sea, sailing around the southern tip of South America and north to California. This was an easier but more expensive way to go, and it involved some nine or ten months of hazardous sailing. The third way was to sail south to the east coast of Panama, travel across the isthmus, and then sail north to California. This was shorter than sailing around South America, but travelers faced the danger of diseases carried by insects in Panama.

Life on the Gold Fields. At first, miners found gold lying on or near the surface in the mountains and rivers of central California. ***Prospectors*** staked out a claim and then tried to obtain gold by digging out gravel and washing it. The heavy gold particles settled out, but the sandy gravel washed away. A miner might obtain only one ounce of gold, worth $16, in one day. Getting rich was not easy; in a ten-hour day, a miner could wash perhaps fifty pans of dirt. But because a few miners "struck it rich," others continued searching in hopes of also making a big find.

A rough, wild manner of life developed as people flocked to the gold country. Fights

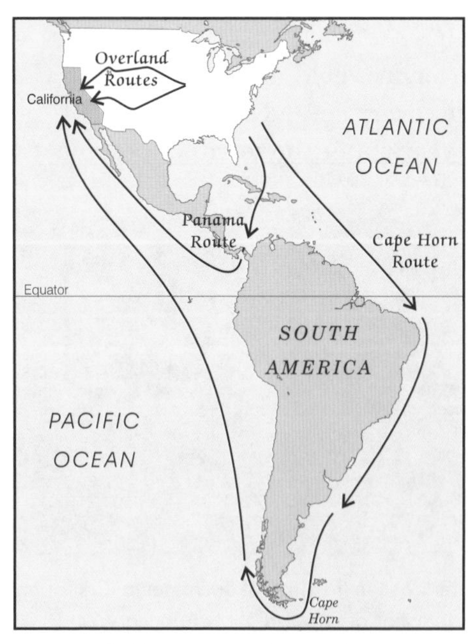

Routes to California During the Gold Rush

Gold seekers crossing the isthmus of Panama. Others traveled by overland routes, and some sailed all the way around Cape Horn.

Three methods of gold mining: Top left: the pan; ***top right:*** the cradle; ***bottom right:*** the "Long Tom."

Methods of Mining. Prospectors used a number of methods to obtain gold, which often appeared in streams as dust, flakes, or nuggets. Panning was perhaps the simplest method. Miners would fill a pan about three-fourths full of soil, hold it underwater, and move it in a circular manner to wash the sand and lighter pebbles over the edge. They continued rotating and jerking the pan until only the heaviest sand with gold particles remained.

Another device was the cradle, which rested on rockers and had a hopper in which the miner placed gold-bearing sand and gravel. He poured water over the gravel while slowly rocking the cradle. Sand but not stones washed through holes in the hopper and onto a canvas apron below the hopper. Some gold stuck to the apron while the sand washed away onto a series of slats called riffles.

Another device was a "Long Tom," a trough that was 12 feet (3.6 m) long. As water poured through the trough, miners shoveled gravel into it. The gravel was filtered out by a screen near the end of the trough, with the bigger stones staying on top of the screen and the fine, gold-rich sediments falling through onto a series of riffles below.

Yet another device was the sluice, a much longer trough into which gravel was shoveled. It had a series of riffles to trap the gold as water washed through. As a miner raked out the gravel, the sand that contained gold remained behind. Some miners dug tunnels and searched for gold underground. In any case, mining was hard work and several miners often worked together.

broke out over claims, and robbery and murder increased. Many who found gold would spend their wealth in drinking and riotous living. Prices rose exorbitantly, with potatoes and eggs priced at $1 apiece and a live chicken at $16. Boots that sold for $2.50 in New York cost $20 in San Francisco. Even renting a shack cost $100 per week! Miners paid in gold dust at the rate of $16 per ounce.

Some men discovered that serving the needs of the miners was much more profitable than mining. One of these was a young man named Levi Strauss, who made trousers from a tough fabric and used rivets to reinforce the stress points. These trousers wore so well that they were soon in great demand. Thus began Levi Strauss and Company, whose trousers later became known as blue jeans or Levi's.

These gold seekers lived for earthly wealth. The Bible warns against the dangers of greed and the vanity of riches. Paul wrote in 1 Timothy 6:10 that "the love of money is the root of all evil" and that by covetousness, some have "pierced themselves through with many sorrows." The latter part of this verse became the bitter experience of many people in California.

Statehood of California

Rapid Growth. Because of the great influx of gold seekers, California grew at a tremendous rate. Towns developed quickly,

Life in San Francisco, 1853. Around 1853, one writer said, "A short experience of the mines had satisfied most of the citizens of San Francisco that . . . hard work was not easy—sorry truisms for weak or lazy men. They . . . found that much greater profits with far less labor were to be found in supplying the necessities of the miners. . . .

"There were no homes at this period in San Francisco. . . . An immense majority of the people took their meals at restaurants, boarding houses, and hotels. . . . Many of these were indeed miserable hovels, which showed only bad [food], . . . dirt, discomfort, and high prices. . . . At night, they lay from half a dozen to twoscore in a room—on the floor, in rows of cots, or . . . [in] filthy bunks fastened to the weatherboards from floor to ceiling, in which were immense swarms of fleas and other troublesome vermin. . . .

"There is perhaps no place in the world where money is so little regarded as in San Francisco. A man spends there like a prince, as he gains like one. . . . At all public and private entertainments, immense sums were squandered. Trade might be dull, . . . rents might rise or fall and people be really insolvent; still they spend money on all sides. . . .

"Ever since the first great immigration, many of the inhabitants carried some weapons of defense secretly about them. . . . The number of duels, and especially of sudden personal affrays, was fearfully great. The general population of San Francisco . . . drank largely of intoxicating liquors. . . . Men thought as little of their blood and lives as of their money and, to gratify high swelling passion, would madly waste them all alike. . . .

"The scum and froth of its strange mixture of peoples, of its many scoundrels, rowdies, and great men, loose women, sharpers, and few honest folk, are still nearly all that is visible. . . . It may be said that nearly all came to the city only as devout worshippers of Mammon; scarcely one to find a home."

with wooden buildings including hotels and saloons going up almost overnight. In San Francisco, some people even lived on ships that were abandoned when their crews went to seek gold! Sacramento, later the capital of California, grew from four houses to ten thousand people, and San Francisco soon had fifty thousand people. By the end of 1849, California had many more than the sixty thousand people necessary to become a state.

The people of California drew up a constitution and applied for statehood that same year. This application again caused a struggle over slavery in the new territories. (The story of that struggle is told in Chapter 15.) But in 1850, California entered the Union as a free state.

Travel and Communication. California was isolated from the rest of the United States by a vast unsettled stretch of almost 2,000 miles (3,219 km). Travel and communication over this stretch were slow and difficult. Though the stagecoaches of the Overland Mail carried letters by 1857, each trip required twenty days or more. These stagecoaches also carried passengers, but travel was dangerous and exhausting. The coaches were robbed by highwaymen and plagued with accidents. A faster method of communication was needed.

Pony express riders faced many dangers. This one is being pursued by an Indian. The structure to the left is an Indian burial platform.

In 1860, the **pony express** began to provide better mail service to California. In this system, expert horsemen galloped 10 to 15

Western Trails and Routes

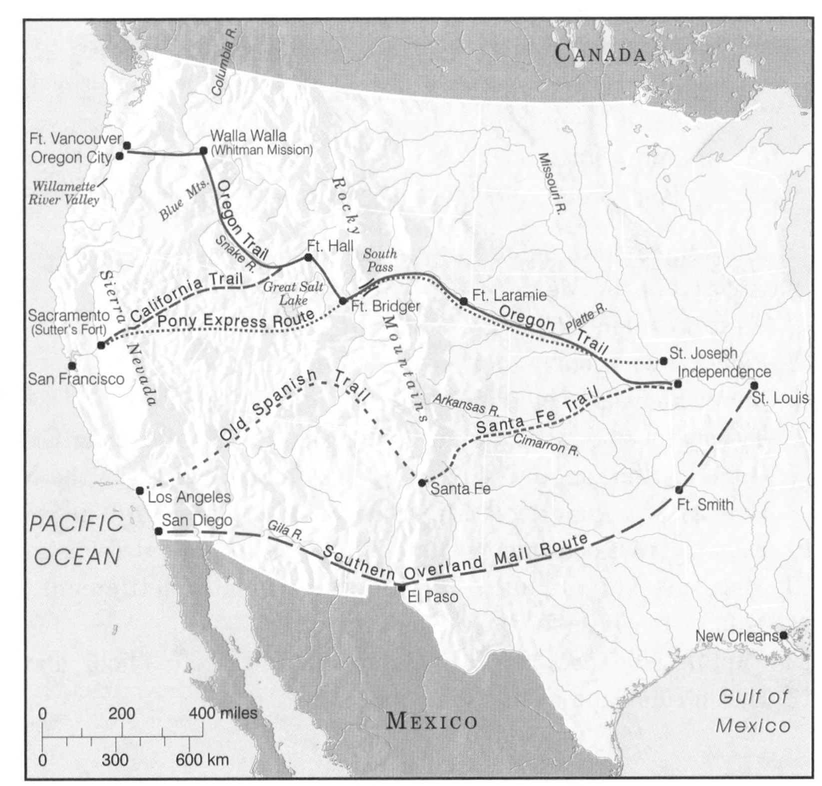

miles (16–24 km) from one station to another, changing horses at each station. One rider would travel about 100 miles (161 km) and then pass the mail pouch to the next rider. By this method, mail could travel between Missouri and California in about ten days. The riders faced the dangers of storms, heat and cold, and attacks by bandits, Indians, and wild animals. The pony express operated only about eighteen months before telegraph lines reached California and put it out of business.

Focus for Thought

12. What three main routes did miners from the East take to travel to California?
13. Give several details of life in California during the gold rush.
14. How did California become a state so quickly?
15. a. Why was the pony express established, and how did it operate?
    b. How long did it last, and why did it end?

Historical Highlights

A. Matching: People

a. Davy Crockett
b. James K. Polk
c. Jedediah Smith
d. Jim Bowie
e. John Frémont
f. John Sutter
g. Kit Carson
h. Marcus Whitman
i. Sam Houston
j. Santa Anna
k. Stephen Austin
l. Stephen Kearny
m. Winfield Scott
n. Zachary Taylor

1. Men who died in defending the Alamo (two answers).
2. General in the Mexican War who was elected president in 1848.
3. First president of the Lone Star Republic.
4. Well-known mountain man.
5. Man who began colonizing Texas.
6. Discoverer of South Pass; first American known to enter California by land.
7. General who conquered New Mexico and California in the Mexican War.
8. General who conquered Mexico City in the Mexican War.
9. Expansionist president when United States gained Texas and California.
10. Missionary to Indians in Oregon who promoted settlement there.
11. Man near whose fort gold was discovered.
12. Captain who led a revolt in California and wrote a book about the West.
13. Harsh ruler and military leader of Mexico.

B. Matching: Terms

a. Bear Flag Republic
b. forty-niners
c. Free-Soil Party
d. Gadsden Purchase
e. Lone Star Republic
f. manifest destiny
g. Mexican Cession
h. mountain men
i. Oregon Trail
j. pony express
k. prospectors
l. rendezvous
m. Treaty of Guadalupe Hidalgo

1. Idea that the United States was intended to spread over the whole North American continent.
2. Hardy fur traders and explorers in the West.
3. Improved system for delivering mail to California.
4. Name given to California when it became independent.
5. Land obtained from Mexico to build a southern railroad.
6. Route used by settlers traveling to the Northwest.
7. People who rushed to find gold in 1849.
8. Land gained through the Mexican War.
9. Political party that opposed slavery in 1848.
10. Meeting place for fur traders to sell their furs and buy supplies.
11. Agreement that ended the Mexican War in 1848.
12. People who seek valuable minerals.
13. Name used for independent Texas.

C. Matching: Places

a. Alamo
b. Buena Vista
c. Fort Laramie
d. Great Salt Lake
e. Oregon Territory
f. Platte River
g. Rio Grande
h. San Jacinto
i. Snake River
j. South Pass
k. Sutter's Fort
l. Vancouver Island
m. Walla Walla
n. Willamette River valley
o. 49° N latitude

1. Place in central California near which gold was found.
2. Body of water in Utah.
3. Border between the United States and Canada to the Pacific.
4. Place in northern Mexico where Zachary Taylor defeated the Mexicans.
5. Final destination of Oregon settlers.
6. Land extending south of 49° N and remaining entirely British.
7. Location of the battle that won independence for Texas.
8. Fort near the Whitman Mission.
9. Stopping place in Wyoming, along the Oregon Trail.
10. River in present-day Nebraska that the Oregon Trail followed for almost 600 miles (966 km).

11. Old mission near San Antonio, Texas, that fell to the Mexicans.
12. Place where the Oregon Trail crossed the Rockies.
13. River that formed the disputed boundary between Texas and Mexico.
14. Area from which the states of Oregon, Washington, and Idaho were formed.
15. River that the Oregon Trail followed across Idaho.

D. Multiple Choice

Write the letter of the best answer.

1. What was the main attraction that drew American settlers to Oregon?
   a. freedom of religion
   b. bounty of the land
   c. social discontent
   d. gold
2. Why did the United States obtain so much territory during the presidency of James Polk?
   a. The United States bought land through the Mexican Cession.
   b. The United States made the Gadsden Purchase.
   c. The mountain men opened the West by exploring it.
   d. The president and many others believed in manifest destiny.
3. Why was Texas not accepted into the United States when it first applied for admission?
   a. The president of that time did not support manifest destiny.
   b. Texas had rebelled against the Mexican government.
   c. There was conflict over slavery in Texas, and fear that war would break out with Mexico.
   d. Texas was part of the Mexican Cession.
4. Which one of the following was included in the Mexican Cession?
   a. Gadsden Purchase
   b. California
   c. Texas
   d. Oregon Country
5. What was Marcus Whitman's greatest contribution to gaining the Oregon Country for the United States?
   a. He conducted a successful mission among the Indians there.
   b. He persuaded authorities that the British and the Americans should occupy the area jointly.
   c. He influenced many United States settlers to move into the area.
   d. He encouraged the mountain men to keep the British out of the area.

E. Deeper Discussion

1. Why did Americans believe in manifest destiny?
2. Why did the Mexicans hold ill feelings toward the United States after the Mexican War?
3. How did the Mexican War contribute to the Civil War?
4. What contributed to the lawlessness and violence of the mining towns in California during the gold rush?
5. Using a topical Bible, look up New Testament references to gold and riches. How should the Christian relate to a gold rush?

F. Chronology and Geography

1. On your map entitled "Territorial Growth of the United States," draw lines showing the Texas Annexation, the Mexican Cession, the Gadsden Purchase, and the Oregon Territory. Label these areas, and color each a different color.
2. On a large map of the United States, follow the route of the Oregon Trail through the present states. (A map in an encyclopedia or a road atlas may help.) Note also the California Trail, as well as the alternate routes at various places. Do modern highways follow the same routes? Over what kind of terrain did the Oregon Trail pass?
3. Answer these questions.
   a. What were the advantages and disadvantages of each of the three routes to California?
   b. Why was the Pacific Coast settled before other areas of the West?

Thousands of California miners lived in crude cabins.

Unit 5

Times of Trouble, 1850–1877

Chapters in Unit 5

Henry Clay, standing right of center, addresses Congress to promote what became the Compromise of 1850. This measure helped to delay the Civil War.

15 "A House Divided": The 1850s

1. Divisive Issues
   - Causes of Disagreement
2. Divisive Events
   - The Compromise of 1850
   - New Controversies
3. Division and Secession
   - Division
   - Secession

"Every kingdom divided against itself is brought to desolation; and every city or house divided against itself shall not stand."

Matthew 12:25

"A House Divided": The 1850s

Focus for Reading

After the Mexican War, the United States entered a period of conflict and division during the 1850s. Sectional differences between the North and the South brought one crisis after another, each one stirring deeper feelings of bitterness and antagonism. By 1860, both North and South had drawn lines and taken positions that seemed irreconcilable without war. Finally when Abraham Lincoln was elected president, a number of Southern states seceded from the Union.

What issues divided the two sections? What events prompted the Southern states to secede? These questions are answered in three sections.

1. Divisive Issues
2. Divisive Events
3. Division and Secession

1. DIVISIVE ISSUES

A number of strong differences separated the North and the South. Although it may seem that slavery was the main issue, in reality deeper causes than slavery separated the two sections. Slavery became the problem that revealed the deeper fissures between the sections, and it became interwoven with all of them.

Causes of Disagreement

States' Rights. As you learned in Chapter 13, the sections of the nation differed in geography, people, and economy. To some extent, these differences had existed since colonial times, but developments in the first half of the 1800s magnified them. One of the disagreements was over interpreting the Constitution. Men such as Hamilton, the Federalists, and later the Whigs wanted a strong federal government and weak state governments. But those like Jefferson and the Democrats promoted stronger state governments.

John C. Calhoun's theory of states' rights led him to formulate his theories of nullification and secession by 1830. (See Chapter 12.) In the 1850s, the South strongly promoted states' rights while the North favored a strong federal government. The issue of which government should have supreme power was one of the main factors leading to the Civil War.

Differing Economies. The South remained agricultural while the North became more industrialized. The North wanted tariffs to encourage industry, but the South wanted free trade. The South believed the North used the federal government to further its ends at the expense of Southerners. They saw the Northern policies as a threat to their Southern way of life.

Control of the Federal Government. For years, Southerners had dominated the federal government through the Democratic Party and Southern presidents. Also, the South maintained a balance of power in the Senate through an equal number of free and slave states. But the North grew much more rapidly in its population and power, even though the Three-fifths Compromise allowed three-fifths of the slaves to be counted for representation. With the higher population already giving the North an advantage in the House, the South feared that soon the North would also have greater power in the Senate. Then the North could overrule whatever the South wanted.

Relationship of Slavery to Other Issues. The dispute over states' rights became especially sharp as men debated the spread of slavery. Should slavery be confined to areas where it already existed, or could it be taken to new territories? Southerners believed it should be allowed in new territories if the people there wanted it. But Northerners believed that the Founding Fathers had only tolerated slavery, expecting it to die out soon, and so would not want it to spread.

According to the Southern point of view, the states were sovereign and could therefore decide whether they wanted slavery; the federal government had no authority to forbid it. But according to the Northern viewpoint, the federal government did have power to decide where slavery should be allowed. This clash over slavery and states' rights was a key issue in the division of the nation.

Slavery also related to the differing sectional economies. The Northern economy was based on manufacturing and trading whereas the Southern economy was based on producing cotton by slave labor. Abolishing slavery would have little effect on the North, but it would threaten the whole economic system of the South. The aristocratic lifestyle of the planters could not continue without slaves. To Southerners, their entire way of life was at stake in the slavery dispute.

Finally, slavery related to control of the federal government because that control was foundational to maintaining slavery. If Northern abolitionists gained control of the government (both House and Senate), they might force the South to comply with their wishes. So the South struggled to maintain its power in the Senate. If it appeared that the North would win control, Southerners would have little choice but to leave the Union.

Thus the immediate issue involving all the controversies was slavery, though the underlying causes were deeper. According to James 4:1, strife comes from the "lusts that war in your members." One of these lusts was the love of money, which was a prime reason for holding slaves. Another was people's wrong desire to have their own way. With both Northerners and Southerners using wrong methods to get their way, the strife could only grow worse.

Slavery divided the South from the North and accented all the other differences. Slavery also caused divisions in churches; for example, the Baptists, the Presbyterians, and the Methodists all split into Northern and Southern wings. This divided spirit prevailed in the nation through the 1850s.

Focus for Thought

1. Compare the North and the South before 1860. Name the section that
   a. was more agricultural.
   b. had more people.
   c. emphasized states' rights.
   d. had fewer people, even though counting three-fifths of the blacks.
   e. favored a strong federal government.
   f. had earlier dominated the federal government through the Democratic Party.
   g. was more industrial and favored tariffs.
2. Explain how slavery related to
   a. states' rights.
   b. differing economies of North and South.
   c. control of the federal government.

2. DIVISIVE EVENTS

As you saw in Chapter 14, the land gained by the Mexican War reopened the thorny issue of slavery in new territories. Compromise had settled the issue formerly, as in the Missouri Compromise, and it would settle the issue again. But new controversies continued to arise.

The Compromise of 1850

The Mexican War had gained vast new lands for the United States, but this raised the question of whether slavery would be permitted there. As early as 1846, Congressman David Wilmot had proposed the Wilmot Proviso (pruh VY zoh), which stated "that . . . neither slavery nor involuntary servitude shall ever exist in any part" of the Mexican Cession. The House passed this measure repeatedly, but the South defeated it every time in the Senate, where their power was equal to that of the North.

Then in 1849, California applied for admission to the Union as a free state—and a new storm of dissension broke out. The South was adamantly opposed because another free state would upset the balance in the Senate. Some radicals said that the South would then need to choose either to secede or to surrender. This issue became a matter of life and death for the Union.

Henry Clay, the Great Compromiser, came up with another plan to save the Union. His proposal contained the following four points. (1) Allow California to enter as a free state. (2) Divide the rest of the Mexican Cession into New Mexico Territory and Utah Territory, and let the settlers there decide the issue of slavery for themselves. (3) End the slave trade, but not slavery itself, in Washington, D.C. (4) Enact a Fugitive Slave Law that would provide for runaway slaves to be returned to their masters.

Congress debated Clay's proposals for months. One group of speakers included John C. Calhoun, Daniel Webster, and others of the older generation. Another group was of the younger generation—William Seward, **Stephen Douglas**, and **Jefferson Davis**. Seward opposed the compromise as he spoke of a "higher law" than the Constitution, which made all men free. Douglas favored the compromise, and Davis promoted slavery. But as long as Zachary Taylor remained president, the compromise did not pass.

In July 1850, President Taylor died and **Millard Fillmore** succeeded him as president.

The Great Compromiser. Henry Clay (1777–1852) became known as the Great Compromiser for his role in devising major political compromises. As a representative from Kentucky, Clay was a war hawk who promoted war with Britain in his first term. After the War of 1812, he was one of the peace commissioners who helped draw up the Treaty of Ghent that ended that war. Again elected to the House in 1815, he promoted his "American System." The first great compromise he achieved was the Missouri Compromise of 1820, which resolved the question of slavery in the Louisiana Territory.

Clay ran for president five times (1824, 1832, 1840, 1844, and 1848), but he never attained to that office. As a senator, he contributed to the Compromise Tariff of 1833, which calmed the nullification crisis. His last great contribution was the Compromise of 1850, which held the nation together for another decade. Clay did not live to see the Union divided; he died two years after this compromise was approved.

Left: Millard Fillmore (1800–1874) was the thirteenth president of the United States. He served from 1850 to 1853 and was a Whig. ***Right:*** Commodore Matthew C. Perry came to Japan in July 1853. As a result of his visit, the Japanese signed a treaty of "peace, friendship, and trade with the United States."

After this, the compromise passed essentially as Clay had proposed it, and became known as the Compromise of 1850. People rejoiced and shouted, "The Union is saved!" But later events would show that the slavery issue had only been put off one more time.

Four relatively peaceful years followed the Compromise of 1850. Near the end of his term, Millard Fillmore sent Commodore **Matthew C. Perry** to the Japanese with a letter requesting that they open to American trade. Japan had been closed for hundreds of years to foreigners and to Christians in particular. In 1854, Japan signed a treaty opening two of its ports to the United States. Now American merchants as well as Christian missionaries could enter Japan. But Fillmore's presidency had ended by then, for **Franklin Pierce** won the election of 1852.

New Controversies

Fugitive Slave Law. Many Northerners strongly opposed the Fugitive Slave Law provided by the Compromise of 1850. They

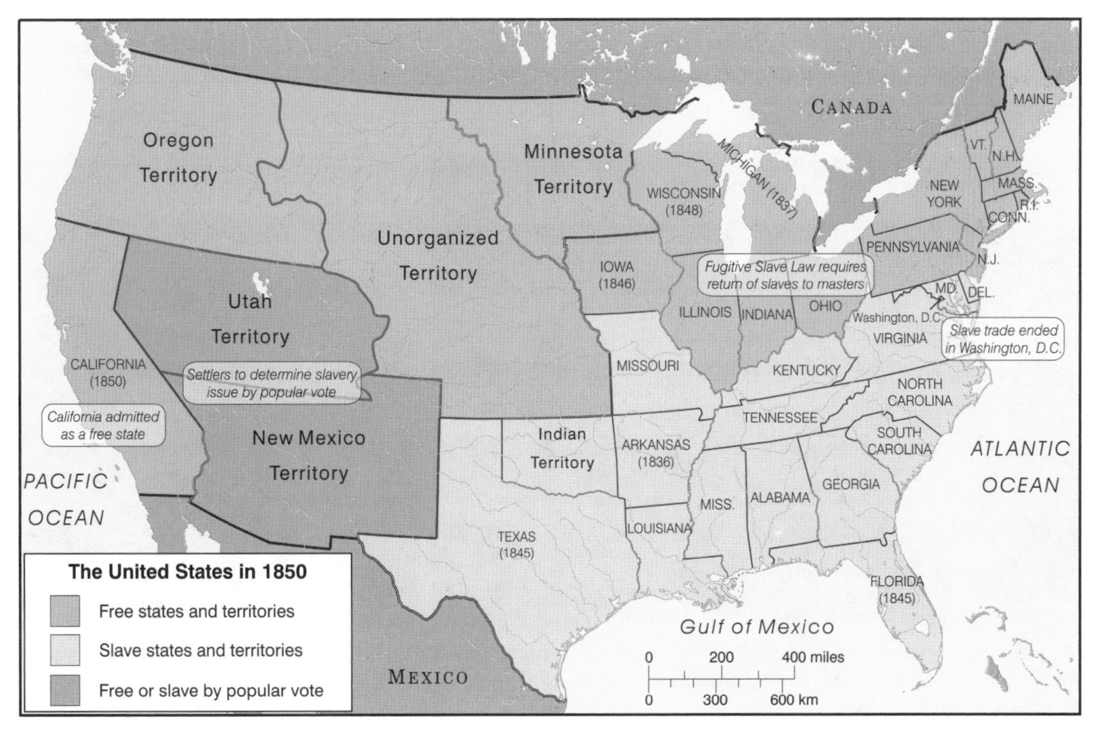

The United States After the Compromise of 1850

$100 REWARD!

RANAWAY

From the undersigned, living on Current River, about twelve miles above Doniphan, in Ripley County, Mo., on 2nd of March, 1860, A NEGRO MAN, about 30 years old, weighs about 160 pounds; high forehead, with a scar on it; had on brown pants and coat very much worn, and an old black wool hat; shoes size No. 11.

The above reward will be given to any person who may apprehend this said negro out of the State; and fifty dollars if apprehended in this State outside of Ripley county, or $25 if taken in Ripley county.

APOS TUCKER.

Left: In Washington, D.C., a chained group of slaves is herded by a man holding a whip. In the distance is the Capitol, which had no dome at the time. The Compromise of 1850 ended the slave trade in this city. ***Right:*** This poster offers a reward for the return of a runaway slave.

believed it was wrong to return blacks to slavery, and they agreed with Mr. Seward about a "higher law" of freedom for all. Sometimes when slave catchers tried to return slaves, mobs would interfere and set the captives free.

Many abolitionists helped the slaves to escape in spite of stiff penalties. They developed such an effective system that it became known as the ***Underground Railroad***. Quakers and other abolitionists were "conductors," and their houses became "stations" with secret places for hiding runaways. The conductors helped the slaves to move from one station to another until they reached Canada, where they were free. As many as seventy-five thousand slaves may have escaped by the Underground Railroad.

Some people became famous for their efforts to help slaves to freedom. **Levi Coffin**, a Quaker who was called the "president

Left: Runaway slaves arrive at a "station" of the Underground Railroad in Indiana. Major routes passed through Indiana, Ohio, and western Pennsylvania. ***Right:*** The Magee House in New York, which served as a "station" of the Underground Railroad.

of the Underground Railroad," helped as many as three thousand slaves to gain freedom. Some former slaves traveled back into the South to help free other slaves. Former slave Harriet Tubman, known as "the Moses of her people," led about three hundred slaves to freedom, including her parents.

How did Mennonites relate to abolition? The Mennonites in general neither owned slaves nor took part in helping them to escape. For example, the Virginia Conference did not allow the ownership of slaves. One source says, "The rule was simply that Mennonites and Amish were not slaveholders."

Southerners became bitter because of all the slaves that were escaping to the North. They said that Northerners were not keeping their part of the Compromise of 1850. Some Northern states even passed personal liberty laws that obstructed the enforcement of the Fugitive Slave Law. This issue drove the sections still further apart.

Protest Against Slavery. *In 1688, four Quakers (including three of Mennonite origin) wrote the following protest against slavery. This is one of the earliest and clearest objections to slavery in American history. It was registered with the Quaker church government because some Quakers of that time owned slaves.*

These are the reasons why we are against the traffic of [slavery]. . . . We hear that most Negroes are brought hither against their will and consent, and that many of them are stolen. Now though they are black, we cannot conceive there is more liberty to have them [as] slaves, as it is to have white ones. There is a saying that we shall do to all men, like as we will be done ourselves, making no difference of what generation, descent or color they are. And those who steal or rob men, and those who buy or purchase them, are they not all alike? . . . But to bring men hither, or rob and sell them against their will, we stand against. In Europe there are many oppressed for conscience sake, and here there are those who are oppressed which are of a black color. And we who know that men must not commit adultery [cause others to commit adultery by] separating wives from their husbands, and giving them to others, and some sell the children of those poor creatures to other men. . . . What thing in the world can be done worse towards us than if men should rob or steal us away and sell us for slaves to strange countries, separating husbands from their wives and children? . . . And we who profess that it is not lawful to steal must likewise avoid purchasing such things as are stolen, but rather help stop this robbing and stealing if possible. . . .

If once these slaves (which they say are so wicked and stubborn men) should join themselves, fight for their freedom, and handle their masters and mistresses like they did handle them before, will these masters and mistresses take the sword and war against these poor slaves? . . . Or have these Negroes not as much right to fight for their freedom as you have to keep them slaves? . . . Our good friends and acquaintances in our native country [think it to be a] fearful thing that men should be handled so in Pennsylvania.

Garret Hendericks   Derick op den Graeff
Francis Daniel Pastorius   Abraham op den Graeff

Harriet Beecher Stowe (1811–1896) wrote *Uncle Tom's Cabin*. She hoped the book would help to end slavery peacefully, but it increased the tensions that brought on the Civil War.

Uncle Tom's Cabin. In 1852, the publication of *Uncle Tom's Cabin*, written by **Harriet Beecher Stowe**, added more fuel to the controversy. In this book, a Christian slave named Tom worked under three different masters. When he refused to give information about two escaped slaves, he was beaten so cruelly that he died soon afterward. The book also tells about Eliza Harris, who crossed the Ohio River on ice floes to get away from her pursuers and then escaped to Canada by way of the Underground Railroad.

In the North, the book became wildly popular; three hundred thousand copies sold in one year. Its portrayal of slaves as normal humans stirred up strong feelings against slavery and the Fugitive Slave Law. Southerners reviled the author and her book, claiming that it gave an unfair picture of slavery. *Uncle Tom's Cabin* served to harden public opinion on both sides.

Kansas-Nebraska Act. In Congress, the ugly quarrel about slavery began anew in 1854 with a bill introduced by Stephen Douglas. He proposed that the unorganized part of the Louisiana Purchase, called the Nebraska Territory, be organized as two parts: the Nebraska Territory and the Kansas Territory. Why would such a simple proposal cause conflict?

First, Senator Douglas believed that the United States should expand and not allow slavery to hinder that expansion. He believed in ***popular sovereignty***—allowing the citizens in a territory to decide about slavery for themselves. He reasoned that popular sovereignty was the best way to defuse the slavery issue without hindering progress. Second, Douglas promoted a transcontinental railroad to the Pacific, and he wanted it to begin in the central part of the country—preferably Chicago, since he was from Illinois.

In order to achieve these goals, Douglas proposed first to organize the Nebraska Territory so that a railroad could be built across it. Then, to appease the South, his bill called for popular sovereignty to apply in the new territories. The problem was that in the Louisiana Territory, the slavery question had already been decided by the Missouri Compromise! In effect, Douglas's proposal would cancel the provision in the Missouri Compromise by which slavery was forbidden north of 36°30'.

The Kansas-Nebraska Act was acceptable to the South, and it passed in April 1854. But the new law stirred a storm of protest by Northerners. They thought the Missouri Compromise had effectively limited slavery, but Douglas's bill would allow it to expand almost without limit. This act divided the Union more sharply than ever.

"Bleeding Kansas." Since the people in

Franklin Pierce (1804–1869) was the fourteenth president of the United States. He served from 1853 to 1857 and was a Democrat.

each territory could make their own decision about slavery, both proslavery and antislavery people began flocking to Kansas. Soon an election was held for a territorial government, and many proslavery Missourians crossed the border to vote in Kansas—with the result that a proslavery government was established there. But the antislavery settlers in Kansas refused to accept its authority and set up a free government at Topeka.

This situation soon led to violence. In 1856, five proslavery men attacked and burned the antislavery town of Lawrence. In retaliation, a radical named **John Brown** led an assault in which five proslavery men were killed at Pottawatomie Creek. Fighting escalated until, by October, about two hundred people were killed and much property was destroyed; hence the name "Bleeding Kansas." Authorities brought the violence under control, but it broke out again when Kansas applied for statehood in 1858. The issue was finally settled in 1861 when Kansas entered the Union as a free state.

Focus for Thought

3. a. What was the Wilmot Proviso?
   b. How was the South able to defeat it?
4. What caused the dispute in 1850 over slavery?
5. Give the four provisions of the Compromise of 1850. After each, write *N* if it favored the North, *S* if it favored the South, or *C* if it was a compromise to satisfy both sides.
6. What significant agreement was made with Japan in 1854?
7. In what ways did the Fugitive Slave Law bring division?
8. a. How did *Uncle Tom's Cabin* help to increase Northern sympathy for black slaves?
   b. How did Southerners respond to the book?
9. a. How did the Kansas-Nebraska Act open additional land for slavery?
   b. What were two effects of this act?

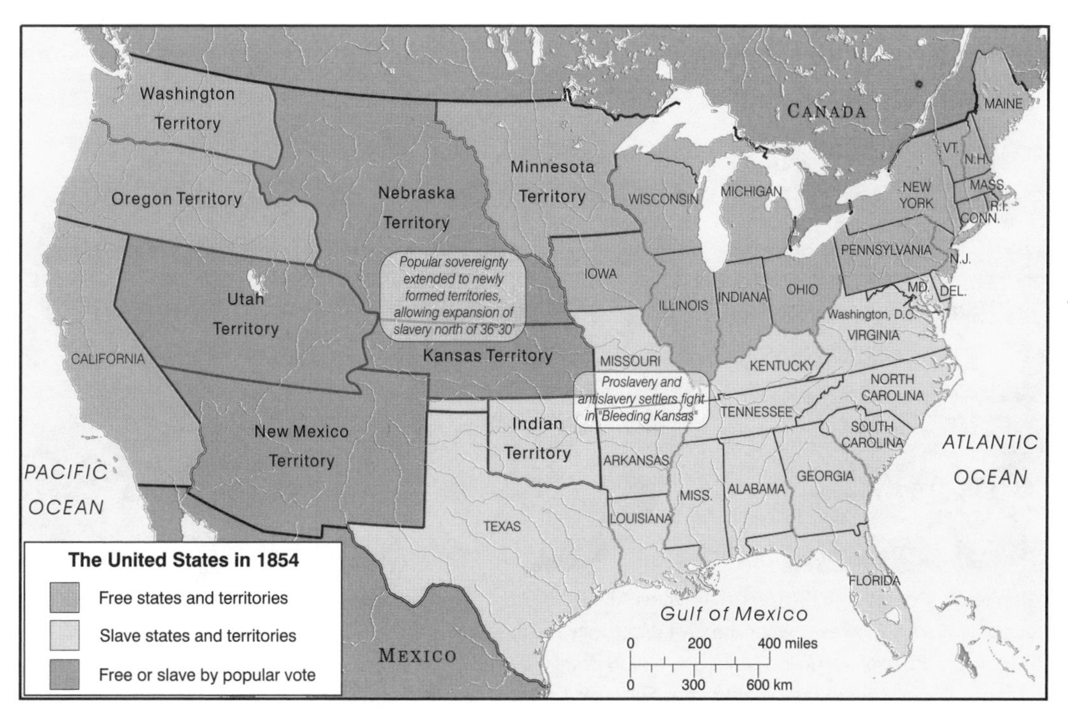

The United States After the Kansas-Nebraska Act

3. DIVISION AND SECESSION

Though various compromises eased the discord between the North and the South, conflict broke out afresh after each agreement, and each new struggle brought greater strife. After a decade of such quarreling, Southern states decided they had had enough—they seceded from the United States. Thus the Union became "a house divided."

Division

Splits in Political Parties. The Kansas-Nebraska Act divided political parties into various fragments that either supported or opposed the new law. One new party that arose was the Republicans, from which the modern Republican Party developed. Founded in Wisconsin in 1854, this party specifically opposed extending slavery into the territories. The Republicans stood for many of the old Whig policies, such as a strong federal government and internal improvements. Consequently, many Whigs and Free Soilers joined Republican ranks, including a lawyer from Illinois named **Abraham Lincoln**.

The nation's disunity showed clearly in the 1856 election. **James Buchanan** ran for the Democrats, John Frémont for the Republicans, and ex-president Millard Fillmore for a group called the American Party. James Buchanan easily won the election.

Caning of Sumner. The bitter feelings erupted into violence in Congress itself. In 1856, Senator **Charles Sumner** gave a speech in which he blamed the South for the troubles in Kansas and made some scornful remarks about a senator from South Carolina. Three days later, Representative Preston Brooks, also of South Carolina, walked up to Sumner's desk and beat him with a cane until he was unconscious. To the North, Sumner was a hero and a victim of Southern proslavery forces. But Brooks was a hero in the South, and he received many canes to replace the one he had destroyed in beating Sumner. This incident was but a foretaste of greater violence to follow.

Dred Scott Decision. In 1857, a case regarding a slave named **Dred Scott** came before the Supreme Court. Scott's master was from Missouri, but he had taken Scott to Illinois and then to Wisconsin—north of

Left: Stephen A. Douglas (1813–1861), known as "the Little Giant," argued that the people of each state should decide for themselves about slavery. However, when the Civil War broke out, he supported the Union. ***Middle:*** James Buchanan (1791–1868) was the fifteenth president of the United States. He served from 1857 to 1861 and was a Democrat. ***Right:*** Dred Scott (1795?–1858), whose suit for freedom went to the United States Supreme Court. A new owner freed Scott about two months after the court dismissed his case.

the Missouri Compromise line—for several years. After his master brought him back to Missouri, Scott sued for his freedom because of the time he had lived in free territory. The outcome of this case would have tremendous implications regarding the slavery issue.

The Court's ruling essentially dismissed Scott's case. In writing for the majority, Chief Justice **Roger Taney** (TAW nee) declared that Scott was not a citizen of the United States and therefore could not bring suit in a federal court. Further, Taney wrote that since Scott was property, his master could take him anywhere in the United States. Congress could not prohibit slavery in the United States because that would violate slaveholders' property rights; and therefore, the Missouri Compromise was unconstitutional. The Supreme Court had ruled in favor of the South.

Naturally, the South was jubilant because now slavery could spread without hindrance. But Northerners bitterly opposed the Dred Scott decision. Whereas slavery had formerly been limited to the South and freedom was the rule, now it seemed that freedom was limited and slavery would become the rule. Many Northerners began thinking that only the Republican Party could stop the spread of slavery.

Lincoln-Douglas Debates. In Illinois, the Republicans chose Abraham Lincoln to run against Democrat Stephen Douglas for the Senate in 1858. Lincoln and Douglas made their views public in a series of seven debates from August to October. The contrast between the two men was striking. Lincoln was a tall, gangling man who spoke in a high-pitched but sincere voice. He wore simple clothes and a stovepipe hat that made him look even taller. Douglas, a short, well-dressed, and graceful man, was a powerful speaker.

Of course, much of the debate centered on the slavery issue. Lincoln opposed the spread of slavery and argued that slavery was wrong, while Douglas stood for popular sovereignty.

The fifth of the Lincoln-Douglas debates, which brought Abraham Lincoln to national prominence. It was held at Knox College in Galesburg, Illinois, on October 7, 1858.

Douglas went on to win the election, but Lincoln became a nationally known figure. In one of his speeches, he warned the nation that "a house divided against itself cannot stand. I believe this government cannot endure half slave and half free."

John Brown's Raid on Harpers Ferry. John Brown, the radical abolitionist from Kansas, believed that God had called him to free the slaves. To achieve this goal, Brown planned to raid a federal armory at Harpers Ferry, Virginia (today in West Virginia), and to arm the slaves with weapons captured there. Brown and a handful of supporters captured the armory in October 1859, but his wild scheme went awry. The plotters were quickly surrounded by Colonel Robert E. Lee and the United States Marines, who stormed the building and captured Brown.

John Brown was tried, convicted of treason, and hanged. Some in the North considered him a martyr and even wrote a song about him. But Southerners despised Brown

John Brown (1800–1859) on his way to be hanged for treason. In this idealized picture, Brown bends to kiss a black child held up by his mother; but a historical source says that never actually happened.

and considered his raid an example of the extreme measures that abolitionists would use to free the slaves.

John Brown's experience illustrates the truth of the Bible verse that says, "He that is hasty of spirit exalteth folly" (Proverbs 14:29).

Secession

Election of Abraham Lincoln. Four men ran for the presidency in 1860. The Republican candidate was Lincoln, who had become popular in the North by giving speeches in a number of states. Northern Democrats nominated Stephen Douglas, while Southern Democrats nominated John Breckinridge, Buchanan's vice president. John Bell ran for the Constitutional Union Party, a group that promoted saving the Union and ignoring slavery.

The South threatened to secede if Lincoln won the election, for he stood against the spread of slavery. Lincoln had stated, however,

Abraham Lincoln in February 1860. This photograph was taken by Mathew Brady, a famous Civil War photographer.

that he did not favor immediately abolishing slavery in states where it already existed, but he thought the slaves should be freed at some later time. When the votes were tallied, it became clear that Abraham Lincoln would be the next president.

Secession of Southern States. Without waiting to see what Lincoln would do, South Carolina voted to secede from the Union shortly after his election. By February 1861, Mississippi, Florida, Alabama, Georgia, Louisiana, and Texas (in that order) had also seceded. Buchanan was still president, but he thought the federal government had no authority to do anything about the secession. Would Lincoln feel the same way, or would he try to preserve the Union by force? Virginia, North Carolina, Tennessee, and Arkansas waited to see what the answer would be.

Meanwhile, the seceded states formed the Confederate States of America at Montgomery, Alabama, in February 1861. The Confederate leaders modified the United States Constitution for their own use, clearly stating that slavery was allowed and that the states were sovereign. Jefferson Davis became the president, and Alexander Stephens became the vice president.

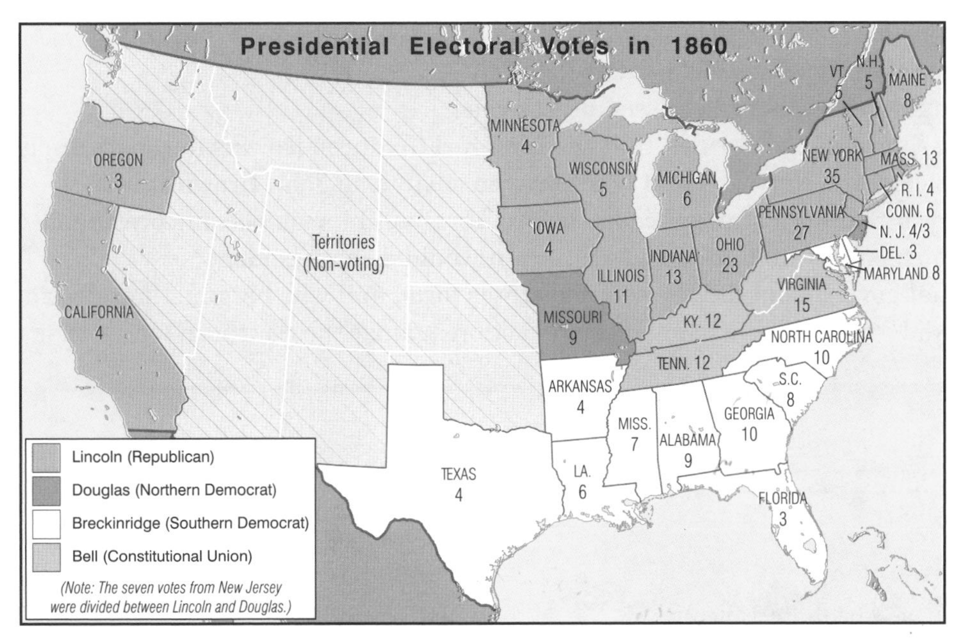

The 1860 Presidential Election

Jefferson Davis (1808–1889) served as president of the Confederate States of America from February 1861 until 1865.

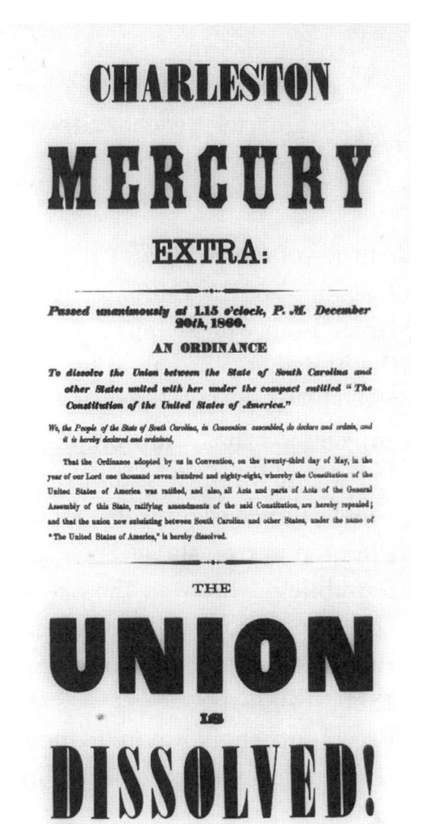

CHARLESTON

MERCURY

EXTRA:

Passed unanimously at 1.15 o'clock, P. M. December 20th, 1860.

AN ORDINANCE

To dissolve the Union between the State of South Carolina and other States united with her under the compact entitled "The Constitution of the United States of America."

We, the People of the State of South Carolina, in Convention assembled, do declare and ordain, and it is hereby declared and ordained,

That the Ordinance adopted by us in Convention, on the twenty-third day of May, in the year of our Lord one thousand seven hundred and eighty-eight, whereby the Constitution of the United States of America was ratified, and also, all Acts and parts of Acts of the General Assembly of this State, ratifying amendments of the said Constitution, are hereby repealed; and that the union now subsisting between South Carolina and other States, under the name of "The United States of America," is hereby dissolved.

THE

UNION

IS

DISSOLVED!

Announcement of South Carolina's secession in the Charleston *Mercury* in 1860.

Focus for Thought

10. What modern political party was founded in the 1850s?
11. What incident of violence occurred in Congress because of the slavery issue?

12. Give the basis on which
    a. Dred Scott sued for his freedom.
    b. the Supreme Court dismissed Scott's case.
    c. the Supreme Court ruled that the Missouri Compromise was unconstitutional.
13. What were the Northern and Southern viewpoints on John Brown's raid?
14. a. Which Southern states seceded before Abraham Lincoln became president?
    b. Which ones waited to see what Lincoln would do as president?
    c. What government did the seceded states form, and who became their president?
15. Why did President Buchanan take no action against the Southern states that seceded?

Historical Highlights

A. Matching: People

a. Abraham Lincoln
b. Charles Sumner
c. Dred Scott
d. Franklin Pierce
e. Harriet Beecher Stowe
f. Henry Clay
g. James Buchanan
h. Jefferson Davis
i. John Brown
j. Levi Coffin
k. Matthew C. Perry
l. Millard Fillmore
m. Roger Taney
n. Stephen Douglas

1. Author of *Uncle Tom's Cabin.*
2. President of the Confederate States of America.
3. Black man whose appeal for freedom was rejected by the Supreme Court.
4. Senator who was caned by Preston Brooks.
5. "President of the Underground Railroad."
6. Introduced the Compromise of 1850.
7. President when the Compromise of 1850 passed.
8. Chief Justice of Supreme Court who wrote for the majority in the Dred Scott decision.
9. Planned to free slaves through an armed uprising.
10. Republican who won the presidency in 1860.
11. United States president when Southern states began to secede.
12. Promoter of popular sovereignty; Northern Democratic candidate for the Senate in 1860.
13. President when Japan opened ports to Americans.
14. Gained permission for the United States to trade with Japan.

B. Matching: Terms

a. Compromise of 1850
b. Confederate States of America
c. Fugitive Slave Law
d. Kansas-Nebraska Act
e. popular sovereignty
f. Republican Party
g. *Uncle Tom's Cabin*
h. Underground Railroad
i. Wilmot Proviso

1. Political group that opposed the spread of slavery.
2. Requirement stating that runaway slaves must be returned.
3. Secret system for helping slaves escape to Canada.
4. Proposal that allowed slavery to spread into new areas.
5. Book that strengthened antislavery feelings in the North.
6. States that seceded from the Union.
7. Proposal to forbid slavery in the Mexican Cession.
8. Proposal introduced after California requested admission as a free state.
9. Idea that people living in an area should decide for themselves about slavery.

C. Multiple Choice

Write the letter of the best answer.

1. How did abolitionists help to move the nation toward the Civil War?
   a. They aroused ill feelings between the North and the South.
   b. They caused the slaves to become restless and rebellious.
   c. They promoted sending black slaves back to Africa.
   d. They opposed the idea that blacks were inferior beings.
2. Why did the Compromise of 1850 fail to overcome the sharp disunity in the nation?
   a. It failed to deal with the major points of conflict.
   b. The South was not satisfied with the final decision.
   c. It favored one side.
   d. It did not settle the bitter dispute over slavery.
3. In what way did popular sovereignty extend slavery?
   a. It allowed slavery to spread into any part of the nation.
   b. It allowed the Dred Scott decision to take effect.
   c. It allowed slavery to spread into new areas if the people there wanted it.
   d. It allowed the South to vote for the extension of slavery.
4. What issue prompted the rise of the Republican Party?
   a. the Compromise of 1850
   b. the Kansas-Nebraska Act
   c. the Dred Scott decision
   d. John Brown's raid
5. Which concept eventually climaxed in Southern secession?
   a. popular sovereignty
   b. nullification
   c. states' rights
   d. aristocracy
6. What was the immediate cause for some Southern states to secede from the Union?
   a. Abraham Lincoln, the Republican candidate, won the presidential election.
   b. Southerners were tired of being harassed by abolitionists.
   c. Southerners wanted Jefferson Davis to be their president.
   d. The Compromise of 1850 did not work.

D. Deeper Discussion

1. a. Explain popular sovereignty.
   b. How did Senator Douglas think popular sovereignty would defuse the slavery quarrel?
   c. Why did it fail to work that way?
2. How did the Dred Scott decision favor the South's view of slavery?
3. How did the South justify its secession?

4. a. What changes did the Confederate States of America make to the United States Constitution?
   b. Why did they make these changes?
5. Galatians 5:15 says, "But if ye bite and devour one another, take heed that ye be not consumed one of another." Explain how this warning went unheeded by the North and the South.

E. Chronology and Geography

1. The following list gives events leading to the secession of the Southern states. Arrange the list in the proper order, and supply the date for each event.

   Charles Sumner caned
   Compromise of 1850 passed
   Dred Scott decision causes contention
   Fugitive Slave Law enacted
   John Brown raids Harpers Ferry
   Kansas-Nebraska Act passed
   Lincoln and Douglas debate issues
   Lincoln elected president
   Other Southern states secede
   Republican Party founded
   South Carolina secedes on December 20
   Uncle Tom's Cabin published
   Violence erupts in "Bleeding Kansas"
   Wilmot Proviso proposed but defeated

2. a. List the seven original states of the Confederacy in the order of secession.
   b. Where was the first capital of the Confederacy?
   c. Which four slave states did not secede immediately?
   d. Why might they have waited longer to secede?

So Far This Year

A. Multiple Choice

Write the letter of the correct answer for each description.

1. Idea that the United States should spread over the whole North American continent.
   a. Mexican Cession
   b. manifest destiny
   c. Oregon fever
   d. California gold rush
2. Land gained by the Mexican War.
   a. the Gadsden Purchase
   b. manifest destiny
   c. the Mexican Cession
   d. the Treaty of Guadalupe Hidalgo
3. Hardy fur traders and explorers of the West.
   a. forty-niners
   b. rendezvous
   c. prospectors
   d. mountain men
4. Expansionist president from 1845 to 1849.
   a. James Polk
   b. Sam Houston
   c. Zachary Taylor
   d. Winfield Scott
5. Man who began colonizing Texas.
   a. John Sutter
   b. Stephen Austin
   c. Sam Houston
   d. Marcus Whitman
6. Missionary who encouraged settlement of Oregon.
   a. Marcus Whitman
   b. John Frémont
   c. John Sutter
   d. Stephen Austin
7. Man near whose fort gold was discovered.
   a. John Frémont
   b. James Marshall
   c. John Sutter
   d. Stephen Kearny
8. Mail system connecting California to the East.
   a. gold rush
   b. pony express
   c. Oregon Trail
   d. forty-niners
9. Treaty that ended the Mexican War.
   a. joint occupation
   b. Gadsden Purchase
   c. Treaty of Guadalupe Hidalgo
   d. Mexican Cession
10. Area from which the states of Oregon, Washington, and Idaho were formed.
   a. Mexican Cession
   b. Oregon Territory
   c. Gadsden Purchase
   d. California Territory
11. President elected in 1848, who had been a general in the Mexican War.
   a. Zachary Taylor
   b. James Polk
   c. Winfield Scott
   d. Sam Houston
12. General who conquered Mexico City in the Mexican War.
   a. Stephen Kearny
   b. Santa Anna
   c. Zachary Taylor
   d. Winfield Scott
13. River that formed the disputed boundary between Texas and Mexico.
   a. Platte River
   b. Snake River
   c. Rio Grande
   d. Colorado River

14. Discoverer of the South Pass and first American known to enter California by land.
    a. Kit Carson
    b. Jim Bridger
    c. John Frémont
    d. Jedediah Smith
15. Old mission near San Antonio, Texas, that fell to the Mexicans.
    a. the Alamo
    b. San Jacinto
    c. Buena Vista
    d. Fort Laramie
16. People with whom the Oregon Country was shared from 1818 to 1846.
    a. Spanish
    b. British
    c. Russians
    d. French

B. Matching: Terms 1

17. Traveling preacher in the West.
18. Effort to stop the use of strong drink.
19. Machine for removing seeds from cotton.
20. Elimination of slavery.
21. Region dependent on cotton.
22. Large farm that produced one main crop and used slave labor.
23. Change from producing handmade goods at home to producing machine-made goods in factories.

a. abolition
b. circuit rider
c. cotton gin
d. Cotton Kingdom
e. Industrial Revolution
f. plantation
g. temperance movement

C. Matching: Terms 2

24. Government divided into three branches.
25. Branch of government that makes laws.
26. Government by elected representatives.
27. Ways by which government branches limit each other.
28. Group of men who elect the president.
29. Branch of government that enacts and enforces laws.
30. Government divided between states and national government.
31. Branch of government that decides cases about laws.

a. checks and balances
b. Electoral College
c. executive
d. federal
e. judicial
f. legislative
g. republic
h. separation of powers

D. Completion

Write the correct name or date for each description.

32. Inventor of the telegraph.
33. Brought textile manufacturing to America.
34. Inventor of the cotton gin.
35. Published the "blue-backed speller."
36. Built the first successful steamboat.
37. Years of the Mexican War.
38. Date for the Constitutional Convention.
39. Date when the Bill of Rights was added to the Constitution.
40. Date when the United States government under the Constitution began.

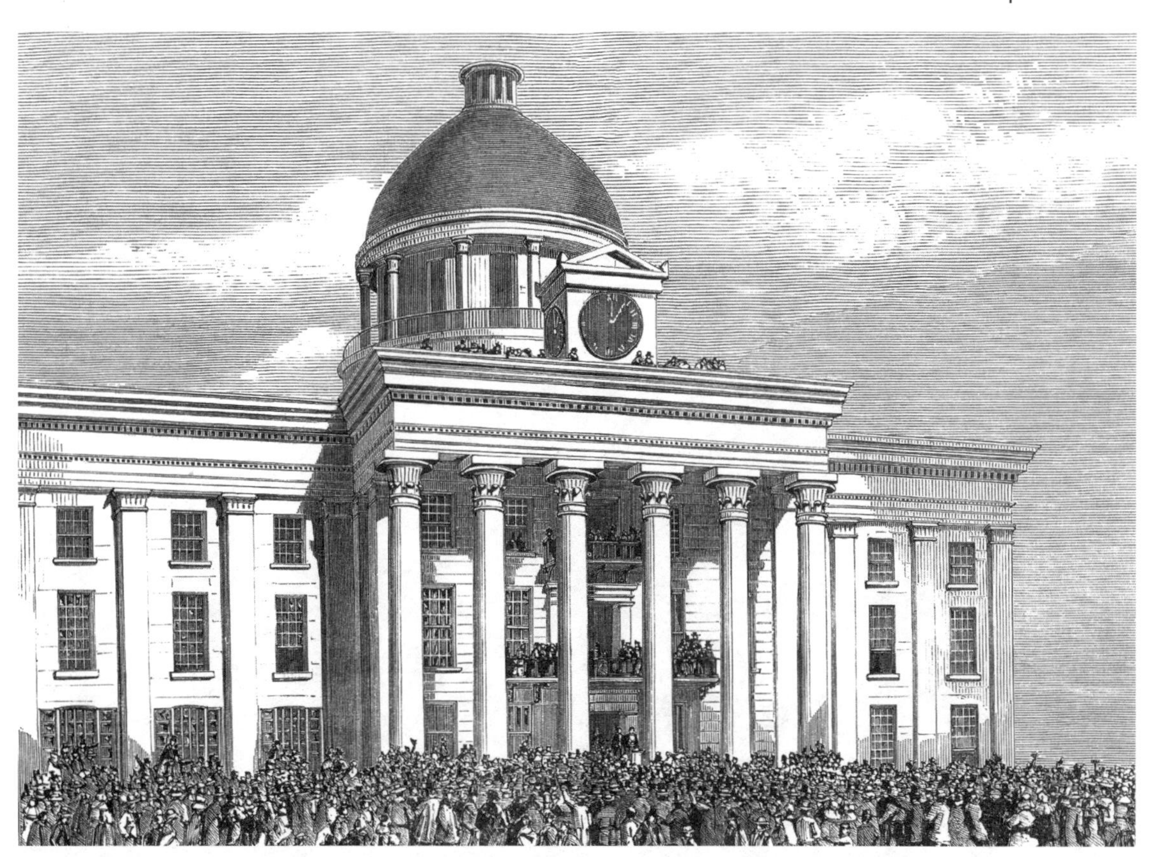

Inauguration of Jefferson Davis in February 1861. The location was Montgomery, Alabama, the first capital of the Confederate States of America.

Abraham Lincoln's inauguration on March 4, 1861. The Capitol was being enlarged at the time; its huge cast-iron dome was not completed until 1863.

16 The Civil War

	1861	
March 4		Lincoln inaugurated
April 12		Fort Sumter fired upon
July 21		First Battle of Bull Run
	1862	
February 6		Fall of Fort Henry
February 16		Fall of Fort Donelson
March–July		Peninsular Campaign
March 9		Battle between *Monitor* and *Merrimack*
April 6–7		Battle of Shiloh
April 25		Fall of New Orleans
August 29–30		Second Battle of Bull Run
September 17		Battle of Antietam
September 22		Emancipation Proclamation issued
December 13		Battle of Fredericksburg
January 1	1863	Emancipation Proclamation becomes effective
May 1–4		Battle of Chancellorsville
July 1–3		Battle of Gettysburg
July 4		Fall of Vicksburg
November 19		Gettysburg Address
	1864	
May–June 1864		Wilderness Campaign
May 5–6		The Battle of the Wilderness
May 8–19		Battle of Spotsylvania Court House
June 3–12		Battle of Cold Harbor
June 20, 1864–April 2, 1865		Siege of Petersburg
September 2		Fall of Atlanta
September 19–October 19		Sheridan's raid
November 8		Lincoln re-elected
November 15–December 21		Sherman's March to the Sea
December 21		Fall of Savannah
	1865	
April 2		Fall of Richmond
April 9		Lee surrenders at Appomattox Court House
April 14		Lincoln assassinated
	1866	

"And, behold, every man's sword was against his fellow, and there was a very great discomfiture."
1 Samuel 14:20

The Civil War

Focus for Reading

When Southern states seceded from the Union in 1861, war broke out soon afterward. This Civil War (also known as the War Between the States) dragged on for four bloody years until the North won the war and preserved the Union. What happened during the Civil War? What were the costs and results of this war? How did nonresistant Christians fare amid the strife? These questions are answered in three sections.

1. The Civil War, Part 1: 1861–1862
2. The Civil War, Part 2: 1863–1865
3. Costs and Results of the Civil War; Experiences of Nonresistant People

1. THE CIVIL WAR, PART 1: 1861–1862

War began in 1861 over Southern secession. At first, both North and South believed the war would be short, with the South winning independence or the North forcing the states of the Confederacy to return to the Union. This war divided not only the nation but also states, churches, communities, and families, so that friend fought friend, father fought son, and brother fought brother. The bitterness and heartache caused by the Civil War lasted many years.

The War Begins, 1861

Lincoln's Inauguration. Many people wondered what Lincoln would do about the secession of the Southern states. In his inaugural address on March 4, 1861, Lincoln declared, "In your hands, my dissatisfied fellow

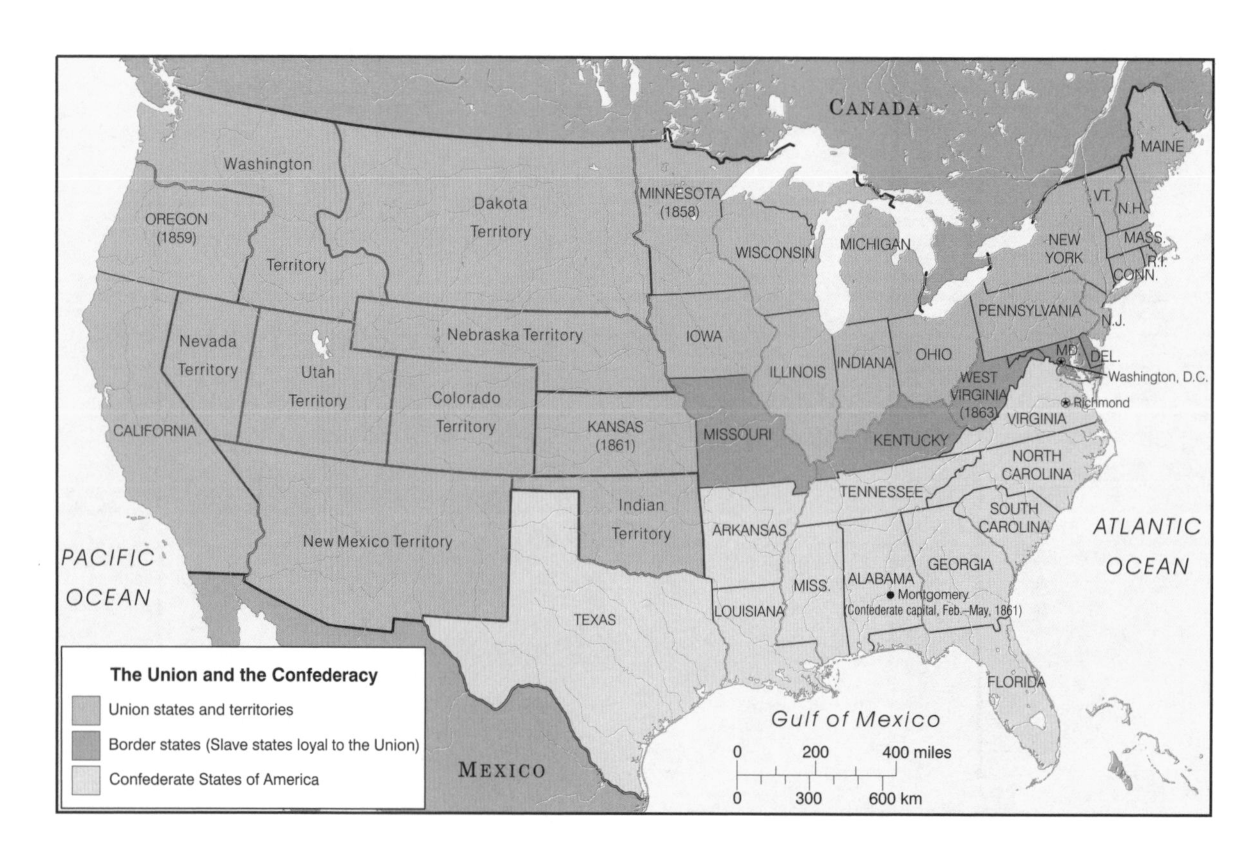

Fort Sumter, site of the first battle in the Civil War. This picture shows the fort as it appears today.

countrymen, and not in mine is the momentous issue of civil war." If war broke out, he said, it would be started by the citizens and not the government. In a closing plea for unity, he said, "We are not enemies, but friends. We must not be enemies. Though passion may have strained, it must not break our bonds of affection."

Fall of Fort Sumter. In spite of these gracious words, Lincoln soon faced severe troubles. The Confederate States had taken over most federal forts and property in the South; but Fort Sumter at Charleston, South Carolina, was an exception. When its commander refused to give up the fort in April 1861, Confederate forces bombarded it for more than thirty hours until it surrendered. The Civil War had begun.

Retreat of the Union army toward Washington, D.C., after the First Battle of Bull Run on July 21, 1861. Note the panic and confusion in the scene.

Shortly afterward, Virginia, Arkansas, Tennessee, and North Carolina joined the Confederacy. President Lincoln called for seventy-five thousand volunteers for ninety days to help put down the insurrection. The president believed that the Union was perpetual and that secession was therefore illegal. His primary goal in fighting was to preserve the Union.

The First Battle of Bull Run. After Virginia seceded, the Confederates moved their capital to Richmond. Since it was not far from Washington, many Northerners thought the Union army should capture Richmond and end the rebellion. So Union forces headed across the Potomac River into Virginia in July. In a carnival atmosphere, many citizens of Washington went out to watch the battle as if they were on a picnic.

About 20 miles (32 km) from Washington lay the town of Manassas Junction, with Confederate troops stationed along a creek called Bull Run, just north of the town. On July 21, Union soldiers attacked the Confederates and at first drove them back. But when the Confederates made a counterattack, the "Federals" panicked, broke ranks, and fled pell-mell toward Washington. Many feared that Washington would fall within hours, but the "Rebels" were too disorganized to pursue. Thus ended the First Battle of Bull Run.

This victory of the South was a great shock to the North. It made the South feel confident that they could beat the "Yankees," but it also strengthened the resolve of the North. Both sides realized, however, that the war would not end with one battle, and so they prepared for a longer war.

The Outlook for War. The Confederate States, like the American colonies in the Revolution, had only to fight a defensive war. They hoped to win enough battles so that the North would grow weary of fighting and give up. They also hoped to gain assistance from foreign nations, especially Britain and France.

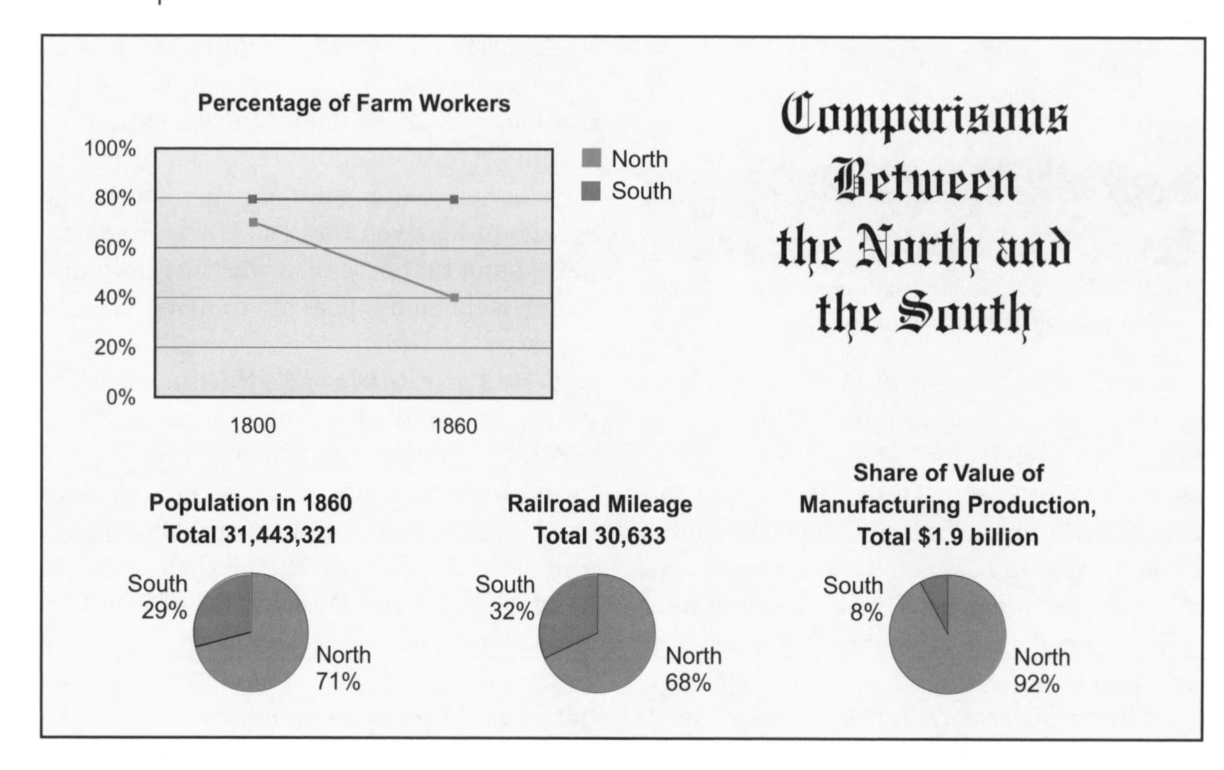

But the North had to conquer the South before the Union could claim victory. The Union's plan included three points: to blockade Southern ports so that cotton could not be shipped out or supplies be brought in, to divide the South by taking control of the Mississippi River, and to capture the Confederate capital of Richmond.

Of the two sides, the North had far greater resources. It had about 22 million people to the South's 9 million, which included 3.5 million slaves. The North also had more than 80 percent of the factories and almost 70 percent of the railroads. But the Confederates were defending their own territory, they knew the land better, and their generals were more capable—especially the noted **Robert E. Lee**. Still, "the race is not to the swift, nor the battle to the strong" (Ecclesiastes 9:11). The overruling hand of God would determine the outcome of the war.

Robert E. Lee (1807–1870), general of the Confederate army in the Civil War. This photograph was taken in April 1865 (after Lee's surrender) by Mathew Brady.

Border States. Four slave states remained in the Union: Delaware, Maryland, Kentucky, and Missouri. These were called border states because they lay along the boundary between the North and the South. President Lincoln worked hard to keep these border states in the Union.

A new state emerged from the war. When Virginia joined the Confederacy in 1861, its northwestern counties voted against secession. These counties separated from Virginia and joined the Union in 1863 as West Virginia.

The South Endures, 1862

Fighting in the West. In February 1862, General **Ulysses S. Grant** captured Fort Henry and Fort Donelson, two important

Confederate forts in Tennessee. Heading south toward Mississippi, Grant was in southern Tennessee when Confederate forces surprised him on April 6, and the Battle of Shiloh began. The Union troops seemed to be defeated by the end of that day; but on the next day, reinforcements helped to drive back the Confederates. Twenty-three thousand men were killed or wounded in this battle—a number that was shocking to the South as well as the North.

About the same time, Union ships under **David G. Farragut** headed for New Orleans. Under heavy fire, Farragut sailed his ships past the forts guarding the city. Then he turned his guns on New Orleans and forced it to surrender on April 25. Farragut was also able to conquer several other cities. But he could not gain control of the entire Mississippi River, for Vicksburg (in the state of Mississippi) held out against him. So the Union did not achieve the objective of dividing the South at that time.

Fighting at Sea. Union ships tried to conquer or blockade Confederate ports. Fast Southern blockade-runners could avoid them at first; but as more ships joined the blockade and more Southern ports fell, fewer Southern ships could get through. Then the South could no longer ship its cotton or buy needed supplies.

Battle of the *Monitor* (foreground) and the *Merrimack* (center) on March 9, 1862. This battle was the first between ironclad ships and also the first between ships moving entirely by steam power. The *Monitor* was nicknamed "a cheese box on a raft."

An important naval battle occurred in March 1862. Having used iron plates to cover the sides of a salvaged Union ship called the *Merrimack*, the Confederates renamed it the *Virginia* and sent it to destroy Union warships guarding the entrance to the James River. The *Merrimack (Virginia)* easily sank two of the wooden Union ships. But the North had secretly built its own ironclad ship, called the *Monitor*, and it went out to meet the *Merrimack* on the next day. The two ships bounced cannonballs off each other's thick sides for two hours, but finally they both retreated without either claiming victory. With this battle, the day of wooden warships ended and the age of ironclads began.

The Peninsular Campaign. In March 1862, General **George McClellan** landed a large Union force on the peninsula between the James River and the York River. Then he fought his way slowly up the peninsula until by late May he was only 6 miles (10 km) from Richmond. On May 31, McClellan was stopped by the Confederates, and there was little fighting for the next three weeks. Then on June 25, Robert E. Lee began a series of attacks that became known as the Seven Days' Battles, in which he forced McClellan to retreat down the peninsula. The Northern attempt to take Richmond had failed.

Invasion of Maryland. Lee's next move was northward. He defeated a Union army in the Second Battle of Bull Run, near the same battlefield of a year earlier. Then Lee invaded the North by crossing the Potomac River and entering Maryland. But now General McClellan of the Union army gained an incredible advantage. One of his soldiers discovered papers that turned out to be Lee's complete battle plans!

McClellan pursued Lee, and on September 17 they fought a battle near Sharpsburg, Maryland, along the Antietam Creek (an TEE tuhm). The armies battled each other through a cornfield and across a stone bridge over the Antietam Creek. (A nearby church building of

Left: The stone bridge over Antietam Creek, called Burnside's Bridge today. In the Battle of Antietam, Ambrose Burnside and his men (fighting under General McClellan) spent hours trying to cross the bridge but were held back by 400 soldiers from Georgia. ***Middle:*** The church building of the nonresistant Dunkers was struck by dozens of bullets during the Battle of Antietam. It was destroyed by a storm in 1921 and rebuilt in 1962. ***Right:*** President Lincoln came to Antietam and met with General George B. McClellan after the battle. About a month later, Lincoln replaced McClellan with Ambrose Burnside as commander of the Army of the Potomac.

the nonresistant Dunkers was riddled with bullet holes.) This was the bloodiest single-day battle of the war, leaving about seven thousand men dead and seventeen thousand wounded. Afterward Lee retreated across the Potomac and into Virginia. The North considered the Battle of Antietam a victory because it repelled Lee's invasion.

The Emancipation Proclamation. President Lincoln had wanted to set the slaves free, but he was waiting until the Union won a victory before doing so. Lincoln hoped that such a move would prevent Britain from recognizing the Confederacy as a nation, since the British opposed slavery. It would also broaden the war into a fight to free the slaves, which Lincoln hoped would motivate Northerners to continue the war until they won.

Presenting of the Emancipation Proclamation to Lincoln's Cabinet. Lincoln issued the proclamation after Lee was forced to retreat at Antietam.

The victory at Antietam provided the opportunity Lincoln wanted. On September 22, 1862, Lincoln issued the ***Emancipation Proclamation***. This proclamation became effective on January 1, 1863, when all the slaves in states still "in rebellion against the United States" were declared to be free. Of course, the proclamation could not free the slaves in the states of the Confederacy until the Union forces conquered those states. And it did not affect the border states, because they were not in rebellion. (Those slaves were liberated in 1865 when the Thirteenth Amendment outlawed all slavery.)

The Emancipation Proclamation had several important effects. It succeeded in preventing British recognition of the Confederacy. It gave Northerners a new zeal for the war because now they were also fighting against slavery. And its provision for recruiting blacks significantly strengthened the Union forces. Nearly 180,000 black soldiers served in the remainder of the war, and they made a major contribution to its outcome.

Continued Southern Resistance. In December 1862, General Ambrose Burnside led Union forces into Virginia and attacked Lee at Fredericksburg. But Lee's soldiers

found shelter behind a stone wall on high ground, and they repelled one Union assault after another. At last Burnside called off the attack and retreated. Northerners were discouraged because it appeared that no Union general could defeat Lee. The Confederacy appeared so strong that it might wear out the North after all. Another year would tell.

General Robert E. Lee (with field glasses) at the Battle of Fredericksburg, December 13, 1862.

Focus for Thought

1. On what basis did Lincoln consider secession to be illegal?
2. a. What two things was the South hoping to do in the Civil War?
   b. What were the three points in the plan of the North?
3. What were the advantages
   a. of the North?
   b. of the South?
4. Name the border states in the war, and also the new state that emerged.
5. What two effects did the Battle of Antietam have?
6. a. What was the provision of the Emancipation Proclamation?
   b. In what three ways did it help the Northern cause?

2. THE CIVIL WAR, PART 2: 1863–1865

By the end of 1862, the Confederacy had resisted the Union with such success that the South appeared able to win the war. But in 1863 the Union forces won several major victories, and the next year they went on campaigns so destructive that the South was crushed. Finally in 1865, the Civil War ended and the Union was saved.

The Tide Turns, 1863

The Battle of Chancellorsville. Early in May 1863, a Union general named Joseph Hooker engaged in a major battle with Lee's army near Chancellorsville, Virginia. In this battle, a noted Confederate general named **Thomas (Stonewall) Jackson** was accidentally shot by his own men and died soon afterward. The Confederates won the battle even though they lost thirteen thousand men.

Thomas J. (Stonewall) Jackson (1824–1863) earned his famous nickname in the First Battle of Bull Run by "standing like a stone wall."

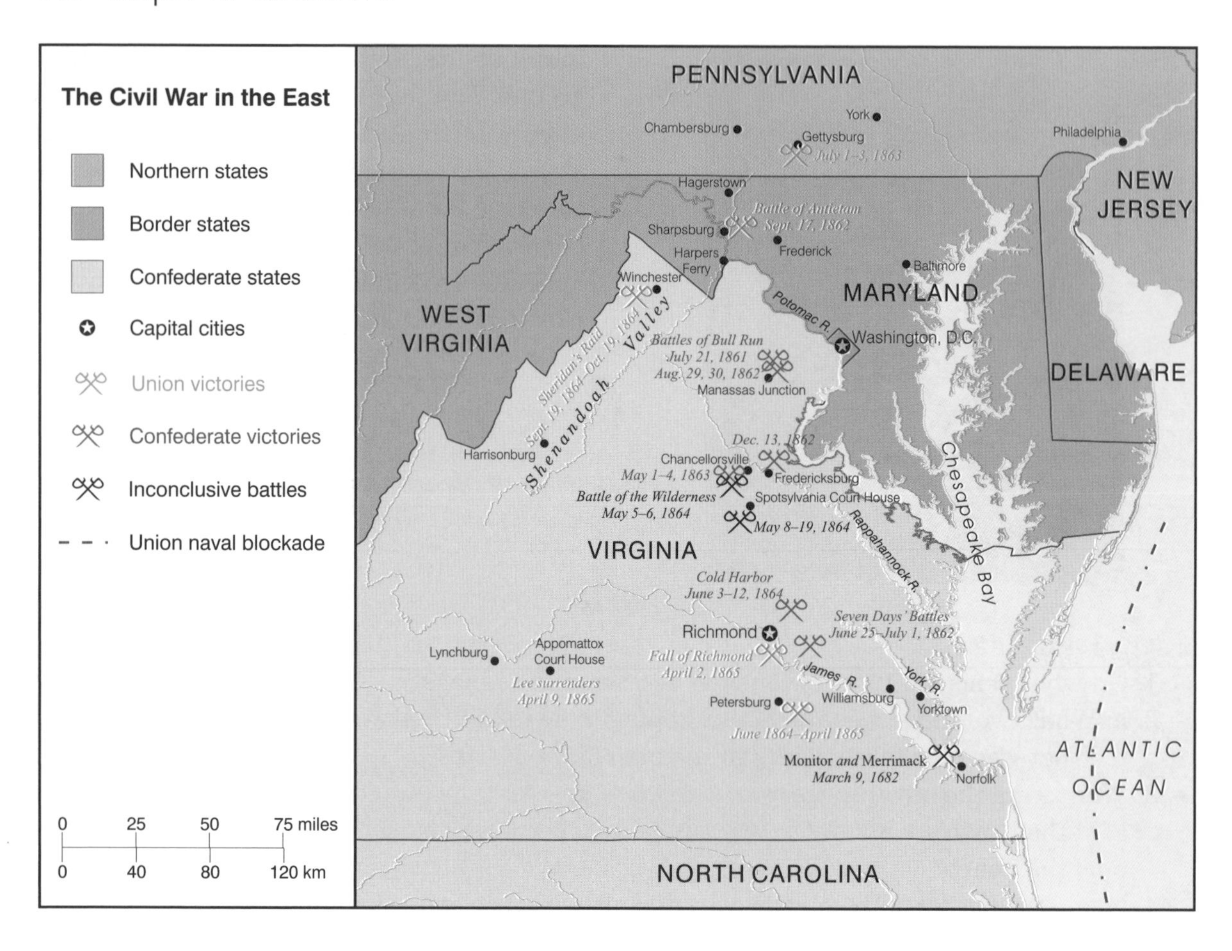

Hooker's army then retreated north across the Rappahannock River.

The Battle of Gettysburg. Emboldened by success, Lee again invaded the North, this time marching into southern Pennsylvania. His army raided the area for supplies and captured the cities of Chambersburg and York. Then on the first three days of July, one of the greatest battles in the Civil War was fought at Gettysburg.

By the evening of July 1, Union troops under **George Meade** held a position on top of Cemetery Ridge just south of Gettysburg. Confederates held an opposing line on Seminary Ridge, about a mile to the west. On July 2, the Confederates attacked both the left and right ends of the Union line, but they were driven back. So Lee decided to attack the center of the Union line the next day.

The Confederates began their attack on July 3 by firing artillery at the Federals for two hours. Then fifteen thousand soldiers under General **George Pickett** made a charge against the Union line, marching directly across the open field below Cemetery

The Battle of Gettysburg raged from July 1 to July 3, 1863, around Gettysburg, Pennsylvania. These cannons sit in the field near the "high-water mark" of the Confederate advance.

Ridge. But the Union guns caused such destruction that in less than an hour the Confederate army was devastated. Pickett's Charge, as it became known, had turned into a disastrous failure.

On July 4, Lee's army retreated toward the Potomac with a train of wagons 17 miles (27 km) long, some of them bearing wounded men whose cries could be heard a mile away. Lee's army was beaten, having suffered over twenty thousand casualties in the battle. Gettysburg became known as the "high-water mark of the Confederacy" because it marked the northernmost limit of the Confederate advance into Union territory. After the battle there, the Confederate army declined in strength until it was totally defeated.

The Gettysburg Address. In November 1863, President Lincoln was invited to take part in a dedication ceremony for a national cemetery at Gettysburg. The first speaker was Edward Everett, a noted orator of the time, who made a speech lasting over two hours. Then Lincoln delivered his address of less than three hundred words, including the comment that "the world will little note, nor long

On November 19, 1863, President Lincoln spoke briefly at a dedication ceremony for a military cemetery at Gettysburg. His succinct address summarized the idea of democracy and captured the essence of the national spirit of the United States.

The Gettysburg Address

Four score and seven years ago our fathers brought forth on this continent a new nation, conceived in Liberty, and dedicated to the proposition that all men are created equal.

Now we are engaged in a great civil war, testing whether that nation, or any nation so conceived and so dedicated, can long endure. We are met on a great battlefield of that war. We have come to dedicate a portion of that field, as a final resting place for those who here gave their lives that that nation might live. It is altogether fitting and proper that we should do this.

But, in a larger sense, we can not dedicate—we can not consecrate—we can not hallow—this ground. The brave men, living and dead, who struggled here, have consecrated it, far above our poor power to add or detract. The world will little note, nor long remember what we say here, but it can never forget what they did here. It is for us, the living, rather, to be dedicated here to the unfinished work which they who fought here have thus far so nobly advanced. It is rather for us to be here dedicated to the great task remaining before us—that from these honored dead we take increased devotion to that cause for which they gave the last full measure of devotion—that we here highly resolve that these dead shall not have died in vain—that this nation, under God, shall have a new birth of freedom—and that government of the people, by the people, for the people, shall not perish from the earth.

Noted Union Generals in the Civil War: First: Major General George B. McClellan (1826–1885), commander of the Union army in 1861 and 1862. Lincoln replaced him because McClellan was too cautious on the battlefield. ***Second:*** Ulysses S. Grant (1822–1885) became general of all the Union armies in 1864. His fighting style was much more aggressive than that of previous Union generals. ***Third:*** Philip H. Sheridan (1831–1888) is remembered for his campaign of devastation in the Shenandoah Valley. ***Fourth:*** William T. Sherman (1820–1891) led his troops on the destructive March to the Sea in 1864.

remember what we say here." But Lincoln was mistaken; his Gettysburg Address has become a classic for its simplicity, brevity, and force of expression.

The Fall of Vicksburg. Vicksburg, along the Mississippi, still held out against the Union. General Grant besieged the city from May until July, making a series of attacks and bombarding it heavily. At last on July 4, 1863, Vicksburg surrendered—one day after the Union victory at Gettysburg. The North had finally succeeded in gaining control of the Mississippi and dividing the South.

The North Strikes Hard, 1864

A New Union General. After Grant's successes in the West, Lincoln put him in charge of the whole Union army in March 1864. Up to this point, the aim of the North had been merely to force the South back into the Union. However, Grant decided that now the South must be crushed completely. He accomplished this by attacking Lee in Virginia while **William T. Sherman** led a campaign against Atlanta, Georgia.

The Wilderness Campaign. Grant attacked Lee on May 5, 1864, at nearly the same place as the Battle of Chancellorsville a year before. This was called the Battle of the Wilderness. Then he moved to Spotsylvania Court House and fought there from May 8 to 19. The armies met again and fought from June 3 to 12 at Cold Harbor, north of Richmond. Some sixty thousand men were killed or wounded in about a month of fighting. But Grant struck again, this time south of Richmond at Petersburg. Grant besieged this town for the next ten months.

Sheridan's Raid. In July 1864, General Jubal Early of the Confederates led a raid that reached right to the outskirts of Washington, D.C. General Early soon returned to his base in the Shenandoah Valley of Virginia, but he had caused great alarm in the Northern capital. The Union had to do something about this threat.

The Shenandoah Valley supplied much food for Southern armies, in addition to being a hideout for Confederate raiding bands. So General Grant assigned **Philip Sheridan** to attack Early and to "eat out Virginia clear and clean . . . so that crows flying over it . . . will have to carry their provender with them." Sheridan's men drove out the Confederate raiders by October, and then they destroyed practically everything of value in the Shenandoah Valley—houses, barns, mills, crops, and stores of hay and grain. They killed or captured thousands of cattle, hogs, and sheep.

"The tender mercies of the wicked are cruel" (Proverbs 12:10). Sheridan's raid caused

> *Here is one description of the devastation in Sheridan's raid.*
>
> The atmosphere . . . has been black with the smoke of a hundred conflagrations, and at night a gleam brighter and more lurid than sunset has shot from every verge. The completeness of the devastation is awful. Hundreds of nearly starving people are going north.
>
> I rode down the Valley . . . beneath great columns of smoke which almost shut out the sun by day, and in the red glare of bonfires which, all across that Valley, poured out flames and sparks heavenward and crackled mockingly in the night air; and I saw mothers and maidens tearing their hair and shrieking to Heaven in their fright and despair, and little children, voiceless and tearless in their pitiable terror.
>
> —*Quoted in* A Stillness at Appomattox

great suffering for hundreds of innocent people, including defenseless Mennonites and Dunkers who did not support the Confederates. The Shenandoah Valley was so devastated that many people had to flee because so little was left to live on.

The Fall of Atlanta. In May 1864, General Sherman led an army from Chattanooga, Tennessee, toward Atlanta, Georgia. Sherman fought a series of battles on the way and then besieged Atlanta until it surrendered. The Union forces raised their flag over this Southern stronghold on September 2.

Re-election of Lincoln. Many Northerners were opposing the war by 1864, especially during the summer as casualties mounted higher and higher. It was not sure whether Lincoln would be able to defeat the former general George McClellan, whom the Democrats had nominated as their presidential candidate. But David Farragut captured Mobile, Alabama, in August; and Sherman took Atlanta in September. The outlook changed, and Lincoln won his second election to the presidency.

Sherman's March to the Sea. General Sherman, like Grant, believed that the South had to be crushed. On November 15, 1864, Sherman's army of about sixty thousand men left Atlanta and marched toward the seaport of Savannah. The army destroyed almost everything in a swath 50 miles (80 km) wide, burning houses and other buildings, taking anything they wanted, and tearing up railroad tracks. One of their specialties was "Sherman neckties"—rails heated and then bent in a loop around trees or telegraph poles. Upon taking Savannah on December 21, Sherman telegraphed to Lincoln, "I beg to present you, as a Christmas gift, the city of Savannah."

The War Ends, 1865

Surrender at Appomattox. Back at Petersburg, Virginia, Grant made a strong

Union soldiers destroy railroad tracks in the South. Wrecked railroads and bridges meant that food and other supplies could not easily reach people. Much suffering was a result.

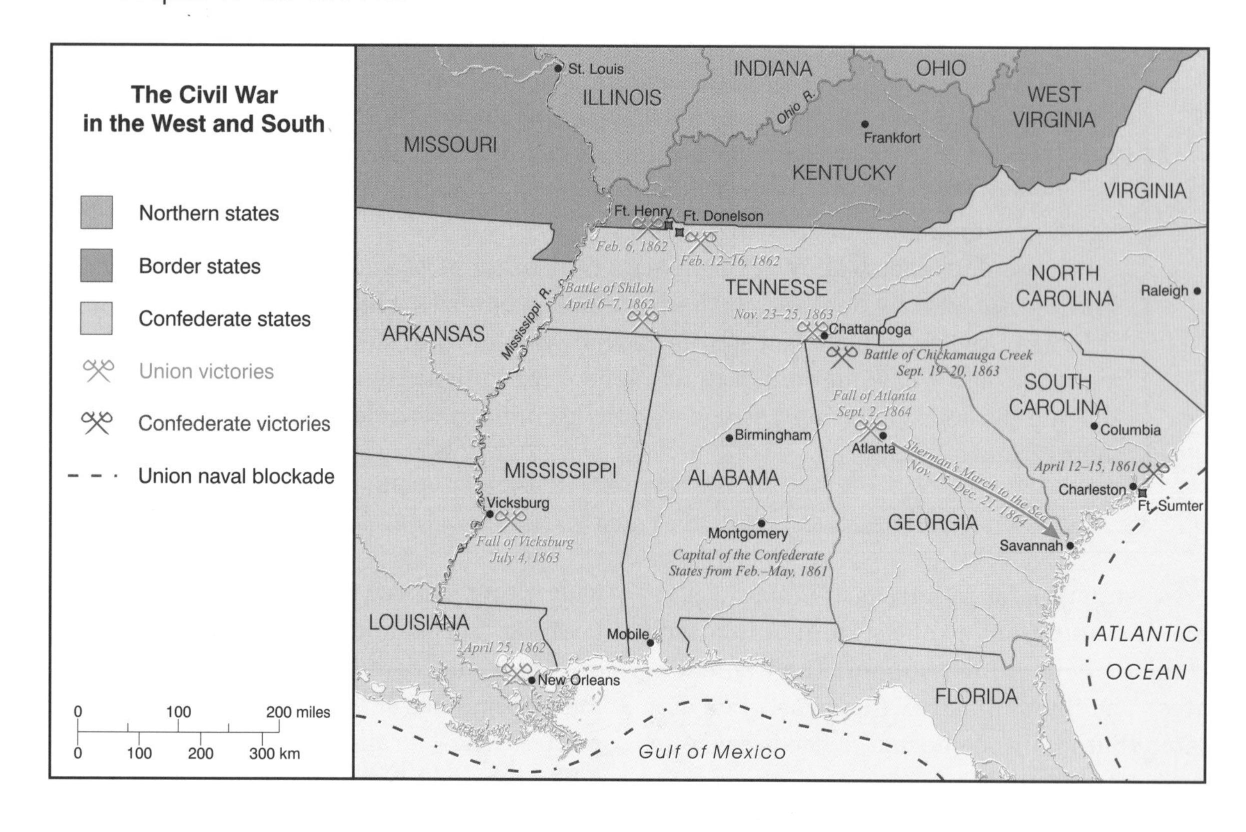

attack on Lee's forces on April 2. The Confederates retreated that night, leaving the way open to Richmond. Citizens of Richmond fled; and within hours, Lincoln himself visited the city and sat down in Jefferson Davis's study. As the president walked the streets, bands of blacks surrounded him, calling him the "Great Messiah" and "Father Abraham."

Lee and his men hurried westward from Richmond, hoping to join a Confederate army still in North Carolina. But Union forces cut them off near a town in Virginia called Appomattox Court House. With no hope of victory, Lee realized that "there is nothing left for

Left: On Sunday night, April 2, 1865, the citizens of Richmond burned its factories, arsenals, and mills before fleeing from the city. Union soldiers took control of Richmond the next day. ***Right:*** President Lincoln in Richmond early in April 1865. The blacks crowded around him, calling him "Father Abraham" and shouting, "Glory to God!" One man knelt before Lincoln, but the president told him to kneel to God only.

On April 9, 1865, Lee surrendered to Grant in the home of Wilmer McLean of Appomattox Court House. Grant paroled Confederate soldiers, gave them a day's rations, and let them keep their horses and mules for use in planting crops.

me to do but go and see General Grant, and I would rather die a thousand deaths."

On April 9, 1865, General Lee met with General Grant in Appomattox Court House. Grant offered generous terms of surrender, as Lincoln had directed. All the Confederate soldiers would be paroled and allowed to return to their homes, and they could take their horses along for planting crops. Grant further promised food for Lee's hungry, ragged soldiers. Lee accepted the terms, and thus ended the great, tragic Civil War.

Lincoln Assassinated. On April 14, 1865, Lincoln visited Ford's Theater in Washington, D.C. While he watched a play, an actor named **John Wilkes Booth** shot the president from behind and then jumped to a floor some distance below. On the way down, the actor's boot spur caught and he broke his leg. Booth managed to flee but was later tracked down and killed in Virginia.

President Lincoln died the morning after the shooting. His body lay in state for viewing in the White House, and afterward it was carried by a special train to its resting place in Springfield, Illinois. Millions of people viewed Lincoln's body as the train stopped at various places along the way.

Even Southerners perceived that they had lost a friend in Lincoln. He had planned to make the Southern states' restoration to the Union as easy as possible and had said as much in his second inaugural address. "With malice toward none; with charity for all; with firmness in the right, as God gives us to see the right, let us strive on to finish the work we are in; to bind up the nation's wounds; to care for him who shall have borne the battle and for his widow, and his orphan—to do all which may achieve and cherish a just and lasting peace among ourselves, and with all nations." In contrast, other Northern leaders wanted to punish the South severely. The work of repairing and reconciling the divided nation had only begun, and now it was in the hands of men less charitable than Lincoln.

Abraham Lincoln (1809–1865) was the sixteenth president of the United States. He served from 1861 to 1865 and was a Republican. This photo was taken in 1864. Because of the war and the duties of office, he looks considerably older than when he was photographed in 1860. (See page 324.)

Focus for Thought

7. Why is Gettysburg known as the "high-water mark of the Confederacy"?
8. Why was the fall of Vicksburg a major triumph for the North?
9. a. How did the Northern aim of the war change in 1864?
   b. Give one example of how this was carried out.
10. a. Why did Grant order the destruction of the Shenandoah Valley in 1864?
    b. What were the results?
11. What did Sherman's men do on their March to the Sea?
12. a. Where and when did General Lee surrender to General Grant?
    b. Give two details of Grant's generous terms of surrender.
13. a. When and how was Lincoln assassinated?
    b. How was Lincoln's death a great loss for the South?

3. COSTS AND RESULTS OF THE CIVIL WAR; EXPERIENCES OF NONRESISTANT PEOPLE

When war shatters a nation, it comes at a terrible price; and the Civil War surely proved this to be true. War also ushers in fundamental changes in nations and peoples, and in this too, the Civil War was no exception. The effects of these changes are evident to this day.

For nonresistant people, the Civil War brought the first experience with the military draft. This war also brought more direct sufferings to nonresistant people, especially in the South, than any previous war had done. The story of nonresistance during the Civil War should challenge and strengthen our own convictions.

Costs of the Civil War

Destruction in the South. Great devastation occurred in the South because most of the battles were fought there. Raids such as Sherman's and Sheridan's desolated large areas. Southern cities lay in ruins, bridges were burned, and railroads were destroyed.

In addition, the war had greatly reduced the number of men available to maintain Southern farms and buildings. With the Union blockade, Southerners had suffered shortages of basic items like clothing and salt; people had to make clothes from carpets and curtains. Besides all these things, Confederate paper

The South lay in ruins after the Civil War. Left: The burned part of Richmond, Virginia. ***Right:*** A railroad at Atlanta, Georgia.

money lost so much value that by the end of the war, people paid $300 for a barrel of flour and $200 for a pair of shoes.

By contrast, the North hardly suffered at all. Little fighting took place there, and Northern factories hummed steadily to produce war supplies. But prices did rise because the government printed large amounts of paper money. (This is inflation, a decline in the value of money because too much of it is available.) Also, the North imposed the first income tax to help finance the war.

High Casualties. Over six hundred thousand men died in the Civil War, many from disease. One reason so many died was because the Civil War was the first "modern war." It was the first war in which soldiers used deadly weapons that could fire much faster than the old muzzle-loading guns of earlier wars. Another reason was the concept of "total war" that developed in 1864, by which soldiers and civilians alike were destroyed. In addition, certain military tactics caused massive loss of life, such as the charges at Fredericksburg and Gettysburg.

Yet another reason so many died was because of the doctors' limited understanding of disease germs. When a person suffered a wound, he often died of infection even if the wound was promptly bandaged. In spite of this, many people did try to help wounded soldiers. One of these was **Clara Barton**, who later helped to found the American Red Cross.

Clara Barton (1821–1912) earned the title "Angel of the Battlefield" for her services to wounded men on Civil War battlefields. In 1881, she helped to found the American Red Cross and served as its president.

High Moral Costs. The Civil War brought bitterness and hatred to many hearts. It also caused selfishness, greed, corruption, and immorality. War always cheapens human life and dignity. The cost to society is serious and long-lasting.

Results of the War

The End of Slavery. Although the Civil War was not fought specifically to free the slaves, the end of slavery was one major result. The Emancipation Proclamation declared that slaves in the states of the Confederacy were free, and in 1865 the Thirteenth Amendment to the Constitution outlawed slavery throughout the nation. This brought on a struggle that has lasted more than a century as blacks found their place in American society.

The Establishing of Federal Supremacy. The question of states' rights had been answered clearly. Never again could states claim to have more power than the Union. The supremacy of the federal government was clearly established, with national interests taking precedence over the interests of the states.

A Need for Reconstruction. The South had to be rebuilt, the divided reconciled, the bitterness and hatred left behind. But with Lincoln dead, that difficult work had to move forward under the direction of other men. The story of Reconstruction is told in the next chapter.

Nonresistance in the North

The Call for Volunteers. Before the Civil War, nonresistant people of the 1800s had faced little challenge about their beliefs. The War of 1812 and the Mexican War had both been fought by volunteers. When Lincoln called for volunteers in 1861, some Mennonite young men were caught up in the patriotism of the time and went off to war. Most of these had not become members of the church.

The armies of both the North and the South consisted of volunteers at first, and men eagerly enlisted. Note the rewards offered for joining the armed forces.

The Draft. When the number of volunteers ran low, Lincoln instituted the first ***draft*** in United States history. If a drafted man did not want to serve, he could hire a substitute or pay a ***commutation fee*** of $300. Thus the law did make a way for ***conscientious objectors*** to avoid military service, but the price was high. Three hundred dollars was about a year's wages!

A few Mennonites and Amish petitioned the government to recognize their conscientious objection. For example, bishop John Brenneman of Ohio wrote to President Lincoln beseeching him that he would "favor us . . . and not allow us to be forced or compelled to take up arms." Some paid the commutation fee of $300, and some paid from $300 to $1,000 to hire a substitute. Others realized that hiring a substitute to fight for them was wrong and that they were responsible for his death if he was killed. A number of men moved to Canada or went into hiding for a time, and some claimed physical disability.

President Lincoln was considerate of the conscientious objectors. When 46-year-old Jacob Overholt, a Mennonite father, was sent to a camp with drafted soldiers, President Lincoln wrote an order for his release upon learning that Overholt had a family of twelve children. This example shows how God can work on behalf of His people in time of war.

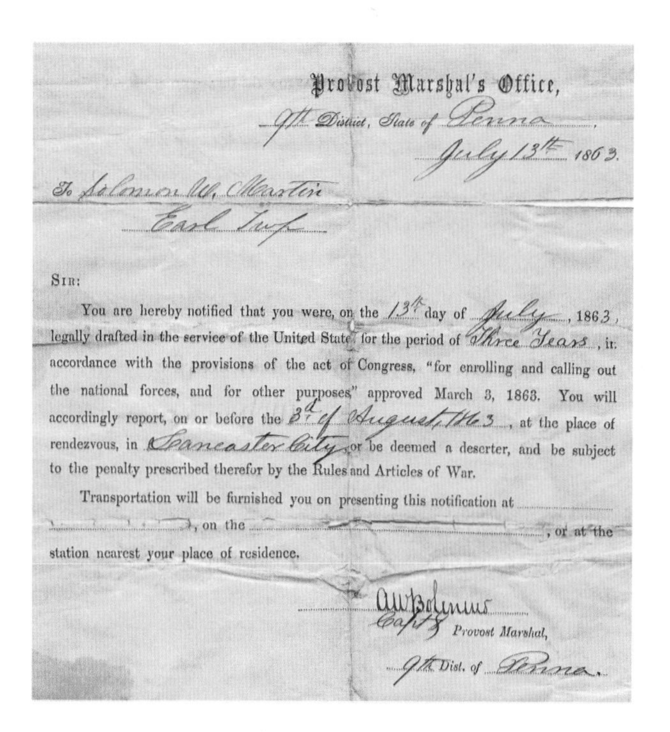

Provost Marshal's Office,
9th District, State of Penna,
July 13th 1863.

To Solomon W. Martin
Earl Twp

SIR:

You are hereby notified that you were, on the 13th day of July, 1863, legally drafted in the service of the United States for the period of Three Years, in accordance with the provisions of the act of Congress, "for enrolling and calling out the national forces, and for other purposes" approved March 3, 1863. You will accordingly report, on or before the 3d of August, 1863, at the place of rendezvous, in Lancaster City, or be deemed a deserter, and be subject to the penalty prescribed therefor by the Rules and Articles of War.

Transportation will be furnished you on presenting this notification at ________, on the ________, or at the station nearest your place of residence.

A W Bolenius
Capt
Provost Marshal,
9th Dist. of Penna.

No 260

Received at Lancaster, on the 3 day of August, 1863, from Solomon W. Martin who was drafted into the service of the United States, on the 13 th day of July 1863, from the 9th Congressional District of the State of Pennsylvania, the sum of three hundred dollars ($300) to obtain, under Section 13 of the "Act for enrolling and calling out the National forces and for other purposes," approved March 3, 1863, discharge from further liability under that draft.

Earl Twp

Alex H. Hood
Receiver of Commutation Money.

Draft exemption documents for Solomon Martin of Lancaster County, Pennsylvania. He paid the $300 commutation fee to gain exemption.

Some nonresistant people in the Gettysburg area suffered in more ways than by having their possessions taken. The following accounts give two examples.

Three Confederate soldiers killed Isaac Strite (a Dunker) when he refused to tell them where he had hidden his money. They were about to kill his wife too, but a daughter told them that money was hidden in the grandfather clock. The Confederates split open the door, took the money, and left. Later some Union soldiers caught up with them and hanged them.

Three Confederates appeared at Michael Hege's door, asking for money. He gave them his purse, but they forced their way into the house and lined up the family at gunpoint. Then they took Michael into a bedroom, where he opened a chest in which money was stored. After the soldiers took the money, one of them pointed his gun at Michael and declared, "We'll send you to another land!" But another soldier jumped between Michael and the would-be murderer, saying, "This man shall *not* be shot!" The soldiers then left without harming anyone.

The Gettysburg Invasion. Lee's invasion of the region around Gettysburg was a severe trial to Mennonites and Dunkers in the Chambersburg area. The Confederates helped themselves to whatever food they could find in people's homes, as well as to horses, cattle, hay, grain, hogs, and chickens. They also took fence rails to burn in their campfires. The Mennonites hid their valuables and sent many of their horses elsewhere to keep them from being stolen.

Nonresistance in the South

The Draft. One Sunday morning in June 1861, a Confederate captain came to Weavers Church in Virginia and announced that all the men between eighteen and forty-five must report for military service the following week. The men then had two choices: they could evade the draft and risk death, or they could enlist in the army and be unfaithful to Christ.

Some men yielded to the point of serving as cooks or wagon drivers in the army. Others chose to evade the draft. These men hid in the mountains or in secret hiding places at their homes. One family had a trap door in a bedroom under which lay a secret chamber where a number of men hid for a time. Others tried to escape into West Virginia or Pennsylvania.

The state of Virginia made a provision allowing conscientious objectors to avoid military service by paying a $500 commutation fee or hiring a substitute. While this law was being discussed in the Confederate Congress, someone read the article on nonresistance in the Mennonite confession of faith. One congressman asked, "Is there anyone . . . that knows anybody like that? Do they live it out?" Another congressman replied, "Yes, they are my next-door neighbors, and they live it to the letter." Hearing this, the first declared, "Any people who live like that ought not to be asked to fight."

The $500 fee was a heavy burden for most of the men to pay. But the church members helped each other, and then the men were free.

Shortages, Disease, and Plundering. In the South, the battles raged right around the nonresistant Mennonites and Dunkers. Food and salt were constantly in short supply. Lawlessness increased, and John Kline, a Dunker elder, was murdered in 1864. Churches closed because of the turmoil of war. On top of all this, a great diphtheria epidemic caused numerous deaths.

Then came Sheridan's raid in the fall of 1864. Nonresistant people suffered the plunder of their homes and the loss of their barns,

The notorious Libby Prison in Richmond. Of the 50,000 men held here by the Confederates, 72 were conscientious objectors from the Shenandoah Valley of Virginia. These men were imprisoned for six horrible weeks and were freed upon payment of $500.

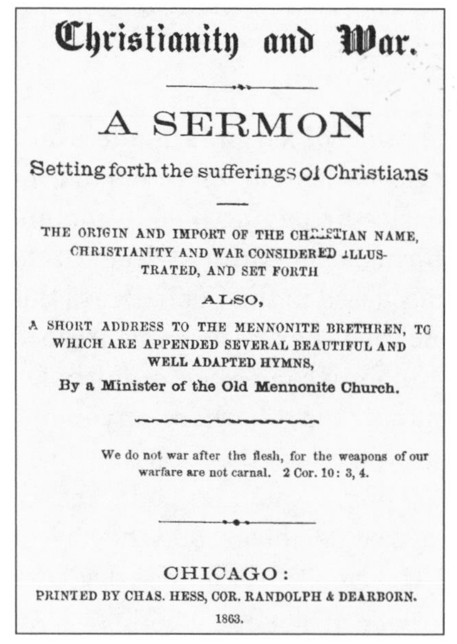

Christianity and War.

A SERMON

Setting forth the sufferings of Christians

THE ORIGIN AND IMPORT OF THE CHRISTIAN NAME, CHRISTIANITY AND WAR CONSIDERED ILLUSTRATED, AND SET FORTH

ALSO,

A SHORT ADDRESS TO THE MENNONITE BRETHREN, TO WHICH ARE APPENDED SEVERAL BEAUTIFUL AND WELL ADAPTED HYMNS,

By a Minister of the Old Mennonite Church.

We do not war after the flesh, for the weapons of our warfare are not carnal. 2 Cor. 10: 3, 4.

CHICAGO:

PRINTED BY CHAS. HESS, COR. RANDOLPH & DEARBORN.

1863.

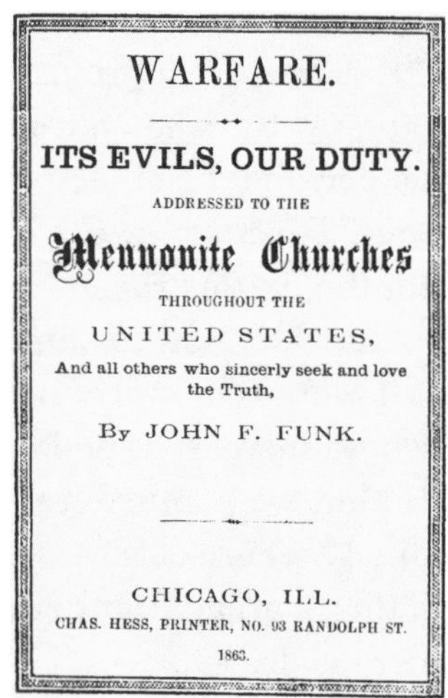

WARFARE.

ITS EVILS, OUR DUTY.

ADDRESSED TO THE

Mennonite Churches

THROUGHOUT THE

UNITED STATES,

And all others who sincerly seek and love the Truth,

By JOHN F. FUNK.

CHICAGO, ILL.

CHAS. HESS, PRINTER, NO. 93 RANDOLPH ST.

1863.

These are the title pages of two publications on nonresistance, written by John Brenneman and John Funk during the Civil War.

crops, and livestock. The Mennonites were so destitute that few had enough food to last through the following winter. Consequently, about a fourth of them moved north after Sheridan left.

> In 1862, a group of over seventy Mennonite men tried to escape into West Virginia, but five men held them up and ordered them to give up their arms. The men pulled out their Bibles—the only weapons they had! They were captured and imprisoned at Richmond.
>
> Another group of eighteen men was caught, robbed of their horses and $6,000, and taken to a cold, damp prison in Harrisonburg. In spite of these hardships, they prayed, sang hymns, and even wrote a poem about their experiences.

Nonresistance Asserted

The war afforded an excellent opportunity to address the doctrine of nonresistance. **John Funk** published *Warfare, Its Evils, Our Duty* in 1863 to strengthen nonresistant beliefs. Also in 1863, John Brenneman published *Christianity and War*, which taught that those who follow Christ can take no part in war. A year later, John Funk began publishing the *Herald of Truth*, a periodical that also promoted nonresistance.

The Civil War was a severe test to the nonresistant churches. Many members were faithful to the Bible doctrines that they professed, but others failed. Hiring a substitute certainly violated the Scriptural teaching of loving one's neighbor as himself. Still, the Mennonite Church did maintain the teaching and practice of nonresistance in this war. As Brenneman put it, their faith had been "put to the trial." The challenge for us is this: Would we stand true if we faced a similar trial? God is as faithful today as He was then.

Focus for Thought

14. What were some effects of the Civil War
    a. on the South?
    b. on the North?
15. Name three major results of the war.
16. In what ways did nonresistant people respond to the draft
    a. in the North?
    b. in the South?
17. Besides hardships relating to the draft, what sufferings did the war bring to nonresistant people
    a. in the North?
    b. in the South?
18. What was done by Mennonite leaders of the 1860s to strengthen the church's stand on nonresistance?

Columbianna County
~~Allen County~~ Ohio, August the 19th 1862.
A Petition to Mr Abraham Lincoln, President of the united States.
We the undersigned Heartily wish unto our Most Nobel President, Grace, Mercy, & Peace from God the Father, & of the Lord Jesus christ.
May the Good Lord abundantly Bless the President, with Wisdom & knowl= edge from on high, and Enable him to Rule this our Great Nation with Prudence, We would Humbly Pray the President, not to Consider us too Burdensome, By Presenting to him this our week & Humble Peti= tion, theirby Humbly Praying & Beseeching him, to take into Consideration our Sore Distress. We would heerwith inform the President, that their is a People Scattered & Living, Mostly in the Northern Parts of the united States; Pennsylvania, Virginia, Ohio, Indianna, & Some few in Illinois, & Iowa, Called Mennonites; who are greatly Distressed at the Present time on acount of the war. As it is against their Confession of Faith, and also against their Conscience, to take up arms their= with to Distroy Human Life. the President must not mistake us

Excerpt from the draft of a letter requesting that the Mennonites be exempted from military service. The letter was written by John M. Brenneman to President Lincoln in 1862.

Historical Highlights

A. Matching: People

a. Clara Barton
b. David G. Farragut
c. George McClellan
d. George Meade
e. George Pickett
f. John Funk
g. John Wilkes Booth
h. Philip Sheridan
i. Robert E. Lee
j. Stonewall Jackson
k. Ulysses S. Grant
l. William T. Sherman

1. Led a Confederate charge against Union forces at Gettysburg.
2. Devastated the Shenandoah Valley in 1864.
3. Union general in Battle of Antietam; Lincoln's opponent in election of 1864.

4. Chief Union general at the end of the Civil War.
5. Conquered New Orleans and Mobile for the Union.
6. Assassinated President Lincoln.
7. Conquered Atlanta and led the destructive March to the Sea.
8. Commander of Union armies at Gettysburg.
9. Noted Confederate general who was shot by his own men.
10. Published the *Herald of Truth* and a pamphlet on nonresistance.
11. Cared for wounded soldiers and helped to found American Red Cross.
12. General of the Confederate armies whose surrender brought the war to an end.

B. Matching: Terms

a. border states
b. commutation fee
c. Confederates
d. conscientious objectors
e. draft
f. Emancipation Proclamation
g. Federals
h. Gettysburg Address
i. ironclad
j. Pickett's Charge
k. "Rebels"
l. Thirteenth Amendment
m. Union
n. "Yankees"

1. People who believe it is wrong to take part in warfare.
2. Delaware, Maryland, Kentucky, Missouri.
3. Terms for Southern soldiers (two answers).
4. Terms for Northern soldiers (three answers).
5. Compulsory enrollment in a military force.
6. Money paid to avoid military service.
7. Statement declaring that slaves in the Confederacy were free.
8. New type of ship that changed naval warfare.
9. Measure that permanently outlawed slavery.
10. Attack on the Union army at Gettysburg.
11. Speech given in the dedication of a cemetery at Gettysburg.

C. Matching: Places and Dates

a. Antietam
b. Appomattox Court House
c. Atlanta
d. First Battle of Bull Run
e. Chancellorsville
f. Fort Sumter
g. Gettysburg
h. Richmond
i. Savannah
j. Shenandoah Valley
k. Shiloh
l. Vicksburg
m. West Virginia
n. April 12, 1861
o. January 1, 1863
p. April 9, 1865
q. April 14, 1865

1. City whose capture aided Lincoln's re-election in 1864.
2. Date when the Civil War began.
3. Battle that was a turning point in the war.
4. Victory that gave Lincoln an occasion to issue the Emancipation Proclamation.
5. City at the end of Sherman's destructive March to the Sea.
6. Date when the Civil War ended.

7. Area destroyed by Sheridan's raid, where Mennonites lived.
8. Battle where Stonewall Jackson lost his life.
9. Date when Lincoln declared that the slaves in the Confederacy were free.
10. Place where the Civil War began.
11. Place where Lee surrendered to Grant.
12. Battle showing that the war would be long and hard.
13. New state formed from Virginia.
14. Bloody battle in Tennessee.
15. Confederate capital.
16. Mississippi stronghold whose fall directly followed the Battle of Gettysburg.
17. Date of Lincoln's assassination.

D. Deeper Discussion

1. Explain why the Civil War lasted four years even if the North had definite advantages over the South.
2. In relation to the Civil War, Lincoln quoted Psalm 19:9: "The judgments of the LORD are true and righteous altogether." What is the connection?
3. a. Why did the Emancipation Proclamation declare freedom only for slaves in the Confederacy?
   b. Why did Lincoln wait until after a Union victory to issue the proclamation?
4. How was Lincoln's assassination a blow to the South as well as to the North?
5. What are some factors that made the Civil War especially destructive and tragic?

E. Chronology and Geography

1. On your map entitled "The States of the United States," draw the borders of the eleven states admitted between 1836 and 1863. (See maps on pages 317 and 334.)
   a. Label the states with their names and dates of admission.
   b. Color these states a different color, and add this color to the legend.
   c. Memorize the names and locations of these states.
2. a. List the eleven states that joined the Confederacy.
   b. How many states did the Union retain?
   c. In general, which of the three sections of the country stayed in the Union, and which seceded?
3. a. How did fighting on their own land give Southerners an advantage in the Civil War?
   b. How did it become a disadvantage by the end of the war?
4. Why did the Union's capture of Vicksburg weaken the South?
5. Place the following events in chronological order, giving the date for each one. The time line for this chapter may help you.

   Battle of Antietam
   Battle of Chancellorsville
   Battle of Gettysburg
   Battle of Shiloh
   Battle of the ironclads
   Emancipation Proclamation
   Fall of Atlanta
   Fall of Richmond
   Fall of Vicksburg
   First Battle of Bull Run
   Gettysburg Address
   Lincoln's assassination
   Lincoln's re-election
   Sheridan's raid
   Sherman's March to the Sea
   Surrender at Appomattox Court House

Many cities in the South, such as Charleston, South Carolina, lay in ruins after the war. Houses, barns, factories, bridges, and railroads needed to be rebuilt during Reconstruction.

17 Reconstruction

1860

Emancipation Proclamation becomes effective (January 1) 1863

Andrew Johnson becomes president 1865

1865

Civil War ends (April 9); Lincoln assassinated (April 14) **1865**

Reconstruction Act passed; United States purchases Alaska 1867

Fourteenth Amendment ratified 1868

Johnson impeached and acquitted; Ulysses S. Grant elected president 1868

1870

Last of Southern states readmitted; Fifteenth Amendment ratified 1870

Ku Klux Klan Act passed 1871

Amnesty Act passed; Grant re-elected 1872

1875

Rutherford B. Hayes elected president 1876

Compromise of 1877 approved; Reconstruction ends 1877

1880

1. Presidential Reconstruction
   - The Need for Reconstruction
   - Presidential Policies for Reconstruction
   - Effects of Presidential Reconstruction
2. Congressional Reconstruction
   - The Reconstruction Acts
   - Reconstruction Governments
   - Johnson's Administration
   - Grant's Administration
3. The End of Reconstruction
   - Southern Redemption
   - Reconstruction Ends
   - The New South

"A brother offended is harder to be won than a strong city: and their contentions are like the bars of a castle."

Proverbs 18:19

Reconstruction

Focus for Reading

"How are the mighty fallen in the midst of the battle!" (2 Samuel 1:25). As David mourned over Jonathan, so thousands of people in the United States mourned over husbands, fathers, brothers, and sons lost in the Civil War. Besides, the nation itself had been torn asunder. What could be done to "bind up the nation's wounds," as Lincoln had said, and bring restoration and healing?

Not everyone agreed on what was best. Bitter feelings between the North and South continued, and this led to quarreling and violence as various factions tried to carry out their own plans. Thus the Reconstruction period that followed the Civil War was a time of turbulence and upheaval. Three sections in this chapter describe the Reconstruction.

1. Presidential Reconstruction
2. Congressional Reconstruction
3. The End of Reconstruction

1. PRESIDENTIAL RECONSTRUCTION

President Lincoln and his successor controlled the first phase of Reconstruction, which lasted from 1865 through 1867. For that reason, this period is called Presidential Reconstruction. The presidents' plan was to use a lenient approach that would restore the South to the Union as quickly as possible. But some Northern congressmen believed that a lenient approach neither punished the South enough nor helped the freed slaves enough. They opposed the new president and eventually wrested control of Reconstruction from him.

The Need for Reconstruction

Devastation in the South. Wherever armies had fought, the South lay in ruins. Cities were burned and railroads torn up, and thousands of men who might have helped to restore things were dead. One reporter described Charleston, South Carolina, as a ruin of "vacant houses, of widowed women, of rotting wharves, of deserted warehouses, of weed-wild gardens, of miles of grass-grown streets,

A soldier returning home after the war receives a joyful welcome. However, life would never be the same for many Civil War veterans. Note that the man's left arm is in a sling.

For some Southern soldiers returning home, there was no home to return to.

A desolate home in the South. With thousands of fathers and young men killed, many Southern families—white and black—were destitute after the Civil War.

of acres of pitiful and voiceful barrenness."

Some plantation owners could not accept the results of the war. A few committed suicide, and some left for places such as Brazil, where they could start over. The majority that stayed found it difficult to relate to freed blacks who were their former slaves. (Slaveholders had lost a total of about $2 billion in human "property.") They could not think of the ***freedmen*** as their equals, and they used various methods to maintain ***white supremacy*** (soo PREHM uh see)—the superiority of whites over blacks.

The Freed Slaves. About 3.5 million slaves had been freed through the war. Most of them were uneducated, and they had no experience in supporting themselves. But most blacks wanted education, jobs, and land. They wanted to reunite families that slavery had divided, and they wanted their own schools and churches. What could be done to help the freedmen become established as responsible citizens?

Restoration of Southern States. The federal government had to deal with the question of secession. Should the states of the Confederacy be considered as conquered enemy territories or as states that had never actually left the Union? Leaders grappled with the problem of how to restore legitimate governments to Southern states and represent them in the federal government, while still ensuring their loyalty to the United States.

Presidential Policies for Reconstruction

Lincoln's Plans. Before the Civil War ended, President Lincoln had developed a lenient plan for reconstruction of Southern states. It proposed that Southerners (except high-ranking Confederate officers) be pardoned and restored to citizenship if they took an oath of loyalty to the United States. When 10 percent of the 1860 (pre-Civil War) voting population in a state had taken this loyalty oath, that state could form a new government. Under this ten percent plan, Louisiana, Tennessee, and Arkansas set up reconstructed governments during the war, after they were conquered by the Union.

Because Lincoln was assassinated, he had not been able to formulate a complete plan for Reconstruction. He believed that the president had authority to direct the restoration of the states, and that the Southern states had never actually seceded. His plan, therefore, was to restore them to the Union in the simplest way possible.

But some congressmen thought Congress had power over Reconstruction, and they considered the states of the Confederacy as conquered enemy territories. They wanted to punish and reform the Southern states before they could rejoin the Union. This group, called the Radical Republicans, opposed Lincoln's ten percent plan even before his assassination. Thus no clear policy for Reconstruction was in force at the time of Lincoln's death.

Johnson's Approach. Lincoln's vice president, **Andrew Johnson**, became president in 1865. Johnson promoted a lenient plan similar to Lincoln's. But his plan omitted the ten-percent provision, and it required wealthy

Southerners to make individual applications for pardons.

Johnson recognized the four states reconstructed under Lincoln's plan. In the other states, he appointed governors who needed to call conventions to amend their constitutions and set up new governments. Johnson later proclaimed that these states must also renounce their secession laws and ratify the Thirteenth Amendment before they could elect representatives to Congress. By the end of 1865, most of the former states of the Confederacy had met these conditions.

Whites continued to look down on blacks and treat them unfairly after the Civil War. Here a freedman in Florida is being sold to pay a fine.

Effects of Presidential Reconstruction

Opposition to Johnson's Plan. The Radical Republicans, led by Senator Charles Sumner of Massachusetts and Representative Thaddeus Stevens of Pennsylvania, opposed the president's plan. They thought it was too lenient on Southern whites, whom they viewed as unrepentant rebels. These Republicans feared that if the same Southern leaders continued in power, they would keep the freedmen from becoming equal with whites. The Radicals thought they themselves should have control of Reconstruction.

The Radicals found another reason to reject President Johnson's plan when the restored Southern states sent representatives to Congress in December 1865. Those representatives included many former members of the Confederate Congress, four former Confederate generals, and even Alexander Stephens, the vice president of the Confederacy! Northern congressmen were so displeased that they would not seat the Southern congressmen.

Left: Thaddeus Stevens (1792–1868), a Radical Republican in the House of Representatives, led the impeachment proceedings against Andrew Johnson. Stevens wanted to use strong measures to remake the South. ***Right:*** Charles Sumner (1811–1874), Senate leader of the Radical Republicans. He promoted freedom and voting rights for blacks. (Sumner had suffered a caning before the Civil War; see Chapter 15.)

Congress refused to recognize the states readmitted under Presidential Reconstruction. A group called the Joint Committee on Reconstruction was established to study Southern conditions and propose a different plan for readmitting Southern states. Congress intended to take charge of Reconstruction.

Difficult Times for Blacks. When the Joint Committee issued its report, many Northern people were disturbed by conditions in the South. It was common for black people to be insulted, whipped, and even killed by whites. Blacks might be murdered for such things as not removing a hat, using disrespectful language, or refusing to call a white man "master." The law seldom punished whites for these crimes.

Blacks faced various forms of legal ***discrimination***. Southern states passed laws called black codes, which were designed to control

After the Civil War, many blacks lived in extreme poverty as sharecroppers, farming the land of white men for a share of the crops. Often their living conditions were little different from when they had been slaves.

blacks and "keep them in their place." These included laws that prohibited them from owning guns, voting, holding public office, and serving on juries. If a black man quit a job, he would lose any pay that was still due. These laws made Northerners think the South was trying to evade the Thirteenth Amendment and still keep blacks in a kind of slavery.

Blacks also faced financial difficulties. The greatest desire of many was to farm their own land, but how could they get land? Their cry was, "Forty acres and a mule!" They hoped the government would give them land, but this did not happen. Instead, many blacks took part in ***sharecropping***, a system in which planters divided their vast lands into small plots each rented by a black family. The planter often provided cabins, tools, and seeds while the black families raised the crops. Then the black family paid their rent by giving the owner a share of the harvest.

Though sharecropping was better than slavery, the system kept blacks in poverty. Destitute freedmen often had to borrow money for food and supplies. If the harvest was poor, the sharecropper would only be deeper in debt at the end of the year. Sharecropping also encouraged production of cash crops, such as cotton (which wore out the soil), rather than food crops. Many blacks became trapped in the sharecropping system.

The Freedmen's Bureau. Before Lincoln died, Congress had established the Freedmen's Bureau to help the blacks. This bureau gave millions of rations of food, clothing, medicine, and seeds to poor people, and it helped former

Top: The Freedmen's Bureau provided millions of meals for the old, sick, and destitute in the South, both black and white. ***Middle:*** The Freedmen's Bureau set up over 4,300 schools for blacks. In this industrial school at Richmond, Virginia, black women are learning to sew. ***Bottom:*** Elementary school of the Freedmen's Bureau at Richmond, Virginia. By 1876, about 40 percent of black children in the South were attending school. Many of the teachers were white women from the North.

slaves to find jobs. It also set up special courts for blacks who were not able to obtain justice in other Southern courts.

In addition, the Freedmen's Bureau provided schools for thousands of blacks, young and old, who wanted to read. One teacher, Charlotte Forten, wrote, "I never before saw children so eager to learn. . . . They come here [to school] as other children go to play. The older ones, during the summer, work in the fields from early morning until eleven or twelve o'clock, and then come to school . . . as bright and as anxious to learn as ever. . . . Many of the grown people are desirous of learning to read."

In 1866, Congress passed a bill authorizing the Freedmen's Bureau to continue its aid to freedmen. But President Johnson vetoed the law, believing that it favored blacks unfairly. The same year, Congress passed the Civil Rights Act, which provided that all people born in the United States, including blacks but not Indians, were United States citizens whose rights could not be restricted. President Johnson also vetoed the Civil Rights Act, saying it made the federal government too strong.

But Congress overrode Johnson's veto on April 9—the first time Congress enacted a major law over a presidential veto. Later, Congress also overrode the veto of the Freedmen's Bureau.

Although these measures were good, no law has the power to change social attitudes such as those between whites and blacks. This truth would become clearly evident in the years that followed. The only real solution is the new birth and the love of God in people's hearts.

The Fourteenth Amendment. Radicals feared that even with the new legislation, the rights of blacks would not be secure. So Congress drew up the Fourteenth Amendment to the Constitution. This amendment states that all persons (except Indians) born in the United States are citizens. It says that no state may deprive any citizen of his right to vote or of "life, liberty, or property, without due process of law."

President Johnson opposed the Fourteenth Amendment. He urged the Southern states to reject it, even though Congress said they must ratify the amendment to be readmitted to the Union. Only one Southern state, Tennessee, ratified the amendment in 1866.

Conflict over the Fourteenth Amendment became an issue in the 1866 Congressional elections. Republicans won this election by such a wide margin that they had more than two-thirds of the seats in both the House and the Senate. This meant they could pass any law regardless of the president's veto. With the Republicans in control, Congressional Reconstruction was at hand.

Focus for Thought

1. Give three reasons why Reconstruction was needed.
2. What were the two main points in Lincoln's ten percent plan?
3. a. How was President Johnson's plan similar to Lincoln's?
   b. How was it different?
4. For what reasons did the Radical Republicans oppose President Johnson's plan for Reconstruction?
5. a. What difficulties were blacks facing in the South?
   b. How did the sharecropping system work?
6. What did the Freedmen's Bureau accomplish?
7. What are the terms of the Fourteenth Amendment?

2. CONGRESSIONAL RECONSTRUCTION

Having rejected Presidential Reconstruction, the Radical Republicans used their majority in Congress to carry out their own plans for the South. These congressmen took a harsher approach than that of President Johnson. When he made efforts to obstruct the Radicals, they tried to remove him from office. At last Johnson's term ended, and a Republican became president.

Andrew Johnson (1808–1875) was the seventeenth president of the United States. He served from 1865 to 1869 and was a Democrat. He was the first president to be impeached and the only president to later become a senator.

The Reconstruction Acts

Not all the Republicans were radical, but they all wanted the South to accept the consequences of the war and to ratify the Fourteenth Amendment. To accomplish this, Congress passed the Reconstruction Act in March 1867. President Johnson vetoed this bill, but Congress easily overrode his veto.

The Reconstruction Act divided the South into five military districts each governed by a Union general. Soldiers kept order and enforced civil rights within each district. Voters in each state were to elect delegates to a constitutional convention, which would write a new state constitution. It had to include a guarantee that blacks could vote. When a state had ratified the Fourteenth Amendment and Congress had approved its constitution, it could be readmitted to the Union and military rule would end.

Congress had to pass additional Reconstruction Acts to deal with problems in the first one. Military rule lasted about a year in most of the states; and in June 1868, Arkansas became the first state to be readmitted. By July 1868, enough states had ratified the Fourteenth Amendment so that it became a part of the Constitution. Finally in July 1870, Georgia became the last state to be readmitted, and military rule ended.

Reconstruction Governments

Republican Control of the South. Under the new state governments, freedmen in the South could vote and hold government offices. They usually supported Republican candidates because the Republican Party had won many privileges for them. A number of whites could not vote, for the new state constitutions prohibited some former Confederates from voting or holding office. In this way, many black Republicans won offices in the new state governments and even in the federal government. For example, in 1870 **Hiram Revels** became the first black man elected to the United States Senate. But whites still held

A number of blacks served as Congressmen during the Reconstruction. In this picture, Hiram Revels of Mississippi (1822–1901), the first black senator, is seated on the left. The others are representatives from South Carolina, Georgia, Alabama, and Florida.

Blacks gained the privilege of serving on juries after the Civil War.

most of the power in state governments.

Many Northerners, black and white, went to the South after the war, hoping to aid in rebuilding the South or to profit in some way from the Reconstruction. They came to farm, to teach, or to operate businesses. Some came merely to seek wealth and power. Southern whites scornfully referred to these Northerners as ***carpetbaggers*** to suggest that they could pack all their belongings in a carpetbag (cheap suitcase made of carpet material). A number of carpetbaggers became powerful in the Reconstruction governments and even served as governors.

Some Southern whites became Republicans who took part in the Reconstruction governments. Other Southerners hated these even more than the carpetbaggers and called them ***scalawags***. These three groups—blacks, carpetbaggers, and scalawags—controlled the Southern governments during Reconstruction.

Accomplishments of Reconstruction Governments. The new state governments made some progress in helping the South. They improved local governments, allowed more people to vote, and provided more schools. Reconstruction governments also spent money to rebuild railroads, restore levees along rivers, and repair other war damages. They encouraged the building of hospitals and factories.

To pay for all this, Reconstruction governments raised taxes, especially property taxes. This angered many whites, who had never before paid such high taxes. The states also went deep into debt to pay for improvements. But some of the money was wasted through corruption. In one case, a man received $9,000 for building a bridge that had cost only $500. In another, the South Carolina legislature voted a $1,000 bonus for its speaker, who had lost that amount in betting on a horse race!

Blacks received the right to vote after the Civil War. The first three men in the line symbolize the black craftsman (note the tools in his pocket), the city dweller, and the soldier.

Not all the officials were dishonest. Besides, the same kind of corruption also flourished in the North, and many whites who condemned the carpetbag governments did similar things themselves. Proverbs 17:23 comments on such wrongdoing: "A wicked man taketh a gift out of the bosom to pervert the ways of judgment." The increase in this kind of corruption was a direct result of the Civil War.

Johnson's Administration

Impeachment and Acquittal. Many of the Radicals believed President Johnson obstructed them by not properly enforcing the laws they had passed. To restrict his power, Congress passed the Tenure of Office Act, which said the president could not dismiss any Cabinet member without the Senate's approval.

The secretary of war in the president's Cabinet was **Edwin Stanton**, who had been appointed by Lincoln and who sympathized with the Radicals. President Johnson did not

Edwin Stanton (1814–1869), the secretary of war under Lincoln and Johnson. President Johnson dismissed him from office to test the new Tenure of Office Act. Congress then impeached Johnson.

think the Tenure of Office Act was constitutional, so he deliberately violated the new law by dismissing Secretary Stanton. Radicals seized upon this as a way to remove the president from office.

The House of Representatives voted to impeach President Johnson on eleven charges of "high crimes and misdemeanors," mainly for violating the Tenure of Office Act. In impeachment cases, the Constitution provides that the Senate shall try the accused to determine his guilt or innocence. President Johnson's impeachment trial lasted from March until May 1868, with the Senate acting as jury and Chief Justice Salmon Chase presiding.

The Republican majority believed that Johnson would easily be convicted by the necessary two-thirds vote. But seven Republicans sided with Johnson and voted "not guilty." One of them, **Edmund Ross** of Kansas, cast the deciding vote to acquit the president. Had Johnson been convicted, the delicate balance of power in the federal government would have been upset. This could easily have started a practice of impeaching any president who did not agree with Congress.

Purchase of Alaska. President Johnson did more than struggle with the Radicals during his administration. He saw that those involved in Lincoln's assassination were punished. Also, his secretary of state, **William Seward**, arranged in 1867 to buy Alaska from Russia for $7.2 million. People called it "Seward's Icebox" and "Seward's Folly"; but the House finally did approve the purchase, and Alaska became a United States possession. This proved to be a historic bargain, for Alaska later became a source of gold, oil, and other kinds of wealth.

Left: Impeachment trial of Andrew Johnson. Removing the president from office required the votes of 36 of the Senate's 54 members. Only 35 voted against him. ***Right:*** Edmund Ross (1826–1907), the Republican senator who cast the deciding vote to acquit President Johnson. Ross was harshly criticized for his stand and was never again elected to the Senate.

William H. Seward signing the treaty to purchase Alaska from Russia, March 1867. Many people called it "Seward's Folly" or "Seward's Icebox."

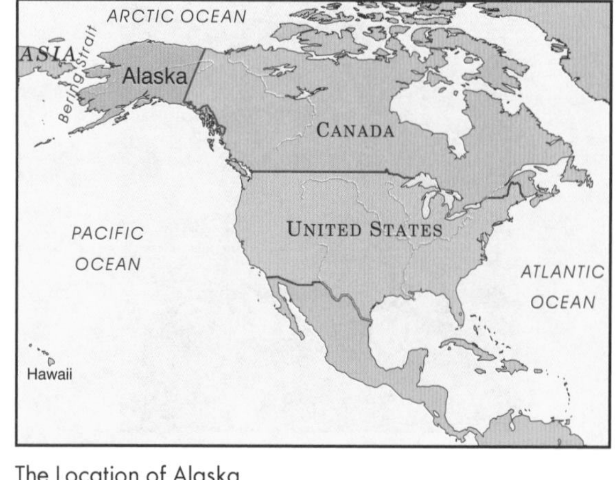

The Location of Alaska

Grant's Administration

Election of 1868. **Ulysses S. Grant** had become a military hero in the Civil War. In 1868, he ran for the presidency as a Republican and won the election. Four years later he was elected to a second term. Grant served from 1869 to 1877.

Corruption was especially rampant during Grant's two terms. High government officials granted favors to businesses in return for money, and various scandals broke out. This corruption again was due to the demoralizing influence of the war, as well as to the rapid expansion of the nation. Deuteronomy 16:19 says, "Thou shalt not wrest judgment; thou shalt not respect persons, neither take a gift: for a gift doth blind the eyes of the wise, and pervert the words of the righteous."

The Fifteenth Amendment. In 1869, Congress submitted the Fifteenth Amendment to the states for ratification. It preserves the right of blacks to vote, saying that no citizen can be denied voting privileges because of his race. This amendment, along with the Thirteenth and the Fourteenth, came about because of the Civil War and its effects.

Four Southern states—Georgia, Mississippi, Texas, and Virginia—were still not readmitted when the Fifteenth Amendment was passed. Congress required them to also ratify this amendment to be readmitted. All four had done so by 1870, and then the Union was complete once more.

March of blacks in honor of the Fifteenth Amendment. This march was held in New York City in 1870 to celebrate black people's right to vote.

Ulysses S. Grant (1822–1885) was the eighteenth president of the United States. He served from 1869 to 1877 and was a Republican.

The Civil War Amendments

Amendment 13

Section 1. Neither slavery nor involuntary servitude, except as a punishment for crime whereof the party shall have been duly convicted, shall exist within the United States, or any place subject to their jurisdiction.

Section 2. The Congress shall have power to enforce this article by appropriate legislation.

Amendment 14

Section 1. All persons born or naturalized in the United States, and subject to the jurisdiction thereof, are citizens of the United States and of the state wherein they reside. No state shall make or enforce any law which shall abridge the privileges or immunities of citizens of the United States; nor shall any state deprive any person of life, liberty, or property, without due process of law; nor deny to any person within its jurisdiction the equal protection of the laws.

Section 2. Representatives shall be apportioned among the several states according to their respective numbers, counting the whole number of persons in each state, excluding Indians not taxed. But when the right to vote at any election for the choice of electors for President and Vice President of the United States, representatives in Congress, the executive and judicial officers of a state, or the members of the legislature thereof, is denied to any of the male inhabitants of such state, being twenty-one years of age, and citizens of the United States, or in any way abridged, except for participation in rebellion, or other crime, the bases of representation therein shall be reduced in the proportion which the number of such male citizens shall bear to the whole number of male citizens twenty-one years of age in such state.

Section 3. No person shall be a senator or representative in Congress, or elector of President and Vice President, or hold any office, civil or military, under the United States, or under any state, who, having previously taken an oath, as a member of Congress, or as an officer of the United States, or as a member of any state legislature, or as an executive or judicial officer of any state, to support the Constitution of the United States, shall have engaged in insurrection or rebellion against the same, or given aid or comfort to the enemies thereof. But Congress may by a vote of two-thirds of each House, remove such disability.

Section 4. The validity of the public debt of the United States, authorized by law, including debts incurred for payment of pensions and bounties for services in suppressing insurrection or rebellion, shall not be questioned. But neither the United States nor any state shall assume or pay any debt or obligation incurred in aid of insurrection or rebellion against the United States, or any claim for the loss or emancipation of any slave; but all such debts, obligations and claims shall be held illegal and void.

Section 5. The Congress shall have power to enforce, by appropriate legislation, the provisions of this article.

Amendment 15

Section 1. The right of citizens of the United States to vote shall not be denied or abridged by the United States or by any state on account of race, color, or previous condition of servitude.

Section 2. The Congress shall have power to enforce this article by appropriate legislation.

Focus for Thought

8. What were some provisions of the Reconstruction Act of 1867?
9. Name and describe each of the three groups who were involved in the Reconstruction governments.
10. a. What were some accomplishments of the Reconstruction governments?
    b. What were some of their problems?
11. a. Why was President Johnson impeached?
    b. How did his acquittal help to maintain the balance between the branches of the United States government?
    c. What major purchase was made during Johnson's presidency?
12. What is the main provision of the Fifteenth Amendment?

3. THE END OF RECONSTRUCTION

By Grant's second term, Northern interest in Reconstruction waned. Many people believed that the government had done as much for blacks as it could, and that blacks should now be able to succeed on their own. As a result, Southern whites were able to regain control of their state governments. This led to the end of official Reconstruction in 1877.

"When the righteous are in authority, the people rejoice: but when the wicked beareth rule, the people mourn" (Proverbs 29:2).

Southern Redemption

Intimidation of Blacks. Some Southern whites tried to accept blacks as their equals, but others did not. They hated the new state governments, which they called "black Republican" because of their strong support by black voters. Many former Confederates had no legal power to change anything, since they were prohibited from voting. Therefore, whites began forming secret societies to terrorize the blacks. They had two goals: to overthrow the Republican governments and to restore white supremacy.

The strongest of the secret societies was the Ku Klux Klan. Members of the Klan dressed in white robes and hoods to suggest that they were the ghosts of dead Confederate soldiers. Also, Klansmen frightened blacks by setting up burning crosses in front of the homes of blacks. They disrupted Republican meetings and drove black voters away from the ***polls*** (voting places). Klansmen whipped and murdered black people, and they also attacked white people who helped the blacks.

The Klan conducted a reign of terror at some places. In several counties of South Carolina, white bands roamed the countryside at night and drove freedmen from their homes, whipping and murdering them. Blacks became so fearful that, in 1871, thousands of them hid

The Ku Klux Klan, founded about 1865, used threats and violence to intimidate blacks. Klan members wore hoods to conceal their identity.

in the woods at night to avoid attack. Most whites either supported the Klan or were too frightened to say anything against the group.

Finally the Southern states appealed to the federal government for help, and Congress responded by passing several laws called Force Acts. The Ku Klux Klan Act of 1871 declared that if states did not punish the ones guilty of violence, the federal government would. President Grant sent soldiers to keep order in South Carolina, where they arrested hundreds of Klansmen and expelled two thousand from the state. Tough law enforcement soon broke the power of the Klan, and it practically disappeared for several decades.

Though the Klan's power was broken, the damage had been done. The Klan had weakened the Republicans, intimidated the blacks, and demonstrated the weakness of the Reconstruction governments.

Restoration of Control by Whites. White Southerners determined to wrest control of state governments from the "black Republicans," and with time they succeeded. One reason was that young citizens who had not taken part in the Confederacy began to vote. Also, Congress passed the Amnesty Act of 1872, which restored to most ex-Confederates the right to vote and hold office. These white voters supported the Democratic Party in the South. When native white Democrats gained control of a state government, that state was said to be ***redeemed***.

One by one, the Reconstruction governments fell and the states were redeemed: Tennessee in 1869, Virginia and North Carolina in 1870, and Georgia in 1871. The new governments tried to undo the changes brought by the Reconstruction governments. They lowered taxes and reduced government spending, especially on public education. They also made efforts to reduce the power of blacks.

By this time, the North had lost much of its interest in Reconstruction. Most people believed that enough had been done for the South and that the three new constitutional amendments protected black rights. The corruption in Reconstruction governments had further diminished Northern support. Besides, the North was occupied with economic problems of its own, and the westward expansion also drew interest away from the South.

So the process of "redemption" continued. Arkansas, Alabama, and Texas were redeemed in 1874, and Mississippi in 1876. By 1877, the states of Louisiana, South Carolina, and Florida were redeemed, and whites were once more in control of the South.

Reconstruction Ends

Election of 1876. In the presidential election of 1876, the Democratic **Samuel Tilden** received more popular votes than did the Republican **Rutherford B. Hayes**. But when the electoral votes were counted, results were uncertain because of disputing over the count for the unredeemed states. So Congress appointed a special committee to decide the

The Electoral Commission of 1877. This special commission was appointed to decide who would win the disputed election of 1876.

issue. This committee voted in February 1877 that Hayes had won the election.

But the issue was still not settled. Some Democrats talked of marching on Washington and forcing Tilden's inauguration. A number of congressmen talked of preventing the recording of the electoral vote—thus keeping anyone from taking office. In that case, the country would have had no president at all! What could be done?

Compromise of 1877. The Democrats and Republicans negotiated a compromise. If Hayes would make certain promises, the Southern Democrats would accept him as president. They wanted ***home rule***, which meant that Southern state governments would take care of all their own affairs. The result was the Compromise of 1877, in which Hayes promised three things: he would not use federal troops to intervene, he would name a Southerner to his Cabinet, and he would provide money for improvements in the South. This compromise was approved, and Hayes took office on March 4, 1877.

President Hayes promptly fulfilled his promises. He withdrew the last troops from Louisiana and South Carolina, named a Southerner as the postmaster general, and

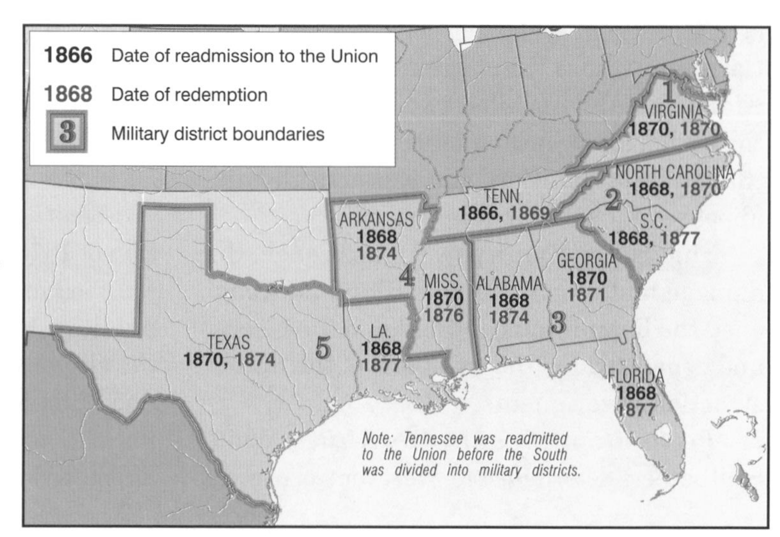

The South After the Civil War

encouraged railroad projects in the South. As a result, the last Reconstruction governments in Louisiana and South Carolina fell—and Reconstruction ended in 1877 as far as the federal government was concerned. Thus harmony was restored between Northern and Southern whites, while blacks were left to fend for themselves.

The New South

The Southern Economy. The South did not regain its former prosperity for years. Not until 1880 did the South produce as much cotton as it had in 1860, and not until 1900 did the tobacco crop exceed the one of 1860. With much of the land divided into small farms, only a few large plantations remained. Cotton, tobacco, rice, and sugar cane were still important, but farmers also raised crops such as fruits and vegetables. A black scientist named **George Washington Carver** did much to get Southern farmers to grow peanuts and other crops instead of wearing out the soil with cotton.

George Washington Carver (1864?–1943), holding a lump of soil in a field at Tuskegee Institute, Alabama. Carver promoted soil conservation and other improved farming practices. He is said to have found over 300 uses for peanuts.

The Mary Pratt Furnace in Birmingham, Alabama. The first blast furnace in this city began operation in 1880, and Birmingham soon became a leading steel center in the South.

The South built more factories to use its abundant resources. For example, Birmingham, Alabama, quickly grew into a large steel-producing town. Lumbering in the vast forests of the South became important, and cotton mills began producing cloth. Nevertheless, for decades the South lagged behind the rest of the nation in prosperity.

A Democratic South. As the whites took power again, they committed themselves to the Democratic Party, which supported white supremacy. The Republican Party grew weaker, and for a long time the South voted strictly for Democrats. It became known as the "solid South" because it stood solidly for the Democratic Party.

Experience of Blacks. After whites redeemed the state governments, they made efforts to restrict blacks. By the 1890s, whites were passing laws that complied with the Fifteenth Amendment while still making it hard for blacks to vote. Some laws required a poll tax, or a tax in order to vote, which was usually too high for blacks to pay. Others required blacks to take literacy tests or to explain parts of the state constitution—both of which many blacks could not do. These things were not required of whites even though many of them also could not read.

Segregation as illustrated in this picture was the accepted practice in the South until the 1960s.

Social ***segregation*** (separation) continued, with "separate but equal" institutions such as schools and hospitals for blacks. However, institutions for blacks often received little support from state governments dedicated to white supremacy, so they were not equal. Many hotels and other public places refused admittance to black people simply because they were black. In the 1890s, states passed so-called Jim Crow laws that enforced segregation. Lynching was common—white mobs would capture a black accused of a crime and hang him without a trial. The Lord sees all such injustices, and someday He will "reward every man according to his works" (Matthew 16:27).

Blacks did make a degree of economic progress. Some became successful through hard work and perseverance, and a middle class of blacks developed. **Booker T. Washington** stands out as an example of this group. By overcoming many obstacles, he obtained an education and later founded the Tuskegee Institute (tuhs KEE gee) in Alabama. His attitude was that blacks should do their best, get an education, and gain respect by being good citizens. Then, he felt, whites would treat them as equals.

Washington was willing to accept social segregation, at least for the immediate future. He did much good for other members of his race by teaching them good work habits and lifestyles and by setting a noble example for them. But things did not work out as he had

Left: History class in the Tuskegee Institute. This school was founded in 1881 to teach practical industrial skills to blacks. George Washington Carver was among its most prominent teachers. ***Right:*** Booker T. Washington (1856–1915) did much to promote harmony between blacks and whites. He was an eminent black leader and founder of the Tuskegee Institute in Alabama.

> *Booker T. Washington wrote the following words in his autobiography,* Up From Slavery.
>
> I learned the lesson that great men cultivate love, and that only little men cherish a spirit of hatred. I learned that assistance given to the weak makes the one who gives it strong; and that oppression of the unfortunate makes one weak. . . .
>
> I . . . resolved that I would permit no man, no matter what his colour might be, to narrow and degrade my soul by making me hate him. With God's help, I believe that I have completely rid myself of any ill feeling toward the Southern white man for any wrong that he may have inflicted upon my race. . . . I pity from the bottom of my heart any individual who is so unfortunate as to get into the habit of holding race prejudice.

hoped, for whites continued to look down on blacks regardless of what they did. If more people—black and white—had been willing to lay aside their prejudice and bitterness, race relations would have greatly improved.

What had Reconstruction accomplished? On one hand, blacks had gained and retained their freedom. The Southern states were restored to the Union, and they were regaining their prosperity. On the other hand, Reconstruction and redemption brought much violence and turmoil, and race prejudice continued. In spite of new industries and new crops, the South still lagged behind the rest of the nation. Yet the South could never again be the same as before the Civil War. It had been reconstructed.

Focus for Thought

13. a. What were the goals and methods of secret societies such as the Ku Klux Klan?
    b. How did the government control the Ku Klux Klan?
14. a. What two things enabled Southern whites to "redeem" their state governments?
    b. What did the new governments do?
15. How did the Compromise of 1877 end Reconstruction?
16. Name four important ways that the South changed after Reconstruction.

Historical Highlights

A. Matching: People

a. Andrew Johnson	f. Hiram Revels
b. Booker T. Washington	g. Rutherford B. Hayes
c. Edmund Ross	h. Samuel Tilden
d. Edwin Stanton	i. Ulysses S. Grant
e. George Washington Carver	j. William Seward

1. Johnson's secretary of state who purchased Alaska from Russia.
2. Lincoln's vice president; impeached when he was president.
3. Secretary of war who was dismissed by President Johnson.

4. President whose two terms were marked by corruption.
5. Man whose vote saved President Johnson from being found guilty.
6. Democratic candidate in disputed election of 1876.
7. Black leader who founded Tuskegee Institute and helped his people.
8. President elected by the Compromise of 1877, which aided redemption.
9. First black man elected to the United States Senate.
10. Black scientist who encouraged Southern farmers to grow peanuts.

B. Matching: Terms 1

a. black codes
b. carpetbaggers
c. Civil Rights Act
d. discrimination
e. Fourteenth Amendment
f. Fifteenth Amendment
g. freedmen
h. Freedmen's Bureau
i. Radical Republicans
j. Reconstruction
k. Reconstruction Act
l. scalawags
m. sharecropping
n. ten percent plan

1. Government agency that aided former slaves after the war.
2. Northerners who went south after the Civil War to help in Reconstruction.
3. Constitutional amendment that guarantees the rights of black people.
4. Law that defined citizenship and provided equal benefit of the law for all citizens.
5. Constitutional amendment granting all citizens the right to vote.
6. President Lincoln's plan for restoring the Southern states.
7. Group that wanted to punish and reform the South.
8. System in which farm workers rent cropland and use a share of the crops to pay the rent.
9. Southern whites who took part in Reconstruction governments.
10. Former slaves.
11. Laws that restricted blacks and kept them subordinate to whites.
12. Rebuilding and restoration of the South after the Civil War.
13. Action based on prejudice against a person.
14. Law that provided military control to enforce Reconstruction.

C. Matching: Terms 2

a. Amnesty Act
b. civil rights
c. Force Acts
d. home rule
e. Jim Crow laws
f. Ku Klux Klan
g. poll
h. redeem
i. segregation
j. Seward's Folly
k. solid South
l. Tenure of Office Act
m. white supremacy

1. Policy allowing Southern states to deal with their own affairs.
2. Belief that whites are superior to blacks.
3. Voting place.
4. Dependable Southern support of Democrats after redemption.
5. To restore government control by whites to a Southern state.
6. Secret society that terrorized blacks.
7. Law forbidding dismissal of Cabinet members without Senate approval.

8. Laws containing measures for dealing with groups that terrorized blacks.
9. Laws requiring segregation of blacks and whites after Reconstruction.
10. Law restoring to most ex-Confederates the right to vote and hold office.
11. Social separation based on race.
12. Term for Alaska.
13. Freedoms and privileges belonging to all citizens.

D. Multiple Choice

Write the letter of the best answer.

1. Which of the following was *not* lost by the South?
   a. religious freedom
   b. slaves
   c. family members
   d. wealth
2. Why did Radicals resist the presidential plans for Reconstruction?
   a. They considered those plans unconstitutional.
   b. The president wanted Congress to control Reconstruction.
   c. They wanted to punish and reform the South.
   d. They thought Southerners themselves should take charge of Reconstruction.
3. What two goals did the Radicals have for the South?
   a. Blacks and whites would be equal.
   b. Sharecropping would continue for blacks and landowners.
   c. Carpetbaggers and scalawags would rebuild the war-torn areas.
   d. Southern states would be restored to the Union as soon as possible.
   e. Republicans would have control of the Southern states.
4. What goal did President Johnson have for the South?
   a. Blacks and whites would be equal.
   b. Southern plantations would be divided and given to the freedmen.
   c. The federal government would provide money for repairing war damages.
   d. Southern states would be restored to the Union as soon as possible.
5. For what reason did Southern states pass black codes?
   a. These codes helped the blacks to gain equality with whites.
   b. These codes aided the blacks economically.
   c. These codes kept blacks in an inferior status.
   d. The Ku Klux Klan promoted these codes.
6. In what two ways was the United States different after the Fourteenth Amendment was added to the Constitution?
   a. The slaves were productive as sharecroppers.
   b. The president could no longer veto legislation.
   c. The federal government had more authority over the states.
   d. The law provided equal rights for blacks and whites.
7. Which one of the following best describes the charges of impeachment against President Johnson?
   a. The charges grew out of personal dislike for the president.
   b. The charges were based on a new law passed mainly to restrict the president.
   c. The president had committed serious crimes worthy of punishment.
   d. The president was incapable of fulfilling the duties of his office.

8. Which political party did the carpetbaggers and scalawags represent?
   a. Republican   b. Democratic
9. What does the Fifteenth Amendment declare?
   a. No person may be held as a slave.
   b. Blacks and whites were equal before the law as citizens.
   c. No citizen (including a black person) may be denied the right to vote.
   d. Poll taxes and literacy tests may not be required for voting.
10. Which one of the following was *not* true of the Ku Klux Klan?
   a. It sought to reverse the changes that Reconstruction was bringing.
   b. Its members supported the Democratic Party.
   c. It was devoted to white supremacy.
   d. Its members frightened black people but did not actually harm them.
11. What contributed to government corruption during Reconstruction?
   a. Whites were considered superior to blacks.
   b. The Civil War had undermined the morals of the nation.
   c. People had an unusually strong love for money.
   d. Officeholders in Reconstruction governments were lazy and inefficient.
12. Why is the beginning of the Hayes administration considered the end of Reconstruction?
   a. The federal government ended its direct involvement in rebuilding the South.
   b. Hayes won the electoral vote but not the popular vote.
   c. Redeemed governments greatly reduced taxes.
   d. Segregation became the normal policy for race relations in the South.

E. Deeper Discussion

1. Which approach to Reconstruction—the presidential plan or the Congressional plan—yielded better results? Explain.
2. a. Why did blacks need so much help after they were free?
   b. What more could have been done to help the freedmen make the transition from slavery to freedom?
   c. Was sharecropping a benefit or a hindrance to blacks? Explain.
3. a. Why were blacks kept in an inferior position even though the Constitution gave them equal standing with whites?
   b. How did whites accomplish this?
4. a. Read Psalm 12:5 and Ecclesiastes 3:16, 17 and 5:8. Who notices each injustice that is never avenged on earth?
   b. What will finally be done about such injustices? (See Revelation 18:5, 6.)
5. How would the balance of power have been upset if President Johnson had been found guilty during his impeachment trial?
6. a. In what respects did Reconstruction succeed?
   b. In what respects did it fail?

F. Chronology and Geography

1. The following list gives some major events during the 1860s and 1870s. Arrange the list in the proper order, and supply the date for each event.

   Amnesty Act passed
   Civil Rights Act passed
   Grant re-elected
   Johnson impeached and acquitted

Civil War ends
Compromise of 1877 approved
Disputed Hayes–Tilden election
Emancipation Proclamation becomes effective
Fourteenth Amendment ratified
Fifteenth Amendment ratified
Ku Klux Klan Act passed
Lincoln assassinated
Reconstruction Act passed
Reconstruction ends
United States purchases Alaska

2. Name the Southern states in the order they were redeemed, and give the year of redemption for each.
3. How did the South make better use of its resources after the war?

Sharecroppers worked hard to plant and harvest their cash crop. Part of the harvested crop belonged to the plantation owner as the rental fee for using his land, but the sharecropper could use or sell the rest of the crop. Sadly, a bountiful harvest was often not possible because much of the soil had lost its fertility by overuse. A poor harvest meant the hardworking sharecroppers had little to live on after the rent was paid. Since many sharecroppers had an open account at the plantation's supply store (which usually charged high prices), they often became indebted to the plantation owner and were forced to work year after year just to pay off their debts.

So Far This Year

A. Matching: Climates

1. Sunny and mild; good for growing oranges and olives.
2. Very warm and moist.
3. Wet and mild; found in Pacific valleys.
4. Cold climate in Canada and Alaska.
5. Climate of four seasons.

a. humid continental
b. humid subtropical
c. Mediterranean
d. subarctic
e. west coast marine

B. Matching: Physical Features

6. Drains about 40 percent of the United States.
7. Rocky region curving like a horseshoe around Hudson Bay.
8. Made up of the Coast Ranges, the Pacific ranges, and the Pacific valleys.
9. Region with high mountains extending from Canada to New Mexico; region includes Great Basin and plateaus.
10. Longest river in Canada.
11. Vast, treeless, grassy land stretching from the Mississippi to the Rockies.
12. Heartland of Canada in Ontario and Quebec.
13. Broad, flat region bordering the Gulf of Mexico and the ocean east of the United States.
14. Made up of the Piedmont, the Appalachian Mountains, and the Allegheny and Cumberland Plateaus.

a. Appalachian region
b. Atlantic Coastal Plain
c. Canadian Shield
d. Great Lakes–St. Lawrence Lowlands
e. Central Plains
f. Mississippi River
g. Mackenzie River
h. Pacific Coast
i. Rocky Mountain region

C. Matching: Explorers

15. Viking who explored the northeastern coast of North America around A.D. 1000.
16. "Admiral of the Ocean Sea" who discovered the New World in 1492.
17. Man who described the new lands as being a new world rather than part of the Orient.
18. Explorer of the northeastern coast of North American for England in 1497.
19. Explorer who discovered in 1513 that a great ocean lay west of America.
20. Captain of five ships, one of which became the first to sail around the world (1519–1522).
21. Explorer who claimed part of America for the Netherlands in 1609.
22. Explorer of the North American coast for France in 1524.
23. Explorer of the St. Lawrence River area for France in 1534.
24. The "father of New France."

a. Vasco de Balboa
b. John Cabot
c. Jacques Cartier
d. Samuel de Champlain
e. Christopher Columbus
f. Francisco de Coronado
g. Leif Ericson
h. Henry Hudson
i. Louis Jolliet
j. Robert de La Salle
k. Ponce de León
l. Ferdinand Magellan

25. Explorer who claimed for France the area drained by the Mississippi River.
26. Jesuits who explored part of the Mississippi River for France (two answers).
27. Explorer who sought the Seven Cities of Cíbola in the Southwest (1540–1542).
28. Explorer who discovered the Mississippi River.
29. Explorer who discovered Florida in 1513 while seeking the Fountain of Youth.

m. Jacques Marquette
n. Hernando de Soto
o. Amerigo Vespucci
p. Giovanni da Verrazano

D. Completion

Write the correct name, term, or date that belongs on each blank.

30. The idea that people living in an area should decide for themselves about slavery is called ___.
31. The ___ Amendment to the Constitution permanently outlawed slavery.
32. The ___ declared that slaves in the Confederacy were free.
33. A secret system that aided escaping slaves was the ___.
34. During the Civil War, Delaware, Maryland, Kentucky, and Missouri were called ___.
35. ___ was president of the Confederate States of America.
36. ___ was president of the Union during the Civil War.
37. ___ was the chief Union general at the end of the Civil War.
38. ___ was the chief general of the Confederate armies.
39. ___ tried to free the slaves through an armed uprising.
40. ___ wrote a book called *Uncle Tom's Cabin*.
41. ___ was a black man whose appeal for freedom was rejected by the Supreme Court.
42. ___ was a Confederate general shot by his own men at the Battle of Chancellorsville.
43. ___ was a Union general who led a destructive March to the Sea.
44. The town of ___ became known as the "high-water mark of the Confederacy."
45. ___ was the place where the Civil War began.
46. The city that served as the Confederate capital was ___.
47. ___ was the stronghold whose fall gave the Union control of the Mississippi.
48. The new state formed from a Confederate state during the Civil War was ___.
49. An early battle that showed the Civil War would be long and hard took place at ___.
50. The Civil War began in the year ___ and ended in the year ___.

Thunder Cape lay on a main route to the Canadian West. This mighty rock symbolizes the expansion of Canada and the forces of nature that so strongly influenced its development.

18 The Development of Canada

1. UPPER AND LOWER CANADA
   - Formation of Upper and Lower Canada
   - Development of Upper Canada
2. BIRTH OF THE DOMINION OF CANADA
   - Struggle for Responsible Government
   - Canada Becomes a Nation
3. GROWTH OF THE DOMINION
   - The Northwest
   - Manitoba
   - British Columbia
   - Further Development

1750

Quebec Act passed 1774

New Brunswick formed 1784

Mennonites settle in Canada 1786

Upper Canada and Lower Canada formed by the Canada Act 1791

Alexander Mackenzie explores to the Pacific 1793

1800

War of 1812 **1812–1814**

Rebellion of 1837

Durham Report submitted 1838

Province of Canada formed by the Act of Union **1841**

Rebellion Losses Bill approved; Parliament buildings burned in Montreal 1849

1850

Reciprocity Treaty implemented 1854

Quebec Conference held 1864

Reciprocity Treaty ended by U.S.; Confederation approved; British Columbia formed 1866

Dominion of Canada formed by the British North America Act **1867**

Rupert's Land and North West Territories obtained; Red River Rebellion 1869

Rupert's Land and North West Territories organized into the Northwest Territories 1870

Manitoba Act passed 1870

British Columbia joins the Dominion 1871

North West Mounted Police formed; Prince Edward Island joins the Dominion 1873

Russian Mennonites arrive in Manitoba 1874

North West Rebellion 1884–1885

Canadian Pacific Railway completed 1885

Yukon Territory formed 1898

1900

Saskatchewan and Alberta become provinces 1905

Newfoundland joins the Dominion 1949

1950

Nunavut becomes a territory 1999

2000

"There is none holy as the LORD: for there is none beside thee: neither is there any rock like our God."
1 Samuel 2:2

THE DEVELOPMENT OF CANADA

Focus for Reading

Although the United States gained independence from Britain through the American Revolution, northern North America remained under British control. In that land, known as Canada, vast regions remained wild and unpeopled except for ambitious explorers, bold fur traders, and Indian tribes. Settlers continued to develop the British colonies in the east, and eventually they united to form a nation. The nation then expanded until it stretched from the Atlantic to the Pacific and north almost to the North Pole. How was British North America settled? How did Canadians establish their nation? What enabled Canada to grow into the large nation it is today? This chapter answers these questions in three sections.

1. Upper and Lower Canada
2. Birth of the Dominion of Canada
3. Growth of the Dominion

1. UPPER AND LOWER CANADA

After the American Revolution, the United States and Canada went separate ways. Sometimes their paths crossed. For example, many Americans moved north to Canada when the United States became independent. The United States invaded Canada during the War of 1812; and before the Civil War, many slaves fled to Canada.

But for the most part, the two nations developed differently. While the United States expanded rapidly, Canada grew at a slower pace. This section explains the early development and settlement of British North America.

Formation of Upper and Lower Canada

The Quebec Act. After the treaty ending the French and Indian War in 1763, the British ruled the thirteen American colonies as well as Newfoundland, Nova Scotia, Prince Edward Island, and Cape Breton Island. They also ruled the French in Quebec. The French were Roman Catholic, spoke French, and followed French laws and customs such as the seigneurial system.

To keep peace with the French colonists, the British passed the Quebec Act in 1774. This act permitted French Canadians to exercise their religion freely and to take part in the government. It also allowed the seigneurial system and French civil laws to continue. Further, the Quebec Act extended the borders of Quebec south to the Ohio River and west to the Mississippi River. This law satisfied most Canadians, especially the French.

But the Quebec Act angered the Americans farther south, and it became one of the Intolerable Acts that contributed to the American Revolution. The Americans hoped the French Canadians would help them overthrow British rule, and for that reason they invaded Canada early in the Revolution. But the French Canadians did not help them and the invasion failed. So Canada remained British after the American Revolution.

Loyalists in Canada. Many Americans had remained loyal to Britain during the Revolution. After the war ended, between forty thousand and fifty thousand of these people, known as United Empire Loyalists, moved to Canada. Many of them settled in Nova Scotia, where they sometimes did not get along with the settlers already there. When the ones living along the St. John River near the Bay

Loyalist "boom town" of Shelburne, Nova Scotia, in 1789. So many Loyalists settled here that in three years the new town had a population of 8,000 people.

of Fundy demanded their own government, Britain established that part of Nova Scotia as the separate province of New Brunswick in 1784.

Thousands of Loyalists also flooded into Quebec. To help them, the governor bought land from the Indians in western Quebec, along the upper St. Lawrence River and along the northeastern shore of Lake Ontario. New townships were surveyed, and Loyalists were transported by boat to the new territory. They cleared the land and built log houses; and by October 1784, four thousand of them were living there.

With so many Loyalist settlers, the region became overwhelmingly English. These people were unhappy with the provisions of the Quebec Act such as French law, the seigneurial system, and the dominance of the Roman Catholic Church. They wanted English law and an elected assembly, and they especially wanted a separate government for their settlements in western Quebec. But many French Canadians opposed these changes.

Accordingly, the British passed the Canada Act (also called the Constitutional Act) in 1791. This act divided Quebec into two parts: Upper Canada (the western English settlements that later became Ontario), and Lower Canada (French Quebec). The boundary between them was the Ottawa River. This act allowed English- and French-speaking people each to use their respective customs. Land in Upper Canada would be freehold, with settlers not paying any rents or duties for their land. But Lower Canada continued to use the seigneurial system until after 1850.

The British hoped that eventually the French Canadians would be so impressed with British ways that they would give up their French ways. But this hope proved vain, for the French continued to cling to their established culture and customs.

Development of Upper Canada

The first lieutenant governor of Upper Canada was John G. Simcoe, who wanted to populate Upper Canada with Loyalists and form a "little Britain." The government built

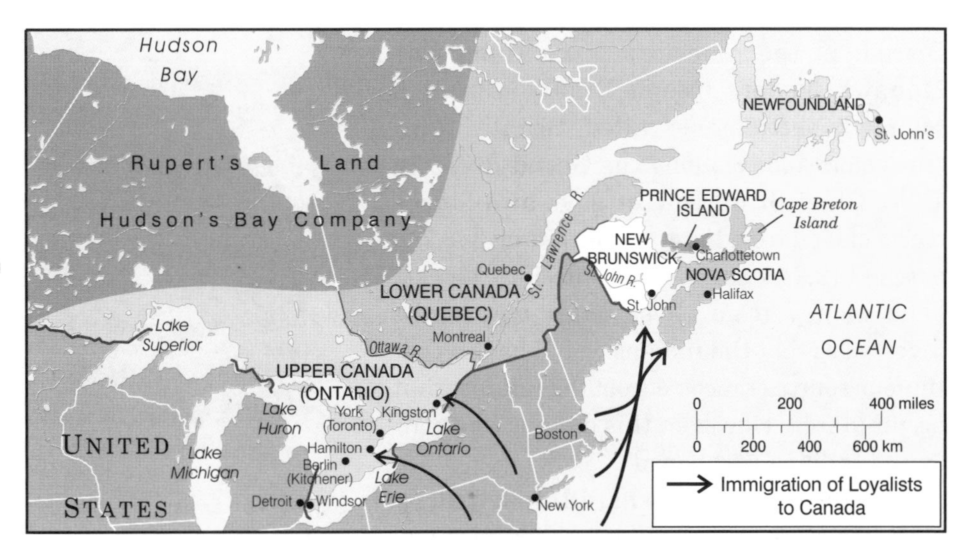

British North America After 1791

Encampment of Loyalists at Cornwall, Upper Canada, in 1784. After the American Revolution, 40,000 to 50,000 Loyalists moved to Canada. This picture shows a new Loyalist settlement only a few days after it was started.

Settlement at York about 1803. It was founded in 1793 as the capital of Upper Canada (now Ontario) and was later named Toronto.

roads and encouraged Loyalists to settle in Upper Canada. Americans could get 200 acres (81 ha) of free land if they took an oath of loyalty to the British government. Soon a stream of settlers moved in, clearing land, building houses, and establishing settlements.

These immigrants came from many places, including the United States, England, Scotland, and Ireland. Americans came from Detroit and from New England. These people began settlements such as Kingston, York, Hamilton, and Windsor along Lakes Ontario, Erie, and Huron. Population increased rapidly in both Upper and Lower Canada.

Mennonites in Canada. An interesting story of Mennonite migration unfolded at this time. It began when the British gave the Mohawk Indians a large tract of land in Upper Canada because they had supported the British in the American Revolution. The Mohawk leader, Joseph Brant, started a Mohawk settlement called Brant's Ford (Brantford today) along the Grand River. In 1798, Chief Brant sold or gave away large tracts of land from his grant, including 352,710 acres (142,848 ha) divided into four blocks. (The money from these sales was to be invested so that the Indians would have a continuous source of income from the interest that accumulated. However, this did not work out as the Indians had hoped.)

An officer named Richard Beasley, along with two other men, agreed to purchase one of these blocks and made a down payment of 600 pounds on the sale price of 8,887 pounds.

About this time, Mennonites in Pennsylvania began considering a move to Canada. Some were concerned about their religious freedom in the United States and thought they might be better off under their former king. Others simply wanted to obtain more farmland. They found it on the Niagara Peninsula. The first Mennonites to arrive in Canada settled at Twenty Mile Creek in 1786. Later, others bought land from Richard Beasley. They cleared land and built homes on the Grand River in Waterloo County. They

This marker describes the first Mennonite settlement in Ontario, Canada.

were the first white people to settle the interior part of present-day southern Ontario. More Mennonites flowed in after 1800. Beasley needed money to pay for the land, of course, so he was happy for these settlers.

These Mennonite pioneers in Canada soon faced a problem that seemed impossible to solve. In 1803, they learned that Beasley had a mortgage on the land. The deeds they held were worthless scraps of paper because Beasley did not hold clear title to the land; he still owed money on it.

At the time, there was a continuing dispute between Chief Brant and the government. Beasley had tried to get the government to give individual mortgages so that the settlers could have clear titles, but that request was denied. Furthermore, the government wanted to take legal action against Beasley because he was not making his interest payments on time. So when the Mennonites questioned him about the matter, Colonel Beasley said that they could gain clear title if they paid 10,000 pounds ($20,000) for the *entire* 60,000 acres (24,300 ha), which was a cheap price for the excellent farmland.

But the settlers despaired—they could never raise such a tremendous amount! They consulted together and sent Samuel Bricker and Joseph Sherk to Pennsylvania to see if they could convince the Mennonites there to come to their aid.

The Mennonites in Lancaster discussed the matter; many did not want to risk their money. But prayers were answered in the form of a business venture called the German Land Company. Some of the shareholders were able to contribute sizeable sums; and together, they managed to raise enough money to purchase the Beasley tract. The $20,000 had to be paid in silver coins, so the women made bags that held one hundred coins each and filled two hundred bags that Samuel Bricker hauled to Canada in a special wagon. The land sale was completed by 1805—and the Mennonite settlement in

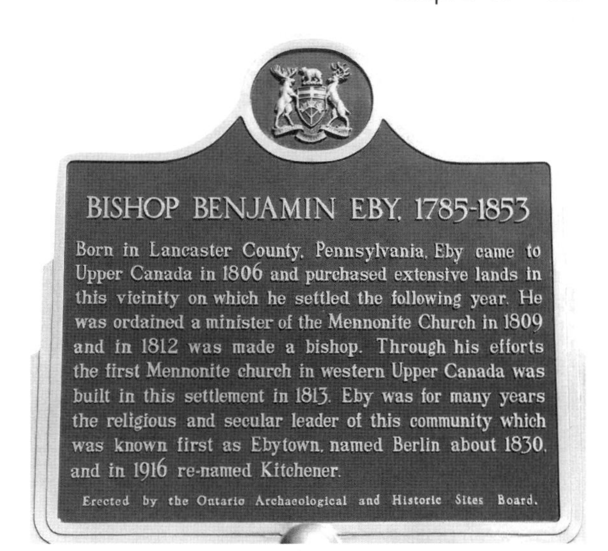

This marker describes the role of Benjamin Eby, a bishop in early Mennonite settlements in Ontario.

Waterloo County was saved! This is a notable example of how Christian brethren can bear "one another's burdens, and so fulfil the law of Christ" (Galatians 6:2).

The Lord blessed these efforts. The shareholders of the German Land Company profited by selling the remaining land in the large tract they now owned. Many more Mennonites arrived after this, and bought land. Soon a log church was built. The village of Ebytown, founded in 1806, became known as Berlin and was renamed Kitchener during World War I. From 1786 to 1825, about two thousand Mennonites moved to Upper Canada.

Canada in the War of 1812. During the War of 1812, attacking Canada seemed like a good way to expand the United States and attack Britain at the same time. The Americans invaded Canada from Detroit, west of Lake Erie, and from New York by way of the Niagara Peninsula between Lakes Erie and Ontario. The British Colonel **Isaac Brock**, with Indian help, defeated the Americans at Detroit; but Brock was killed at Queenston Heights on the Niagara Peninsula in 1812. The next year, the Americans burned the Parliament buildings of York, the capital of Upper Canada.

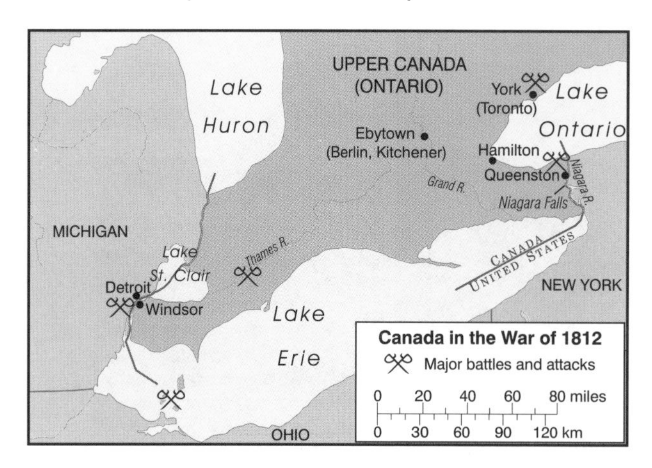

In October and November 1813, American forces attacked Lower Canada but suffered defeat. On Lake Erie, Oliver Hazard Perry defeated the British in September, and later United States troops defeated the British at the Battle of the Thames. But American forces were defeated on the Niagara Peninsula in 1814; and by the end of that year, the Treaty of Ghent had ended the war.

Though neither side officially won the War of 1812, this conflict had important effects on Canada. It brought greater prosperity because of increased British military spending. The war also gave Canadians a stronger sense of nationalism as they worked together to defend their country. On the other hand, many Canadians became bitter because of the invasions by United States armies. Yet through a series of agreements between the United States and Britain, relations stayed generally peaceful between Canada and its neighbor to the south.

Focus for Thought

1. What were four important provisions of the Quebec Act?
2. What effects did the Loyalists have on the parts of Canada where they settled?
3. a. What was the aim of the Canada Act of 1791?
   b. Why was this aim not fulfilled?
4. a. What problem was experienced by Mennonites who bought land from Richard Beasley?
   b. How did they solve the problem?
5. What were some ways that the War of 1812 affected Canada?

2. BIRTH OF THE DOMINION OF CANADA

After the War of 1812, the provinces in Canada grew in population, but they also developed problems in getting along with their British colonial government. The British eventually provided a better system of government for Upper and Lower Canada, but the provinces continued to operate as a disunited group of colonies. By the 1860s, various influences brought the provinces to agree that they should unite into one nation.

Struggle for Responsible Government

Problems in Colonial Government. Each province in Canada had a government consisting of a governor, an Executive Council, a Legislative Council, and a Legislative Assembly. The English governor controlled the province, assisted by his appointed Executive Council. The Legislative Council was the upper lawmaking body, whose members were appointed for life. The Legislative Assembly was the lower law-making body, elected by the people.

In each province, the government was dominated by a small group of upper-class Loyalists (Tories). This group was commonly known as the Family Compact because the members often gave positions of power and influence to their families and friends. Members of the Family Compact promoted British traditions and

CANADIAN PROVINCIAL GOVERNMENT

Branch	Status	Function
Lieutenant governor	Always an Englishman	Head of province
Executive Council	Appointed by governor	Assistant to governor
Legislative Council	Appointed for life	Upper law-making body
Legislative Assembly	Elected by the people	Lower law-making body

interests. They were convinced that only they could properly exercise government power, and that the common people should support them. But most common people resented the Family Compact because it allowed them little voice in the government.

After the War of 1812, many people came to Canada from Ireland, Scotland, and England. These immigrants brought their British ways with them, and thus British ways rather than American ways prevailed in Canada. But in Lower Canada, the French Canadians looked on the English-speaking settlers with suspicion. The French habitants were afraid they would lose their farms to English industrialization. Above all, they worried that their French language and culture would lose out to those of the English.

Rebellion of 1837. Because of these problems, reform movements developed in the colonies to produce ***responsible government*** (self-government in local affairs). Up to this time, the government had been responsible (answerable) mainly to the British rulers, not to the people. Reformers wanted more democracy in the government instead of ***oligarchy*** (AHL ih gahr kee), or rule by a small group. They wanted to pass laws that the majority of colonists wanted, and to have the common people in charge of the government. Newspaperman **Joseph Howe** led the reform movement in Nova Scotia.

The Reform Party also developed in Upper Canada, with **William L. Mackenzie** among its strongest leaders. He attacked the Family Compact so forcefully that in 1826, young men of the Family Compact destroyed his newspaper printing shop. But this only served to bolster Mackenzie's support among the common people. He and his party demanded such reforms as having the Legislative Council elected by the people, and by 1835 his party had a majority in the Assembly of Upper Canada.

But trouble was brewing. Sir Francis Bond Head, the lieutenant governor of Upper Canada, dissolved the Reform-dominated Assembly and ordered a new election in 1836. This election resulted in a strong Tory majority because of Sir Bond Head's manipulation. Shocked by this turn, some radical reformers such as Mackenzie began to plan an outright rebellion to gain reform by force.

Mackenzie started military drills with several groups of men. When the rebels marched on Toronto on December 5, 1837—some of them armed with pitchforks—they were easily repulsed by volunteer soldiers. Mackenzie fled across the Niagara River to New York, but some revolutionary leaders were hanged or exiled for treason. Thus ended the Rebellion of 1837 in Upper Canada.

Unrest also developed in Lower Canada, where the French dominated the Assembly but the English dominated the Council. When a deadlock resulted in 1837, the English decided to move ahead without French cooperation, and the French-controlled Assembly was adjourned indefinitely. Frustrated, **Louis Joseph Papineau** (PAHP un noh) and his supporters, known as Patriotes, decided that their only option was rebellion. Fighting broke out in Montreal in November, but the Patriotes were defeated. The Rebellion of 1837 ended in Lower Canada when Papineau and the other leaders fled to the United States.

The Durham Report. The Rebellion of 1837 convinced the British government that the Canadian provinces were having serious difficulties. Queen Victoria appointed **Lord Durham** (John G. Lambton, Earl of Durham) to investigate the problems. He spent five months in Canada in 1838 and then submitted his "Report on the Affairs of British North America," commonly known as the Durham Report.

Lord Durham made a number of important recommendations. He suggested that the Canadian provinces be given more self-government. He advised making the government more responsible to the people by putting the Executive Council under the authority of the elected Legislative Assembly rather than under the governor. Another important proposal was to unite Upper and Lower Canada into one province. This would make the French a minority in the new province, and then they could no longer obstruct the wishes of the English majority. Lord Durham mistakenly believed that the French would eventually give up their French ways.

The Durham Report was strongly opposed by the Family Compact and by French Canadians, but was enthusiastically endorsed by many reformers. In 1840, the British Parliament passed the Act of Union to join the two Canadas into the Province of Canada. This act took effect in 1841. Upper Canada was now called Canada West, and Lower Canada was called Canada East.

Responsible Government Achieved. Even though the new government was more responsible than before, the governor still held considerable power. He continued to appoint the members of the Legislative and Executive Councils, and the Legislative Council was still responsible to him. But matters changed little by little. Fully responsible government was achieved in Nova Scotia and the Province of Canada in 1848, and in New Brunswick and Prince Edward Island by 1855.

In 1849, the Assembly and the Legislative Council approved a law known as the Rebellion Losses Bill. Its purpose was to pay citizens of Canada East for damages suffered in the Rebellion of 1837. Tories strongly opposed this bill because they did not think the rebels should be paid for their losses. But the governor-general, named Elgin, signed the bill because he believed in responsible government—that is, if the people's representatives passed a law, he should sign it.

Soon a mob of opponents gathered outside the Parliament building in Montreal. They threw sticks and stones at Elgin's carriage, but he escaped safely. Later that day, a mob again converged on the Parliament buildings. They smashed windows, set the buildings on

The Parliament House in Montreal burned on April 25, 1849, after an English-speaking mob rioted against the Rebellion Losses Bill.

fire, and engaged in rioting for several days.

Tories appealed to Britain to withdraw Elgin and disallow the Rebellion Losses Bill. But the British Parliament refused. This showed that it would not intervene in the affairs of the Province of Canada, and also that Parliament approved Elgin's support of responsible government. Now local matters were in the hands of the elected Assembly rather than in the hands of the appointed British officials. Canada had achieved greater self-government—and had taken an important step toward becoming a nation.

Canada Becomes a Nation

The Road to Confederation. A number of factors moved the disjointed Canadian provinces toward union. These included commerce, relations with the United States, and political problems.

The effect of commerce began in 1846, when the British ended the special trade privileges that Canadian provinces had had with Britain. This caused the Canadian economy to suffer as exports dropped. But in 1854, the Canadian provinces worked out the Reciprocity Treaty (rehs uh PRAHS ih tee), which greatly expanded trade with the United States. Grain, lumber, and textile industries grew, and new railroads linked the provinces together. After the Civil War, however, the United States ended this treaty in 1866. It became clear that the provinces should become united to increase trade among themselves.

Relations with the United States also caused the Canadians to think of uniting. They worried that the United States might expand northward into their territory, especially after the purchase of Alaska in 1867. Besides, many Americans were moving into British Columbia to seek gold. The Province of Canada by itself was not strong enough to restrain American settlement in British territory; but if all the Canadian provinces united, they might be able.

Canadians began to talk seriously about unity because they were weary of political problems. According to the Act of Union, Canada East and Canada West were to have equal numbers of representatives in the Legislative Assembly. But this caused deadlock when the English-speaking and French-speaking representatives could not agree. Furthermore, since the Province of Canada had more English speakers than French speakers by the mid-1860s, the English resented the French equality in representation. Such equality did not seem fair at all.

Confederation Achieved. Several statesmen proposed that a ***confederation*** of the Canadian provinces was the answer to these problems. In October 1864, leaders from all the provinces came to a meeting called the Quebec Conference. These "fathers of the Confederation" worked out the Seventy-two Resolutions, or Quebec Resolutions, to specify

BY THE PRESIDENT OF THE UNITED STATES OF AMERICA.

A PROCLAMATION.

Whereas a treaty between the United States of America and her Majesty the Queen of the United Kingdom of Great Britain and Ireland, was concluded and signed by their respective plenipotentiaries at Washington on the 5th day of June last, which treaty is, word for word, as follows:

The government of the United States being equally desirous with her Majesty the Queen of Great Britain to avoid further misunderstanding between their respective citizens and subjects in regard to the extent of the right of fishing on the coasts of British North America, secured to each by article 1 of a convention between the United States and Great Britain, signed in London on the 20th day of October, 1818; and being also desirous to regulate the commerce and navigation between their respective territories and people, and more especially between her Majesty's possessions in North America and the United States, in such manner as to render the same reciprocally beneficial and satisfactory, have, respectively, named plenipotentiaries to confer and agree thereupon—that is to say, the President of the United States of America, William L. Marcy, Secretary of State of the United States, and her Majesty the Queen of the United Kingdom of Great Britain and Ireland, James, Earl of Elgin and Kincardine, Lord Bruce and Elgin, a peer of the United Kingdom, Knight of the most ancient and most noble Order of the Thistle, and governor general in and over all her Britannic Majesty's provinces on the continent of North America, and in and over the island of Prince Edward, who, after having communicated to each other their respective full powers, found in good and due form, have agreed upon the following articles:

ARTICLE 1. It is agreed by the high contracting parties that, in addition to the liberty secured to the United States fishermen by the above-mentioned convention of October 20, 1818, of taking, curing, and drying fish on certain coasts of the British North American colonies therein defined, the inhabitants of the United States shall have, in common with the subjects of her Britannic Majesty, the liberty to take fish of every kind, except shell-fish, on the sea-coasts and shores, and in the bays, harbors, and creeks of Canada, New Brunswick, Nova Scotia, Prince Edward's island, and of the several islands thereunto adjacent, without being restricted to any distance from the shore, with permission to land upon the coasts and shores of those colonies and the islands thereof, and also upon the Magdalen islands, for the purpose of drying their nets and curing their fish: provided that, in so doing, they do not interfere with the rights of private property, or with British fishermen, in the peaceable use of any part of the said coast in their occupancy for the same purpose.

It is understood that the above-mentioned liberty applies solely to the sea fishery, and that the salmon and shad fisheries, and all fisheries in rivers and the mouths of rivers, are herby reserved, exclusively, for British fishermen.

And it is further agreed, that in order

First page of the Reciprocity Treaty of 1854. This treaty boosted trade between Canada and the United States, and it also improved relations between the two countries.

Toronto, Ontario, in 1854. Many Canadian cities expanded rapidly in the middle 1800s, mainly due to the growth of railroads and manufacturing. Contrast this picture with the one of Hochelaga in Chapter 5.

the details of their union. Canada would be a federation somewhat like the United States, with provincial and national governments and with a Parliament like the one in Great Britain.

After the Seventy-two Resolutions were adopted, they needed to be approved by each province and then by the British Parliament. Approval from the provinces did not come easily, especially from Quebec. But finally in 1866, a group of Canadian delegates traveled to London to work out the last details for uniting the provinces. On March 29, 1867, the British Parliament passed the British North America Act to create the Dominion of Canada. Its name was taken from Psalm 72:8: "He shall have dominion also from sea to sea."

The British North America Act joined four provinces: Ontario (Canada West), Quebec (Canada East), Nova Scotia, and New Brunswick. It made allowance for other provinces to be added later. The head of the Dominion would be the British monarch; but since the king or queen would seldom be in Canada, the monarch would be represented by a governor-general.

The Parliament of Canada would consist of an upper house named the Senate (similar to the former Legislative Council) and a lower house named the House of Commons (similar

Delegates at the Quebec Conference in October 1864. These were the men who framed the Seventy-two Resolutions.

Left: Parliament buildings in Ottawa, Canada, around 1880. Ottawa became the capital of the Dominion of Canada. ***Right:*** Sir John A. Macdonald (1815–1891) became the first prime minister of the Dominion of Canada. He served from 1867 to 1873 and again from 1878 to 1891. He is called the "father of present-day Canada" because of his influence in establishing the Dominion of Canada.

to the former Legislative Assembly). Members of the Senate were appointed for life, while members of the House of Commons were elected. The prime minister would be the leader of the majority party in the House of Commons; he would be the actual head of government. A group of men called his Cabinet, chosen from the House of Commons, would aid him in ruling the Dominion.

The Dominion of Canada was to be self-governing but not independent. The British government retained the power to disallow laws of the Dominion Parliament, to control foreign policy, and to amend the British North America Act. In short, the British government could override decisions made by the Canadian government.

The Dominion of Canada officially came into being on July 1, 1867. Its first prime minister was **John A. Macdonald**, and its capital was Ottawa. Canada had only about 3.5 million people and covered just a small part of eastern North America when it became a nation.

Focus for Thought

6. Why did the French Canadians distrust the English-speaking settlers in Canada?
7. A two-part rebellion broke out in 1837.
   a. What sparked the rebellion in Upper Canada? in Lower Canada?
   b. What were the results of these rebellions?
8. What three things did the Durham Report recommend?
9. Why was the passage of the Rebellion Losses Bill an important step in achieving responsible government?
10. Name and describe three factors that moved the Canadian provinces toward uniting as a nation.
11. List the four original provinces in the Dominion of Canada, and the date when they officially became a self-governing nation.

3. GROWTH OF THE DOMINION

The Dominion of Canada had a good beginning. In the decades after its formation, Canada expanded until it included nearly the entire northern part of North America. This section tells the story of that expansion.

The Northwest

Fur Trading. In the late 1700s, a fur-trading partnership called the North West Company was operating in the region north and west of the Great Lakes. Traders from Montreal headed west every year in canoes loaded with merchandise and paddled by strong French Canadians called ***voyageurs*** (voi uh ZHURZ). At Grand Portage, a rendezvous northwest of Lake Superior, the traders would barter with their "wintering partners" for beaver, otter, wolverine, and other pelts. They became fabulously rich through their fur trading.

Canadian trappers on Lake Superior. Fur trappers often traveled by canoe as they roamed the West.

Exploration of the Northwest. This rich fur country had been discovered by explorers like **Peter Pond**, who in 1778 helped to establish the fur trade in the region around Lake Athabasca. Pond inspired a man named **Alexander Mackenzie** to look for the long-sought Northwest Passage. In June 1789, Mackenzie traveled down the Slave River to the Great Slave Lake. From there he followed a river westward, hoping it would lead through the Rocky Mountains; but the river led north to the Arctic Ocean instead. It was later named the Mackenzie River after its discoverer.

In 1793, Mackenzie tried again, this time following the Peace River and eventually working his way over the Continental Divide and out to the Pacific. At the mouth of the Bella Coola River, on the Pacific Coast, Mackenzie wrote on a stone: "Alexander Mackenzie, from Canada by land, the 22nd of July, 1793."

This fur trader sorts fox, beaver, mink, and other furs at Fort Chipewyan in northeastern Alberta.

In 1808, the North West Company sent **Simon Fraser** to explore the river that now bears his name. He followed it to the Pacific. And in 1811, the famous surveyor **David Thompson** traveled to the Pacific by following the Columbia River. Thompson produced an excellent map of the West, and he later helped to survey the border between Canada and the United States.

Merging of Fur Companies. The Hudson's Bay Company competed with the North West Company for the western fur trade. Often, the Hudson's Bay Company built trading posts near the North West Company posts, and this rivalry caused fierce competition. Traders sold liquor to the Indians and even fought each other. But by 1821, the rivals merged under the Hudson's Bay Company. **George Simpson** directed the new company skillfully, treating the Indians fairly and reducing the liquor trade. The Hudson's Bay Company effectively ruled nearly all the land north and west of the Great Lakes.

The Northwest Territories. Prime Minister John A. Macdonald wanted to expand the Dominion to the Pacific Ocean. Of the West he said, "I would be quite willing to leave that

WANTED

A FEW stout and active YOUNG MEN, for the service of the HUDSON'S BAY COMPANY, at their Factories and Settlements in America. The Wages to be given, will depend on the qualifications of each individual: very good hands may expect from £12. to £15. a year, besides a sufficient allowance of oatmeal, or other food equally good and wholesome. Each person must engage by contract for a period of three years, at the end of which, he shall be brought home to Scotland, free of expence, unless he chuses to remain at the Settlements of the Company, where THIRTY ACRES of GOOD LAND will be granted, in *perpetual feu*, to every man who has conducted himself to the satisfaction of his employers. Those who are thus allowed to remain as settlers after the expiration of their service, may have their Families brought over to them by the Company at a moderate freight. Every man who chuses to make an allowance to his relations at home, may have any part of his wages regularly paid to them, *without charge or deduction.* No one will be hired, unless he can bring a satisfactory character for general good conduct, and particularly for honesty and sobriety; and unless he is also capable of enduring fatigue and hardship. Expert Boatmen will receive particular encouragement. Those who are desirous of engaging in this service, will please to specify their names, ages, and places of abode, as also their present station and employments, and may apply to

The Hudson's Bay Company competed with the North West Company in the fur trade. This poster advertises for young men from Scotland who are interested in work and adventure in the Canadian West.

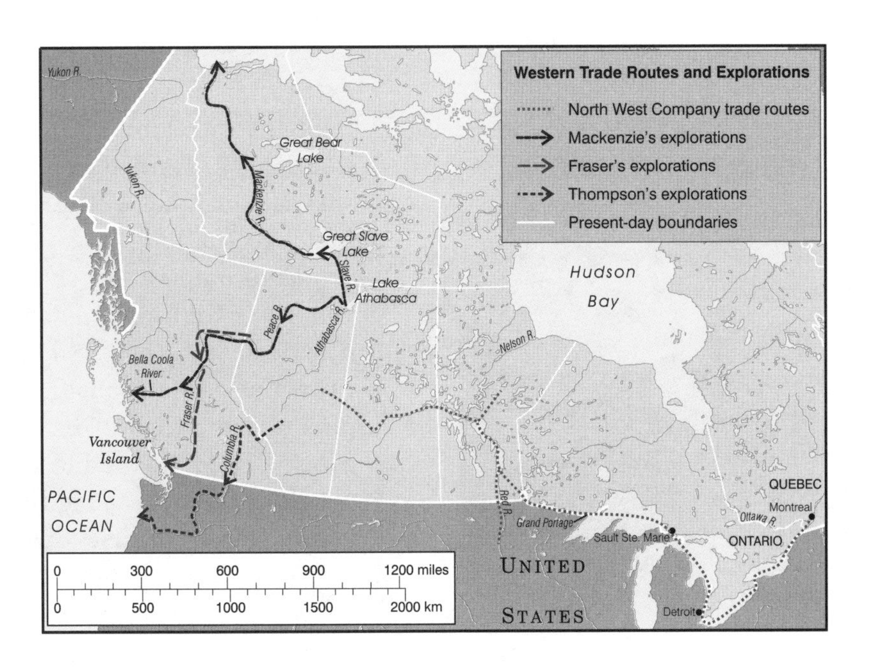

Encampment of the Henry Y. Hind Expedition on the Red River, 1858. The Province of Canada sent this expedition to explore Rupert's Land and to prepare the way for future Canadian control. Canada purchased Rupert's Land from the Hudson's Bay Company in 1869.

whole country a wilderness for the next half century, but I fear that if Englishmen do not go there, Yankees will." Macdonald took the first step in 1869, when the Dominion of Canada paid $1.5 million to the Hudson's Bay Company for Rupert's Land, its territory around the Hudson Bay. The same year, the Dominion gained possession of the land lying north, west, and south of Rupert's Land. The Dominion organized the two regions as the Northwest Territories (called the North West Territories at first).

Manitoba

The Red River Rebellion. The Red River valley, a region called Assiniboia (uh sihn uh BOY uh), lies west of Lake Superior. In this area lived the Métis (may TEES), a people of mixed French and Indian ancestry. They spoke French, were Roman Catholics, and made their living by hunting buffalo. The westward expansion of Canada intruded into the lives of these people in the 1800s.

Since Assiniboia was included in Rupert's Land, it became part of Canada when the Dominion purchased Rupert's Land in 1869. The Métis became alarmed when English-speaking settlers began arriving in their area.

Settler's house in Manitoba, about 1862. On the road is a Red River cart drawn by an ox.

Red River Carts. The Métis used a peculiar two-wheeled cart known as a Red River cart. These carts were built entirely of wood and could carry as much as 1,000 pounds (454 kg). The wheels were about 5 feet (1.5 m) in diameter and were extra wide so as not to sink into the mud. Instead of iron rims, the wheels had rims of tanned hide. The cart was held together with pegs, wedges, and pieces of hide.

Their outstanding characteristic was their high-pitched squeaking, described as "a thousand fingernails drawn across a thousand panes of glass," which could be heard far away. The Métis did not grease the wooden axles, because the grease would catch prairie dust, which would wear away the axles!

Louis D. Riel (1844–1885) was the leader of two Métis rebellions. He was hanged after the second rebellion, which increased tensions between the French and English in Canada.

Fort Garry, the location of the Red River Rebellion of 1870. The city of Winnipeg grew up at the site; many Métis and Indians still live in the area.

They were even more upset when government surveyors divided the land into townships with thirty-six sections of 1 square mile (2.59 km^2) each. Their divisions ignored the property lines of the Métis, whose farms extended in long strips away from the Red River, like those in Quebec. Most Métis were ***squatters*** who had never had their land surveyed and did not hold legal title to their properties.

In 1869, a Métis leader named **Louis Riel** (ree EHL) organized a committee to stand up for the rights of the Métis. William McDougall had been sent as governor of the Northwest Territories, but Riel's followers kept him from crossing the border between the United States and Canada. Then Riel took over Fort Garry (later Winnipeg), the main outpost of the Hudson's Bay Company in the region. Next, he presented a list of rights to the Canadian government, demanding protection of the Métis's rights to their land and religion. Finally, Riel set up his own government in the Red River region.

The Red River Rebellion soon turned violent. Riel's men captured a number of Canadians who had come to oppose him, among them a radical named Thomas Scott. This man attacked a guard and let it be known that he would kill Riel at his first opportunity. So the Métis tried Scott, condemned him to death, and executed him by firing squad. This action stirred up strong protest elsewhere in Canada, where Scott, who was a Protestant, was viewed as a martyr.

Formation of Manitoba. In 1870, the Canadian Parliament passed the Manitoba Act to create Manitoba as the fifth province. This act incorporated nearly all the Métis demands and granted them about 1.4 million acres (567,000 ha) of land. But the Manitoba Act also provided for a militia at Fort Garry to keep peace in Manitoba. Fearing retribution, Riel fled to the United States, and the Red River Rebellion ended.

The North West Mounted Police. Manitoba and the rest of Rupert's Land faced other difficulties, especially in relation to the Indians. A scourge of smallpox took the lives of Indians by the hundreds. But the man-made scourge of alcohol was even worse. Degenerate dealers made large profits by trading high-alcohol whiskey (which the Indians called "firewater") for the Indians' furs.

To try to stop this sinful disgrace, the Canadian government formed the North West Mounted Police in 1873, often called "Mounties." About three hundred of these men in scarlet jackets were to police the entire Northwest! But their dignity and fairness won the respect of both white men and Indians. By the

Parade of the North West Mounted Police at Calgary, Alberta, in 1901. The "Mounties" were established in 1873 to stop the whiskey trade and maintain law and order in the Canadian Northwest.

The Whiskey Trade. One missionary reported in 1873, "In this traffic very many Indians were killed, and also quite a number of white men. Within a few miles of us, forty-two able-bodied men were victims among themselves, all slain in drunken rows [quarrels]. Some terrible scenes occurred when whole camps went on the spree . . . shooting, stabbing, killing, freezing, dying. . . . The poor red man was in a fair way toward extinction, just because some white men, coming out of Christian countries, . . . were now ruled by lust and greed."

One of the callous traders who lived at Fort Whoop-Up wrote in a letter, "My partner . . . got to putting on airs and I shot him and he is dead—the potatoes is looking well."

end of 1874, the Mounties could report that the whiskey trade throughout that whole section of the country had been stopped.

Next, the Mounties set out to negotiate a treaty with the Indians, who were in danger of starving because of the dwindling buffalo herds. The Canadians dealt with them as citizens by working through police rather than armies. (This was unlike the United States, where the government treated Indian tribes as foreign nations and worked through armies.) In a series of treaties through 1877, the Indians peacefully gave up their lands to the government in return for money and supplies. These dealings between the Mounties and the Indians showed that "wisdom is better than weapons of war" (Ecclesiastes 9:18).

British Columbia

After the United States and Great Britain divided the Oregon Country in 1846, the Hudson's Bay Company found its western headquarters on United States territory. So the company moved its headquarters from Fort Vancouver, along the Columbia River, to Fort Victoria—on Vancouver Island. The British formed the colony of Vancouver Island in 1849.

In 1858, the discovery of gold along the Fraser River triggered a gold rush in British Columbia. **James Douglas**, the governor of Vancouver Island, determined to prevent the lawlessness associated with the California gold rush. So he imposed license fees on the miners and enforced British laws on the mainland. When he requested that a government be established there, the British created the new colony of British Columbia in late 1858, with Douglas himself as governor.

After this gold rush, a greater discovery of gold was made near Cariboo Lake. Within about a year, over $2.5 million worth of gold had been taken from the Cariboo strike. But travel to the Cariboo region was difficult because of the rugged terrain. So Governor Douglas built the Cariboo Road, which extended 480 miles (772 km) from the Fraser River to the Cariboo region. This road led along steep canyons and across foaming rivers. In some places it was chiseled out of sheer canyon walls, and in others it rested on foundations built along cliffs. This monumental

Gold mining in the rugged Cariboo region in 1867 or 1868. The miners dug up gold-bearing soil and washed it through a sluice to separate the gold from the ore.

achievement greatly simplified travel to the Cariboo region and helped to increase settlement there.

In 1866, Vancouver Island and British Columbia were joined to become the Crown Colony of British Columbia. But thousands of miles separated this colony from the Canadian provinces to the east. The Dominion was concerned that British Columbia might join the United States—and rightly so, for some British Columbians were talking of that very thing. As an incentive to join the Dominion, the Canadian government promised to build a railroad within ten years to link British Columbia to the eastern provinces. British Columbia accepted this promise and joined the Dominion in 1871.

Further Development

Prince Edward Island. The tiny colony of Prince Edward Island continued to stay aloof from the other provinces. But more and more people favored joining the Dominion; and in 1873, Prince Edward Island enthusiastically became a province of Canada. In fact, the governor-general remarked that the Prince Edward Islanders seemed to think it was Canada that had joined their province!

The Canadian Pacific Railway. Before the great western plains could be settled, a better means of transportation was needed. The Canadian government already planned to build the Canadian Pacific Railway, a transcontinental railroad to link British Columbia with the eastern provinces. The project was delayed, however, when John A. Macdonald lost his position because of a political scandal. But he returned to power in 1878, having proclaimed a National Policy to strengthen Canada. This included tariffs to protect Canadian business, construction of more railroads, and further settlement of the Northwest beyond Manitoba.

The Dominion resumed work on the Canadian Pacific Railway in 1881, and completed it in 1885. This transcontinental railroad stretched about 2,900 miles (4,667 km) across Canada, linking Montreal and Toronto with Vancouver. The line crossed a vast stretch of trackless prairie and passed through the rugged terrain of the Rockies in British Columbia. Finally the Canadians could say, "All aboard for the Pacific!"

The North West Rebellion. The Canadian Pacific Railway caused another disturbance among the Métis—this time in the

Métis and Indian prisoners at Regina, Saskatchewan, in 1885. They were captured in the North West Rebellion.

valley of the Saskatchewan River. Tension increased as the builders worked their way across the plain, for the Dominion did not recognize the property rights of the Métis. Finally in 1884, Louis Riel returned and led the North West Rebellion against the Canadian government. But the Mounted Police and the Canadian militia defeated the rebels in 1885. Some of the leaders, including Riel, were hanged; and a number of others were imprisoned.

The North West Rebellion had significant consequences. While the Métis did receive title to their lands, they became bitter because of Riel's execution. This incident deepened the resentment between French Canadians and the English citizens.

Settlement of the Plains. Multitudes of immigrants were arriving in Canada by 1900, with many of them moving to the great prairies of the West. Among them were Russian Mennonites who left their native land because Russia had passed a law requiring service in the armed forces in the 1870s. (Previously, Russia had exempted the Mennonites from military duty.) When Canada offered them complete exemption from military service as well as the right to affirm instead of swearing oaths, almost seven thousand migrated to Manitoba after 1874.

These Mennonites established villages much like the ones in Russia, and later some moved west into what is now Saskatchewan and Alberta. After World War I, Hutterite immigrants also came to Canada, as well as many additional Russian Mennonites fleeing the new Communist government. By 1905, so

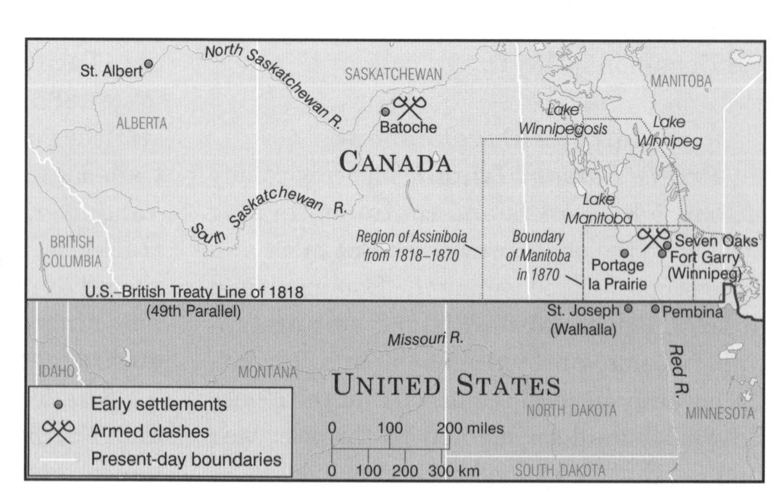

The Red River and North West Rebellions

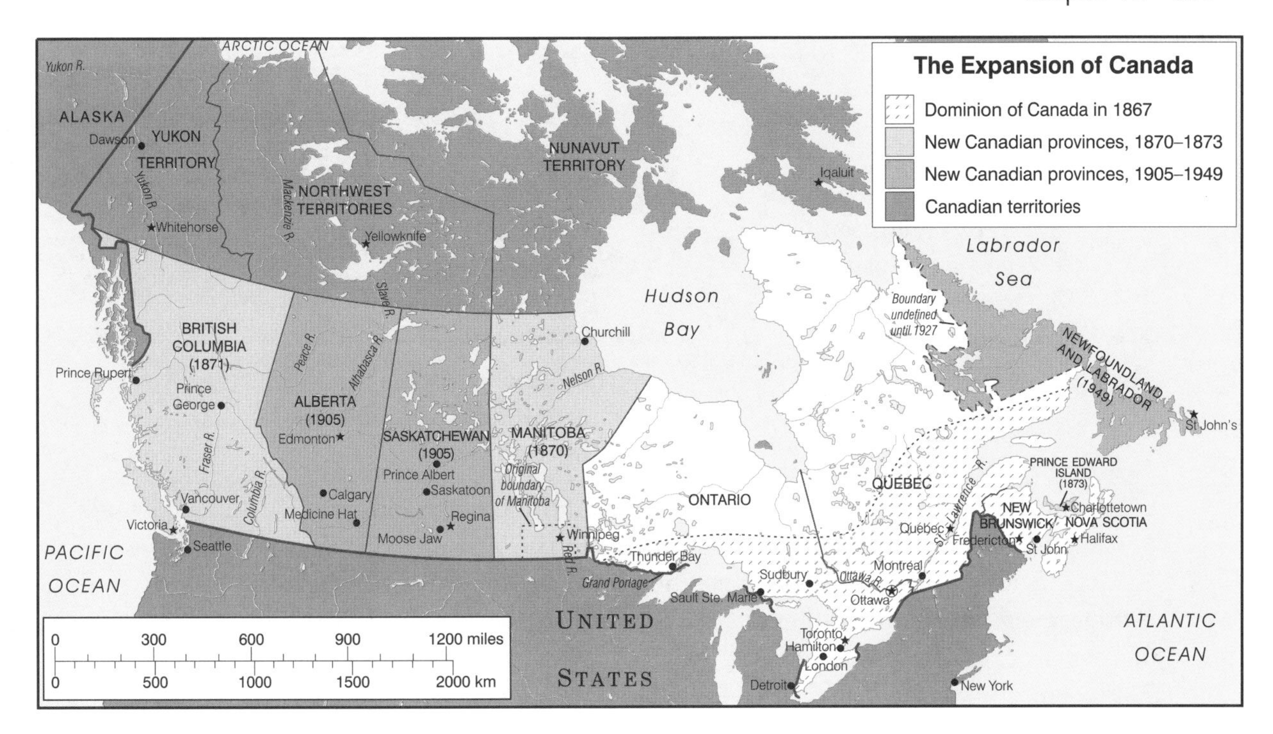

many people had settled on the plains that the Dominion created the provinces of Saskatchewan and Alberta. That year the Dominion of Canada finally stretched across the continent from Atlantic to Pacific.

Gold was discovered in 1896 along a small tributary of the Klondike River in the Northwest Territories. Prospectors rushed in, and soon an estimated thirty-five thousand people lived in the area. In 1898, the Yukon Territory was formed.

The last province added was Newfoundland, which today is called Newfoundland and Labrador. It joined the Dominion in 1949.

In 1999, the Canadian government set aside the eastern part of the Northwest Territories as a separate territory named Nunavut (NOO nuh voot). The new territory was formed so that the Inuit, who make up most of the population, could have more self-government. The name Nunavut means "Our Land."

Focus for Thought

12. a. What did Alexander Mackenzie hope to find in the Northwest?
    b. What three rivers did he explore?
13. Describe how the Northwest Territories came to be part of the Dominion of Canada.
14. What did the Red River Rebellion gain for the Métis?
15. What were two important accomplishments of the North West Mounted Police?
16. a. Why can it be said that British Columbia had its beginnings in furs and gold?
    b. What did a transcontinental railroad have to do with British Columbia?
17. What were the results of the North West Rebellion of 1885?
18. List the four provinces that joined the Dominion after British Columbia, and the dates when they joined.

Historical Highlights

A. Matching: People

a. Alexander Mackenzie
b. David Thompson
c. George Simpson
d. Isaac Brock
e. James Douglas
f. John A. Macdonald
g. Lord Durham
h. Joseph Howe
i. Louis J. Papineau
j. Louis Riel
k. Métis
l. Peter Pond
m. Simon Fraser
n. William L. Mackenzie

1. First prime minister of Canada.
2. Explorer who established the fur trade around Lake Athabasca.
3. Canadian colonel who defeated Americans in the War of 1812.
4. Métis leader of the Red River Rebellion and the North West Rebellion.
5. Reformers who led rebellions in 1837 (two men).
6. Leader of reform in Nova Scotia.
7. Famous surveyor who explored the Columbia River.
8. Explorer who in 1808 followed a river (later named after him) to the Pacific Ocean.
9. British noblemen who wrote a famous report that recommended responsible government for Canada.
10. Explorer who followed a river (later named after him) to the Arctic Ocean and also reached the Pacific by land in 1793.
11. People of mixed French and Indian ancestry.
12. Skillful director of the combined North West Company and Hudson's Bay Company.
13. Governor of British Columbia who built the Cariboo Road.

B. Matching: Canadian Government

a. Cabinet
b. Executive Council
c. House of Commons
d. Legislative Assembly
e. Legislative Council
f. Parliament
g. prime minister
h. Senate

1. Leader of the majority party in the House of Commons, and actual head of the Dominion government.
2. Elected law-making body in the Dominion government.
3. Upper house of the colonial government, its members appointed.
4. Council in the colonial government that assisted the governor.
5. Group of men assisting the prime minister in the Dominion government.
6. Legislative branch of the Dominion, including both upper and lower houses.
7. Lower law-making body of the colonial government, its members elected.
8. Upper law-making body of the Dominion, its members appointed.

C. Matching: Terms 1

a. Act of Union
b. Canada Act
c. Durham Report
d. Family Compact
e. oligarchy
f. Patriotes
g. Quebec Act
h. Rebellion of 1837
i. Reform Party
j. responsible government
k. Tories
l. United Empire Loyalists

1. Supporters of Papineau in the Rebellion of 1837.
2. United two provinces into the Province of Canada.
3. Rule by a small group of people.
4. Party that opposed the Family Compact.
5. Uprisings in Upper and Lower Canada against the Family Compact.
6. People who left the United States because they wanted to stay under British rule.
7. Law passed in 1774 that attempted to reconcile the French to British rule.
8. Divided the province of Quebec into Upper and Lower Canada.
9. Recommended changes in the government of the Canadian provinces.
10. Government controlled by the people rather than by aristocrats.
11. Another name for Loyalists.
12. Small group of wealthy men who controlled Canadian government.

D. Matching: Terms 2

a. British North America Act
b. confederation
c. fathers of the Confederation
d. Hudson's Bay Company
e. Manitoba Act
f. National Policy
g. North West Company
h. North West Mounted Police
i. North West Rebellion
j. Quebec Conference
k. Rebellion Losses Bill
l. Reciprocity Treaty
m. Red River Rebellion
n. Seventy-two Resolutions
o. squatters
p. voyageurs

1. Trade agreement with the United States.
2. Law that stirred up a riot and demonstrated support for responsible government.
3. Union of provinces under a single government.
4. Program that included tariffs, railroad construction, and settlement of the Northwest.
5. People who settle on unoccupied land without legal title to it.
6. Métis rebellion in 1885 in the Saskatchewan River valley.
7. Strong French-Canadian canoe paddlers.
8. Law that created the province of Manitoba.
9. Métis rebellion in 1869 that led to the establishment of Manitoba.
10. Competing fur companies that merged in 1821 (two answers).
11. Law that created the Dominion of Canada.
12. Details for the Confederation drawn up at the Quebec Conference.
13. Men sent to stop the whiskey trade and to deal with the Indians.
14. Meeting where the Confederation was proposed and planned.
15. Men who worked out the plan for the Confederation.

E. Matching: Places

a. Alberta
b. Assiniboia
c. British Columbia
d. Canada East
e. Canada West
f. Canadian Pacific Railroad
g. Cariboo Road
h. Dominion of Canada
i. Lower Canada
j. Manitoba
k. New Brunswick
l. Newfoundland
m. Northwest Territories
n. Nova Scotia
o. Ontario
p. Ottawa
q. Prince Edward Island
r. Province of Canada
s. Quebec
t. Saskatchewan
u. Upper Canada

1. Provinces that formed the Dominion of Canada (four answers).
2. Other names for the province of Ontario (two answers).
3. Other names for the province of Quebec (two answers).
4. Province on the west coast; first settled through a gold rush.
5. Land in the Red River region.
6. Provided transcontinental travel.
7. Province that began through a rebellion.
8. Provinces that grew out of settlement of the plains (two answers).
9. Confederation of the British North American provinces.
10. Improved transportation during the gold rush in British Columbia.
11. Union of Upper and Lower Canada.
12. Small province that joined the Dominion in 1873.
13. Province that did not join the Dominion until 1949.
14. Rupert's Land and land north, west, and south of it; became part of Canada in 1869.
15. Capital of the Dominion of Canada.

F. Matching: Dates

a. 1774
b. 1791
c. 1841
d. July 1, 1867
e. 1870
f. 1871
g. 1873
h. 1898
i. 1905
j. 1949
k. 1999

1. Yukon Territory formed after a gold rush.
2. Canada's birthday.
3. Prince Edward Island joins the Dominion.
4. Manitoba becomes a province.
5. Quebec Act passed.
6. British Columbia becomes a province.
7. Province of Canada formed by the Act of Union.
8. Nunavut formed from the Northwest Territories.
9. Upper Canada and Lower Canada formed by the Canada Act.
10. Alberta and Saskatchewan become provinces.
11. Newfoundland joins the Dominion.

G. True or False

Write whether each statement is true (T) *or false* (F).

1. Every year the "wintering partners" traded with the voyageurs at Montreal.
2. The French people of Lower Canada were eager to adopt English ways and industrialize Canada.
3. The oligarchy of Upper Canada sought to introduce responsible government.
4. The Durham Report recommended responsible government.
5. Reciprocity with the United States helped Canada to prosper after 1854.
6. The Fraser River gold rush was noted for its law and order in contrast to the California gold rush.
7. The British Parliament created the nation called the Dominion of Canada.
8. The Dominion of Canada was to be independent of Great Britain.
9. Prime Minister John A. Macdonald promoted a transcontinental railroad to bind the provinces together.
10. The Red River Rebellion led to the formation of Manitoba.
11. The Mounted Police brought law and order to the prairies.
12. Louis Riel's execution helped to calm the strife between the French and English peoples of Canada.

H. Deeper Discussion

1. a. Why did Canada remain British?
   b. Why did it not revolt as the United States had or join the United States?
2. a. How is government in the Dominion of Canada similar to that of the United States?
   b. How is it different?
3. a. Why did the French not become assimilated into the British society of Canada?
   b. How did this help to make the Métis issue so divisive?
4. Why were the Canadians so successful in their approach to the British Columbia gold rushes, the whiskey trade, and their relations with the Indians?
5. How does Habakkuk 2:15, 16 aptly describe the wickedness of the whiskey trade with the Indians?

I. Chronology and Geography

1. The following list gives major events in Canadian history. Arrange the list in the proper order, and supply the date for each event.

   British Columbia formed
   British Columbia joins the Dominion
   Confederation approved
   Dominion of Canada formed by the British North America Act
   Durham Report submitted
   Manitoba Act passed
   Newfoundland joins the Dominion
   North West Rebellion
   Prince Edward Island joins the Dominion
   Province of Canada formed by the Act of Union
   Rebellion of 1837
   Red River Rebellion
   Saskatchewan and Alberta join the Dominion

2. On your map entitled "Exploration of North America," draw red lines to show the explorations of Mackenzie, Fraser, and Thompson. Label these lines.

3. Trace Map B (including the borders of the provinces and territories) and label it "Provinces and Territories of Canada."
   a. Label the ten provinces and three territories. Give admission dates for the provinces that were admitted after 1867.
   b. Use four different colors to represent the following areas: (1) four original provinces, (2) provinces admitted from 1870 to 1873, (3) provinces admitted from 1905 to 1949, (4) three territories.
   c. Make a legend to show what each color represents.
   d. Memorize the names and locations of the provinces and territories.

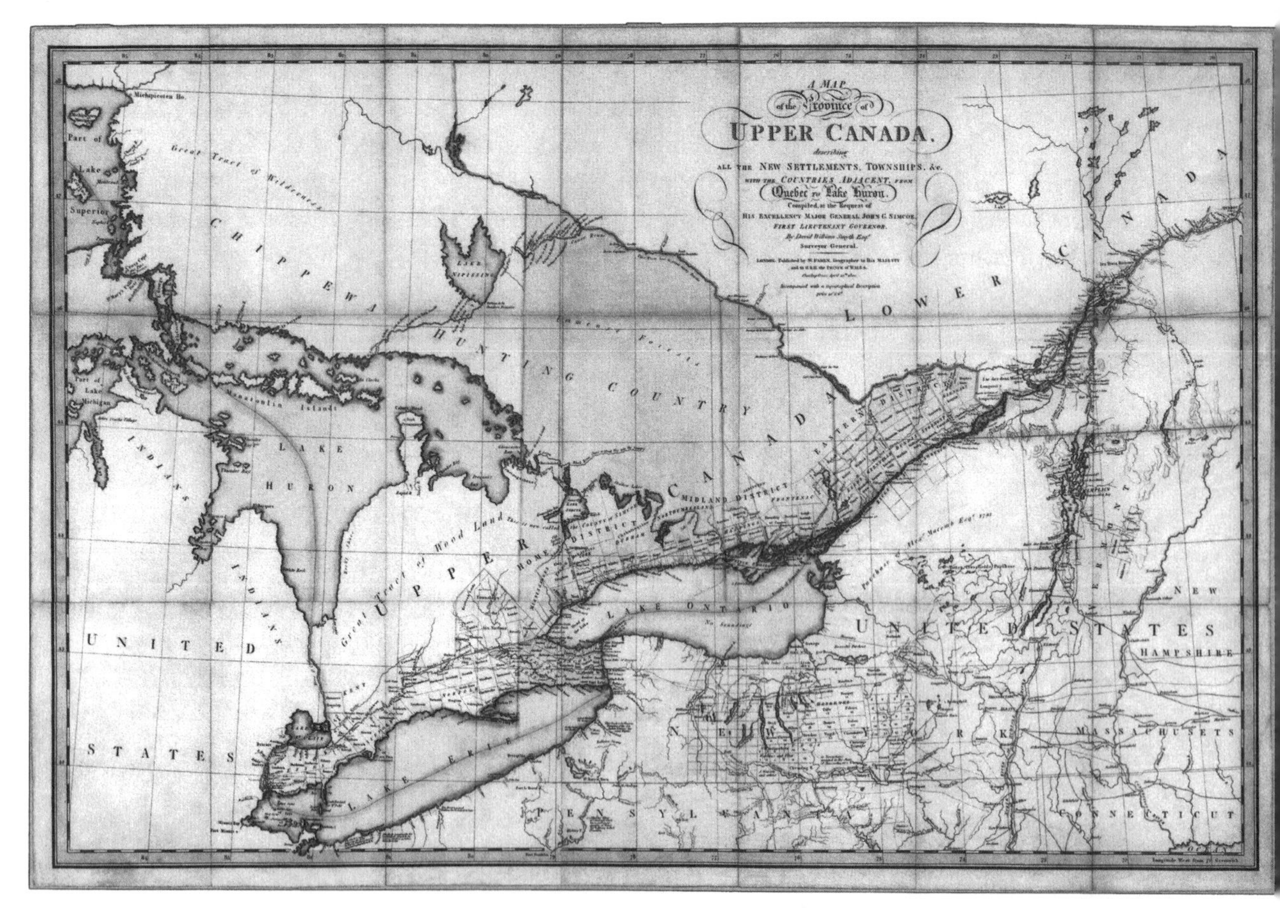

The Canada Act of 1791 divided the province of Quebec into Upper Canada and Lower Canada. This map shows Upper Canada and parts of Lower Canada and the United States about 1800.

BY THE QUEEN.

A PROCLAMATION

For Uniting the Provinces of Canada, Nova Scotia, and New Brunswick into One Dominion under the Name of CANADA.

VICTORIA R.

WHEREAS by an Act of Parliament passed on the Twenty-ninth Day of March One thousand eight hundred and sixty-seven, in the Thirtieth Year of Our Reign, intituled " An Act for the Union of Canada, Nova Scotia, and New Brunswick, and the " Government thereof, and for Purposes connected therewith," after divers Recitals, it is enacted, that " it shall be lawful for the Queen, by and with the Advice of Her Majesty's most Honorable " Privy Council, to declare by Proclamation that on and after a Day therein appointed, not being " more than Six Months after the passing of this Act, the Provinces of Canada, Nova Scotia, and " New Brunswick shall form and be One Dominion under the Name of Canada, and on and after " that Day those Three Provinces shall form and be One Dominion under that Name accordingly:" And it is thereby further enacted, that " such Persons shall be first summoned to the Senate as " the Queen, by Warrant under Her Majesty's Royal Sign Manual, thinks fit to approve, and " their Names shall be inserted in the Queen's Proclamation of Union:" We therefore, by and with the Advice of Our Privy Council, have thought fit to issue this Our Royal Proclamation, and We do Ordain, Declare, and Command, that on and after the First Day of July One thousand eight hundred and sixty-seven the Provinces of Canada, Nova Scotia, and New Brunswick shall form and be One Dominion under the Name of Canada. And We do further Ordain and Declare, that the Persons whose Names are herein inserted and set forth are the Persons of whom We have, by Warrant under Our Royal Sign Manual, thought fit to approve as the Persons who shall be first summoned to the Senate of Canada.

FOR THE PROVINCE OF ONTARIO.	FOR THE PROVINCE OF QUEBEC.	FOR THE PROVINCE OF NOVA SCOTIA.	FOR THE PROVINCE OF NEW BRUNSWICK.
JOHN HAMILTON,	JAMES LESLIE,	EDWARD KENNY,	AMOS EDWIN BOTSFORD,
RODERICK MATHESON,	ASA BELKNAP FOSTER,	JONATHAN M'CULLY,	EDWARD BARRON CHANDLER,
JOHN ROSS,	JOSEPH NOËL BOSSÉ,	THOMAS D. ARCHIBALD,	JOHN ROBERTSON,
SAMUEL MILLS,	LOUIS A. OLIVIER,	ROBERT B. DICKEY,	ROBERT LEONARD HAZEN,
BENJAMIN SEYMOUR,	JACQUE OLIVIER BUREAU,	JOHN H. ANDERSON,	WILLIAM HUNTER ODELL,
WALTER HAMILTON DICKSON,	CHARLES MALHIOT,	JOHN HOLMES,	DAVID WARK,
JAMES SHAW,	LOUIS RENAUD,	JOHN W. RITCHIE,	WILLIAM HENRY STEEVES,
ADAM JOHNSTON FERGUSON BLAIR,	LUC LETELLIER DE ST. JUST,	BENJAMIN WIER,	WILLIAM TODD,
ALEXANDER CAMPBELL,	ULRIC JOSEPH TESSIER,	JOHN LOCKE,	JOHN FERGUSON,
DAVID CHRISTIE,	JOHN HAMILTON,	CALEB R. BILL,	ROBERT DUNCAN WILMOT,
JAMES COX AIKINS,	CHARLES CORMIER,	JOHN BOURINOT,	ABNER REID M'CLELAN,
DAVID REESOR,	ANTOINE JUCHEREAU DUCHESNAY,	WILLIAM MILLER.	PETER MITCHELL.
ELIJAH LEONARD,	DAVID EDWARD PRICE,		
WILLIAM MACMASTER,	ELZEAR H. J. DUCHESNAY,		
ASA ALLWORTH BURNHAM,	LEANDRE DUMOUCHEL,		
JOHN SIMPSON,	LOUIS LACOSTE,		
JAMES SKEAD,	JOSEPH F. ARMAND,		
DAVID LEWIS MACPHERSON,	CHARLES WILSON,		
GEORGE CRAWFORD,	WILLIAM HENRY CHAFFERS,		
DONALD MACDONALD,	JEAN BAPTISTE GUÉVREMONT,		
OLIVER BLAKE,	JAMES FERRIER,		
BILLA FLINT,	Sir NARCISSE FORTUNAT BELLEAU, Knight,		
WALTER M'CREA,	THOMAS RYAN,		
GEORGE WILLIAM ALLAN.	JOHN SEWELL SANBORN.		

Given at Our Court at Windsor Castle, this Twenty-second Day of May, in the Year of our Lord One thousand eight hundred and sixty-seven, and in the Thirtieth Year of Our Reign.

God save the Queen.

Proclamation of Confederation issued by Queen Victoria in May 1867. It united the four Canadian provinces as the Dominion of Canada and set July 1, 1867, as the official beginning of the Dominion.

UNIT 6

TIMES OF CHANGE, 1859–1920

Chapters in Unit 6

Prairie fires were one of the hazards of homesteading in the West. The dry grass ignited easily in the fall, and great walls of flame would sweep across the prairie.

19 The Last Frontier

1. The Miners and Railroaders
   - The Mining Frontier
   - The Transcontinental Railroad
2. The Indians
   - The Indian Wars
   - Recognition for the Indians
3. The Cattlemen and Homesteaders
   - The Cattle Kingdom
   - Homesteading in the West

1840

Pikes Peak gold rush; Comstock Lode discovered in Nevada 1859

1860

Nevada becomes a state; Sand Creek massacre in Colorado 1864

Sioux War 1865–1867

Transcontinental railroad completed; George Westinghouse invents air brake 1869

Russian Mennonites settle in Kansas 1873–1874

Joseph Glidden invents barbed wire 1874

Black Hills gold rush 1875–1876

Colorado becomes a state; Battle of the Little Bighorn 1876

1880

Time zones created 1883

Dawes Act passed 1887

Montana, Washington, North and South Dakota become states 1889

Idaho and Wyoming become states; Wounded Knee massacre 1890

Utah becomes a state 1896

1900

Oklahoma becomes a state 1907

Arizona and New Mexico become states 1912

1920

Indians become citizens 1924

Indian Reorganization Act passed 1934

1940

"For he that will love life, and see good days, let him refrain his tongue from evil, and his lips that they speak no guile: let him eschew evil, and do good; let him seek peace, and ensue it."

1 Peter 3:10, 11

THE LAST FRONTIER

Focus for Reading

By the mid-1800s, a line of states from Louisiana to Iowa lay along the west bank of the Mississippi River. Settlements also prospered in California, along the Pacific shore far to the west. In between lay the "Great American Desert" (roughly the area between the Missouri River and the Sierra Nevada), which was inhabited mostly by Indians, trappers, and a few isolated pioneers. This unsettled region became the last American frontier.

During and after the Civil War, waves of people headed westward for gold, for cattle ranching, and for homesteading. The "iron horse" traversed newly laid tracks across plains, deserts, and mountains. The Indians, caught in the midst of this westward scramble, fought vainly to preserve their land and way of life. By 1890, the United States Census Bureau could report that "the unsettled area has been so broken into by isolated bodies of settlement that there can hardly be said to be a frontier line." What was the last frontier? Who were the people that settled there? What was it that drew them on? This chapter tells the story of the last frontier of the Great American West.

1. The Miners and Railroaders
2. The Indians
3. The Cattlemen and Homesteaders

1. THE MINERS AND RAILROADERS

Miners were often the forerunners of western settlement. The miners themselves usually stayed at the same place for only a year or two before joining the rush to a new gold strike. But in their wake came farms, towns, and settled communities.

Although the West obviously needed better transportation, circumstances prevented the building of a transcontinental railroad. But with the miners moving into the West and new towns springing up, the need for such a railroad became acute by the 1860s. The story of the first transcontinental railroad is an epic of the West.

The Mining Frontier

Gold Rushes. Hundreds of miners searched the West, hoping to discover gold or silver. In 1858, prospectors found gold in the Rocky Mountains near present-day Denver. The next spring found multitudes of "fifty-niners" traveling west with "Pikes Peak or Bust" lettered on their packs and wagons.

But they were disappointed; little gold was to be found. Soon thousands of miners were heading east again, with their wagons now proclaiming "Busted." Proverbs 28:22 says, "He that hasteth to be rich hath an evil eye, and considereth not that poverty shall come upon him."

Wherever large groups of miners went, they were followed by farmers, carpenters, and merchants; and for this reason, cities such as Denver grew rapidly. Companies began working the mines with machinery to extract the ores in the ***mother lodes*** (main veins of ores). In the 1870s, gold and silver strikes in Leadville and Cripple Creek, Colorado, brought in more people. Because of this rapid growth, Colorado became a state in 1876.

Meanwhile, fabulous discoveries of gold and silver were made on the eastern slopes of the Sierra Nevada. Here, in 1859, a number of miners found bluish quartz that contained almost pure gold and silver. They had

Left: "Fifty-niners" struggled through the Rocky Mountains during the Pikes Peak gold rush in 1859. As many as 100,000 people headed for Colorado to seek gold. Over half of them returned in disappointment. ***Right:*** Virginia City, Nevada, in 1866. Located near the Comstock Lode, this was a typical boom town that sprang up when gold or silver was discovered.

stumbled upon the Comstock Lode, one of the richest strikes ever. This lode included the "Big Bonanza," a pocket of silver measuring 600 by 400 by 70 feet (183 by 122 by 21 m)! Over the next three decades, the Comstock produced over $300 million worth of gold and silver. Miners also made other strikes in surrounding regions; consequently, Nevada became a state in 1864.

The last great gold rush in the United

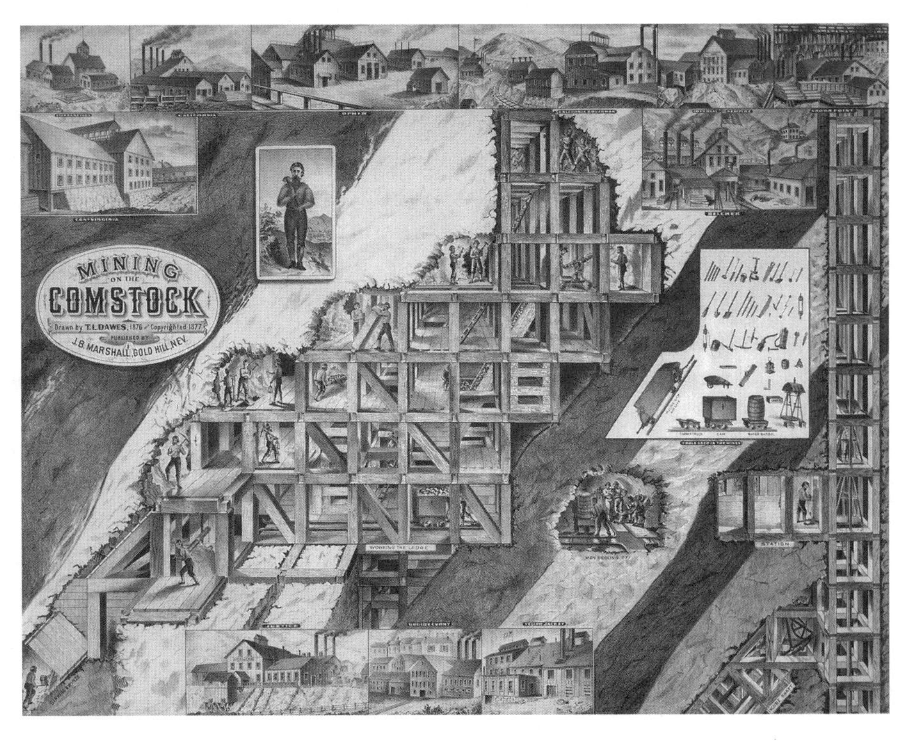

This illustration shows miners at work in the underground tunnels of the Comstock Lode. The small pictures portray mining tools and various mills associated with the mines. Mining had become a big business instead of being carried on by individual prospectors.

States took place in the Black Hills of the Dakota Territory. Miners began arriving in 1875, but many were arrested because the Black Hills had been promised to the Indians by a federal treaty in 1868. When the flood of miners continued, the Indians fought to retain their land. The government tried to reach a settlement with the Indians but could not. New laws forced the Indians to give up much of their land in 1877. The Black Hills were opened to the miners, who rushed in by the thousands.

Life on the Mining Frontier. Most mining camps sprang up along a similar pattern. First, miners rushed to stake their claims and lived in an assortment of tents and other makeshift dwellings. These first prospectors usually wanted only to seek gold; but as people of low character moved in, hotels, saloons, and gambling halls sprang up. Gamblers and criminals flocked in to prey on the opportunities for easy riches. Truly, "the love of money is the root of all evil"!

Open violence in mining camps usually did not last long. After a large number of people arrived, the miners would hold a meeting to set up laws about claims and about crimes like robbery and murder. Often they set up ***vigilance committees*** whose members, called vigilantes (vihj uh LAN teez), meted out swift and stern justice—usually by hanging. These mining camps exemplified the tendency of Americans to govern themselves when there was no established government.

End of the Mining Frontier. Gradually the era of the prospector came to an end. Mining was taken over by large companies, which used machines to extract the gold and silver that prospectors could not reach. Copper and petroleum were also important minerals, but they did not generate rushes as had the gold and silver strikes.

When mining camps developed into permanent towns, the people would establish organized governments there. Then the region would request territorial status, as Nevada did in 1861. After the territory had a population of sixty thousand people, its next step was statehood. Montana, Washington, and the Dakotas became states in 1889, and Idaho and Wyoming in 1890.

Example of Vigilante Justice

Sometimes the outlaws and the officers of law were the same people. One example is Henry Plummer, who was sheriff of Bannack and Virginia City in Montana. Plummer had a gang of men who would mark coaches that left the mining camps loaded with gold. When the coach drivers asked Plummer how to get safely out of the mining camp, he obligingly told them how to fall into his trap. His men then waylaid and robbed the marked coaches, and Plummer would rush to the scene to "investigate."

This gang used any means possible, including murder, to keep their plot hidden. However, a group of vigilantes uncovered the scheme when they captured a number of suspected outlaws. In 1864, Plummer was hanged, like Haman, on a gallows he himself had built to hang a horse thief. Twenty-one other villains were also hanged, and the rest of the gang slunk quietly away.

The Transcontinental Railroad

Plans for the Railroad. Already before the Civil War, many Northerners thought a railroad should be built to link the eastern part of the nation to California and the other western settlements. But the idea was blocked through Southern opposition, and the Civil War further hindered these plans.

The Overland Stage

The Stagecoach. Before the railroad came, the best way to travel in the West was by stagecoach. John Butterfield operated the Overland Stage, which provided the first official mail service by land to California. His route was called the Butterfield Overland Mail Route, but some people called it the Oxbow Route because it curved like a bow from Missouri southwest through Texas and then northwest to San Francisco. This service began in 1858, and it took twenty-four or twenty-five days to cover the 2,800 miles (4,506 km). Later stagecoaches traveled a central route (along the Platte River), which was 600 miles (966 km) shorter.

Passengers aboard the stage paid up to $600 for a twenty-day journey. On the trek, they braved dust, lost sleep, helped to push in deep mud, and walked alongside in deep sand. When crossing the Rockies, they endured hairpin curves as well as descents so steep that the brakes smoked! The driver, called a "jehu," sat high up on a box to guide his team of horses (six in all) as they jolted and lurched along the rough roads.

Freight traveled by freight wagons. A business known as Wells, Fargo & Co. operated large stagecoach and freighting enterprises in the West. Teams of a dozen mules or oxen pulled wagons hauling up to 5 tons (4,500 kg) of supplies. If mule-drawn, a "muleskinner" rode on one of the mules to guide the team; if ox-drawn, a "bullwhacker" walked alongside the oxen, cracking his whip over their heads to keep them plodding on. The freight wagons usually traveled in long caravans, with a wagon master as the "general" to direct them. At night the wagons formed a corral for protection, and the "bullwhackers" greased their axles and then crawled under the wagons to sleep. It was all very slow and arduous, but there was no other means of travel in the West before the building of railroads.

When the Southern states seceded, the North was free to proceed with a transcontinental railroad. An engineer named Theodore Judah proposed that the railroad be built along a central route, directly through the Sierra Nevada. He persuaded four Sacramento businessmen to back his plan, and in 1861 the Central Pacific Railroad Company was formed. Then Judah went to Washington to seek government support for the project.

Congress passed the Pacific Railroad Act in 1862. According to this law, the Central Pacific was to build a railroad from California eastward. From Omaha, Nebraska (the point farthest west of the eastern railroads), a company called the Union Pacific was to build west to meet the Central Pacific line. The law also provided the necessary right-of-way for the railroads, for land grants along the route, and for loans to finance the project.

Work on the Railroad. In 1863, the Central Pacific started to build a railroad eastward from California through some of the most rugged territory in the country. All the rails, spikes, and locomotives had to be shipped around South America or across Panama. Workers were in short supply because of the nearby gold fields; so **Charles Crocker**, the general manager, hired many Chinese laborers. Crocker solved trouble with the Indians by handing out boarding passes to the Indian chiefs. These allowed the chiefs to ride on the train whenever they pleased.

Crossing the Sierras was an immense challenge. Because of snowslides in the high mountains, the Central Pacific built 37 miles (60 km) of roofing called snowsheds over the rails. The workers cut through high ridges or blasted tunnels through them, and they built long wooden trestles across ravines. All these difficulties held construction to an extremely slow pace. Remember, workers had no loaders, graders, or big trucks—only their muscles, their mules, and blasting powder!

To speed progress, the Central Pacific decided to start laying track in the more level country east of the Sierras. Finally in the spring of 1868, the Central Pacific finished the tracks across the mountains so that it was possible to travel by rail from Sacramento, California, to Reno, Nevada. Now the great race with the Union Pacific was on. Whichever company laid the most track would receive the most financial aid from the government.

Workers for the Union Pacific began laying track from Omaha, but they also faced the

Work on the last mile of the Central Pacific Railroad. Note the Chinese laborers in the picture. Also note the use of blasting powder in the background.

Laying track for the Union Pacific Railroad in Nebraska. Because of the "work train" method, the Union Pacific was able to lay 260 miles (418 km) of track through the Platte River valley in an eight-month period in 1866.

difficulty of obtaining supplies. For a time, all building materials had to be hauled up the Missouri River by steamboat. Many former soldiers began working for the Union Pacific after the Civil War, thus relieving the initial shortage of laborers.

The Union Pacific began the work by laying out a path for the railway; then the graders used plows, scrapers, picks, and shovels to make it level. Finally the track layers came along, placing the ties, laying the track, and spiking down the rails.

The Union Pacific developed the "work train" to speed the job of laying track. This efficient method used a train with cars for sleeping, for eating, and for carrying the workers' personal belongings. The train also included flatcars carrying supplies for building the railroad. The work train was the first train to ride the newly laid track; it followed the men as they moved westward.

The Union Pacific faced problems with the Plains Indians, who resented the railroad dividing their buffalo range. These Indians sometimes attacked the work crews or ripped up the tracks. When the Indians went on the warpath, workmen hastily grabbed guns from the work train to defend themselves.

Completion of the Railroad. In May 1869, the Union Pacific and the Central Pacific

Completion of the transcontinental railroad at Promontory, Utah Territory, May 10, 1869. After the last spike was driven, locomotives of the two railroad companies touched cowcatchers amid joyous celebration. Samuel S. Montague of the Central Pacific (left) shakes hands with Grenville M. Dodge of the Union Pacific (right) in the center of the photograph.

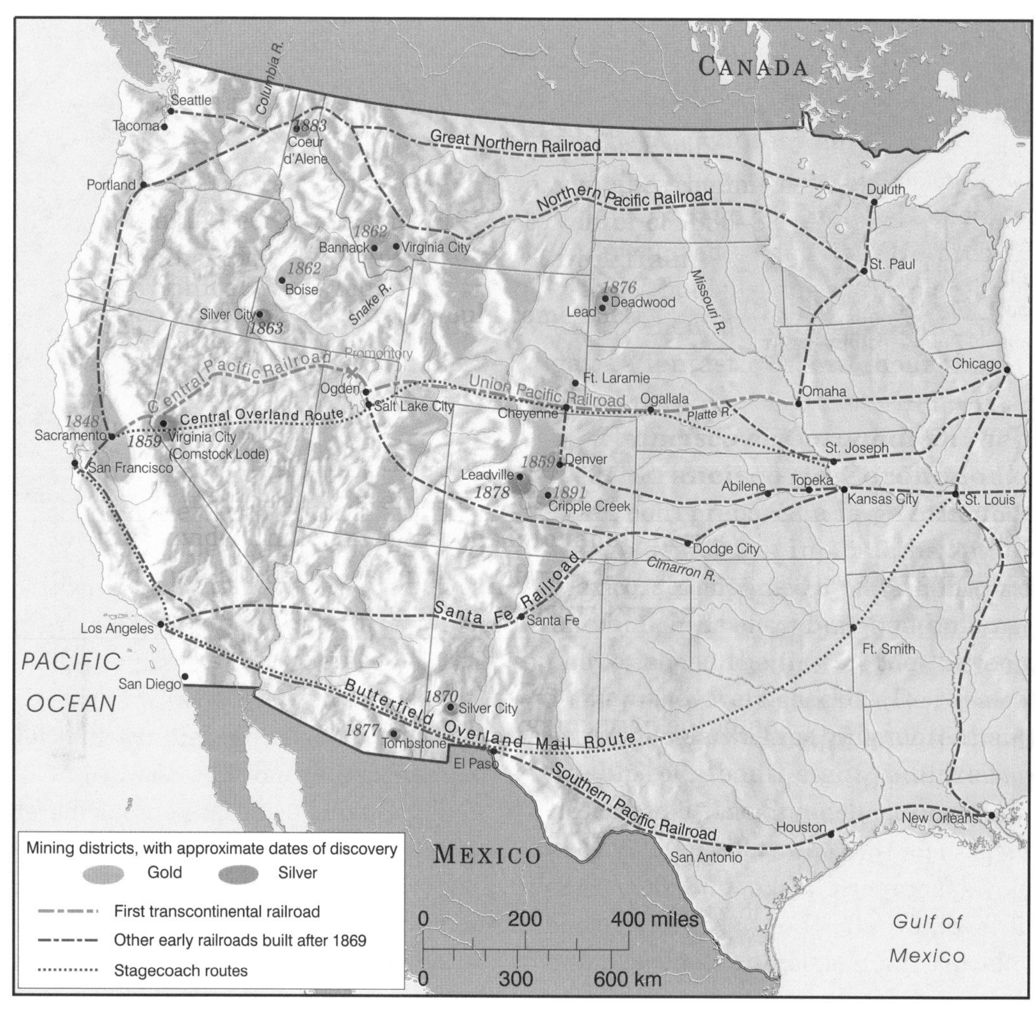

The Mining Frontier and the Transcontinental Railroads

met at Promontory, Utah. With two locomotives facing each other on the tracks, officials for the Central Pacific and the Union Pacific joined the lines with a final railroad spike made of gold. Then the special spike was replaced with a regular one, and the two engines crept forward until they touched. The long-awaited railroad spanned the continent at last. The Union Pacific had laid 1,086 miles (1,748 km) of track, and the Central Pacific had laid 689 miles (1,109 km).

> **The Golden Spike.** The final spike, made of gold and weighing 18 ounces (510 g), was inscribed with the following words: "May God continue the unity of our country, as this railroad unites the two great oceans of the world." (Note the spirit of manifest destiny.) The spike is now at Stanford University in California.

Effects of the Railroad. After the first transcontinental railroad was completed, railroad companies built four others by 1893. Soon a rail network linked the once-remote sections of the West, and a person could travel from coast to coast in about eight days. There were problems, of course, such as railroad accidents and delays due to bad weather. But railroads greatly improved travel, shipping, and mail delivery, and thus they helped to tie the nation together.

Railroads themselves were big business,

Standard Time Zones. Before 1883, the time in each town of the United States was set by the local position of the sun at noon. This resulted in much confusion as a person traveled from one town to another. The Pennsylvania Railroad in Philadelphia used a time five minutes slower than New York's time and five minutes faster than Baltimore's! Some states had more than twenty different times—Michigan had twenty-six and Wisconsin thirty-eight. This caused difficulty for passengers and shippers, and it resulted in disastrous accidents.

In 1883, the American Railway Association held a convention at which railroad superintendents adopted a standard time plan. They set up time zones with boundaries near Philadelphia, Pennsylvania; Memphis, Tennessee; Denver, Colorado; and Fresno, California. At noon on November 18, 1883, all the railroads began using the new time. Some people railed against the change, saying it was a lie and was un-Christian; but gradually the new time came into general use. According to one story, the attorney general of the United States refused to accept the standard time. But one afternoon he went to the Washington station to catch a train to Philadelphia, and found himself eight minutes and twenty seconds too late!

and they contributed to the growth of other industries, such as steel companies. New developments constantly improved the railroads, such as the air brake invented by **George Westinghouse** in 1869. (Formerly each car was braked by its own brakeman, with the result that trains came to a jolting, clattering stop.) In 1883, the American Railway Association divided the United States into four time zones. This helped to prevent railroad accidents, and the uniform time also made things more convenient for society in general.

Scene in an immigrant waiting room of the Union Pacific Railroad station in Omaha, Nebraska. Railroads promoted settlement of the West by encouraging Europeans to move to America and by selling land near the railroad at cheap prices. They also provided transportation to these lands. At this railroad station, they even offered to fill lunch baskets for 25 cents!

Railroads brought many immigrants to the western plains. These passengers are enduring the long, wearisome journey across the country.

The railroads promoted settlement through the land grants they had received and now wanted to sell. These lands they advertised heavily in the East and in Europe, and people responded in great numbers. Among the immigrants were thousands of Russian Mennonites, who fled from Russia to escape military service. Many of these came to Kansas during 1873 and 1874. They brought with them their hard "Turkey Red" winter wheat, which flourished in America and helped to make Kansas a chief wheat-growing state.

The "iron horse" had helped to conquer the Great American West.

Focus for Thought

1. How did miners help the West to become settled?
2. a. How did vigilance committees mete out justice?
   b. What American tendency did this illustrate?
3. Why did prospecting by individuals give way to mining by large companies?
4. Why was there a need for a transcontinental railroad?
5. a. What were some difficulties faced by the builders of the transcontinental railroad?
   b. Where and when was the first transcontinental railroad completed?
6. What were three effects of railroads in the West?

2. THE INDIANS

Miners and railroads spread across the West, and permanent white settlements soon followed. This threatened the Indians and their way of life. The result was the Indian wars, which lasted from the 1850s to the 1880s and ended with the Indians being forced to live on reservations.

The Indian Wars

Causes of the Wars. A number of things contributed to the Indian wars. In the days of Andrew Jackson, the United States government had removed Indians to lands across the Mississippi River because it was thought that whites would never settle there. But as whites moved west and needed land for transportation routes, the government policy changed from "removal" to "concentration"—that is, the Indians were concentrated on reservations even though many did not want to go on reservations. Furthermore, greedy whites often settled on land that had been promised to the Indians. Then war broke out.

The greatest cause of war was the white man's threat to the Indian way of life. As gold rushes and railroads brought in more and more whites, the open plains were settled and the buffalo disappeared. So the Indians fought to preserve their way of life.

Misunderstandings and bad attitudes also brought war. Many whites made no difference between peaceful and warlike Indians, and readily broke their promises to Indians. Corrupt government officials often mistreated the Indians, cheating them out of necessary supplies to fill their own pockets.

Cultural differences played a large part in the struggle. Whites wanted Indians to "walk the white man's road" (learn to live like white men), but many Indians refused to cooperate.

Basically, it was the white man's greed for gold, land, and other riches of the West that caused the Indian wars.

Battles in the Southwest. The Indian wars took place in the Southwest, on the Central Plains, and in the Northwest. In the Southwest, the Navajo and Apache fought desperately against the white men from 1861 to 1864. The Navajo were subdued by Kit Carson and his forces, and thousands of them then took the "long walk" of 300 miles (483 km) to a reservation along the Pecos River in eastern New Mexico. Hundreds died on the way, and many more died because of the climate, disease, and starvation on the desolate land of the reservation. Finally in 1868, the Navajo chiefs signed a treaty in which they promised never to fight the United States, and they were allowed to return to a portion of their homeland in Arizona, which had become a reservation for them. The Navajo kept their promise, and they remain in Arizona to this day.

The Apache fought on in numerous skirmishes and raids, some led by Mangas Coloradas and **Cochise** (koh CHEES). When Mangas Coloradas sought peace in 1863, he was captured and murdered by his captors. Cochise continued to fight, but in 1872 he agreed to go on a reservation. Other bands of warriors sometimes left the reservations and raided settlements, so that fighting with the Apache continued for a time. The last great Apache chief, **Geronimo**, (juh RAHN uh moh) was finally subdued in 1886.

Battles on the Plains. Some of the greatest Indian conflicts took place on the Plains. Among the first was the Minnesota Sioux (SOO) uprising of 1862. The First Treaty of Fort Laramie (1851) had assigned the Sioux to small reservations. When the federal government forced them to sell some of these lands, the Sioux rebelled. They slaughtered hundreds of settlers and caused as many as

Sioux chief Red Cloud (1822–1909) addressing an audience in New York in 1870. He said, "We cannot take [riches] away with us out of this world, but we want to have love and peace.... If this is so, I would like to know why the commissioners who are sent out there do nothing but rob to get the riches of this world away from us."

Geronimo (1829–1909) was a feared Apache warrior. He and his band terrorized the southwestern United States and northern Mexico in the 1870s and 1880s. Geronimo was captured in 1886 and became a prisoner of war at forts in Florida and the Oklahoma Territory. He later became a rancher in Oklahoma.

These settlers stopped for lunch in their flight from the Sioux massacre of 1862 in Minnesota. In this uprising, 800 white settlers were killed and 30,000 fled.

thirty thousand to flee their homes. But a militia caught several thousand Sioux, released their white captives, and condemned over three hundred Indians to be hanged. However, President Lincoln allowed the sentence to be executed on only thirty-eight of them.

Another episode, the Sand Creek massacre, took place in Colorado in 1864. A chief named **Black Kettle** and a band of 500 Cheyenne and Arapaho camped along Sand Creek, thinking themselves safe because they had sought peace. But early in the morning of November 29, 1864, a band led by Colonel John Chivington surrounded the encampment and massacred an estimated 450 Indians—men, women, and children. Black Kettle raised an American flag and then a white truce flag, but his gestures were useless. The heartless Chivington had said, "I have come to kill Indians, and believe it is right and honorable to use any means under God's heaven to kill Indians."

After that, the Cheyenne and other tribes of the southern plains accepted reservations in the Indian Territory (Oklahoma) under a treaty signed at Medicine Lodge Creek in 1867. Such a treaty held out the hope that negotiation, rather than force, could settle the problems with the Indians. In spite of this, fighting continued.

The Sioux war of 1865–1867 broke out to the north in Wyoming and Montana, after the government tried to build forts on some of the best Sioux hunting grounds. The Indians were led by Chief **Red Cloud**; and in a battle fought in December 1866, they killed all of Captain William Fetterman's eighty-man force. However, in 1868 the Sioux agreed to the Second Treaty of Fort Laramie. It stated that the Sioux would go on a reservation in Dakota Territory, but they would be allowed to continue hunting on their old hunting grounds along the Powder River, off the reservation.

Another Sioux war began in 1876 after gold miners had invaded the Black Hills in Dakota. Angered by this influx, Indians led by **Sitting Bull** and **Crazy Horse** moved west and joined forces with a group of Indians in Montana. They were opposed by Lieutenant Colonel **George Custer**, who attacked an Indian encampment of about seven thousand along the Little Bighorn River in June 1876. The Indians had perhaps eighteen hundred warriors while Custer had only about six

Left: Lieutenant Colonel George A. Custer (1839–1876) is best known for his defeat in the Battle of the Little Bighorn, also referred to as "Custer's Last Stand," on June 25, 1876. ***Right:*** Sitting Bull (1834?–1890) of the Hunkpapa Sioux. He and Crazy Horse led the Indians to victory at the Battle of the Little Bighorn in 1876.

hundred. Custer divided his men into three groups; he and all the 200 soldiers in his group were killed. The Indians won a great victory in the Battle of the Little Bighorn, also known as "Custer's Last Stand."

Yet this victory brought defeat, for the United States now attacked the Indians in earnest. In October 1876, two thousand Sioux surrendered when Colonel **Nelson Miles** caught them, but Sitting Bull and some followers escaped to Canada. Miles then tracked down the Sioux under Crazy Horse and defeated them in Montana during a January blizzard. By spring of 1877, thousands of Sioux and Cheyenne came into the Indian agencies to surrender, including Crazy Horse himself. By the end of that year, the power of the Plains Indians was broken and most of them were on reservations.

Chief Joseph. When he surrendered, Chief Joseph said, "I am tired of fighting. Our chiefs are killed. . . . It is cold and we have no blankets. . . . Hear me, my chiefs! I am tired; my heart is sick and sad. From where the sun now stands I will fight no more forever." When Chief Joseph died in exile in 1904, it was said that he died of a broken heart.

Battles in the Northwest. In 1877, the Nez Perce tried to keep white settlers out of their territory in the Wallowa Valley of Oregon. But after a Nez Perce raid left 18 whites dead, their **Chief Joseph** decided they had to flee. Fighting off the army in a series of battles, 150 Nez Perce braves and 550 others headed across the Bitterroot Mountains toward Canada. They covered 1,700 miles (2,736 km) and outwitted the best of the United States army. But only about 35 miles (56 km) from Canada, the Nez Perce were trapped by Colonel Miles.

Chief Joseph surrendered when he was promised that he and his people could go to a reservation near their homeland. But the Nez Perce were sent instead to Indian Territory (Oklahoma), hundreds of miles from home, and many of them died there. Finally the government allowed the remaining few to return to a reservation near their native land.

Final Incident at Wounded Knee. The Indian wars came to an end with Geronimo's surrender in 1886. But one more tragedy

Surrender of Chief Joseph (1840?–1904) of the Nez Perce, 1877. He led his people on a 1,700-mile (2,736-km) flight toward Canada but was caught not far from the border.

Chief Big Foot was leader of the Indian band at Wounded Knee in 1890. These are the only Indians of that band that survived the slaughter.

occurred in 1890, after an Indian "messiah" named Wovoka began promoting his Ghost Dance religion. If the Indians followed his precepts and danced the Ghost Dance, he said, the great buffalo herds destroyed by the white men would come back. The Indians' land would be restored, and the dead Indians would come back to life.

White men became uneasy about the frenzied dancing among the Indians, especially on the Sioux reservations in South Dakota. Sitting Bull had returned from Canada; and since some considered him to blame, they arrested him. But a scuffle broke out and Sitting Bull was killed. This prompted one band of Indians to flee toward another reservation, but they surrendered when the army caught up with them and surrounded them at a place called Wounded Knee. As the soldiers searched the Indians for weapons on December 29, 1890, someone fired his gun and fighting erupted. The army used rifles and machine guns to shoot down men, women, and children—leaving more than two hundred Sioux dead.

We might wonder how a righteous God could allow such injustices, but we must remember that He is always in control and His ways are higher than our ways. The prophet Habakkuk long ago asked a similar question of God. Then God reassured the prophet by revealing His greater plans, and Habakkuk wrote, "Yet I will rejoice in the LORD, I will joy in the God of my salvation." (See Habakkuk 3:17, 18.)

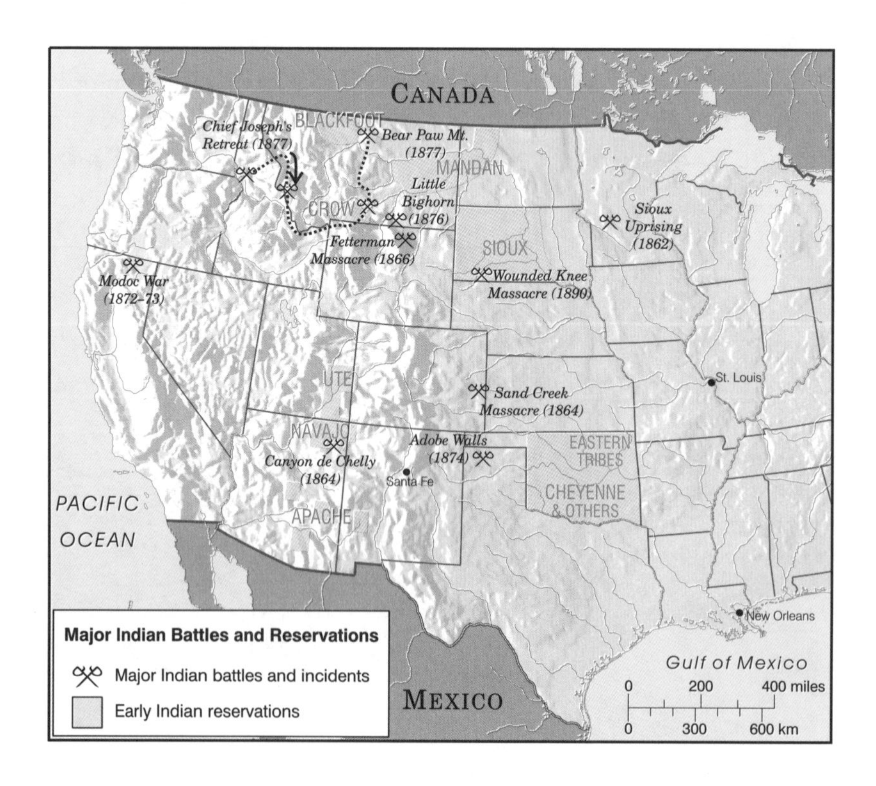

These Chiricahua Apache have just arrived at the Carlisle Indian School in the 1880s.

The Carlisle Indian School. Captain Richard Henry Pratt worked with considerable success among the Indians. Pratt believed the answer to the Indian problem was to educate the Indians so that they would conform to the white man's ways, rather than isolating them on reservations. Then they could blend into white society.

With the help of Carl Schurz (the secretary of the interior), Pratt obtained an unused army barracks at Carlisle, Pennsylvania; and in 1879 he set it up as a boarding school for Indians. Then Pratt visited the Rosebud Indian Reservation in South Dakota, where he persuaded Chief Spotted Tail to send his sons to the new school. Young Ota Kte ("Plenty Kill") volunteered to go and prove to his father that he was brave. At Carlisle he received a new name, Luther Standing Bear. This was in line with the school's goal of completely changing the Indians. Their traditionally long hair was cut short, and they dressed in uniforms instead of Indian clothes.

At the school, students were kept on a strict schedule and were forbidden to use their native languages. They learned reading, writing, and mathematics as well as shop skills like blacksmithing for boys and homemaking skills for girls. The students would go on "outings" in summer; they lived with white families and practiced their new skills. In the twenty-four years that Captain Pratt supervised the school, 4,903 Indians from 77 tribes attended there. The Carlisle Indian School closed in 1918 after thirty-nine years of operation.

Chiricahua Apache after four months at the Carlisle Indian School in the 1880s.

Left: Classroom in the Carlisle Indian School. On the blackboard are math problems related to farming. ***Right:*** Two Sioux Indian chiefs shake hands in 1891. On the left is American Horse, and on the right is the better-known Red Cloud. Their clothing shows some influence from the white man's culture. A few years before Red Cloud died, he and his wife were baptized as Christians and took the names John and Mary.

Recognition for the Indians

By the late 1880s, attitudes toward the Indians were changing. Whites began trying to help the Indians rather than killing them. Congress passed the Dawes Act in 1887, which divided the reservations into farms for the Indian families. In this way, the tribal system would be broken up and the Indians could be helped to become responsible citizens. The government granted citizenship to all Indians in 1924.

But the Dawes Act did not work out well, for the Indians were accustomed to functioning in tribal groups rather than as separate families. In 1934, the Indian Reorganization Act promoted a return to tribal organization among the Indians.

Other efforts were also made to help the Indians. In 1879, the Carlisle Indian School opened to teach Indians how to function as individuals in American society. Its success spawned other Indian schools, and these did much to help the Indians "walk the white man's road."

Focus for Thought

7. What were three main causes of the Indian wars?
8. a. Name the Indian tribes and their leader who camped at Sand Creek in 1864 after seeking peace with the whites.
   b. Who attacked them, and how many Indians were killed?
9. How did the Sioux victory at the Battle of the Little Bighorn finally lead to their defeat?
10. a. Why was Sitting Bull arrested in 1890?
    b. Where did an Indian massacre take place soon afterward?
11. Explain what the Dawes Act provided for the Indians, and why this law did not work well.
12. Besides the Dawes Act, what three things showed a change in white people's attitudes toward Indians?

3. THE CATTLEMEN AND HOMESTEADERS

With the West mostly emptied of buffalo, the Central Plains lay open for herds of another kind—cattle and sheep. The story of the cattle frontier is one of the most colorful tales of the West.

Many settlers in the West had come to farm. The great abundance of open land drew millions of easterners and immigrants to the plains. This influx populated the expanses of the West and ended the frontier.

The Cattle Kingdom

Beginning of Cattle Herding. After the Spanish introduced cattle to America, the descendants of their cattle roamed Texas and the Southwest for many generations. These were tough, wild cattle known as longhorns. In the 1850s, **Charles Goodnight**, Richard King, and others began building ranches and herding these cattle. But the main product was hides, for both the East and California were too far away to provide a market for beef.

The needed link finally emerged when railroads extended into Missouri and Kansas. Ranchers in Texas realized that they could make large profits by sending their cattle to market by rail. So they decided to drive thousands of cattle north to railroad towns where they could be shipped to large cities elsewhere in the nation. Thus began the era of the "long drive."

The first drive was made during 1865 and 1866 to Sedalia, Missouri. This drive was not altogether successful because of opposition from Indians, as well as from crop farmers who did not want cattle tramping across their land. So **Joseph McCoy**, an Illinois meat dealer, devised a better plan. He built stockyards with loading chutes along the Kansas-Pacific Railroad at Abilene, Kansas. Then he persuaded a number of cattlemen to drive their cattle there instead of to Missouri. At Abilene, 35,000 steers were loaded in 1867, and 1.5 million in the years 1868 to 1871.

Cattle Herding on the Open Range. Livestock roamed freely on the ***open range***, with cattle from different ranches mingling together. To identify them, each rancher had his cattle branded with the distinctive mark of his ranch. Cowboys rounded up the cattle each spring, separated them by brand, and branded the calves. They had another roundup in the fall to separate the steers ready for market. The following spring, the cowboys drove those cattle up the trail to the north.

A herd on the trail numbered from 1,000 to 3,000 or more cattle, with about one cowboy per 150 animals. The cowboys drove the cattle 10 to 15 miles (16–24 km) each day, with a chuck wagon accompanying them to provide

Loading cattle at Abilene, Kansas. In the late 1800s, cowboys drove thousands of cattle to Abilene and other towns to be loaded on railroad cars.

Calf branding at a spring roundup in 1888. There were two main roundups each year—in the spring and in the fall. Calves were branded in the spring.

Mealtime at a fall roundup in 1887. Cattle were rounded up in the fall to be driven to market. Here cowboys in South Dakota eat lunch in front of two chuck wagons.

meals. One famous trail was the Chisholm Trail (CHIHZ uhm), which ran from San Antonio, Texas, to Abilene and other northern points. When the herd reached the ***cattle town***, the animals were loaded on railroad cars and shipped to Kansas City, St. Louis, or Chicago.

The cowboy faced many difficulties along the trail. Flooding rivers had to be forded, and wolves or thunderstorms could cause the cattle to stampede. Angry Indians or farmers needed to be pacified or fended off. Because of his work, a cowboy needed special clothing: high boots, leather chaps to protect his legs, and a wide-brimmed hat to shield him from the hot sun. He became an expert at riding, using ropes, and handling cattle. But the rough, ungodly life of many cowboys was such that this work was not suitable for a Christian.

Driving cattle across rivers was a major difficulty of the "long drive." Deep water might frighten the cattle and cause them to swim in circles, or they might get mired in quicksand.

Expansion of the Cattle Domain. As railroads extended farther west, settlements moved west also. First Abilene and then Ellsworth, Newton, and Dodge City became the leading cattle towns. Many thousands of cattle passed through the stockyards there. When the herds arrived, the town went wild as cowboys engaged in boisterous celebrating. These towns, like the western mining towns, gained a reputation for coarseness and violence.

Later Charles Goodnight and others crossed the tough longhorns with other breeds to produce cattle with the endurance of a longhorn but having more tender meat. Cattle raising spread northward to Wyoming, Montana, and the Dakotas; and huge cattle ranches developed as they had in Texas. The XIT Ranch in Texas had about 150,000 cattle and 150 cowboys, and measured about 30 miles by 200 miles (48 by 322 km). This one was unusually large, but the ranches were all of impressive size. A small number of cattle kings ruled a vast domain.

End of Open-range Cattle Herding. Cattle ranching changed after 1874, when **Joseph Glidden** invented barbed wire. Whereas suitable fencing materials were scarce before, cattlemen could now fence off their land to protect their water and pastures.

Joseph Glidden invented barbed wire in 1874. Barbed wire helped to end the open range and changed the West forever.

The XIT Ranch eventually used 1,500 miles (2,414 km) of barbed wire! The day of the open range and cattle roundups was coming to a close.

Because of the profits in cattle raising, more and more investors set up ranches in the West. They placed so many cattle on them that the western plains were overgrazed. Cattle prices fell in 1885, but it was weather that brought the greatest setback. Many cattle froze in the bitter winter of 1885–86, and the hot, dry summer that followed was also hard on cattle.

The winter of 1886–87 dealt the final blow. Snow came in November, and late January brought a howling blizzard followed by temperatures as low as –68° F (–56° C). Thousands of cattle starved when they could no longer paw through the snow for grass, and their carcasses lay piled along the fences and in canyons. The animals that survived were little more than skeletons.

This hard winter ruined many cattlemen, and it permanently ended the era of open-range cattle herding. Ranching continued, but ranchers had smaller herds and raised hay to feed them in winter. The wild, free days of the cowboy were over.

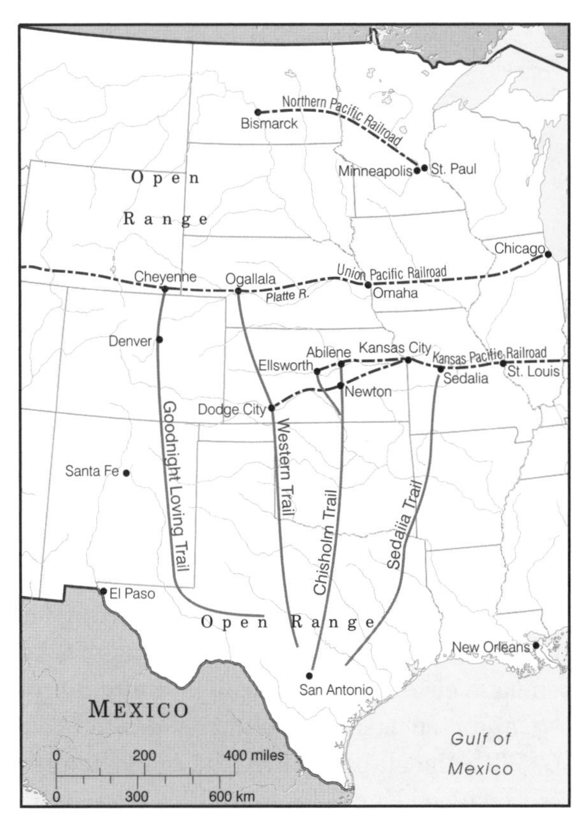

Cattle Trails and Towns

Homesteading in the West

The Homestead Act. For many years, westerners had been demanding cheap land from the ***public domain*** (land owned by the government). Congress finally passed the Homestead Act in 1862, which allowed any citizen of age twenty-one or older to file a claim on a quarter section (160 acres, or 65 ha). Married couples could file for 320 acres (130 ha). To gain possession, a settler had to live on the land for five years, make improvements such as building a claim shanty, and begin cultivating the land. If public land was for sale, a settler could ***preempt*** (pree EHMPT) a certain portion by settling on the land. Then he would have the first chance to buy it for $1.25 per acre.

Life on a Homestead. The ***homesteader*** first needed to select his land; he chose land close to water if possible. Then he marked his claim by staking its boundaries or plowing a furrow. Next he went to the land office to file

A sod house, likely in Nebraska in 1887. A "soddy" was cool in summer and warm in winter. But dirt sifted from the ceiling, mice might live in the thatch, and snakes might burrow into the walls. This family used the elkhorns to dry their clothes.

his claim and pay the $14 fee. This in itself could be a task, for often the land office was jammed with other homesteaders applying for claims—maybe even his claim! Trying to take someone else's claim was called ***claim jumping***, and it sometimes led to violence.

With the claim secure, the homesteader next fashioned a dwelling. But few trees grew on the plain, so he might live in a tent, brush house, or dugout—a hole in a bank with a front wall of sod. A homesteader could also build a sod house from blocks of the tough prairie sod. But a "soddy" was dirty and infested with insects, and it often leaked in rainstorms. If lumber could be brought in by rail, the homesteader might build a claim shanty of wood.

If the claim was not near a stream or river, the settler dug a well by hand, going deeper and deeper until he struck water—or failed. Wells might reach a depth of 200 feet (61 m) or more, so the farmer shoveled dirt into a bucket and lifted it out with a winch. Danger lurked in a well: the sides might collapse, poisonous gases might get into it, or someone might fall in.

The settler needed to get a crop planted in good time. This included breaking the tough sod with a breaking plow and then planting the seed. Often the first year's crop failed to do well, or some calamity destroyed it. Many farmers planted one main crop—wheat; and if that failed, they failed too. Raising a variety of crops, such as oats and potatoes, provided something to eat and a hedge against disaster.

Money was often in short supply. Seed, building materials, livestock, and farming implements all cost money; and if a settler did not have it, he borrowed money or simply did without things. Some farmers lost out and headed back East, or they found jobs in one of the growing towns.

Natural calamities were another test of courage. The extreme climate of the plains brought scorching heat in summer and brutal cold in winter. Fuel for winter heat was a common problem—settlers sometimes had to burn corncobs or twist hay into sticks to provide a

In this picture, wolves roam in a forsaken railroad town in Kansas. Homesteading was so difficult that some settlers gave up and went back East.

Account of a Grasshopper Plague on August 6, 1874

There was not a hint of a cloud in the sky that day until along about four o'clock in the afternoon. Then the sky suddenly became hazy and speedily darkened until, in a matter of a few minutes, it was so dark that it not only frightened me but did something to the chickens. I can't say they were frightened. But they hastened to their roosts as fast as they could. . . . Then with a whizzing, whirring sound, the grasshoppers came from the northwest in unbelievable numbers. They lit on everything. I was covered from head to foot. When they hit my face or hands, the impact was like missiles; and at once the insects began to eat. The ground was covered, in some spots to a depth of three to four inches, and trees along the creek were so loaded with grasshoppers that large limbs were broken off. The insects fell into the creek and drowned, and the dead insects were in such numbers that they formed a dam and the water turned brown and our cattle and horses would not drink it. Even fish died in the foul water.

It was only a few minutes that darkness prevailed. Then the hoppers were all out of the sky and eating. The chickens came out of the hen house and gorged themselves on hoppers. . . . We had about fifteen acres of corn, which older settlers said would make fifty bushels an acre. The hoppers landed about four o'clock. By dark there wasn't a stalk of that field of corn over a foot high left in the entire field. I slept in a straw stack. That night the hoppers ate my straw hat, or most of it, leaving me only a part of the brim and a part of the crown. They seemed to like sweaty things and ate around the sweatband of my hat. They gnawed the handles of pitchforks and other farm tools that had absorbed perspiration, and they ate the harness on the horses or hanging in the barn. They ate every leaf off the trees and every green thing on our farm except the grass.

—Written by a Mennonite boy of Kansas

brief respite from the cold. People caught in a blizzard might freeze to death, and cattle could suffocate as ice built up on their heads until they could not lift them.

Prairie fires sometimes raced across the plains, destroying everything in their path. Farmers protected their fields by lighting a backfire or plowing a fire break. Tornadoes, hail, and other vicious storms might destroy a farmer's crops and his dreams with them. Among the worst disasters were the plagues of grasshoppers—huge clouds of hopping, buzzing insects that left nothing green behind. One farmer returning to the East put a sign on his wagon, lamenting, "From Kansas, where it rains grasshoppers, fire, and destruction."

Success of the Homesteads. In spite of the many obstacles, thousands of homesteaders survived. New crops and technology were a great help to them. Hard wheat flourished on the prairies, and new milling processes

A detail from a photograph of James Oliver's improved hard-steel plow, on display in the Henry Ford Museum at Dearborn, Michigan. This plow cut through the tough prairie sod and helped to make farming possible in the West.

Oklahoma land rush on April 22, 1889. Thousands of people scrambled across the border on foot, on bicycles, on horseback, and in wagons or trains.

The towns of Guthrie and Oklahoma City had 10,000 inhabitants each by the evening of April 22, 1889. This picture shows the "tent city" at Guthrie.

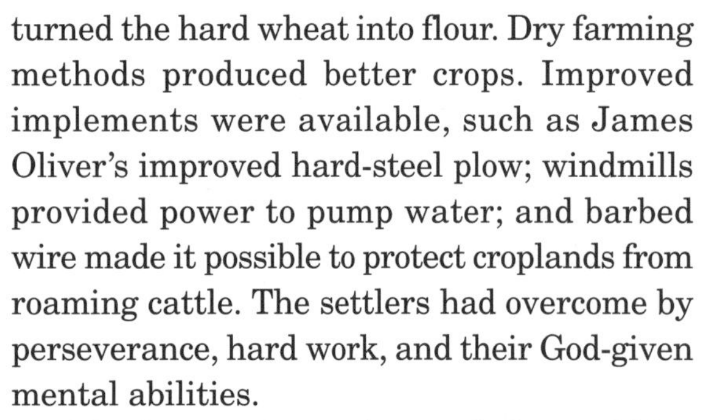

turned the hard wheat into flour. Dry farming methods produced better crops. Improved implements were available, such as James Oliver's improved hard-steel plow; windmills provided power to pump water; and barbed wire made it possible to protect croplands from roaming cattle. The settlers had overcome by perseverance, hard work, and their God-given mental abilities.

The last region to be settled was Oklahoma. This had been reserved as Indian Territory, but white people would settle there anyway until the government drove them out—and then they would sneak back in! At last the government decided to open a section of Indian Territory for white settlement. On April 22, 1889, over fifty thousand people gathered along the border; and when soldiers fired their guns at noon, the settlers rushed in to stake their claims. Towns such as Guthrie mushroomed overnight.

A similar land rush occurred in 1893, when about one hundred thousand people raced into the Cherokee Strip—first come, first served! Some were called "sooners" because they rushed in ahead of the appointed time to make their claims; so Oklahoma became the Sooner State in 1907.

Utah entered the Union in 1896, and New Mexico and Arizona in 1912. Thus, the organization of the forty-eight contiguous states was completed.

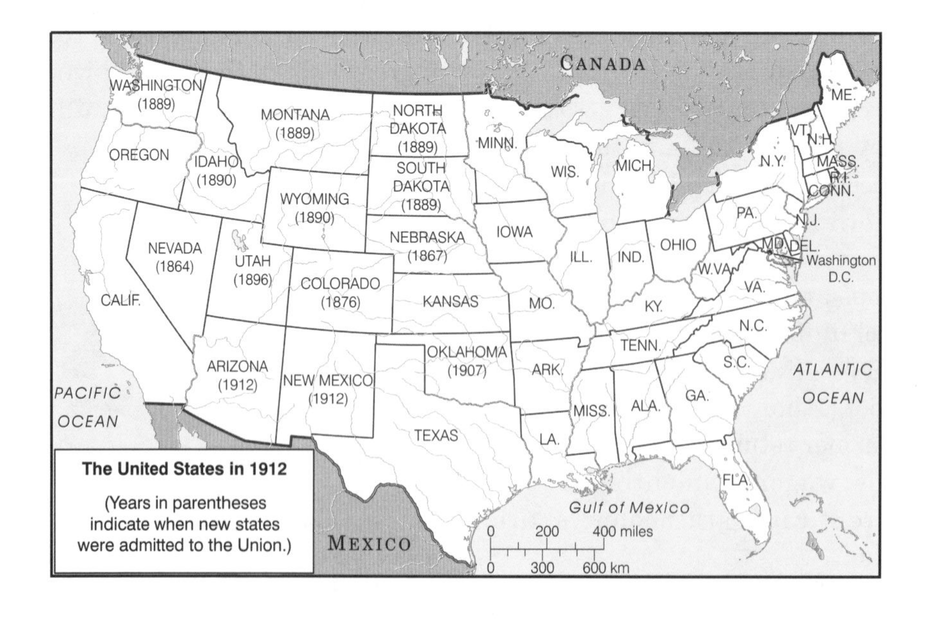

The United States in 1912

(Years in parentheses indicate when new states were admitted to the Union.)

Focus for Thought

13. a. Why were hides the main product of early ranches in Texas?
    b. What caused this to change later?
14. What were some difficulties that cowboys experienced as they drove cattle to a cattle town?
15. Describe two things that brought an end to open-range cattle herding.
16. What were some provisions of the Homestead Act?
17. a. Describe some difficulties of homesteading.
    b. What enabled the homesteaders to survive?
18. a. How was the settlement of Oklahoma carried out?
    b. Who were the "sooners"?

Historical Highlights

A. Matching: People 1

a. Charles Crocker
b. Charles Goodnight
c. George Custer
d. George Westinghouse
e. Joseph Glidden
f. Joseph McCoy
g. Nelson Miles

1. Man who invented barbed wire in 1874.
2. Colonel who lost the Battle of the Little Bighorn.
3. Man who invented the air brake for trains in 1869.
4. One of the first cattle ranchers in Texas.
5. Colonel who defeated the Sioux and Nez Perce during 1876 and 1877.
6. Man who built stockyards at Abilene, Kansas.
7. Railroad director who hired Chinese workers.

B. Matching: People 2

a. Black Kettle
b. Chief Joseph
c. Cochise
d. Crazy Horse
e. Geronimo
f. Red Cloud
g. Sitting Bull

1. Apache leader who went on a reservation in 1872.
2. Cheyenne and Arapaho leader whose people were massacred at Sand Creek.
3. Indian leaders at the Battle of the Little Bighorn (two answers).
4. Last great Apache leader, who surrendered in 1886.
5. Nez Perce leader who went on a long flight with his people before capture.
6. Sioux leader whose warriors killed all of Captain Fetterman's troops.

C. Matching: Terms 1

a. cattle town
b. Central Pacific
c. Dawes Act
d. Ghost Dance religion
e. Indian Reorganization Act
f. mother lode
g. open range
h. reservation
i. Union Pacific
j. vigilance committee
k. winter of 1886–87
l. work train

1. Belief that Indians and buffalo would come back.
2. Main vein of ore.
3. Place to which cattle were driven by cowboys.
4. Unfenced grazing land.
5. Main feature of efficient track-laying method.
6. Group that meted out swift and stern justice.
7. Law that divided Indian reservations into family farms.
8. Railroad that laid track east from California.
9. Place where Indians were compelled to live.
10. Helped to end open-range cattle herding.
11. Railroad that laid track west from Nebraska.
12. Law that promoted a return to tribal organization of Indians.

D. Matching: Terms 2

a. claim jumping
b. Homestead Act
c. homesteader
d. "long drive"
e. Pacific Railroad Act
f. preempt
g. public domain
h. Second Treaty of Fort Laramie
i. sod house

1. Land owned by the government.
2. Law that allowed settlers to claim 160 acres (65 ha) for farming.
3. To settle on (public land) so as to have the first chance to buy it.
4. Taking of land already claimed by someone else.
5. Law authorizing a transcontinental railroad.
6. Dwelling built with blocks of prairie turf.
7. Person who claimed land and settled on it for five years.
8. Indian treaty of 1868 with the Sioux.
9. The taking of cattle over a trail to a cattle town.

E. Matching: Places

a. Abilene
b. Black Hills
c. Chisholm Trail
d. Comstock Lode
e. Pikes Peak
f. Promontory
g. Wounded Knee

1. Route of cattle herds moving north to Kansas.
2. Place where last Indian war took place.
3. Place where transcontinental railroad joined.

4. Part of Dakota Territory promised to Indians, where a gold rush occurred.
5. Rich gold and silver strike in Nevada.
6. Famous cattle town in Kansas.
7. Place in Colorado where a gold rush occurred in 1859.

F. Deeper Discussion

1. How did the mining camps illustrate the tendency of Americans to govern themselves?
2. a. Why could Indians and whites seemingly not live together in peace?
   b. Why could the Indians not hold out against the whites?
3. a. In Habakkuk 1:1–4, the prophet asked God how He could tolerate such violence and evil in the land. When God told Habakkuk that the Chaldeans would punish Judah, the prophet wondered how God could punish the Judeans by using people more wicked than they (1:12–17). How do Habakkuk's questions relate to the Indian wars?
   b. What was God's answer to Habakkuk (2:14, 20) and Habakkuk's response to that (3:17–19)? How does this help us to put the Indian wars in proper perspective?
4. What made barbed wire so important in the West?
5. Why did the boom towns of the West become such dens of evil and violence?

G. Chronology and Geography

1. Match the states to the years of their admission into the United States. Some dates will be used more than once.
   a. North and South Dakota
   b. New Mexico
   c. Colorado
   d. Nevada
   e. Arizona
   f. Utah
   g. Montana
   h. Washington
   i. Wyoming
   j. Oklahoma
   k. Idaho
   l. Nebraska

   1864
   1867
   1876
   1889
   1890
   1896
   1907
   1912
2. Give the correct year for each item.
   a. Homestead Act and Pacific Railroad Act.
   b. Completion of transcontinental railroad.
   c. Battle of the Little Bighorn.
   d. Dawes Act.
3. On your map entitled "The States of the United States," draw the borders of the thirteen states admitted between 1864 and 1912. (See map on page 426.)
   a. Label the states with their names and dates of admission.
   b. Color the states admitted between 1864 and 1896 one color, and those admitted in the 1900s another color. Add both colors to the legend.
   c. Memorize the names and locations of these states.

So Far This Year

A. Matching

1. Northerners who went south to help in Reconstruction.
2. System in which farm workers rent cropland and use a share of the crops to pay the rent.
3. Southern whites who took part in Reconstruction governments.
4. Rebuilding of the South after the Civil War.
5. Seward's Folly.
6. Social separation based on race.
7. Amendment that granted citizenship to blacks.
8. Amendment granting all citizens the right to vote.
9. Laws that restricted blacks.
10. Former slaves.

a. Alaska
b. black codes
c. carpetbaggers
d. Fourteenth Amendment
e. Fifteenth Amendment
f. freedmen
g. Reconstruction
h. scalawags
i. segregation
j. sharecropping

11. Write the date of founding for each colony or settlement.

a. Georgia	1607
b. Jamestown	1620
c. Pennsylvania	1681
d. Plymouth	1733

B. Completion

Write the correct name for each description.

12. President who was impeached in 1868.
13. Former Civil War general who became president.
14. President appointed after a disputed election and the Compromise of 1877.
15. Black leader who founded Tuskegee Institute.
16. Founder of Maryland.
17. Two leaders of the colonial religious revival.
18. Quaker who received a land grant as payment for a debt.
19. Leader of Jamestown who established a policy of "no work, no food."
20. Founder of Rhode Island who insisted on freedom of conscience.
21. Religious revival of the 1700s.
22. Federalist leader and first secretary of the treasury.
23. Two men who explored the Louisiana Purchase from 1804 to 1806.
24. Man who opened the Wilderness Road into Kentucky.
25. Chief justice who strengthened the Supreme Court.

C. Multiple Choice

Write the letter of the correct answer.

26. Those who wanted to purify the Church of England from within were
    a. Pilgrims.
    b. Puritans.
    c. Quakers.
    d. Scotch-Irish.

27. A group that withdrew from the Church of England and settled in New England was the
    a. Pilgrims.
    b. Puritans.
    c. Quakers.
    d. Scotch-Irish.
28. A legal document granting the right to settle an area and establish a government there was
    a. the Mayflower Compact.
    b. a charter.
    c. a legislature.
    d. a constitution.
29. An agreement signed by Pilgrims and Strangers to make "just and equal laws" was
    a. the Mayflower Compact.
    b. a charter.
    c. the Act of Toleration.
    d. a constitution.
30. A Maryland law that granted religious freedom was
    a. the Mayflower Compact.
    b. a charter.
    c. the Act of Toleration.
    d. a constitution.
31. The owner of an English colony was called
    a. an indentured servant.
    b. a charter.
    c. a duke.
    d. a proprietor.
32. The political party in favor of limited government and strict interpretation of the Constitution was
    a. the Federalists.
    b. the Whigs.
    c. the Democratic-Republicans.
    d. the Nationalists.
33. The treaty that ended the War of 1812 was
    a. the Treaty of Ghent.
    b. the Jay Treaty.
    c. the Adams-Onís Treaty.
    d. the Pinckney Treaty.
34. The agreement that gained Florida in 1819 was
    a. the Treaty of Ghent.
    b. the Jay Treaty.
    c. the Adams-Onís Treaty.
    d. the Pinckney Treaty.
35. The idea that states are supreme over the federal government is called
    a. sectionalism.
    b. the spoils system.
    c. judicial review.
    d. states' rights.
36. A declaration about involvement of European and American nations in each other's affairs was the
    a. Monroe Doctrine.
    b. Missouri Compromise.
    c. Era of Good Feelings.
    d. Emancipation Proclamation.
37. Practice in which the winner of an election rewards his supporters with government positions is called
    a. sectionalism.
    b. the spoils system.
    c. judicial review.
    d. states' rights.

Immigrants contributed to the rapid growth of industries and cities after the Civil War. Manhattan's Lower East Side in New York City was a popular immigrant destination; Mulberry Street is shown here about 1900.

20 The Industrial Age

1. Change in Industry and Agriculture
   - New Technology
   - New Business Methods
   - New Developments in Labor
   - New Developments in Farming
2. Change in Society
   - The Golden Door
   - The Rise of the City
   - Intellectual and Religious Change
   - Changes in the Mennonite Church
3. Change in Politics
   - The Political Issues
   - The Presidents

1850

Drake drills the first successful oil well 1859

1860

Transatlantic cable laid 1866

1870

Standard Oil founded 1870

Great Chicago Fire 1871

Alexander Graham Bell patents the telephone 1876

Rutherford B. Hayes becomes president 1877

Thomas Edison patents the light bulb 1879

1880

James A. Garfield elected president 1880

Garfield assassinated; Chester A. Arthur becomes president 1881

Grover Cleveland elected president 1884

Statue of Liberty dedicated 1886

Benjamin Harrison elected president 1888

1890

Grover Cleveland elected to second term 1892

Panic of 1893

Coxey's Army marches on Washington 1894

William McKinley elected president 1896

1900

"Labour not for the meat which perisheth, but for that meat which endureth unto everlasting life, which the Son of man shall give unto you: for him hath God the Father sealed."

John 6:27

THE INDUSTRIAL AGE

Focus for Reading

From 1865 through 1900, the United States industrialized rapidly. Bigger, better, faster, more efficient—this was the second Industrial Revolution. It brought dramatic changes to the United States and laid the foundation for modern times. Along with changes in industry came changes in farming, politics, and society in general. What contributed to the advances in industry and farming? What were some changes in society in the final decades of the 1800s? Who were the presidents, and what issues did they face? Three sections in this chapter answer these questions.

1. Change in Industry and Agriculture
2. Change in Society
3. Change in Politics

1. CHANGE IN INDUSTRY AND AGRICULTURE

At the close of the Civil War in 1865, the industrial output of the United States still did not attain to that of great European nations. But by 1900, the United States had become one of the greatest manufacturing nations in the world. Along with this industrial progress came a revolution in agriculture that enabled farmers to produce much more food in much less time than ever before. These changes had great and lasting effects on the United States.

New Technology

An important reason for the prosperity of the United States was the ***free enterprise*** system by which it operated. Free enterprise includes the private ownership of property, free markets, and a minimum of government regulation. It allows people to reap the profits of their efforts, and this motivates them to be as productive as possible. But because of man's evil nature, free enterprise allows rich people to engage in "the oppression of the poor, and violent perverting of judgment and justice" (Ecclesiastes 5:8). The civil government is responsible to restrain such evils (Romans 13:4).

Americans constantly wanted to do things faster and better, and they invented many devices to fill that demand. When a man developed a new invention, he obtained a ***patent*** that gave him the sole right to produce that item for seventeen years. This helped to assure the inventor that others would not make unfair profits on his work.

The Corliss steam engine at the Philadelphia Centennial Exposition in 1876. With a height of 40 feet (12 m) and a weight of 700 tons (635 M.T.), this 2,500-horsepower engine symbolized the might of American industry. The picture shows the moment when President Grant started the great engine.

Cyrus W. Field (1819–1892) made five attempts in ten years before successfully laying a transatlantic telegraph cable in 1866. This picture shows cable being laid from the ship *Niagara* in the first attempt (1857).

Telegraph lines tied the nation together by 1862; and in 1866, Cyrus W. Field successfully completed an underwater telegraph cable across the Atlantic Ocean. The Western Union Company was the largest telegraph company, with over 400,000 miles (643,710 km) of lines that sent over 40 million messages in 1883.

The telephone brought another revolution to communications. It was patented in 1876 by **Alexander Graham Bell**, who formed the Bell Telephone Company in 1877. Eventually the American Telephone and Telegraph Company took over, and by 1900 well over a million telephones were in use. The telephone quickly became an important business tool.

In the late 1800s, electricity began replacing steam as the primary energizer of industry. **Thomas Alva Edison** probably did more than any other person to bring this about. He invented hundreds of electrical devices; but he realized that if people were to benefit from his inventions, they would need a steady source of electricity. So he set about to provide a complete electrical system, with generating stations and transmission wires. Edison designed the Pearl Street Station as a central power station for New York City, and it went into operation in 1882. From this small beginning, electric power stations spread to many cities across the nation.

Night scene along Grand Street, New York City, in 1889. Electric lights made it safer and easier to travel city streets at night.

Left: Thomas Edison (1847–1931) and his phonograph. This photograph was taken in 1877 after he had worked on the machine for 72 hours without stopping. ***Right:*** A replica of the Edison light bulb in the Menlo Park Laboratory at Greenfield Village, Dearborn, Michigan.

Thomas A. Edison. Born in 1847, young Edison first lived in Milan, Ohio, and then in Port Huron, Michigan. As a boy, he liked to experiment with chemicals; when he was only six, he burned down his father's barn "just to see what it would do." (He was punished with a whipping from his father.) Edison did poorly in school, so his mother taught him at home. He later sold magazines and candy on trains; and one day when he experimented with chemicals in a baggage car, some phosphorous was upset by a jolt and started a fire in his "laboratory."

Edison later became a telegraph operator, and his first inventions were improvements to the telegraph. He then established a research laboratory at Menlo Park, New Jersey. Here he worked on many different projects, but the electric light bulb is probably the best known. After hundreds of failures, Edison finally developed a bulb that shone for as long as forty hours. He applied in November 1879 for a patent on his invention; and by New Year's Eve of 1880, Menlo Park was aglow with his electric lights.

Edison became an extraordinarily successful inventor, with over one thousand patents to his credit. People called him a genius, but he said, "Genius is 1 percent inspiration and 99 percent perspiration." He showed what he meant by working day and night—sometimes more than one hundred hours in a week! Edison lived until 1931, long enough to see the fiftieth anniversary of his electric lamp. But he was an agnostic, saying that one could not know if God existed. Edison illustrates the truth that God can use even those who deny Him to provide many benefits for others.

New Business Methods

New Forms of Business Organization. The ***corporation*** became an important type of business organization. The new corporations were owned by many people instead of just one or several. To raise capital to operate, they began selling ***shares of stock*** to investors, who actually owned the company. The corporations paid part of their profits to the stockholders in the form of ***dividends***.

As time passed, some corporations purchased other corporations, and these industrial giants grew so large that a new form of organization was needed. So some businessmen and lawyers created the ***trust***, which is a combination of related businesses, such as oil producers and refineries. A board of trustees manages the whole group of corporations as one company.

Some people objected to the trusts, saying they were too large and restricted competition instead of encouraging a free market. They viewed a trust as a ***monopoly***, a company that has complete control over a certain product and can therefore charge high prices without fear of competition. In reality, though, prices generally declined during the late 1800s, and the trusts did not control 100 percent of the market—they always had some competition.

Andrew Carnegie, an immigrant from Scotland, built up the corporation that became the United States Steel Corporation. To control the whole process of steel production, Carnegie bought iron-ore mines, ore ships, rail lines, and a business that processed coal for steel making. Carnegie's steel company helped make the United States the largest steel producer in the world. When U.S. Steel was formed in 1901, it was the first billion-dollar company in the United States.

Steel mill at Pittsburgh, Pennsylvania.

John D. Rockefeller made a fortune through his Standard Oil Company, founded in 1870. Rockefeller bought out his competitors; and like Carnegie, he tried to control every phase of oil production. By 1880, Standard Oil controlled 90 percent of the oil business in the United States. Standard Oil was the first trust, and it became a pattern for other trusts.

New Methods of Manufacturing and Marketing. Factory output was greatly increased by ***mass production***, which included

Left: Andrew Carnegie (1835–1919), a Scottish immigrant, helped to make the United States the greatest steel producer in the world. ***Right:*** John D. Rockefeller (1839–1937), head of the Standard Oil company. He became the richest man in the world, and in his later years he gave millions of dollars to religious, educational, and medical institutions.

Workers at National Cash Register in Dayton, Ohio, in 1902. As the United States became more industrialized, increasing numbers of people worked in industries rather than as farmers or craftsmen.

Drake's Oil Well. In certain places along Oil Creek in northwestern Pennsylvania, oil bubbled out of the ground in oil springs. The Pennsylvania Rock Oil Company was formed in 1854 to develop this as a source of oil. In 1858, this company sent Edwin L. Drake to Titusville, Pennsylvania, to drill for oil.

People laughed at the effort and called it "wild and woolly," saying, "You don't mean to tell me that Drake thinks he can get oil out of solid rock?" But Drake plunged ahead anyway. First he tried to dig a well, but water flowed into the hole. So Drake drove in an iron pipe with a battering ram, and then he drilled with steam power. Drake eventually ran out of money; but his company would not send him more, and the president gave him orders to return home.

Instead of quitting, Drake borrowed money and kept drilling. Then on Saturday, August 27, 1859, the drill slipped into a crack at 69.5 feet (21 m) down; so all the workers went home. But on Sunday, William Smith, the driller, visited the well and lowered a container down the pipe. It came up with oil! Smith's son ran out, shouting, "They've struck oil! They've struck oil!"

Large-scale oil production began with Edwin Drake's oil well at Titusville, Pennsylvania, in 1859. The picture shows Drake (right front) with other men at the well in 1861.

Thus Drake succeeded after long persistence. Instead of the few gallons per day that had been taken from the oil springs, he now obtained as much as eight to ten barrels each day. From this small beginning, the oil industry grew until it developed into large oil companies worth millions of dollars.

the use of interchangeable parts and assembly lines. In an assembly line, each item passes from one worker to another, and each person adds one part until the product is complete. This is much more efficient than having each worker make one complete item at a time.

With factories so productive, businessmen had to find new ways to sell their products. So they began advertising in newspapers and magazines—something that was considered "ungentlemanly" before the Civil War. Companies distinguished their products by putting them into appealing packages and using brand names, such as Kellogg's Corn Flakes and Ivory soap. They also began using slogans, such as "When it rains, it pours" (Morton salt).

American manufacturers began using advertisements like this one (dated 1898) to market their many products.

New kinds of stores sold the mass merchandise now available. One kind was the department store; Alexander Stewart built the first of these in New York in 1848. Another kind was chain stores, which included A&P grocery stores, Woolworth five-and-ten-cent stores, and J. C. Penney clothing stores. Chain stores had annual sales in the millions of dollars.

Some businesses began selling goods by mail. Aaron Montgomery Ward first did this in the 1880s by sending out catalogs; and Sears, Roebuck and Company was soon doing the same. By the early 1900s, mass marketing had almost completely replaced the old-time general store.

New Developments in Labor

Growth of Labor Unions. Working conditions in factories were sometimes unhealthy. Buildings had poor lighting and inadequate ventilation, workers toiled as long as twelve hours a day, and industrial accidents claimed many limbs and lives. Children worked long hours at dangerous jobs, such as picking slate out of coal for fifty or sixty cents a day.

Because of these things, some workers banded together to form ***labor unions***. Two of the first national unions were the Knights of Labor (1869) and the American Federation of Labor (1886). Unions demanded higher pay, better working conditions, an eight-hour workday, and the end of child labor. To achieve their ends, they used ***collective bargaining***, in which union leaders negotiated with employers for the whole group. Labor unions also used ***strikes***, in which they refused to work until their demands were met.

Strikes sometimes became violent, with rioting and even murder. In 1886, the Haymarket Riot left eight people dead in Chicago. Also near Chicago, workers in 1894 went on strike against the Pullman Palace Car Company, a manufacturer of railroad cars. This strike stopped the trains running into Chicago, including mail trains. Finally President Cleveland sent soldiers to end the strike and get the mail trains running again.

Labor Unions and the Christian. True Christians cannot join labor unions for several reasons. First, labor unions use force in dealing with employers, thus violating the Scriptural teaching of nonresistance. The Bible

Steel making at Pittsburgh, Pennsylvania, in 1886. Industrial jobs were often hard and dangerous, and employees worked long hours.

The Pullman Strike. United States cavalry escorted the first train to leave the Chicago stockyards on July 10, 1894. The strikers were members of the American Railway Union.

Top: Harvesting on a large farm of the late 1800s. From 3,000 to 65,000 acres (1,215 to 26,320 ha) of wheat grew on these huge farms in Dakota Territory. On one such farm, 1,000 people worked to harvest the wheat crop in 1884.

Middle: An early combine on a farm in Oregon. Such machines were so large that 20 or 30 horses were needed to pull them. Because of mechanized farming, the average time required to produce a bushel of wheat dropped from three hours in 1830 to half an hour in 1896.

Bottom: This steam-powered tractor pulls a plow and seeder in South Dakota, in about 1907. The man standing by the rear wheel of the tractor gives an idea of the wheel's huge size.

also teaches us to "be obedient to them that are your masters according to the flesh" (Ephesians 6:5). Christians should seek to do their work "heartily, as to the Lord" (Colossians 3:23) instead of trying to do as little as possible for as much money as they can get.

The Bible does direct businessmen to "give unto your servants that which is just and equal" (Colossians 4:1). Following the Bible way brings peace and harmony between business owners and their workers.

New Developments in Farming

Change in the Nature of Farming. Around 1800, most farmers produced little more than what their families needed (subsistence farming). They made most of their own clothing, tools, and other necessities, and they sold only a few farm products to buy the things they could not make.

Gradually farming changed from an occupation depending on hand labor to one depending largely on machines. Machines eventually did almost all the farmer's work. Horse-drawn plows, harrows, and disks greatly simplified the work of tilling the soil. Other new machines included hay rakes, hay balers, corn planters, corn binders, and corn shellers. Mechanical reapers and threshing machines were common by the 1870s; and by the 1880s, combines were cutting and threshing grain in a single operation.

All these inventions enabled a few men to do work that formerly had required many. For example, the combine replaced three hundred men with just four men, and the corn sheller replaced fifty men with one. This mechanization allowed farmers to cultivate much more land in much less time than before.

As farm machines grew in size and complexity, horses were no longer sufficient to operate them. Steam tractors were one new source of power, but they were not very practical because of the time it took to build up steam pressure. Tractors with gasoline engines proved to be much more versatile. The Hart-Parr company was among the first to build gasoline-powered tractors (about 1903).

Better Farming Methods. Various men promoted techniques that contributed to greater farm productivity. William D. Hoard founded *Hoard's Dairyman*, a national magazine that promoted better dairying practices. Men like **Luther Burbank** and **George Washington Carver** introduced new crops and new uses for old crops such as the peanut.

The federal government and the education system also encouraged better farming methods. The United States Department of Agriculture was established in 1862. That same year, Congress passed the Land-Grant Act, by which government-owned land was granted to individual states for establishing colleges of agriculture. Farmers could then attend the colleges for scientific instruction in farming. Farmers also learned to care for their soil by fertilizing it and using methods to prevent erosion.

New Farm Organizations. The very success of American farmers brought them hardships in the late 1800s. Farmers sent so many products to market that prices declined steadily. For example, wheat fell from a dollar a bushel in the 1870s to fifty cents by the 1890s. This was due to the law of ***supply and demand***—prices rise when a product is scarce, but they fall when the product is plentiful. Yet the farmers' expenses for things like equipment and fertilizer remained high.

Farmers began to band together to help their situation. The first national farm organization was the Patrons of Husbandry, or the Grange, founded by Oliver Kelley in 1867. This organization grew so rapidly that almost every state had Granges by 1873, and total membership was over 750,000. One way the Granges helped farmers was by forming ***co-operatives***—associations that bought things cheaply in large quantities and then sold them to farmers at a discount.

Granger meeting in the woods near Winchester, Illinois, in 1873.

The Grange was later overshadowed by Farmers' Alliances, which began springing up in the late 1870s. This organization grew until it had about 2 million members, and eventually the Farmers' Alliances developed into a political movement that campaigned for radical changes. By 1892, the Farmers' Alliances formed the nucleus of the Populist Party, a new political group that brought national attention to many of the farmers' ideas.

Christians should be careful about belonging to cooperatives lest they be "unequally yoked together with unbelievers" (2 Corinthians 6:14). If a group uses force or political means to achieve its purposes, a believer should have no part in it at all.

Focus for Thought

1. Give at least two inventions or developments that promoted industrial growth in relation to communications.
2. How did Thomas Edison help people to benefit from the many electrical devices that he invented?
3. How did Andrew Carnegie and John D. Rockefeller contribute to industrial growth in the United States?
4. Describe three new methods that developed for selling the abundance of merchandise produced by factories.

5. Give three details indicating that many laborers worked in unfavorable conditions.
6. a. What four things were demanded by labor unions?
   b. What Scriptural principles are violated by membership in a labor union?
7. a. Describe several ways in which machines helped to make farmers more productive.
   b. How did the farmers' success cause hardships for them?

2. CHANGE IN SOCIETY

In the decades after the Civil War, American society changed dramatically. Multitudes of immigrants thronged to American shores for new opportunities. Cities grew and then expanded even more as the United States became increasingly urban. New ideas and philosophies developed in the late 1800s, strongly influencing thought and behavior in the twentieth century. The winds of change also affected Mennonite churches as they sought to deal properly with the new ideas.

The Golden Door

The "New Immigration." The "old immigration" included people who had come to America between 1776 and the 1880s, mainly from western and northern Europe. By the 1890s, a new wave of immigrants was flooding into the United States. Most of these people came from eastern and southern Europe. This was the "new immigration," and it lasted until the 1920s.

One reason for this flood of newcomers was the many opportunities in America. Hundreds of factory jobs were available, and dozens of trades, professions, and businesses were also open. In addition, immigrants were attracted by the prospects of education, land ownership, freedom of worship, and a democratic society.

These opportunities stood in sharp contrast to conditions in the immigrants' home countries. Overcrowding in Europe meant less land to farm, and this along with lower prices for farm products meant that farming no longer provided an adequate living. Religious persecution, wars, and compulsory military service caused other people to flee. For example, thousands of Russian Mennonites came to North America in the 1870s when they no longer received exemption from military service. And persecution in Russia brought almost 3 million Jews to the United

Left: Emigrants waiting to leave Europe. ***Right:*** These immigrants are traveling in the steerage, which is the lowest, dirtiest place on a ship. Many could not afford anything better. They needed to carry their own food, bedding, and other necessities for the journey.

States between 1880 and 1914.

The majority of "new immigrants" arrived in New York City, where they gazed in wonder at the Statue of Liberty as they sailed into the New York harbor. Then they went to Ellis Island, where they were examined by doctors and questioned by officials. Having been accepted, most of the immigrants settled in cities because they could not afford land and because factories in the city offered employment. Many newcomers found homes in sections of cities with names like Little Italy or Chinatown, where they lived with others from their native country.

Opposition From Americans. Some Americans disliked the immigrants and considered them inferior (especially those from Asia). They were afraid the newcomers with

The Statue of Liberty. Raising her torch over the New York harbor, the Statue of Liberty has become a symbol of freedom around the world. Entitled "Liberty Enlightening the World," the statue was completed in 1886 and presented to the United States as a gift from the French people. The statue stands on a pedestal and reaches a height of 305 feet (93 m) above ground level. Designed by Frédéric Bartholdi, the Statue of Liberty has a copper skin supported by a framework that combines flexibility with firmness.

President Grover Cleveland dedicated the Statue of Liberty on October 28, 1886. One hundred years later, it was extensively remodeled and then rededicated by President Ronald Reagan on July 3–6, 1986. This statue has become a symbol of hope for millions of immigrants. In 1883, the poet Emma Lazarus wrote about the statue in a poem entitled "The New Colossus," and the poem was later placed on a plaque at its base. Some of its lines are as follows: " 'Give me your tired, your poor, / Your huddled masses yearning to breathe free, / The wretched refuse of your teeming shore. / Send these, the homeless, tempest-tost to me. / I lift my lamp beside the golden door!' "

Ellis Island. Ellis Island was established by the federal government in 1892 to handle the vast flow of immigrants into New York. The facility was designed to process up to five thousand people per day, but on some days as many as ten thousand passed through! In all, more than sixteen million people entered the United States there.

The officials at Ellis Island were responsible to decide whether immigrants could legally enter the United States. Doctors examined each immigrant, and marked the immigrants' coats with chalk if they had a physical problem. Other officials questioned the immigrants about their work skills and finances. People were not admitted if they were criminals, sick, or insane, or if they were likely to become a "public charge." About 2 percent of all immigrants were sent back home. Sometimes a family would be separated because one or more family members were denied entry. Children as young as ten were sent back to Europe alone, and of course those sent back had nowhere to go. In desperation, some tried to swim ashore and drowned. A journalist described the immigrants' experience at Ellis Island as "the nearest earthly likeness to the final day of judgment, when we have to prove our fitness to enter heaven."

Ellis Island was closed as an immigration center in 1954. It was later restored, and in 1990 it opened as a museum.

Immigrants crowding the deck of the Atlantic liner SS *Patricia* in 1906.

Ellis Island, New York, in 1905.

Italian immigrant family at Ellis Island, about 1910.

The Statue of Liberty in 1886, the year of its dedication. It was designed by Frédéric A. Bartholdi (1834–1904) of France. Lady Liberty's right hand holds a torch symbolizing the light of liberty, and her left hand holds a tablet inscribed with the year 1776. Her crown has seven spikes to symbolize the light of liberty shining to the seven seas and seven continents. At her feet lies a broken chain to symbolize freedom from tyranny.

In this building on Ellis Island, immigrants were checked for fitness to enter the United States.

their strange ways would change the American way of life. Workers resented immigrants because they worked for low wages at nearly any job, and that tended to keep wages down for everyone.

Labor unions and other groups campaigned for laws restricting immigration. So Congress passed the Chinese Exclusion Act in 1882, which barred Chinese workers from entering the United States for ten years. This was one of the first laws designed to restrict immigration. Such a movement to limit immigration is called ***nativism***.

Contributions of Immigrants. Because of the thousands of immigrants, the United States became a great ***melting pot*** in which many different peoples mingled together. Immigrants brought a great diversity of culture in language, food, art, and music. They contributed their labor by taking jobs in factories, by working in mines, and by farming the prairies. They and their children sometimes became noted leaders in politics, business, science, and education. Thus the immigrants helped in many ways to build America.

Elevated train in New York City. Notice also the horse-drawn trolley at the street level. These forms of transportation contributed to city expansion by making it possible for people in the suburbs to work in the city.

The Rise of the City

Growth of Cities. The population of American cities rose tremendously in the latter 1800s. Between 1880 and 1900, Chicago tripled its size and grew to over 1.5 million people; and New York City expanded from under 2 million to almost 3.5 million people. Other large cities had similar increases.

One reason for this explosive growth was immigration. Also, many factories were located in cities, and provided work for people from far and near. Another reason was good transportation, especially railroads. Towns located on rail lines usually grew more rapidly than others. Growth was especially fast in a city like Chicago, since it provided a link between railroads and ships.

New building techniques allowed cities to grow even more. The height of buildings had earlier been limited because thick walls of masonry were needed to support their weight. But in the latter 1800s, engineers began to build soaring skyscrapers with steel skeletons

Ten Largest U.S. Cities in 1900	Population
New York City	3,437,202
Chicago	1,698,575
Philadelphia	1,293,697
St. Louis	575,238
Boston	560,892
Baltimore	508,957
Cleveland	381,768
Buffalo	352,387
San Francisco	342,782
Cincinnati	325,902

Source: 1996 World Almanac

The Brooklyn Bridge was labeled the "eighth wonder of the world" when it first opened in 1883. At that time, it was the longest suspension bridge in the world. The Brooklyn Bridge is still in use today.

Building skyscrapers in New York City, about 1895. These tall buildings with steel skeletons allowed cities to expand upward to great heights.

and thin walls serving merely as a skin. The first skyscraper was completed in Chicago in 1885. These tall buildings enabled cities to expand upward as well as outward.

City Problems. The growth of cities brought many problems. One of them was poor water—sometimes a result of getting water from the same river where the city sewage was dumped! Another problem was poor sanitation, with garbage piling up on the streets and sewage running in the gutters. These unsanitary conditions contributed to epidemics of tuberculosis, typhoid fever, and other diseases.

Still another threat was fire, since many buildings were made of wood. When a fire raged out of control, it sometimes destroyed a large part of a city because fire-fighting equipment was too primitive to cope with it. By 1900, some cities had fire departments with

Scene at the Randolph Street Bridge during the Great Chicago Fire of 1871. This picture illustrates the plague that fire can be in a large city of wooden buildings.

The Great Chicago Fire. One of the most memorable city fires is the Great Chicago Fire of October 8, 1871. According to a popular story, it started when a cow owned by a Mrs. O'Leary kicked over a lantern in her barn. Whether or not this is true is uncertain. The fire fanned out rapidly because of dry conditions and the many wooden buildings. It consumed eighteen thousand buildings worth $200 million over an area of 4 square miles (10 km^2). Three hundred people perished, and ninety thousand were left homeless.

professional firemen rather than volunteers.

Slums were one of the worst aspects of cities. Thousands of slum dwellers lived together in run-down buildings that often had no plumbing, no heat, poor lighting, and inadequate ventilation. Many families lived in tenements—buildings that stood perhaps five stories high, were several hundred feet long, and housed five hundred or more people. Some slums had over fifty-seven thousand people in an area of forty-five city blocks—over three hundred thousand per square mile!

Crime thrived in the cities. Gambling, drinking, and other vices abounded. It was common for thieves to "break through and steal," and murders were frequent. Corruption prevailed as city officials accepted bribes for ignoring criminal activity or for granting special favors to businesses. These officials were usually part of the city's ***political machine***—an organized group controlled by a powerful "boss" who often used dishonest

The crowded, filthy conditions of tenements contributed to crime and violence in large cities. This photograph, entitled "Bandits' Roost," was taken by Jacob Riis. It pictures tenements in New York City in about 1888.

An early "fire engine" races to a fire in New York City. Steam-powered pumps were a great improvement over the hand pumps and bucket brigades that were used formerly.

means to gain his ends. Political machines and their bosses controlled New York, Philadelphia, Boston, Chicago, and other cities.

Reform Campaigns. Reformers tried to help the poor people in large cities. In 1889, **Jane Addams** established a settlement house named Hull House in the slums of Chicago. Here she tried to help the poor by giving classes in things such as English, cooking, and sewing, and by providing medical and dental services for children. Soon other settlement houses sprang up in cities across the land.

Reformers attacked liquor and alcoholism because they blamed strong drink for poverty and crime. Many women joined a group called the Woman's Christian Temperance Union, founded in 1874 to fight the saloons and reduce political corruption.

These reform movements were promoted largely by women. They crusaded for the things already mentioned, as well as for women's right to vote and to receive the same pay as men. Susan B. Anthony and Elizabeth Stanton were two prominent leaders of the campaign for women's rights. In contrast to such ideas, the Bible teaches that women are to be "keepers at home" (Titus 2:5) and to be "subject . . . to their own husbands" (Ephesians 5:24).

Intellectual and Religious Change

New Philosophies. New ideas gradually took over as people rejected God's Word in favor of human reasoning. Two of the new philosophies were ***Darwinism*** and ***socialism***. In 1859, Charles Darwin published *The Origin of Species*, which promoted the theory of evolution. Darwin wrote that all living things had a natural origin (rather than being created by God) and that they gradually evolved into the species existing today. Darwinism gained wide acceptance in the United States, especially among educators.

Socialism had its roots in the ideas of Karl Marx of Germany. Socialists wanted to establish a classless society in which the government owned and controlled business production and the distribution of wealth. In the late 1800s, influential men wrote books that caused socialism to gain popularity in America.

Revivalism. The latter 1800s brought a third religious "great awakening" to America. This ***revivalism*** placed more emphasis on conversion than on discipleship, and its songs focused on religious experiences and feelings rather than on obedience and cross-bearing.

Dwight L. Moody became the foremost evangelist of this movement. He took his crusade to the cities, where multitudes were attracted by his sermons and the songs of his

Dwight L. Moody preaching in New York in 1876. Moody conducted great revivals in the United States and England.

Dwight L. Moody. Dwight Lyman Moody (1837–99) was born in East Northfield, Massachusetts, and was converted through a Sunday school teacher. He became a successful shoe salesman in Chicago and also established a mission Sunday school there. Moody gave up business in 1860 and became active in preaching, tract distribution, and prayer meetings. The Chicago fire of 1871 destroyed his home and his church.

In 1873, Moody and Ira D. Sankey sailed for England and conducted two years of revivals there. Returning to the United States, Moody held revivals from 1875 to 1878. It is thought that he traveled over 1,000,000 miles (1,609,300 km) and reached as many as 100 million people in his career. Moody also established two boarding schools in Northfield, Massachusetts, and the organizations that later became Moody Bible Institute and Moody Press.

Moody did much to popularize Christianity. He believed that all men are sinners by nature and need the blood of Christ for salvation. He was a great storyteller and often told Bible stories in everyday language. Moody made numerous pithy statements like the following: "God never made a promise that was too good to be true." "It is better to be a little too strict than too liberal." "The devil tempts most men, but a lazy man tempts the devil." He was a firm believer in the Bible, for "if it is not in the Bible, it is not worth believing. But if it is in the Bible, there can be no question about believing it." However, Moody did not uphold the Bible doctrines of nonresistance and outward nonconformity to the world.

song leader, Ira D. Sankey. Thousands in England and America heard Moody's preaching in the 1870s and the 1880s, and Protestant churches added millions to their membership.

A Social Gospel. A Protestant movement known as the ***social gospel*** emerged in the late 1800s. This was an effort to improve present social conditions instead of urging people to prepare for future bliss in heaven. Its adherents attacked evils such as saloons, poverty, and corrupt government. **Charles Sheldon** wrote the book *In His Steps* to promote the social gospel. His book became immensely popular, and millions of copies were sold.

Left: John F. Funk (1835–1930) contributed greatly to Mennonite publishing and also promoted Sunday schools, revival meetings, and mission work. ***Right:*** John S. Coffman (1848–1899) helped to bring revival meetings into the Mennonite Church, and he promoted Mennonite publishing.

Changes in the Mennonite Church

For decades the Mennonite Church had rejected new things such as Sunday school, evangelistic meetings, and prayer meetings. (See Chapter 13.) Because these innovations began in churches that did not practice nonconformity and nonresistance, the Mennonites were afraid their church would go in the wrong direction if they accepted these things. They wanted to be sure changes were good before they accepted them.

But in the late 1800s, the Mennonite Church began accepting some of the practices that had come into Protestant churches in the 1820s and 1830s. These included Sunday schools, mission work, and evangelistic meetings. Other changes included use of the English language, four-part singing, and new patterns of organization. Often the changes began in the Midwest and spread to the East.

Sunday School. Mennonites had earlier resisted Sunday school because it was often conducted by laymen working independently of any church. The lessons were produced by non-Mennonite writers, and they were in English, whereas Mennonite services were in German. Also, different church groups often mingled together in the "Union" Sunday schools.

However, Sunday school was gradually accepted after the first permanent Mennonite Sunday school began in 1863. This was partly because leaders were concerned that young people were being lost to the Mennonite Church through other Sunday schools. The new Sunday schools were taught in the Mennonite meetinghouse and with the approval of the church. By the 1870s, Mennonites were producing some of their own Sunday school materials through the publishing work of John F. Funk. By 1890, Sunday school was well established in many Mennonite congregations.

Revivalism. Revivalism came to the Mennonite Church primarily through the work of **John S. Coffman,** who was influenced by

Mennonite Publishing Company, Elkhart, Indiana. This business was started by John F. Funk and his brother in 1867, and in 1908 it was sold to the Mennonite Publishing House in Scottdale, Pennsylvania.

Left: Elkhart Institute, founded in 1894 at Elkhart, Indiana. In 1903, it was moved to Goshen and renamed Goshen College. ***Right:*** The Mennonite Home Mission, in Chicago, Illinois, was started by Menno S. Steiner in 1893 in the building shown. The workers held Gospel services and provided medical care. Other activities included Sunday school, children's meetings, kindergarten, sewing school, clothing distribution, and home visitation.

Moody's revivals. Coffman held "protracted meetings" in which he preached evangelistic sermons nightly for a week and invited listeners to respond for salvation. This evangelist traveled widely, holding revivals in many congregations from 1881 to 1899. He even wrote the song "O Weary Wanderer" to use as an invitation hymn. Coffman's work helped to bring many young people into the church and to make "protracted meetings" acceptable to Mennonites.

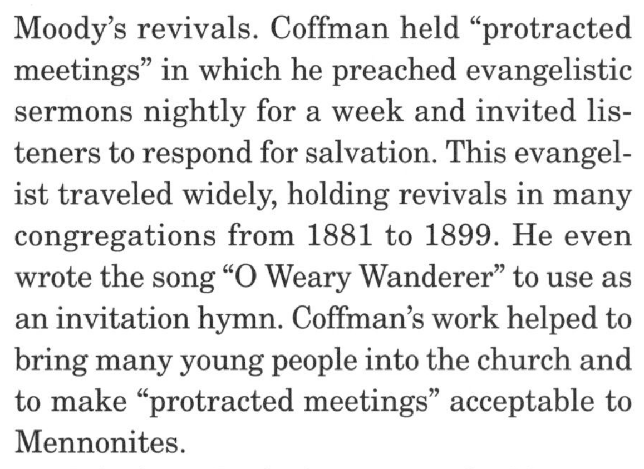

Missions. In the late 1890s, the Mennonite Church began mission work as well. The first Mennonite city mission began in Chicago in 1893. Local or "home" missions developed in the 1890s; and in 1896, the Lancaster County Sunday School Mission was established to open new outreaches in the area of Lancaster, Pennsylvania. The first foreign mission opened in 1899 with a mission in India.

New Organizations. The Mennonite Church formed a number of new organizations in the latter 1800s. At Elkhart, Indiana, church leaders organized a mission board that eventually became the Mennonite Board of Missions and Charities. The Mennonite General Conference held its first biannual meeting in 1898, with bishops from various conferences working together to direct the church. And in 1895, the Elkhart Institute at Elkhart, Indiana, became the first Mennonite institution of higher education. Later it became Goshen College.

These changes sent shock waves through the Mennonite Church. They caused schisms that became known as Old Order divisions because some people wanted to keep the old order of things. One Old Order group was led by Jacob Wisler of Indiana, who started a new group in 1872. In Lancaster County, Pennsylvania, bishop Jonas Martin led an Old Order group that began in 1893. The issues included preaching in the English language, Sunday school, and other matters of smaller importance.

The changes in the church had some positive effects. Mennonite publishing work produced periodicals and books such as Daniel Kauffman's *Manual of Bible Doctrine*, which helped to unify and strengthen the church.

Young people gained more Bible knowledge, and more young people became Christians and joined the church before marriage. The church maintained a higher level of spiritual life and morality, especially through teaching against tobacco and alcohol. Mission work developed into a more active outreach to the world. Many of these changes still benefit the church today.

Daniel Kauffman (1865–1944) at his typewriter circa 1913. He served as editor of the *Gospel Herald* for many years but is best known for his work *Doctrines of the Bible*.

Focus for Thought

8. a. What things in the United States attracted a flood of immigrants?
   b. In what ways did the United States benefit from immigrants?
9. Give three reasons for the rapid population growth of American cities.
10. What improvements did reformers try to make in large cities?
11. What were two new ideas that brought changes to the thinking of American people in the late 1800s?
12. Describe the revivalism and the social gospel of the latter 1800s.
13. Give at least three changes that took place in the Mennonite Church during this period.

3. CHANGE IN POLITICS

From 1877 to 1897, the Democratic and Republican political parties alternated in their control of the presidency and of Congress. The White House was occupied by a series of relatively weak presidents, none of whom served two consecutive terms. By the 1890s, many rural people became alienated from the two major parties and formed a new Populist Party with radically new ideas.

"For promotion cometh neither from the east, nor from the west, nor from the south. But God is the judge: he putteth down one, and setteth up another" (Psalm 75:6, 7).

The Political Issues

Three major political issues in the late 1800s were civil service reform, tariffs, and business regulation. Civil service reform had to do with the way government employees were appointed. Since the days of Jackson, this had been done by the spoils system: the party that won the presidency filled government offices with its supporters. Political machines in cities and states operated in the same way—bosses handed out offices to their supporters. But the spoils system involved much corruption; and besides, it filled many government offices with men poorly qualified for them.

Some men in both parties wanted to replace the spoils system with a civil service merit system. Their goal was to appoint government workers on the basis of what they could do rather than whom they supported.

High tariffs were still in place to protect manufacturers from competition by taxing imports, even though the manufacturers were no longer "infants" that needed protection. Many Democrats favored lower tariffs, while Republicans generally supported higher tariffs. Supporters argued that high tariffs encourage new industries and help to make America self-sufficient. Opponents argued that tariffs raise prices and protect inefficient businesses, thus hurting American consumers.

As corporations grew, some people began thinking the federal government should regulate nationwide businesses such as railroads. These people were afraid the giant trusts would become monopolies that would control the markets and raise prices while cheating their workers and giving poor service. As a result, the government began passing laws by 1890 to regulate business operations.

Left: Rutherford B. Hayes (1822–1893) was the nineteenth president of the United States. He served from 1877 to 1881 and was a Republican. ***Right:*** James A. Garfield (1831–1881) was the twentieth president of the United States. He served as president for only a few months in 1881 and was a Republican.

The Presidents

Rutherford B. Hayes. Rutherford B. Hayes had come into office through a disputed election (see Chapter 17). Hayes pushed for civil service reform, but he made little progress against the spoils system. Because of corruption, Hayes removed Chester A. Arthur from his position as collector of the New York customhouse. (That customhouse collected most tariffs, since most imports came into the United States through New York.) Hayes decided not to run again for the presidency when his term was over.

James A. Garfield. Republican James A. Garfield, with Chester A. Arthur as his vice president, was elected in 1880. But on July 2, 1881, a man shot Garfield from behind as he waited at a Washington train station. The assassin, Charles Guiteau, was bitter because he had been turned down for a government job. (He was later hanged.) Garfield calmly fought death for two months, but he died on September 19.

Chester A. Arthur. As the vice president in 1881, Arthur became president upon the death of Garfield. Arthur promoted civil service reform, and in 1883 Congress established the United States Civil Service Commission of three men. They were to give examinations to prospective government employees and select the ones best qualified for the job. The new law established the merit system for about 10 percent of government jobs, but it allowed the president to expand the number of jobs subject to the merit system. Arthur served only one term because the Republicans did not renominate him in 1884.

Grover Cleveland (first term). After a bitter campaign in 1884, the Democrats

Left: Chester A. Arthur (1829–1886) was the twenty-first president of the United States. He served from 1881 to 1885 and was a Republican. ***Right:*** Grover Cleveland (1837–1908) was the twenty-second and twenty-fourth president of the United States. He served as a Democrat from 1885 to 1889 and again from 1893 to 1897. This photograph shows Cleveland during his second administration.

regained the White House for the first time since 1856. The winner was Grover Cleveland, a former governor of New York. Cleveland promoted civil service reform and opposed the growth of government spending. In 1887, Cleveland signed the Interstate Commerce Act, which established the Interstate Commerce Commission (ICC) to regulate railroads and interstate transportation.

Cleveland strongly promoted lower tariffs; in fact, he devoted his entire State of the Union message in 1887 to this subject. But the Republicans opposed lower tariffs, so this became a major issue in the election of 1888—which Cleveland lost.

Left: Benjamin Harrison (1833–1901) was the twenty-third president of the United States. He served from 1889 to 1893 and was a Republican. ***Right:*** William McKinley (1843–1901) was the twenty-fifth president of the United States. He served from 1897 to 1901 and was a Republican.

Interesting Facts About Five Presidents

- **Rutherford B. Hayes.** During his term in office, Hayes had the first telephone installed in the White House. His wife was known as "Lemonade Lucy" because she refused to serve alcoholic beverages in the White House.
- **James A. Garfield.** This man was the last of seven presidents born in a log cabin.
- **Chester A. Arthur.** He was known as "Elegant Arthur" because of his fancy clothing. At one time he owned eighty pairs of trousers!
- **Grover Cleveland.** Cleveland was noted for his honesty. As president, he did what he thought was right, not just what was convenient. He vetoed over four hundred bills in his first term—more than double all the vetoes of all the presidents before him. Cleveland took a wife in 1886, thus becoming the only president to be married in the White House.
- **Benjamin Harrison.** Grandson of William Henry Harrison, he had campaigned under the slogan "Grandfather's hat fits Ben." Electric lights were installed in the White House during his term in office.

Benjamin Harrison. Benjamin Harrison took a cautious, moderate approach to the presidency. He came to office with a Republican majority in both houses of Congress. This was the "Billion Dollar Congress," the first to spend $1 billion in a single peacetime session. Congress did this because of an unusual problem—government revenues exceeded expenditures.

In 1890, this Congress passed the Sherman Antitrust Act, which allowed the government to attack businesses that it considered monopolies. Another act, the McKinley Tariff Act, raised tariffs to yet higher levels. But the McKinley Tariff Act was unpopular because it raised prices, and it caused a rising tide of discontent in some parts of the nation. Farmers in the South and West banded together and formed the Populist Party, based on the Farmers' Alliances.

Fiery, radical speakers promoted socialistic ideas, calling for an income tax and for government ownership of railroad, telegraph, and telephone systems. They promoted new laws that would favor organized labor by restricting immigration and setting shorter working

Coxey's Army on the way to Washington, D.C., in 1894. Numbering about 500, these unemployed men hoped to pressure the government into providing jobs through a road-building program.

hours. They agitated for a more democratic government with more control by the people. It was a farmers' rebellion.

Grover Cleveland (second term). Even though the Populist Party captured over 1 million votes in 1892, Grover Cleveland regained the presidency. He thus became the only president to serve two nonconsecutive terms. But his second term was beset by difficulties. Only two months after Cleveland took office, the country fell into a deep depression known as the Panic of 1893. By the year's end, five hundred banks had failed and fifteen thousand businesses had closed. This caused 3 to 4 million workers to be out of jobs by 1894.

That year a ragtag group of hungry, unemployed men, called Coxey's Army, arrived in Washington, D.C. They had come to protest financial conditions and call for government measures of relief. But the army disbanded when police arrested the leader, Jacob Coxey, for trespassing on the Capitol lawn. Many strikes occurred in the nation, such as the Pullman Strike of 1894. Cleveland wanted to lower tariffs, and Congress passed a bill to that effect; but the president did not like it, because it fell far short of his goal. Cleveland's second term was not very successful.

The Election of 1896. The Democrats nominated young **William Jennings Bryan** as their presidential candidate in 1896. The Populists also supported Bryan, bringing the Democrats and Populists together. Bryan, a stirring orator, traveled over 18,000 miles (28,967 km) and made over six hundred speeches in his campaign across the country.

One of the main issues at this time was "free silver"; that is, the free (unlimited) coining of silver dollars on the basis that 16 troy ounces (497.6 g) of silver was equal to 1 troy

William Jennings Bryan (1860–1925), known as "the Commoner," was a supporter of free silver. Bryan was the Democratic nominee for the presidency in 1896, 1900, and 1908; but he lost each time.

ounce (31.1 g) of gold. Democrats and Populists supported free silver because they thought a larger money supply would help the economy. But this was at a time when large amounts of silver were coming from mines in the West. It was the oversupply of this silver that contributed to the Panic of 1893.

The Republicans nominated **William McKinley** of Ohio, who opposed free silver and favored the gold standard for money. He carried on a "front-porch" campaign in which he met groups that traveled to his home in Canton to hear the speeches he made from his front porch.

When the election was over, McKinley had won with a majority of over six hundred thousand popular votes. The Populists all but disappeared after that. Republicans occupied the White House from 1897 to 1933, with the exception of Woodrow Wilson, who served two terms as a Democrat from 1913 to 1921.

Focus for Thought

14. a. What problems resulted from the spoils system that had long been used in government?
    b. What is meant by a civil service merit system?
15. a. Why did some people favor high tariffs?
    b. Why did others want to reduce tariffs?
16. Why did some people think that railroads and other giant businesses should be regulated by the federal government?
17. What things did the Populist Party promote?
18. What things made President Cleveland's second term difficult?

Historical Highlights

A. Matching: People

a. Alexander Graham Bell
b. Andrew Carnegie
c. Charles Sheldon
d. Dwight L. Moody
e. George Washington Carver
f. Jane Addams
g. John D. Rockefeller
h. John S. Coffman
i. Luther Burbank
j. Thomas A. Edison
k. William Jennings Bryan

1. Man who wrote *In His Steps* to promote the social gospel.
2. Democrat who supported free silver in the 1896 presidential election.
3. Famous evangelist who preached in America and England.
4. Man who started revival meetings in the Mennonite Church.
5. Reformer who founded the Hull House in Chicago.
6. Man whose steel company made the United States a leading steel producer.
7. Inventor of the electric light bulb and many other electrical devices.
8. Man who founded Standard Oil as the first trust.
9. Men who introduced new uses or varieties of plants (two names).
10. Inventor of the telephone.

B. Matching: Presidents

Each choice should be used twice.

a. Rutherford B. Hayes
b. James A. Garfield
c. Chester A. Arthur
d. Grover Cleveland
e. Benjamin Harrison
f. William McKinley

1. In office when the Sherman Antitrust Act and the McKinley Tariff Act were passed.
2. In office for only a few months before being assassinated.
3. Came into office through a disputed election.
4. Only president who served two nonconsecutive terms.
5. Was opposed by William Jennings Bryan and the Populist Party in 1896.
6. Became president in 1881 when the previous president was assassinated.
7. In office during the Panic of 1893.
8. Removed the collector of the New York Custom House from office.
9. Had Chester A. Arthur for his vice president.
10. In office at the time of the "Billion Dollar Congress."
11. In office when the Civil Service Commission was established.
12. Supported the gold standard and conducted a "front-porch" campaign.

C. Matching: Terms 1

a. collective bargaining
b. cooperative
c. corporation
d. dividends
e. free enterprise
f. labor union
g. mass production
h. monopoly
i. patent
j. share of stock
k. strike
l. supply and demand
m. trust

1. Exclusive right to make and sell an invention.
2. Organization of workers agreeing to require certain things of employers.
3. Large business owned by many people.
4. Related businesses combined into one large organization.
5. Company that has no competition because it controls a certain market.
6. Scarce product + high demand = high price; abundant product + low demand = low price.
7. Refusal to work until labor demands are met.
8. Negotiation of union leaders with employers for wages and working hours.
9. System that includes private ownership of property, free markets, and a minimum of government regulation.
10. Profits that corporations pay to stockholders.
11. One portion of a corporation, which is purchased by an investor.
12. System for making large numbers of products by using interchangeable parts and assembly lines.
13. Group of people who purchase things in large quantities to obtain lower prices.

D. Matching: Terms 2

a. Civil Service Commission
b. Darwinism
c. Interstate Commerce Act
d. McKinley Tariff Act
e. melting pot
f. nativism
g. "new immigration"
h. political machine
i. Populist Party
j. revivalism
k. Sherman Antitrust Act
l. social gospel
m. socialism

1. Organized group controlled by a powerful "boss."
2. Theory that living things had a natural origin and that they gradually evolved into the species existing today.
3. People from eastern and southern Europe who moved to the United States in the years 1890 to 1920.
4. Place where people of many different nationalities mingle together.
5. Movement to limit immigration.
6. Karl Marx's theory proposing a classless society and government ownership of businesses.
7. Religious movement emphasizing conversion more than discipleship.
8. Measure that raised taxes on imports and became unpopular for raising prices.
9. Group that developed from Farmers' Alliances and promoted radical changes.
10. Religious movement designed to improve present social conditions.
11. Measure that established the Interstate Commerce Commission to regulate railroads.
12. Group that checked the qualifications of prospective government employees.
13. Measure allowing the government to attack businesses that it considered monopolies.

E. Deeper Discussion

1. Why were new ways of selling necessary during the Industrial Revolution of the late 1800s?
2. Read Ephesians 6:5–9 and Colossians 3:22–4:1, and answer the following questions.
   a. How is the worker ("servant") to serve his employer ("master")? Be specific, and give both negative and positive ways.
   b. How is the employer to treat his workers? Why?
3. Discuss the economic problems caused by labor unions.
4. How did the law of supply and demand affect farmers?
5. Does immigration hinder the nation, as nativists say, or does it benefit the nation?
6. a. How does the social gospel fall short of true Christianity?
   b. How should Christians respond to the social gospel?

F. Chronology and Geography

From memory, list the presidents from Washington through McKinley, along with the dates of their terms in office. Remember that an elected president's term begins in the year after the election.

On September 26, 1913, the tugboat *Gatún* made the first trial passage through the Gatún Locks in the Panama Canal. Here the *Gatún* is going through the first of three locks while thousands of people witness the historic occasion.

21 World Power

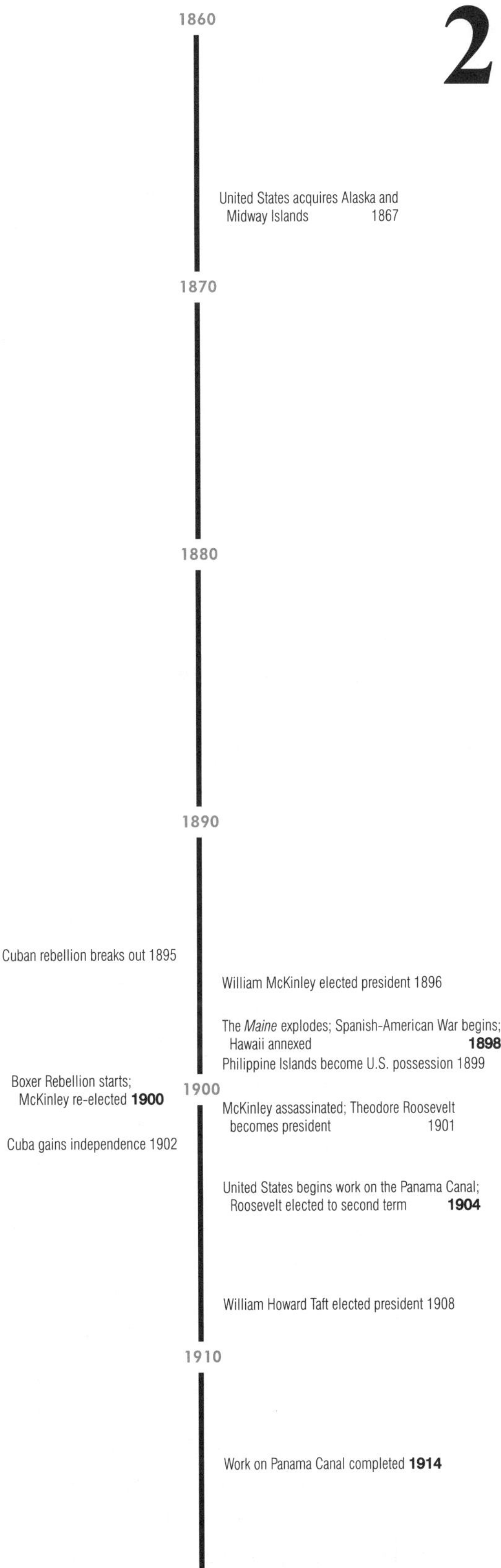

1. EXPANSIONISM AND THE SPANISH-AMERICAN WAR
    - From Isolationism to Imperialism
    - The Story of Hawaii
    - The Spanish-American War
2. THE OPEN DOOR IN THE FAR EAST
    - Foreign Influence in China
    - The Open Door Policy
    - Relations With Japan
3. THE "BIG STICK" IN LATIN AMERICA
    - Events After the Spanish-American War
    - The Panama Canal
    - Dealings With Other Latin American Nations

"The LORD maketh poor, and maketh rich: he bringeth low, and lifteth up."

1 Samuel 2:7

World Power

Focus for Reading

Before the Civil War, the United States had grown from a string of states along the Atlantic to a nation that spanned North America. Then for a generation after the war, Americans concentrated on developing their nation and its resources while giving little attention to expansionist ideas. But by the 1890s, a new generation had risen that wanted to gain possession of land outside North America. By treaty, by purchase, and by conquest, the United States obtained new lands and pushed its way onto the world scene as a major power. Three sections in this chapter tell the story of that expansion and its consequences.

1. Expansionism and the Spanish-American War
2. The Open Door in the Far East
3. The "Big Stick" in Latin America

1. EXPANSIONISM AND THE SPANISH-AMERICAN WAR

Securely isolated from world turmoil by two great oceans, the United States avoided entanglements with other nations for many years. But by 1900, Americans had developed new ambitions that changed this policy. One incident was the Spanish-American War, which the Americans won in less than four months but which wrought some great changes. The United States emerged from this war as a world power.

From Isolationism to Imperialism

Isolation. For thirty years after the purchase of Alaska in 1867, the United States developed the land it already had instead of gaining more territory. Americans were busy with Reconstruction, western expansion, Indian wars, and the growth of industries and cities. Many of them wanted to isolate the United States and have little to do with foreign nations, especially European nations. This concept is called ***isolationism***. Supporters of the idea believed that the United States should not expand to any territory beyond its own continent.

This does not mean that the United States never took interest in other lands. Besides Alaska, for example, the United States in 1867 also acquired the Midway Islands in the Pacific. In 1889, the United States, Great Britain, and Germany agreed to work together to protect the Samoa Islands. The part of these islands that belonged to the United States became American Samoa in 1900.

Expansion. A new spirit affected many Americans in the 1890s. With the frontier vanishing in the West, these people clamored for possessions overseas, for greater military might, for world power, and even for war. They embraced ***imperialism*** (an ambition for empire building), and they looked abroad for other lands to add to their territory.

The expansionists favored imperialism for a number of reasons. They were of a new generation that had not experienced the Civil War. These Americans saw that more foreign trade could boost business production and provide markets for American goods. They thought the United States should civilize and uplift the people they considered primitive and heathen. They wanted the United States to become a world power by building a strong merchant fleet and navy. To support these fleets, the United States would need island bases where ships could refuel and from which the United States could project its naval might.

Both isolationism and imperialism belong to the system of this world. Christian people do not isolate themselves and seek their own interests; neither do they have a covetous spirit that seeks possessions and power.

The Story of Hawaii

Growth of Interest in Hawaii. In the 1800s, the United States became actively interested in Hawaii, a group of Pacific islands about 2,000 miles (3,219 km) west of the United States. American ships had begun stopping at Hawaii in the 1780s for water and supplies as they crossed the sea in trading with China. A number of Americans settled in Hawaii by the 1820s, and their descendants became wealthy and powerful as they managed great sugar plantations.

The United States recognized that Hawaii was important for trade and for its location in the Pacific. In 1875, the United States and Hawaii signed a treaty that permitted Hawaiian sugar to be sold to the United States without a tariff. This led to a large increase of sugar exports from Hawaii to the United States, and great prosperity for the plantation owners.

A ceremony for the annexation of Hawaii was held on August 12, 1898. Hawaii became a United States possession on this date, and about two years later it became a territory with a governor.

Annexation of Hawaii. Because of various developments in the 1890s, planters in Hawaii requested annexation to the United States. After President McKinley expressed support for the idea, Congress annexed Hawaii in 1898. It was organized as a territory of the United States in 1900; and in 1959, Hawaii became the fiftieth state of the Union.

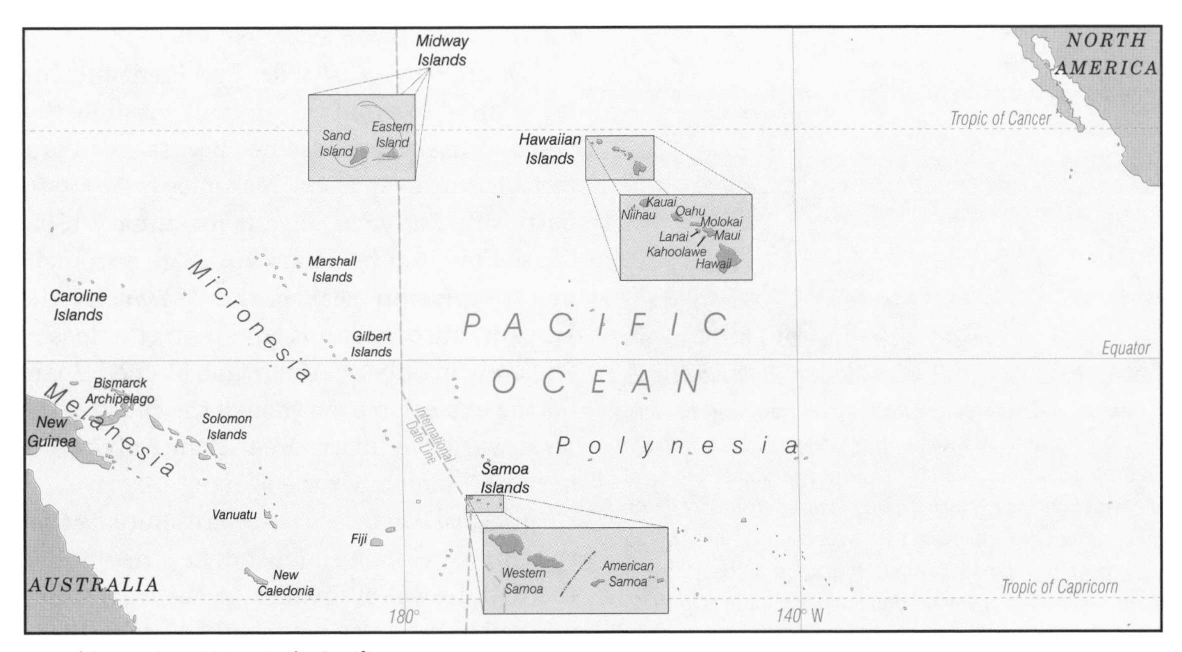

United States Acquisitions in the Pacific

863,956
WORLDS CIRCULATED YESTERDAY
The World.
"Circulation Books Open to All."
VOL. XXXVIII. NO. 13,336.
NEW YORK, THURSDAY, FEBRUARY 17, 1898.

MAINE EXPLOSION CAUSED BY BOMB OR TORPEDO?

Capt. Sigsbee and Consul-General Lee Are in Doubt---The World Has Sent a Special Tug, With Submarine Divers, to Havana to Find Out---Lee Asks for an Immediate Court of Inquiry---260 Men Dead.

IN A SUPPRESSED DESPATCH TO THE STATE DEPARTMENT, THE CAPTAIN SAYS THE ACCIDENT WAS MADE POSSIBLE BY AN ENEMY.

Dr. E. C. Pendleton, Just Arrived from Havana, Says He Overheard Talk There of a Plot to Blow Up the Ship--Zalinski, the Dynamite Expert, and Other Experts Report to The World that the Wreck Was Not Accidental---Washington Officials Ready for Vigorous Action if Spanish Responsibility Can Be Shown---Divers to Be Sent Down to Make Careful Examinations.

Top: USS *Maine* entering the Havana harbor in January 1898. The battleship was sent to protect Americans from harm in riots. **Middle:** Sensational newspaper headlines proclaim the news about the explosion of the *Maine* in February 1898. Americans began clamoring for war with Spain, saying "Remember the Maine!" **Bottom:** Wreckage of the *Maine* in the Havana harbor. The wreckage remained there until 1912, when it was taken out to sea and sunk.

The Spanish-American War

Revolt in Cuba. Americans had long wanted to possess Cuba, an island only 90 miles (145 km) from Florida. But Spain maintained its harsh rule over the island, even though the people made a number of fruitless attempts to gain independence. Then in 1895, a revolution broke out that directly affected the United States. American businessmen had invested millions of dollars in Cuban mines and plantations, and now the revolt threatened their investments as parts of Cuba were laid waste. Also, American citizens in Cuba were endangered and mistreated.

Then the Spanish sent Valeriano Weyler to be governor-general in Cuba. The ruthless Weyler set out to crush the rebellion by destroying eastern Cuba. He moved children and old people into fenced cities, where he left them to die without enough food or proper sanitation.

When these stories appeared in United States newspapers, Americans were filled with wrath against Spain and sympathy for the Cubans. Further, Americans did not like a Spanish colony so near their borders. They remembered their own revolution a century before, and they felt sorry for the oppressed Cubans. Warmongers stirred up popular feeling in favor of war with Spain.

Declaration of War. President McKinley wanted to avoid war if at all possible. But when military force seemed necessary to protect Americans in Cuba, McKinley ordered the battleship *Maine* to Havana in January 1898. On the night of February 15, 1898, a tremendous explosion rocked the *Maine* in the Havana harbor, and it sank with the loss of 260 crew members. Americans blamed Spain for the explosion even though the cause of the blast was never discovered. Their rallying cry became "Remember the *Maine*!"

In April, Congress passed resolutions that recognized Cuban independence, demanded the withdrawal of Spanish troops from Cuba, and authorized the president to use military force to end the Cuban conflict. The Spanish were willing to meet some of these demands, but they would not give Cuba its independence. Spain declared war on April 24, and the United States responded by declaring war on April 25. The Spanish-American War had begun.

War in the Philippines. Curiously, the first fighting of the war took place not in Cuba but on the Philippine Islands, which Spain had governed for centuries. Commodore **George Dewey** had earlier been ordered to attack the Spanish base in the Philippines if war started. So he promptly headed for Manila Bay, where a large Spanish fleet lay. His ships entered the harbor the evening of April 30.

Early on the morning of May 1, the Americans attacked the Spanish and destroyed most of their fleet without losing one man or ship of their own. Then Dewey blockaded Manila until August 1898, when the city was captured by Americans with the help of Filipino rebels led by Emilio Aguinaldo (ah gee NAHL doh). The victory over Spain in the Pacific was complete.

Capture of Cuba and Puerto Rico. In June 1898, a group of American forces landed near Santiago to attack the Spanish in Cuba. Their plan was to capture the high ridges around Santiago and then take command of the city. But many of the soldiers became sick with malaria and yellow fever; indeed, more died from disease than from battle in Cuba.

By July 1, the Americans had driven back the Spanish and taken San Juan Hill above Santiago. One charge was led by **Theodore Roosevelt**, whose group of volunteers was

American troops boarding ships at Tampa, Florida, for the voyage to Cuba. Lack of organization and limited rail service produced railcar jams that stretched inland for 50 miles (80 km).

In the Battle of Manila Bay on May 1, 1898, six ships under the command of Commodore George Dewey (1837–1917) defeated ten Spanish ships and then blockaded the Manila harbor.

Theodore Roosevelt and the Rough Riders made a charge that helped to win the Battle of San Juan Hill. Roosevelt is in the center, with glasses.

Surrender of Santiago. The Spanish general Toral surrendered Santiago, Cuba, to the American general Shafter on July 17, 1898.

President McKinley watches as the Spanish representative signs the peace treaty after the Spanish-American War. The Treaty of Paris was signed on December 10, 1898, and ratified by the United States Senate on February 6, 1899.

called the Rough Riders. This battle at San Juan Hill made Roosevelt a national hero. Meanwhile, the United States navy had trapped the Spanish fleet in the Santiago harbor. When the Spanish ships tried to escape, the American ships destroyed them. Santiago surrendered on July 17.

The United States also attacked the Spanish island of Puerto Rico, in the Caribbean Sea. Under General Nelson A. Miles, American troops captured the island with little resistance.

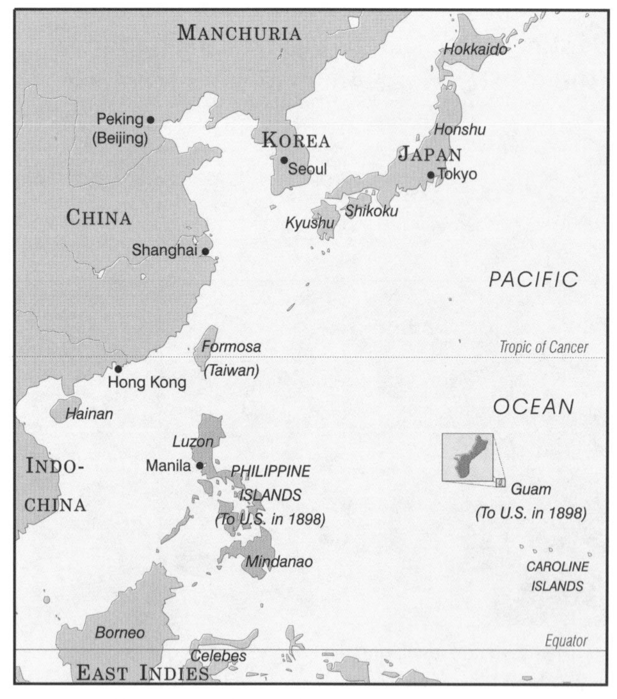

United States Acquisitions in the Pacific From the Spanish-American War

Conclusion and Effects of the War. On August 12, Spain agreed to stop fighting, grant independence to Cuba, and give Puerto Rico and a Spanish island in the Pacific Ocean to the United States. The fighting ended less than four months after the declaration of war.

The terms of the peace treaty were negotiated in Paris. Spain agreed to accept $20 million for the Philippines and to give the island of Guam to the Americans. This fulfilled its promise to give a Pacific island to the United States. The peace treaty was signed on December 10, 1898; and after a long debate between imperialists and anti-imperialists, the Senate ratified the treaty in February 1899. Now the Philippine Islands were a possession of the United States.

The Filipinos hoped to receive independence immediately, but the Americans did not think they were ready for it. So Emilio Aguinaldo and his rebels began fighting once more, this time against the United States. Some seventy thousand Americans went to battle against the Philippine guerrillas, and an estimated 600,000 Filipinos were killed in the next three years. Aguinaldo was finally

Mennonites in the Philippines. On January 7, 1982, four conservative Mennonite families arrived in the Philippines and began to work as missionaries at Dasmarinas, in the province of Cavite. Services were held in one of their homes at first, but in July 1983 a church building was erected. The work expanded in the following years; and by the year 2000, there were four places of worship: the original site at Dasmarinas, Lumban in Laguna, Calasiao in Pangasinan, and Sapang Palay in Bulacan.

Mennonites in Puerto Rico. A Mennonite mission began in Puerto Rico in 1943 when Mennonite conscientious objectors were invited to serve on that island during World War II. These men provided medical, educational, and agricultural services there. The Mennonite Board of Missions established a church and a hospital in Puerto Rico in 1947, and by 1978 there were eighteen Mennonite congregations on the island. However, there were very few conservative Mennonites in Puerto Rico by the year 2000.

captured in 1901. He took an oath of loyalty to the United States, and the conflict ended about a year later.

Americans did many things to help the Filipinos. They established a health bureau and sanitation programs. They founded schools and prepared teachers. They taught the Filipinos new farming methods, and they built roads, bridges, and irrigation systems. The United States purchased sugar, hemp, and other goods from the Philippines. Americans also tried to prepare the Filipinos for independence by helping them to take part in their own government. The Philippines finally became independent in 1946, after World War II.

Having defeated Spain in the Spanish-American War, the United States could reign supreme in the Caribbean and wield its power in the Far East. American forces were strong enough to uphold the Monroe Doctrine on their own. But instead of returning to isolationism, the nation continued on its course of increasing involvement in world affairs.

Focus for Thought

1. What was the difference between isolationists and imperialists in America?
2. What two things caused the growth of American interest in Hawaii?
3. For each date, tell what happened to move Hawaii toward becoming a state of the United States.
   a. 1875 b. 1898 c. 1900 d. 1959
4. a. In the Spanish-American War, why did the United States attack the Philippines when the main issues involved Cuba?
   b. In what two other places were battles fought?
5. Answer these questions about the results of the Spanish-American War.
   a. What was to be the status of Cuba?
   b. What two territories did the United States gain outright?
   c. For which territory did the United States pay $20 million?
6. What things did Americans do to help the Filipinos?
7. What were some major effects that the Spanish-American War had on the United States?

2. THE OPEN DOOR IN THE FAR EAST

After the Spanish-American War, the United States became a major power in the Far East. Because of American business interests in China, developments in that country became a great concern to Americans. Other nations were moving in and dividing China among themselves. So the United States used various means to protect its trade with China.

Foreign Influence in China

Inroads by Foreign Nations. For centuries, China had been a powerful, advanced empire. The Chinese considered their culture superior to that of Western nations, so they carefully restricted Western influence in their country. For example, foreigners could trade only in the port city of Canton on the east coast. But the Chinese had not experienced an industrial revolution. Compared with the powerful European nations of the 1800s, China was a backward country.

In this, certain European nations saw an opportunity to expand their trade with China and to enlarge their empires. These nations, called the Powers, included Great Britain, France, Germany, and Russia, along with Japan. When the British defeated China in the Opium Wars of 1839 and 1856, they took control of Hong Kong and gained trading privileges in five Chinese cities.

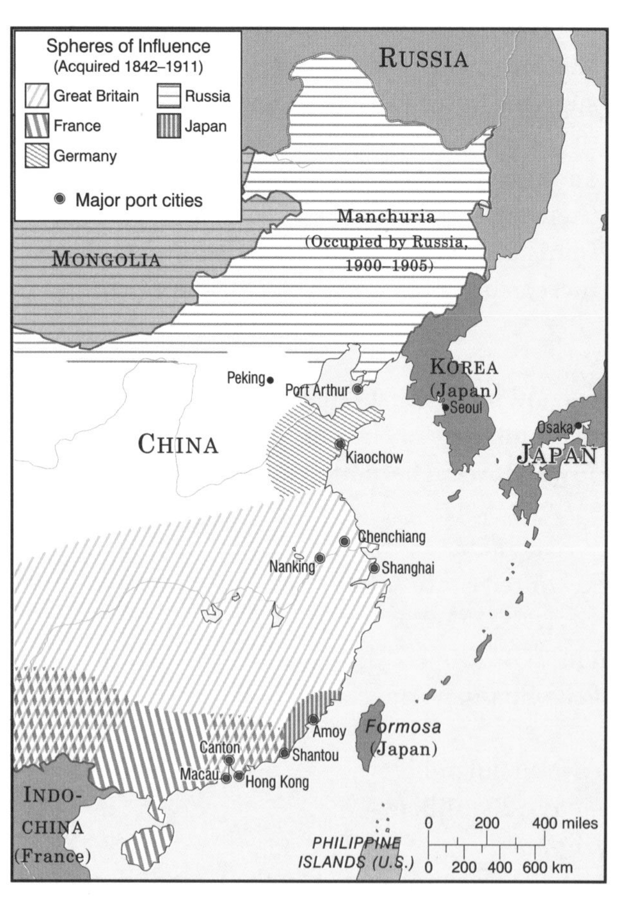

Spheres of Influence in China

After the second Opium War, the Chinese opened even more cities to foreign trade and allowed Christian missionaries to enter China. The French gained trading privileges in southern China and the Russians in Manchuria to the north. Then Japan fought a war against China during 1894 and 1895. Japan forced China to recognize Korean independence and to give Formosa (Taiwan) to Japan. The Powers appeared ready to divide China into many small parts.

After the war with Japan, China was so weak that foreign powers established ***spheres of influence*** within China. These spheres of influence were areas in which a foreign nation controlled the port cities and trade. Great Britain, France, Russia, and Germany all claimed spheres of influence in China, with other nations also trying to get their share. The United States was afraid that these developments would limit its own trade with China.

Relations With the United States. Ever since the United States had developed trade with China in the late 1700s, China and the United States had maintained an important relationship. Having gained possession of the Philippines, the United States now had a gateway to China that could become highly profitable. Alarmed at the rapid breakup of China, the United States moved to preserve that country and its own interests in China.

John Hay (1838–1905) was the secretary of state under presidents William McKinley and Theodore Roosevelt. He developed the Open Door Policy of dealing with China.

The Open Door Policy

The United States did not take part in the dividing of China; instead, it worked to preserve fair trade with China. In September 1899, McKinley's secretary of state, **John Hay**, sent diplomatic notes to the Powers involved in China. Hay proposed several principles that would keep China open to trade with all nations equally—hence the name Open Door Policy. Britain agreed to these principles, but the other nations gave only partial support. Nevertheless, John Hay proclaimed that his policy had been accepted.

The Open Door Policy was a help not only to businessmen but also to missionaries seeking to extend God's kingdom. "Behold, I have set before thee an open door" (Revelation 3:8).

The Boxer Rebellion. In China, more and more people resented the inroads of Western influence. Especially in northern provinces, many Chinese joined secret societies known collectively as Boxers (because they practiced boxing in their training). These Boxers rampaged through parts of China in 1900, killing hundreds of foreigners and their Chinese associates. They tore up railroads—a hated symbol of foreign dominance—and in Peking, the capital, they assaulted foreign diplomats in their homes. Hundreds of Christians were killed in

A Chinese "Boxer." Members of this Chinese secret society were called Boxers because they practiced boxing and other physical exercises. Their opposition to Western influences in China led to the Boxer Rebellion.

this uprising, called the Boxer Rebellion.

To protect their citizens and diplomats in China, the Powers banded together with about twenty thousand soldiers and attacked China. These forces defeated the Chinese and marched into Peking, where they rescued the diplomats and restored order. Would the victorious nations now divide China among themselves?

To keep that from happening, John Hay issued another Open Door note in July 1900. This one indicated that the United States opposed any further division of China. Instead, the Chinese government was required to punish the Boxers and to pay heavy ***reparations*** (rehp uh RAY shuhnz), or money demanded for war damages. These actions marked a bold advance in United States involvement in world affairs.

Relations With Japan

The Russo-Japanese War. The United States and Japan were on friendly terms for about fifty years after Commodore Perry opened the Japanese market in 1854 (see Chapter 15). Japan had agreed to the Open Door Policy if the other powers also agreed. But Japan did not want Russia to control Manchuria, for the Japanese needed the rich resources of that region. In 1904, Japan went to war against Russia; and to the surprise of other nations, Japan prevailed in one battle after another.

Many people in the United States grew concerned over this development. Japan might become so powerful in the Far East that it would threaten American interests there. Therefore, American diplomats arranged peace talks between the Japanese and Russians, and the resulting treaty ended the war and gave Japan special privileges in Manchuria and Korea. By 1910, the Japanese had annexed Korea altogether.

Japanese delegates arriving at Portsmouth, New Hampshire, for a conference on the Russo-Japanese War. For his role in helping to end this war, President Roosevelt won the Nobel Peace Prize in 1906. He was the first American to win a Nobel prize.

Cooling of Relations With Japan. The Japanese considered the treaty unfair, and they blamed the United States. Around the same time, Americans began to resent the many Japanese people coming to the United States (called the "yellow peril"), and they passed special laws to restrict Asian immigration. The Japanese were displeased with these laws as well. By 1908, however, the two nations had reached an understanding known as the "gentlemen's agreement," which limited the migration of Japanese workers to the United States.

To impress the Japanese—and the world—with American military might, President Roosevelt had sent the "Great White Fleet" on a long tour in 1907. The gleaming white ships were received in peace by nations around the world, even Japan. But though the two nations reached seeming agreement on most issues, they remained at odds on several points—with disastrous consequences in World War II.

Focus for Thought

8. Why could European nations take advantage of China in the 1800s?
9. What was the main purpose of the Open Door Policy?
10. Why did the Boxer Rebellion break out?
11. Why was the Open Door Policy an important development in United States history?
12. Why were Americans concerned over Japan's success in the Russo-Japanese War?
13. For what two reasons did relations cool between the United States and Japan?

3. THE "BIG STICK" IN LATIN AMERICA

"Speak softly and carry a big stick." This quotation from Theodore Roosevelt summarizes his approach to foreign policy, particularly in Latin America. For good or ill, the United States continued to take an active part in the affairs of other nations.

Events After the Spanish-American War

Assassination of President McKinley. In 1900, President William McKinley won election to a second term. But in September 1901, a man shot the president as he shook hands with visitors. McKinley lingered about eight days and then passed away. This reminds us that God is sovereign over the rulers of the earth.

McKinley was replaced by Theodore Roosevelt, his vice president. Roosevelt became especially active in dealing with Latin American countries.

Problems in Cuba. Though free from Spanish rule, Cuba was plagued with troubles. Its government was unstable, its economy had collapsed, and public services were nonexistent. Because of these problems, President McKinley had sent in an army that occupied Cuba until 1902. The Americans helped the sick, the poor, and the homeless; and they built schools, roads, and hospitals. They established better sanitation and helped eliminate the dreaded yellow fever.

The Cubans adopted a constitution for self-government in 1901, in which they agreed to several conditions required by the United States. One of these was that the United States could intervene whenever necessary to preserve Cuban independence, and another was that the United States could obtain land in Cuba for naval stations. Cuba became independent in 1902, and the American troops withdrew.

American investments increased, and trade between the two countries grew rapidly. Eventually the United States built a large naval base at Guantánamo Bay in Cuba, which it maintains to this day. Yet relations between the two countries were not always smooth because Cubans resented American involvement in their affairs.

Dealings With Puerto Rico. The United States set up a civil government for Puerto Rico in 1900. Puerto Ricans became American citizens in 1917; and in 1952, Puerto Rico adopted its own constitution and became a self-governing commonwealth of the United States. But Puerto Rico had no voting members in Congress, and its citizens could not vote in elections for American presidents. Puerto Rico is still a commonwealth today; however, its people are considering whether to keep things as they are, become a state of the Union, or become independent.

The United States has done much to aid Puerto Rico by building roads and schools and by introducing health programs to control disease. The elimination of tariffs encouraged a flourishing trade with the United States in

This Red Cross camp for orphans in Cuba (1899) is an example of American efforts to help the nations conquered in the Spanish-American War. Clara Barton is in the center of the ring of children.

In Puerto Rico during the 1940s, thousands of slum buildings such as these were torn down and replaced with better housing.

sugar, coffee, tobacco, and bananas. In addition, thousands of tourists visit Puerto Rico to enjoy this land of mild climate, verdant mountains, and lush valleys.

The Panama Canal

Plans for the Panama Canal. Men had long dreamed of building a canal across Central America. Now that the United States had gained territories in the Pacific and the Far East, it became even more important to have a shorter route between the Atlantic and Pacific Oceans. A canal would save thousands of miles as well as much time and money. The French had already made a heroic attempt in the 1880s to build a canal across Panama. But after spending millions of dollars and moving tremendous amounts of earth, they abandoned the effort because of disease and other difficulties. However, Americans believed that they could succeed where the French had failed.

Important steps had to be taken before a canal could be started. The United States first needed to obtain land through which to build a canal. Since Panama was then a part of Colombia, John Hay negotiated a treaty for a strip of land across Panama. The Colombian senate rejected the treaty, but in 1903 a group of Panamanians who wanted the canal revolted against their government. President Roosevelt sent ships to support them and helped the revolt to succeed.

The United States recognized Panama's independence and quickly negotiated a canal treaty with the new nation. This treaty granted the United States a canal zone 10 miles (16 km) wide across Panama for payment of $10 million and annual rent of $250,000. But Colombia protested this action, and the United States later made amends by paying $25 million to Colombia.

Construction of the Panama Canal. Work on the Panama Canal began in 1904. The first step was to reduce the threat of yellow fever and malaria. William Gorgas attacked the mosquitoes that spread these diseases. It took eighteen months to eliminate the threat of yellow fever in Panama.

Then the Americans prepared to dig the "big ditch." They hired thousands of workers, built railroads, and brought in huge earthmoving machines. Actual construction on the canal began in 1907. The man chiefly responsible for digging the canal was **George Washington Goethals** (GOH thuhlz). Perhaps the

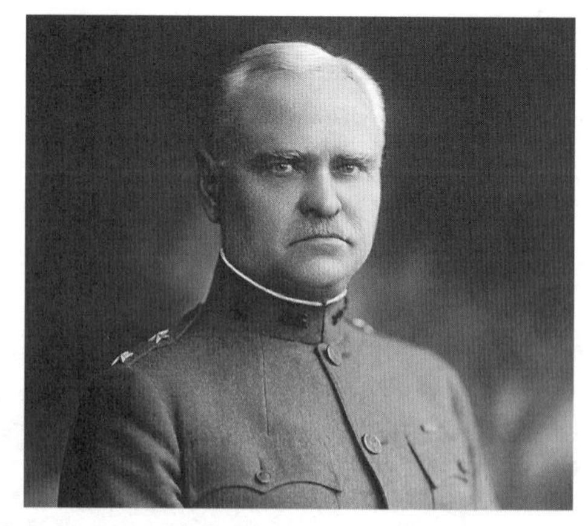

George W. Goethals (1858–1928) directed the building of the Panama Canal from 1907 to its completion in 1914. He overcame many difficulties and completed the canal ahead of schedule.

Malaria and Yellow Fever. Two of the most deadly tropical diseases are malaria and yellow fever. An attack of malaria begins with chills and violent shivering. Next comes a burning fever and thirst, followed by a drenching sweat. The fever leaves the patient feeling drained in body and spirit. He often suffers from terrible depression. One case of malaria does not produce immunity; instead, recurring attacks might come all through life.

Yellow fever also begins with shivering, fever, and thirst; but it is accompanied by severe headaches and pain in the legs and back. The victim becomes restless; and then as the symptoms subside, he begins to turn yellow. Often the disease is fatal; but if a person survives yellow fever, he becomes immune for life.

Americans encountered the scourge of yellow fever when they governed Cuba. One of them was **William Gorgas,** an army surgeon who had contracted the dread disease but had survived with immunity. As head of a sanitation commission in Cuba, he was a good man to fight the disease. Many people thought yellow fever was caused by unclean conditions such as garbage and other filth, but Carlos Finlay and some other physicians thought mosquitoes transmitted yellow fever. The sanitation commission decided to do experiments to test Dr. Finlay's theory.

In the experiments, several brave volunteers allowed themselves to be bitten by mosquitoes that had bitten yellow fever sufferers. The volunteers promptly contracted yellow fever, and a number of them died as a result. Further tests provided strong proof that mosquitoes transmit yellow fever.

William Gorgas started a campaign against mosquitoes in Havana. Wherever he found stagnant water, he drained it, covered it, or poured oil on the surface. He drained swamps or spread oil over the water, and he isolated yellow fever patients behind wire screens. Havana was free of yellow fever by October 1901, whereas the city had known fourteen hundred cases in 1900. Gorgas used the same methods to make Panama safe for workers on the Panama Canal. Without his labors, the American effort to build the canal might have been no more successful than previous attempts.

William C. Gorgas (1854–1920).

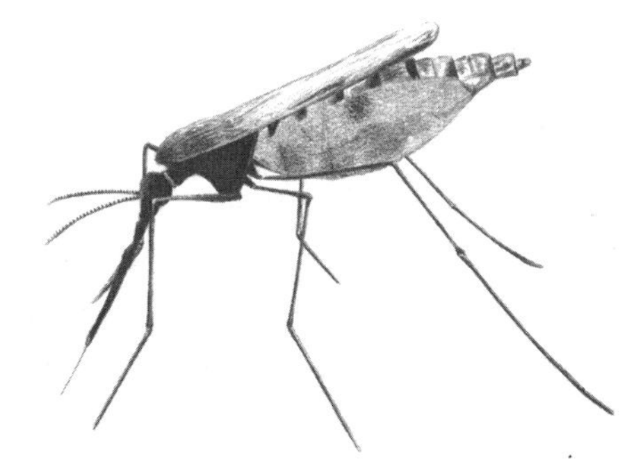

The *Anopheles* mosquito is a major carrier of malaria and yellow fever. In recent years, malaria is on the increase because many mosquitoes have become resistant to pesticides. Throughout history, malaria has likely taken more lives than any other disease.

Making the Gaillard Cut required the removal of 210 million cubic yards (161 million m^3) of earth. The cut must be dredged frequently to remove earth from mudslides—as much as 1 million cubic yards (765,000 m^3) in a year.

President Roosevelt sits at the controls of a steam shovel at the Panama Canal in 1906. This huge machine could dig up 5 cubic yards of earth in one scoop—about 8 tons! It was operated by ten men; and in good conditions, it could load a railcar in eight minutes.

Miraflores Locks under construction in 1912. When completed, each lock had a depth of about 70 feet (21 m). Ships as much as 1,000 feet (305 m) long are pulled or guided by small locomotives through the locks.

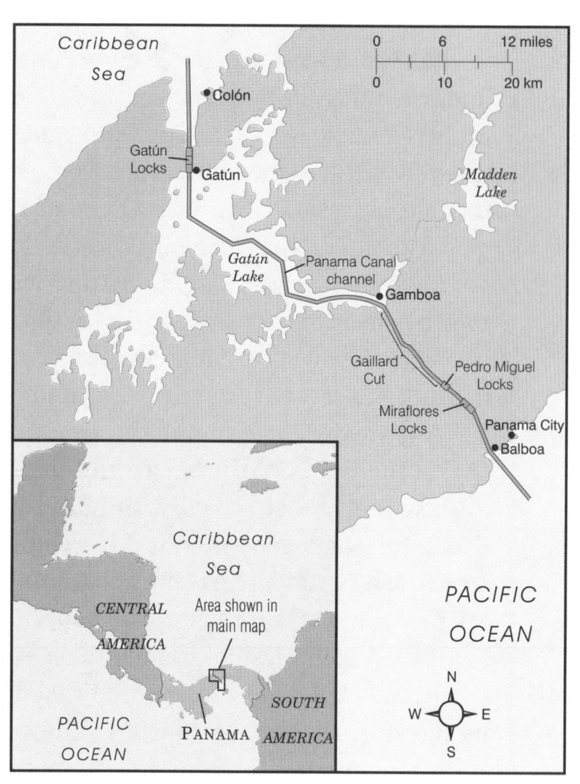

The Panama Canal

greatest challenge was making the Gaillard Cut (gihl YAHRD) through the continental divide, where landslides repeatedly filled the cut with tons of new mud. The completed cut was 8 miles (13 km) long, and its width was 500 feet (152 m).

A great amount of water was needed to operate the canal, so the Chagres River (CHAH grehs) was dammed to create Gatún Lake (gah TOON). To raise and lower ships the 85 feet (26 m) between Gatún Lake and the two oceans, six sets of huge locks were built. The water levels in the locks closest to the ends of the canal vary because of the daily ocean tides, which range from 2 feet (0.6 m) to 12½ feet (3.8 m).

The canal was officially completed in 1914 when the president pressed a button in Washington, D.C., that set off an explosion to release water from Gatún Lake into the locks and the Gaillard Cut. In August 1914, the steamer *Ancon* made the first transit of the canal. Man had accomplished another astounding feat by using his God-given abilities.

On August 15, 1914, the SS *Ancon* became the first ship to make a complete passage through the Panama Canal. This photograph shows the ship in the Gaillard Cut as it traveled from the Atlantic Ocean to the Pacific.

Today ships travel through the Panama Canal in eight hours, saving over 7,800 miles (12,552 km). The canal gives passage to about 13,500 ships per year, or an average of about 37 per day.

With time, the Panamanians wanted to take over the canal themselves. So in 1978, the United States agreed to give Panama control of the canal on January 1, 2000.

Dealings With Other Latin American Nations

The Roosevelt Corollary. Because of the Panama Canal and other interests, the United States under Theodore Roosevelt began taking an active part in the affairs of Latin America. Roosevelt was especially concerned lest European nations find excuses to move in. For example, some Latin American nations borrowed large sums from European countries and then could not repay their debts. What if the Europeans decided to send military forces against those nations?

According to the Monroe Doctrine, European nations were to stay out of the Western Hemisphere. Since his nation took that position, President Roosevelt thought the United States should keep order in Latin America so that Europeans would have no reason to move in. This extension of the Monroe Doctrine is called the Roosevelt Corollary (KOR uh lehr ee). (A corollary is a natural result or consequence.)

On this basis, the United States intervened a number of times in the affairs of its southern neighbors. Americans took over the finances of Haiti from 1915 to 1934, and of the Dominican Republic from 1916 to 1924, to force payment of their debts. The United States Army also intervened in Nicaragua from 1912 to 1933. Not surprisingly, many Latin Americans resented what they viewed as bullying by their powerful neighbor to the north. But the United States saw it as being helpful to those countries.

Dollar Diplomacy. After **William Howard Taft** became president in 1909, he began a policy called "dollar diplomacy" because he encouraged Americans rather than Europeans to invest in Latin America. He hoped this would help to stabilize those countries while at the same time keeping out the Europeans. In this way, the United States tried to influence the countries without actually

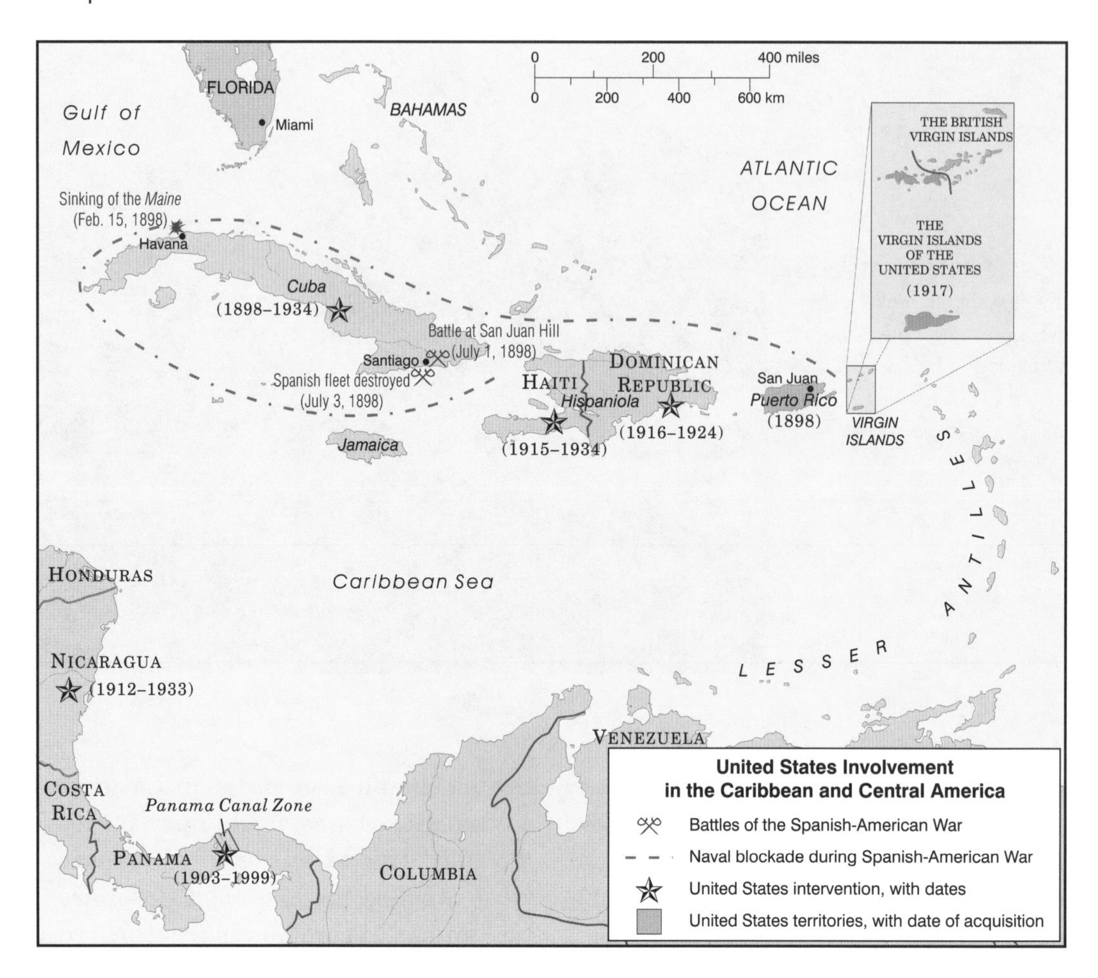

controlling them, and tried to prevent violence and bring economic improvement.

Intervention in Mexico. Before the 1920s, the United States had made great investments in Mexico. But a period of violence and revolution started there in 1910. A harsh dictator had ruled for over thirty years, bringing prosperity to Mexico through foreign investment. But many Mexicans remained poor and disliked the presence of the foreigners, so they revolted against their government.

The United States intervened in 1914 by sending an army to occupy Veracruz for several months. Then in 1916, a Mexican rebel named Pancho Villa (VEE yah) raided New Mexico and killed at least eighteen Americans. The United States responded by sending General John J. Pershing to capture Villa. His men scoured northern Mexico for almost a year without success—which increased the Mexicans' resentment against the United States because they saw Villa as a hero. This was just one of the many problems that world power brought to the United States.

Focus for Thought

14. a. In what ways did the United States help to improve Cuba?
    b. Why did Cubans become resentful toward the United States?
15. What were the three steps by which Puerto Rico became a self-governing commonwealth of the United States?
16. a. Why did the United States need the Panama Canal?
    b. What were two problems that had to be overcome in building the Panama Canal?
17. What was the reasoning behind the Roosevelt Corollary?
18. What did President Taft hope to accomplish through "dollar diplomacy"?
19. On what two occasions were United States troops sent to Mexico between 1910 and 1920?

Historical Highlights

A. Matching: People

You will use some letters twice.

a. George Dewey
b. George Washington Goethals
c. John Hay
d. Theodore Roosevelt
e. William Gorgas
f. William Howard Taft
g. William McKinley

1. President who used "dollar diplomacy" in Latin America.
2. Man chiefly responsible for digging the Panama Canal.
3. President during the Spanish-American War.
4. Overcame yellow fever and malaria by controlling mosquitoes in Cuba and Panama.
5. Man who promoted the Open Door Policy.
6. Defeated the Spanish fleet in the Philippines during the Spanish-American War.
7. President who used the "big stick."
8. President assassinated in 1901.
9. Man who negotiated with Colombia for land to build the Panama Canal.

B. Matching: Terms

a. Boxer Rebellion
b. imperialism
c. isolationism
d. Open Door Policy
e. reparations
f. Roosevelt Corollary
g. sphere of influence

1. Policy of having little to do with foreign nations.
2. United States policy of intervening in the affairs of Latin America.
3. Desire to gain control of foreign territories.
4. Basis for American relations with countries in the Far East.
5. Area in China in which a foreign nation controlled the trade and port cities.
6. Uprising in China in 1900.
7. Money demanded from a defeated nation for war damages that it caused.

C. Matching: Places

Match the following territories acquired by the United States to their descriptions.

a. Cuba
b. Guam
c. Hawaii
d. Midway Islands
e. Philippines
f. Puerto Rico
g. Samoa

1. Group of Pacific islands about 2,000 miles (3,219 km) west of the United States; annexed in 1898.
2. Pacific islands acquired in 1867.
3. Spanish island in the Pacific that was ceded to the United States in 1898.
4. Pacific islands shared with Britain and Germany; American part annexed in 1900.
5. Far East islands conquered in the Spanish-American War and purchased for $20 million.
6. Spanish island in the Caribbean that was ceded to the United States in 1898.
7. Caribbean island that the United States conquered and gave independence in 1902.

D. Multiple Choice

Write the letter of the correct answer.

1. By becoming imperialistic, the United States was breaking what tradition?
   a. capitalism
   b. socialism
   c. federalism
   d. isolationism
2. Which one of these was *not* part of American empire building in the late 1800s and early 1900s?
   a. Canada
   b. Hawaii
   c. Cuba
   d. Panama Canal
3. Which one of these island possessions was acquired before the Spanish-American War?
   a. Guam
   b. American Samoa
   c. Midway Islands
   d. Puerto Rico
4. Which one of these was *not* a reason that some Americans began favoring imperialism?
   a. A new generation came into power that had not experienced the Civil War.
   b. The United States was busy developing the land it already had.
   c. Foreign trade could boost business production and provide markets for American goods.
   d. The United States had the ability to become a world power by building a strong merchant fleet and navy.
5. Which of these tell why the United States went to war with Spain in 1898?
   a. Americans had long wanted to possess Cuba.
   b. The revolution in Cuba threatened American business investments.
   c. American citizens in Cuba were endangered and mistreated.
   d. Americans remembered their own revolution a century before and sympathized with the Cubans.
   e. All the reasons above.
6. Which one of these was not a *new* challenge that arose when the United States became a world power?
   a. Cuban political chaos
   b. building the Panama Canal
   c. corruption in politics
   d. Open Door Policy in China
   e. Dominican Republic not paying its debts

E. Deeper Discussion

1. What effects did the change from isolationism to imperialism have on the United States?
2. How might the war with Spain have been prevented?
3. Even though the United States did much good in the Philippines, Cuba, and Panama, why did their people still want to be independent?
4. How did the Open Door Policy mark a turning point in United States foreign policy?
5. Deuteronomy 10:18, 19 says that God "loveth the stranger, in giving him food and raiment. Love ye therefore the stranger: for ye were strangers in the land of Egypt."
   a. How were immigrants in America like the strangers to which this passage refers?
   b. This direction was given to the children of Israel, who had lived in the land of Egypt. How does it apply to many people in America?
   c. How should Christians relate to strangers, such as immigrants and other foreigners?
6. Why did Latin Americans resent United States policy under the Roosevelt Corollary and the "dollar diplomacy"?

F. Chronology and Geography

1. Give the following dates.
   a. The Spanish-American War, from the United States declaration of war to the signing of the peace treaty.
   b. The Boxer Rebellion.
   c. The work on the Panama Canal by the United States, from start to finish.
2. Answer with names listed in Part C.
   a. Which places are located in the Pacific Ocean?
   b. Which places are located on the Atlantic side of the Americas?
   c. Which places are United States territories today? Which one has become a state?
   d. Find all these places on a world map. Be prepared to show their locations in class.

So Far This Year

A. Matching: People and Terms

1. Inventor of the telegraph.	a. abolition
2. Man who brought textile manufacturing to America.	b. circuit rider
3. Publisher of the "blue-backed speller."	c. Cotton Kingdom
4. Man who built the first successful steamboat.	d. Eli Whitney
5. Inventor of the cotton gin.	e. Industrial Revolution
6. Elimination of slavery.	f. Noah Webster
7. Change from producing handmade goods at home to producing machine-made goods in factories.	g. Robert Fulton
	h. Samuel F. B. Morse
8. Effort to stop the use of strong drink.	i. Samuel Slater
9. Region dependent on cotton.	j. temperance movement
10. Traveling preacher in the West.	

B. Matching: Presidents

11. First president, 1789–1797.	a. Andrew Jackson
12. First president to die in office.	b. George Washington
13. Son of a former president.	c. James Madison
14. Vice president under Andrew Jackson.	d. James Monroe
15. President during War of 1812; served from 1809 to 1817.	e. John Adams
16. First vice president to fill the position of a president who died in office.	f. John Q. Adams
	g. John Tyler
17. President during the Era of Good Feelings.	h. Martin Van Buren
18. President who represented the common man.	i. Thomas Jefferson
19. Second president; Federalist; 1797–1801.	j. William H. Harrison
20. Leader of Democratic-Republicans; third president, 1801–1809.	

C. Completion

Write the correct name or term for each description.

Terms

21. System for making large numbers of products by using interchangeable parts and assembly lines.
22. Scarce product + high demand = high price; abundant product + low demand = low price.
23. People from eastern and southern Europe who moved to the United States in the years 1890 to 1920.
24. Religious movement designed to improve present social conditions.
25. Movement to limit immigration.
26. Religious movement emphasizing conversion more than discipleship.
27. Economic system that includes private ownership of property, free markets, and a minimum of government regulation.
28. Karl Marx's theory proposing a classless society and government ownership of business.
29. Belief that living things had a natural origin and that they gradually evolved into the species existing today.

Presidents

30. Served from 1889 to 1893; was in office when the Sherman Antitrust Act was passed.
31. Was opposed by William Jennings Bryan in 1896; supported the gold standard and conducted a "front-porch" campaign.
32. Came into office through a disputed election; served from 1877 to 1881.
33. Was assassinated only a few months after becoming president in 1881.
34. Was the only president to serve two nonconsecutive terms.
35. Became president in 1881 when the previous president was assassinated.

Other Persons

36. Famous evangelist of the latter 1800s who preached in America and England.
37. Evangelist who started revival meetings in the Mennonite Church.
38. Inventor of the telephone.
39. Inventor of the electric light bulb.
40. Founder of Standard Oil Company, the first trust.
41. Man whose company helped make the United States a leading steel producer.

D. True or False

Write whether each statement is true (T) *or false* (F).

42. The Homestead Act allowed settlers to claim 160 acres (65 ha) of land for farming.
43. Charles Goodnight was one of the first Texas cattle ranchers.
44. The Dawes Act authorized a transcontinental railroad.
45. Joseph McCoy invented barbed wire in 1874.
46. Joseph Glidden built stockyards at Abilene, Kansas.
47. The transcontinental railroad was joined at Promontory, Utah, in 1869.
48. Sitting Bull was an Indian chief killed in the Sand Creek massacre.
49. The colonel defeated at the Battle of the Little Bighorn was George Custer.
50. In the "long drive," cowboys moved cattle north by railroad to Kansas.
51. Chief Joseph was an Apache leader who surrendered in 1886.
52. Wounded Knee was the site where one of the last Indian battles took place.

These children worked at a cotton mill in North Carolina in 1908. The mill had about 40 employees in all, of which 10 were children.

22 Progressive Reform

1900

Theodore Roosevelt becomes president 1901

William McKinley assassinated 1901

Roosevelt elected to second term 1904

1905

Earthquake shatters San Francisco; Pure Food and Drug Act passed 1906

William Howard Taft elected president 1908

1910

Roosevelt Dam dedicated 1911

Woodrow Wilson elected president 1912

Progressive Party begins; the *Titanic* sinks 1912

Federal Reserve Act passed 1913

Sixteenth and Seventeenth Amendments ratified; Underwood Tariff Act passed 1913

World War I begins **1914**

1915

Wilson re-elected 1916

Eighteenth Amendment ratified 1919

Nineteenth Amendment ratified 1920

1920

"The way of man is not in himself: it is not in man that walketh to direct his steps."

Jeremiah 10:23

PROGRESSIVE REFORM

Focus for Reading

Americans felt confident of their future as they entered the 1900s, and they prospered in the first decade of the new century. But not everyone was satisfied with conditions in the nation. Reformers attacked corruption in government, the power of big business, slums in the cities, and a host of other real or imagined woes. These reformers, labeled progressives, held a strong influence because they had a champion in the White House: Theodore Roosevelt. This president, along with William Howard Taft and Woodrow Wilson, are all considered progressives.

Historians refer to the period from about 1900 to 1917 as the Progressive Era. What were the goals of these reformers? How did they try to improve government, society, and the economy? What did Roosevelt, Taft, and Wilson accomplish? Chapter 22 answers these questions in three sections.

1. The Progressive Movement
2. Progressives in Power: Theodore Roosevelt and William Howard Taft
3. Another Progressive in Power: Woodrow Wilson

1. THE PROGRESSIVE MOVEMENT

The overall goals of progressive reformers were to remove corruption from government, to make government more democratic, and to make the United States a better place in which to live and work. However, their reliance on the government to carry out their aims tended to increase the size of the government and expand its power to control the lives of the people. This prepared the seedbed for government power to grow even more in the future.

If things have worked well over a long period of time, it is wise to be slow about changing them. "My son, fear thou the LORD and the king: and meddle [associate] not with them that are given to change" (Proverbs 24:21).

Progressive Goals

Progressive reformers were not a separate political party. Instead, they represented a diverse group of Democrats, Republicans, and others who wanted to use government power to improve American society. They linked progress to reform; hence the name *progressives*. These reformers wanted to make improvements in three main areas: government, business, and society.

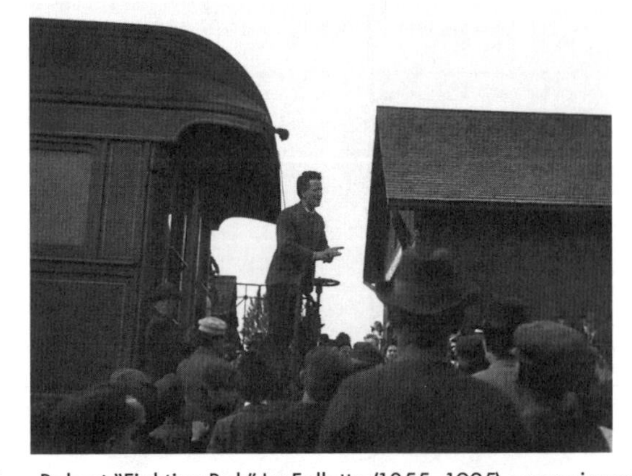

Robert "Fighting Bob" La Follette (1855–1925) campaigned for governor of Wisconsin in 1900. La Follette's reforms in Wisconsin made his state a "laboratory of Progressivism."

Reform in Government. Progressives believed that if the government were first reformed, then good government could reform both business and society. They wanted to purge the government of corruption, and they especially wanted the government to serve society as a whole rather than serving special-interest groups such as big businesses. This would make the government more democratic, they thought, by being more responsive to the will of the people.

To achieve this goal, progressives promoted the direct election of United States senators by the people, rather than having them chosen by the state legislatures as the Constitution specified. They believed this would eliminate the problem of corrupt state legislatures accepting money from large corporations to elect the senator preferred by businessmen.

Other progressive changes included the ***initiative***, the ***referendum*** (rehf uh REHN duhm), and the ***recall***. The initiative would allow voters to introduce new laws to the legislature; the referendum would allow voters to approve or reject laws passed by the legislature; and the recall would allow voters to remove unsatisfactory public officials from office.

Reform in Business. Many businesses had grown large and powerful. Progressives said that businessmen oppressed their workers by not paying them enough and by making women and children work long, toilsome hours. In 1900, the average man working in a factory earned less than ten dollars a week; a woman earned perhaps six dollars; and children received even less. That was barely enough even in those days. Besides, working conditions were harsh and many accidents occurred. When a worker was hurt on the job, he often paid the medical bills himself.

This little girl worked as a spinner in a cotton mill in Georgia.

These children in a labor parade were crusading to "Abolish child slavery."

Authors called ***muckrakers*** wrote books and articles that pointed out evils in society. They especially focused on big business. For example, Ida Tarbell denounced John D. Rockefeller's business practices. Though muckrakers tended to overemphasize the evils of big business, they convinced many Americans of the need for reform in business.

To achieve business reform, progressives wanted to give the government power to regulate businesses and to break up the ones that became too large. They campaigned for laws to limit the working hours of women, to ban child labor, and to improve working conditions. They promoted workers' compensation laws, which made employers liable for injuries their workers received on the job. They sought minimum-wage laws to raise the wages of working people. Some even believed that businesses such as railroads should be owned or directly controlled by the government.

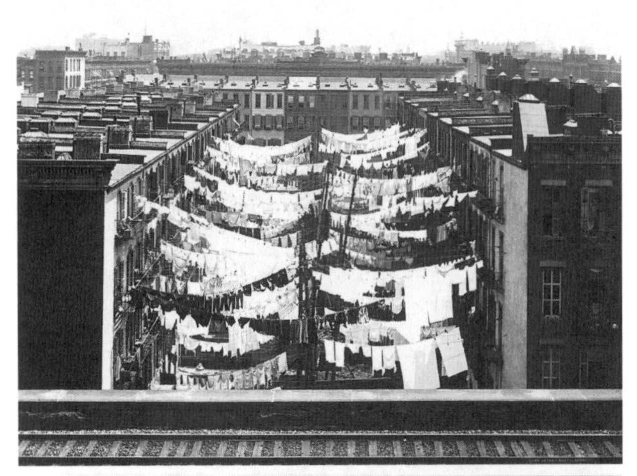

Progressives worked to reform the living conditions of poor people in cities. ***Top:*** The yard of a tenement in New York City. ***Bottom:*** The back of a tenement in New York City.

To provide an income, this mother and her four children, ages 3 to 14, make flower wreaths in their tenement home in New York City.

Reform in Society. Muckrakers called attention to the problems of immigrants, city slums, rundown tenements, and corruption in city government. In response, progressives began promoting building codes, zoning laws, and other laws to regulate tenements. Some reformers promoted conservation—they believed that the nation was wasting its natural resources and that the government should take action to protect these resources before they vanished. Others were prohibitionists—they wanted to pass laws making alcoholic beverages illegal. Many women campaigned for women's rights, especially in the area of women's suffrage (the right to vote).

Progressives noted that in 1900, 2 percent of the people owned 60 percent of the nation's wealth. To address this "problem," progressives advocated a graduated income tax that would tax the rich more heavily than the poor, thus supposedly helping to redistribute money in society. However, blacks and American Indians received little attention. In fact, the plight of blacks actually seemed to grow worse as illiteracy and segregation continued.

Public schools also became more progressive in their teaching. Led at first by John Dewey, progressives emphasized using schools to reform society. They promoted child-centered teaching that focused on the interests of children rather than adults. Progressive educators abandoned the teaching methods and strict discipline of the old schools. They

taught more subjects such as sewing and cooking instead of the "three *R*'s." They emphasized thinking skills rather than learning by memorization.

Such a child-centered approach runs directly contrary to a number of Scriptures. "Train up a child in the way he should go: and when he is old, he will not depart from it" (Proverbs 22:6). "The rod and reproof give wisdom: but a child left to himself bringeth his mother to shame" (Proverbs 29:15). Cities generally became progressive sooner than rural areas, but these ideas took root in the 1800s and came into full bloom in the 1900s.

Advance of Progressive Reform

Reform in Cities. Progressives began by reforming at the local and state levels and then seeking national reform through the federal government. Cities were an obvious target for reform. In Ohio, for example, progressive mayors made significant changes in cities like Cleveland and Toledo. Mayor Tom Johnson of Cleveland ended the control of corrupt politicians over the city streetcar system, bringing the fare down to three cents. Samuel Jones reformed Toledo, establishing a minimum wage for city employees and providing playgrounds for children.

Cities also adopted building codes and zoning ordinances. In New York City, stricter building codes were passed after a fire at the Triangle Shirtwaist factory in 1911. The factory was located on the top three floors of a ten-story building; and after a fire started on the eighth floor, scores of workers (mostly young immigrant women) were trapped inside. A total of 146 people died, more than 40 of them by leaping from windows.

Reform in States. Progressive reformers began to influence state governments. Robert La Follette (luh FAHL uht), elected governor of Wisconsin in 1900, was one progressive leader. Wisconsin became the first state with a direct primary election; the state also passed laws for conservation, higher taxes on corporations, and the first state income tax. La Follette's "Wisconsin Idea" became a model for numerous other states. Progressive reforms were also made in New York, California, and New Jersey.

By 1914, eleven states had adopted new methods such as the initiative and the referendum. States also passed laws that limited

Before safety laws were passed to give guidelines for working conditions, much of the sewing industry was carried out in sweatshops. These crowded factories flourished because many workers were willing to work long hours for low wages in poor working conditions.

working hours, set minimum wages, and provided workers' compensation. At least twenty-six states had prohibited alcoholic beverages and gone "dry" by 1917. Progressives also pressured states to pass compulsory school attendance laws. If states already had such laws, they lengthened the school year and extended the number of years children were required to go to school.

But progressives felt that city and state reforms did not go far enough—they wanted the federal government to pass similar laws for the whole nation. With Theodore Roosevelt in the White House, they had a chance to accomplish that.

How should the people of God view the progressive movement? The progressives did some good, such as reducing corruption in politics and relieving the oppression of poor people. But these reformers were wrong in thinking that government power is the key to solving the problems of society. Government power can also cause problems; and besides, man's greatest problem is his sinful nature. True social improvement comes only as people's hearts are changed by the power of God.

Focus for Thought

1. What people took part in the progressive movement?
2. What three reforms did the progressive reformers promote
   a. in government?
   b. in business?
   c. in society?
3. What changes did the reformers make in education?
4. Write *federal*, *state*, or *local* for each blank.
   Progressives usually began reforming at the ___ level of government. From there they went to the ___ level and finally to the ___ level.
5. Name at least three state reforms that progressives accomplished.

2. PROGRESSIVES IN POWER: THEODORE ROOSEVELT AND WILLIAM HOWARD TAFT

President Theodore Roosevelt was a dynamic leader who used his office to advance progressive reform. Roosevelt extended the power of the presidency, attacking problems in society and assuming the responsibilities of world power. But his chosen successor, William Howard Taft, was not as strong a president as Roosevelt had been. By 1912, the two leaders had parted ways, splitting the Republican Party and paving the way for a Democrat to become president.

The "Square Deal"

A Popular President. At forty-two, Theodore Roosevelt became the youngest president in American history. He had been the assistant secretary of the navy under McKinley before the Spanish-American War. When the war began, Roosevelt resigned his commission and helped form the Rough Riders (see Chapter 21).

A national hero after the war, Roosevelt eventually became the vice president and then advanced to the presidency after McKinley was assassinated. He served from 1901 to 1909, having been re-elected in 1904 by a wide majority. President Roosevelt and his family of six children endeared themselves to the American people. With this kind of popularity, it was fairly easy for Roosevelt to

Left: Theodore Roosevelt (1858–1919) was the twenty-sixth president of the United States. He served from 1901 to 1909 and was a Republican. The family members, from left to right, are as follows: Quentin, Mr. Roosevelt, Theodore Jr., Archie, Alice, Kermit, Mrs. Roosevelt, Ethel. ***Right:*** Sagamore Hill, Theodore Roosevelt's home at Oyster Bay on Long Island, New York.

achieve progressive reform.

A Strong President. Theodore Roosevelt believed the president could do whatever was not forbidden by the Constitution. He exercised strong leadership in foreign policy, and he began a new, active approach in domestic policy. Instead of waiting for Congress to act, Roosevelt started the practice of promoting his own program of new laws for Congress to pass.

The president referred to his program of reform as the "Square Deal." By this label, Roosevelt indicated his desire to give everyone fair treatment, whether rich or poor, businessman or laborer. Later presidents followed this pattern of having a legislative program and giving it a name.

Dealings With Business. President Roosevelt set out to limit the power of businesses that he thought were getting too big. One of the first "square deals" was his handling of a coal strike in 1902. In May, about 140,000 coal miners in the United Mine Workers union walked off the job, demanding higher wages, an eight-hour day, and recognition of the union by the mine owners.

The mine owners refused to budge. As the strike dragged on into the fall months, coal prices began to soar. Fearing that trouble would break out, Roosevelt invited both the union leaders and the mine owners to a conference in Washington, D.C., in October. But the owners refused to even talk to the union leaders, and they requested that Roosevelt settle the strike by using force against the miners. Instead, Roosevelt declared that he would use federal troops, not to break the strike, but to operate the mines!

The mine operators quickly reached an agreement whereby the miners would go back to work, and both workers and owners would submit their grievances to a commission appointed by the president. The commission granted the workers a nine-hour day and a 10 percent wage increase, while allowing the owners to raise coal prices by 10 percent.

Scene during the 1902 coal strike, when Theodore Roosevelt's arbitrators met with miners and mine operators.

President Roosevelt basked in public praise for settling the strike, but he had started a questionable practice. For the first time, a president had personally intervened in employer–employee affairs, and that would be repeated many times afterward. Thus he greatly expanded the power of the president and the federal government to intervene in private business matters.

President Roosevelt became known as a "trustbuster" because he used federal power to break up huge businesses called trusts (see Chapter 20). While he recognized that some trusts were good, he thought the bad ones should be broken up by using the Sherman Antitrust Act of 1890. In 1902, Roosevelt's attorney general filed an antitrust lawsuit against Northern Securities Company, an enormous railroad combination, and it was dissolved in 1904. The president went on to break up about forty other companies, including Standard Oil and the American Tobacco Company. Overall, however, the number of large companies increased during the Roosevelt years.

The president did not believe that all big businesses were bad, but that the government should regulate them if it did not break them up. Therefore, he pressured Congress to create a new department in his Cabinet in 1903, the Department of Commerce and Labor. In his second term, the Hepburn Act of 1906 greatly increased the powers of the Interstate Commerce Commission (ICC) to regulate transportation and set freight rates for railroads.

Also in 1906, a muckraker named Upton Sinclair published a book titled *The Jungle*, which exposed revolting practices in meatpacking industries. After Roosevelt read the book, he ordered an investigation that produced a shocking report about the meatpackers. He then prevailed upon Congress to take action on the matter.

The result was two laws passed in 1906. The Meat Inspection Act required that sanitation laws be enforced in meatpacking plants and that meat shipped between states be federally inspected. The Pure Food and Drug Act prohibited shipment of impure or mislabeled products in interstate commerce.

Support for Conservation. President Roosevelt thought the government should take an active part in conserving natural resources. In 1902, Congress passed a law providing funds to build dams for waterpower and irrigation projects. The Roosevelt Dam in Arizona, dedicated by Theodore Roosevelt himself in 1911, is an example of such a project. The president also created several new national parks and game preserves, as well as numerous national monuments and bird refuges.

Roosevelt and his chief forester, Gifford Pinchot (PIHN shoh), wanted to make the American people aware of conservation needs. In 1908, the president called a special conference on conservation, which was attended by businessmen, state governors, and federal officials. This conference led to the National Conservation Commission as well as to numerous state commissions for conservation. By these means, Theodore Roosevelt changed conservation from a private affair to a public issue under the authority of the federal government.

President Roosevelt and naturalist John Muir on a peak in Yosemite National Park. Both men promoted the conservation of natural resources and the establishing of national parks.

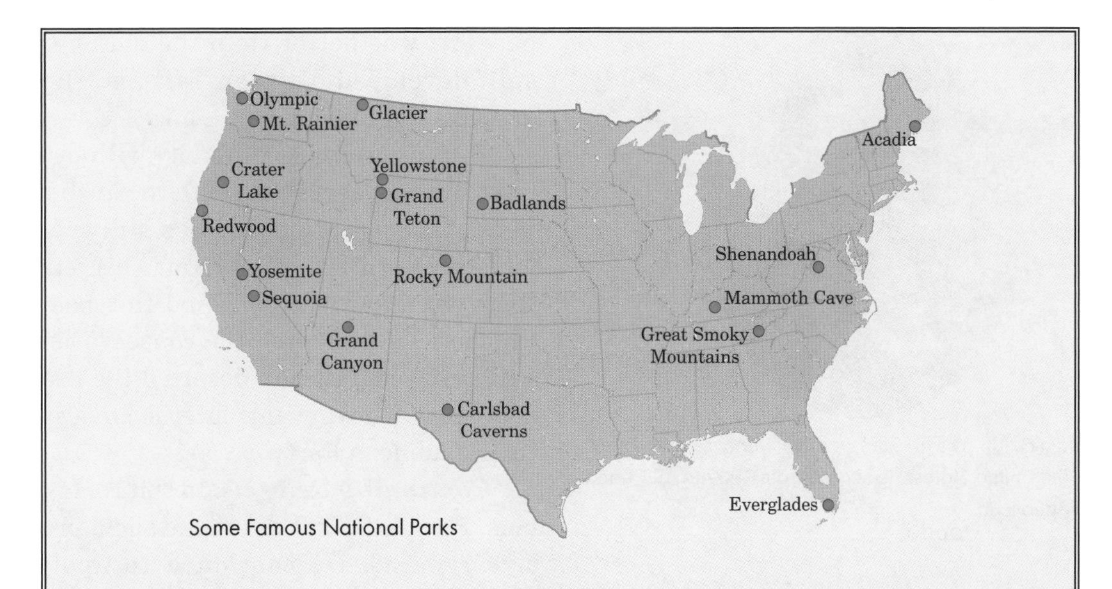

Some Famous National Parks

National Parks. Thousands of people visit United States national parks every year. Among the most famous parks are the Grand Canyon in Arizona, Yellowstone in Wyoming, and the Great Smoky Mountains in the Appalachians. These parks are huge areas set aside by the government to preserve their unique natural features or historical associations. Yellowstone was the first national park, set aside in 1872 during President Grant's term. Sequoia and Yosemite National Parks, in California, were created in 1890, while Benjamin Harrison was president. In 1899, President McKinley added Mount Rainier, in Washington. Ten more national parks were added by 1920. These last ones included Crater Lake (1902), in Oregon; Mesa Verde (1906), in Colorado; and Acadia (1919), in Maine.

Historical parks include Independence Hall in Philadelphia, the Statue of Liberty, and many battlefield parks. National monuments are similar to national parks but are smaller in size and significance. By 2000, the national park system included more than 375 areas with over 130,000 square miles (336,700 km^2).

Worldly-minded conservationists want to take care of the earth because "this is all we have." Christians know that the earth will pass away, but they still try to be good stewards of it because that is what God commanded (Genesis 1:28–30).

The Taft Presidency

Election of William Howard Taft. President Roosevelt wanted William Howard Taft, a good friend, to be his successor. He believed that Taft would continue to further the reforms that had been started. Taft, who weighed more than 300 pounds (136 kg), was the largest man to become president. He did not really want to be president, but would rather have been a Supreme Court justice. Still, Taft went on to defeat Democrat William Jennings Bryan and serve as president from 1909 to 1913.

Alienation of the Progressives. Taft soon ran into trouble with the progressive reformers. Though intending to carry on Roosevelt's program, he believed that he should have a Constitutional basis for his actions. He also did not move as quickly or push as

William H. Taft (1857–1930) was the twenty-seventh president of the United States. He served from 1909 to 1913 and was a Republican.

hard as Roosevelt had. But the progressives were impatient—they did not want to wait for Taft. This caused tension between them and the president.

One of the first areas of difficulty was tariff revision. Many wanted protective tariffs reduced because large American companies no longer needed them. In 1909, Congress did consider tariff revision and passed the Payne-Aldrich Tariff—but this law contained few changes and no reduction of tariffs. Progressives expected the president to veto the bill, but Taft signed it because he thought the new law was better than the old one. So a split developed between Taft and the progressive Republicans.

Taft also ran into difficulty with progressives over conservation. Gifford Pinchot, the hero of conservationists, was still the chief forester. But Pinchot and Taft's secretary of the interior had a dispute, and Taft dismissed Pinchot. This angered the conservationists, who believed Taft had deserted the progressive cause. These events later led to a split in the Republican Party.

Continuing Reforms. In spite of his troubles, President Taft did make some progressive reforms. He continued to apply the Sherman Antitrust Act to break up large trusts; in fact, Taft broke up more trusts than Roosevelt had. He also signed the Mann-Elkins Act of 1910, which gave greater authority to the Interstate Commerce Commission, including expanded power to regulate railroad rates.

Also during the Taft administration, Congress passed the Sixteenth Amendment to allow for an income tax. This amendment was necessary because the Supreme Court had declared prior income tax laws unconstitutional. In addition, the Seventeenth Amendment was passed during his term to

Great Disasters. Two famous disasters took place during the Roosevelt–Taft years. In 1906, a great earthquake shattered the city of San Francisco. Fire raged through buildings for three days and destroyed 4 square miles (10 km^2). With a magnitude of 8.3 on the Richter scale, the quake killed over five hundred people and left hundreds of thousands homeless. (The upper limit of the Richter scale is 10.)

In April 1912, the luxury liner *Titanic* sank after striking an iceberg while trying to cross the Atlantic in record time. This disaster cost over fifteen hundred lives, but it led to stricter safety standards, such as requiring enough lifeboats for all passengers. It also demonstrated the limitations of man's technology; one man had boasted that God Himself could not sink the *Titanic*. A search expedition discovered the hulk of the ship on the ocean floor in 1985.

Disasters such as these may not be God's direct judgment in every case, but they should cause men to hear the voice of God.

Destruction caused by the San Francisco earthquake in 1906.

provide for direct election of senators.

But the progressive Republicans wanted to push reform faster than Taft did. The president seemed to agree more and more with conservative Republicans, thus widening the split within the party. By 1912, the party had divided, paving the way for a Democrat to win the presidential election.

Focus for Thought

6. a. Why did Theodore Roosevelt label his program the Square Deal?
   b. What pattern did this establish?
7. What is significant about Roosevelt's handling of the coal strike in 1902?
8. a. How did Roosevelt deal with a number of trusts?
   b. What three acts of 1906 increased the power of federal government to regulate trade between states?
9. What did President Roosevelt do to promote conservation of natural resources and to make conservation a national issue?
10. Why did President Taft hesitate to act as aggressively as Roosevelt had?
11. What progressive reforms did President Taft accomplish?

3. ANOTHER PROGRESSIVE IN POWER: WOODROW WILSON

A party called the Progressive Party split away from the Republican Party by 1912. Led by Theodore Roosevelt, this party challenged both President Taft and the Democrats. But since the Republicans were divided, the Democrats won the election. They continued the progressive reforms begun under Roosevelt.

The "New Freedom"

Woodrow Wilson won the 1912 election by a large majority of electoral votes. He became only the second Democrat to win the presidency after the Civil War. Interestingly, Taft became chief justice of the Supreme Court in 1921, where he served until 1930 in the position he had always desired. Taft was the only former president to serve later on the Supreme Court.

Woodrow Wilson (1856–1924) was the twenty-eighth president of the United States. He served from 1913 to 1921 and was a Democrat.

As president, Woodrow Wilson introduced a program of reform called the "New Freedom," and he worked energetically to have it enacted into law. He used every power at his disposal to get his wishes accomplished. The president wanted to lower tariffs, reform the banking system, and attack business trusts. By 1917, Wilson had reached many of his goals.

Tariff Reforms. Wilson wanted to reduce tariffs to make businesses more competitive and to increase foreign trade. The Underwood Tariff Act of 1913 reduced tariff rates from an average of 41 percent to about 26 percent. Some products, such as iron, steel, and sugar, were even placed on the free list, which meant no tariff at all would be charged on them. The Underwood Tariff Act was the first major reduction of tariffs after the Civil War.

To make up for the revenue lost through lower tariffs, the government would need more money from other sources. Therefore, the Underwood Tariff contained a provision for an income tax under the newly ratified Sixteenth Amendment. Some people object to income taxes, but Christians should willingly and honestly pay the taxes levied by the government. Paul wrote, "Render therefore to all their dues: tribute to whom tribute is due; custom to whom custom; fear to whom fear; honour to whom honour" (Romans 13:6, 7). It is the Christians' responsibility to pay taxes, and the government is then responsible for its use of tax revenue.

Banking Reforms. Reform in banking was one of the greatest achievements of Wilson's presidency. Bank reformers wanted to create a money supply that would expand or contract with the needs of the economy. They hoped in this way to eliminate the panics that struck the banking system periodically and caused banks to close. Actually, the panics occurred because the banks kept only a small amount of cash on hand to meet their obligations. Then when too many customers demanded cash at the same time, banks had to close because they did not have enough.

In 1913, Congress passed the Federal Reserve Act to create a central banking system called the Federal Reserve System. This act divided the nation into twelve banking districts with a privately controlled federal reserve bank in each district. The Federal Reserve Board, with seven members appointed by the president, was to supervise the Federal Reserve System.

The Federal Reserve Act greatly increased government control over the nation's banking system. Federal reserve banks began issuing federal reserve notes (printed by the United States Treasury) to serve as cash. In this way the Federal Reserve System regulates the money supply and controls the growth of the economy. Also, the Federal Reserve Board can control interest rates by raising or lowering the rates on money lent to member banks. Thus the Federal Reserve Act gave the federal government great power over the economy.

Business Reforms. President Wilson also moved to regulate the trusts. In 1914, Congress established the Federal Trade Commission (FTC) to enforce fair trade practices. It included a five-man commission to

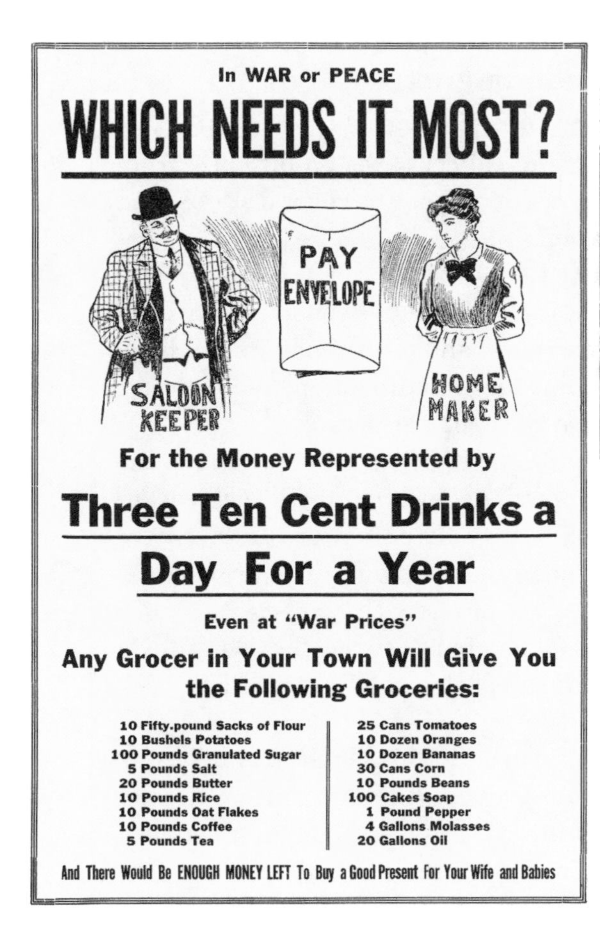

Left: Prohibition poster. The temperance movement brought about the passage of the Eighteenth Amendment in 1919, which led to nationwide Prohibition. The amendment was repealed in 1933. ***Right:*** Women's suffrage parade in Washington, D.C., in 1913. Such demonstrations helped to bring about the passage of the Nineteenth Amendment in 1920, which granted women in the United States the right to vote.

investigate companies and constrain them to stop any unfair methods of competition. Then in 1914 Congress passed the Clayton Antitrust Act, which strengthened the old Sherman Antitrust Act but exempted unions from antitrust laws. Federal laws like these were intended to encourage competition, but they did not always fulfill that goal.

Wilson's administration saw the passing of other laws relating to business and farmers. In 1916, the Adamson Act established an eight-hour day for railroad workers on interstate railroads, as well as time-and-a-half pay for more than eight hours. Thus began federal regulation of hours and wages in private business. The Federal Farm Loan Act (1916) aided farmers by making it easier for them to obtain loans. This law favored one specific group—farmers—and it too would not be the last of its type.

Effects of the Progressive Movement. President Wilson narrowly won re-election in 1916. By then he had accomplished many of his goals, but foreign affairs interrupted his reform program—World War I broke out in Europe in 1914. This war diverted the nation's attention from internal reform to world affairs. Reform zeal faded after the war.

Nevertheless, President Wilson and other progressive reformers had achieved a number of important measures. They had established the idea that the government was responsible for the health and safety of its citizens, and they had added four new amendments to the Constitution. They included the Sixteenth, allowing an income tax; the Seventeenth, providing for the direct election of senators; the Eighteenth, which outlawed alcoholic beverages but was later repealed; and the Nineteenth, which gave women the right to vote. These measures had profound effects that have changed American government and society to this day.

Progressive Amendments

Amendment 16

The Congress shall have power to lay and collect taxes on incomes, from whatever source derived, without apportionment among the several states, and without regard to any census or enumeration.

Amendment 17

The Senate of the United States shall be composed of two senators from each state, elected by the people thereof, for six years; and each senator shall have one vote. The electors in each state shall have the qualifications requisite for electors of the most numerous branch of the state legislatures.

When vacancies happen in the representation of any state in the Senate, the executive authority of such state shall issue writs of election to fill such vacancies: *Provided,* That the legislature of any state may empower the executive thereof to make temporary appointments until the people fill the vacancies by election as the legislature may direct.

This amendment shall not be so construed as to affect the election or term of any senator chosen before it becomes valid as part of the Constitution.

Amendment 18

Section 1. After one year from the ratification of this article the manufacture, sale, or transportation of intoxicating liquors within, the importation thereof into, or the exportation thereof from the United States and all territory subject to the jurisdiction thereof for beverage purposes is hereby prohibited.

Section 2. The Congress and the several states shall have concurrent power to enforce this article by appropriate legislation.

Section 3. This article shall be inoperative unless it shall have been ratified as an amendment to the Constitution by the legislatures of the several states, as provided in the Constitution, within seven years from the date of the submission hereof to the states by the Congress.

Amendment 19

The right of citizens of the United States to vote shall not be denied or abridged by the United States or by any state on account of sex.

Congress shall have power to enforce this article by appropriate legislation.

Focus for Thought

12. What three main areas did President Wilson want to reform?
13. a. What changes did the Underwood Tariff Act make in tariffs?
    b. What did this act provide for new revenue?
14. How did the Federal Reserve Act give the federal government power to control the economy?
15. What did the federal government do in 1914 to regulate the trusts?
16. Which amendment to the Constitution provided for
    a. women's suffrage?
    b. direct election of senators?
    c. prohibition of alcoholic beverages?
    d. an income tax?

Historical Highlights

A. Matching: Presidents

Each choice will be used more than once.

a. Theodore Roosevelt b. William Howard Taft c. Woodrow Wilson

1. President from 1913 to 1921.
2. The largest president.
3. President from 1901 to 1909.
4. Only president to become a justice of the Supreme Court.
5. President from 1909 to 1913.
6. President who promoted the Square Deal.
7. President who promoted the New Freedom.
8. A Democrat.

B. Matching: Terms

Not all the choices will be used.

a. Clayton Antitrust Act
b. Department of Commerce and Labor
c. Federal Reserve Act
d. Federal Trade Commission
e. initiative, referendum, recall
f. Meat Inspection Act
g. muckraker
h. New Freedom
i. progressive movement
j. Progressive Party
k. Pure Food and Drug Act
l. Square Deal
m. Underwood Tariff Act

1. Woodrow Wilson's reform program.
2. Theodore Roosevelt's reform program to treat everyone equally.
3. Law of 1913 that reduced taxes on imports and provided for an income tax.
4. First laws regulating the quality of goods shipped between states (two answers).
5. Agency set up to enforce fair trade practices.
6. Crusade promoting reform and change.
7. Group that nominated Theodore Roosevelt for president in 1912.
8. Law of 1914 that aimed to strengthen the Sherman Antitrust Act against big business.
9. Established a central banking system in 1913.
10. New department of the Cabinet set up in 1903 to regulate big business.
11. Measures for democratic reforms promoted by progressives.
12. Author of books or articles pointing out evils in society.

C. Matching: Constitutional Amendments

One choice will be used more than once.

a. Sixteenth Amendment
b. Seventeenth Amendment
c. Eighteenth Amendment
d. Nineteenth Amendment

1. Amendment that allowed women to vote.
2. Amendment that was later repealed.
3. Amendment that allowed an income tax.
4. Amendment that provided for the direct election of senators.
5. Amendment that prohibited alcoholic beverages.

D. Deeper Discussion

1. a. How did progressive reformers think they could solve problems in society?
   b. How did progressive educators depart from a Biblical premise?
2. a. Why was a third political party formed in 1912?
   b. What were the effects of this party?
3. a. Why did the progressives make so many amendments to the Constitution?
   b. What were the effects?
4. a. What should be the Christian's attitude toward conservation? Give Bible verses to support your thinking.
   b. How is this approach different from that of the progressives?
5. What should be the Christian's attitude toward taxation? Again, give Bible verses to support your thinking.

E. Chronology and Geography

Make a time line of the Progressive Era (1900–1920). On your time line, list the presidents by their year of election, the five laws (acts) listed in Part B, and the Constitutional amendments. Be sure to scale your time line correctly. Title it "The Progressive Era, 1900–1920."

The World.

Weather Forecast: UNSETTLED. "Circulation Books Open to All." "Circulation Books Open to All." Weather Forecast: UNSETTLED.

VOL. LII. NO. 18,501. Copyright, 1912, by The Press Publishing Co. (The New York World). NEW YORK, TUESDAY, APRIL 16, 1912. PRICE ONE CENT in Greater New York and Jersey City. TWO CENTS outside of Greater New York, Jersey City and on trains.

GREAT TITANIC SINKS; MORE THAN 1.500 LOST; 866 WOMEN AND CHILDREN KNOWN TO BE SAVED; SCORES OF NOTABLES NOT ACCOUNTED FOR

THE LOST LINER, HER POSITION AND THAT OF OTHER SHIPS WHEN SHE HIT ICEBERG

The TITANIC
LENGTH—882 FT.
BEAM —92 FT.
DEPTH — 94 FT.
DISPLACEMENT 45,000 TONS
VALUE (ESTIMATED) $10,000,000—

WHITE LINES ON SIDE of STEAMSHIP INDICATE LOCATION of BULKHEADS ...

① "VIRGINIAN", 170 MILES from SCENE of the COLLISION, STEAMS to her AID and IS the FIRST VESSEL to REACH SPOT.
② "CARPATHIA" ③ "BALTIC" ④ "OLYMPIC" ⑤ "PARISIAN" and ⑥ "CALIFORNIA" ALL PUT on FULL STEAM to REACH STRICKEN BOAT.
⑦ "CARPATHIA" TAKES PASSENGERS from LIFE BOATS and PUTS BACK for NEW YORK.

White Star Official Admits the Greatest Disaster in Marine History — J. J. Astor Rumored Lost, but Bride Saved — Text of Olympic's Fateful Message—Partial List Is Received.

HOPE THAT MANY WILL BE FOUND ON WRECKAGE.

Virginian and Parisian Reach Scene Too Late—They Are Joined by Other Steamers. Which Find Only Debris—Capt. Smith Believed to Have Gone Down with Ship—The Saved Suffer Severely from Exposure, After Floating in the Lifeboats for Eight Hours.

More than fifteen hundred souls, men, women and children, were lost, it is feared, in the wreck of the White Star liner Titanic, latest and greatest ship of the seas, which collided with an iceberg at 10.25 P. M. Sunday night and sank off the Banks of Newfoundland at 2.20 A. M. yesterday, less than four hours after she had struck.

Capt. Haddock of the Olympic sent this despatch by wireless to the White Star line last evening:

"Carpathia reached Titanic position at daybreak. Found boats and wreckage only. Titanic sank about 2.20 A. M., in 41.46 North, 50.14 West. All her boats accounted for, containing about 675 souls saved, crew and passengers included. Nearly all saved women and children. Leyland liner Californian remained and searching exact position of disaster. LOSS LIKELY TOTAL 1,800 SOULS.

The exact text of this despatch was closely guarded until after midnight by Vice-President Franklin of the White Star line, who received it at 7 o'clock. It gave the first definite news of the sinking of the Titanic and of the great loss of life.

But it is believed that the words "loss likely total 1,800 souls" is an error due to the ignorance of Capt. Haddock and the rescued passengers of the total number of persons aboard.

There were, according to the ship's manifest, 325 first cabin, 285 second cabin, and 710 steerage, a total of 1,320 passengers, and a crew of 860. This would make 2,180 persons aboard and some late comers not on the passenger lists are believed to have brought the total up to 2,200. Deducting 675 from this, the lost would only number 1,505, which Mr. Franklin believes to be correct.

A wireless despatch from the Olympic was picked up by a Boston operator late last night, in which it was stated that the Carpathia was on her way to New York with 866 passengers rescued from the Titanic. The rescued, the despatch read, were mostly women and children, and the despatch concluded:

"Grave fears are felt for the safety of the balance of the passengers and crew."

The disparity between this number of rescued, 866, and the 675 mentioned in Capt. Haddock's despatch to the White Star line was explained on the theory that the Carpathia might have picked up some more passengers in lifeboats

Front page of a New York newspaper, *The World,* for April 16, 1912.

President Wilson asking Congress for a declaration of war on Germany, on April 2, 1917.

23 The United States and World War I

1. NEUTRALITY IN WORLD WAR I
   - The War in Europe
   - Neutrality in the United States
   - The Road to War
2. INVOLVEMENT IN WORLD WAR I AND THE PEACE CONFERENCE
   - The Home Front
   - The American Army in France
   - The Paris Peace Conference
   - The League Campaign
   - Effects of World War I
3. NONRESISTANCE IN WORLD WAR I
   - At Home
   - In the Army
   - After the War

1880

Triple Alliance formed 1882

1890

1900

Triple Entente formed 1907

1910

Austria-Hungary declares war on Serbia; World War I begins **1914**

Lusitania sinks 1915

Woodrow Wilson re-elected; preparedness parades held 1916

United States declares war on Germany **1917**

Armistice ends World War I (November 11) **1918**

Paris Peace Conference held; Treaty of Versailles signed **1919**

1920

Mennonite Central Committee formed 1920

1930

"For thus saith the LORD; We have heard a voice of trembling, of fear, and not of peace."

Jeremiah 30:5

THE UNITED STATES AND WORLD WAR I

Focus for Reading

Ever since the Monroe Doctrine was proclaimed in 1823, the United States had followed a policy of not interfering in the affairs of European nations. Many Americans wanted to continue this policy when a number of European nations began fighting in 1914. Woodrow Wilson even won re-election in 1916 after campaigning on the slogan "He kept us out of the war." How did the United States come to depart from its former policy? What happened when Americans became involved in the war? How did nonresistant Christians fare amid the great outburst of patriotic fervor? Three sections in this chapter address these questions.

1. Neutrality in World War I
2. Involvement in World War I and the Peace Conference
3. Nonresistance in World War I

1. NEUTRALITY IN WORLD WAR I

According to Daniel 7, God sees earthly nations as ravenous beasts. This characteristic is vividly evident in the fighting that broke out in 1914 among European nations. But Americans steadfastly declared that they would have nothing to do with it—this was a European war. President Wilson proclaimed that America would remain neutral, and he tried to stay on a neutral course even as the war dragged on into its second and third year. Finally the president decided that the United States had little choice but to enter the war.

The War in Europe

Seedbed for Conflict. One cause of this war was the competition among European nations to build empires. After Germany defeated France in the Franco-Prussian War, the Prussians united the German Empire by 1871. (See "The Last Lesson in French" in Rod and Staff's Seventh Reader.) Germany, Italy, Great Britain, and France all sought to extend their empires by taking colonies in Africa and Asia. Russia and Austria-Hungary tried to take land near them in Europe, especially from the Ottoman Empire in Turkey.

All these efforts caused intense rivalries and bitter enmity. The French hated the Germans because in 1871 they had taken over Alsace-Lorraine—which the French considered their territory. Thus in 1914, the French still longed for vengeance on the Germans.

A second cause of war was the harsh rule in these empires. The leaders were from dynasties that had governed Europe with absolute authority for centuries. Their oppressed peoples, especially in Austria-Hungary, longed to be free. The spirit of rebellion smoldered particularly in the Balkan countries, which became known as the "powder keg of Europe."

Another cause of war was militarism. Because the empires competed with each other, they worked to build up powerful armed forces. They raised huge armies, stocked increasingly powerful weapons, and launched immense navies. Germany in particular began building a navy to match Britain's unrivaled ships.

Yet another cause is that the powerful European nations began forming military alliances. In 1882, Germany, Austria-Hungary, and Italy formed a union called the Triple Alliance. By 1907, France, Russia, and Great Britain had formed an alliance called the

Triple Entente (ahn TAHNT). Besides these unions, some of the stronger nations agreed to protect weaker nations from attack. For example, Russia promised to defend Serbia, and Britain agreed to protect Belgium.

Thus Europe became two armed camps arrayed against each other. Yet until 1914, the European nations had avoided a major war by diplomatic negotiations. But when those efforts failed that year, vast armies set out to destroy each other and anything in their paths.

Outbreak of Fighting. The spark that ignited the conflict came on June 28, 1914, when **Francis Ferdinand** visited Sarajevo (sar uh YAY voh) in Bosnia. Ferdinand was the archduke of Austria-Hungary and the heir to the throne. As he rode through the city in an open car, some Serbs shot and killed the archduke and his wife.

This incident led quickly to war. Austria-Hungary blamed Serbia for the killing and made harsh demands of that small nation. When Serbia did not meet all the demands, Austria-Hungary declared war on July 28, 1914. Russia soon sent its army to protect Serbia. German leader Kaiser **Wilhelm II** then led Germany into the war. Allied with Austria-Hungary, Germany declared war on Russia and then on Russia's ally, France.

Hoping to quickly subdue France, the Germans tried to evade French defenses by attacking France through neutral Belgium. This brought the British into the war, since they had pledged to protect Belgium. In just a few weeks, Europe became a huge battlefield on which the Central Powers (Germany, Austria-Hungary, Bulgaria, and Turkey) fought the Allies (Great Britain, France, Russia, Italy, and some others). Thus began the Great War, which was later called World War I.

A Solid Deadlock. No one envisioned the bloody stalemate that would soon follow. The Germans drove swiftly through Belgium and struck at the heart of France. But in September the French stopped the German advance at the Marne River. Both sides built elaborate defenses along a line called the Western Front, which extended from Switzerland across France through part of Belgium to the North Sea.

Troops on both sides dug trenches and built fortifications of barbed wire and sandbags. Behind the trenches they positioned their artillery (heavy guns and cannons) that could rain destruction on the opposing trenches. Deadly machine-gun fire added to the great numbers of casualties.

Both Francis Ferdinand, archduke of Austria-Hungary, and his wife were shot only a few minutes after this photograph was taken.

Allied soldiers going "over the top" of their trench to begin an assault on enemy trenches in World War I. This was a common part of trench warfare.

Europe During World War I

Since both sides were about equal in strength, the Western Front changed little for over three years. From time to time each side would make massive assaults against the other, gaining perhaps a few yards or several miles—only to bog down or retreat again. Some campaigns left as many as four hundred thousand to five hundred thousand soldiers dead or wounded on each side. Flamethrowers and poison gas added to the horror. As the war dragged on, it claimed millions of lives in a terrible conflict with no end in sight.

German soldiers in France wearing gas masks. Poison gas was a new weapon of modern warfare.

Neutrality in the United States

President Wilson declared United States neutrality in August 1914, though the nation probably never was truly neutral in the war. Many Americans sympathized with the Allies for a number of reasons.

Economic Involvements With the Allies. The Allies as well as the Germans needed war materials that American businesses could supply. But the British blockaded the ports of the Central Powers so that other nations could not trade with them. The British also stopped neutral ships and searched them for ***contraband of war***, goods headed toward an enemy nation to support its war effort. The British defined contraband of war so broadly that the term included almost anything, even food. They confiscated cargoes and sometimes did not even pay for them.

Americans had always defended ***freedom of the seas***—the right of any merchant ship to sail the ocean in peace or war. They objected to Britain's actions, which violated international law; but the British replied that since they were fighting for their lives, the law did not apply. So the Americans found it almost impossible to trade with the Central Powers, but they sold weapons, ammunition, and many other things to the Allies.

By 1915, the Allies desperately needed money to finance their war; so the United States granted huge loans to them. Much of this money came back to America to purchase military supplies. If the Allies lost the war, those who had loaned the money would lose it; so this naturally caused their sympathy for the Allies to grow even stronger.

Submarine Attacks by the Germans. To gain an advantage at sea, the Germans began using submarines, a weapon that they called the *Unterseeboot* ("undersea boat"). In February 1915, they declared a war zone around Great Britain, and their "U-boats" began sinking almost any ship within the zone—whether Allied or neutral. This caused Americans to become greatly upset with the Germans.

The wisest thing for Americans to do was to stay off ships subject to German attack. But Americans wanted to maintain their rights as neutrals, especially against Germany. So when the *Lusitania*, a British liner, set out for Britain with nearly 2,000 people aboard (and with ammunition for the Allies), numerous Americans were on it. On May 7, 1915, a German U-boat sent a torpedo into the *Lusitania*, and the great liner sank in only eighteen minutes. Nearly 1,200 people died, among them 128 Americans.

A German U-boat at sea. In order to starve Britain into surrender, German submarines sank many cargo ships headed for British seaports.

The *Lusitania* disaster caused an uproar in the United States. Many people wanted to

The *Lusitania*. Its sinking in 1915 was a major provocation that brought the United States into World War I.

Escape from a ship torpedoed by a German submarine, about 1917. Note the people in the lifeboat and the man sliding down the rope.

declare war, but Wilson only demanded that Germany apologize, pay for the damages, and promise to stop attacking passenger ships. The Germans agreed to apologize and to pay for damages, but they promised to stop sinking ships without warning only if Allied ships followed the rules of international law. However, the British would not agree to change their methods of warfare, so the issue of submarine attacks remained unsettled.

Preparedness in the United States. By 1916, an election year, multitudes of Americans were thinking their nation should prepare to fight Germany. President Wilson had tried to avoid entering the war, but now war seemed imminent. Huge ***preparedness*** parades were held in cities across the nation, and Wilson also promoted the idea to help his re-election campaign. He won the election by a narrow margin, having campaigned on the slogan "He kept us out of the war." But this slogan would not be true a year later.

Preparedness parade on Pennsylvania Avenue in Washington, D.C. These parades favored supporting the Allies and going to war against Germany.

The Road to War

President Wilson hoped the neutral United States could help to work out a peace treaty between the warring nations. Germany agreed to negotiate in December 1916, but it was a forlorn hope. When the opposing sides met, they could not agree on the terms for peace.

Soon afterward, the Germans announced that they would resume unrestricted submarine warfare. As of February 1, 1917, U-boats would sink without warning all ships in the declared war zone. The Germans knew this would probably bring the United States into the war, but they hoped a strong U-boat campaign would cut off supplies to the Allies and win the war before the United States could make much difference.

Soon another issue arose. The British intercepted a telegram sent to Mexico in which Arthur Zimmermann, the German foreign minister, proposed an alliance with Mexico and Japan if the United States entered the war. It promised that if the Germans won, they would restore Texas, New Mexico, and Arizona to Mexico. When the Zimmermann telegram was made public on March 1, 1917, Americans were outraged. The clamor for war with Germany grew louder than ever.

Since German submarines were already sinking American ships, President Wilson needed no further cause for declaring war. He called Congress into a special session on April 2, 1917, and asked for a declaration of war on Germany. The House and the Senate both passed the war resolution by April 6, and the president signed it immediately. On April 6,

1917, the United States went to war with Germany—a war that was supposed to "make the world safe for democracy" and to "end all wars."

"And ye shall hear of wars and rumours of wars: see that ye be not troubled: for all these things must come to pass" (Matthew 24:6).

Focus for Thought

1. a. What were four main causes of the war in Europe?
   b. What incident led to the outbreak of fighting?
   c. Name the nations that made up the Central Powers, and those that made up the Allies.
2. Summarize what happened along the Western Front for over three years.
3. How did the following things influence the United States in favor of the Allies?
   a. economic involvements
   b. German submarine warfare
   c. preparedness
4. What two main issues finally brought the United States into the war?
5. What were the two stated reasons for the United States to enter World War I?

---

2. INVOLVEMENT IN WORLD WAR I AND THE PEACE CONFERENCE

United States participation in World War I touched the life of almost every citizen in the country. American civilians provided supplies and weapons, and American troops bolstered the Allied effort and helped to defeat the Central Powers.

After the war, President Wilson promoted lofty ideals for world peace; but the Allies did not share his vision. Then after Wilson achieved some of his goals in Europe, his own nation rejected the work he had done. Bitterly disappointed and suffering poor health, Woodrow Wilson served out the rest of his term as best he could.

The Home Front

To build up United States military might, Congress passed the Selective Service Act in May 1917 to draft men into the armed forces. Nearly 3 million men were drafted by random selection, and these along with 2 million volunteers served during the eighteen months of United States involvement in World War I.

Men could be exempted from military service for physical or professional reasons, as well as for religious beliefs. But conscientious objectors were exempted only from combatant service, not from ***noncombatant*** (nonfighting) duty. This proved to be a great trial for Mennonites and other nonresistant people.

To meet the need for supplies and weapons, the federal government established various agencies to make the nation as productive as possible. These agencies supervised factory production, managed the food supply, and bought up large supplies of wheat, sugar, and other crops. The government even set up an administration to supervise the railroads.

Newton D. Baker, secretary of war, drew the first U.S. military draft number for World War I. The first number drawn at random out of a bowl by the blindfolded Baker was 246. Potential draftees with this number were the first to be called.

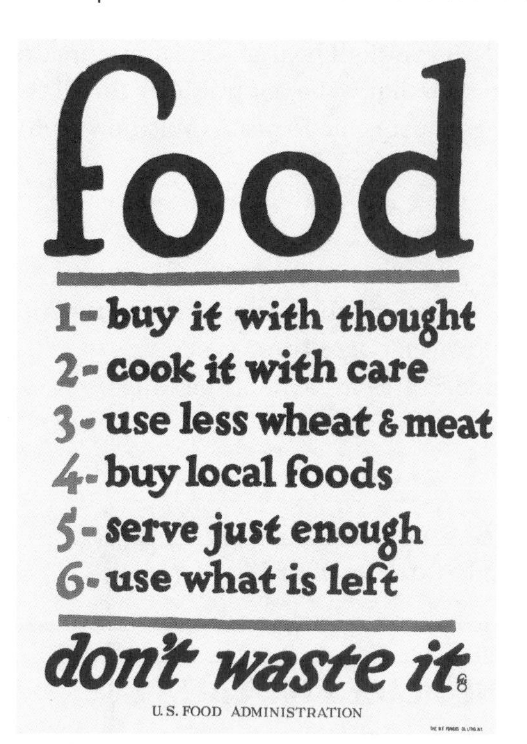

The U.S. Food Administration encouraged food conservation with posters such as this one.

The men standing in line are senators waiting to purchase Liberty Bonds.

The government encouraged farmers to plant more field crops and to raise "victory gardens" of vegetables. American housewives were urged to cook frugally and to can their own fruits and vegetables. People observed "wheatless Mondays," "meatless Tuesdays," and "porkless Saturdays" to conserve wheat and meat.

The war cost America around $35 billion, of which about $11 billion was loaned to other nations. This total came to about $2 million per hour during the time the United States was involved! One way the government paid this staggering price was by raising taxes. Income taxes were increased, a tax on "excess profits" was enacted, and a 25 percent inheritance tax was levied. The government also raised money by selling Liberty Bonds to be repaid with interest after fifteen or thirty years. With slogans, speeches, advertisements, and bond drives, the government rallied the support of the American people for the war cause.

The American Army in France

To help the Allies, the United States sent the American Expeditionary Force to France under the leadership of General **John J. Pershing**. Soldiers began arriving in Paris by July 1917—the first American troops ever sent to fight in Europe—and over the following months, thousands of other soldiers came. Although they did little fighting in 1917, the

John J. Pershing (1860–1948) was the United States general who led the American Expeditionary Force in World War I.

United States troops arriving at Brest, France. In all, about 2 million American soldiers served in Europe in World War I.

German prisoners after the battle at Saint-Mihiel. These are some of the 15,000 German prisoners that Americans captured there.

influx of new troops greatly encouraged the Allies.

American soldiers reached the battlefield in the spring of 1918, soon after a massive German assault in which the Allies were driven back to the Marne River. The Americans helped to win a battle that kept the enemy from crossing the river, and then they pushed the Germans back in the Battle of Belleau Wood (BEHL oh). In July 1918, the Allies stopped another German attack in the Second Battle of the Marne. This halted the German advance and became the turning point in the war.

Now the Allies began a steady advance, and that summer they gradually pushed the Germans toward Germany. Over a million Americans took part in the final assault, which was called the Meuse-Argonne campaign because it took place in the Meuse valley and Argonne region of France. The Allies drove the Germans back to their last line of defense, called the Hindenburg Line; and by November 1, the German armies were in retreat all along the Western Front.

The Central Powers gave up one by one. Bulgaria surrendered in September, Turkey in October, and Austria-Hungary on November 3. Finally the Germans decided to seek peace.

Traffic congestion behind American lines in the Argonne region. With over 800,000 Americans taking part in the Meuse-Argonne offensive, there was a great demand for men and supplies. The vehicles in the picture could move no faster than 2 miles per hour (3 km/h).

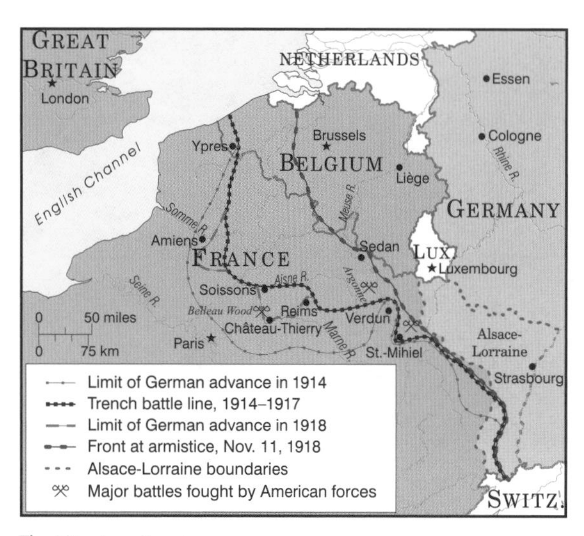

The Western Front

(Kaiser Wilhelm II fled to the Netherlands.) On November 8, 1918, a German delegation met with Ferdinand Foch (FAHSH), the French commander-in-chief, in a railroad car. There the Germans heard the Allied terms for an ***armistice*** (AHR mih stihs)—an agreement to stop fighting.

The Allies made a number of demands. Among other things, the Germans would need to withdraw from all occupied territory, including the land west of the Rhine, and to give up Alsace-Lorraine. These terms were harsh; but since the Germans had no other choice, they signed the armistice on November 11. The war officially ended at eleven o'clock on the eleventh day of the eleventh month. Wild celebrations burst out in Europe and in the United States as people heard that the Great War was over.

The Paris Peace Conference

President Wilson had earlier prepared the Fourteen Points, in which he summarized his ideals for world peace. Such peace would be achieved by open agreements between nations, complete freedom of the seas, removal of trade barriers, and reduction of military forces. Most important was his fourteenth point, which

The World.

GERMANS SIGN THE ARMISTICE; HOSTILITIES STOP AT 6 A. M. TO-DAY; SOCIALIST REBELS TAKE BERLIN; EX-KAISER AND HEIR IN HOLLAND

The world rejoiced when World War I ended at 11:00 A.M. on November 11, 1918. The headline says 6:00 A.M. because that was the time in New York.

Allied leaders, called the "Big Four," met at the Paris Peace Conference in May 1919. From left to right, they are David Lloyd George (Britain), Vittorio Orlando (Italy), Georges Clemenceau (France), and Woodrow Wilson (United States).

Signing of the peace treaty in the Hall of Mirrors, Versailles, on June 28, 1919. The German delegate is seated with his left hand on the treaty. The distorted windows in the background are reflections in the mirrors on the wall.

called for a "general association of nations" to provide peaceable means of settling disputes. It was based on the idea that if the nations would unite, they could prevent war. This idea is false, of course, because war is a product of man's evil nature.

In January 1919, President Wilson himself traveled to the Paris Peace Conference (actually held in the nearby city of Versailles) to promote his ideals. He was the first president to travel to Europe while in office. Over thirty nations attended the conference, but neither Germany nor Russia was represented. Most decisions were made by the leaders of four nations: Great Britain, France, Italy, and the United States. These leaders were referred to as the "Big Four."

It soon became clear that the other three members of the Big Four did not fully support Wilson's ideals. They had suffered greatly in the war, and they intended to punish the Germans severely. So President Wilson decided to start with his most important point: an association of nations to maintain peace. A committee formulated a plan for such an association, later called the League of Nations, and the proposal was presented to the peace conference in February.

The primary goal of the League would be to maintain peace and to promote cooperation among nations. Disputes between nations could be submitted to a Permanent Court of International Justice; and if any nation did not cooperate, the others were to stop trading with it. The member nations pledged to protect the "territorial integrity" and "political independence" of one another.

By June 1919, the delegates had worked out the Treaty of Versailles (vur SY). This treaty incorporated the League of Nations, but it also laid severe penalties on the Germans. They were required to pay reparations of over $30 billion, and their colonies were distributed among the Allies. Japan took Germany's islands in the Pacific, Britain and France took the colonies in Africa, and Alsace-Lorraine was returned to France.

In addition, the Treaty of Versailles greatly reduced the size of the German army, navy, and merchant fleet. Germany would not be allowed to build tanks, warplanes, or battleships. The Germans objected strongly to these harsh terms. But since there was little else to do, they signed the Treaty of Versailles on June 28, 1919.

The League Campaign

Back in America, President Wilson faced strong opposition to the Treaty of Versailles. The Senate had to ratify the treaty before it

In 1919, President Wilson (standing inside the automobile) campaigned in Los Angeles. He was trying to gain American support for the Treaty of Versailles and the League of Nations.

could go into effect, but many senators opposed its terms. The greatest problem was with the League of Nations. Many senators wanted to continue isolationism as spelled out in the Monroe Doctrine, rather than becoming so deeply involved in the affairs of other nations. Opponents also believed that by joining the League, the United States would give up some of its independence because it might have to provide troops to help the League enforce its decisions.

Wilson went on a nationwide tour to gain public support for his ideas. He traveled over 8,000 miles (12,874 km) and delivered at least thirty-seven speeches. But the strain was so great that the president became ill and had to return to Washington before completing the tour. Soon afterward, Wilson suffered a stroke that partly paralyzed his left side and permanently damaged his ability to perform official duties.

When the Treaty of Versailles finally came up for a vote, it was defeated twice in November 1919 and once more in March 1920. This effectively ended President Wilson's dreams for world peace. The United States did not join the League of Nations, nor did it agree to the Treaty of Versailles. Instead, it made separate peace treaties with the Central Powers by 1921.

Effects of World War I

The costs of World War I were enormous. In financial terms, the total has been estimated at $400 billion. But because of the economic collapse in the 1930s, much of the money borrowed by warring nations was never repaid.

World War I left many Americans disillusioned. The goals they had fought for were not realized. The war did not make the world safe for democracy or end war. Besides, an epidemic of influenza in 1918 and 1919 caused

Some wounded soldiers of World War I are being treated in a damaged church building in France.

Europe After World War I

about 30 million deaths worldwide, with 550,000 of these in the United States.

Like all wars, this one had a harmful effect on the nation's moral standards. Thousands of young men adopted tobacco use and coarse language in their term of military service. Many women started working in factories during the war and continued to do so afterward. Some had to go to work because their husbands were killed in battle. For

Ruins of Vaux, France, in July 1918.

These women were employed to make fuses in an arms factory during World War I.

these and other reasons, the 1920s became a period of the most rapid breakdown of morals that the nation had ever experienced.

World War I is generally considered a turning point in history. It marked the end of the old empires and the beginning of modern nations. Moreover, the failure of the League of Nations and the harshness of the Treaty of Versailles helped to bring on World War II just twenty years later—and the effects of these wars are still felt today. Yet through it all, God was in control, using the "wrath of man" to praise Him by accomplishing His purposes (Psalm 76:10).

Focus for Thought

6. How was the American Expeditionary Force in Europe a "first" for America?
7. Briefly describe what happened at the four main places where Americans helped the Allies in 1918.
8. How and when did World War I come to an end?
9. How were the Fourteen Points to bring peace to the world?
10. How did the Treaty of Versailles meet the goals
    a. of President Wilson?
    b. of the other members of the Big Four?
11. a. How did President Wilson try to get the American public to support his ideas?
    b. What became of his efforts?
12. In what way was World War I a turning point in history?

3. NONRESISTANCE IN WORLD WAR I

World War I was a great trial to Mennonites and other nonresistant groups. It severely tested their loyalty to Christ and His kingdom. It tested their understanding and practice of true nonresistance in a number of important ways, both at home and in the army camps.

At Home

Relating to the Military Draft. After the United States declared war in 1917, the Mennonites made efforts to clarify their position of nonresistance. On August 29, about 180 ordained men from sixteen Mennonite conferences met at the Yellow Creek Church near Goshen, Indiana. They drafted a statement rejecting all forms of military service, combatant or noncombatant, but saying that young men should report to the authorities when drafted.

The men at the Yellow Creek meeting also set up a War Problems Committee, which was composed of three ministers from Pennsylvania and Indiana. The War Problems Committee went to Washington to speak with **Newton D. Baker**, the secretary of war. He could tell them little more than that conscientious objectors (COs) should report to army camps, where they would be segregated from the other men and be given noncombatant duties. But this was of little help because noncombatant service was still part of the military effort and so was unacceptable to the Mennonites. Soon a number of nonresistant young men found themselves in army camps, where they were sorely tried for their convictions.

Relating to Patriotism. The intense patriotism stirred up by the war brought severe tests for nonresistant people. When their young men refused to fight, they were called "cowards, slackers, parasites, scoundrels, traitors, and individuals not worthy of holding American citizenship." In one case, a

The following is an excerpt from the statement signed at Yellow Creek Church. Some authorities viewed the statement as a violation of the Espionage Act; and as a result, a number of the church leaders who signed it were called before federal authorities in Washington, D.C.

"We hold that Christian people should have no part in carnal warfare of any kind or for any cause. Our attitude on the question of military service is correctly stated in that clause of the Selective Draft Law enacted May 18, 1917, which provides for exemption for members of every church 'whose existing creed or principles forbid its members to participate in war in any form and whose religious convictions are against war or participation therein.' We deeply regret, however, that this exemption is practically nullified (save in the matter of bearing arms) in the further provision empowering the government to impress nonresistant people into noncombatant service. . . .

"This position has been uniformly held by our forefathers from Reformation times . . . even to the extent of martyrdom and banishment by those governments enjoining military service upon their citizens, and for which cause they gratefully accepted the hospitality and the guarantee of religious liberty of this land, historical records bearing ample witness to these facts. . . .

"We are grateful for the exemption clause for nonresistant people in the new Selective Draft Law, and hereby express the hope that when the powers that be fully understand our position with reference to military service, this clause referring to noncombatant service may be accordingly modified. . . .

"With a fervent prayer to the Almighty God that He may bless and so direct the rulers of our land that we may lead a quiet and peaceable life, . . . we humbly subscribe our names to these declarations and pledge our powers in devotion to the principles herein set forth."

CO released from an army camp found this sign in his front yard: "Sam Yoder, a slacker, ashamed of the U.S. uniform, is home, lives here. We are ashamed of him. Leave, for the people don't want you." People whose sons were killed in France became especially bitter toward those whose young men would not even join the army.

Camp Sherman at Chillicothe, Ohio. Numerous conscientious objectors were sent to this camp.

Conscientious objectors at Camp Sherman, Ohio. Philemon Frey is in the front row on the right.

Because of strong anti-German feelings, people were especially hostile against the German-speaking Mennonites. Anything German—periodicals printed in German, church services conducted in German, and teaching the German language in schools—all were suspect. In one case, John Franz, a Mennonite pastor in Montana, almost suffered a lynching, partly because his church used German. His abductors took him out to a lonely place and strung a rope from a tree. But John grabbed the rope and would not let go. Finally the local sheriff, who was among the captors, took John to the county jail. Then a trial was held, and the church members had to post a high bond before John was released.

The government was suspicious of Mennonites because they taught Biblical nonresistance. Some Mennonite ministers were fined for encouraging their people not to buy Liberty Bonds. The government confiscated 150 copies of a tract entitled *Nonresistance*. It became hazardous for Mennonites to speak openly against warfare.

Relating to the American flag was another issue for nonresistant people. Those who did not display or salute the flag seemed suspiciously unpatriotic. In one case in Ohio, mobs went about and placed flags on Mennonite church buildings. Saluting the flag was a particular problem for Amish and Mennonite children in public schools. One man, Ora Troyer, was arrested and sentenced to twenty-five days in jail for refusing to let his daughter salute the flag.

Relating to War Finances. Mennonites believed in paying taxes as the Bible teaches, but Liberty Bonds were a different matter. If a person bought them, was he not helping to finance the war of his own free will? Therefore, Mennonites generally refused to buy them even though they faced intense pressure to do so. Patriotic citizens painted Mennonite houses and church buildings yellow. On one meeting house in Illinois, the words "WE ARE SLACKERS" were painted on one side and "WE BUY NO BONDS" on the other. Some nonresistant people were tarred and feathered, such as Daniel Diener and two others in Kansas.

These people's loyalty to their faith challenges us to be loyal as well. We do not know what is in store for us, but we must build firm convictions to stand for the truth, regardless of consequences. We also need to be faithful in expressing nonresistance today; for if we fail in times of peace, we will hardly be able to stand when severe testing comes.

In the Army

Nonresistant Men in Camp. When a Mennonite young man was drafted, he had to go to the army training camps and stand for his own convictions—usually all alone. Though the official policy of the War Department was to treat COs leniently, the officers at camp usually hoped to persuade them to give up and join the army. So the COs generally were not segregated as promised, but were treated harshly. Officers interrogated them relentlessly to see if they really were sincere. They were asked about their past life, their church attendance, and so forth.

The strongest conflict usually focused on three things: wearing the uniform, working in noncombatant service, and drilling for war. Since a man who put on a uniform was identifying with the army, a faithful CO refused to wear it. This brought much persecution in the form of threats and tricks. For example, a CO might have his clothes taken and then be told that he would have nothing to wear unless he put on the uniform. Others had uniforms put on them by force.

Most COs realized that it was wrong to drill. One young man, upon observing the cruel methods being taught at drill, concluded that he could have no part in such an organization, even noncombatant service. But work in the army camps posed a dilemma: Would it be right for a CO to cook, or clean, or garden, or do any other work for the military? Some did these things, but others realized that such work was still a part of the war effort. Therefore, many refused to do any work that involved them with the army.

COs in camp suffered much ridicule and mockery. They were also beaten, or held under a cold shower, or scrubbed with lye and a stiff brush, or dunked in a filthy sewage tank. Mock trials and executions were sometimes held, in which COs were lined up and "shot" by a firing squad whose guns were loaded with blanks.

COs who persisted in disobeying orders were sent to the guardhouse (camp prison), where they were treated brutally. Some had to stand with outstretched arms for hours, and some were beaten so severely that they suffered broken bones. Faithful COs did not fight back, but rather tried to show love and forgiveness according to the example of Christ (1 Peter 2:21).

Nonresistant Men in Prison. A CO who refused to compromise might face a military trial called a court-martial. These trials were usually conducted by military officials with little sympathy for COs, and the outcome was sometimes a long prison sentence, regardless of the CO's testimony. One man said, "I did not regard the order [given me] as a lawful order, because I could not obey it without violating the dictates of my conscience and the plain teachings of God's higher law. . . . I know the teachings of Christ my Saviour. He taught us to resist not evil, to love our enemies, to do good to them that hate us." This man, Maurice Hess, was sentenced to twenty-five years in the prison at Fort Leavenworth, Kansas.

The prisons were brutal places where nonresistant men had to live with criminals of all sorts. Those who still refused to work in prison were punished harshly. Some were put on a diet of bread and water for several weeks. Maurice Hess had to stand handcuffed to the iron bars of his cell gate for nine hours a day, and then sleep on the concrete floor at night. The COs were released after the war, but with a dishonorable discharge.

Other Experiences. Two developments eventually made things easier for COs, but they came almost too late to be very helpful. In March 1918, the Furlough Act allowed men in the army to work at civilian jobs such as farming. This law was extended in June to include conscientious objectors, and that same month the War Department set up a Board of Inquiry to review CO cases.

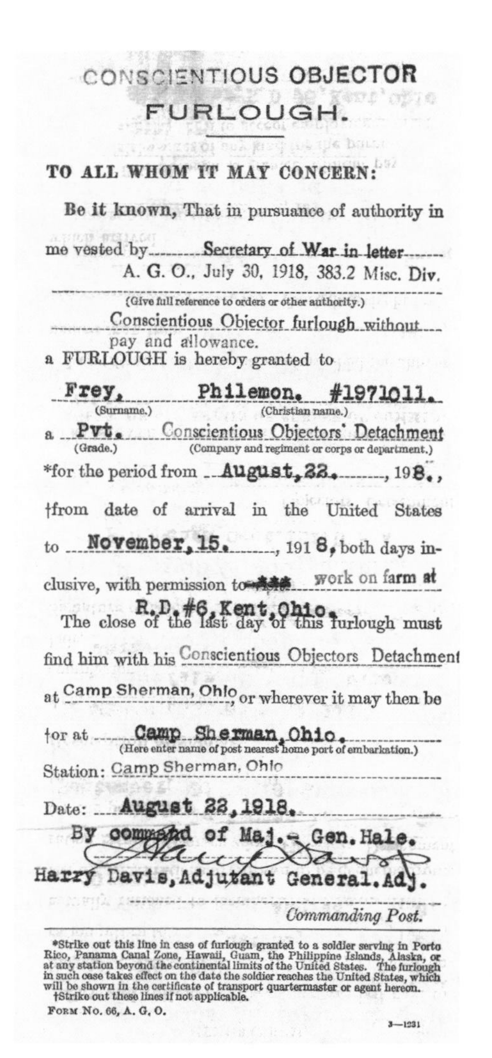

CONSCIENTIOUS OBJECTOR
FURLOUGH.

TO ALL WHOM IT MAY CONCERN:

Be it known, That in pursuance of authority in me vested by Secretary of War in letter A. G. O., July 30, 1918, 383.2 Misc. Div.
(Give full reference to orders or other authority.)
Conscientious Objector furlough without pay and allowance.
a FURLOUGH is hereby granted to
Frey, Philemon. #1971011.
(Surname.) (Christian name.)
a Pvt. Conscientious Objectors' Detachment
(Grade.) (Company and regiment or corps or department.)
*for the period from August, 22., 1918.,
†from date of arrival in the United States
to November, 15., 1918, both days inclusive, with permission to work on farm at R.D.#6, Kent, Ohio.
The close of the last day of this furlough must find him with his Conscientious Objectors Detachment at Camp Sherman, Ohio, or wherever it may then be
†or at Camp Sherman, Ohio.
(Here enter name of post nearest home port of embarkation.)
Station: Camp Sherman, Ohio
Date: August 22, 1918.
By command of Maj.-Gen. Hale.
Harry Davis, Adjutant General. Adj.
Commanding Post.

*Strike out this line in case of furlough granted to a soldier serving in Porto Rico, Panama Canal Zone, Hawaii, Guam, the Philippine Islands, Alaska, or at any station beyond the continental limits of the United States. The furlough in such case takes effect on the date the soldier reaches the United States, which will be shown in the certificate of transport quartermaster or agent hereon.
†Strike out these lines if not applicable.
Form No. 66, A. G. O.
3—1231

Philemon Frey was a conscientious objector from Ohio who received a furlough on August 22, 1918. The furloughs were a great blessing because the young men could leave the army camps to work on farms.

Martyred for Their Faith. Four Hutterite young men received some of the worst treatment of any conscientious objectors. David, Joseph, and Michael Hofer, along with their brother-in-law Jacob Wipf, were sentenced to twenty years in prison. (The three Hofer brothers were married and had children.) They were taken to the notorious Alcatraz Prison in San Francisco Bay, where they were stripped of most of their clothing and put in a dark and filthy dungeon. For over four days, they received no food and only half a glass of water every twenty-four hours. With their hands above their heads, they were chained to bars so high that their feet barely touched the floor. They were also beaten with clubs.

For the next four months, they were held in solitary confinement with only one hour on Sundays for exercise. In November 1918, they were transferred to the Fort Leavenworth prison. The four men marched at bayonet point from the railway station to the prison; then they had to remove most of their outer clothing and stand outside for two hours in the middle of the night. At five in the morning, they were again forced to stand outside. Both Joseph and Michael became sick and were sent to the military hospital. Their wives were notified and arrived only when their husbands were almost dead.

Joseph died on November 29, and Michael died on December 2. As a final insult, Joseph's body was dressed in the military uniform he had refused to wear. A Mennonite preacher named Jacob Minninger said, "If ever I saw a person die as a real Christian and pass from this life to a better world, it was Joseph Hofer." The other two remained in prison and were later released. Military officials denied some of these actions, but there is no doubt that the brutality of the prison treatment contributed to the deaths of the Hofer brothers. They had given their lives for their faith.

The Board of Inquiry questioned COs thoroughly to see if they were sincere. They were asked if they engaged in smoking, drinking, or other vices. They had to answer "what if" questions, such as what they would do if someone broke into their house and threatened or harmed someone. If the board determined that a CO was sincere, he was furloughed into alternate service such as farm-work programs.

When a young man received a furlough, he went into service on a farm in America or under the American Friends (Quaker) Service Committee doing relief work in France. About 60 percent of the COs did alternate work in this way. Around 30 percent remained in the camps until the end of the war, and perhaps 10 percent were imprisoned.

The church was able to help some of the young men in the camps. A number of ministers visited the camps to encourage them, and sometimes they even held Communion services with the young men. This was a great comfort to the lonely, persecuted COs. Ministers also made appeals to government officials, and they carried messages between the men and their parents.

After the War

Participation in Relief Work. The experiences of World War I stirred the Mennonites to a greater interest in service and in relief work. In 1917, they established the Mennonite Relief Commission for War Sufferers (MRCWS). This commission supported the Quaker relief work in France and also sent men to Armenia and the Middle East.

Clayton Kratz, an MCC representative, stands by a dead horse in Ukraine. As many as 12,000 horses died from the lack of feed, and people also perished in the famine. Kratz later vanished and apparently died at the hands of the Communists.

Top: Mennonites helped to feed starving Russians at relief kitchens such as this one in the Trans-Volga district. ***Bottom:*** Mennonites also helped Russians by sending tractors to help rebuild agriculture. These Fordson tractors are plowing in Ukraine in 1922.

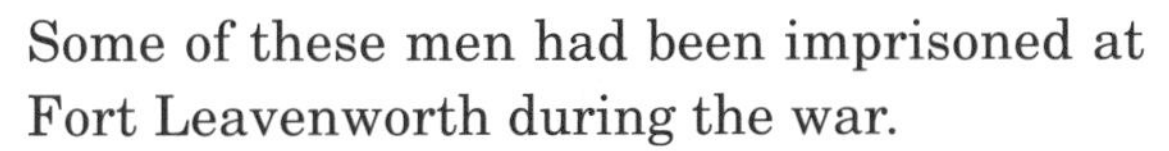

Some of these men had been imprisoned at Fort Leavenworth during the war.

Also, the Mennonite Central Committee (MCC) was formed in July 1920 as a relief organization representing various Mennonite groups. The MCC was initially set up for aid to Russia, where the people suffered much destruction of property during the communist revolution. One young man, Clayton Kratz, gave his life in this work. Captured by the Communists, he disappeared and was never heard from again.

Preparation for Future Conflicts. World War I helped the nonresistant people to be better prepared for World War II. They came to see that even noncombatant service was unacceptable for members of their groups. After an appeal to the government, a program of voluntary service was instituted which helped the conscientious objectors of World War II to avoid the difficulties that the COs of World War I had faced when they upheld their convictions while living in military camps. Nonresistant groups also began producing more literature to give clear teaching on nonresistance.

Many Christians were strengthened by the testimonies of the conscientious objectors. The COs who had suffered were willing to forgive the ones who had wronged them. When one of John Franz's captors apologized for his part in the attempted lynching, John replied with a smile, "I forgive you from my heart."

Focus for Thought

13. a. What was the first provision that the government made for conscientious objectors?
    b. Why was this provision unacceptable to nonresistant people?
14. Give at least three specific reasons why Mennonites suffered at the hands of patriotic people around them.
15. Why did Mennonites generally refuse to buy Liberty Bonds?
16. What three main areas of testing did conscientious objectors face in the army camps?

17. What happened when a conscientious objector refused to compromise?
18. What legal provision was made for conscientious objectors in June 1918?
19. What were two important effects of World War I on Mennonites?

World War I involved nearly every American in some way. These schoolchildren in New York City exhibit a head of cabbage raised in their school's war garden. This 1½-acre garden yielded over $500 worth of produce.

Historical Highlights

A. Matching: Terms 1

a. armistice	f. Selective Service Act
b. contraband of war	g. Triple Alliance
c. freedom of the seas	h. Triple Entente
d. noncombatant	i. Western Front
e. preparedness	j. Zimmermann telegram

1. Battle line extending through Switzerland, France, and Belgium.
2. Agreement to stop fighting.
3. Law providing for a military draft.
4. Union of Russia, France, and Great Britain.
5. Fulfilling military duties but not actually fighting.
6. Goods headed toward an enemy nation to support its war effort.
7. Right of any merchant ship to sail the ocean in peace or war.
8. Item proposing an alliance of Germany with Mexico and Japan.
9. The state of being prepared to fight if necessary.
10. Union of Germany, Austria-Hungary, and Italy.

B. Matching: Terms 2

a. Allies
b. Central Powers
c. Fourteen Points
d. Furlough Act
e. League of Nations
f. Liberty Bonds
g. American Expeditionary Force
h. Mennonite Central Committee
i. Treaty of Versailles
j. War Problems Committee

1. Items sold to help pay for the war.
2. Union of Germany, Austria-Hungary, Bulgaria, and Turkey.
3. United States army sent to France.
4. Woodrow Wilson's ideas for world peace.
5. Agreement that punished Germany harshly and proposed a League of Nations.
6. Law that allowed drafted men to work in civilian jobs.
7. Mennonite organization set up for relief work in Russia.
8. Organization designed to maintain world peace.
9. Group that appealed for government recognition of the Mennonite's stand on nonresistance.
10. Union of Russia, France, Great Britain, and Italy.

C. People, Places, Dates

a. April 6, 1917
b. Francis Ferdinand
c. John J. Pershing
d. July 28, 1914
e. Kaiser Wilhelm II
f. Newton D. Baker
g. November 11, 1918
h. Versailles
i. Woodrow Wilson

1. Date when World War I began.
2. Date when United States entered World War I.
3. Date when World War I ended.
4. President during World War I.
5. Secretary of war.
6. General of the American Expeditionary Force in France.
7. Archduke of Austria-Hungary.
8. Place where the peace treaty with Germany was signed.
9. Leader of Germany during World War I.

D. Deeper Discussion

1. Could the United States have remained genuinely neutral in World War I? Why or why not?
2. a. What was the main idea behind the League of Nations?
   b. Why does this idea not work?
3. A military officer once made a statement to this effect: "The man behind a typewriter is in the war just as surely as the man behind a machine gun." Why is this true?
4. Read 1 Peter 2:19–25; 4:12–19.
   a. How did these verses apply to nonresistant people in World War I?
   b. How did nonresistant people put these principles to practice?
5. How did World War I lead to World War II?

E. Chronology and Geography

The Treaty of Versailles dealt with Germany, but other treaties related to the other Central Powers. These treaties divided parts of the old empires of Russia, Germany, and Austria-Hungary into nine new nations, which are listed below.

1. Match the numbers on the map to the following countries.

   a. Austria

   b. Czechoslovakia

   c. Estonia

   d. Finland

   e. Hungary

   f. Latvia

   g. Lithuania

   h. Poland

   i. Yugoslavia

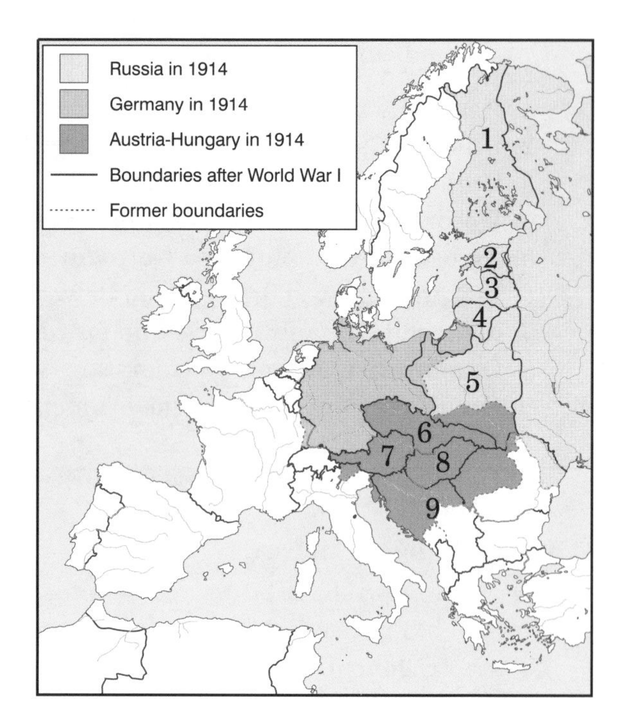

2. Compare this map with a modern map of eastern Europe since the fall of communism. Be prepared to discuss how these nine countries have changed since the early 1920s.

So Far This Year

A. Matching: Terms

Write the correct term for each description. Not all the choices will be used.

Boxer Rebellion	Isolationism	Pure Food and Drug Act
Eighteenth Amendment	New Freedom	Seventeenth Amendment
Federal Reserve Act	Nineteenth Amendment	Sixteenth Amendment
Federal Trade Commission	Open Door Policy	Square Deal
imperialism	progressive movement	Underwood Tariff Act

1. Policy of having little to do with foreign nations.
2. Uprising in China in 1900.
3. Theodore Roosevelt's reform program to treat everyone equally.
4. Constitutional amendment that prohibited alcoholic beverages.
5. Crusade promoting reform and change.
6. Law of 1913 that reduced import taxes and provided for an income tax.
7. Constitutional amendment that allowed an income tax.
8. Woodrow Wilson's plans for reform.
9. Desire to gain control of foreign territories.
10. Basis for American relations with countries in the Far East.
11. Measure that established a central banking system in 1913.
12. Constitutional amendment that provided for the direct election of senators.
13. Constitutional amendment that allowed women to vote.

B. Matching: People, Places, and Dates

Write the correct answer for each description. Not all the choices will be used.

Guam	Theodore Roosevelt	1898
Hawaii	William Howard Taft	1900
Philippines	William McKinley	
Puerto Rico	Woodrow Wilson	

14. President during the Spanish-American War.
15. President of the Square Deal and the "big stick"; served from 1901 to 1909.
16. Spanish islands in the Far East conquered by the United States and purchased for $20 million.
17. Year the Spanish-American War was fought.
18. Spanish island in the Caribbean ceded to the United States after the Spanish-American War.
19. President who served from 1909 to 1913 and later became a Supreme Court justice.
20. Pacific islands lying about 2,000 miles (3,219 km) west of the United States; annexed in 1898.
21. Democratic president elected after a split in the opposing party; served from 1913 to 1921.
22. Spanish island in the Pacific ceded to the United States in 1898.

C. True or False

Write whether each statement is true (T) *or false* (F). *If it is false, write the word or phrase that should replace the underlined part.*

23. Manifest destiny refers to the idea that the United States should spread over the whole North American continent.
24. Zachary Taylor was the expansionist president from 1845 to 1849.
25. Land that the United States gained by the Mexican War was called the Gadsden Purchase.
26. Marcus Whitman was the man who began colonizing Texas.
27. The treaty that ended the Mexican War was the Treaty of Guadalupe Hidalgo.
28. The Oregon Trail was a mail system to connect California with the East.
29. The general who conquered Mexico City in the Mexican War was Winfield Scott.
30. John Fremont owned a fort in California near which gold was discovered in 1848.
31. The forty-niners were hardy fur traders and explorers of the West.
32. The Colorado River formed the disputed boundary between Texas and Mexico.
33. Popular sovereignty was the idea that people living in a territory should decide for themselves about slavery.
34. The Fourteenth Amendment to the Constitution permanently outlawed slavery.
35. Jefferson Davis served as president of the Confederate States of America.
36. Abraham Lincoln was the Union president during the Civil War.
37. Ulysses S. Grant was the chief general of the Confederate armies.
38. Missouri was a border state.
39. *Uncle Tom's Cabin,* written by Harriet Beecher Stowe, contributed to the Civil War.
40. The Civil War lasted from 1861 to 1865.
41. Fort Sumter was the place where the Civil War began.
42. John Brown was a black man whose appeal for freedom was rejected by the Supreme Court.
43. The town of Antietam was known as the "high-water mark of the Confederacy."
44. West Virginia was a new state formed from a Confederate state during the Civil War.
45. The Emancipation Proclamation declared that, beginning in 1863, slaves in the states of the Confederacy would be free.
46. The Underground Railroad aided slaves in escaping from the South.

D. Dates

Write the correct years for these descriptions.

47. Years when the French and Indian War began and ended.
48. Years when the Revolutionary War began and ended.
49. Year when Mennonites first came to America.
50. Year of the Constitutional Convention.
51. Year when the government under the Constitution began operating.
52. Year when the Bill of Rights was added to the Constitution.

UNIT 7

MODERN TIMES, 1920–2000

Chapters in Unit 7

Dust storm in Oklahoma in 1936. The man who took this picture said the air was so full of dust that he could hardly breathe.

24 Prosperity and Hardship

1900

Wright brothers' first successful flight 1903

Ford Model T introduced 1908

1910

1920

Warren G. Harding elected president; Prohibition goes into effect 1920

Harding dies; Calvin Coolidge becomes president 1923

Coolidge elected to second term 1924

Scopes trial held 1925

Charles Lindbergh makes first solo transatlantic flight 1927

Herbert Hoover elected president 1928

Great Depression **1929–1939**

Stock market crashes (October 29) 1929

1930

First New Deal begins; Twentieth Amendment ratified; Twenty-first Amendment ratified 1933

Severe drought causes the Dust Bowl 1934–1937

Second New Deal begins 1935

Roosevelt re-elected 1936

1940

1. The Roaring Twenties
   - Politics
   - Society
   - Business
2. The Great Depression
   - The Crash of 1929
   - The Great Depression
   - The Hoover Years
3. The "New Deal"
   - Election of Roosevelt
   - Programs of the New Deal
   - End of the New Deal

"In the day of prosperity be joyful, but in the day of adversity consider: God also hath set the one over against the other, to the end that man should find nothing after him."

Ecclesiastes 7:14

PROSPERITY AND HARDSHIP

Focus for Reading

The 1920s were a decade of such prosperity and pleasure seeking, such contrast and change, that the decade has been labeled the "Roaring Twenties." These boom years came to an abrupt end with the stock market crash of 1929 and the Great Depression that followed. President Franklin D. Roosevelt tried to fight the Depression with his New Deal—a program that profoundly influenced the course of American history. Three sections in this chapter tell the story of these turbulent decades.

1. The Roaring Twenties
2. The Great Depression
3. The "New Deal"

1. THE ROARING TWENTIES

The 1920s are called "roaring" because of the galloping prosperity and the rapid pace of change in this decade. The motto in politics was "normalcy," but in society it seems that the watchword was "change." Unfettered business brought prosperity as never before. But the whole structure rested on a shaky foundation; and when the foundation gave way, a great economic crash followed.

Politics

Three Republican presidents served in the 1920s: **Warren G. Harding** (1921–1923), **Calvin Coolidge** (1923–1929), and **Herbert Hoover** (1929–1933). These men opposed progressive-type reforms and believed rather that the government should place few limits on businesses so that they would make maximum profits. This approach provided the basis for much of the prosperity in the 1920s.

Presidency of Warren G. Harding. Warren G. Harding was elected upon his promise to restore ***normalcy*** to America. He promoted tax reduction, and Congress passed bills to

Left: Warren G. Harding (1865–1923) was the twenty-ninth president of the United States. He served from 1921 to 1923 and was a Republican. ***Middle:*** Calvin Coolidge (1872–1933) was the thirtieth president of the United States. He served from 1923 to 1929 and was a Republican. ***Right:*** Herbert Hoover (1874–1964) was the thirty-first president of the United States. He served from 1929 to 1933 and was a Republican.

lower income taxes as well as to raise tariffs. Businessmen applauded these changes; and by 1922, after the slump that followed the war, wages were rising and unemployment was falling.

Troubles began to surface in 1923 as the Senate investigated some of the men who belonged to Harding's Cabinet. For respite, the president left Washington and went traveling across the country. But he became ill along the way; and on August 2, 1923, Harding died, apparently of a heart attack.

A number of scandals came to light soon afterward. Investigators found that Albert Fall, Harding's secretary of the interior, had illegally accepted $400,000 to lease government oil reserves to private companies. This incident became known as the Teapot Dome Scandal because one of the oil reserves was at Teapot Dome, Wyoming. Fall was fined $100,000 and sent to prison. Several scandals were also discovered in other departments, though there was no evidence that Harding himself had been involved.

Presidency of Calvin Coolidge. The next president was Calvin Coolidge, Harding's vice president. He was known as "Silent Cal" because he spoke so little. Coolidge made sure that the corruption of the Harding administration was uprooted. He was elected to another term in 1924.

Coolidge continued to favor business. He cut government spending and reduced the national debt from $24 billion to $16 billion. His philosophy was "to spend less than you make, and to make more than you spend." He further reduced income taxes but maintained high tariffs. This period of booming business became known as "Coolidge Prosperity."

Presidency of Herbert Hoover. In 1928, Herbert Hoover won the presidential election by an overwhelming majority. The Republicans' slogan was "A chicken in every pot and a car in every garage." Hoover said, "We in America today are nearer to the final triumph over poverty than ever before in the history of any land." He would soon be disillusioned.

During Hoover's administration, the Federal Farm Board was established to help farmers, many of whom were not sharing in the prosperity of the times. Hoover also began a more friendly policy toward Latin American nations, retreating from Roosevelt's policy of intervention. However, the president spent much of his time in dealing with the Great Depression, which is discussed in the second part of this chapter.

Society

New Technology. With inventions such as vacuum cleaners and washing machines available, Americans had more leisure time in the 1920s than ever before. Electric lights contributed to this by enabling people to continue their activities after dark. Even grocery shopping took less time. Since food could be kept in refrigerators, housewives did not need to go shopping as often.

Probably no invention changed American life as much as the automobile, which **Henry Ford** made affordable to the average citizen. He introduced the Model T in 1908, and eventually he was able to reduce its price from $825 to as low as $290. Almost anyone could afford a car at that price. Motor vehicle registration

Henry Ford and his first car, built in 1896.

The Model T. The Ford Model T became the standard American car in the early decades of the 1900s. Henry Ford said the car was available in any color as long as it was black! The Model T had to be started by hand cranking, which was usually quite a chore. (A self-starter was a more expensive option.) The driver would set the spark and the throttle levers, pull the choke cable, and give the crank a sharp turn. Sometimes the engine backfired and the handle spun backward, resulting in a broken arm called a "Model T fracture." When the engine did start, the driver had to hop into the car and try to keep it running by adjusting the throttle and spark levers. But often the engine sputtered and choked off, especially in cold weather. Back to the crank!

Once the Model T was running, the driver had to take charge of its complicated controls. They included three pedals (low speed, reverse, and brake) and a lever that could be placed in three different positions (high gear, neutral, and transmission brake). The Model T had only about twenty horsepower, and its top speed was 45 miles (72 km) per hour. The car could be repaired easily with things such as hairpins, baling wire, and chewing gum. Its owners affectionately called it their "Tin Lizzie" and said, "The Model T is a good car—a rattling good car!"

By 1927, General Motors and other manufacturers had outclassed the Model T with the Buick and other models that were more comfortable, more stylish, and easier to operate. So Ford shut down his production line for eighteen months and finally unveiled his new Model A. The Model T was history.

rose from 1.25 million in 1913 to over 23 million in 1929.

The car "put America on wheels" and gave people a new sense of freedom. Sunday drives became popular, and people went on long vacations—the whole United States was within their range. Rural people could go to the city, enjoy city life, and then return to their farms. In fact, many people began living in the country and working in the city.

The automobile contributed to the growth of a larger middle class of people. New terms such as *spare tire* and *used car* entered the

New Model T cars at the Ford Motor Company. By using mass production, Henry Ford made automobiles available to the common people.

Ford sedan of 1923. The automobile hastened the pace of change in American society.

nation's vocabulary. But the automobile also brought problems such as accidents and traffic jams.

The airplane introduced more changes. **Wilbur and Orville Wright** made the first successful flight at Kitty Hawk, North Carolina, in December 1903 with their heavier-than-air machine. Airplanes were in commercial use by 1927, when William E. Boeing began flying mail and passengers between San Francisco and Chicago. The same year, **Charles Lindbergh** made the first solo flight across the Atlantic Ocean.

Decline of Morals. The 1920s brought widespread rebellion against established standards. Young people rebelled against their parents. Increasing numbers of women cut their hair and used cosmetics, and hemlines rose to the knees. Women also began to use tobacco and alcohol more freely. The popular jazz music of the age emphasized freedom of expression and the breaking of traditions. To be sure, many people continued in the old ways, and they were shocked at the changes they saw.

The twenties were an age of hero worship and pursuit of entertainment. Americans watched movies in theaters, listened to the radio at home, and became devoted to professional sports. Movie stars and sports champions became national celebrities. Some people did sensational things to gain attention, such as standing on the wing of a flying airplane or sitting on top of a very high flagpole.

Nativism. World War I left many Americans with a strong distrust for "radicals,"

Top left: The Wright brothers' first flight was on December 17, 1903. In this historic photograph, Orville Wright is flying the airplane and Wilbur Wright is running at the side. The airplane traveled a distance of 120 feet (37 m) in 12 seconds.

Top right: Charles A. Lindbergh (1902–1974) used the *Spirit of St. Louis* to make the first nonstop solo flight across the Atlantic Ocean on May 20 and 21, 1927. He flew the 3,600 miles (5,793 km) from New York to Paris, France, in 33.5 hours.

Middle right: Airplanes at the Chicago Airport in 1928.

Bottom right: Ford Trimotor of the middle 1930s. By this time, four major airlines and several smaller ones provided passenger service for hundreds of thousands of people every year.

In this Prohibition scene, a public safety director in Philadelphia hacks a barrel of beer.

J. Edgar Hoover (1895–1972) in 1932.

whom they blamed for the war. This led to a widespread antagonism toward foreigners, blacks, Catholics, and Jews. The Ku Klux Klan revived, and the Red Scare developed because Americans feared Communists (called Reds). Immigrants were blamed for communism, unemployment, and lawlessness. As a result, Congress passed a restrictive immigration law in 1921; and in 1924, the National Origins Act further restricted immigration.

The Age of Prohibition. The Eighteenth Amendment made alcoholic beverages illegal after 1919. But ***Prohibition*** caused more problems than it solved. People made liquor in secret, and bootleggers sold it illegally. The government simply did not have enough officers to stop the trade.

In big cities such as Chicago and New York, the illegal trade in liquor was taken over by gangsters. They operated brazenly and bribed the police, and violence sometimes erupted between rival gangs. Newspapers published sensational accounts of the gangsters' deeds, and people admired "successful" criminals as heroes. This went on until the middle 1920s, when **J. Edgar Hoover** and the Federal Bureau of Investigation (FBI) began taking strong action to enforce federal laws.

Prohibition was largely a failure. This was not because of the law itself but because many

J. Edgar Hoover and the FBI. In the 1920s, criminals were heroes and children sometimes played "gangster." J. Edgar Hoover set out in 1924 to change that—to make criminals the villains and law enforcement officers the heroes. This he did through his management of the Federal Bureau of Investigation (FBI). Under Hoover, the FBI began identifying criminals by their fingerprints, and it maintained the largest fingerprint file in the world. Hoover also developed highly successful methods for training officers of the law and for capturing and prosecuting criminals. His efforts did much to reduce the status of criminals and to heighten respect for the law and its officers. Hoover served as FBI director for forty-eight years, until his death in 1972.

Scopes trial in Dayton, Tennessee, July 1925. Clarence Darrow stands with his back to the table (center), and John T. Scopes sits at the table behind him.

Americans—especially politicians—were hypocritical. They claimed to support Prohibition, but they drank liquor in secret. This illustrates Romans 8:7, which says that "the carnal mind is enmity against God: for it is not subject to the law of God, neither indeed can be." No law can overcome sinful desires, even in those responsible to enforce the law.

Modernism and Fundamentalism. By the 1920s, many intellectuals were accepting beliefs called ***modernism***. These included Darwin's theory of evolution, the rejection of anything supernatural, and the idea that science is the only source of truth. Along with modernism came secular humanism, which teaches that man rather than God is the highest being in the universe. By contrast, the humanism of the Enlightenment (in the colonial period) at least recognized God as the Creator.

Leading Protestants began a movement called ***fundamentalism***, which opposed modernism and defended a number of basic Bible doctrines. These included (1) the infallibility and inerrancy of the Scriptures, (2) the virgin birth of Christ, (3) the miracle-working power of Christ, (4) the redemptive sacrifice of Christ, and (5) the bodily resurrection of Christ. Fundamentalists distributed millions of pamphlets proclaiming the truth of these doctrines.

In 1925, the clash between modernism and fundamentalism came to a head in the Scopes trial held at Dayton, Tennessee. The American Civil Liberties Union (ACLU) wanted to challenge Tennessee's law against teaching evolution in public schools. So it was made to appear that John Scopes had taught evolution, and he was duly arrested and brought to trial.

The prosecuting attorney was a former presidential candidate, William Jennings Bryan (a believer in Creation); and the defense attorney was Clarence Darrow (a famous agnostic). In the trial, Darrow ridiculed Bryan for his beliefs, and he used the latest scientific evidence to support evolution. It included the Java man (now acknowledged as fully human) and the Piltdown man (today recognized as a hoax). Hordes of newsmen recorded the proceedings, and their scornful reports about the "ignorant" creationists were blazed across the nation.

In the end, Darrow had Scopes plead guilty and thus lose the case. But this event actually served to promote evolution, for it made belief in Creation seem ignorant while evolution appeared to be enlightened and scientific. Since then, the teaching of evolution has been accepted and taught as fact in public schools throughout America, while the teaching of Creation in public schools has become illegal.

Concerning those who reject Bible truth, Paul wrote, "Professing themselves to be wise, they became fools" (Romans 1:22). Creation gives abundant testimony of an omnipotent Creator. "For the invisible things of him from the creation of the world are clearly seen, being understood by the things that are made, . . . so that they are without excuse" (Romans 1:20).

The Response of Mennonites to Modernism and Fundamentalism. Modernism was rejected by most Mennonite leaders of that time. Especially outspoken was **George R. Brunk, Sr.,** who founded the *Sword and Trumpet* in 1929 to champion the cause of truth. The struggle had become acute at Goshen College (Indiana) in 1923, when this Mennonite college was closed for a year because of the inroads of modernism. Later events showed that if a church promotes higher education, it will eventually lose its separation from the world.

Although Mennonites had many of the same concerns as the fundamentalists, the Mennonites believed important doctrines that fundamentalists did not stress. In particular, Mennonites supported nonresistance and nonconformity to the world. They responded to the attacks of modernists by clearly stating in the Garden City Confession of Faith (1921) that the Bible is the inerrant and infallible Word of God. Mennonite leaders also began putting more details of their decisions and rules of discipline into writing.

George R. Brunk, Sr. (1871–1938), was a well-known conservative leader of the Mennonite Church in the 1920s.

Business

The Booming Business of the 1920s. Several key industries fueled the business boom of the Coolidge years, including the automobile industry, the construction business, radio companies, and electric companies. The automobile industry in particular helped other businesses to prosper, especially those that supplied what automobile manufacturers needed. To make an automobile required steel for the car body, rubber for the tires, glass for the windows, paint, and other supplies. Car dealerships sprang up, and service stations provided gasoline, oil, and repair parts. By the end of the 1920s, about 3 million Americans worked in industries related to the automobile.

The automobile contributed to a construction boom as many people built new houses in suburbs. This in turn contributed to a real estate boom that caused a sharp increase in land prices. Huge skyscrapers also

Newton's Garage on Long Island, New York, between 1910 and 1920. With the automobile came the need for new businesses such as gas stations and garages. Note the tow truck in front of this garage.

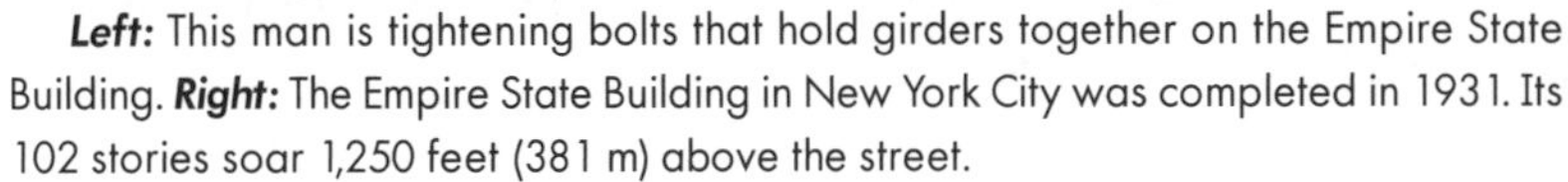

Left: This man is tightening bolts that hold girders together on the Empire State Building. ***Right:*** The Empire State Building in New York City was completed in 1931. Its 102 stories soar 1,250 feet (381 m) above the street.

soared skyward, among them the Empire State Building in New York City. When its 102 stories were completed in 1931, this building was the tallest in the world.

The Booming Stock Market. In 1928, the stocks of large companies increased rapidly in value, with the result that those who traded in stocks made large profits. Many people began trying to make money by speculation (the hope of selling stocks at a profit) rather than by simply receiving dividends on their investments. More and more stocks changed hands as people heard of the fortunes to be made in the booming stock market.

Many people bought stocks on credit. They would obtain possession by paying only a small part of the price, wait until the value of the stocks rose, and then sell the stocks. The difference was usually enough to pay off the original price and leave a generous profit besides. There was little danger as long as stocks increased in value. But if prices fell, the purchaser might owe more than the value of his stocks. In the late twenties, however, experts were predicting that stocks would rise and never go down again. So the risky speculation seemed to be safe.

Exceptions to the Prosperity. Not everyone was so prosperous. Many farmers did not do well in this decade, even though the sale of milk and ice cream rose significantly. Growers of wheat, corn, and cotton saw their prices drop. People in coal mining, textile industries, and shoe and leather manufacturing also suffered. But most people felt confident that the good times had come to stay.

Focus for Thought

1. In the 1920s, how did the three Republican presidents think the government should deal with businesses?
2. Describe some effects of the automobile on American life.

3. What were some evidences of declining morals in the 1920s?
4. What were some problems resulting from Prohibition?
5. a. What is modernism?
   b. What were the five points emphasized by fundamentalism?
6. What was the general effect of the Scopes trial?
7. a. How did the stock market contribute to the business boom of the 1920s?
   b. What people did not share in the prosperity?

2. THE GREAT DEPRESSION

The booming prosperity of the 1920s was not as secure as it seemed. Underlying weaknesses led to a crash in 1929 that ushered in the Great Depression. This depression lasted a full decade and brought the worst economic conditions that had ever existed in the United States. Many people suffered through the Depression, and it had major effects on the life of the nation.

The Crash of 1929

Crash of the Stock Market. The rise in stock prices could not continue forever. Stocks declined in September 1929, but experts still predicted that the market would rebound. However, prices began falling dramatically on October 18, and stockbrokers demanded that investors put up more money for stocks purchased on credit. Frightened investors sold almost 13 million shares on October 24 to cover their loans. Stock prices dropped steeply, and panic spread.

A group of wealthy bankers tried to head off the crash by investing millions of dollars in stocks, and they succeeded temporarily. But on "Black Tuesday," October 29, the stock market crashed as investors sold over 16 million shares. By the middle of November, stocks on the New York Stock Exchange had lost $26 billion in value.

Many common people who had bought stocks on credit were ruined, as were many wealthy investors. Multitudes saw their assets vanish before their eyes, and general prosperity disappeared with the assets. Proverbs 23:5 describes it this way: "Riches certainly make themselves wings; they fly away as an eagle toward heaven." The stock market collapse of October 1929 ushered in the Great Depression.

Causes of the Crash. Overproduction was one reason for the crash and the Depression that followed. Too many houses, offices, and factories had been built for the demand, and the market for automobiles was flooded. Americans had already borrowed and purchased as much as they could afford. When they began buying less, factories laid off many workers—who then had no income and could buy even less.

Scene in a Stockbroker's Office. "In that broker's office, as in hundreds of other offices from one end of the land to the other, one saw men looking defeat in the face. One of them was slowly walking up and down, mechanically tearing a piece of paper into tiny and still tinier fragments. Another was grinning shamefacedly. . . . Still another was sitting motionless, as if stunned, his eyes fixed blindly upon the moving figures on the screen, those innocent-looking figures that meant the smash-up of the hopes of years."

Another reason was the unhealthy farm economy. Because prices of farm products stayed low through the 1920s, farmers had difficulty paying the loans on their properties. When many farmers went bankrupt, the banks holding the loans also failed. Over five hundred banks went out of business during 1928 and 1929, mostly in rural areas.

But the main reason for the crash was the overuse of credit. People could easily borrow money to purchase things they wanted, such as furniture, automobiles, and houses. Easy credit also encouraged speculation as people put down a little money to buy stocks in hopes of making quick profits. This speculation pushed the prices of stocks much higher than the true value of the companies they represented.

This "buy now, pay later" approach always has its day of reckoning. To pay the loan, a borrower must work to earn money that he has already spent—which means he cannot buy as many new goods. When enough people have borrowed enough money, business slackens as borrowers work to pay off debts instead of buying more goods. The result is often hardship as demand drops, businesses fail, and workers lose their jobs. But finally the economy recovers and demand increases again. This swing between prosperity and decline in the economy is called the ***business cycle***.

The stock market crash, then, was simply a readjustment of the economy. But for investors, it was a harsh reality. Those who had bought stocks on credit were required to pay the value that those stocks had at the time of purchase. But since they received much less for those stocks than they had paid, many investors lost everything they had.

Changes in stock prices from September 3 to November 13, 1929

Stock	Sept. 3	Nov. 13
AT&T	304	197 1/2
General Electric	396 1/4	168 1/8
General Motors	72 3/4	36
Montgomery Ward	137 7/8	49 1/4
Radio	101	28
U.S. Steel	261 3/4	150
Westinghouse	289 7/8	102 5/8
Woolworth	100 3/8	52 1/4

Note: Stock prices are shown as mixed numbers; 168 1/8 means 168 1/8 dollars per share ($168.125).

The Great Depression

A Prolonged Depression. Earlier depressions had never lasted long, but the Great Depression went on year after year. One reason was that the Depression became worldwide, partly because Congress approved the Smoot-Hawley Tariff in 1930. This extremely high tariff was harmful to foreign trade because other nations retaliated by increasing tariffs on American goods. The government's efforts to end the Depression may actually have prolonged it.

As stock prices continued to fall, many investors lost so much money that they could not repay their bank loans. People became worried about their savings in banks, and thousands hurried to withdraw their money. Soon one bank after another was closing its doors; a total of about five thousand banks failed during the years 1930 to 1932. Anyone who had not withdrawn his money simply lost it.

Over one hundred thousand businesses failed during the years 1929 to 1932. This meant that many workers lost their jobs as well as their savings. Unemployment soared to 25 percent of workers, and many workers who kept their jobs took pay cuts. When people could not pay their loans, they lost their houses as banks foreclosed on them. (The banks took possession of the houses because they were security for the loans.)

Left: Run on a bank during the Great Depression. When a bank was rumored to be closing, depositors rushed there to withdraw their money. ***Right:*** When this picture was taken in 1936, this migrant mother and her seven children were living in a lean-to tent in California. They survived on frozen vegetables from the fields and on birds that the children killed. The mother had just sold the tires off her car to buy food.

Hardships in the Great Depression. When people lost their homes, some moved in with relatives, some lived in shacks built of tin and crates, and others lived in rusted car bodies. Thousands of men became hoboes, traveling about and begging for food or taking any work they could find. Hoboes often rode freight trains illegally to travel from one area to another.

Farmers were especially hard hit. Many had borrowed money when land values were higher; and now that prices for farm products were falling, these farmers could not pay their loans. So the banks foreclosed on farmers too.

Left: In the Great Depression, destitute people stood in long bread lines like this one in New York City, waiting for food from a mission or soup kitchen. ***Right:*** Destitute men wait in a bread line at a soup kitchen in San Francisco, California, in 1933.

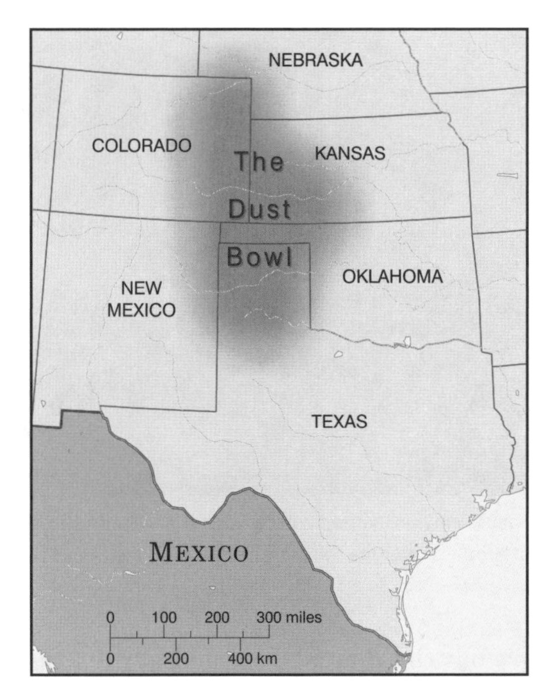

The Dust Bowl

Dust storm in Kansas, May 1937. In the background are dust clouds, not rain clouds.

This reminds us of the verse that says, "The rich ruleth over the poor, and the borrower is servant to the lender" (Proverbs 22:7).

The prices of grain and other farm products fell drastically. Then from 1934 to 1937, some parts of Kansas and nearby states went through a period of extremely hot and dry weather. Winds picked up the dirt and caused enormous dust storms that obscured the sun for hours. Dust blew in huge piles that made roads impassable. The drought was so severe that this area was called the Dust Bowl.

Plight of a Missouri family of five in 1937. Many families in the Dust Bowl headed for California. This photograph is entitled "Broke, baby sick, and car trouble."

However, not all Americans went through such hardships. If 25 percent of workers were unemployed, 75 percent still had jobs. People learned to cope with hardship, and some actually found satisfaction in getting along with less. A few even prospered in these years. For example, some men had sold their stocks when prices were high, so they had plenty of money to invest when prices were low during the Depression.

The Hoover Years

The President's Efforts. President Hoover thought people should help themselves rather than depending on the government. He believed that business would improve if left alone. Yet the president did make some efforts to relieve the Depression. Hoover tried to persuade businessmen not to lay off workers and not to reduce wages and prices. Yet companies needed to do these things in order to earn enough to remain in business. Since President Hoover's efforts interfered with the normal business cycle, they tended to make things worse instead of better.

In 1930, Hoover asked Congress for money to finance public-works projects, which would

Hoover Dam, completed in 1936, was built to provide jobs during the Depression. Its height is 726 feet (221 m), its length is 1,244 feet (379 m), and the thickness of its base is 660 feet (201 m). The concrete used to build the dam could pave a two-lane highway from New York City to San Francisco.

Bonus Army on the steps of the Capitol in Washington, D.C. A riot erupted after the Senate failed to pass the Bonus Bill.

provide more jobs for people. This money was used for projects such as the Supreme Court building and an office building for the Senate. The most notable project was the Hoover Dam. Built across the Colorado River, the dam served to control flooding, provide water for irrigation, and produce electricity. But these projects did little to relieve the overall effect of the Depression.

The Citizens' Discontent. Many Americans thought President Hoover was doing too little about the Depression. Their discontent was magnified by the Bonus Army incident of 1932. That year a group of about fifteen thousand World War I veterans arrived in Washington, demanding immediate payment of a bonus that the government had promised to pay them in 1945. When Congress rejected their appeal, most of the veterans went home, but about two thousand stayed. Finally the president called out the army against them. Using tear gas, bayonets, and tanks, troops drove out the Bonus Army and burned their shanties. This action appeared heartless to many people, and it caused more of them to turn against Hoover.

Effects of the Depression. The Great Depression left its mark on many Americans. The hundreds of business failures caused people to lose confidence in businessmen, who had been widely respected before. People also lost confidence in themselves, since hard work no longer seemed enough to guarantee success in life. And some who had lived in poverty developed an unhealthy concern for earthly security. We do need to be thrifty and make reasonable provisions for the future, but these people went to extremes in their ambition for money and possessions.

Proverbs 30:8, 9 says, "Give me neither poverty nor riches . . . lest I be full, and deny thee, and say, Who is the LORD? or lest I be poor, and steal, and take the name of my God in vain." The opposites in this passage are illustrated by the Roaring Twenties and the Great Depression. Only a solid trust in God will keep us from being shaken by the economic changes of this world.

Focus for Thought

8. a. When did the stock market crash?
   b. What were some reasons for the crash and the Depression that followed?

9. Briefly explain how business cycles operate.
10. Why did many banks fail during the Depression?
11. What were two ways in which farmers suffered because of the Depression?
12. How did President Hoover respond to the Depression?
13. Describe several effects that the Great Depression had on Americans.

3. THE "NEW DEAL"

In 1932, **Franklin D. Roosevelt** was elected to the presidency. Many people saw him as the man who could save the nation from its Depression. President Roosevelt started a large number of government programs to improve the economy. His "New Deal" did more than fight the Depression; it changed the very nature of the United States government.

Election of Roosevelt

Franklin D. Roosevelt, the Democratic candidate, won the presidential election of 1932. This man radiated hope and confidence to a Depression-weary people, and he promised a New Deal for America.

At that time, a newly elected president waited until March of the next year to take office, while the previous president finished his term as a ***lame duck***. The lame-duck period was so long because of slow transportation in the early days. That changed in 1933, when the Twentieth Amendment moved the inauguration date to January 20.

Another change was made to the Constitution in 1933. That year Congress passed the Twenty-first Amendment to repeal the Eighteenth Amendment and bring an end to Prohibition. The attempt to eliminate strong drink by law had ended in failure.

Franklin D. Roosevelt (1882–1945) was the thirty-second president of the United States. He served from 1933 to 1945 and was a Democrat.

The new president took office on March 4, 1933. In his inaugural address, Roosevelt tried to cheer the nation with these words: "The only thing we have to fear is fear itself." He declared that he would ask Congress for power to fight the Depression, which he called an emergency "as great as . . . if we were in fact invaded by a foreign foe." The president immediately went to work on this commitment.

Programs of the New Deal

The First New Deal. President Roosevelt called Congress into special session from March 9 to June 16, 1933. This period became known as the Hundred Days, or the first New Deal. During this time, Roosevelt gained Congressional support for one measure after another to fight the Depression.

One of the first items approved by Congress was the Banking Act. It authorized the government to examine all banks and allow only sound banks to continue operating. But many banks had little business because multitudes of people no longer trusted banks. So Roosevelt went on national radio for his first "fireside chat." He explained his plans and asked people to put their money back into banks, assuring them that the banks would

The Civilian Conservation Corps (CCC) employed young men to build dams, plant trees, and fight forest fires. Some CCC camps were used during World War II in the CPS program for conscientious objectors.

be safe. This did restore a measure of confidence, and banking slowly recovered. Roosevelt used fireside chats many times to gain support directly from the people.

To further restore confidence in banks, Congress set up the Federal Deposit Insurance Corporation (FDIC) to insure bank deposits. The FDIC guaranteed that if a bank failed, each depositor's money would be repaid up to $5,000. Congress also established the Securities and Exchange Commission (SEC) to help prevent illegal and unsound practices in the stock market.

Poster showing support for policies of the National Recovery Administration (NRA). This agency regulated things such as wages, working hours, and prices of goods. Businesses that participated could display the NRA "Blue Eagle" to show their support.

The New Deal also included a variety of government relief programs. Some of the main ones are described below.

1. The Civilian Conservation Corps (CCC). In the CCC, young men from ages seventeen to twenty-five lived in camps and worked at conservation projects such as planting trees, controlling soil erosion, and fighting forest fires. The CCC plan later became the basis of Civilian Public Service, a program of alternate service for nonresistant young men during World War II.

2. The Federal Emergency Relief Administration (FERA). Under this agency, money was given to the states to distribute directly to needy people. This federal welfare program was the first one of its kind.

3. The Agricultural Adjustment Administration (AAA). This agency tried to raise the prices of farm products by restricting farmers' output. For example, $100 million was paid to cotton growers to plow up 10 million acres (4 million ha) of young cotton plants, and two hundred thousand sows and six million piglets were killed. Many people were appalled at this wanton destruction, especially since large numbers were going hungry at the time.

4. The National Recovery Administration (NRA). To improve the economy, this agency was to draw up rules of fair business practices for each industry, and to establish the amount that each industry should produce. Its goal was to eliminate improper competition, to boost employment, and to promote cooperation between the government and industry.

5. The Public Works Administration (PWA). This agency managed a program that

provided relief for people by putting them to work instead of simply giving them money. Men were employed at public works such as roads, schools, courthouses, dams, and bridges. One of the largest projects was the Golden Gate Bridge in California.

6. The Tennessee Valley Authority (TVA). Under this program, the government tried to relieve poverty in the Tennessee River valley by building dams on the Tennessee River and its tributaries. The dams would control flooding and produce electricity, which the government would sell to the people. Many citizens objected strongly to this government ownership of a utility company, thinking it was not fair for the government to compete against private electric companies.

Generators at the Pickwick Dam built by the Tennessee Valley Authority (TVA). These four enormous generators could produce 144,000 kilowatts of electricity.

But the Depression continued in spite of these government programs. Indeed, a considerable number of people were opposing the New Deal. Republicans and some Democrats charged that the president was making the government too strong. They said the government was spending too much, destroying people's independence through relief, and threatening freedom. Later the Supreme Court declared some of the new measures unconstitutional, such as the National Recovery Administration.

The Second New Deal. The Democrats gained several new Congressional seats in 1934, which encouraged Roosevelt to introduce further New Deal measures. His second New Deal began in 1935 and lasted through 1939. Some programs and laws established during that period are still in effect.

7. The Works Progress Administration (WPA). This was another relief agency that put people to work. It was similar to the Public Works Administration, but the WPA also focused on smaller projects. For example, the WPA employed people to improve state parks and hired artists to paint murals in post offices. But unemployment remained high; the government could not provide jobs for everyone.

8. The Rural Electrification Administration (REA). This agency helped to bring electricity to rural areas. It was especially appreciated by farm families, who could finally enjoy the same conveniences as city people.

9. The National Labor Relations Act. This law guaranteed workers the right to join unions and take part in collective bargaining. It also listed unfair practices that employers could not use, such as refusing collective bargaining. Unions became more powerful than

These WPA workers are laying a water main in Alabama in 1936. The Works Progress Administration provided work for unemployed men in various construction projects such as road building.

These workers are stringing electric lines in a rural area. The Rural Electrification Administration (REA) expanded electrical service in rural areas, where only about 10 percent of farms had electricity before the agency was founded in 1935.

ever, and union membership reached more than 8 million by 1941.

10. The Federal Insurance Contributions Act (FICA). This social security program was passed in 1935. It provided a fund to which workers contribute a certain percent of their pay, and employers contribute an equal amount. When the worker retires, he receives payments out of the fund. This act also provided unemployment compensation, aid to dependent children, and public health programs.

The social security program is still in effect today. What happens is that workers contribute money which is then paid to those who have retired. Thus, social security is basically a program in which the government takes money from younger people who work to support older people who no longer work. The Bible teaches that if elderly parents need financial help, their children should support them directly.

Social security minimizes the importance of providing for oneself and one's family. It encourages people to retire and receive their payments, rather than continuing to work as

Left: Poster promoting the social security program. ***Right:*** People in California waiting to receive their government relief checks in 1937. Social Security and welfare programs began with the New Deal. By the end of the 1900s, officials were making efforts to curb such programs because the funds paid out were rising faster than the funds coming in.

long as they are able. Finally, it promotes a trust in earthly security rather than in God. Christians should seek to stay clear of such entanglements.

End of the New Deal

Roosevelt's Second Term. In 1936, the Republicans chose Governor Alfred Landon of Kansas as their presidential candidate. He won the widespread favor of wealthy businessmen, who by this time despised Roosevelt. But the president was strongly supported by people who had received government relief, as well as by many farmers, union members, blacks, and young people. This Democratic ***coalition*** (koh uh LIHSH uhn), or alliance, re-elected Roosevelt by a large majority of votes.

The economy improved somewhat during 1936 and 1937; but by the end of 1937, it took a dramatic turn for the worse. Thus it was that the New Deal wound down by 1939. In spite of all the billions of dollars spent, Roosevelt had not ended the Depression. Many New Deal programs continued into the 1940s; but one by one they were discontinued, and few new programs were begun.

Effects of the New Deal. The New Deal brought major changes to America. No doubt some groups gained by its programs, but this was at the expense of many others—especially businessmen. The government became much more powerful than ever before. It could now intervene freely in the economy, and it held extensive control over industries, banks, and money.

Many people began to depend on government support. And the government began a policy of spending more money than it received (deficit spending), which later became a tool in trying to improve economic conditions during downturns. This set a pattern for decades to come, and the resulting national debt increased until many citizens became alarmed. Christians should not be unsettled by such changes in government; for they are citizens of the heavenly kingdom, whose principles will never change.

Focus for Thought

14. Describe the two Constitutional amendments that Congress passed in 1933.
15. Name the New Deal act or agency that matches each description.
    a. Supervised the building of dams to control flooding and produce electricity.
    b. Tried to improve the economy by regulating business practices and establishing the amount that each industry should produce.
    c. Employed people at projects such as the building of roads, dams, and bridges.
    d. Gave workers the right to join unions and to bargain collectively.
    e. Insured bank deposits.
    f. Tried to raise prices of farm products by paying farmers to destroy crops and livestock.
    g. Helped to bring electricity to many farms.
    h. Employed people in projects such as improving parks and painting murals.
    i. Authorized the government to examine banks and allow sound banks to continue operating.
    j. Provided money for retired workers and for unemployment compensation, aid to children, and public health programs.
    k. Gave money to states to distribute directly to needy people.
16. How did it become evident that the New Deal was not effective?
17. List two important effects of the New Deal.

Historical Highlights

A. Matching: People

a. Calvin Coolidge
b. Charles Lindbergh
c. Franklin D. Roosevelt
d. George R. Brunk
e. Henry Ford
f. Herbert Hoover
g. J. Edgar Hoover
h. Warren G. Harding
i. Wilbur and Orville Wright

1. Published the *Sword and Trumpet* to oppose modernism.
2. Served as vice president under Harding and as president from 1923 to 1929.
3. Made cars available to most people by introducing the Model T.
4. Was elected president in 1932; introduced the New Deal.
5. Made the first successful flight with a heavier-than-air machine in 1903.
6. Made the first solo flight across the Atlantic Ocean in 1927.
7. Was president when the Great Depression began; served from 1929 to 1933.
8. Was president from 1921 to 1923; died in office.
9. Served as director of the Federal Bureau of Investigation.

B. Matching: Terms

a. business cycle
b. coalition
c. Dust Bowl
d. foreclose
e. fundamentalism
f. Great Depression
g. Hundred Days
h. lame duck
i. modernism
j. New Deal
k. normalcy
l. Prohibition
m. Scopes trial
n. secular humanism
o. Twentieth Amendment
p. Twenty-first Amendment

1. Group of government programs designed to end the Depression.
2. Man-centered philosophy in which the existence of God is denied.
3. Period when alcoholic beverages were outlawed in the United States.
4. Set of beliefs including the theory of evolution, rejection of the supernatural, and acceptance of science as the only source of truth.
5. Periodic swing between prosperity and decline in the economy.
6. Person finishing a term after another is elected to replace him.
7. Condition desired by Americans after World War I, which included a less troubled life and less involvement in European affairs.
8. Measure that repealed the Eighteenth Amendment and ended Prohibition.
9. To take property serving as security for a loan.
10. Temporary alliance of various groups to accomplish a certain thing.
11. Movement to assert basic truths of the Bible and oppose modernism.
12. Event in 1925 when fundamentalists and modernists clashed over evolution.
13. Measure that reduced the lame-duck period to less than three months.
14. Region of severe drought in the 1930s.
15. Special session of Congress in 1933 when many new programs were approved.
16. Long economic downturn from 1929 to 1939.

C. Agencies and Programs

The following initials (acronyms) designate agencies and programs established in the 1920s and 1930s, which are still in existence today. Give the full name of each one, and briefly describe its function.

1. FBI
2. FDIC
3. FICA
4. REA
5. SEC
6. TVA

D. Deeper Discussion

1. Give similarities and differences between the beliefs of Mennonites and of fundamentalists.
2. What contributed to the rapid social changes and the rebellion against traditions in the 1920s?
3. How was the prosperity of the 1920s based on a shaky foundation?
4. Read Proverbs 23:4, 5 and 30:8, 9.
   a. How do these verses apply to the boom times of the 1920s, the stock market crash, and the Great Depression?
   b. How might these Scriptures apply to us?
5. Why did the Great Depression continue for a whole decade?
6. How should Christians relate to government programs?

E. Chronology and Geography

1. Tell what important events took place at the following times.
   a. 1903 b. 1927 c. October 1929
2. Name the three Republican presidents who served in the 1920s, and give the dates of the terms they served in office. Remember that an elected president's term begins in the year after the election.
3. How did the geography and climate of the Plains contribute to the Dust Bowl?

So Far This Year

A. Matching

Not all the choices will be used.

1. United States president during World War I.
2. Year when World War I began.
3. Agreement that punished Germany harshly and proposed a League of Nations.
4. American president's ideas for world peace after World War I.
5. Nations that fought on one side in World War I, including Russia, France, Great Britain, and Italy.
6. Nations that fought on the other side in World War I, including Germany, Austria-Hungary, Bulgaria, and Turkey.
7. Year when World War I ended.
8. International organization designed to maintain world peace.
9. Year when the United States entered World War I.

a. 1914
b. 1917
c. 1918
d. 1919
e. Allies
f. Central Powers
g. Fourteen Points
h. John J. Pershing
i. League of Nations
j. Treaty of Versailles
k. Woodrow Wilson

B. Completion

Write the correct name or term that belongs on each blank.

10. Northerners who went south to help in Reconstruction were called ___.
11. Southern whites who took part in Reconstruction governments were known as ___.
12. ___ describes the rebuilding and restoration of the South after the Civil War.
13. In a system called ___, farm workers rent cropland and use a share of the crops to pay the rent.
14. Former slaves freed during and after the Civil War were called ___.
15. A term that describes social separation based on race is ___.
16. Laws that restricted blacks after the Civil War were known as ___.
17. The constitutional amendment that granted blacks the right to vote was the ___ Amendment.
18. The constitutional amendment that granted citizenship to blacks was the ___ Amendment.
19. ___ was a territory purchased in 1867 and known as "Seward's Folly."
20. The black leader who founded Tuskegee Institute was ___.

C. Matching: Presidents

21. President when the Compromise of 1850 passed; 1850–1853.
22. President when Japan opened ports to Americans; 1853–1857.
23. President when Southern states began to secede; 1857–1861.
24. President during the Civil War; 1861–1865.
25. President impeached in 1868; 1865–1869.
26. Former Civil War general who became president; 1869–1877.
27. President chosen after a disputed election in 1876; approved the Compromise of 1877; served from 1877 to 1881.
28. President assassinated a few months after taking office in 1881.

a. Abraham Lincoln
b. Andrew Johnson
c. Benjamin Harrison
d. Chester Arthur
e. Franklin Pierce
f. Grover Cleveland
g. James Buchanan

29. Took office in 1881 after the former president was assassinated; 1881–1885.
30. Only president to serve two nonconsecutive terms; 1885–1889 and 1893–1897.
31. President when the Sherman Antitrust Act and the McKinley Tariff Bill passed; 1889–1893.
32. President elected in 1896; opposed by William Jennings Bryan.

h. James Garfield
i. Millard Fillmore
j. Rutherford B. Hayes
k. Ulysses S. Grant
l. William McKinley

D. Multiple Choice

Write the letter of the correct answer.

33. A law that allowed settlers to claim 160 acres (65 ha) of land for farming was
    a. the Dawes Act.
    b. the Homestead Act.
    c. the Pacific Railroad Act.
34. A law that divided Indian reservations into family farms was
    a. the Dawes Act.
    b. the Homestead Act.
    c. the Pacific Railroad Act.
35. The man who invented barbed wire in 1874 was
    a. Joseph McCoy.
    b. Charles Goodnight.
    c. George Westinghouse.
    d. Joseph Glidden.
36. A colonel defeated at the Battle of the Little Bighorn was
    a. George Custer.
    b. Sitting Bull.
    c. Crazy Horse.
    d. Nelson Miles.
37. The first transcontinental railroad was joined at
    a. Wounded Knee, South Dakota.
    b. Pikes Peak, Colorado.
    c. Promontory, Utah.
38. The last great Apache leader, who surrendered in 1886, was
    a. Chief Joseph.
    b. Black Kettle.
    c. Geronimo.
    d. Sitting Bull.
39. One of the first cattle ranchers in Texas was
    a. Joseph McCoy.
    b. Charles Goodnight.
    c. Joseph Glidden.
    d. Charles Crocker.
40. A term that refers to cowboys taking cattle north to cattle towns is
    a. "long drive."
    b. Comstock Lode.
    c. open range.
    d. homesteading.

USS *West Virginia* in flames after the attack on Pearl Harbor. A small boat is rescuing a seaman from the burning ship. Note the two men on the high platform near the center.

25 The United States and World War II

1915

Treaty of Versailles signed **1919**

1925

1935

Spanish Civil War 1936–1939

Rome-Berlin Axis made 1936

World War II begins with German invasion of Poland (September 1) **1939**

Battle of Britain 1940–1941

Franklin D. Roosevelt elected to third term 1940

United States declares war on Japan (December 8) **1941**

Battle of Stalingrad; Americans land in North Africa 1942

Allies invade Sicily and Italy 1943

Roosevelt elected to fourth term 1944

Allies invade France on D-day (June 6); Battle of the Bulge; Battle of the Philippine Sea; Battle of Leyte Gulf 1944

Roosevelt dies; Harry S. Truman becomes president 1945

1945

Allies celebrate victory over Germany on V-E Day (May 8); Japan surrenders and World War II ends on V-J Day (September 2); United Nations founded **1945**

Truman elected to second term 1948

China becomes communist; NATO formed 1949

Warsaw Pact formed 1955

1955

1. Prelude to United States Participation
    - The Advent of Dictators
    - The Rising Tide of Aggression
    - World War II in Europe and Asia
    - The United States Enters the War
2. United States Participation in World War II
    - The Home Front
    - The War in Europe
    - The War in the Far East
3. Results of World War II; Experiences of Nonresistant People
    - Costs of the War
    - Peacemaking After the War
    - Consequences of the War
    - Nonresistance in World War II

"Fear and a snare is come upon us, desolation and destruction."

Lamentations 3:47

THE UNITED STATES AND WORLD WAR II

Focus for Reading

In 1941, the United States entered once more into a world war. This war proved to be much longer, costlier, and deadlier than the first world war. In its worldwide scope, its devastation, its millions of deaths, and its ongoing consequences, World War II was the most destructive war in human history. What provoked such a struggle just twenty years after World War I? How was the United States drawn into the war? What was the outcome of the war, and what were its effects? How did nonresistant Christians fare amid the conflict? These questions are addressed in three sections.

1. Prelude to United States Participation
2. United States Participation in World War II
3. Results of World War II; Experiences of Nonresistant People

1. PRELUDE TO UNITED STATES PARTICIPATION

Jesus' words in Matthew 24 seem to indicate that wars will continue until He returns. Yet after World War I, hopes ran high for a permanent peace. The League of Nations and several agreements to limit armed forces held promise of a future without war. But the picture changed in the 1930s as fighting erupted once more in Europe. World War II had begun.

The Advent of Dictators

Most Europeans enjoyed prosperity in the middle 1920s, but the worldwide economic depression brought hardships by the end of the decade. This made conditions ripe for the rise of radical leaders who promised the people riches, might, and glory. When these men took control of nations, they became dictators who ruled with absolute power.

Lenin and Stalin in Russia. In November 1917, Russia came under the control of Communists led by V. I. Lenin and known as Bolsheviks (BOHL shuh vihks). ***Communism*** was a system based on the socialistic ideas of Karl Marx, and its followers tried to set up Communist governments through revolution. The Bolsheviks crushed their opponents in 1921; and in 1922, Russia became the Union of Soviet Socialist Republics (USSR).

In 1924, **Joseph Stalin** became one of the leaders of the Soviet Union, and by 1929 he assumed complete control. Stalin imprisoned millions of people in concentration camps for daring to disagree with him. Christians in the Soviet Union were persecuted mercilessly, since atheistic communism allowed no freedom of speech or religion.

Mussolini in Italy. After World War I, Italy was plagued with economic woes. Into the chaos stepped **Benito Mussolini** (moo suh LEE nee) and his Fascist Party (FASH ihst). ***Fascism*** was a political system that

Joseph Stalin (1879–1953) ruled as Communist dictator of the Soviet Union during World War II.

Benito Mussolini (1883–1945) ruled as Fascist dictator of Italy during World War II.

Adolph Hitler (1889–1945) ruled as Nazi dictator of Germany during World War II.

emphasized nationalism and ***totalitarian*** (toh tal ih TAIR ee uhn) control, that is, a single authority with absolute control over every aspect of life. The Fascists opposed the Communists, though many of their methods were similar.

Mussolini came to power in 1922 and later made himself dictator of Italy. Like Stalin, Mussolini ended civil rights, ended free speech, and engaged in a campaign of terror to stamp out opposition. He began trying to expand Italian power and build an empire in the Mediterranean region.

Hitler in Germany. The National Socialist German Workers' Party, abbreviated Nazi (NAHT see), was formed in 1920. One of its leaders was **Adolf Hitler**, who declared that the German race was superior to all others—especially Jews. Hitler said the inferior races must be exterminated or serve the Germans. He wanted Germany to expand eastward by taking territory from the Soviet Union and other people of the Slavic race.

In 1933, Hitler became the chancellor (prime minister) of Germany. The nation soon came under the complete sway of Hitler and ***Nazism***. The Nazis eliminated the people's freedoms, especially those of Jews and other minorities. They took control of the nation's newspapers and schools. Hitler began seeking to expand Germany—an ambition that led to World War II.

Boycott of a Jewish store in 1933. The German words say, "Germans! Defend yourselves! Do not buy from Jews!" The Nazis placed such signs in front of Jewish-owned businesses. Later, the Nazis confiscated the businesses and personal property of the Jews.

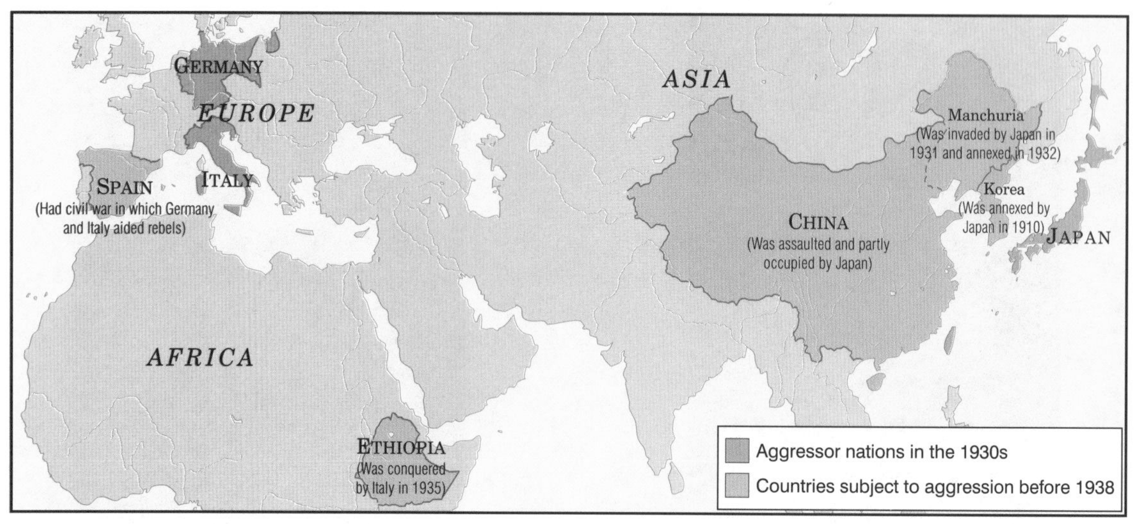

Aggression in the 1930s

Militaristic Leaders in Japan. By the 1930s, the Japanese needed more raw materials such as coal, oil, and iron ore for industrialization. They knew these materials were available in nearby colonies held by nations such as Britain and France. Military leaders began to dream of an Asian empire that could supply Japan's factories with all the resources they wanted. Already in 1931, Japan invaded Manchuria, in northern China. Their ambitions would lead eventually to conflict with the United States.

The Rising Tide of Aggression

In the 1930s, military actions by Japan, Italy, and Germany led toward World War II. Japan made repeated assaults on China, and by 1938 it occupied much of eastern China. In 1935, Italian forces under Mussolini used planes and tanks to overwhelm the African nation of Ethiopia. When the Spanish Civil War began in 1936, Germany and Italy aided the rebels with men and supplies. The aggressors tried out weapons and tactics that they would use later, in World War II.

After he took power, Hitler began to rearm Germany in violation of the Treaty of Versailles. In 1936, he marched his troops into the Rhineland, which lay west of the Rhine River on the French border. The Treaty had specified that this land was to be ***demilitarized*** (kept free of soldiers and weapons). But Hitler's violation went unpunished because a spirit of ***appeasement*** (uh PEEZ muhnt) prevailed in Europe. After the ordeal of World War I, other nations preferred having peace at almost any price rather than fight Germany again.

The same year, Hitler and Mussolini made

Rally of Nazi troops at Nuremberg, Germany, in November 1935. This picture shows how Hitler rearmed Germany and built up its military might.

an agreement to work together. Mussolini described it as the "Rome-Berlin Axis" on which the world was supposed to turn. Japan joined the agreement in 1940, and it became known as the Rome-Berlin-Tokyo Axis. Germany, Italy, and Japan became the Axis powers.

Hitler took control of Austria in 1938 and of Czechoslovakia in 1939. His next target was Poland. In planning his attack on that country (which Britain and France had pledged to defend), Hitler made a surprise move. He entered into a nonaggression treaty (agreement not to attack each other) with his rivals, the Communists of the Soviet Union. In this treaty, Germany and the Soviet Union became allies and agreed not to fight each other. Another part of the treaty remained secret: Germany and the Soviet Union agreed to divide Poland between them. This would free Hitler from having to fight the Soviet Union in addition to Britain and France should war break out when he invaded Poland.

These German soldiers break down a barrier at the Polish border. They did this in connection with the invasion of Poland on September 1, 1939.

World War II in Europe and Asia

Early Conquests. World War II began with Hitler's invasion of Poland on September 1, 1939. The Germans used the ***blitzkrieg*** (BLIHTS kreeg), or "lightning war," a new style of fighting in which German planes and tanks swiftly took control of one region after another. Great Britain and France declared war on September 3, but they could do little against the Germans. Poland fell by late September after Soviet troops invaded from the east. Germany and the Soviet Union then divided Poland between themselves.

The Germans continued their advance, conquering Denmark in April 1940 and Norway by June. As Hitler's armies pushed toward France, they quickly defeated the Netherlands and then Belgium. The British tried to intervene, but they were almost trapped by the Germans and had to evacuate their army by ferrying 338,000 soldiers across the English Channel at Dunkirk, France. The Germans marched into Paris on June 14; and on June 22, France surrendered to Germany in the same railroad car, on the same spot, where the Germans had surrendered in World War I. Now Great Britain was the only major obstacle to Hitler's control of Europe.

The Battle of Britain. In July 1940, Hitler's *Luftwaffe* (air force) began attacking Britain in preparation to invade that country. Bombs fell day and night on British military installations and cities, especially London. But **Winston Churchill**, the British

St. Paul's Cathedral stands amid the flames and smoke of burning buildings during the bombing of London in December 1940.

Sir Winston Churchill (1874–1965) was the prime minister of England during much of World War II. When he became prime minister, he stated, "I have nothing to offer but blood, toil, tears, and sweat."

prime minister, encouraged his people to keep fighting the Germans regardless of the cost. The British Royal Air Force fought persistently, using a new device—radar—that enabled them to detect enemy planes before they arrived. British guns shot down more than a thousand German planes in this struggle, called the Battle of Britain; and by May 1941, Hitler gave up the idea of invading Britain.

Other German Advances. Bulgaria, Hungary, and Romania joined the Axis in 1941. Hitler's forces defeated Yugoslavia and then Greece in April; and in May 1941, the British-controlled island of Crete fell to the Germans. This seriously threatened British power in the Mediterranean Sea.

Hitler then decided to attack the Soviet Union despite their nonaggression treaty. A German force of nearly 2 million troops marched into the Soviet Union in June 1941, and by December they were within sight of Moscow. (The Soviets joined the Allies about this time.) But God had planned an unusually severe winter, which would soon take its toll of the German army.

"Woe to thee that spoilest, . . . and dealest treacherously; . . . when thou shalt make an end to deal treacherously, they shall deal treacherously with thee" (Isaiah 33:1).

The United States Enters the War

The United States had made efforts to remain neutral as the battles raged in Europe and Asia. Neutrality laws were passed to prevent involvement in the war, but gradually the United States began to help the Allies by selling them supplies. Then, as the Germans neared Moscow, an event in the Pacific Ocean brought the United States into World War II on the side of the Allies.

The Japanese wanted to further expand their empire and to guarantee a supply of much-needed oil. Accordingly, they planned to attack the Dutch East Indies, British Malaya, and the Philippines. But the Americans' powerful Pacific Fleet, based at Pearl Harbor in Hawaii, threatened the Japanese plans. So they planned to destroy the Pacific Fleet by a surprise attack.

The garrison at Pearl Harbor, on Oahu, was unprepared when the attack came on December 7, 1941. That Sunday morning, 350 Japanese planes bombed Pearl Harbor and other military installations on Oahu. Eight American warships were sunk or disabled, over 300 planes were damaged or destroyed, and more than 3,000 Americans were wounded or killed.

People in the United States were outraged by the attack on Pearl Harbor. In a speech to

World War II in Europe and North Africa

Scene at Pearl Harbor during the Japanese attack on December 7, 1941. The explosion at the right is the USS *Shaw* blowing up.

Congress the next day, President Roosevelt referred to December 7 as "a date which will live in infamy" and asked for a declaration of war. That same day Congress declared war on Japan, and the United States entered World War II.

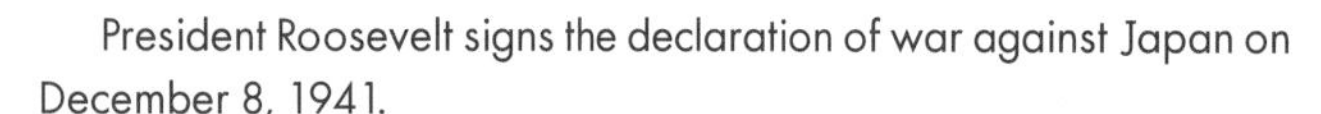

President Roosevelt signs the declaration of war against Japan on December 8, 1941.

Focus for Thought

1. Name the three major dictators who became involved in World War II, along with the country each one controlled, the date he came to power, and the kind of political party he represented.
2. a. Why was Hitler not punished for violating the Treaty of Versailles?
   b. What nation did the Germans take over in 1938? in 1939?
3. What surprise move did Hitler make in 1939, and why did he make it?
4. What event marked the beginning of World War II, and when did it happen?
5. a. List five countries that the Germans conquered in 1940, and three that they conquered in 1941.
   b. Which European nation resisted German air raids until Hitler gave up the idea of an invasion?
6. a. When and why did the Japanese attack Pearl Harbor?
   b. How did the United States respond to the attack on Pearl Harbor?

2. UNITED STATES PARTICIPATION IN WORLD WAR II

World War II was the greatest conflict that the United States has ever known. Millions of soldiers went to the battlefield, and they needed food, clothing, and weapons. Factories also produced vast numbers of ships, tanks, and airplanes. American soldiers fought in lands around the globe—from Europe and Africa to the Far East. Many fierce battles raged on land, at sea, and in the air before the war ended.

The Home Front

Because of the great demand for military supplies, American factories, both new and old, were devoted to producing war materials and began operating day and night. Millions of new workers were hired, which ended the unemployment of the Depression. The total production of the economy doubled, from under $100 billion in 1939 to over $200 billion in 1945.

Left: These cargo ships are ready to be outfitted for carrying war supplies. The United States built nearly 3,000 such ships during World War II; this photograph was taken in 1944. ***Right:*** Because of the many men needed for the military effort, 4 million more women held jobs in 1945 than in 1941. This woman is working on an airplane engine during the war.

Many of the goods that civilians needed were rationed. The government issued ration stamps to purchase restricted foods, such as meat, butter, and sugar. To conserve gasoline and rubber, all unnecessary travel was discouraged and a "victory speed limit" of 35 miles (56 km) per hour was enacted. Americans conserved energy by using daylight-saving time, which was called "war time."

The war effort had a special impact on the lives of women. With millions of men away, about 4 million additional women entered the work force. These women received the nickname of "Rosie the Riveter" because they did men's work such as welding and riveting on assembly lines. Thus it became common for American mothers to work in factories rather than being "keepers at home" (Titus 2:5).

Government spending soared from 1941 to 1945. To increase revenues, the government raised taxes, especially income taxes,

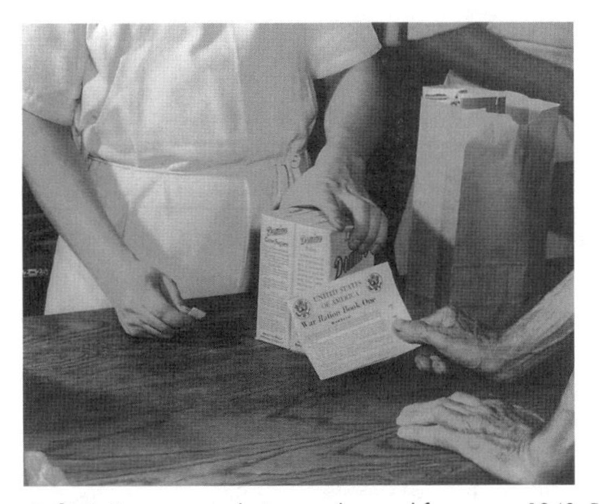

Left: Ration coupon being exchanged for sugar, 1942. ***Right:*** A grocer in New York City rations canned foods to his customers in December, 1942.

Japanese-American people of San Pedro, California, starting for relocation camps in April 1942.

Japanese Internment. After the attack on Pearl Harbor, a wave of anti-Japanese hysteria swept the United States. Especially on the West Coast, Americans clamored to have the Japanese removed from their communities. So in 1942, President Roosevelt ordered the army to move about 110,000 Japanese to "relocation camps" in Colorado, Utah, and other states. Here they were imprisoned behind barbed wire and under armed guard—even though about 70,000 of them were American citizens. Other people took the homes and farms of these Japanese. The government later repaid them for their losses, but this was small compensation for the great injustice done to these people.

and sold war bonds. Yet the national debt swelled from about $49 billion to almost $260 billion by the end of the war.

The War in Europe

In 1942, the situation did not look good for the Allied nations (the United States, Great Britain, the Soviet Union, and China). Axis powers controlled Europe from the English Channel to the heart of the Soviet Union and from Norway to North Africa. German U-boats dominated much of the North Atlantic, and Japanese forces controlled the South Pacific, including Guam and Wake Island, which were possessions of the United States.

The Battle of the Atlantic. As in World War I, German U-boats sank hundreds of ships that were carrying supplies to Britain. So the Allies formed convoys of merchant ships protected by warships. They located submarines by using sonar, and then they destroyed many of them. By mid-1943, the Allies had essentially won the Battle of the Atlantic.

This poster urges secrecy. Warring countries try to keep their plans secret to avoid losing men and equipment, and to keep their enemies from gaining an advantage over them.

Allied Victories in the Soviet Union and the Mediterranean Region. Two important battles in 1942 marked a turning point in the war against Germany. One was the Battle of Stalingrad in the Soviet Union after the Germans resumed their eastward advance in 1942. The invaders lost about 240,000 soldiers to fighting, cold, and starvation in that battle. On January 31, 1943, the German army at Stalingrad was forced to surrender, and soon the Soviets were driving back the Germans elsewhere in the Soviet Union.

The other crucial battle took place in North Africa. In October 1942, a British army attacked the Germans and Italians in Egypt and drove them westward. The next month, General **Dwight D. Eisenhower** and his American forces landed in Algeria and Morocco and moved east. Trapped between the British and the Americans, the Axis army in North Africa surrendered in May 1943.

From bases in North Africa, the Allies invaded Sicily and Italy the same year, and Mussolini fell from power in July 1943. (He was rescued from prison by Hitler's men but was assassinated in April 1945.) Mussolini's successor surrendered to the Allies in September, and in 1945 they gained control of all Italy.

Allied Invasion of France. General Eisenhower, supreme commander of the Allied forces in Europe, took charge of the campaign to liberate France. The Allies prepared for it by assembling a vast force of soldiers, supplies, armored vehicles, and landing craft in England. The date of the invasion—called D-day—was June 6, 1944, and the place was the coast of Normandy, a region in northern France.

Early that morning, Allied warships and soldiers attacked the French coast with the largest ***amphibious*** assault (attack by both naval and land forces) in history. The Germans fought back fiercely; and by the end of D-day, the beach was strewn with landing boats, disabled tanks, burned-out trucks, and corpses. The Allies prevailed and then pushed on until they liberated Paris on August 25. Within another month, they drove the remaining Germans out of France.

General Dwight D. Eisenhower speaks to American paratroopers (soldiers who parachute behind enemy lines) just before the invasion of Normandy, France, on June 6, 1944.

Defeat of Germany. While Eisenhower planned a final attack on Germany itself, Hitler suddenly made a strong assault in which the Germans tried to divide a thin line of Allies in Belgium. The Germans drove nearly 60 miles (97 km) into the Allied line, creating a

During the Allied invasion of France, American soldiers waded the last perilous yards to the beach of Normandy after leaving the ship that transported them. Many of these soldiers lost their life because of the Nazi's machine guns. Transport ships continued to bring more soldiers all that day and into the night.

These French civilians rejoiced as American troops entered Paris on August 25, 1944.

bulge that gave the battle its name, the Battle of the Bulge. This conflict in December and January became the largest European battle of World War II. The Allies finally stopped the Germans and then drove them back into Germany. They crossed the Rhine River in March and reached the Elbe River by April 1945.

At the same time, the Soviets had made a powerful attack from the east. They took control of Poland in January 1945 and then marched into Greece, Yugoslavia, Romania, Bulgaria, and Hungary. When the Soviets took Austria in April 1945, they occupied nearly all of eastern Europe. The same month, over a million Soviets made a strong attack that took them to the outskirts of Berlin. American and Soviet troops met along the Elbe River on April 25.

In the final conflict, the Battle of Berlin, the German capital was defended mostly by young boys and old men. Hitler took refuge in an underground bunker, and on April 30 he took his own life. Finally in early May of 1945, the Germans surrendered—and the war in Europe was over! The victorious Allies celebrated May 8 as V-E Day (Victory in Europe).

The Holocaust Revealed. As the Allied forces advanced, they discovered a horrifying reality: the Nazi concentration camps. Prisoners came forth by the tens of thousands—living skeletons that had existed in conditions of unbelievable filth and deprivation. There were many forced labor camps; but several, such as Auschwitz in Poland, were death camps built specifically to destroy people whom Hitler and the Nazis considered inferior—especially Jews.

Death camps were equipped with gas chambers where thousands of people could be killed in one day. Prisoners were transported in boxcars to these camps, where anyone who could work was spared but the rest were sent to the gas chambers. The ***Holocaust*** (HAHL uh kawst), as it became known, destroyed over

German Colonel General Alfred Jodl signed an unconditional surrender at Allied headquarters in Reims, France, on May 7, 1945.

Nazi concentration camp at Theresienstadt. On the far wall is the heartless message "*Arbeit macht frei*" (Work makes free).

Roll call at a German concentration camp. In the front row, two men support a comrade to keep him from falling, since fainting was frequently an excuse for the guards to kill a "useless" prisoner.

Starving men liberated from a concentration camp in Ebensee, Austria.

10 million people in all, of which about 6 million were Jews.

The Holocaust is a sobering reminder of how depraved man can become when he departs from God. Truly the heart of man is "desperately wicked" (Jeremiah 17:9), and those who follow such a course will experience the wrath of God unless they repent. Yet the same God could provide grace for survivors of the Holocaust to forgive their tormentors, as numerous victims would testify in later years.

The War in the Far East

While the battles raged in Europe, the Japanese continued to expand their empire in the Far East. In December 1941, they invaded the Philippines, which was defended by American forces under General **Douglas MacArthur.** On orders from President Roosevelt, MacArthur left the Islands in March 1942 because of the advancing Japanese. The Philippines fell to Japan in early May.

End of Japanese Expansion. The Japanese threatened Australia in May 1942. But an American aircraft carrier force opposed the invasion fleet in the Battle of the Coral Sea. This was the first naval battle fought entirely by planes from aircraft carriers; none of the opposing ships ever came in sight of each other. The Battle of the Coral Sea prevented the invasion of Australia and marked the limit of Japanese expansion to the south.

Early in June 1942, the Japanese sent a fleet to attack the Midway Islands west of Hawaii. This led to the Battle of Midway, in which planes sent by Admiral **Chester Nimitz** sank four Japanese aircraft carriers while their planes were bombing Midway. (There were only nine carriers in the whole Japanese navy.) This battle was a major turning point because Japan's naval power was crippled and also because it ended the Japanese advance in the Pacific war.

Douglas MacArthur (in the front row, wearing sunglasses) returns to the Philippines in October 1944. When MacArthur had left in 1942, he had promised, "I shall return."

It was decided that General MacArthur would drive toward the Philippines through New Guinea while Admiral Nimitz's forces advanced through the central Pacific toward Japan. During 1943 and 1944, the Allies conducted an island-hopping campaign, going from one Pacific island to another as they moved closer and closer to Japan.

Two important naval battles were fought in Philippine waters in 1944. One was the Battle of the Philippine Sea on June 19 and 20, and the other was the Battle of Leyte Gulf (LAY tee) from October 23 through 26. In these battles, the Japanese lost so many ships that their sea and air power were destroyed. The Allies took control of Manila, the Philippine capital, in March 1945.

Defeat of Japan. Allied forces then moved to islands closer to Japan. The first was Iwo Jima (EE woh JEE muh), and the second was Okinawa (oh kih NAH wuh). But the invaders were opposed by thousands of Japanese troops and hundreds of kamikaze (kah mih KAH zee) attacks, in which pilots deliberately crashed their planes into Allied ships. By the time the Allies captured Okinawa in June, they had lost over 55,000 men and the Japanese had lost about 130,000 men.

From the islands, Allies launched destructive bombing raids on Tokyo and other Japanese cities, but Japan would not surrender. General MacArthur hesitated to invade Japan itself, for he estimated that it might cost a million lives. The invasion never took place because the United States had developed the atomic bomb, a new weapon of mass destruction.

The atomic bomb had been built through a secret operation called the Manhattan Project, and a test in New Mexico had proved that it worked. After Franklin D. Roosevelt's death in April 1945, the new president **Harry S. Truman** decided that the atomic bomb should be used to bring the war to an end. The Allies warned the Japanese to surrender or face "a rain of ruin from the air," but they still refused.

A cloud in the shape of a mushroom rose 20,000 feet (6,096 m) above Nagasaki after the second atomic bomb was dropped on Japan.

On August 6, 1945, an American plane dropped an atomic bomb on the city of Hiroshima (heer oh SHEE muh). The bomb exploded with a fireball several million degrees in temperature and a blast that completely destroyed several square miles of the city. As many as 100,000 people (mostly civilians) were killed; but the Japanese still would not surrender. So a second atomic bomb fell

Site directly below the atomic bomb explosion over Hiroshima, photographed in October 1945. The domed building on the right has been preserved in its damaged state and today is called the Atomic Bomb Dome.

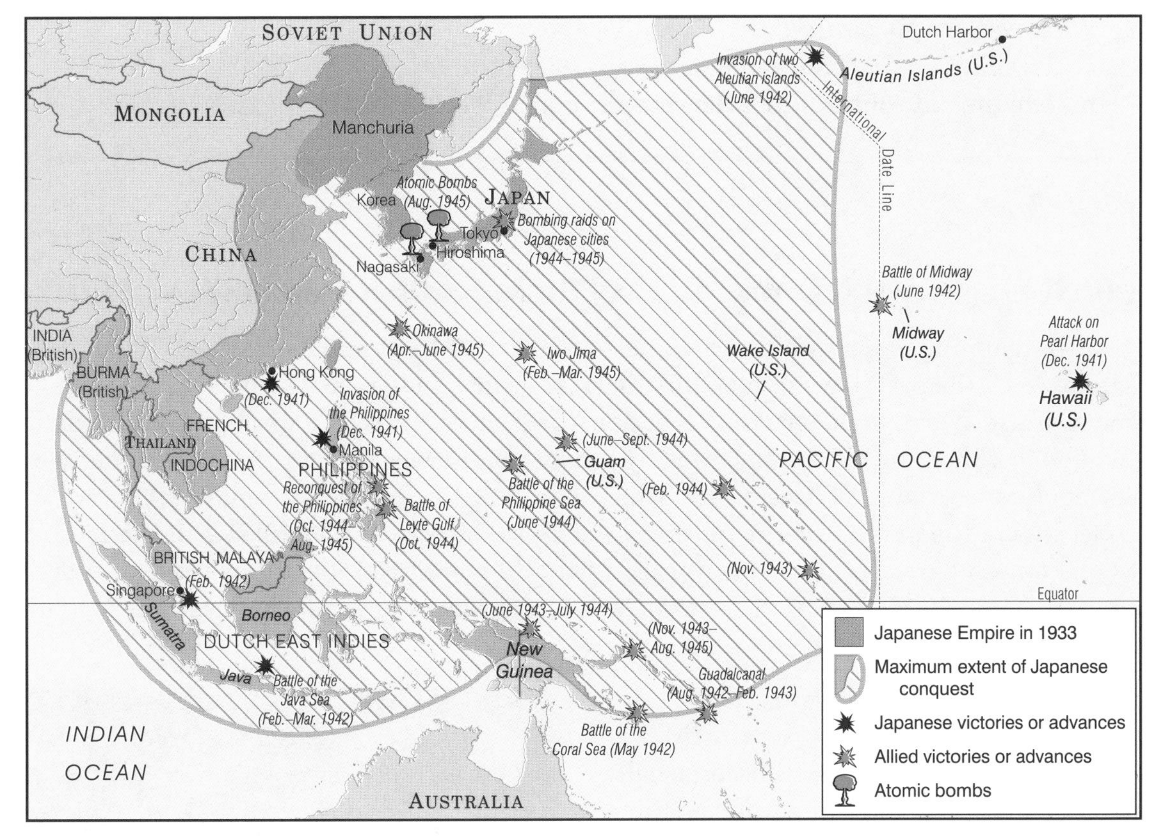

World War II in the Pacific

on Nagasaki (nah guh SAH kee) on August 9, ending about 40,000 lives.

Finally on August 14, the Japanese agreed to the Allied terms of surrender. The surrender ceremony took place on the United States battleship *Missouri* in Tokyo Bay on September 2, 1945, which was declared V-J Day (Victory over Japan). World War II was over at last.

Ceremony at the Japanese surrender aboard the USS *Missouri* on September 2, 1945.

Focus for Thought

7. a. Describe some ways that World War II affected Americans in general.
   b. How did it change the lives of women?
8. What two events in 1942 were turning points in the war against Germany?
9. Give the date and place of the invasion in which the Allies began to liberate France.
10. a. Which conflict was the largest European battle of World War II?
    b. What day did the Allies celebrate as the date of German surrender?

11. What was the Holocaust?
12. a. How did the Allies force Japan to surrender?
    b. Give the date of the surrender and the end of World War II.

3. RESULTS OF WORLD WAR II; EXPERIENCES OF NONRESISTANT PEOPLE

At the planning conference of the United Nations in 1945, President Harry S. Truman said, "You are to be the architects of a better world. In your hands rests our future." But the outcome of World War II was not really a better world. It was rather a world of continuing distrust and ill will, a world overshadowed by the fear of nuclear disaster. As in Jeremiah's day, the leaders were saying, "Peace, peace; when there [was] no peace" (Jeremiah 8:11).

Because of the harsh experiences of conscientious objectors in World War I, the Mennonites and other nonresistant groups worked to obtain more favorable terms from the government for COs in World War II. The result was a program of alternate service called Civilian Public Service.

Costs of the War

World War II was the most destructive war in history. Large areas lay in ruins, especially in Germany and Japan. About 12 million Europeans were uprooted from their homes. Of some 70 million soldiers from all participating countries, about 17 million perished. Millions of civilians died in bombings, massacres, and epidemics. Also, many died in the Holocaust or of starvation. Altogether, the deaths from World War II total about 55 million souls. What a staggering cost!

Displaced persons hold on to a few possessions at a train station in Berlin, Germany, in 1945. They are among the millions of Europeans uprooted by the war.

Top: Aerial view of Würzburg, Germany, after World War II. This city was heavily bombed because of its industrial plants and railway lines. Only a few people survived. ***Bottom:*** Citizens cleaning up at Brühl, Germany, after World War II.

The price of World War II was also exorbitant in financial terms. The total expenses for weapons and war materials came to about $1.15 trillion. The United States spent about $300 billion and Germany about $231 billion. In addition were the losses resulting from burned houses, bombed factories, and other forms of destruction to property, which ran into uncounted millions of dollars.

Peacemaking After the War

Founding of the United Nations. After the war, the victors established the United Nations in 1945 as an international association for keeping peace. The United Nations was organized with six units, of which the General Assembly and the Security Council were foremost. The General Assembly was designed to give every member nation a voice in international affairs.

The Security Council carried the main responsibility for keeping world peace. This unit was made up of five permanent members (the United States, the Soviet Union, Great Britain, France, and China) and six additional members (ten today). Each permanent member received veto power, so that one dissenting vote by a permanent member could block a resolution in the Security Council. The United Nations was granted authority to use military force against nations that broke the peace, with member nations providing the soldiers.

Like the League of Nations, the United Nations is based on the idea that if nations unite, they can prevent war. This idea is a fallacy—war is caused by selfish human nature, and it will continue as long as men are evil. Numerous wars have raged since the United Nations was founded.

Dealings With Germany. The Allies divided Germany into four zones occupied by the Soviet Union, the United States, Great Britain, and France. In 1949, the Soviets set up a Communist government in their zone, which became the German Democratic Republic, or East Germany. The three other Allies combined their zones as the Federal Republic of Germany, or West Germany, in the same year. They gave West Germany full independence in 1955, but the Soviets refused to withdraw from their zone. Germany remained a divided country until 1990.

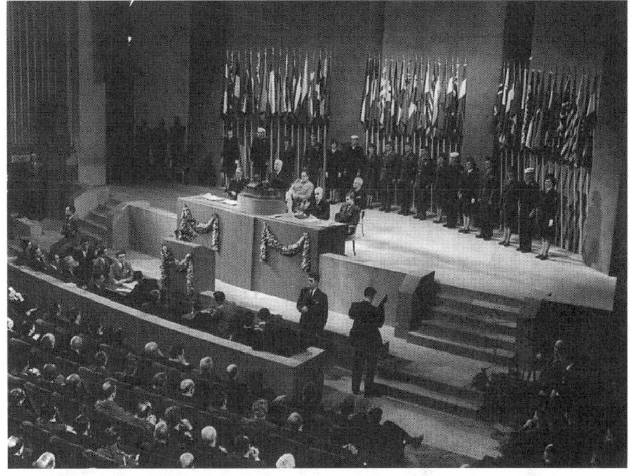

Top: Seal of the United Nations. The design around the edge represents a pair of olive branches, a symbol of peace. ***Bottom:*** President Harry Truman addressing the United Nations in 1946.

In 1945, the Allies set up a tribunal at Nuremberg, Germany, to try Nazi officials involved in the Holocaust and other crimes against humanity. Of the twenty-one men brought to trial, eleven were sentenced to be hanged (though one of them committed suicide before he could be executed). Seven others were sentenced to prison, and three were acquitted. A Nazi official named Adolf Eichmann went into hiding in other lands, but in 1960 he was captured by Israelis and hanged for his part in the Holocaust.

God will finally require justice for all shedding of innocent blood, something that He hates (Proverbs 6:16–19). But the people of God are content to leave such matters in His

Trial of Nazi leaders at Nuremberg, Germany. The 21 defendants sit inside the box with a low partition around it. Eleven of them were sentenced to be hanged, and the others were either acquitted or were imprisoned for varying terms.

hands, for Romans 12:19 declares, "Vengeance is mine; I will repay, saith the Lord."

Dealings With Other Axis Powers. American military forces occupied Japan from 1945 to 1951. For war crimes they brought twenty-five Japanese leaders to trial, of whom seven were executed and the rest were imprisoned. In 1946, the Allies worked out peace treaties with Italy, Romania, Bulgaria, Hungary, and Finland, which had all fought with the Axis. They lost some territory and had to pay reparations. Austria was divided as Germany had been, but it was united and given independence in 1955.

Consequences of the War

New Nations. One result of World War II was the dissolving of large European empires. For example, Italy lost its land in Africa, and the British Empire was weakened so that nations in the Far East, the Middle East, and Africa gained independence in the decades after World War II. Among these were the Philippines (1946), Israel (1948), and Indonesia (1949).

The Cold War. Another major effect of World War II was the ***Cold War***, a conflict in which opposing nations worked against one another without actually fighting. Joseph Stalin had said he would allow free elections after the war, but he ignored those promises. By the end of 1948, Czechoslovakia, Poland, Hungary, Bulgaria, Romania, Albania, Yugoslavia, and East Germany all had Communist governments dominated by the Soviet Union.

Mainland China became communist in 1949, and it seemed likely that Communists might also take control of other countries: Italy, Greece, Austria, and even France. Already in 1946, Winston Churchill had declared that "an ***Iron Curtain*** has descended" across Europe. The United States became the chief defender of the democratic nations, and the Soviet Union the chief defender of the communist nations. Those nations not aligned with either the United States or the Soviet Union were called the Third World.

Thus the world became divided into two armed camps, communist and democratic. In 1949, the United States formed a military alliance called the North Atlantic Treaty Organization (NATO) to unite democratic nations—called the free world—against communist nations. To counter this, the Soviet Union and other communist nations banded together in 1955 to form the Warsaw Pact.

Americans strongly opposed the spread of communism. In 1947, President Truman declared in the Truman Doctrine that the United States would aid any nation fighting communism, and two years later the United States helped to defeat the Communists in Greece. This conflict and several others showed that the Cold War could quickly flare into a "hot" war.

The United States tried to help Europe rebuild after the war. In 1947, Secretary of State George Marshall proposed the Marshall Plan under which the United States contributed $17 billion over four years to help European nations with reconstruction. The United States hoped such aid would help these nations withstand communism.

The Nuclear Age. The Cold War was dangerous because the two most powerful nations

Europe After World War II

in the world, the United States and the Soviet Union, both had nuclear weapons. After the United States developed the atomic bomb in World War II, the Soviets rushed to develop one also, and by 1949 they succeeded. The United States then went on to develop the even more powerful hydrogen bomb, and again the Soviets soon did the same.

Thus the United States and the Soviet Union began competing for superiority in the number and power of their weapons. Each built more and more nuclear bombs and missiles in an effort to keep ahead of the other. The atomic bomb had seemed like a quick and simple way to end World War II in 1945. But the world was now overshadowed with a cloud of fear at the thought of a global nuclear war.

Nonresistance in World War II

Plans for an Alternate Service Program. As the likelihood of war increased in 1939, the historic peace churches diligently sought to spare their young men from hardships like those of COs during World War I. These churches included the Mennonites, the Amish, the Church of the Brethren (Dunkers), and the Friends (Quakers). In 1939, the Mennonite Central Peace Committee was formed to draw up a plan of alternate service. They presented the plan to President Roosevelt in January 1940.

Congress passed a draft law called the Selective Training and Service Act in 1940. Because of efforts by the Quakers, this law contained a clause stating that conscientious objectors should be assigned to "work of national importance under civilian direction." Accordingly, a group of leaders in the historic peace churches set up the National Service Board for Religious Objectors to make plans for alternate service—though conservative Mennonite leaders had grave concerns about letting their young men work under this board. On February 6, 1941, the president signed an executive order that established Civilian Public Service (CPS) as a program of alternate service for COs.

Left: The first Civilian Public Service camp that was operated by Mennonites was at Grottoes, Virginia. It opened in May 1941 and closed in May 1946. ***Right:*** CPS workers file into a camp building, probably to eat a meal. The CPS program spared nonresistant young men from being compelled to serve in the armed forces.

Top: From 1943 to 1946, some young men in CPS served as smoke jumpers to fight forest fires. The parachute of one man, from the camp near Missoula, Montana, got caught in a tree. ***Bottom:*** These CPS workers are planting seedlings at the Wells Tannery camp in Sideling Hill, Pennsylvania.

Civilian Public Service. CPS was a program in which the government provided work camps and had general oversight of the projects, while the peace churches managed the camps and paid the costs of the men living in them. This program began with the opening of the first camps in May 1941, and it ended in March 1947. It provided alternate service for about 12,000 COs, of whom 4,665 were Mennonites.

COs in the CPS program took part in projects such as soil conservation, building dams, digging ditches, planting trees, and fighting forest fires. Some worked in general hospitals or in mental hospitals. Others volunteered to be "guinea pigs" in experiments for the government. They wore lice-infested clothes to test powders designed to kill lice, and a few even allowed mosquitoes to bite them in tests of new drugs to fight malaria.

Most of the men lived in camps, where they had opportunities to read, have social activities, and pursue hobbies in their spare time. Libraries and educational programs were also made available. But there were some problems. The men had to get along with each other in close quarters. Many grew bored with the work and with camp life. They did not receive pay, so they had to depend on money from their churches for their support.

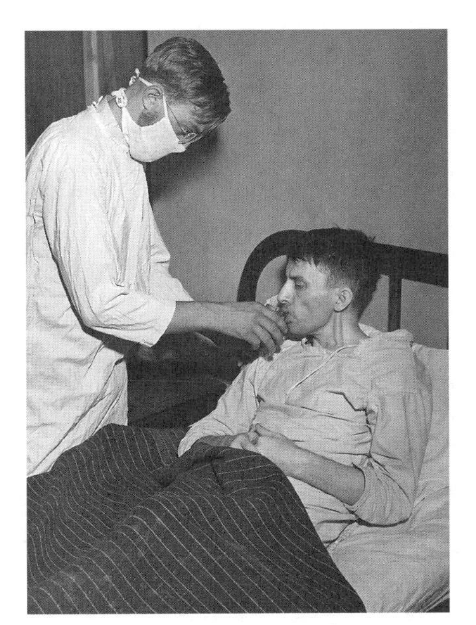

Some CPS workers served in mental hospitals. One was the Cleveland State Hospital at Cleveland, Ohio, where this orderly is shown assisting a patient.

Philemon Frey, who had been a conscientious objector in World War I, preaches at a worship service for young men at a CPS camp in Nebraska.

Providing spiritual nurture for the men proved difficult. It was hard to find enough ministers to hold regular Sunday schools, midweek meetings, and Bible studies. In addition, a camp often contained a mixture of different Mennonite groups as well as other church groups. This made it hard for conservative COs to stand for their convictions.

The experience of young men in Civilian Public Service was much less difficult than that of COs in World War I. The COs of World War II went into special service for up to five

Mennonite Relief Efforts. World War II encouraged the outreach program of the Mennonite Church. Even before the war, the Mennonite Relief Committee sent workers to Spain during the Spanish Civil War. During the war, Mennonite relief workers went to England, France, and Poland. They distributed food, cared for orphans and needy children, and operated homes for children and old people. They aided refugees and those evacuated from bombed cities. A Civilian Public Service unit in Puerto Rico during the war resulted in the establishment of a mission there.

After the war, Mennonite relief workers went to Belgium, the Netherlands, Italy, Germany, Denmark, Austria, and Poland. There they helped in rebuilding, distributing food and clothing, and giving other aid to refugees. In 1947, for example, forty-three Mennonite workers in Germany distributed 4,538 short tons (4,117 M.T.) of food, clothing, and supplies. Mennonites in the United States donated clothing and canned food; the value of the gifts and monetary donations in 1947 was over $3.5 million. This aid was delivered "In the Name of Christ" as a testimony to the recipients. In addition, the Mennonite Central Committee helped to relocate thousands of Mennonites to Paraguay and Canada in the years after the war.

Top left: The Mennonite Central Committee provided soup for hungry schoolchildren in Germany, about 1947. ***Top right:*** This little German boy is thankful for the food that Mennonites in America sent to his war-torn country. His grandmother tried to explain where the food came from. ***Left:*** After World War II, many Mennonites from the Soviet Union sailed to South America to begin a new life in Paraguay. These Mennonite refugees on the ship SS *Volendam* arrive at Buenos Aires, Argentina. From there, they will travel to Paraguay.

years because of their beliefs, and this served to strengthen the convictions of some. But a much larger number of young men in CPS departed from the Biblical principles that they had been taught. Thus the overall effect of CPS was to weaken rather than strengthen nonresistance and nonconformity in the Mennonite Church.

Focus for Thought

13. Describe some costs of World War II.
14. a. Into what four zones was Germany divided after the war?
    b. Why did Germany remain divided after 1955?
15. Describe four important consequences of World War II.
16. What is meant by the Cold War?
17. a. What services were performed by young men in CPS?
    b. What were some difficulties that they faced?

Historical Highlights

A. Matching: People

a. Adolf Hitler
b. Benito Mussolini
c. Chester Nimitz
d. Douglas MacArthur
e. Dwight D. Eisenhower
f. Franklin D. Roosevelt
g. Harry S. Truman
h. Joseph Stalin
i. Winston Churchill

1. Dictator of the Soviet Union.
2. Supreme commander of Allied forces in Europe.
3. American general in the Far East.
4. President during the Great Depression and most of World War II; first president to serve more than two terms.
5. Dictator of Germany.
6. American admiral in charge during the Battle of Midway.
7. Prime minister of Great Britain during World War II.
8. Dictator of Italy.
9. President who replaced Roosevelt and ordered use of the atomic bomb.

B. Matching: Terms 1

a. Allies
b. amphibious
c. appeasement
d. Axis
e. blitzkrieg
f. communism
g. D-day
h. demilitarized
i. fascism
j. historic peace churches
k. Holocaust
l. Nazism
m. totalitarian

1. Free of troops and weapons.
2. Political system of nationalism and totalitarian control in Germany.
3. Date when Allies invaded France in World War II.
4. Policy of maintaining peace by letting an aggressor have his way.
5. "Lightning war" in which German planes and tanks swiftly took control of a region.
6. Pertaining to a combination of naval and land forces.
7. Germany and the nations that helped it in World War II.
8. Having a single authority with absolute control of everything.
9. Hitler's destruction of millions of Jews and others in Europe.
10. Great Britain, the United States, and the nations that helped them.
11. Political system of totalitarian control in Italy.
12. Mennonites, Brethren, and Friends.
13. System based on the socialistic ideas of Karl Marx, in which the government owns most of a nation's land and resources.

C. Matching: Terms 2

a. Civilian Public Service
b. Cold War
c. free world
d. General Assembly
e. Iron Curtain
f. Manhattan Project
g. National Service Board for Religious Objectors
h. North Atlantic Treaty Organization
i. Security Council
j. Third World
k. United Nations
l. Warsaw Pact

1. Body of the United Nations responsible for keeping world peace.
2. Program to build the atomic bomb.
3. Nations not aligned with either the United States or the Soviet Union.
4. Program of alternate service for conscientious objectors.
5. International organization to maintain world peace and security.
6. General name for the United States and other democratic nations.
7. Military alliance formed by Western nations in 1949 to oppose communism.
8. Group that made plans for alternate service in work camps.
9. Military alliance formed by communist nations of Eastern Europe in 1955.
10. Body of the United Nations in which every member nation has a voice.
11. Conflict in which enemy nations worked against each other without actually fighting.
12. Term introduced by Churchill to describe the barrier between communist nations and free nations.

D. Matching: Dates

a. September 1, 1939
b. December 7, 1941
c. December 8, 1941
d. June 6, 1944
e. May 8, 1945
f. September 2, 1945

1. D-day—Allies invade France.
2. V-J Day—World War II ends.
3. "Date of infamy"—Japanese attack Pearl Harbor.
4. V-E Day—Allies celebrate Germany's surrender.
5. World War II begins.
6. United States declares war on Japan.

E. Matching: Battles and Places

a. Battle of Leyte Gulf
b. Battle of Midway
c. Battle of Stalingrad
d. Battle of the Atlantic
e. Battle of the Bulge
f. East Germany
g. Hiroshima
h. Nagasaki
i. Nuremberg
j. Pearl Harbor
k. West Germany

1. Japanese cities devastated by atomic bombs in 1945 (two answers).
2. Battle in the Soviet Union that marked a turning point in the war against Germany.
3. Parts into which Germany was divided (two answers).
4. Place of Japanese surprise attack that brought the United States into the war.

5. Place where Nazi leaders were tried for war crimes.
6. Naval battles in the Pacific that resulted in great losses for Japan (two answers).
7. Hitler's desperate attempt to divide the Allies and save Germany in 1944.
8. Struggle against German submarines that attacked Allied ships.

F. Deeper Discussion

1. Why could the United States not remain neutral in World War II?
2. How was the attack on Pearl Harbor actually the downfall of Japan?
3. How could human beings treat their fellow men as the Jews and others were treated during the Holocaust? (See Ecclesiastes 4:1; Jeremiah 17:9; and Romans 3:10–18.)
4. How were the results of World War II as bad as the problems that caused it?
5. Contrast God's justice with man's justice as demonstrated at Nuremberg, Germany. (See Ecclesiastes 5:8; Romans 12:19; and Revelation 20:11–13.)
6. Why did the Cold War break out after World War II?

G. Chronology and Geography

1. The following list gives some main events leading up to World War II. Arrange the list in the proper order, and supply the year for each event.

   Germany occupies Austria
   Germany occupies Czechoslovakia
   Hitler comes to power in Germany
   Hitler occupies the Rhineland
   Italy invades Ethiopia
   Japan attacks China
   Japan invades Manchuria
   Mussolini comes to power in Italy
   Spanish Civil War
   World War II begins with German invasion of Poland (September 1)

2. a. List the four main Allied nations.
   b. List the three main Axis nations.
3. Tell what geographic features hindered the Allies in each of these cases.
   a. the fighting in North Africa
   b. the liberation of Italy
   c. the D-day invasion of France
   d. the invasion of Germany itself
   e. the Pacific war

Housing project at Levittown, Pennsylvania, in 1959. This project was the work of William Levitt, whose housing developments included as many as 17,000 homes that housed over 80,000 people. Levitt's houses cost less than $8,000 at first.

26 Tranquil Years: America in the 1950s

1945

Harry S. Truman becomes president; United Nations (UN) founded 1945

Truman elected to second term 1948

North Atlantic Treaty Organization (NATO) formed 1949

1950

Korean War begins (June 25) **1950**

Twenty-second Amendment ratified 1951

Dwight D. Eisenhower elected president 1952

Korean War ends (July 27) **1953**

Southeast Asia Treaty Organization (SEATO) formed 1954

1955

Black boycott of buses in Montgomery 1955

Eisenhower re-elected; conflict over the Suez Canal 1956

Sputnik 1 launched by Soviets 1957

Explorer 1 launched by Americans 1958

Alaska and Hawaii become states 1959

John F. Kennedy elected president 1960

1960

1. YEARS OF CONFRONTATION
   - The "Fair Deal"
   - The Korean War
   - Anti-communism
2. YEARS OF PROSPERITY
   - Eisenhower's Administration
   - The Prosperous Years
   - The Civil Rights Movement
3. YEARS OF PEACE
   - Eisenhower's Foreign Policy
   - The Cold War in the 1950s

"We looked for peace, but no good came; and for a time of health, and behold trouble!"

Jeremiah 8:15

Tranquil Years: America in the 1950s

Focus for Reading

The United States was a global power at the end of World War II. Victor in battle and the sole possessor of atomic weapons, America stood a giant among nations. Bright hopes for a secure, peaceful future floated like a mirage on the horizon. But the mirage soon vanished in clouds of anxiety as the Cold War brought on the dread of communism. So strong was this fear that the United States became involved in several foreign wars to oppose the expansion of communism.

Americans prospered financially in the 1950s. Just as they had sought "normalcy" in the decade following World War I, so they did in the decade following World War II. Under the calm surface, however, changes stirred. Blacks began demanding that society treat them the same as white people. Morals deteriorated under the influence of radio and television. More and more youth rebelled against their elders. These changes would bear bitter fruit in the 1960s.

The story of these developments is told in the following three parts.

1. Years of Confrontation
2. Years of Prosperity
3. Years of Peace

1. YEARS OF CONFRONTATION

"When they shall say, Peace and safety; then sudden destruction cometh upon them" (1 Thessalonians 5:3). The thought in this verse matches the mood in America after World War II. Though it was a time of peace and prosperity, people feared that it might suddenly be destroyed by communism or nuclear war—maybe both. In 1950, the Cold War flared into a hot war in Korea as the United States fought to keep Communists from taking over South Korea. A strong anti-Communist movement developed in the United States after this war.

The "Fair Deal"

Truman's Domestic Policy. After Harry S. Truman succeeded Roosevelt in 1945, he proposed an ambitious social program for the United States. Among other things, he wanted to expand the social security program, increase the minimum wage, and provide health care. Few of Truman's proposals became law, although Congress did establish the Atomic Energy Commission to control the use of atomic energy.

Harry S. Truman (1884–1972) was the thirty-third president of the United States. He served from 1945 to 1953 and was a Democrat.

To aid blacks, President Truman set up a committee on civil rights that proposed stronger civil rights laws, and he gained Congressional approval of laws against lynching (mob justice) and poll taxes (taxes paid for the

Interior of the White House during reconstruction. The renovation, which took place while Truman was president, was so extensive that the White House was practically rebuilt.

Rebuilding the White House. By the time Harry S. Truman moved into the White House, the building had deteriorated to the point of being dangerously weak. The head usher told Truman that the whole second floor might fall down, and an engineer told him that the State Dining Room ceiling stayed up from "force of habit." When the leg of a piano broke through to the ceiling of the dining room, President Truman knew the 149-year-old mansion needed major repairs. So he and his family lived elsewhere from 1949 to 1952 while the executive mansion was renovated.

The inside was completely stripped, and a new framework of steel was placed within the exterior walls. Then the White House was rebuilt. Two new basement levels were added (one bombproof), and the mansion went from sixty-two rooms and twenty-six halls to over one hundred rooms and forty halls. On April 22, 1952, the renovated White House again opened for public tours—5,444 people toured it that day! The architect and engineers told President Truman that it was built to last five hundred years.

privilege to vote). Truman ordered the ***desegregation*** (ending of separation by race) of the military forces, and he appointed the first black federal judge in the United States.

After winning the election in 1948, Truman proposed another program of social reforms. Called the "Fair Deal," this program included basically the same ideas that Truman had promoted in 1945. Congress expanded social security and raised the minimum wage from forty cents to seventy-five cents an hour. It also authorized federal aid for slum clearance and low-cost public housing. Truman served as president until 1953.

The Twenty-second Amendment. In 1947, Congress passed the Twenty-second Amendment to the Constitution. This amendment said that no person could be elected president more than twice, as Franklin D. Roosevelt had been. The amendment became part of the Constitution in 1951.

The Korean War

Conflict with communism continued in the Cold War. After World War II, the United States reorganized its military forces to make them more effective. The Defense Department was created in 1947 to supervise all the military services. Congress also established the National Security Council and the Central Intelligence Agency to protect United States military interests.

In 1949, Communist rebels led by Mao Zedong (MOW DZUH DAHNG) took over China, and the ruling Nationalists fled to Taiwan. This communist victory was a bitter blow to the United States, which had a long history of friendship with China. The United States continued to support the Nationalists and refused to recognize the Communist government of China.

Invasion of South Korea. After World War II, the Korean peninsula was occupied by the Soviets in the north and Americans in the south, with the boundary at the thirty-eighth parallel. The occupying forces withdrew by 1949, leaving North Korea with a Communist government and South Korea with a non-Communist government. In 1950, the Communists decided to unite Korea by force. So on June 25, an army of North Korean tanks and soldiers invaded South Korea, and a few days later they captured Seoul (SOHL), the capital.

President Truman took the issue to the United Nations Security Council, which promptly called upon member nations to repel the attack. President Truman then ordered American troops to South Korea, with General Douglas MacArthur in command of all the troops supplied by the United Nations (UN). The president considered this a "police action" and therefore did not ask Congress to declare war.

The Korean War was a UN action, and MacArthur flew the UN flag over his headquarters. Sixteen nations fought in the conflict, with the United States supplying 90 percent of the soldiers. This was the first "world army" deployed by an international organization.

In South Korea, the communist forces kept up their offensive drive until the UN troops held only the southeast corner of the peninsula. There the UN troops formed a defensive line called the Pusan Perimeter. But on September 15, General MacArthur landed another army at Inchon along the west coast of Korea. These forces moved rapidly to Seoul and occupied the city on September 27. Meanwhile, the UN troops of the Pusan Perimeter attacked the North Koreans and drove them northward. Finding themselves attacked from two directions, the communist forces fled; and by October 1, most of South Korea was regained.

General MacArthur's forces landing at Inchon, Korea. These UN troops attacked from the west while others advanced from the south, forcing the North Koreans to retreat.

Chinese Intervention. President Truman authorized General MacArthur to pursue the North Koreans across the thirty-eighth parallel and try to conquer all of Korea. On October 19, UN forces captured the North Korean capital of Pyongyang (PYAWNG yang). From there, some units advanced to the Yalu River on the border of China. The Chinese had warned that if UN forces moved north of the thirty-eighth parallel, they might intervene. But General MacArthur discounted this idea and declared that the war would be over by Christmas.

China did intervene, and soon thousands of Chinese troops were helping North Koreans to drive the UN soldiers back. Their retreat continued until the communist forces again

Retreating UN forces head south across the thirty-eighth parallel after being repulsed by Chinese forces.

Korean refugees flee south to escape the fighting near Kangnung, South Korea, in January 1951. Kangnung receives snow because it is located at about 38°N (as far north as Washington, D.C.).

captured Seoul in January 1951. Then the UN forces counterattacked; they regained Seoul in March 1951, and by June they held a line just north of the thirty-eighth parallel.

Disagreement Over the War. A bloody stalemate now developed. Fighting broke out from time to time, but little was gained and many lives were lost. General MacArthur wanted to do everything necessary to win the war quickly, such as blockading China and even using nuclear weapons. But President Truman did not favor an all-out war that involved China. He was afraid the Soviet Union would come to China's aid, and then World War III might begin.

General MacArthur publicly opposed the idea of a limited war. He voiced his disagreement so strongly that on April 11, 1951, President Truman dismissed him as commander. Many Americans disapproved; and when MacArthur returned to the United States, crowds greeted him as a hero. But a Senate committee investigated the matter and concluded that President Truman was justified in his action. This incident made it clear that the civilian president had power over the armed forces.

President Truman and General MacArthur met on Wake Island, October 15, 1950, for a conference. Although this meeting was amiable, Truman dismissed MacArthur as commander within six months.

Women and children search in the rubble of Seoul, South Korea, looking for fuel or anything usable.

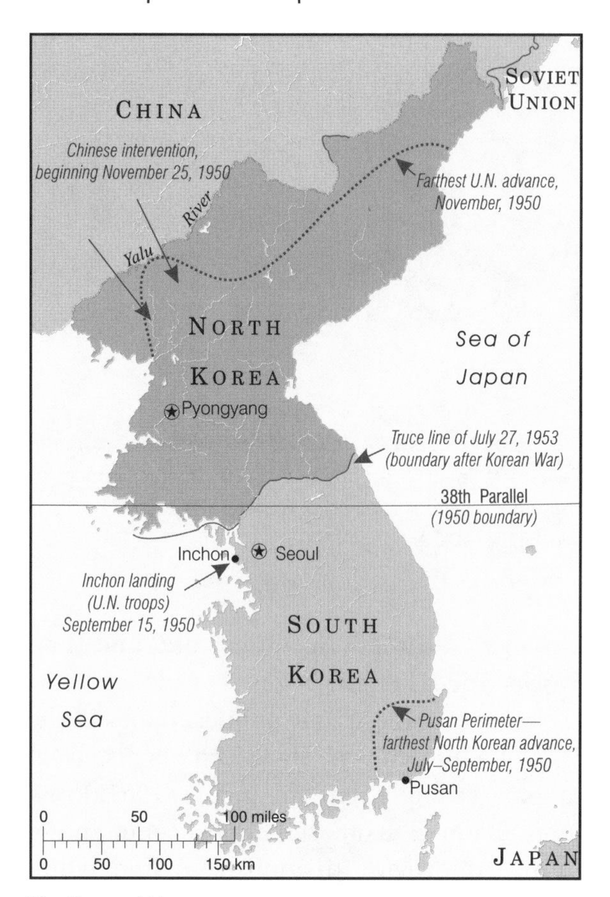

The Korean War

End of the War. The Korean War dragged on until after Dwight D. Eisenhower became president. Finally on July 27, 1953, the two sides agreed to a truce (cease-fire). They established a new border between North and South Korea, with a demilitarized zone 2.5 miles wide (4 km) along the border.

Effects of the War. The Korean War had been costly—about half a million men in the UN armies were wounded or killed. North Korean and communist forces suffered an estimated 1.5 million military casualties. In addition, North and South Korea each suffered about a million civilian casualties; and thousands of homes and factories were destroyed by heavy bombing.

The Korean War had no victor. When it ended, the line dividing Korea remained about where it had been before the war. However, the war showed that the United States intended to oppose communism anywhere in the world, not only in Europe.

Anti-communism

After the Korean War, a great fear of communism swept the United States. China had become communist in 1949, and the Korean War made it clear that the Communists intended to expand their domain. Were they also conspiring to overthrow America? Might some of them even be holding offices in the United States government? Such thoughts filled many Americans with dread.

God's people must remember that their security comes not from the military might of nations, but from God. Psalm 20:7 says, "Some trust in chariots, and some in horses: but we will remember the name of the LORD our God." In a world trembling with fear and uncertainty, Christians can rest in the assurance that God is still in control.

Notable Spy Cases. In 1948, a former State Department official named **Alger Hiss** was accused of being a Communist. Whittaker Chambers, a former Communist, said that Hiss had stolen government secrets and sold them to the Soviet Union in the 1930s. Hiss denied the charges. But Chambers produced supporting evidence, including five rolls of film with pictures of important State Department documents. The pictures included summaries of the material in Hiss's handwriting.

It appeared that Hiss was a spy for the Communists, though that was never fully proven. The government did not charge him with spying, for the statute of limitations had run out (too much time had passed since the crime occurred). So Alger Hiss was charged with perjury (lying under oath) and was sentenced to prison for five years.

Soon other Communist spy activities came to light. Several people, including a couple named Julius and Ethel Rosenberg, were arrested in 1950 for giving atomic secrets to the Soviet Union. The Rosenbergs were found

What is Communism? Communism is a system based on the ideas of the German philosopher Karl Marx. (See Chapter 20.) Marx taught that throughout history there has been a class struggle between those who own the means of production (capitalists) and those who do not (workers). He believed that as capitalists became increasingly rich, the workers would grow poorer. Then one day the workers would rise up, overthrow the capitalists, and establish a free, classless society in which everyone had equal wealth and recognition.

Marx's ideas held widespread appeal because they offered a new vision for man. Marxism, and subsequently communism, presented a kind of faith that replaced God with man. But when man rejects God and His revelation, he distorts the truth and promotes falsehood. "There is a way that seemeth right unto a man, but the end thereof are the ways of death" (Proverbs 16:25).

Marxist ideas gave rise to the Bolshevik Revolution in Russia, by which the Soviet Union was established. The modern term *communism* refers to the application of Marxist ideas in the Soviet Union and other countries that became communist. In those nations, the Communist Party was able to seize power and crush all opposition. Communist leaders then tried to expand their power by promoting revolutions in non-communist countries.

In practice, a Communist government owns and manages all the factories and farms in a nation. This has produced wealth and freedom only for the Communist leaders. The rest of the people are an impoverished, oppressed society with all aspects of life under government control. Religious freedom is not permitted, since the Communist Party is an atheistic, humanistic organization. Often a dictator exercises great power, and secret police enforce his will through terror, torture, and murder. This is why people in the free world feared communism as they did.

guilty and were executed in 1953.

In this climate of suspicion, a Wisconsin senator named Joseph McCarthy started a campaign in 1950 in which he publicly accused prominent individuals of being Communists. He made similar accusations against hundreds of people in the next several years, ruining many reputations but never proving any of his charges. In 1954, the Senate officially condemned McCarthy, and his influence quickly faded. The term *McCarthyism* came to describe the practice of defaming someone by making unfair public accusations against him.

Julius and Ethel Rosenberg after being found guilty by a jury in 1951. They were electrocuted in 1953 despite widespread protests that their trial was unfair.

Focus for Thought

1. How did President Truman try to help black people?
2. What did the Twenty-second Amendment provide for?
3. Why were Americans distressed at China's fall to communism?

4. How and when did the Korean War begin?
5. a. Why did President Truman want to fight only a limited war in Korea?
   b. What happened when General MacArthur disagreed with the president?
6. Describe two effects of the Korean War.
7. Why were Americans afraid that Communists might take over America?

2. YEARS OF PROSPERITY

Dwight D. Eisenhower, a Republican, won the presidential election of 1952; and Richard M. Nixon served as his vice president. Eisenhower served two terms, lasting through the rest of the 1950s. He presided over America in a time of peace and prosperity. Yet there were social stirrings, especially among blacks, which would lead to troubled times in the years ahead.

Eisenhower's Administration

America was a prosperous, growing nation during President Eisenhower's two terms (1953–1961). Because of a "baby boom," the United States population climbed by almost 28 million from 1950 to 1960. In Eisenhower's second term, two new states joined the Union: Alaska in January 1959, and Hawaii in August 1959. Then there were fifty states.

Dwight D. Eisenhower (1890–1969) was the thirty-fourth president of the United States. He served from 1953 to 1961 and was a Republican.

Eisenhower expanded some social programs of Roosevelt's New Deal. He extended social security to cover 10 million additional people, and he raised the minimum wage to one dollar per hour. He established the Department of Health, Education, and Welfare in his Cabinet in 1953 to oversee federal aid to children, the sick, and the needy.

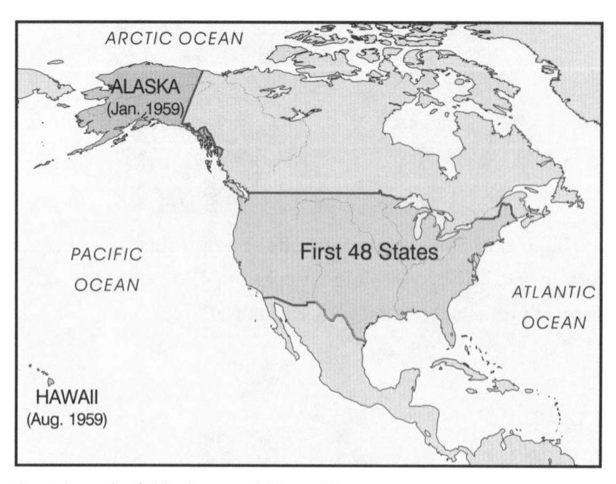

Statehood of Alaska and Hawaii

The Interstate Highway Act was passed in 1956. This law stated that the federal government would pay most of the cost of a new 40,000-mile (64,371-km) network of interstate highways. Also, the United States and Canada worked together to build the St. Lawrence Seaway. Completed in 1959, the new seaway allowed larger ships to travel between the Atlantic Ocean and the Great Lakes.

The Prosperous Years

Many Americans enjoyed wealth and prosperity in the 1950s. Rising wages and productivity pushed more and more families into

This UNIVAC computer of 1959 was developed from the ENIAC model of the 1940s.

the middle class—defined at the time as those with incomes over $5,000 a year after taxes were deducted. These families could afford to buy bigger houses, better appliances, and new furniture.

Advances in Technology. New technology produced better and cheaper products. Synthetic fabrics, such as nylon, began replacing natural fibers; and plastics replaced wood and metal. The first electronic digital computer, ENIAC, was built in 1946. It took up 1,800 square feet (167 m^2) of floor space, used eighteen thousand vacuum tubes, and could do several hundred calculations per minute.

The development of the transistor made pocket-sized radios possible. But it was television that became one of the strongest new influences. The number of television sets increased so rapidly that 90 percent of American families had one by 1960. Television brought commercial advertisements, political candidates, professional sports, and many other things right into American homes. Ungodly entertainment was piped directly into millions of living rooms. One man connected with the industry wrote, "Television in the main is being used to distract, delude, amuse, and insulate."

Medical science advanced. In 1953, Dr. Jonas Salk introduced a vaccine for polio, a disease that had crippled thousands of people. Development of antibiotics helped control disease, and the life expectancy of Americans approached seventy years. Though rising, this still fell within the "threescore years and ten" of Psalm 90:10.

A Mobile Society. Some of the greatest changes in society took place because Americans were more mobile. Since they could drive to their jobs, many moved out to the suburbs of large cities. This led to vast suburban housing developments consisting of houses built by mass production. Such housing developments were whole new communities, complete with schools, churches, and parks.

Americans bought more and bigger cars. The number of automobiles rose from 49 million in 1950 to 73.8 million in 1960. Automobiles became more expensive, rising from an average $1,270 to $1,822 during the decade. Federal and state governments built hundreds of miles of better highways to accommodate the increased traffic.

As Americans took to the road, more services became available for them. The first Holiday Inn motel was built in 1952, and soon other motel chains developed. Chains of fast-food restaurants also sprang up. The McDonald's chain began in 1955 and grew to several

Road construction delays rush-hour traffic in New York City, 1951. From 1950 to 1960, the number of automobiles on American highways surged by over 24 million.

hundred locations by 1960. By the late 1990s, there were over 8,000 McDonald's restaurants in the United States, and 23,000 in 111 countries around the world!

Conformists and Nonconformists. The fifties were a decade of social conformity. In the housing developments, houses looked very similar and people followed similar lifestyles. Wives stayed at home and took care of the children while husbands worked for large corporations. These companies offered regular work, a steady income, and a retirement plan. People wanted security after the tension of the war years; they wanted to raise a family and enjoy a good life.

Not everyone was so willing to fit in. Especially among the youth, a group labeled the "beat generation," or beatniks, rebelled against the older generation's devotion to material things. In the mid-1950s, a singer named Elvis Presley popularized a new kind of music called rock-and-roll. The strong, irregular rhythm of this music, along with the degenerate themes of the songs, helped to further break down morals in America. Rock-and-roll is one of the "wicked imaginations" devised by those who are "inventors of evil things" (Proverbs 6:18; Romans 1:30).

Federal troops escorted black students to the Central High School at Little Rock, Arkansas, in 1957.

The Civil Rights Movement

In 1953, President Eisenhower appointed **Earl Warren** as the chief justice of the Supreme Court. The Warren Court, as it was known, presided over sweeping changes in the American judicial system. It became an ***activist court;*** that is, the Warren Court began to make rulings that were the equivalent of laws passed by Congress. Instead of merely deciding how the current laws applied to specific cases, the Court began to issue orders that had the force of new laws. This approach was to have profound effects in the following decades.

Beginning of the Civil Rights Movement. One of the first areas where the Court's new direction became evident was in civil rights. Increasingly, black Americans resented unfair and unequal treatment by whites, and they challenged laws and customs that kept the races segregated. The drive to give blacks equal status with whites is called the ***civil rights movement***.

A case known as *Brown v. Board of Education of Topeka* arose in 1951 and eventually came before the Supreme Court. This case involved a black man who wanted to send his daughter to an all-white school. At issue was the idea of separate but equal facilities, which were allowed by laws then in force. These laws stated that schools should be separated according to race, but they were still to provide equal education.

On May 17, 1954, the Warren Court delivered its unanimous decision: segregation of black and white children in public schools was unconstitutional. The Court said, "Separate educational facilities are inherently unequal." This major ruling was known as the Brown Decision.

As a result, many states that had segregated facilities for education took action to integrate their schools. But in 1957, a crisis arose in Little Rock, Arkansas, when nine black children enrolled in an all-white school.

A mob tried to keep the blacks from attending, but President Eisenhower sent soldiers to Little Rock to enforce the law. Federal troops protected the black students throughout the school year.

Other Developments in Civil Rights. Black people soon won further victories. On December 1, 1955, a black woman named **Rosa Parks** took a seat on a bus in Montgomery, Alabama. She sat near the front of the black section (the back seats); but when the front section filled up, the driver ordered some of the blacks to give their seats to whites. Rosa Parks refused to move, so she was arrested.

Soon a black minister named **Martin Luther King, Jr.**, organized a boycott in which black people refused to ride on Montgomery buses until they received the same treatment as whites. The boycott lasted about a year and nearly put the bus company out of business. Finally in November 1956, the Supreme Court ruled that segregation on buses was unconstitutional, and the city desegregated its buses.

Martin Luther King, Jr., and his followers became bolder in their struggle for civil rights. Instead of physical violence, King promoted the use of nonviolent resistance to bring about changes. His methods included boycotts, protest marches, and civil disobedience (disobeying laws that the protesters considered wrong). This is quite different from what Jesus meant when He instructed His followers to "resist not evil" (Matthew 5:39). Nonviolent resistance is still resistance, so it is inconsistent with Biblical nonresistance.

Focus for Thought

8. Give some details about the following developments of the 1950s.
   a. the growing middle class
   b. improved technology
   c. television
   d. medical advances
   e. greater mobility
9. Describe the social conformity of the 1950s.
10. How did the Supreme Court change after Earl Warren became chief justice?
11. a. What was the main idea of the Brown Decision?
    b. What effect did it have on schools?
12. a. What was the approach of Martin Luther King, Jr., in seeking rights for blacks?
    b. How is this different from Biblical nonresistance?

3. YEARS OF PEACE

The Korean War continued for half a year after Dwight D. Eisenhower became president, but the United States did not become directly involved in any other war during his presidency. Nevertheless, the nation continued to be drawn into foreign affairs around the globe. Perhaps the greatest concern was the Cold War between the United States and the Soviet Union.

Eisenhower's Foreign Policy

When Eisenhower became president, he and John Foster Dulles, his influential secretary of state, wanted to chart a new course in foreign policy. President Truman had promoted the mere ***containment*** of communism (keeping it from spreading). But Dulles wanted to liberate countries already under Communist rule.

Dulles also wanted to place more emphasis

on nuclear weapons; so in 1954, he introduced a strategy called ***massive retaliation***. Its goal was to prevent war by threatening a nuclear attack on the Soviet Union if the Soviets attacked any American ally. In this way, nuclear weapons became a central part of the Cold War.

The idea of liberating countries under Communist rule did not work out well. In 1956, Hungary rebelled against the Soviet Union and installed a more democratic ruler. When the Soviet army attacked, Hungarian freedom fighters resisted but the United States did little to help them. Soviet troops executed the new leader and killed thousands of Hungarians, while 150,000 refugees fled to neighboring countries. About 20,000 of these refugees were accepted into the United States.

President Eisenhower depended on the spy activities of the Central Intelligence Agency (CIA) in pursuing United States goals in other lands. The CIA helped to overthrow governments that the United States viewed as pro-Communist. It began sending U-2 spy planes to fly at high altitudes over the Soviet Union and photograph Soviet military installations. The U-2 could soar as high as 80,000 feet (24,383 m), and special cameras could take pictures so sharp that they showed the painted lines in a parking lot 14 miles (23 km) below.

The Cold War in the 1950s

Trouble in Southeast Asia. The country of Vietnam, in Southeast Asia, was divided at the seventeenth parallel in 1954. Its northern part came under the Communist rule of Ho Chi Minh (HOH CHEE MIHN), and the southern part retained the Vietnamese emperor. In 1956, an anti-Communist named Ngo Dinh Diem (NGOH DIHN DYEHM) overthrew the emperor and made himself president.

The next year, a Communist group called the Viet Cong started a guerrilla war against South Vietnam. Small bands would make hit-and-run attacks, striking here and there at unexpected places. The United States gave millions of dollars each year in the late 1950s to help South Vietnam fight the guerrillas.

Laos (LAH ohs), a country which borders Vietnam, also faced a threat from Communist guerrillas. Here too the United States poured in aid by the millions of dollars. The CIA made efforts to set up a Laotian government that was friendly to the United States. But Laos remained a trouble spot in Southeast Asia.

Why did the United States pay so much attention to these small far-off countries? Leaders feared that if one nation fell to communism, nearby nations would also fall like a row of dominoes. This was called the ***domino theory***.

In order to maintain stability in the region, the United States formed the Southeast Asia Treaty Organization (SEATO) in 1954 as a defense alliance. This organization included the United States, France, Great Britain, Australia, New Zealand, the Philippines, Thailand, and Pakistan.

Conflict in the Middle East. Egypt had received a promise from Great Britain and the United States to help finance the construction of the Aswan High Dam across the Nile River. But because of Egypt's growing ties with communist countries, this financial aid was canceled in July 1956. Egypt responded by seizing control of the Suez Canal, which had previously been operated by a private company. The leaders predicted that tolls from ships using the canal would pay for the dam in five years. That action prompted Israel to invade Egypt; and since the canal was a vital link for European oil supplies, the British and French also sent troops to the area. The Soviet Union threatened to send nuclear missiles against Britain and France if they did not withdraw. Finally in November, a United Nations peace-keeping force put an end to the conflict and restored international access to the canal.

Because of this incident, Congress passed

a resolution approving the Eisenhower Doctrine. This gave the president authority to send armed forces to any nation in the Middle East that requested military aid against a communist attack.

Cuba's Fall to Communism. The United States had been supporting the rule of Fulgencio Batista, the oppressive dictator of Cuba, largely because of American investments in that country. Then in 1959, **Fidel Castro** overthrew the Batista government. But instead of allowing greater freedom, Castro refused to hold elections and persecuted his opponents as ruthlessly as the Batista regime had done. About seven hundred thousand Cubans fled from the island, mostly to the United States.

Castro seized $1 billion worth of American business and property investments in Cuba. He declared himself a Communist, became a Soviet ally, and accepted Soviet aid. President Eisenhower was greatly concerned about a communist nation only 90 miles (145 km) from the southern shores of the United States. He cut off diplomatic relations with Cuba in January 1961.

The Arms Race and Space Race. The military competition continued between the United States and the Soviet Union. In this ***arms race***, each nation tried to have more nuclear weapons than the other, and both built missiles capable of carrying nuclear warheads thousands of miles. Their hydrogen bombs had the power to do massive destruction around the world. The idea of a Soviet nuclear attack became a constant worry to many Americans. People made fallout shelters in their basements, and public schools held air-raid drills.

The ***space race*** began in October 1957 when the Soviet Union launched *Sputnik 1*, the first manmade satellite, into orbit around the earth. The satellite weighed 184 pounds (83 kg) and carried a radio transmitter. Later that year the Soviets launched *Sputnik 2*, which weighed over 1,100 pounds (499 kg) and carried a small dog into space.

This scientific advance came as a shock to Americans. The United States had its own rocket program under Wernher von Braun, a rocket scientist who had formerly worked for the Nazis. American officials decided to launch a satellite of their own as quickly as possible; but on the first attempt, the rocket exploded on the launching pad.

At last in January 1958, Braun's team launched America's first space satellite, *Explorer 1*. It weighed only 31 pounds (14 kg), but an American satellite was in orbit. Also in 1958, the United States set up the National Aeronautics and Space Administration (NASA) to direct the American space program. The United States now began competing with the Soviet Union for dominance in space.

Rising and Falling Hopes for Peace. The Soviet dictator Joseph Stalin died in 1953 and was succeeded by **Nikita Khrushchev** (KROOSH chehf). In 1955, President Eisenhower met with Khrushchev in a ***summit meeting*** (meeting between heads of state) at Geneva, Switzerland, to discuss disarmament

Some people built shelters for protection against fallout (radioactive particles falling from the sky), which is the most widespread danger resulting from a nuclear explosion. This basement fallout shelter has enough food and water for two weeks, together with a radio, backup lights, and first-aid supplies.

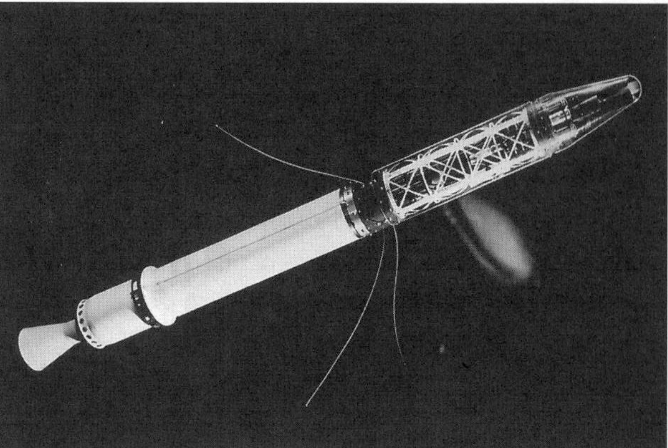

Sputnik 1, the first Soviet satellite, and *Explorer 1*, the first American satellite.

and other issues. This meeting brought a slight lessening of Cold War tensions.

American and Soviet leaders held several more meetings. One was in 1959, when Vice President **Richard M. Nixon** met with Khrushchev in Moscow. Another was in September 1959, when Khrushchev traveled to the United States for a conference with Eisenhower. The easing of tensions continued, and the two leaders agreed to a summit meeting at Paris in 1960.

Then suddenly the rising hopes for peace were dashed. On May 1, 1960, the Soviets shot down a U-2 spy plane and captured its pilot, along with several films showing Soviet military bases. During the Paris summit in May, Khrushchev lashed out so angrily against American spying that the meeting ended in confusion. Lasting peace had seemed so near, but now the hope was gone. In this atmosphere, Eisenhower's administration came to a close.

Focus for Thought

13. How was Eisenhower's foreign policy different from the containment of communism that President Truman had promoted?
14. a. Why did American leaders work so hard against communism in Southeast Asia?
    b. What actions were taken to oppose communism?
15. a. Why did Israel, Britain, and France go to war against Egypt in 1956?
    b. What was stated in the Eisenhower Doctrine?
16. How did Cuba become a communist nation?
17. a. Describe the arms race.
    b. Tell about the first successful satellite that the Soviets launched, and the first one that the Americans launched.
18. a. How did Cold War tensions ease somewhat in the 1950s?
    b. What spoiled the apparent progress?

Historical Highlights

A. People

a. Alger Hiss
b. Douglas MacArthur
c. Dwight D. Eisenhower
d. Earl Warren
e. Fidel Castro
f. Harry S. Truman
g. Martin Luther King, Jr.
h. Nikita Khrushchev
i. Richard M. Nixon
j. Rosa Parks

1. General in the Korean War who was dismissed by President Truman.
2. Vice president under Dwight D. Eisenhower who met with Khrushchev.
3. Dictator who took over Cuba in 1959 and made it a communist nation.
4. Black minister who led the civil rights movement and promoted nonviolent resistance.
5. President who served from 1945 to 1953, after Franklin D. Roosevelt.
6. Black person arrested for not yielding a bus seat to a white person.
7. President during most of the 1950s; served from 1953 to 1961.
8. Leader of the Soviet Union who succeeded Joseph Stalin.
9. Chief justice when the Supreme Court became more activist in the 1950s.
10. Former state department official accused of Communist activities and imprisoned for perjury.

B. Terms 1

a. arms race
b. Central Intelligence Agency
c. containment
d. demilitarized zone
e. domino theory
f. Eisenhower Doctrine
g. Korean War
h. massive retaliation
i. space race
j. summit meeting

1. Conference between heads of state.
2. Policy by which the president could send armed forces to countries of the Middle East that requested help against communism.
3. Idea that if one nation in a region falls to communism, nearby nations will also fall.
4. United States spy organization.
5. Place where no military activity is allowed.
6. Competition between the United States and the Soviet Union in building up a supply of weapons.
7. Threat of responding with nuclear weapons in case of attack on an American ally.
8. Policy of trying to keep communism from spreading.
9. Competition in which the United States and the Soviet Union tried to outdo each other in achievements in outer space.
10. Conflict in which UN forces opposed communist aggression.

C. Terms 2

a. activist court
b. civil rights movement
c. desegregation
d. Fair Deal
e. *Brown v. Board of Education of Topeka*
f. Department of Health, Education, and Welfare
g. Interstate Highway Act
h. National Aeronautics and Space Administration
i. Twenty-second Amendment

1. Drive to give blacks equal status with whites.
2. Measure passed in 1956 to build a network of interstate highways.
3. Agency established in 1958 to direct the American space program.
4. Ending of separation by race.
5. Department of the Cabinet established to oversee federal aid.
6. President Truman's program of social reforms.
7. Measure limiting a president's administration to two terms.
8. Inclined to make decisions that are the equivalent of new laws.
9. Case in which separate but equal facilities for blacks were declared unconstitutional.

D. Places and Dates

Not all the choices will be used.

a. Alaska
b. Cuba
c. Hawaii
d. North Korea
e. South Korea
f. Vietnam
g. June 25, 1950
h. 1945–1953
i. 1953–1961
j. July 27, 1953
k. 1956
l. 1959

1. Communist nation that invaded its neighbor in 1950.
2. States added to the Union during Eisenhower's administration (two answers).
3. Years of the Truman administration.
4. Nation that was invaded by its communist neighbor in 1950.
5. Years of the Eisenhower administration.
6. Nation aided by the United States in opposing Communist guerrillas.
7. Beginning and ending dates of the Korean War (two answers).
8. Year when two new states were admitted to the Union.

E. Deeper Discussion

1. Why did the United States consider it important to oppose communism everywhere in the world, even in faraway places such as Southeast Asia?
2. Why did the United States and the Soviet Union engage in an arms race?
3. How might an activist Supreme Court upset the delicate balance of powers in the American system of federal government?
4. Evaluate the goals and methods of the civil rights movement.

F. Chronology and Geography

1. The United States became a global power after World War II.
   a. What defense alliance did the United States form in Europe? in Southeast Asia?
   b. List six nations in whose affairs the United States became directly involved.
2. Review all the presidents and their terms from George Washington through Dwight D. Eisenhower by writing from memory their names and the dates they were in office. (Remember that an elected president's term begins in the year after the election. Also note that presidents before Franklin D. Roosevelt were inaugurated on March 4, and those after him on January 20.)
3. Label Alaska and Hawaii (and their dates of admission) on your map entitled "The States of the United States." Color them the same color as the other states admitted in the 1900s. Be sure you know the names and locations of all the states.

So Far This Year

A. Matching: Terms

a. appeasement
b. Allies
c. Axis
d. business cycle
e. Civilian Public Service
f. Cold War
g. Great Depression
h. Holocaust
i. Iron Curtain
j. modernism
k. Nazism
l. New Deal
m. North Atlantic Treaty Organization
n. Prohibition
o. Third World
p. Twentieth Amendment
q. Twenty-first Amendment
r. United Nations

1. Set of beliefs including the theory of evolution, rejection of the supernatural, and acceptance of science as the only source of truth.
2. Government programs designed to end the Depression.
3. Period when alcoholic drinks were outlawed.
4. Long economic downturn from 1929 to 1939.
5. Periodic swing between prosperity and decline in the economy.
6. Measure that ended the ban on alcoholic drinks.
7. Measure that shortened the lame-duck period after presidential elections.
8. Germany and the nations that helped it in World War II.
9. Political system of nationalism and totalitarian control in Germany.
10. International organization to maintain world peace.
11. Hitler's destruction of millions of Jews and others in Europe.
12. Conflict in which enemy nations opposed each other without fighting.
13. Policy of maintaining peace by letting an aggressor have his way.
14. Military alliance formed by Western nations in 1949 to oppose communism.
15. Great Britain, the United States, and the nations helping them in World War II.
16. Program of alternate service for conscientious objectors in World War II.
17. Nations not aligned with either the United States or the Soviet Union.
18. Barrier to communication and travel between communist nations and free nations.

B. Completion

Write the correct name or date for each description.

19. Made the first successful flight with a heavier-than-air machine in 1903.
20. Made cars available to the masses by introducing the Model T.
21. President from 1921 to 1923; died in office.
22. Took office after the death of the previous president; served from 1923 to 1929.
23. President when the Great Depression began; served from 1929 to 1933.
24. President during the Great Depression and most of World War II; first president to serve more than two terms.
25. Supreme commander of the Allied forces in Europe in World War II.
26. American general in the Far East who helped to liberate the Philippines.
27. President who replaced Roosevelt and ordered use of the atomic bomb.
28. Date when World War II began.
29. Date when Pearl Harbor was attacked.
30. Date of the D-day invasion of France.
31. Date when World War II ended (V-J Day).

C. Filling the Blanks: American Government

Not all the choices will be used.

Articles of Confederation
Bill of Rights
checks and balances
constitution
executive
Electoral College
federal
impeach
James Madison
judicial
legislative
monarchy
republic
separation of powers
Thomas Jefferson
~~veto~~

32. As a limit to the power of Congress, the president may ___ a law that Congress has passed.
33. A written plan of government is called a ___.
34. The "father of the Constitution" and fourth president of the United States was ___.
35. A ___ is a nation with a government by elected representatives and without a king or queen.
36. The first ten amendments to the Constitution, added in 1791, are called the ___.
37. The limits that the different government branches place on each other are called ___.
38. The branch of government that decides cases about laws is the ___ branch.
39. The term ___ describes the division of government into three branches.
40. The branch of government that proposes new laws is the ___ branch.
41. The ___ is the group of men who actually elect the president.
42. In a ___ system of government, powers are divided between the states and the national government.
43. The branch of government that enacts and enforces laws is the ___ branch.
44. Congress may ___ a president, or bring him to trial for misconduct in office.

D. True or False

Write whether each statement is true (T) *or false* (F). *If it is false, write the word or phrase that should replace the underlined part.*

45. The <u>Federalists</u> were a political party that favored strict interpretation and limited government.
46. The <u>Monroe Doctrine</u> was a declaration about involvement of European and American nations in each other's affairs.
47. The <u>Treaty of Ghent</u> ended the War of 1812.
48. The <u>Adams-Onís Treaty</u> settled differences with Spain in 1795.
49. <u>Sectionalism</u> is the idea that states are supreme over the federal government.
50. The <u>spoils system</u> refers to the practice in which the winner of an election rewards his supporters with government positions.
51. The term <u>judicial review</u> describes the Supreme Court's power to declare a law unconstitutional.
52. The Missouri Compromise settled the issue of slavery in <u>1850</u>.
53. <u>Alexander Hamilton</u>, a Federalist leader, was the first secretary of the treasury.
54. <u>Meriwether Lewis and William Clark</u> opened the Wilderness Road to Kentucky.
55. <u>John Marshall</u> was an important chief justice who strengthened the Supreme Court in the early 1800s.

March on Washington in August 1963. More than 200,000 people took part in this demonstration to gain civil rights for black Americans.

27 Turbulent Years: America in the 1960s

1. CRISIS AND TRAGEDY
   - Kennedy and the Cold War
   - Kennedy and the "New Frontier"
   - Assassination of President Kennedy
2. CHANGE AND UPHEAVAL
   - Johnson and the "Great Society"
   - Social Changes in the 1960s
3. DISCORD, WAR, AND NONRESISTANCE
   - Johnson and the Vietnam War
   - Nixon and the Vietnam War
   - Nonresistance

1950

I-W program begins 1952

1955

1960

John F. Kennedy elected president 1960

Berlin crisis; Twenty-third Amendment ratified 1961

Supreme Court decisions end prayer and Bible reading in public schools 1962

John Glenn becomes first American to orbit the earth; Cuban missile crisis 1962

Kennedy assassinated; Lyndon B. Johnson becomes president 1963

Johnson re-elected; Twenty-fourth Amendment ratified; Tonkin Gulf Resolution 1964

1965

Medicare and Medicaid established; bombing of North Vietnam begins 1965

Miranda ruling on criminal's rights 1966

Twenty-fifth Amendment ratified 1967

(June) Tet Offensive in Vietnam 1968

Martin Luther King, Jr., assassinated (April); Robert Kennedy assassinated; Richard M. Nixon elected president 1968

1970

Invasion of Cambodia; protests at Kent State and other universities 1970

Twenty-sixth Amendment ratified 1971

Nixon re-elected 1972

United States withdraws from Vietnam; military draft ends **1973**

South Vietnam, Laos, and Cambodia fall to the Communists 1975

1975

"Their feet run to evil; . . . wasting and destruction are in their paths. The way of peace they know not; and there is no judgment in their goings."

Isaiah 59:7, 8

Turbulent Years: America in the 1960s

Focus for Reading

In the 1960s, America dealt with crises abroad and turmoil at home. Of the three presidents inaugurated in the 1960s, one was assassinated, one chose not to run for re-election, and one later resigned from office. Society changed so drastically that it seemed "the foundations [were] destroyed." As general society declined in morals, rebellion and rioting broke out.

Where was the nation headed? Since the people had rejected Bible truth and replaced it with humanistic teachings, they were headed for ruin. Proverbs 14:34 says, "Righteousness exalteth a nation: but sin is a reproach to any people." These turbulent years illustrate that truth.

Three sections in this chapter discuss the turbulent events of the 1960s.

1. Crisis and Tragedy
2. Change and Upheaval
3. Discord, War, and Nonresistance

1. Crisis and Tragedy

When John F. Kennedy became president in the early 1960s, many Americans held the prospect of dreams fulfilled and hopes realized. These hopes faded as the United States faced crises in Berlin, Cuba, and Vietnam. Then a shocking assassination brought Kennedy's life to an abrupt end.

Kennedy and the Cold War

In November 1960, **John F. Kennedy** (age forty-three) became the youngest man in United States history to win a presidential election. (Theodore Roosevelt took office at forty-two, but that was due to McKinley's assassination.) Kennedy made speeches that inspired the multitudes. People saw him as a symbol of youth, vigor, charm, and idealism. He and his Republican opponent, Richard M. Nixon, had debated with each other on television, the first such national debates in a presidential campaign. Kennedy won the election by a narrow margin.

John F. Kennedy (1917–1963) was the thirty-fifth president of the United States. He served from 1961 to 1963 and was a Democrat. He was the youngest man ever elected president.

The Peace Corps. President Kennedy supported the containment of communism, but he wanted to do more than oppose it with military force. He believed that if living conditions were improved in poor countries of the world, they would be strengthened against communism. So he established the Peace Corps (KAWR) in March 1961 to "promote world peace and friendship."

In the Peace Corps program, American volunteers went to other lands to live and work. They helped the people to gain an education as well as to improve their farming and mechanical skills. This program is still in operation today, with volunteers serving in more than one hundred countries.

The Bay of Pigs Invasion. Americans saw the communist country of Cuba as a constant threat. With secret support from the United States, a group of Cuban exiles prepared to invade Cuba. They hoped the Cuban people would rise up and help them overthrow Fidel Castro. In April 1961, about thirteen hundred exiles came ashore at the Bay of Pigs, on Cuba's southern shore. But the local people did not help them, and Castro's forces soon killed ninety of the invaders and captured the rest. Americans had to pay over $50 million in food and medical supplies to get them released.

The Crisis in Berlin. Located in communist East Germany, Berlin was a divided city with the eastern part communist and the western part democratic. Thousands of people in East Germany were escaping from communism by going to East Berlin and then crossing to West Berlin. In June 1961, Soviet leader Nikita Khrushchev announced that the Soviet Union might cut off the access that Western nations had to West Berlin. Kennedy responded by threatening military action if the Soviets did that.

Khrushchev did not carry out his threat, so the immediate crisis was defused. However, the Communists built the Berlin Wall in August 1961 to stop the exodus of people from East Germany. This was a concrete wall topped with barbed wire and watched by guards who had orders to shoot anyone that tried to cross it illegally.

President Kennedy on a platform overlooking the Berlin Wall, June 1963. Kennedy made a famous speech in which he declared, *"Ich bin ein Berliner"* (I am a Berliner) and invited the world to Berlin to see what communism did.

The Arms Race and Space Race. The United States and the Soviet Union continued their efforts to keep ahead of each other in military power. President Kennedy also built up the stock of conventional (nonnuclear) weapons, following his strategy of ***flexible response***. He did this so that the United States could respond to threats around the world without depending mainly on nuclear weapons.

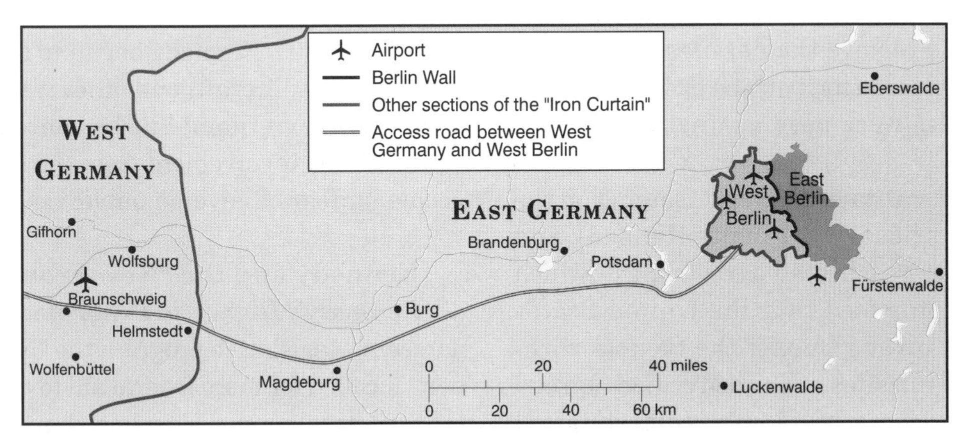

Berlin: Divided City Surrounded by East Germany

President Kennedy, with John Glenn behind him, looks inside the *Friendship 7* capsule in which Glenn orbited the earth on February 20, 1962.

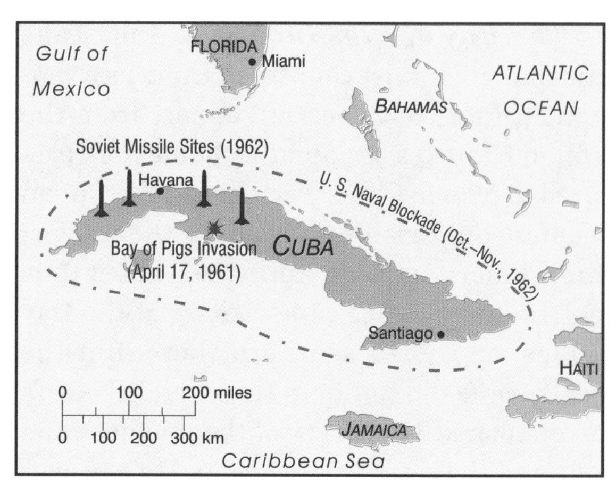

The Cuban Missile Crisis

The Soviets surprised the United States when in April 1961 they put the first man into orbit around the earth. The United States sent Alan Shepard into space for a few minutes in May 1961; and in February 1962, **John Glenn** became the first American astronaut to orbit the earth. The space race came to a climax in July 1969, when two American astronauts became the first men to walk on the moon.

The Cuban Missile Crisis. In October 1962, an American spy plane over Cuba took pictures of Soviet missile bases that could launch a nuclear attack on the United States. President Kennedy promptly demanded that the Soviets remove the missiles. He threatened a nuclear attack on the Soviet Union if the missiles were used against the United States.

For several days the world teetered on the brink of nuclear war. Finally Kennedy and Khrushchev reached an agreement in which Kennedy promised that the United States would not invade Cuba if the Soviets withdrew the missiles. (Kennedy also agreed secretly to remove American missiles stationed in Turkey.) The Soviets withdrew their missiles, and the world breathed a sigh of relief because a major war had been averted.

This incident actually led to improved relations with the Soviet Union. A telephone "hot line" was installed from Washington to Moscow so that the leaders could have direct communication whenever necessary. Also, a treaty on nuclear tests was approved in July 1963. This agreement outlawed the testing of nuclear weapons in space, in the atmosphere, and under water. The treaty was signed by all the major nations except France and China.

United States Involvement in Vietnam. In Southeast Asia, Viet Cong guerrillas supported by the Communist government of North Vietnam (capital: Hanoi) continued to attack the non-Communist government of South Vietnam (capital: Saigon). The United States had been sending financial aid to South Vietnam since the 1950s. Kennedy began to send military advisers, aircraft, and other war materials to South Vietnam; but he concealed the extent of this involvement from the American people for fear of adverse public reaction.

Kennedy and the "New Frontier"

Kennedy's Domestic Program. Kennedy named his legislative program the "New Frontier." It called for more federal aid to education, medical care for the elderly, urban renewal, and help for the poor. But since Congress was dominated by Republicans, it failed to enact Kennedy's proposals.

Congress added two amendments to the Constitution in the early 1960s. The Twenty-third Amendment (1961) gave the people of Washington, D.C., the right to vote in presidential elections. The Twenty-fourth Amendment (1964) ended the poll tax (tax for voting) in federal elections.

The Civil Rights Movement. Black people continued to struggle for equality with whites. Some tried to force change by defying laws that discriminated against blacks. In 1961, both black and white people (called freedom riders) deliberately rode on buses through the South to challenge segregation on interstate buses. The blacks would get off at bus terminals and use facilities such as restrooms and water fountains reserved for whites. Angry whites greeted the freedom riders with violence. In Alabama, a bus was burned at Anniston and the freedom riders were assaulted in Birmingham. As a result, the Interstate Commerce Commission issued an order prohibiting "racial discrimination in interstate facilities."

In 1963, Martin Luther King, Jr., began nonviolent protest marches to end segregation in the shops, restaurants, and hotels of Birmingham, Alabama. But local police used high-pressure fire hoses, electric cattle prods, and fierce dogs to disperse the black marchers. When television broadcast the scenes of violence across the nation, shocked Americans sympathized with the blacks.

President Kennedy began to promote a stronger civil rights act in June 1963. The following August, Martin Luther King, Jr., organized the March on Washington, in which over two hundred thousand people gathered at the Lincoln Memorial. There King made a famous speech in which he said, "I have a dream," and he described his vision of equality and freedom for all people, regardless of race.

Assassination of President Kennedy

On November 22, 1963, President Kennedy sat in an open car as his motorcade drove through Dallas, Texas. Suddenly gunshots rang out and several bullets struck the president. He was pronounced dead in less than an hour.

The nation and the world were stunned. A suspect named Lee Harvey Oswald was soon captured; but two days later, as Oswald was

Martin Luther King, Jr., is the fourth from the left in the front row of the March on Washington on August 28, 1963. He has a white paper in his suitcoat pocket.

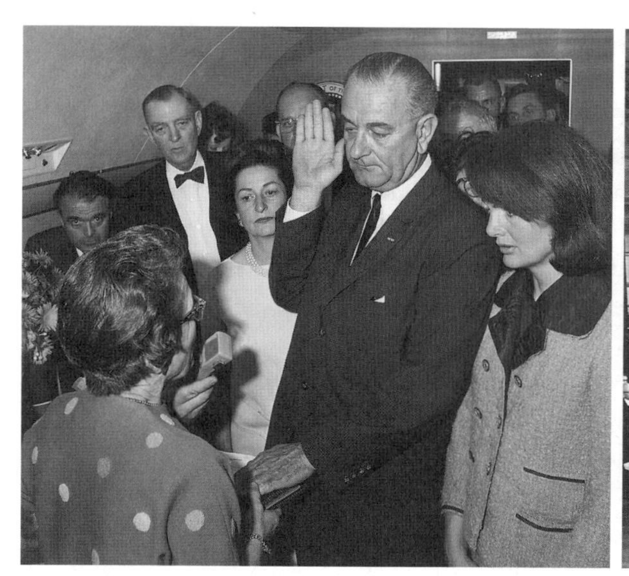

Left: Lyndon B. Johnson takes the oath of office aboard the presidential plane, *Air Force One*. To Johnson's right is his wife, Lady Bird, and to his left is Kennedy's widow, Jacqueline. ***Right:*** The funeral of President John F. Kennedy was held in the rotunda of the Capitol. Kennedy was assassinated on November 22, 1963.

transferred from the city jail to the county jail, a man named Jack Ruby shot and killed him. So it became difficult to determine who had actually killed the president.

Vice President **Lyndon B. Johnson** was sworn in as the new president, and Kennedy was buried in Arlington Cemetery. President Johnson appointed the Warren Commission, headed by Chief Justice Earl Warren, to investigate the assassination. In 1964, this commission ruled that Oswald alone was responsible for shooting the president. But fifteen years later, a Congressional committee reexamined the evidence and concluded that Kennedy was probably killed through a conspiracy.

Focus for Thought

1. What was President Kennedy's goal in establishing the Peace Corps?
2. Why did the Communists build the Berlin Wall?
3. Who was the first American to orbit the earth, and when did he accomplish this?
4. Explain what caused the Cuban missile crisis, and how it was resolved.
5. How did white people oppose the blacks' campaign for equal rights in the early 1960s?
6. How was John Kennedy's presidency cut short?

2. Change and Upheaval

President Johnson proposed to continue Kennedy's policies, and he succeeded in having many new laws passed to change society. But social upheaval brought great change to America as national morals continued to decay.

Lyndon B. Johnson (1908–1973) was the thirty-sixth president of the United States. He served from 1963 to 1969 and was a Democrat.

Johnson and the "Great Society"

President Kennedy had been working on several major proposals, such as a civil rights bill and a tax cut. After he was assassinated, a national mood of unity prevailed and Congress approved a number of Kennedy's proposals. President Johnson declared his "War on Poverty" in January 1964, and in May he called for a "Great Society," the title he gave to his social programs.

That summer President Johnson signed the Civil Rights Act of 1964, the most sweeping legislation since the Reconstruction period. This act outlawed racial discrimination in public places and set up an Equal Employment Opportunity Commission (EEOC) to see that employers did not discriminate against blacks and other minority groups. Congress also passed an act that devoted nearly $1 billion to various antipoverty programs, such as a food stamp program to help poor people buy groceries.

Johnson easily won the presidential election in November 1964, and soon even more Great Society programs were passed. In 1965, Medicare was established to provide health care for the elderly, and Medicaid for poor people under age sixty-five. The Elementary and Secondary Education Act expanded government assistance to schools. And in 1966, the Model Cities Act provided money to improve urban areas.

New laws gave blacks more rights. By August 1965, a Voting Rights Act eliminated reading tests as a requirement for voting. Johnson also began a policy of ***affirmative action***, by which companies working for the federal government were required to employ a certain percentage of blacks and other minorities.

Other laws dealt with the environment. Americans became increasingly concerned about pollution, especially after a book called *Silent Spring* was published in 1962. This book pointed out the dangers of DDT and other chemicals used as pesticides. (DDT was banned in 1972.) In 1965, the Clean Air Act called for controls to reduce automobile pollution, and the Clean Rivers Restoration Act was passed to control water pollution.

Johnson established two new agencies in his Cabinet. One was the Department of Housing and Urban Development (HUD), created in 1965 to help poor people with housing and to help cities deal with problems such as slums. The other new agency was the Department of Transportation (DOT), created in 1966 to promote safe and efficient transportation by land, water, and air.

The Twenty-fifth Amendment was added

Congress approved one major civil rights bill in 1964 and another in 1968. Here President Johnson signs the one passed in 1968.

to the Constitution in 1967. It defines presidential disability and specifies when a vice president should assume the presidency.

Like the New Deal, the Great Society caused a sharp increase in government spending and in the national debt. It resulted in a "welfare shift" as federal revenues were diverted from other purposes into welfare programs. These programs encourage people to depend on government handouts when they would be well able to "work with [their] own hands" as the Bible teaches.

Social Changes in the 1960s

Major Supreme Court Decisions. The Supreme Court continued its activist approach in the 1960s, making several rulings that changed long-standing traditions in America. These decisions related to separation of church and state, civil rights, and criminals' rights.

The cases involving separation of church and state related to public schools. In decisions of 1962 and 1963, the Court ruled that public schools could not hold sessions of Bible reading and prayer even if a student could choose not to take part. One of these decisions resulted from a case involving Madalyn Murray O'Hair, an atheist who objected to daily Bible reading and prayer in the school where her son attended. But her son later joined a Protestant church and apologized for the damage that his mother had

Revival

Despite the widespread decline of the 1960s, a significant number of people continued to uphold traditional values and standards. When some church leaders allowed looser morals in their churches, dozens of members "voted with their feet" and started going to more fundamental churches. Especially after the Supreme Court ruled against prayer in public schools, concerned parents began sending their children to private religious schools.

Among the Mennonites and Amish, many new schools opened as parents became alarmed over the secularism and evolutionary teaching in public schools. But sometimes conflict developed because of laws relating to education. In 1965, school officials in Iowa tried to pick up Amish children and take them to a public school because the one-room schools they attended did not have certified teachers. The children ran to hide in cornfields, and pictures of this brought public sympathy for the Amish. Their case came before the Supreme Court in 1972, and the Court ruled in favor of the Amish on the basis of religious freedom. This decision provided a strong boost for Amish and Mennonite schools.

The Mennonite Church degenerated seriously in the 1950s and '60s as most leaders no longer tried to maintain separation from the world. Dress standards declined, the use of radio and television was accepted, and eventually the church even tolerated divorce and remarriage. A number of leaders and lay members opposed this worldward trend and tried to maintain Biblical practices. When their efforts failed, they withdrew and organized conservative congregations. Most of the new congregations also started Christian schools.

One of the new movements was the Conservative Mennonite Fellowship (CMF), which began in 1957 with one congregation in Ontario and two in Ohio. Other congregations joined the CMF during the done by getting the Bible out of public schools.

Public schools were also affected by a decision involving civil rights. Many schools had all white or all black students, but the Court required that schools be integrated to have a mix of whites and blacks. To achieve this, school buses began bringing children from one neighborhood to another. Many parents objected strongly because their children had to go on long bus rides to schools in strange communities. But the Supreme Court continued to endorse busing as a way to bring about desegregation.

An important decision about criminals' rights was handed down in the case *Miranda v. Arizona* (1966). Chief Justice Warren wrote that before a suspect is questioned about a crime, he must be informed of his right to remain silent and to have a lawyer present. To many Americans, this decision seemed to give the criminal so many rights that it actually encouraged crime.

Social Uprisings. By the mid-1960s, many blacks were rejecting the nonviolent methods of Martin Luther King, Jr. Some became so radical in demanding their rights that from 1965 to 1968 they staged massive riots in Los Angeles, Chicago, and Detroit. The rioters would continue an uproar for several days, with looting, setting fires, breaking windows, and throwing rocks at policemen.

Then in April 1968, Martin Luther King, Jr.,

1960s. The group set up a publication board and founded Messiah Bible School, today located at Carbon Hill, Ohio. In 1964, the CMF began a mission in Guatemala.

Other conservative leaders in Ontario, Virginia, and Pennsylvania withdrew from their conferences in 1959 and 1960 and formed what became known as the Nationwide Mennonite Fellowship (NWF). This group established missions in the Dominican Republic, Mexico, Nigeria, and the Philippines. Also affiliated with the NWF are Lamp and Light Publishers of Farmington, New Mexico; Rod and Staff Publishers of Crockett, Kentucky; and Grace Press of Ephrata, Pennsylvania.

The Eastern Pennsylvania Mennonite Church emerged in the late 1960s. Five conservative bishops organized the Mennonite Messianic Mission in 1966, and in 1968 they withdrew from the Lancaster Conference and established the Eastern Pennsylvania Mennonite Church (EPMC). This group has a publication board and supervises missions in Guatemala, the Bahamas, and Paraguay. The EPMC also operates the Numidia Bible School at Numidia, Pennsylvania.

Numerous other groups and congregations have participated in the conservative revival movement. By promoting Biblical churches, Christian schools, and sound literature, this revival has been a great blessing in the degenerate society of today.

Rod and Staff Publishers at Crockett, Kentucky is a conservative Mennonite publisher that produces a variety of Christian periodicals, storybooks, doctrinal books, and school textbooks. This work began in 1960 at Crockett, Kentucky.

Sit-in at Howard University in Washington, D.C., 1968. Black students demanded more control over policies, courses, and faculty at the university.

Results of the rioting in Detroit, Michigan, July 1967. The National Guard was called to restore order in the city.

was shot and killed by a white man named James Earl Ray. (He confessed the crime but later claimed innocence.) Because of King's death, an epidemic of rioting broke out in over one hundred cities. It seemed that the whole nation was going to pieces.

Large numbers of young people in the 1960s rebelled against traditional values and authority (which they called "the establishment"). Many entered the ***counterculture*** and became "hippies," who adopted long hair for men, wore faded blue jeans, and used mind-altering drugs such as marijuana, LSD, and heroin. Some lived in communes where they emphasized personal freedom, listened to rock music, and promoted their own version of "love" and "peace."

The rebellious lifestyle of these youth was encouraged by the popular music of the time. Singers such as Elvis Presley were especially famous, along with rock groups such as the Beatles from England. In 1969, the Woodstock music festival brought three hundred thousand young people to a farm in upstate New York for three days of revelry and rock music.

A group known as feminists also clamored for change. They protested because women rarely held positions of leadership and because working women received less pay for doing the same work as men. Feminists established the National Organization for Women (NOW) in 1966, and they began campaigning for a Constitutional amendment to guarantee women the same rights as men.

The feminist movement clearly violates the order established by God. The Bible states that "the head of the woman is the man" (1 Corinthians 11:3), and it directs women to be "keepers at home" (Titus 2:5). Women generally find their greatest fulfillment in being wives and mothers, as even non-Christian women came to admit in later decades.

Focus for Thought

7. Which part of Johnson's Great Society
   a. provided health care for poor people?
   b. provided health care for the elderly?
   c. provided money to improve cities?
8. What were some concerns about the Great Society programs?

9. What was the outcome of the Supreme Court cases involving
   a. separation of church and state?
   b. civil rights in relation to schools?
   c. criminals' rights?
10. How were the methods used in the riots of the late 1960s different from the methods promoted by Martin Luther King, Jr.?
11. What were some expressions of rebellion among youth of the 1960s? of women?

3. Discord, War, and Nonresistance

United States involvement in Vietnam expanded dramatically in the mid-1960s. This divided Americans as nothing had done since Civil War days. In 1973, the United States finally withdrew from Vietnam, thus ending the longest military operation in its history.

Johnson and the Vietnam War

Escalation of the Conflict. President Johnson, like Kennedy, believed in the containment of communism. In August 1964, Johnson announced that North Vietnamese boats had fired on an American warship patrolling the Gulf of Tonkin off the coast of North Vietnam. Congress promptly approved the Tonkin Gulf Resolution, which authorized the president to use military force in Vietnam. But Johnson wanted to maintain a limited war because he feared Chinese involvement as had happened in the Korean War.

From February 1965 until the end of 1968, American planes dropped bombs on military targets in North Vietnam, which was supporting the Viet Cong. Increasing numbers of ground troops were sent until the number of Americans in Vietnam reached 538,300 by the end of 1968. Deaths in battle rose also, from over 1,300 in 1965 to over 14,000 in 1968. But despite the enormous costs in money and men, the United States made little progress in Vietnam.

Troops boarding helicopters during the Vietnam War. United States armed forces used helicopters extensively in this war.

On January 30, 1968, the Communists launched the Tet Offensive (Tet is the Vietnamese New Year), in which they struck Saigon and other cities in South Vietnam. The Americans and South Vietnamese counterattacked, driving the Communists back and greatly weakening the North Vietnamese army. Feeling sure that victory was near, United States generals asked for 200,000 more troops to follow up their success. But Johnson turned down their request, though he ordered that the bombing continue.

Opposition in America. People in the United States were shocked by the Tet Offensive. People realized that the Communists were much stronger than they had thought, and they felt deceived because Johnson had concealed the extent of American involvement. This was the first war that was televised, and Americans were upset by the scenes of bloodshed and destruction that they saw.

Young men especially protested the war. They complained that they were too young to vote (voting age was twenty-one) but old enough to fight (draft age was eighteen). Riotous antiwar demonstrations were held at

Top: Refugees in Vietnam during the Tet Offensive. Many fled across the bridge that spanned the river at Hue. ***Bottom:*** After Communists bombed the bridge, others fled by using a boat to cross between the remaining sections.

colleges and other places. Many young men burned their draft cards or fled to a foreign country, especially to nearby Canada. Some even declared themselves to be conscientious objectors. Later the Twenty-sixth Amendment (1971) lowered the voting age to eighteen.

Antagonism against President Johnson became so strong that in 1968, he announced that he would not seek re-election. The most likely candidate to run instead was Robert Kennedy, brother of the former president. But on June 6, 1968, Kennedy was shot and killed by Sirhan Sirhan, an Arab who resented Kennedy's support for Israel. **Hubert H. Humphrey**, the vice president, was chosen as the Democratic candidate.

Election of Richard M. Nixon. The Republicans nominated Richard M. Nixon, who campaigned for law and order and promised to end the war in Vietnam. Just before the election, President Johnson announced that North Vietnam was ready to begin peace talks and that he would halt the bombing of North Vietnam. This made the election close. But in January 1969, Nixon took office as the new president.

Nixon and the Vietnam War

Vietnamization. President Nixon's goal was to achieve "peace with honor" in Vietnam rather than withdrawing in defeat. When American negotiators met with the North Vietnamese in early 1969, they proposed that North Vietnam and the United States both withdraw their troops from South Vietnam. But the talks failed because the North Vietnamese insisted that United States troops be withdrawn unconditionally.

That year Nixon began the process of "Vietnamization," or giving full responsibility for the war to South Vietnam. From the spring of 1969 to the fall of 1972, the number of American soldiers in Vietnam dropped from

Military police and anti-Vietnam demonstrators at the Pentagon, 1967. A young woman taunts one of the policemen by offering him a flower.

over half a million to only sixty thousand.

Continued Fighting and Protests. Even while seeking peace, Nixon expanded the Vietnam War. In April 1970, he sent bombers into neighboring Cambodia, hoping to cut off communist supply lines. Then later that month, he proclaimed that American soldiers would invade Cambodia to "clean out major enemy sanctuaries."

This announcement sparked wild protests, especially on college campuses. The worst of these occurred at Kent State University in Ohio, where a riot erupted in May 1970. Students broke windows and threw rocks at police and National Guardsmen, who had been called out to keep order. The harassment continued until several National Guardsmen fired into a group of students. Four students were killed, including two uninvolved women on their way to classes.

Soon an epidemic of violence swept the nation's campuses. The National Guard had to deal with riots on twenty-one campuses in sixteen states. In 1971, Nixon once more expanded the war with an invasion of Laos, again to destroy communist supply lines.

Protesting against the government is common among unbelievers, but it should not be found among nonresistant people. Although they may petition the government to show consideration for their beliefs, they must never take part in any action that involves force or violence.

Withdrawal From Vietnam. By the fall of 1972, American and North Vietnamese representatives were again discussing terms of peace. When negotiations failed once more, Nixon ordered another attack on North Vietnam. Bombs fell continuously on Hanoi for twelve days in December; and by January 1973, the North Vietnamese were willing to resume peace talks.

Nixon was inaugurated for a second term in January 1973. On January 27, delegates from the United States, North Vietnam, South Vietnam, and the Viet Cong signed a peace treaty in Paris. It stated that a cease-fire would begin immediately, that United States troops would withdraw within sixty days, and that North Vietnam would return all its prisoners of war. At long last, the United States was out of the war in Vietnam.

Former prisoners of war cheer as their airplane takes off from North Vietnam. They were released as part of the peace agreement ending the Vietnam War.

Effects of the Vietnam War. This war had lasted nearly a decade—from the Tonkin Gulf Resolution in 1964 to the cease-fire in 1973. It was the longest conflict in which Americans had ever fought, and it had cost America at least $150 billion. Over three hundred thousand Americans were wounded and fifty-eight thousand were killed. North and South Vietnam together suffered over a million military deaths and over a million civilian deaths. The 6.7 million tons (6 billion kg) of American bombs had devastated Vietnam, and one-third of the surviving people were refugees.

The war had bitter and divisive effects in America. Returning soldiers were treated with contempt rather than honor. Americans had previously felt proud because the United States had never been defeated in fighting for its ideals of democracy and peace. That image was shattered by the Vietnam War and its disgraceful end.

Years passed before the United States overcame the bitterness of Vietnam. In 1973,

The Vietnam War

These "boat people," fleeing from Communist Vietnam, were rescued by an American ship in the South China Sea. The man climbing the ropes is one of 29 people taken from one wooden boat. He is carrying his possessions in his mouth.

Congress passed the War Powers Act, which limited the president's power to go to war without consulting Congress. It was not until the 1980s that the American people began to take a greater interest in the Vietnam War and its veterans.

South Vietnam surrendered to North Vietnam on April 30, 1975. Saigon, its former capital, was renamed Ho Chi Minh City. During that same year, Cambodia and Laos also fell to the Communists. The new leaders in Cambodia exterminated over a million of their own people. In South Vietnam, 1.5 million people used small boats to flee from the Communists. About 1 million of these refugees settled in the United States.

End of the Military Draft. President Nixon promoted an all-volunteer army; and in June 1973, the military draft ended. The armed forces of the United States have since consisted of volunteers only. A law passed in 1980 required young men reaching the age of eighteen to register in case of a future draft.

The Vietnam Veterans Memorial, located in Washington, D.C., is a monument inscribed with the names of thousands of Americans who died in the Vietnam War. This memorial was completed in 1982.

Nonresistance

Nonresistant people continued to express their beliefs during the years of the Korean War and the Vietnam War. The following paragraphs describe the experiences of conscientious objectors in that period.

During the Korean War. The Civilian Public Service system and the World War II draft ended in 1947. A new program started in 1952, during the Korean War, and it continued until 1974. In this program, conscientious objectors were placed in the Selective Service classification I-W (the I is a Roman numeral), and they performed what was known as I-W service. The men would serve two years in civilian work ("alternate service")

These I-W men are serving under the Pax program. They are helping with a housing project for refugees at Enkenbach, Germany.

maintenance

kitchen

housekeeping

electrical

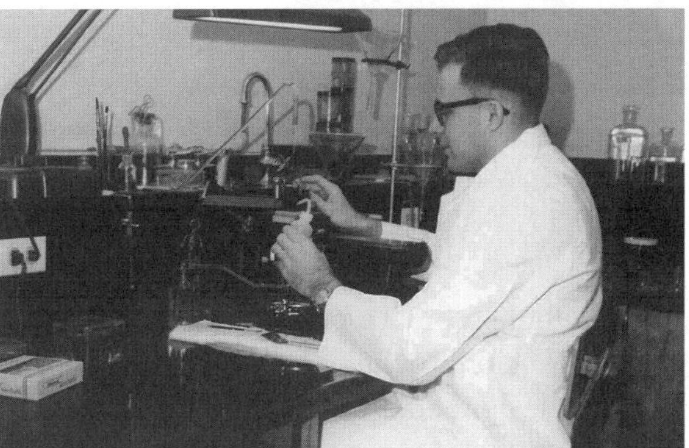

laboratory

Conscientious objectors in I-W service could work at different jobs in an approved facility such as a hospital.

for the government or an approved nonprofit agency. Over the years, about fifteen thousand Mennonite men served in the I-W program.

The young men worked in three types of programs. One was Pax Service, in which single men went overseas to do relief work in nations devastated by war or natural disaster. Another type was voluntary service (VS), in which the men usually worked in groups called VS units at places such as children's homes or old people's homes. A third type was service at an approved public or private agency such as a hospital or an experimental farm.

The I-W program gave great flexibility to the COs, but it exposed many young men to grave spiritual dangers. They often worked in strange settings far away from home, where they faced numerous temptations. Some COs were overcome by worldly allurements and never returned to the faith they had professed.

During the Vietnam War. The I-W program continued during the Vietnam War. As before, young men from different religious groups were mixed together. They often had little spiritual oversight, and considerable numbers gave up their profession. Many church leaders did little to counteract this downward trend.

Church leaders who did have a concern tried to provide a safe setting for their young men. They established VS units in hospitals, children's homes, or old people's homes. Young men in these units were carefully supervised and lived as much like a family as possible. VS units did much to encourage faithfulness in the young men, and they started the practice of young people going into voluntary service even when there was no military draft.

Focus for Thought

12. How did President Johnson gain authority to take military action in Vietnam?
13. Why did Americans begin opposing the Vietnam War after the Tet Offensive?
14. a. What was President Nixon's goal regarding the Vietnam War?
    b. How did he expand the war in 1970 and 1971?
15. a. What were three results of the Vietnam War?
    b. How was the outcome of the war a victory for the Communists?
16. a. Describe three types of I-W service that were available to conscientious objectors.
    b. What were some spiritual dangers to young men in the I-W program?
    c. What was one immediate effect and one long-term effect of the VS units?

Historical Highlights

A. Matching: People

a. Earl Warren
b. Hubert H. Humphrey
c. John F. Kennedy
d. John Glenn
e. Lyndon B. Johnson
f. Richard M. Nixon

1. Johnson's vice president who lost the 1968 election.
2. President when United States troops were withdrawn from Vietnam.
3. Vice president who succeeded John Kennedy as president in 1963 and was re-elected in 1964.
4. Chief justice who wrote that criminal suspects must be informed of their rights.
5. First American astronaut to orbit the earth.
6. President elected in 1960 and assassinated in 1963.

B. Matching: Terms 1

a. affirmative action	f. I-W service
b. counterculture	g. New Frontier
c. Cuban missile crisis	h. Tet Offensive
d. flexible response	i. Tonkin Gulf Resolution
e. Great Society	j. Viet Cong

1. Communist attack on South Vietnam in 1968.
2. Title of President Johnson's social programs.
3. Measure that gave President Johnson power to use military force in Vietnam.
4. Youth who rebelled against established values and violated social customs.
5. Name of Kennedy's domestic program.
6. Policy requiring companies to hire a certain percentage of people considered the victims of discrimination, such as women and blacks.
7. Incident in which Soviet weapons threatened United States security.
8. Communist guerrilla fighters in South Vietnam.
9. Program for conscientious objectors from the 1950s to the 1970s.
10. Policy of having both conventional and nuclear weapons for dealing with military threats.

C. Matching: Terms 2

a. Civil Rights Act of 1964	f. Voting Rights Act
b. Department of Housing and Urban Development	g. Twenty-third Amendment
c. Department of Transportation	h. Twenty-fourth Amendment
d. Medicaid	i. Twenty-fifth Amendment
e. Medicare	j. Twenty-sixth Amendment

1. Agency in the Cabinet responsible for things such as highway and waterway programs.
2. Measure that defined presidential disability and stated when a vice president should take over the presidency.
3. Measure that allowed people of Washington, D.C. to vote in presidential elections.
4. Measure that eliminated reading tests as a requirement for voting.
5. Program that funded health care for elderly people.
6. Measure that ended the poll tax in federal elections.
7. Agency established in 1965 to provide shelter and improve cities.
8. Measure that outlawed racial discrimination in public places.
9. Measure that lowered the voting age to eighteen.
10. Program that funded health care for poor people under age sixty-five.

D. Matching: Places and Dates

a. Berlin Wall	e. 1963
b. Cuba	f. 1964
c. North Vietnam	g. 1968
d. South Vietnam	h. 1973

1. Small communist land supported by China and the Soviet Union.
2. Year when John F. Kennedy was assassinated and Lyndon B. Johnson succeeded him.
3. Non-communist land in which the United States fought a long war.
4. Year when President Johnson won re-election and the Tonkin Gulf Resolution was passed.

5. Barrier between communist and democratic areas.
6. Year when the United States withdrew from Vietnam.
7. Island where Soviet missiles threatened the United States.
8. Year when Richard Nixon was elected president.

E. Deeper Discussion

1. Why was the United States so concerned about saving West Berlin and South Vietnam from communism?
2. Why did society change so drastically in the 1960s?
3. Why did blacks use violent methods to gain their ends in the middle and late 1960s?
4. Why was the Vietnam War so divisive?
5. According to the domino theory, if one nation falls to communism, neighboring nations will also fall. (See Chapter 26.) Did the domino theory prove true in Southeast Asia after American forces withdrew from Vietnam? Explain.
6. During the Vietnam War, some Mennonites promoted being a "witness to the state" by urging the government to follow principles of right and wrong. Why is such an approach a departure from New Testament nonresistance?

F. Chronology and Geography

1. Give the years for the following events.
   a. election of John F. Kennedy
   b. Kennedy administration
   c. Tonkin Gulf Resolution
   d. Johnson administration
   e. beginning of the Nixon administration
   f. United States withdrawal from Vietnam
   g. end of the military draft
2. Match the numbers on the map to the names below. (Countries are marked with larger numbers and cities with smaller numbers.)
   a. Cambodia
   b. China
   c. Laos
   d. North Vietnam
   e. South Vietnam
   f. Hanoi
   g. Saigon

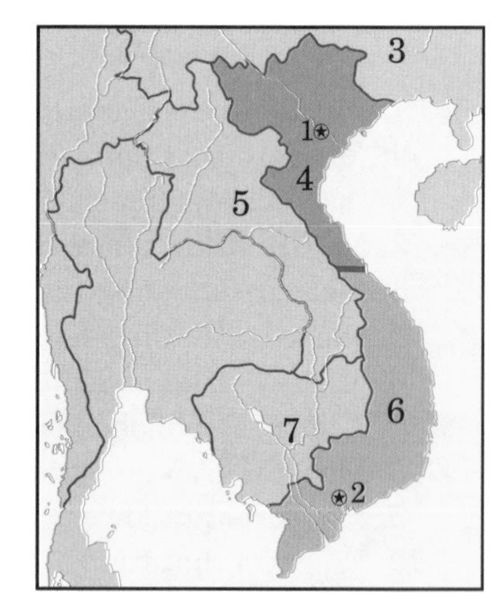

Launch of Apollo 17 at 12:33 A.M., December 7, 1972. This was the last lunar mission of the Apollo program.

28 Recent Years: America From 1970 Into the 2000s

1960

Richard M. Nixon inaugurated; first man to walk on the moon 1969

1970

Watergate offices burglarized; Nixon re-elected 1972

Vice president Spiro Agnew resigns; Gerald R. Ford becomes vice president 1973

Nixon resigns; Ford becomes president 1974

Vietnam falls to Communists 1975

United States observes bicentennial (July 4);1976

James E. (Jimmy) Carter elected president **1976**

United States opens diplomatic relations with Communist China 1979

Ronald Reagan elected president 1980

1980

Sandra Day O'Connor appointed to Supreme Court 1981

Reagan wins re-election 1984

Space shuttle *Challenger* explodes 1986

George H. W. Bush elected president 1988

1990

Communist governments of Eastern Europe overthrown 1989–1990

Persian Gulf War; Soviet Union dissolves and Cold War ends **1991**

Twenty-seventh Amendment ratified; William J. "Bill" Clinton elected president 1992

Clinton wins re-election 1996

Clinton impeached and acquitted 1998

2000

George W. Bush elected president 2000

Terrorists attack the World Trade Center and the Pentagon 2001

2010

1. Challenges of the 1970s
   - The Nixon–Ford Years, 1969–1977
   - The Carter Years, 1977–1981
2. Developments of the 1980s
   - The Reagan Era, 1981–1985
   - The Reagan Era, 1985–1989
3. Events of the 1990s
   - The Bush Administration, 1989–1993
   - The Clinton Presidency, 1993–2001
   - American Society

"Righteousness exalteth a nation: but sin is a reproach to any people."

Proverbs 14:34

RECENT YEARS: AMERICA FROM 1970 INTO THE 2000S

Focus for Reading

The United States experienced both failure and success in the final decades of the twentieth century. In the 1970s, a president resigned, the economy stagnated, and the United States lost prestige among other nations. Economic distress continued in the first part of the 1980s, but then began the longest peacetime business expansion in American history. In the early 1990s, the Cold War ended as communism collapsed in Eastern Europe and the Soviet Union dissolved. By the late 1990s, advances in technology—especially computers—were affecting American life in ways never known before.

What will happen in the future? Though the world may fear, Christians know that God holds the future. Jesus said, "Peace I leave with you, my peace I give unto you. . . . Let not your heart be troubled, neither let it be afraid" (John 14:27). He said also, "I will come again" (John 14:3). We do not know when that will be, but we need to trust in God and heed His Word so that we may be found watching when Christ returns.

Three sections in this chapter cover the events from 1970 to 2000.

1. Challenges of the 1970s
2. Developments of the 1980s
3. Events of the 1990s

1. Challenges of the 1970s

In the early years of the 1970s, President Richard M. Nixon accomplished some notable things in his foreign policy. He was re-elected in 1972, but a scandal called Watergate forced him to resign in 1974. Gerald R. Ford served the remainder of Nixon's term; and in the 1976 election, he was defeated by James E. Carter, Jr. The Carter administration was plagued by inflation, an energy crisis, and a hostage crisis. Thus the 1970s were a decade of numerous challenges for the United States.

Richard M. Nixon (1913–1994) was the thirty-seventh president of the United States. He served from 1969 to 1974 and was a Republican. Nixon was the only president to resign from office.

The Nixon–Ford Years, 1969–1977

A dramatic event took place six months after Richard M. Nixon's inauguration. On July 20, 1969, the Apollo 11 spacecraft landed on the moon. As astronaut **Neil A. Armstrong** stepped out of the lunar lander, he said, "That's one small step for [a] man, one giant leap for mankind." He and Edwin E. Aldrin, Jr., left a plaque on the moon that read in part, "We came in peace for all mankind."

Nixon's Foreign Policy. President Nixon and his adviser, **Henry Kissinger**, are credited with a number of successes in foreign affairs. The first one was the ending of American involvement in the Vietnam War (Chapter 27). In 1972, Nixon visited China, the first

Edwin E. Aldrin, Jr., walking on the surface of the moon, July 20, 1969.

American president to do so. After a week of talks, Nixon and the Chinese leaders agreed to increase trade and cultural interchange between the two nations. This visit helped to restore relations with China that had been broken since 1949. (See Chapter 26.)

Later in 1972, Nixon flew to Moscow to sign a treaty of arms reduction with the Soviet leader Leonid Brezhnev (LAY oh nihd BREHZH nehf). Negotiations that had produced the treaty were called Strategic Arms Limitation Talks, or SALT I. Though strongly anti-Communist, Nixon wanted to reduce tension with the Soviets. He called his approach ***détente*** (day TAHNT), a French word meaning "relaxing of tension between rivals."

In the Middle East, Israel had taken possession of Egypt's Sinai Peninsula, Jordan's West Bank, and Syria's Golan Heights in the Six-Day War (1967). These nations wanted their land back, but Israel refused to give it up. In October 1973, Egypt and Syria attacked Israel on Yom Kippur, the Day of Atonement. President Nixon ordered an airlift to supply Israel with military equipment, and this helped Israel to drive off its opponents. A cease-fire soon ended the war.

President Nixon met with Chinese leader Mao Zedong (also spelled Mao Tse-tung) in February 1972. This meeting helped to restore relations between China and the United States.

Arab nations of the Organization of Petroleum Exporting Countries (OPEC) were upset with the United States for helping Israel. They retaliated by banning oil exports to the United States, which brought fuel shortages and caused oil prices to rise nearly fourfold.

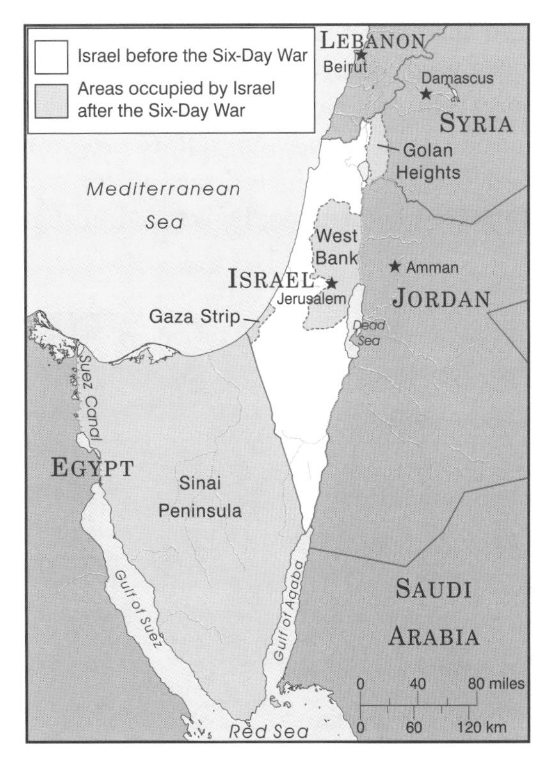

Territories Occupied by Israel After the Six-Day War

American service stations ran out of gasoline, and people waited in long lines at places where fuel was available.

Nixon's Domestic Accomplishments. At home, Nixon's basic philosophy was to reduce the power of the federal government. He wanted to decrease government regulation and allow businesses more freedom. He also wanted to give state and local governments more authority, an idea that he called "New Federalism."

President Nixon had to deal with problems pertaining to energy and pollution. Because of the oil shortage, Congress passed laws to conserve energy by means such as reducing the speed limit to 55 miles per hour (89 km/h). The government helped to build a great pipeline to bring oil 789 miles (1,270 km) from northern Alaska to ports in the southern part of the state. Because of popular pressure to deal with environmental pollution, the Environmental Protection Agency (EPA) was established in 1970 to control pollution.

One of the greatest problems of the 1970s was the economy. President Nixon had balanced the budget in 1969, but after that the government again spent much more money than it collected. Nixon tried to reduce spending and cut back on some welfare programs; when Congress budgeted money for some things that he disliked, he refused to spend that money. An especially severe problem was inflation (rising prices and declining money value). Prices increased over 14 percent from 1969 to 1971.

Watergate and Nixon's Fall. President Nixon campaigned for re-election in 1972. In June of that year, five of his supporters were caught burglarizing the Democratic offices in the Watergate building in Washington, D.C. When Nixon was questioned about the matter, he claimed that he knew nothing about it. The president was re-elected in November by an overwhelming majority.

A committee was appointed to investigate the burglary, and a number of Nixon's top aides resigned in 1973 because of their involvement in the Watergate affair. On top of this, Nixon's vice president, **Spiro Agnew**, was accused of tax fraud and of receiving bribes. He confessed to tax evasion, resigned from office, and was replaced by **Gerald R. Ford** in December.

As the Watergate investigation continued in 1974, tape-recorded conversations made it clear that Nixon had tried to cover up the

The committee appointed by the Senate to investigate the Watergate break-in.

Richard M. Nixon leaves the White House after his resignation on August 9, 1974. Nixon is on the right, and the newly appointed President Ford is on the left.

Gerald R. Ford (1913–) was the thirty-eighth president of the United States. He served from 1974 to 1977 and was a Republican.

Gerald R. Ford being sworn in as president on August 9, 1974. Mrs. Ford stands in the background.

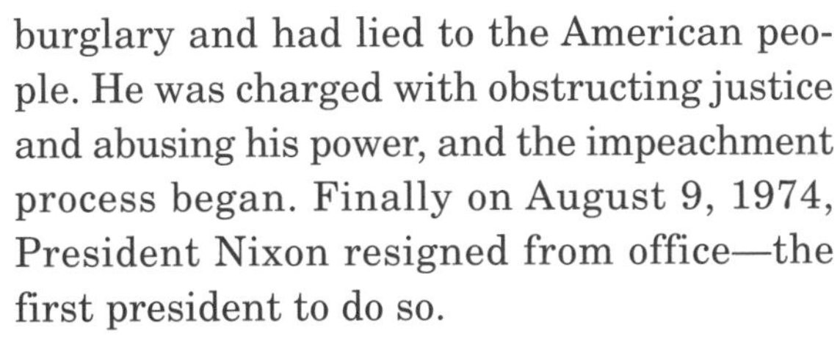

burglary and had lied to the American people. He was charged with obstructing justice and abusing his power, and the impeachment process began. Finally on August 9, 1974, President Nixon resigned from office—the first president to do so.

Administration of Gerald R. Ford. President Ford was the first unelected president, since he had not been elected as vice president. He wanted to heal the wounds caused by the Watergate affair as well as the Vietnam War. So within thirty days of taking office, he pardoned Nixon for any wrongdoing that he might have committed during his presidency. Many people were upset because they thought that Nixon should have been punished in some way for his part in the scandal.

President Ford used various means to fight inflation, which was around 12 percent in 1974. But the economy declined so much that in 1976, the dollar could purchase only as much as 25 cents had purchased in 1940. Ford vetoed fifty-three Congressional bills in order to reduce government spending and to control the size of the government (by limiting the number of new positions, workers, and programs).

On July 4, 1976, the United States observed its two hundredth birthday, or bicentennial. The occasion was celebrated with parades, ceremonies, fireworks, huge flags, and the striking of the Liberty Bell. The United States had endured for two hundred years.

President Ford announcing the pardon of Richard M. Nixon.

Bicentennial parade in Washington D.C.

James E. (Jimmy) Carter (1924–) was the thirty-ninth president of the United States. He served from 1977 to 1981 and was a Democrat.

The Carter Years, 1977–1981

President Ford ran for another term in 1976, but he was defeated by **James E. (Jimmy) Carter,** a Democrat and former governor of Georgia. This was the first man from the Deep South to be elected president since Zachary Taylor in 1848. Carter preferred to be called "Jimmy," and he took a casual, informal approach to the presidency.

Carter and Economic Problems. Two of the greatest challenges that President Carter faced were the energy supply and a stagnant economy. By the late 1970s, the United States consumed more oil than ever before while its own oil production dropped. Another oil shortage developed, and again long lines of cars waited for gasoline.

To deal with the crisis, President Carter established a new Department of Energy in 1977. He promoted a program to boost oil production and encourage development of other energy sources such as nuclear power. But in 1979, an accident occurred at the Three Mile Island nuclear plant near Harrisburg, Pennsylvania. Because of a malfunction, a nuclear reactor was severely damaged and some radioactive steam was released into the outside air. People were stricken with panic at the thought of a nuclear meltdown. This did not happen, but the incident caused a fear of nuclear power that greatly hindered its development as a source of energy.

President Carter also battled inflation, which rose to 13 percent in 1979. That year he tightened the money supply to restrict inflation, but this caused interest rates to soar. Then people no longer bought as many major items, such as houses and cars; and many workers were laid off. The combination of business stagnation and rising prices became known as "stagflation."

President Carter declared that the problem was "a crisis of the American spirit" and that the people had "lost confidence in the future." But much of the problem was due to policies of the government itself. Spending increased so much that the government debt neared $60 billion in 1980.

President Carter's Foreign Policy. In foreign policy, Carter promoted human rights. He wanted to see that other nations gave their citizens basic freedoms and avoided such

Aerial view of the Three Mile Island nuclear power plant near Harrisburg, Pennsylvania. The two cooling towers that have no steam ascending were part of the reactor unit that malfunctioned in 1979.

Menachem Begin of Israel (left), Anwar el-Sadat of Egypt (right), and Jimmy Carter (center) met at Camp David in 1978 to discuss ways to bring peace between Israel and Egypt.

things as torture and unjust imprisonment. This was in line with his profession of being a Christian.

President Carter worked to gain peace among nations. He held a conference in which he brought the leaders of Egypt and Israel together, and the two former enemies signed a peace plan in March 1979. The United States established diplomatic relations with Communist China in the same year. And in July, President Carter and Soviet leader Leonid Brezhnev signed the SALT II treaty, which limited nuclear missiles. (But this treaty was never officially ratified.)

Carter's foreign policy began to unravel later in 1979. The Soviet Union invaded Afghanistan in December to keep a Communist government in power there, and Carter responded by cutting sales of American grain to the Soviet Union. He also called for a boycott of the 1980 Olympic games in Moscow. But these things had little effect on the Soviet Union.

This development shows once more that a civil government cannot operate on New Testament principles. President Carter seemed to think that the Soviets would respect the United States if he showed respect to them, but it failed to work that way.

Early in 1979, a radical Muslim known as the Ayatollah Khomeini (eye uh TOH luh koh MAY nee) overthrew the government of Iran, and the shah (king) was allowed to come to the United States. In November, militant students took control of the United States embassy in Tehran (teh RAHN) and took sixty-six Americans hostage. The Iranians said they would hold the hostages until the shah was brought back to Iran for trial.

Carter tried in various ways to free the hostages, but all his efforts failed. This crisis did great harm to Carter's popularity in the United States. He was defeated in the election of 1980, and the Iranians released the hostages on January 20, 1981—the day President Carter left office.

Focus for Thought

1. What was President Nixon able to accomplish
   a. with China?
   b. with the Soviet Union?
2. What resulted after Nixon supported Israel in the 1973 Yom Kippur War?
3. a. Why did President Nixon resign from office in 1974?
   b. Why did President Ford pardon Nixon soon afterward?

4. What date of special historical significance did Americans celebrate during Ford's presidency?
5. What were two serious problems in American business during Carter's presidency?
6. What were some of Carter's accomplishments in foreign affairs?
7. In what two places did Carter's foreign policy fail to work?

2. Developments of the 1980s

During the 1980s, conservative political ideas prevailed again, and the United States moved from economic decline to prosperity. Government regulation decreased; and with more freedom, business boomed. The Cold War continued, but respect for the United States was restored as the nation firmly resisted its opponents. By the end of the decade, communism in Europe suffered a major decline.

The Reagan Era, 1981–1985

Former California governor **Ronald W. Reagan** won the presidential election of 1980. At sixty-nine years of age, he was the oldest man ever to become president.

New Directions in Government and Business. Ronald Reagan planned to make major changes in the way the government operated. In his inaugural address, he said, "Government is not the solution to our problem; government is the problem." Reagan planned to return more power to the states and give individuals more freedom. He wanted to remove economic restrictions and let the market regulate the economy.

Reagan helped to rebuild confidence in America and its leadership by ending the informal practices of Carter and taking a more formal and assertive approach. A would-be assassin shot Reagan in March 1981, but he recovered quickly and soon went back to work. The president responded firmly to an illegal strike by air traffic controllers in August 1981. When they refused to return to work, he fired eleven thousand controllers and hired others to replace them.

To stimulate the economy, Reagan promoted tax cuts and reduced government spending. He expanded the ***deregulation*** (removal of government regulation) of business, which President Carter had begun. Deregulated industries included airlines, trucking companies, and banks. The government also quit trying to break up companies

President Reagan delivering his inaugural address on January 20, 1981.

Ronald Reagan (1911–2004) was the fortieth president of the United States. He served from 1981 to 1989 and was a Republican. Reagan was the oldest man ever to be elected as president.

that were considered monopolies, such as IBM and AT&T.

The economy did not improve immediately. Instead, conditions became even worse for a time, and people blamed the problem on "Reaganomics," Reagan's program for restoring the economy. So many workers lost their jobs that the unemployment rate reached 10 percent by December 1982. But finally Reagan's policies began to work. Inflation fell to below 4 percent, and unemployment to less than 8 percent by 1984. Interest rates declined, business improved, and investment increased. This recovery lasted through the rest of the 1980s.

New Directions in Foreign Policy. President Reagan wanted to increase military spending so that the United States could take a stronger stand against enemies. He believed in peace through strength, and he thought the Soviets were taking advantage of détente to benefit themselves. Reagan began a policy of more firmly resisting the Soviet Union, which he called an "evil empire." In 1981, he announced plans to increase the number of bombs, missiles, and other weapons.

President Reagan intervened in places where the interests of the United States were affected, especially in Latin America and the Middle East. In Nicaragua, a group known as Sandinistas took control and tried to spread communist revolution in Central America. Reagan did what he could to help fighters called Contras to oppose the Sandinistas. In October 1983, he sent armed forces to the Caribbean island of Grenada to oppose a Communist takeover there. They evacuated seven hundred United States citizens from the island and overthrew the Cuban-backed government.

American forces also became involved in the Middle East. After Israel invaded Lebanon to drive out ***terrorists*** there, fighting broke out between factions within Lebanon. In April 1983, a bomb blew up the American embassy in Beirut (bay ROOT), killing 63 people. Reagan then sent troops to Lebanon in September 1983 as part of an international peacekeeping force. But in October, terrorists set off an explosion that killed 241 American soldiers and wounded 71 others. In February 1984, Reagan ordered that the troops be withdrawn from Lebanon.

The 1984 Election. Ronald Reagan and his vice president, **George H. W. Bush**, ran for re-election in 1984. The Democratic nominee, Walter Mondale, chose **Geraldine Ferraro** as his vice-presidential candidate; she was the first woman to run for high office. Reagan and Bush won the election by a wide margin.

The Reagan Era, 1985–1989

Domestic Affairs in Reagan's Second Term. About a year after Reagan's second term began, a tragedy shocked the United States. On January 28, 1986, the space shuttle *Challenger* lifted off but exploded seventy-three seconds later. All seven people on board were killed.

Space shuttle *Challenger* in space with the doors of its cargo bay open. This shuttle exploded on January 28, 1986, during takeoff.

President Reagan presenting his tax-cut plan to Americans. He reduced personal income taxes by the largest amount in United States history.

Reagan promoted further tax cuts; and in October 1986, he signed the most significant tax reform law in forty years. This law relieved many low-income people from paying any income tax at all. The economy continued to flourish, and the stock market rose. Yet government spending increased markedly; in 1987 Reagan submitted the first $1 trillion budget to Congress. The government debt rose until it reached nearly $3 trillion by 1989.

President Reagan appointed several new judges to the Supreme Court. In 1981, he appointed **Sandra Day O'Connor** as the first woman justice. William Rehnquist became the chief justice in 1986; and by the end of 1987, Reagan had appointed two other new justices. These appointments helped to make the Supreme Court more conservative and less activist.

President Reagan and Sandra Day O'Connor. She was the first woman to serve as a justice of the United States Supreme Court.

Foreign Affairs. In Reagan's second term, struggles continued in the Middle East and in Central America, but relations with the Soviet Union improved. Mikhail Gorbachev (GAWR buh chawf) became the Soviet president in 1985. He took steps to make Soviet politics and society more open (a policy he called *glasnost*) and to rebuild the deteriorating Soviet economy (a plan called *perestroika*). Gorbachev took a more moderate approach in dealing with the United States; for example, he said the Soviet Union would abide by the arms limits set in the SALT II agreement even though it had not been ratified.

Reagan and Gorbachev held several summit meetings in which they discussed ways to reduce arms. But Reagan refused to give in on a plan known as Strategic Defense Initiative (SDI). The purpose of this plan, popularly called "Star Wars," was to have weapons orbiting in space to destroy any missiles attacking the United States. The Soviets opposed the

On December 8, 1987, Reagan and Gorbachev signed a treaty that banned intermediate-range missiles. This was the first time the two nations agreed not only to limit but also to reduce the amount of nuclear weapons.

development of such a system. Finally in December 1987, Reagan and Gorbachev signed a historic agreement to remove all intermediate-range nuclear missiles in Europe.

In Central America, Reagan continued to favor the Contras in Nicaragua. But Congress banned direct government aid to them in 1984, so Reagan encouraged private organizations and other nations to help the Contras. During 1985 and 1986, Reagan agreed to sell arms to Iran because he believed Iran could use its influence to America's advantage in the Middle East. An official named Oliver North used profits from the sale of these arms to help the Contras in Nicaragua even though such aid was illegal.

President Reagan and Congress thoroughly investigated this matter, known as the Iran-Contra affair, and North was fired from his job. Reagan himself apparently had not known about using the profits to help the Contras, but he took responsibility for it; and for this reason the Iran-Contra affair did little long-term harm to his popularity.

The 1988 Election. Vice President George H. W. Bush ran for president in 1988. His Democratic opponent was Michael Dukakis. Bush planned to continue Reagan's policies and promised not to raise taxes, and he easily won the election. No vice president since Martin Van Buren (1836) had been elected as the next president.

Focus for Thought

8. a. What things did Reagan do to improve the economy?
   b. How well did this approach work?
9. What were Reagan's goals in his foreign policy?
10. Name two countries where Reagan intervened, and tell why he intervened.
11. What was the effect of Reagan's appointments to the Supreme Court?
12. In what ways did American relations with the Soviet Union improve in Reagan's second term?
13. Briefly explain what happened in the Iran-Contra affair.

3. Events of the 1990s

The 1990s witnessed the fall of Communist governments in Eastern Europe, the breakup of the Soviet Union, and the end of the Cold War. Except for the early years, prosperity reigned in America throughout the decade. But society continued its downward course as "evil men and seducers [became] worse and worse" (2 Timothy 3:13). God alone knows the future, and He will continue to provide for His people as He has done in the past.

The Bush Administration, 1989–1993

While George H. W. Bush was president, he focused so much on foreign affairs that some criticized him for neglecting domestic problems. There is no doubt, however, that remarkable events took place in foreign nations in the early 1990s.

End of the Cold War. In an unexpected series of events, Communist governments in Eastern Europe fell one after another. When these countries in Eastern Europe realized that Soviet leader Gorbachev would not intervene in their political affairs, they revolted against their Communist rulers. By the end of 1989, the Communists had lost control of Poland, Czechoslovakia, Hungary, and Romania; and the same happened in Bulgaria and Albania over the next several years. The Communist military alliance, the Warsaw Pact, was dissolved in 1991.

George H. W. Bush (1924–) was the forty-first president of the United States. He served from 1989 to 1993 and was a Republican.

The people of East Germany also overthrew their Communist government in 1989. President Reagan had challenged the Soviets in 1987 to tear down the Berlin Wall; and in late 1989, it came down section by section. People from East Germany thronged into West Germany, and the Germans were soon demanding a reunified nation. By the end of 1990, East and West Germany were one nation again.

With the rise of these new, free governments in Eastern Europe, the Cold War was over. Communist governments around the world had fallen except in Cuba, North Korea, and China. President Bush continued to improve relations with the Soviet Union, reaching agreement in 1991 to reduce long-range nuclear weapons. But later that year, the Soviet Union itself fell into disorder and then broke apart. Its former republics each became independent nations, with Russia as the largest one.

Intervention in Latin America and the Middle East. George H. W. Bush readily used military force when he considered it necessary to protect American interests. In 1989, he dispatched soldiers to Panama to overthrow dictator Manuel Noriega (nawr YAY gah), who was then brought to the United States for trial on charges of international dealing in illegal drugs.

In 1990, Iraq invaded the neighboring nation of Kuwait. This was a threat to the United States, for it endangered Saudi Arabia and the United States oil supply. President Bush and other world leaders assembled a coalition of thirty-nine nations to oppose Iraq, and the Security Council of the United Nations declared trade restrictions against Iraq. Hundreds of thousands of soldiers went to the Persian Gulf region to keep Iraq from invading Saudi Arabia.

The Security Council gave the coalition members permission "to use all necessary

President Bush meeting American troops in the Persian Gulf region, 1991.

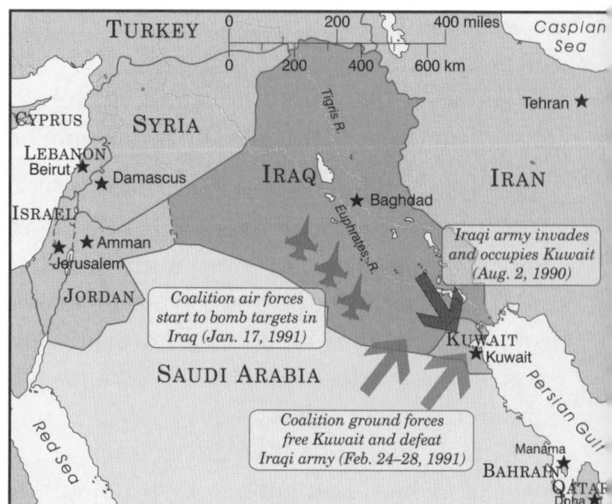

The Persian Gulf War

means" to expel Iraq from Kuwait if Saddam Hussein (hoo SAYN), the Iraqi leader, would not withdraw by January 15, 1991. When he refused, coalition air forces (mostly Americans) began bombing Iraq on January 17. Then on February 24, coalition ground troops invaded Kuwait, freed it from Iraqi domination, and moved into Iraq itself. The ground war lasted only one hundred hours before Bush ordered the attack to end, and Hussein agreed to UN terms. This conflict became known as the Persian Gulf War.

Domestic Accomplishments. President Bush wanted to balance the budget without raising taxes, but he found this difficult. Eventually he agreed to raise a number of taxes, including some income taxes, despite his promise during his presidential campaign that he would oppose any new taxes. He lost much support in doing so.

In general, Bush took a moderate approach to political matters. He signed the Americans With Disabilities Act in 1990, which outlawed discrimination against people with physical and mental disabilities. Also, the Immigration Act of 1990 raised the number of immigrants allowed into the United States annually.

The Twenty-seventh Amendment was added to the Constitution during the Bush administration. It prohibited Congress from making salary changes for its members until after the next Congressional election. This amendment was ratified in 1992.

The 1992 Election. Bush ran for reelection in 1992 but was defeated by **William J. (Bill) Clinton**, a liberal Democrat and the governor of Arkansas. Clinton was the first of the post-World War II generation to become president.

The Clinton Presidency, 1993–2001

President Clinton promoted a number of liberal social policies. He campaigned for a law to provide medical insurance for millions of uninsured Americans, but his effort failed. Clinton also promoted free trade. He supported the North American Free Trade Agreement (NAFTA), which allowed duty-free trade with Canada and Mexico. The Senate approved NAFTA in November 1993.

In 1996, President Clinton ran for a second term. He was opposed by Republican Robert (Bob) Dole, a World War II veteran; but Clinton won the election.

After the Cold War, the United States tended to intervene in the affairs of other nations for humanitarian reasons. George H. W. Bush had sent troops to Somalia in 1992 to restore order so that food might be sent to

President Bush signed the Americans With Disabilities Act in 1990. Among other things, this law stated that sidewalks and public buildings were to be made accessible to disabled people, such as by having ramps for wheelchairs.

William (Bill) Clinton (1946–) was the forty-second president of the United States. He served from 1993 to 2001 and was a Democrat. Clinton was the second president to be impeached, but he was not removed from office.

President George W. Bush (1946–) was the forty-third president of the United States. He took office in 2001 and was a Republican.

starving people there. President Clinton sent in more soldiers but then withdrew all troops in 1994. He also sent troops to Bosnia as part of an agreement to end fighting there. In 1999, he ordered the bombing of Kosovo, a province of Yugoslavia, because of its oppression of ethnic Albanians.

Clinton's presidency was clouded with scandal for most of his years in office. Some of this had to do with earlier business dealings, some with political issues, and some with moral matters. In 1998, the House of Representatives impeached the president, charging him with perjury and obstruction of justice. He was only the second president to be impeached; the first was Andrew Johnson in 1869. But the Senate did not have the two-thirds majority required to convict the president. So Clinton, like Johnson before him, remained in office.

The 2000 Election. In 2000, the two main candidates for the presidency were Vice President Albert (Al) Gore (Democrat) and Texas governor George W. Bush (Republican). When the election was held, the winner remained unclear for seven weeks because the vote in Florida was so close. A recount confirmed that Bush had won Florida, but the Democrats wanted the votes to be re-counted by hand in certain districts. Finally the United States Supreme Court ruled that the recounting of votes could not continue, and George W. Bush was declared the winner.

This election was historic in several ways. It was the most disputed election since 1876. It was the first time since 1888 that the winner received a majority of electoral votes even though his opponent received a majority of popular votes. And it was only the second time in United States history that the new president was the son of a former president.

American Society

The number of Americans continued to grow. The 1990 census showed a population of 248 million; and by the end of the decade, it was nearing 270 million. This was due to increased immigration, longer life expectancy, and natural increase. The population center continued to shift westward as more and more people moved to the South and the West. The population was also aging, with the median age rising to a record high of over thirty-five years in 2000.

Deteriorating Families. By Biblical standards, American society deteriorated

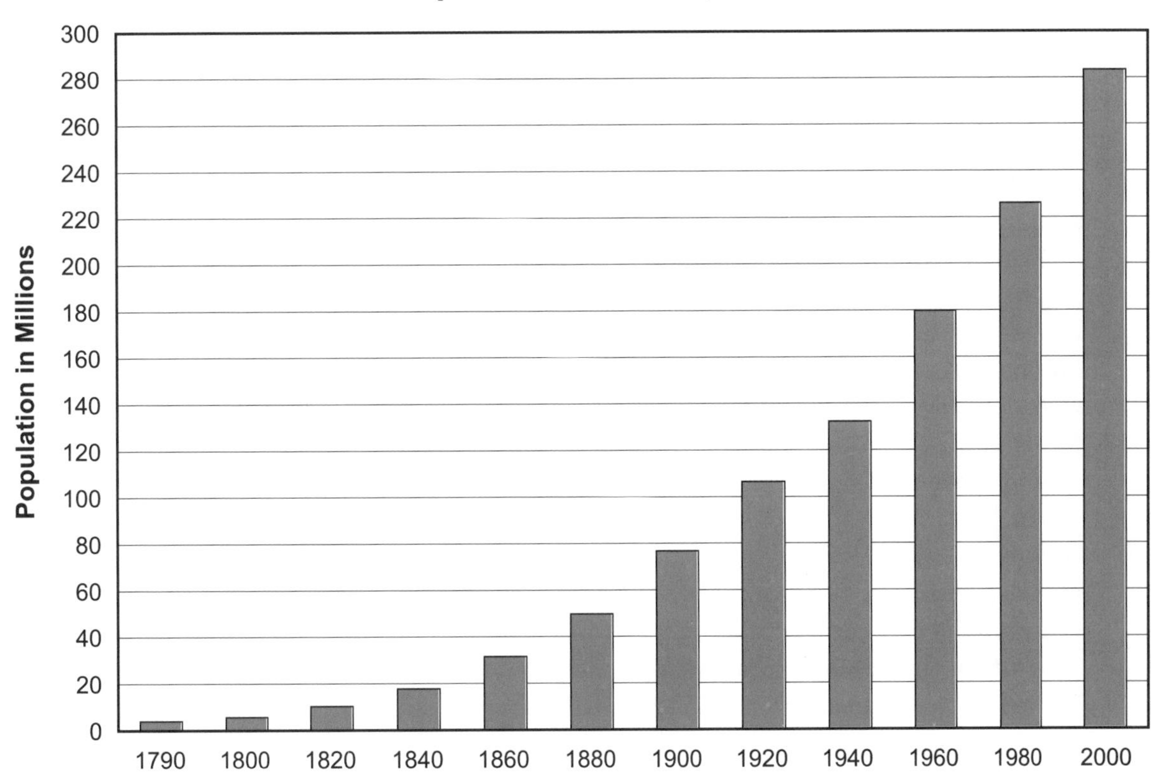

rapidly in the closing decades of the 1900s. Congress passed the Equal Rights Amendment in 1972, which specifically gave the same rights to women as to men; but the amendment expired in 1982 when not enough states ratified it. However, feminists continued to challenge Biblical standards for society, and they looked with scorn on women who stayed at home to care for their children. Increasing numbers of women went to work until they made up 47 percent of the labor force by 2000.

Divorce rates climbed steeply until they reached a rate of 4.1 divorces per 1,000 in population. Nearly half of all marriages ended in divorce. The Bible clearly says, "What therefore God hath joined together, let not man put asunder" (Matthew 19:6).

Crime, Drug Abuse, and Terrorism. Crime increased dramatically from 1960 to 1990. Violent crimes, such as murder and robbery, increased fivefold in those thirty years. The rise in crime brought an increase in the prison population, which reached nearly 2 million in 2000.

Drug abuse contributed to many of the crimes. People committed crimes to obtain money for narcotics, and the illegal drug trade caused many other crimes. The government fought the drug scourge, especially during the 1980s when Nancy Reagan, President Reagan's wife, promoted her slogan of "just say no" to drugs. But the campaign had only limited success. In a survey of 1996, 24 percent of eighth graders, 38 percent of tenth graders, and 40 percent of twelfth graders admitted to using illegal drugs.

Drug use and immorality contributed to the spread of a new disease called acquired immune deficiency syndrome (AIDS). This disease attacks the body's immune system, leaving it vulnerable to many other diseases.

Canada in the Twentieth Century

As the twentieth century dawned, the Dominion of Canada consisted of seven provinces and two territories. Sir Wilfrid Laurier (LAWR ee ay) was serving as prime minister. Under his leadership, from 1896 to 1911, Canada expanded in size, population, and production. Saskatchewan and Alberta became new provinces in 1905, and immigration swelled the population by 30 percent from 1901 through 1911. Manufacturing expanded, 10,000 miles (16,093 km) of railroad were added, and the prairie provinces became the "granary of the nation."

World War I helped to bring about Canada's independence from the United Kingdom. Canada went to war against Germany when Britain did, since its relations to foreign countries were tied to those of Great Britain. About 600,000 Canadians fought in World War I; and because of this heavy contribution, Canada received a greater voice in the war effort. Representatives from Canada were among those who signed the Treaty of Versailles.

In 1931, the Statute of Westminster established the British Commonwealth of Nations, which recognized each of the self-governing dominions of Britain as independent nations equal with Great Britain. This is usually considered the beginning of Canada's actual independence from Britain.

During the 1930s, Canada experienced a depression similar to that in the United States. Wheat prices fell to 60 cents a bushel, drought turned the western prairies into a dust bowl, and demand for Canadian exports fell. Economic hard times continued through the 1930s in spite of numerous government programs.

Canada declared war on Germany on September 10, 1939, becoming the first American nation to enter World War II. This time Canada took part in the conflict because it chose to do so, not just because of ties to Great Britain; and a million Canadians fought in the war. Canada joined the United Nations in 1945 and the North Atlantic Treaty Organization (NATO) in 1949.

Canada prospered after World War II. Its mineral resources were developed, including oil and natural gas in Alberta and iron ore in Labrador. A million immigrants arrived from Europe. The St. Lawrence Seaway was completed in 1959 to improve transportation between the Great Lakes and the Atlantic Ocean. In 1962, the Trans-Canada Highway linked Canada from coast to coast. In 1965, Canadians rejoiced to have a new flag with a maple leaf as its symbol. And in 1967, Canada held a huge world's fair in Montreal to celebrate the hundredth anniversary of its confederation.

Canada experienced economic problems in the 1970s and 1980s. However, in the western provinces, oil brought significant profits to Alberta and British Columbia. In 1989, a free trade agreement went into effect between the United States and Canada. In 1993, Canada ratified the North American Free Trade Agreement (NAFTA) with the United States and Mexico.

Canadian unity continued to pose problems. French Canadians began to assert their views more in the 1960s, seeking more self-government for Quebec. The Parti Québecois (kay beh KWAH) won provincial elections in Quebec in 1976; their goal was to make Quebec an independent nation. However, that proposal was defeated in a referendum held in 1980.

In 1982, the Constitution Act gave Canada the right to amend its own Constitution. This made Canada completely independent of the British legislature. The Meech Lake accord was proposed in 1987 as a constitutional amendment to get Quebec to endorse the new Constitution. It recognized Quebec as a distinct society within Canada, but it had to be ratified by all ten of the provinces. Manitoba and Newfoundland would not ratify the agreement, for they thought it gave too much power to Quebec.

This encouraged Quebec to promote separatism again. Canada held a referendum on independence in 1992, and Quebec held one in 1994; but voters defeated each one, and Quebec remained Canadian. However, many French Canadians in Quebec were still committed to independence.

The government spent millions of dollars in battling AIDS, but it continued to spread.

Violence also occurred in other areas. In 1993, terrorists bombed the World Trade Center, in New York City. In April 1995, a bomb destroyed much of a large federal building in Oklahoma City, Oklahoma, killing 168 people. And in the latter 1990s, students in several parts of the country took guns to school and shot down their teachers and fellow students. Citizens became so fearful for their safety that many obtained permits to carry weapons for self-defense.

Entertainment. One thing that contributed to the violence was the kind of entertainment that many Americans enjoyed, especially the youth. Television, movies, and video games promoted violence and immorality. This influence, along with the teaching of evolution and the general rejection of Biblical morals, produced a group of people who glorified themselves and violence.

Music and art continued to deteriorate. Rock music became increasingly popular, and its later forms further promoted violence and shameful behavior. Paintings and movies were designed with an emphasis on destruction and lawlessness in order to shock the audience.

Religion and Education. Churches also degenerated. Many began accepting practices directly forbidden in the Bible, which included ordaining women preachers and those who engaged in immoral practices. This decline definitely affected society; for when churches no longer uphold the light of truth, the world becomes darker with sin and error.

More and more Americans went to school, but the general quality of education deteriorated. Test scores declined even though textbooks were made easier so that more pupils could receive passing grades. This was because people rejected God and accepted humanistic, progressive ideas. Disorder and lack of discipline also contributed. Computers and other modern inventions provided entertainment rather than solid education.

In response to the decline, citizens across the country demanded that public schools get "back to the basics." A number of schools returned to traditional methods such as teaching phonics in reading and drilling math facts, and their pupils' scores rose significantly. The number of private schools increased, especially Christian schools, and many parents began teaching their own children in home schools.

The Environment and Technology. Many Americans became increasingly concerned about preserving the environment. Issues such as global warming, acid rain, and depletion of the ozone layer became prominent. Environmentalists often exaggerated the dangers so that people would get excited and support their campaigns.

Technology also changed society. The first personal computer was introduced in 1977, and computers soon occupied desks in offices and homes across the land. By the late 1990s, many computer users were connected to the Internet, which made it easier than ever before to obtain materials portraying violence and indecency. In America, 98 percent of homes had television, and many had devices to record and play videotapes.

Terrorism and the Twin Towers

On the morning of September 11, 2001, terrorists launched a major attack on the United States by hijacking four commercial airliners. They crashed two of them into the 1,350-foot (411-m) Twin Towers of the World Trade Center, in New York City. The resulting fire produced such intense heat that both buildings collapsed within two hours, causing the death of about 2,800 people. Besides the two towers, which were directly hit, at least eight nearby buildings partially or totally collapsed, and numerous other buildings were damaged.

On the same morning, hijackers crashed another airliner into the southwestern part of the Pentagon, the five-sided military headquarters near Washington, D.C. This attack destroyed or damaged 2,000,000 square feet (186,000 m^2) of office space and killed a total of 189 people who were either in the plane or in the building. A fourth hijacked plane crashed into the ground in southwestern Pennsylvania after passengers attacked the hijackers. This plane may have been heading for the White House in Washington, D.C.

The terrorist attacks instantly changed the nation. Americans were outraged that anyone should commit such terrible crimes against their country. A spirit of intense patriotism burst forth, and flags appeared everywhere—on poles, in windows, and even on vehicles. Signs proclaiming "God Bless America" became popular across the land.

On the evening of September 11, President George W. Bush made a speech in which he strongly denounced the terrorists. He declared that America would make no distinction between the terrorists and the nations that sheltered them. It seemed obvious that terrorist leader Osama bin Laden was the mastermind of the attacks, and he was in Afghanistan. The president assembled a coalition of anti-terrorist nations and sent American troops to Afghanistan, where they overthrew the Afghan government and established a more friendly government. But President Bush cautioned that the war on terror might go on for a number of years.

It is not for us to define God's ultimate purposes in allowing men to commit such evils. At least one point is clear: the attacks were a strong reminder that people's security depends on God, not on their own abilities. "Except the LORD keep the city [or the nation], the watchman waketh but in vain" (Psalm 127:1).

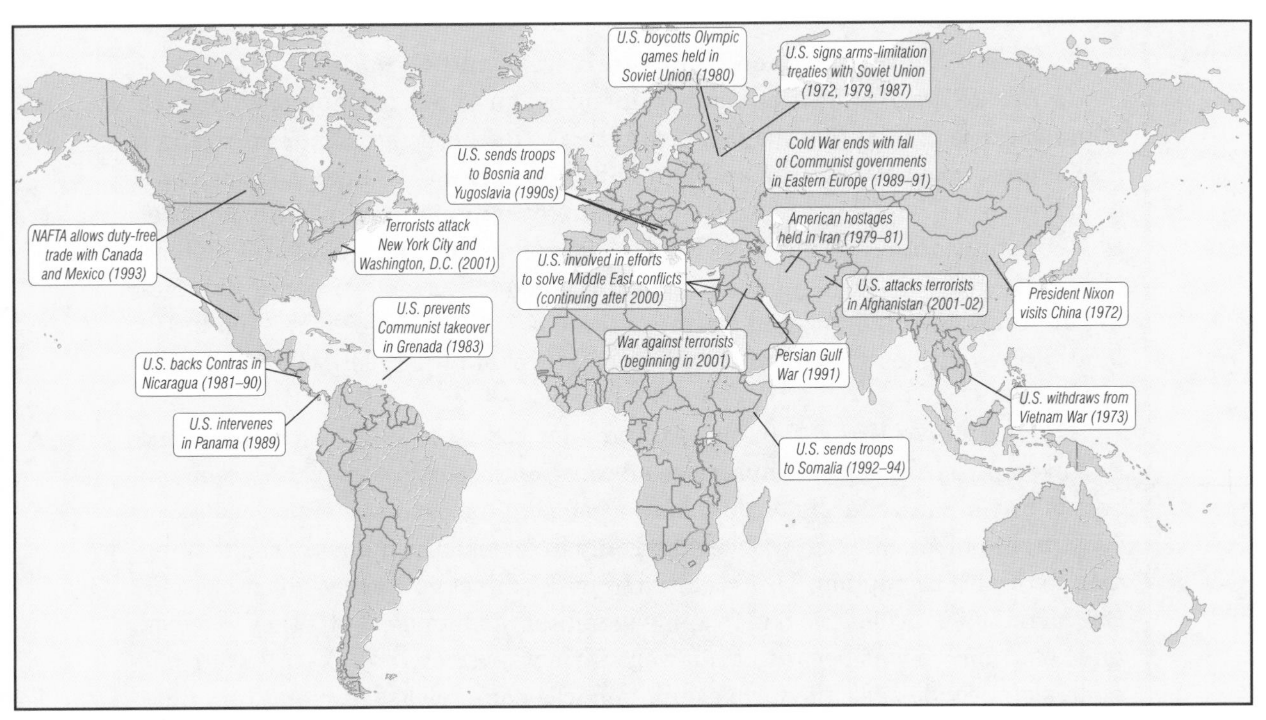

United States Involvement in Foreign Affairs (1970 until after 2000)

This view of New York City features the Brooklyn Bridge, which is one of several bridges that connect the boroughs of Manhattan and Brooklyn. On the right are the Twin Towers of the World Trade Center, which were destroyed by terrorists on September 11, 2001. On that day, frightened people fled on foot across the Brooklyn Bridge from Manhattan. They looked back across the river to see the smoke and flames billowing from the towers. After the towers collapsed, the skyline of New York City looked quite different.

Nonresistance Issues in Russia and Canada

In the 1870s. The Russian government began to discontinue privileges of nonresistance for the Mennonites living there. Rather than compromise their convictions, about 7,000 Russian Mennonites migrated to Canada after a Canadian Order-in-Council in 1873 gave "an entire exemption from military service" to Mennonites immigrating from Russia, as well as the right to affirm instead of swearing oaths. The Mennonites that remained in Russia prospered, expanding in numbers to 120,000 and holding title to 2.5 million acres (1 million ha) of land. However, these Mennonites suffered severely in the Bolshevik Revolution of 1917.

During World War I. Canada's Military Service Act of 1917 included a clause that exempted from combatant service all conscientious objectors who were members of any organized religious denomination that opposed war.

Russian Mennonites in the west had only to furnish the names of their young men to receive exemption. This resulted from the direct guarantee given in 1873. But Mennonites in Ontario had to apply to military tribunals; and if they received an exemption, it was because they were farmers rather than because of their nonresistance. Besides, the farm exemption was not a release from military duty but only a postponement of it.

Mennonites who could not obtain a farm exemption had to report for noncombatant duty. If they refused to wear a military uniform or do noncombatant service, they could be put in guardhouses and court-martialed. Ernest J. Swalm of the Canadian Brethren in Christ (Dunkers) refused to wear a military uniform, but was forced to. Then he was court-martialed and sentenced to two years of hard labor. However, he was released after he had served only about a month of his sentence. Later, the Mennonites worked out an agreement with Canadian authorities in which conscientious objectors received an automatic leave of absence with clear proof of their Mennonite identity.

World War I changed many Canadians' attitudes toward Mennonites from friendly to suspicious and even hostile. All things German raised suspicion. German literature was restricted and even forbidden at times. Canadians resented the military exemptions that the government granted to Mennonites. These attitudes continued after the war, with the result that a law of 1919 forbade Mennonite immigration for a time. This caused a hardship to many of the Mennonites still in Russia who wanted to migrate to Canada in the early 1920s because of the severe persecution they were facing under Communist rule in Russia. The door to Canada seemed closed to them, but when these Russian Mennonites appealed to their Dutch ancestry to show that they were not Germans, the immigration ban was lifted in 1922. From 1923 to 1930, about 20,000 Mennonites moved from the Soviet Union to Canada. But by the end of that period, both Canada and the Soviet Union were closing the door to the Mennonite migrations.

During World War II. The Canadian government again enacted a military draft in World War II. In response, Canadian peace churches formed the Conference of Historic Peace Churches in July 1940. This included Quakers, Brethren in Christ, various groups of Mennonites and Amish, plus Russian Mennonites in Ontario. Representatives of the conference proposed alternate service work for conscientious objectors, and in December 1940, a law provided that such alternate service could be established.

In 1941, five Alternative Service Work (A.S.W.) camps were set up in British Columbia, Alberta, and Ontario. The COs helped to build the Trans-Canada Highway and served as fire rangers in British Columbia in case of Japanese attack. They also engaged in forestry; for example, from May to December of 1942, the A.S.W. men planted 425,000 seedlings in British Columbia.

The Alternative Service program was replaced in May 1943 by a Selective Service program. This provided that a CO come before a local board, which would evaluate his qualifications. The board would then recommend a farm or factory job that he could do. The CO would receive a wage but had to pay a certain amount of it to the government, which gave it to the Red Cross. At the end of the war, the COs were gradually discharged.

In summary, the Canadian government respected the nonresistant position in allowing these alternative service programs. The Conference of Historic Peace Churches expressed gratitude by sending a thank-you note to the prime minister, William Lyon Mackenzie King.

Mennonite Migrations in the 1900s. During and after World War II, the thousands of Mennonites who remained in the Soviet Union endured intense suffering. The Communist government exiled Mennonite church leaders and fathers. As many as half of the fathers were sent to prison or to forced-labor camps, and all the meetinghouses were closed by 1938. As the German army retreated from the Soviet Union in World War II, thousands of these German-speaking Mennonites fled with them. Many were captured by the Soviets and sent back to the Soviet Union; others managed to escape while suffering incredible hardships. For example, one group of 614 Mennonites fled from the Soviet Union in 1943, but only 33 of them arrived safely in the Netherlands in 1945. A number of these people found refuge in Canada, including some of the group of 33. Thousands of others went to Paraguay.

While some Mennonites were moving into Canada, others were moving out. In the 1920s, those in Manitoba and Saskatchewan (of Dutch–Russian origin) faced a crisis concerning their schools. During and after World War I, they had been free to teach their religious beliefs and the German language in their schools. But then the government passed laws that restricted these freedoms. The laws required a display of patriotism, including raising the flag, and they restricted the use of languages other than English as part of a "Canadianization" program.

The Mennonites who resisted this program suffered fines and even jail terms. They investigated various places in the United States, Mexico, and Paraguay; and eventually about 6,000 moved to Mexico and almost 1,800 to Paraguay. These nations guaranteed the Mennonites exemption from military service and the freedom to have their own schools without government control. The determination to have their own schools without interference is a good example for us today.

The concluding words of the New Testament say, "The grace of our Lord Jesus Christ be with you all" (Revelation 22:21). This verse tells us that God will always provide grace for righteous living regardless of conditions around us. God is still reigning, and we can rest assured that He will accomplish His plans in the affairs of the United States and other nations. We must also remember Jesus' promise that He will come quickly. No one knows when that will be, but we should always live in such a way that we are ready for His return.

Having studied this course in North American history, you should have a better understanding of this continent and why things are as they are. You should also be better prepared to face the future and to serve God wherever He calls you. May these goals be accomplished in the life of each student who studies this text, and may God be glorified through it all.

Focus for Thought

14. What events brought the Cold War to an end?
15. Why did President George H. W. Bush send soldiers to Panama? to Iraq?
16. a. After the Cold War, what was the general reason that the United States intervened in the affairs of other nations?
    b. Describe one case in which the United States intervened for this purpose.
17. On what charges was President Clinton impeached in 1998?
18. How did concerned Americans respond to the decline of public schools in the 1990s?
19. How did technology affect society by the end of the 1900s?

Historical Highlights

A. Matching: People

a. George H. W. Bush
b. Geraldine Ferraro
c. Gerald R. Ford
d. Henry Kissinger
e. James E. Carter
f. Neil Armstrong
g. Richard M. Nixon
h. Ronald Reagan
i. Sandra Day O'Connor
j. Spiro Agnew
k. William J. Clinton

1. Vice-presidential candidate in 1984 who was the first woman to run for that office.
2. First woman appointed to the Supreme Court.
3. First unelected president; took office when President Nixon resigned; served from 1974 to 1977.
4. Foreign policy adviser to Richard Nixon.
5. Nixon's vice president who resigned in 1973.
6. First president to resign from office; served from 1969 to 1974.
7. First man to walk on the moon.

8. President who faced economic troubles and the Iran hostage crisis; served from 1977 to 1981.
9. President who brought economic recovery in the 1980s; served from 1981 to 1989.
10. President when the Cold War ended and the Persian Gulf War was fought; served from 1989 to 1993.
11. Post-World War II president; served from 1993 to 2001.

B. Matching: Terms

a. bicentennial
b. Contras
c. deregulation
d. détente
e. Environmental Protection Agency
f. Iran-Contra affair
g. Iran hostage crisis
h. New Federalism
i. North American Free Trade Agreement
j. Organization of Petroleum Exporting Countries
k. Persian Gulf War
l. "Reaganomics"
m. SALT I
n. SALT II
o. stagflation
p. Strategic Defense Initiative
q. terrorist
r. Twenty-seventh Amendment
s. Watergate

1. Scandal in 1972 that led to the resignation of President Nixon.
2. Rising prices along with business stagnation in the 1970s.
3. Reagan's program for restoring the economy.
4. Removal of government controls.
5. Relaxing of tension between rivals.
6. Group of nations that banned oil exports to the United States in 1973.
7. Effort in which Iraqis were driven out of Kuwait in 1991.
8. Nixon's plan to give more authority to state and local governments.
9. Arms reduction agreement signed with the Soviet Union in 1979.
10. Two hundredth anniversary of the United States.
11. One who uses violence and threats to intimidate people, especially for political purposes.
12. Proposal approved by the Senate in 1993, involving Canada, Mexico, and the United States.
13. Proposed system of weapons orbiting in space to destroy missiles attacking the United States.
14. Arms reduction agreement made with the Soviet Union in 1972.
15. Government agency established in 1970 to limit pollution.
16. Group that opposed the Sandinistas in Nicaragua.
17. Incident when Americans were held captive in Tehran in 1979.
18. Measure stating that Congress could not raise its pay until after an election; ratified in 1992.
19. Incident when profits from weapons sold to Iran were used to help Contras in Nicaragua.

C. Matching: Dates

a. 1972
b. 1974
c. 1976
d. 1979
e. 1980
f. 1983
g. 1984
h. 1986
i. 1988
j. 1989
k. 1990
l. 1991
m. 1992
n. 1996
o. 1998

1. Election of George H. W. Bush, the first vice president since 1836 to be elected as the next president.
2. Year of the Watergate break-in, Nixon's visit to China, and his re-election.
3. Persian Gulf War; Soviet Union collapses and the Cold War ends.
4. United States bicentennial year; Jimmy Carter wins election as president.
5. President Reagan elected for his first term.
6. Richard Nixon resigns and Gerald Ford becomes president.
7. President Clinton impeached.
8. President Clinton elected for his first term.
9. President Reagan re-elected.
10. Space shuttle *Challenger* explodes.
11. Three Mile Island nuclear accident and Iran hostage crisis.
12. President Clinton re-elected.
13. United States invasion of Grenada.
14. Germany reunited.
15. United States invasion of Panama.

D. Matching: Places

a. Afghanistan
b. China
c. Czechoslovakia, Hungary, Poland
d. Egypt
e. Germany
f. Grenada
g. Iran
h. Iraq
i. Israel
j. Lebanon
k. Nicaragua
l. Panama
m. Soviet Union
n. Three Mile Island

1. Country aided by the United States in the 1973 Yom Kippur War.
2. Country invaded by the Soviet Union in 1979, which caused American–Soviet relations to deteriorate.
3. Nation visited in 1972 by Richard Nixon, the first United States president to do so; diplomatic relations with the United States restored in 1979.
4. Country where President Reagan sent troops in 1983 to keep peace; bomb killed 241 soldiers; American troops recalled in 1984.
5. Place where a nuclear accident occurred in 1979, causing a fear of nuclear power.
6. Some nations whose Communist governments were overthrown in 1989.
7. Country in Central America where Contras fought the Sandinista government.

8. Country in which militants took American hostages in 1979.
9. Caribbean island invaded by American troops in 1983 to keep it from becoming communist.
10. Nation divided since World War II but reunited in 1990 after its eastern part overthrew its Communist rulers.
11. Nation in Central America that was invaded by United States troops in 1989 to overthrow a dictator accused of dealing in illegal drugs.
12. Nation that invaded Kuwait in 1990 and triggered the Persian Gulf War in 1991, which it lost.
13. Nation that collapsed in 1991.
14. Nation that made peace with Israel in 1979, with encouragement from President Carter.

E. Deeper Discussion

1. a. Why did the United States experience such severe problems in the economy and with energy in the 1970s?
   b. Why did the economy turn around in the 1980s?
2. Trace the developments of the Cold War by answering the following questions.
   a. How did the United States improve relations with China and the Soviet Union in the early 1970s?
   b. What contributed to deepening Cold War tensions in the late 1970s and early 1980s?
   c. Why did the Cold War thaw somewhat in the late 1980s?
   d. How did the Cold War end?
3. What are the underlying causes for the deteriorating conditions in modern society?
4. a. What is the Christian's responsibility to the people in surrounding society? See Ephesians 5:11–13 and Philippians 2:15.
   b. What gives the Christian hope in spite of the decay in society? See John 14:3 and Revelation 22:20, 21.

F. Chronology and Geography

1. Why was the Middle East of such importance to the United States in the latter decades of the twentieth century?
2. On a world map, find the following countries discussed in Chapter 28. Be prepared to show their locations in class.
   a. Nations of the Middle East: Egypt, Iran, Iraq, Kuwait, Israel, Lebanon, Saudi Arabia, Syria
   b. Asian nations: Afghanistan, China, Russia (which is partly in Europe)
   c. European nations: Albania, Bulgaria, the Czech Republic and Slovakia (Czechoslovakia is now divided into these two nations), Germany, Hungary, Poland, Romania, Yugoslavia
   d. Nations of Central America and the Caribbean: Grenada, Nicaragua, Panama
3. List all the American presidents in order with the dates of their terms in office. Remember that an elected president's term begins in the year after the election.

So Far This Year

A. Completion

Write the correct name, term, or date for each description.

1. Case in which separate but equal facilities for blacks were declared unconstitutional.
2. Youth who rebelled against established values and violated social customs.
3. Drive to give blacks equal status with whites.
4. Incident in which Soviet weapons threatened United States security in 1962.
5. Ending of separation by race.
6. Idea that if one nation in a region falls to communism, nearby nations will also fall.
7. President Truman's program of social reforms.
8. Title of President Johnson's social programs.
9. Program for conscientious objectors from the 1950s to the 1970s.
10. Name of President Kennedy's domestic program.
11. Measure that gave President Johnson power to use military force in Vietnam.
12. Constitutional amendment that limited a president's administration to two terms.
13. Constitutional amendment that lowered the voting age to eighteen.
14. Constitutional amendment that defined presidential disability and stated when a vice president should take over the presidency.
15. General in the Korean War who was dismissed by President Truman.
16. First American astronaut to orbit the earth.
17. Black minister who led the civil rights movement and promoted nonviolent resistance.
18. Two states added to the Union in 1959.
19. Years of the Korean War.
20. Year when the United States withdrew from Vietnam.
21. Measure passed in 1956 to build a network of interstate highways.

B. Matching: Presidents

a. Dwight D. Eisenhower
b. George H. W. Bush
c. Gerald Ford
d. Harry S. Truman
e. James E. (Jimmy) Carter
f. John F. Kennedy
g. Lyndon B. Johnson
h. Richard M. Nixon
i. Ronald Reagan
j. William (Bill) Clinton

22. President who served from 1945 to 1953, after Franklin D. Roosevelt.
23. President during most of the 1950s; served from 1953 to 1961.
24. President elected in 1960 and assassinated in 1963.
25. Vice president who became president in 1963 and was elected in 1964; served from 1963 to 1969.
26. President when United States troops were withdrawn from Vietnam; first president to resign; served from 1969 to 1974.
27. First unelected president; in office during the American bicentennial; served from 1974 to 1977.
28. President who faced economic troubles and the Iran hostage crisis; served from 1977 to 1981.

29. President who brought economic recovery in the 1980s; served from 1981 to 1989.
30. President when the Cold War ended and the Persian Gulf War was fought; served from 1989 to 1993.
31. First president born since World War II; served from 1993 to 2001.

C. Multiple Choice

Write the letter of the correct answer.

32. Policy of having little to do with foreign nations.
    a. imperialism c. Roosevelt Corollary
    b. isolationism d. Open Door Policy
33. Basis for American relations with countries in the Far East.
    a. Monroe Doctrine c. Open Door Policy
    b. Roosevelt Corollary d. New Deal
34. Campaign promoting reform and change around the beginning of the 1900s.
    a. progressive movement c. New Freedom
    b. Square Deal d. New Frontier
35. President Roosevelt's reform program to treat everyone equally.
    a. Roosevelt Corollary c. Square Deal
    b. Great Society d. New Freedom
36. Constitutional amendment that provided for the direct election of senators.
    a. Sixteenth Amendment c. Eighteenth Amendment
    b. Seventeenth Amendment d. Nineteenth Amendment
37. Constitutional amendment that prohibited alcoholic beverages.
    a. Sixteenth Amendment c. Eighteenth Amendment
    b. Seventeenth Amendment d. Nineteenth Amendment
38. Constitutional amendment that allowed an income tax.
    a. Sixteenth Amendment c. Eighteenth Amendment
    b. Seventeenth Amendment d. Nineteenth Amendment
39. Constitutional amendment that allowed women to vote.
    a. Sixteenth Amendment c. Eighteenth Amendment
    b. Seventeenth Amendment d. Nineteenth Amendment
40. Law that established a central banking system in 1913.
    a. Federal Reserve Act c. Federal Trade Commission
    b. Underwood Tariff Act d. Pure Food and Drug Act
41. President during the Spanish-American War; served from 1897 to 1901.
    a. Theodore Roosevelt c. William McKinley
    b. Woodrow Wilson d. William Howard Taft
42. Democratic president who promoted the New Freedom program; served from 1913 to 1921.
    a. Theodore Roosevelt c. William McKinley
    b. Woodrow Wilson d. William Howard Taft
43. President who served from 1909 to 1913 and later became a Supreme Court justice.
    a. Theodore Roosevelt c. William McKinley
    b. Woodrow Wilson d. William Howard Taft

44. President with the "big stick"; served from 1901 to 1909.
    a. Theodore Roosevelt
    b. Woodrow Wilson
    c. William McKinley
    d. William Howard Taft
45. Spanish islands in the Far East conquered by the United States in the Spanish-American War and purchased for $20 million in 1898.
    a. Guam
    b. Hawaii
    c. Puerto Rico
    d. Philippines
46. Spanish island in the Caribbean ceded to the United States after the Spanish-American War.
    a. Guam
    b. Cuba
    c. Puerto Rico
    d. Philippines

Guidelines for Neat Maps

1. Use printing, not cursive writing, for all words on the map.
2. As space allows, print all words horizontally except the names of rivers and mountain ranges. A river or mountain range name should follow the course of the river or mountain range.
3. Use all capital letters for the names of countries, states, provinces, and large bodies of water. Capitalize only the first letter of each word for cities, lakes, rivers, and land regions.
4. Color bodies of water blue. Make all coloring strokes horizontal, not vertical or in every direction.
5. To color countries, states, or provinces, use a color that is different from the color of any area beside it. Do not use any color that is too dark for the lettering to show.

Outline Maps

Map A (The United States)

Map B (Canada)

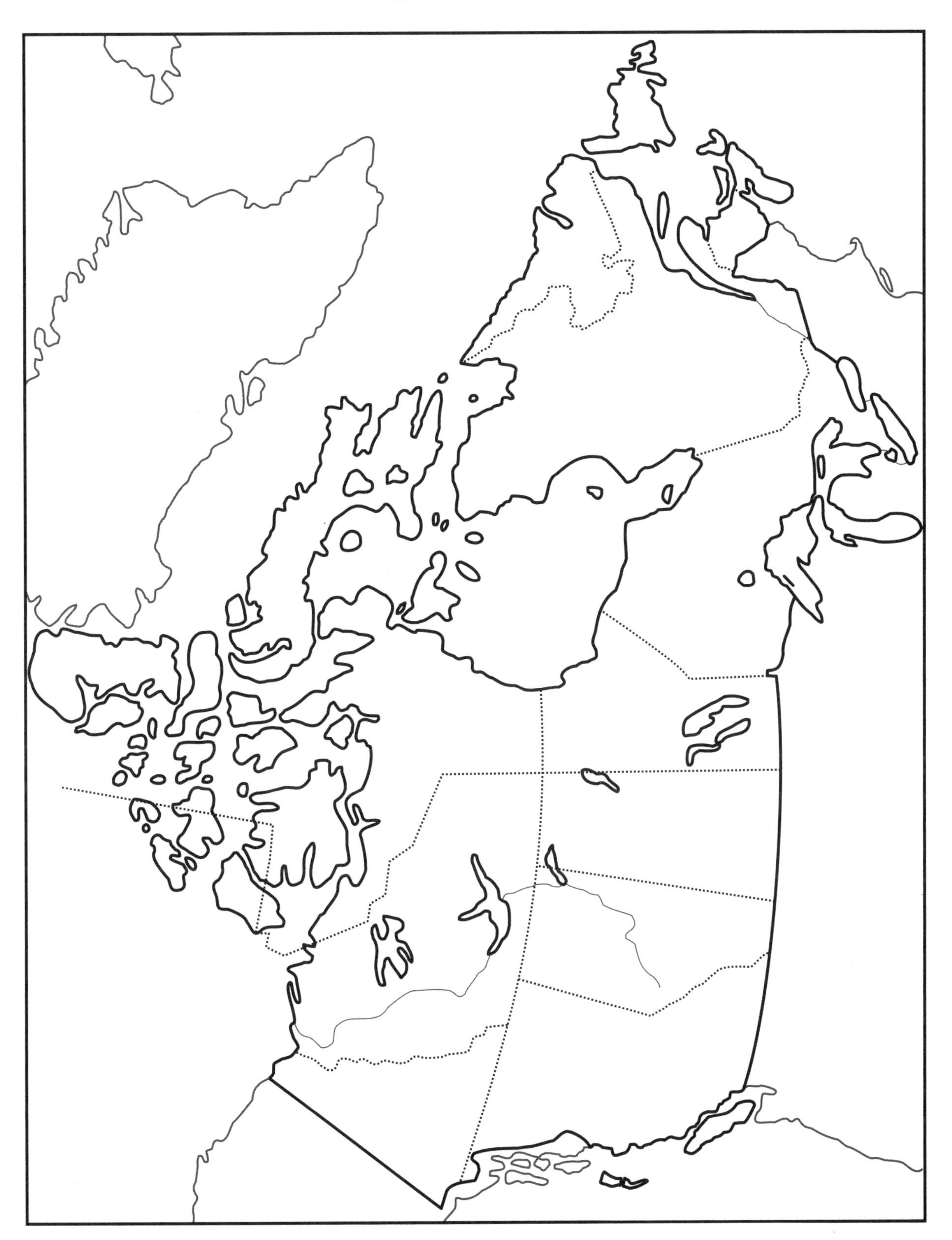

Map C (North America)

Map D (The Thirteen Colonies)

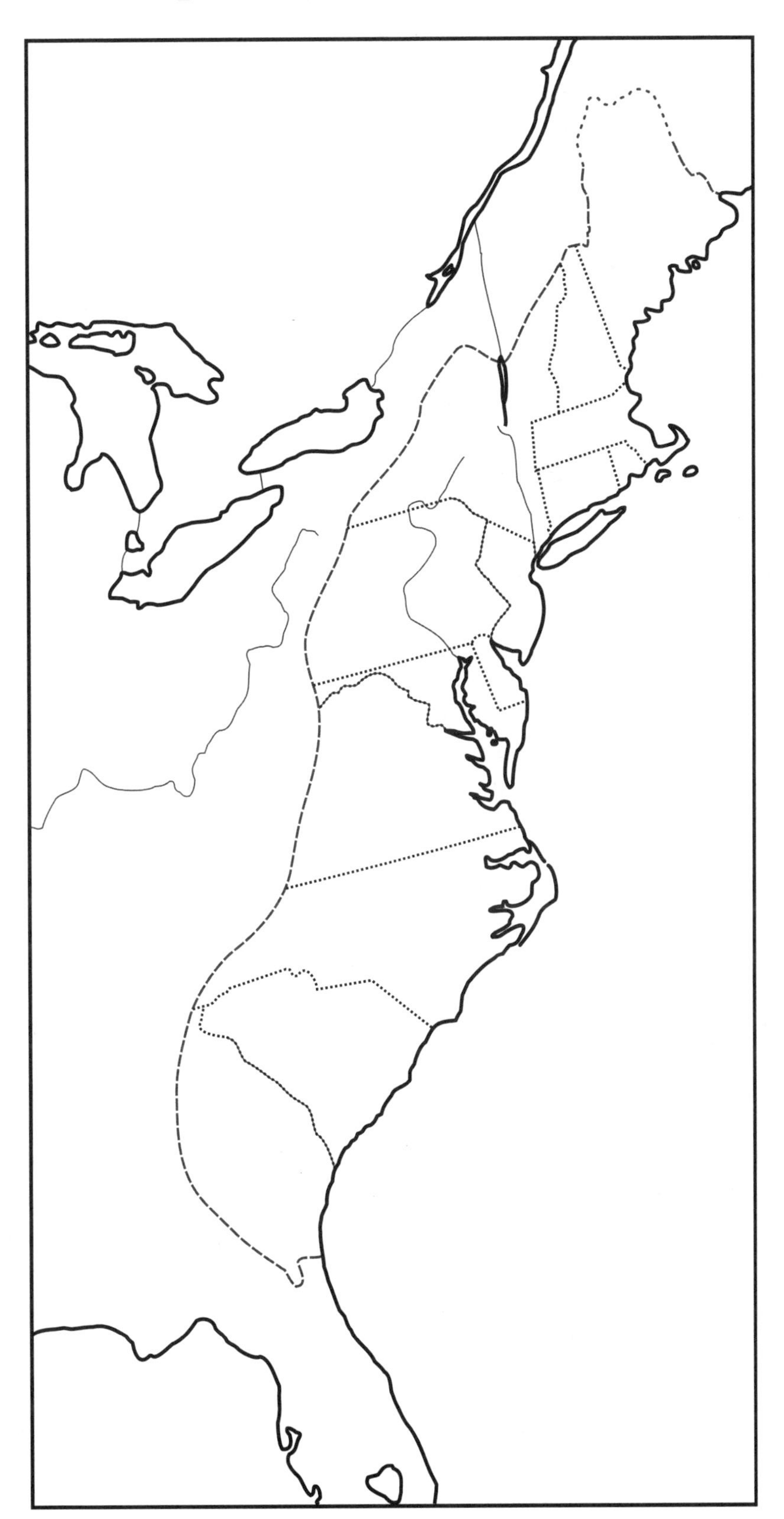

GLOSSARY

This glossary gives the meanings and pronunciations of the vocabulary words listed in each lesson. The numbers in brackets indicate the chapters where words are introduced.

The definitions tell only how the words are used in this book. Use a dictionary if you want to find other meanings for the words.

Many of the words have been respelled within parentheses to show how they are usually pronounced. Accented syllables are printed in capital letters.

abolition (ab uh LIHSH uhn) Elimination of slavery. [13]
absolutism (AB suh loo tihz uhm) System in which one person has complete authority in all matters. [4]
activist court A court inclined to make decisions that are the equivalent of new laws. [26]
affirmative action Policy requiring companies to hire a certain percentage of people considered the victims of discrimination, such as women and blacks. [27]
amphibious Pertaining to a combination of naval and land forces. [25]
appeasement (uh PEEZ muhnt) Policy of maintaining peace by letting an aggressor have his way. [25]
apprentice (uh PREHN tihs) Boy working without pay under a master for a certain time, in order to learn a craft. [7]
arctic Very cold climate where no trees grow and deep soil layers are permanently frozen. [1]
armistice (AHR mih stihs) Agreement to stop fighting. [23]
arms race Competition in which the United States and the Soviet Union tried to outdo each other in building nuclear weapons. [26]
artifact Manmade object, such as a tool or weapon, that is of interest in archaeology. [3]
astrolabe (AS truh layb) Instrument used by medieval sailors to determine latitude, now replaced by the sextant. [2]
basin 1. Low, bowl-shaped area surrounded by higher land. 2. The area drained by a river system. [1]
better class Social group of highest rank in colonial America. [7]
bicameral (by KAM ur uhl) Having a legislature with two houses. [10]
blitzkrieg (BLIHTS kreeg) "Lightning war" of the Germans in World War II, which depended on speed and surprise. [25]
blue laws Regulations on Sunday activities. [7]
bond Certificate of debt to be paid back with interest. [11]
boycott Refusing to buy certain goods as a way to gain what one demands. [9]
breaking plow Large, heavy plow used to turn over prairie sod. [13]
buffer Territory between two enemy nations that helps to reduce the likelihood of conflict. [6]
burgess (BUR jihs) Representative who took part in colonial government. [6]
business cycle Periodic swing between prosperity and decline in the economy. [24]
Cabinet Group appointed as advisers to the president. [10]
camp meeting One of a series of evangelistic meetings held outdoors or in a tent. [13]
capitalist Person who invests money in a project in order to make a profit. [2]
carpetbagger Northerner who went to the South after the Civil War to help in Reconstruction. [17]

cattle town Railroad town to which cattle were driven in the days of the open range. [19]
charter Legal document granting the right to settle and govern a certain region. [6]
checks and balances Methods by which branches of government limit each other's powers. [10]
circuit rider Minister who traveled about, preaching to pioneers. [13]
civil rights movement Movement to give blacks equal status with whites. [26]
claim jumping Taking of land already claimed by someone else. [19]
coalition (koh uh LIHSH uhn) Temporary alliance of various groups to accomplish a certain thing. [24]
Cold War Conflict in which enemy nations worked against each other without actually fighting. [25]
collective bargaining Negotiation of union leaders with employers for wages and working hours. [20]
communism Economic and political system in which most of the land, factories, and resources are owned and controlled by the government rather than by individual citizens. [25]
commutation fee Money paid to avoid military service. [16]
Conestoga wagon (kahn ih STOH guh) Canvas-topped wagon used by American pioneers moving west. [13]
confederation (1) Weak union in which states have more power than the national government. [10] (2) Union of the Canadian provinces under a single government. [18]
coniferous softwood (koh NIHF ur uhs) Kind of trees that bear cones and usually have needles instead of broad leaves. [1]
conscientious objector Person who believes it is wrong to take part in warfare. [16]
constitution Written plan of government. [10]
containment Policy of trying to keep communism from spreading. [26]
contiguous (kuhn TIHG yoo uhs) In contact; adjoining. [1]
Continental Divide High ridge that separates water flowing into the Pacific Ocean from water flowing into the Gulf of Mexico. [1]
contraband of war Goods headed toward an enemy nation to support its war effort. [23]
cooperative Group of people who purchase things in large quantities to obtain lower prices. [20]
corporation Large business owned by many people. [20]
corruption Misuse of a public office for the sake of illegal gain. [8]
counterculture Youth of the 1960s who rebelled against established values and violated social customs. [27]
coureur de bois (koo RUR duh BWAH) "Forest runner" who gathered furs from the Indians and brought them to trading centers. [5]
culture Distinctive set of customs and values associated with a certain group of people. [3]
culture area Region where a number of Indian tribes had basically the same culture. [3]
Darwinism Theory that living things had a natural origin and that they gradually evolved into the species existing today. [20]
deciduous hardwood (dih SIHJ oo uhs) Kind of trees that lose their leaves for part of the year. [1]
deism (DEE ihz uhm) False idea that God created the world and then withdrew from it. [7]
delta Fertile deposit of earth, usually triangular, that builds up at the mouth of some rivers. [1]
demilitarized (dee MIHL ih tuh ryzd) Free of troops and weapons. [25]
deregulation Removal of government regulation. [28]

desegregation Ending of separation by race. [26]

détente (day TAHNT) Relaxing of tension between rivals. [28]

discrimination Action based on prejudice against a person. [17]

dividends Profits that corporations pay to stockholders. [20]

domino theory Idea that if one nation in a region falls to communism, nearby nations will also fall. [26]

draft Compulsory enrollment in a military force. [16]

elastic clause Statement in the Constitution saying that Congress may assume powers not specifically mentioned in the Constitution. [10]

Emancipation Proclamation Statement issued by Abraham Lincoln, which declared that slaves in the Confederacy were free. [16]

Enlightenment Movement of the 1700s in which men began to be "enlightened" by human reasoning rather than by religion; the Age of Reason. [7]

estuary (EHS choo ehr ee) Broad bay at the mouth of a river. [1]

excise tax (EHK syz) Tax levied on certain domestic products. [11]

executive branch Branch of government that enacts and enforces laws. [10]

Fall Line Line at the edge of the Piedmont plateau, where waterfalls occur in rivers descending to the Coastal Plain. [1]

fascism (FASH ihz uhm) Political system of totalitarian control under Mussolini in Italy. [25]

fault Crack or break in the crust of the earth, where earthquakes occur. [1]

federal Kind of government system with powers divided between the states and the national government. [10]

feudalism System of loyalty in Europe during the Middle Ages, by which noblemen of lower rank received land from noblemen of higher rank. [2]

fiord (FYAWRD) Long, narrow bay extending inland in a steep-sided valley. [1]

flexible response Policy of having both conventional and nuclear weapons for dealing with military threats. [27]

flotilla (floh TIHL uh) Group of boats or canoes traveling together. [5]

foreign policy The manner of a nation or national leader in relating to other nations. [12]

Founding Fathers Men who framed the Constitution of the United States. [10]

free enterprise System that includes private ownership of property, free markets, and a minimum of government regulation. [20]

freedman Person who was a former slave. [17]

freedom of the seas Right of any merchant ship to sail the ocean in peace or war. [23]

frontier Edge of a settled area. [4]

frontier raid Sudden attack on an English settlement by French and Indians. [8]

fundamentalism Movement to assert basic truths of the Bible and oppose modernism. [24]

girdling Removing a strip of bark around a tree to kill it. [13]

habitant (ah bee TAHN) Settler who worked a seigneur's land in New France. [5]

headright System in which each person entering an English colony received 50 acres (20 ha) of land. [7]

Holocaust (HAHL uh kawst) Hitler's destruction of millions of Jews and others in Europe. [25]

home rule Policy allowing Southern states to deal with their own affairs after the Civil War. [17]

homesteader Person who claimed western land and settled on it for five years. [19]

hornbook Flat board with a paper protected by a sheet of horn, which showed the alphabet and other basic items and was used in New England schools. [7]

humanism Man-centered philosophy in which values are determined by man rather than by God. [2]

humanitarian Serving to promote human welfare. [6]

humid continental climate Climate with four distinct seasons and a great contrast between summer and winter. [1]

humid subtropical climate Warm and moist climate near the Tropics. [1]

impeach To bring to trial for misconduct in office. [10]

imperialism Ambition to gain control of foreign territories. [21]

impress To force into military service. [11]

indentured servant A person who worked for a certain period of time to pay for his voyage to America. [7]

Industrial Revolution Change from producing handmade goods at home to producing machine-made goods in factories, which began in the late 1700s. [13]

initiative (ih NIHSH uh tihv) Measure allowing voters to introduce new laws to a legislature. [22]

interchangeable parts Parts that can be interchanged because they are made exactly alike. [13]

interior plain Level land lying some distance inland from the ocean. [1]

internal drainage Flowing of water into inland lakes having no outlets to the ocean. [1]

Iron Curtain Barrier to communication and travel between communist nations and free nations. [25]

isolationism Policy of having little to do with foreign nations. [21]

journeyman One who worked for wages after completing an apprenticeship. [7]

judicial branch Branch of government that decides whether laws have been broken or whether laws are constitutional. [10]

judicial review Action in which a court examines a law to determine whether it is constitutional. [10]

justice of the peace Official who was a judge and tax collector in colonial America. [7]

labor union Organization of workers agreeing to require certain things of employers. [20]

lame duck Person finishing a term after another is elected to replace him. [24]

legislative branch Branch of government that proposes new laws. [10]

legislature Group of people appointed to make laws. [7]

loose interpretation Idea that the government should be free to assume powers not specifically described in the Constitution. [11]

lower house Part of legislature elected by voters and having greater power. [7]

Loyalist Colonial American who favored remaining subject to Great Britain. [9]

manifest destiny Idea that the United States was intended by God to spread over the whole North American continent. [14]

manorialism (muh NAWR ee uh lihz uhm) System in which a lord owned a tract of land called a manor, and serfs farmed it for him. [2]

mass production System for making large numbers of products by using interchangeable parts and assembly lines. [20]

massive retaliation Threat of responding with nuclear weapons in case of attack on an American ally. [26]

meaner sort Unskilled persons who did not own land and who were of low rank in colonial America. [7]

Mediterranean climate Warm, dry climate like that of lands around the Mediterranean Sea. [1]

melting pot Place where people of many different nationalities mingle together. [20]

mercantilism (MUR kuhn tee lihz uhm) Idea that colonies should serve for the profit of the mother country. [9]

middle class 1. In the Middle Ages, people who were neither lords nor serfs. 2. In modern times, people who are neither extremely rich nor extremely poor. [2]

middling class Small farmers and craftsmen in colonial America. [7]

minuteman Man of colonial America who was ready to fight on a minute's notice. [9]

mission Spanish outpost established to convert and civilize Indians. [4]

modernism Set of beliefs including the theory of evolution, rejection of the supernatural, and acceptance of science as the only source of truth. [24]

monopoly 1. Exclusive control over the market of a certain product. 2. A person or company that has such control and therefore has no competition. [5, 20]

Monroe Doctrine Proclamation issued in 1823 by James Monroe, stating that European nations were not to interfere in the affairs of American nations and vice versa. [12]

mother lode Main vein of ore. [19]

mountain man One of the hardy fur traders and explorers in the American West. [14]

muckraker Author of books or articles pointing out evils in society. [22]

nationalism Pride in belonging to one's nation; patriotism. [2]

nativism Movement to limit immigration. [20]

naval stores Tar, pitch, and related pine products used to seal cracks in wooden ships. [6]

Nazism (NAHT sihz uhm) Political system of nationalism and totalitarian control under Hitler in Germany. [25]

noncombatant Fulfilling military duties but not actually fighting. [23]

normalcy Condition desired by Americans after World War I, which included a less troubled life and less involvement in European affairs. [24]

nullify To set aside; declare void. [12]

old-field school School located on soil worn out by tobacco growing. [7]

oligarchy (AHL ih gahr kee) Rule by a small group of people. [18]

open range Unfenced grazing land. [19]

pacifism (PAS uh fihz uhm) Policy of settling disputes by nonviolent means rather than by fighting. [6]

palisade (pal ih SAYD) Fence made of vertical poles. [3]

patent Exclusive right to make and sell an invention. [20]

patriot Colonial American who favored independence from Great Britain. [9]

pemmican (PEHM ih kuhn) Dry, crumbled meat mixed with buffalo tallow and pressed into cakes. [3]

permafrost Subsoil that stays permanently frozen. [1]

pig iron Crude iron as it first comes from a blast furnace, formerly cast in oblong blocks called pigs. [7]

pillory Device used to fasten the head and hands of lawbreakers. [7]

plateau Large, elevated area of the same general height. [1]

political machine Organized group controlled by a powerful "boss." [20]

poll Place where voting is done during elections. [17]

pony express System for delivering mail to California during 1860 and 1861. [14]

popular sovereignty Idea that people living in an area should decide for themselves about slavery. [15]

preempt (pree EHMPT) To settle on (public land) so as to have the first chance to buy it. [19]
preparedness (prih PAIR ihd nihs) The state of being prepared to fight if necessary. [23]
presidio (prih SEE dee oh) Fort built to keep order and protect a Spanish mission. [4]
private enterprise System in which individuals have their own property and receive the benefits of their own labor. [6]
Prohibition Period when alcoholic beverages were outlawed in the United States, lasting from 1920 to 1933. [24]
propaganda (prahp uh GAN duh) Material publicized to spread certain ideas, usually with a strong, one-sided emphasis. [9]
proprietor (pruh PRY ih tur) A nobleman who received land in America to be rented or sold after the pattern of the manorial system. [6]
prospector Person who seeks gold or other valuable minerals. [14]
public domain Land owned by the government. [19]
pueblo (PWEHB loh) Indian village of multilevel apartment houses made of stone or adobe. [3]
quitrent (KWIHT rehnt) Money paid yearly to be free from feudal obligations. [7]
ratification The act of giving formal agreement to. [10]
recall Measure allowing voters to remove unsatisfactory public officials from office. [22]
redeem To restore government control by whites to a Southern state after Reconstruction. [17]
referendum (rehf uh REHN duhm) Measure allowing voters to approve or reject laws passed by a legislature. [22]
Reformation Great change in the religious system of Europe, which began around 1500 when Protestants and other groups broke away from the Roman Catholic Church. [2]
Renaissance (REHN ih sahns) Rebirth of learning and culture that began in Europe around 1300. [2]
rendezvous (RAHN duh voo) Meeting place where western fur traders sold furs and bought supplies. [14]
reparations (rehp uh RAY shuhnz) Money demanded from a defeated nation for war damages that it caused. [21]
repeal To withdraw something, especially a law. [9]
republic Government managed by elected representatives. [10]
responsible government Government controlled by the people rather than by aristocrats. [18]
revenue Government income, usually obtained by taxation. [9]
revivalism Religious movement placing strong emphasis on conversion but little emphasis on discipleship. [20]
royal colony Colony owned and managed by the king. [6]
rural Pertaining to the country, as opposed to the city. [1]
saga (SAH guh) A story of Viking adventures dating from the Middle Ages, first handed down orally and later put into writing. [2]
salutary neglect (SAL yuh tair ee) Lax enforcement of laws, which allowed trade to develop in English colonies. [7]
scalawag Southern white who took part in Reconstruction government. [17]
sea dog Pirate supported by the English government in the 1500s. [4]
secede (sih SEED) To withdraw formally from an organization. [12]
sectionalism Devotion to the interests of a local region rather than the whole nation. [12]
segregation Social separation based on race. [17]

seigneur (sayn YUR) Noble who owned land in New France. [5]
seigneurial system (sayn YAWR ee uhl) Form of manorialism transplanted to New France, in which seigneurs owned land and habitants farmed it. [5]
separation of powers Dividing of government into several branches to limit its power. [10]
share of stock One portion of a corporation, which is purchased by an investor. [20]
sharecropping System in which farm workers rent cropland and use a share of the crops to pay the rent. [17]
slave code Set of laws placing restrictions on slaves. [13]
social gospel Religious movement designed to improve present social conditions. [20]
socialism Karl Marx's theory proposing a classless society and government ownership of businesses. [20]
space race Competition in which the United States and the Soviet Union tried to outdo each other in achievements in outer space. [26]
sphere of influence Area in China in which a foreign nation controlled trade and port cities around 1900. [21]
spoils system Practice in which the winner of an election rewards his supporters with government positions. [12]
squatter Person who settles on unoccupied land without legal title to it. [18]
states' rights Idea that states have more power than the federal government. [12]
strict interpretation Idea that the government should exercise only the powers specifically described in the Constitution. [11]
strike Refusal to work until labor demands are met. [20]
subarctic climate Cold climate near a polar region, where coniferous trees grow. [1]
summit meeting Conference between heads of state. [26]
supply and demand Principle that scarcity and high demand cause prices to rise, and abundance and low demand cause prices to fall. [20]
tariff (TAR ihf) Tax levied on certain imports, usually to protect domestic industries. [11]
temperance movement Effort to stop the use of strong drink. [13]
terrorist One who uses violence and threats to intimidate people, especially for political purposes. [28]
tidewater Low-lying region where rivers rise and fall with ocean tides. [1]
topography (tuh PAHG ruh fee) Surface features of a region. [1]
Tory Colonial American who favored remaining subject to Great Britain. [9]
totalitarian (toh tal ih TAIR ee uhn) Having a single authority with absolute control of everything. [25]
town meeting New England assembly for discussions and voting on matters of local government. [7]
township Tract of land granted to a group of people in New England. [7]
travois (truh VOY) Pair of poles drawn by a dog or horse, used by Plains Indians to carry their belongings. [3]
triangular trade System of commerce that involves taking one cargo to a certain place, taking a second cargo from there to another place, and taking a third cargo from there back to the starting point. [7]
tributary River flowing into a larger river. [1]
trust Related businesses combined into one large organization. [20]

trustee Person who cares for property entrusted to him. [6]

turnpike Road for which users pay toll. [13]

Underground Railroad Secret system for helping slaves escape to Canada. [15]

unicameral (yoo nih KAM ur uhl) Having a legislature with only one house. [10]

upper house Part of legislature representing the upper class of citizens but having little power. [7]

urban Pertaining to the city, as opposed to the country. [1]

utopia (yoo TOH pee uh) Ideal society such as that desired by the Puritans and Quakers. [8]

veto (VEE toh) To reject a proposed law. [10]

vigilance committee Group that meted out swift and stern justice in the American West. [19]

voyageur (voi uh ZHUR) Strong French-Canadian canoe paddler of the 1700s and 1800s. [18]

war hawk Bold young congressman who promoted war in the early 1800s. [11]

west coast marine climate Mild, wet climate of the Pacific valleys. [1]

Whig Colonial American who favored a boycott of Great Britain to force recognition of the colonies' rights. [9]

white supremacy (soo PREHM uh see) Belief that white people are superior to blacks. [17]

writs of assistance Search warrants allowing officials to search buildings for smuggled goods. [9]

UNITED STATES OF AMERICA

State	Admitted to Union	Capital	Land Area	Nickname	Population for 2000
1. Alabama	1819	Montgomery	51,718 sq. mi. (133,950 km^2)	The Heart of Dixie	4,447,100
2. Alaska	1959	Juneau	587,878 sq. mi. (1,522,604 km^2)	Last Frontier	626,932
3. Arizona	1912	Phoenix	114,007 sq. mi. (295,278 km^2)	Grand Canyon State	5,130,632
4. Arkansas	1836	Little Rock	53,183 sq. mi. (137,744 km^2)	Land of Opportunity	2,673,400
5. California	1850	Sacramento	158,648 sq. mi. (410,898 km^2)	Golden State	33,871,648
6. Colorado	1876	Denver	104,100 sq. mi. (269,619 km^2)	Centennial State	4,301,261
7. Connecticut*	1788	Hartford	5,006 sq. mi. (12,966 km^2)	Constitution State	3,405,565
8. Delaware*	1787	Dover	2,026 sq. mi. (5,247 km^2)	First State	783,600
9. Florida	1845	Tallahassee	58,681 sq. mi. (151,984 km^2)	Sunshine State	15,982,378
10. Georgia*	1788	Atlanta	58,930 sq. mi. (152,629 km^2)	Empire State of the South	8,186,456
11. Hawaii	1959	Honolulu	6,459 sq. mi. (16,729 km^2)	Aloha State	1,211,537
12. Idaho	1890	Boise	83,574 sq. mi. (216,457 km^2)	Gem State	1,293,953
13. Illinois	1818	Springfield	56,343 sq. mi. (145,928 km^2)	Land of Lincoln	12,419,293
14. Indiana	1816	Indianapolis	36,185 sq. mi. (93,719 km^2)	Hoosier State	6,080,485
15. Iowa	1846	Des Moines	56,276 sq. mi. (145,755 km^2)	Hawkeye State	2,926,324
16. Kansas	1861	Topeka	82,282 sq. mi. (213,110 km^2)	Sunflower State	2,688,418
17. Kentucky	1792	Frankfort	40,411 sq. mi. (104,664 km^2)	Bluegrass State	4,041,769
18. Louisiana	1812	Baton Rouge	47,717 sq. mi. (123,587 km^2)	Pelican State	4,468,976
19. Maine	1820	Augusta	33,128 sq. mi. (85,802 km^2)	Pine Tree State	1,274,923
20. Maryland*	1788	Anapolis	10,455 sq. mi. (27,078 km^2)	Old Line State	5,296,486
21. Massachusetts*	1788	Boston	8,262 sq. mi. (21,399 km^2)	Bay State	6,349,097
22. Michigan	1837	Lansing	58,513 sq. mi. (151,549 km^2)	Wolverine State	9,938,444
23. Minnesota	1858	St. Paul	84,397 sq. mi. (218,588 km^2)	Gopher State	4,919,479
24. Mississippi	1817	Jackson	47,698 sq. mi. (123,538 km^2)	Magnolia State	2,844,658
25. Missouri	1821	Jefferson City	69,709 sq. mi. (180,546 km^2)	Show Me State	5,595,211
26. Montana	1889	Helena	147,047 sq. mi. (380,852 km^2)	Treasure State	902,195
27. Nebraska	1867	Lincoln	77,359 sq. mi. (200,360 km^2)	Cornhusker State	1,711,263
28. Nevada	1864	Carson City	110,567 sq. mi. (286,369 km^2)	Silver State	1,998,257
29. New Hampshire*	1788	Concord	9,283 sq. mi. (24,043 km^2)	Granite State	1,235,786
30. New Jersey*	1787	Trenton	7,790 sq. mi. (20,176 km^2)	Garden State	8,414,350
31. New Mexico	1912	Santa Fe	121,599 sq. mi. (314,941 km^2)	Land of Enchantment	1,819,046
32. New York*	1788	Albany	49,112 sq. mi. (127,200 km^2)	Empire State	18,976,457
33. North Carolina*	1789	Raleigh	52,672 sq. mi. (136,420 km^2)	Tar Heel State	8,049,313
34. North Dakota	1889	Bismarck	70,704 sq. mi. (183,123 km^2)	Flickertail State	642,200
35. Ohio	1803	Columbus	41,328 sq. mi. (107,040 km^2)	Buckeye State	11,353,140
36. Oklahoma	1907	Oklahoma City	69,903 sq. mi. (181,049 km^2)	Sooner State	3,450,654
37. Oregon	1859	Salem	97,052 sq. mi. (251,365 km^2)	Beaver State	3,421,399
38. Pennsylvania*	1787	Harrisburg	45,310 sq. mi. (117,353 km^2)	Keystone State	12,281,054
39. Rhode Island*	1790	Providence	1,213 sq. mi. (3,142 km^2)	Ocean State	1,048,319
40. South Carolina*	1788	Columbia	31,117 sq. mi. (80,593 km^2)	Palmetto State	4,102,012
41. South Dakota	1889	Pierre	77,122 sq. mi. (199,746 km^2)	Mount Rushmore State	754,844
42. Tennessee	1796	Nashville	42,146 sq. mi. (109,158 km^2)	Volunteer State	5,689,283

43. Texas	1845	Austin	266,874 sq. mi. (691,204 km²)	Lone Star State	20,851,820
44. Utah	1896	Salt Lake City	84,905 sq. mi. (219,904 km²)	Beehive State	2,233,169
45. Vermont	1791	Montpelier	9,615 sq. mi. (24,903 km²)	Green Mountain State	608,827
46. Virginia*	1788	Richmond	40,598 sq. mi. (105,149 km²)	Old Dominion	7,078,515
47. Washington	1889	Olympia	68,126 sq. mi. (176,446 km²)	Evergreen State	5,894,121
48. West Virginia	1863	Charleston	24,231 sq. mi. (62,758 km²)	Mountain State	1,808,344
49. Wisconsin	1848	Madison	56,145 sq. mi. (145,416 km²)	Badger State	5,363,675
50. Wyoming	1890	Cheyenne	97,818 sq. mi. (253,349 km²)	Equality State	493,782

One of the 13 original states.

CANADA

Province or Territory	*Admitted to Canada*	*Capital*	*Land Area*	*Population for 2001*
1. Alberta	1905	Edmonton	255,287 sq. mi. (661,193 km²)	2,974,807
2. British Columbia	1871	Victoria	365,900 sq. mi. (947,681 km²)	3,907,738
3. Manitoba	1870	Winnipeg	250,947 sq. mi. (649,953 km²)	1,119,583
4. New Brunswick	1867	Fredericton	28,355 sq. mi. (73,439 km²)	729,498
5. Newfoundland and Labrador	1949	St. John's	156,649 sq. mi. (405,721 km²)	512,930
6. Northwest Territories	1870	Yellowknife	501,570 sq. mi. (1,299,066 km²)	37,360
7. Nova Scotia	1867	Halifax	21,423 sq. mi. (55,486 km²)	908,007
8. Nunavut	1999	Iqaluit	770,000 sq. mi. (1,994,300 km²)	26,745
9. Ontario	1867	Toronto	412,581 sq. mi. (1,068,585 km²)	11,410,046
10. Prince Edward Is.	1873	Charlottetown	2,185 sq. mi. (5,659 km²)	135,294
11. Quebec	1867	Quebec	594,860 sq. mi. (1,540,687 km²)	7,237,479
12. Saskatchewan	1905	Regina	251,866 sq. mi. (652,333 km²)	978,933
13. Yukon Territory	1898	Whitehorse	186,661 sq. mi. (483,452 km²)	28,674

Sources: U.S. Census Bureau (2000) and Statistics Canada Regional Reference Centre (2001).

Presidents of the United States

President	Term of Office	Political Party	Vice President	Church Denomination
1. George Washington	1789–1797	None	John Adams	Episcopalian
2. John Adams	1797–1801	Federalist	Thomas Jefferson	Unitarian
3. Thomas Jefferson	1801–1809	Dem.–Rep.	Aaron Burr George Clinton	Unitarian*
4. James Madison	1809–1817	Dem.–Rep.	George Clinton Elbridge Gerry	Episcopalian
5. James Monroe	1817–1825	Dem.–Rep.	Daniel D. Tompkins	Episcopalian
6. John Quincy Adams	1825–1829	Dem.–Rep.	John C. Calhoun	Unitarian
7. Andrew Jackson	1829–1837	Democratic	John C. Calhoun Martin Van Buren	Presbyterian
8. Martin Van Buren	1837–1841	Democratic	Richard M. Johnson	Dutch Reformed
9. William H. Harrison	1841	Whig	John Tyler	Episcopalian
10. John Tyler	1841–1845	Whig	None	Episcopalian
11. James K. Polk	1845–1849	Democratic	George M. Dallas	Methodist
12. Zachary Taylor	1849–1850	Whig	Millard Fillmore	Episcopalian
13. Millard Fillmore	1850–1853	Whig	None	Unitarian
14. Franklin Pierce	1853–1857	Democratic	William R. D. King	Episcopalian
15. James Buchanan	1857–1861	Democratic	John C. Breckinridge	Presbyterian
16. Abraham Lincoln	1861–1865	Republican	Hannibal Hamlin Andrew Johnson	Presbyterian*
17. Andrew Johnson	1865–1869	Democrat	None	Methodist*
18. Ulysses S. Grant	1869–1877	Republican	Schuyler Colfax Henry Wilson	Methodist
19. Rutherford B. Hayes	1877–1881	Republican	William A. Wheeler	Methodist*
20. James Garfield	1881	Republican	Chester A. Arthur	Disciples of Christ
21. Chester A. Arthur	1881–1885	Republican	None	Episcopalian
22. Grover Cleveland	1885–1889	Democratic	Thomas A. Hendricks	Presbyterian
23. Benjamin Harrison	1889–1893	Republican	Levi P. Morton	Presbyterian
24. Grover Cleveland	1893–1897	Democratic	Adlai E. Stevenson	Presbyterian
25. William McKinley	1897–1901	Republican	Garret A. Hobart Theodore Roosevelt	Methodist
26. Theodore Roosevelt	1901–1909	Republican	Charles W. Fairbanks	Dutch Reformed
27. William H. Taft	1909–1913	Republican	James S. Sherman	Unitarian
28. Woodrow Wilson	1913–1921	Democratic	Thomas R. Marshall	Presbyterian
29. Warren G. Harding	1921–1923	Republican	Calvin Coolidge	Baptist
30. Calvin Coolidge	1923–1929	Republican	Charles G. Dawes	Congregationalist
31. Herbert C. Hoover	1929–1933	Republican	Charles Curtis	Friend (Quaker)
32. Franklin D. Roosevelt	1933–1945	Democratic	John N. Garner Henry A. Wallace Harry S. Truman	Episcopalian
33. Harry S. Truman	1945–1953	Democratic	Alben W. Barkley	Baptist
34. Dwight D. Eisenhower	1953–1961	Republican	Richard M. Nixon	Presbyterian
35. John F. Kennedy	1961–1963	Democratic	Lyndon B. Johnson	Roman Catholic
36. Lyndon B. Johnson	1963–1969	Democratic	Hubert H. Humphrey	Disciples of Christ
37. Richard M. Nixon	1969–1974	Republican	Spiro T. Agnew Gerald R. Ford	Friend (Quaker)
38. Gerald R. Ford	1974–1977	Republican	Nelson A. Rockefeller	Episcopalian
39. James (Jimmy) Carter	1977–1981	Democratic	Walter F. Mondale	Baptist
40. Ronald W. Reagan	1981–1989	Republican	George H. W. Bush	Disciples of Christ
41. George H.W. Bush	1989–1993	Republican	James D. (Dan) Quayle	Episcopalian
42. William (Bill) Clinton	1993–2001	Democratic	Albert (Al) Gore	Baptist
43. George W. Bush	2001–	Republican	Richard B. (Dick) Cheney	Episcopalian

**never joined any church (church preference given)*

MAP INDEX

General Index

N

T

U

V

Photograph Credits

Architect of the Capitol: 36 (#70226), **49** (#70240), **56** (#34113), **182** (#70222), **193** (bottom: #70228), **202** (#70242), **247** (left: #32189)

Auker, Kenneth: 16 (both); **17** (both); **18** (bottom left and right); **19** (top left and bottom left); **20** (all except top left); **21** (second and third), **27** (top left); **59** (left: courtesy Cahokia Mounds State Historical Site); **65** (left), **72** (courtesy Mission San Juan Capistrano); **117** (lower right: Plimoth Plantation, Plymouth, Massachusetts); **171** (top left; top right: courtesy Hans Herr House and Museum), **197** (Ephrata Cloister. Administered by the Pennsylvania Historical and Museum Commission); **226** (right); **229** (right: courtesy Old Fort Harrod State Park); **231** (right: Monticello); **237** (top right); **264** (courtesy Slater Mill Historic Site); **274** (top right: courtesy Stanton Hall); **335**; **338** (top left and middle photos: courtesy National Park Service, Antietam National Battlefield); **340; 487** (top right); **425** and **436** [right] (From the collections of the Henry Ford Museum and Greenfield Village); **620** (bottom right)

Auker, Mary Jane: cover (courtesy Portland Head Light)

Copyright © Corel Corporation: 1, back cover, **10** (photograph by Darrell Templeton), **21** (first), **25, 26** (all), **27** (top right and lower right), **28** (top left and top right), **29** (both), **35, 71, 100** (top left), **153, 165, 617** (top left), **623, 633**

Copyright © Corel Corporation/National Archives of Canada: 8 (#C-043171), **97** (#C-000856), **98** (#C-021404), **99** (#C-011925), **170** (#C-000361), **378** (#C-040358), **382** (top right: #C-040137), **388** (top: #C-046109), **392** (bottom: #C-013965), **393** (right: #C-010514)

© Digital Vision: Dynamic Graphics, Inc.: 13, 19 (top right), **21** (fourth)

FDR Library: 536 (top left: #27-0642a), **540** (top: #27-0873a, bottom: #27-0592a), **542** (top: #27-0757a), **560** (bottom left: #NLR-PHOCO-A-837[103])

George Bush Presidential Library: 626 (bottom: #P17676-19), **627** (#P14777-18)

Gerald R. Ford Library (courtesy of): 619 (top right: #A0004-10, bottom left: #A0627-8A)

Hoover, Samuel: 603

Illustrated London News: 331 (#V1-110), **501** (top: V1-041)

Jimmy Carter Library (courtesy of): 621 (#NLC-WHSP-C-07288-24)

John F. Kennedy Library: 597 (#KN-C29210), **598** (#ST-A13-60-62)

LBJ Library Photo by Cecil Stoughton: 600 (left: #1A-1-WH63)

Library of Congress, Prints and Photographs Division: 18 (top right: LOC # unknown), **23** (LOC # unknown), **28** (bottom: LOC # unknown), **39** (left: LC-USZ62-25245), **43** (LC-USZ62-104244), **44** (LC-USZ62-101614), **46** (top: LC-USZ62-1784, bottom: LC-USZ62-23655), **47** (LC-USZ62-3016), **48** (left: LC-USZ62-3020, right: LC-USZ62-3091), **49** (bottom: LOC # unknown), **55** (LC-USZ62-89908), **59** (right: LC-USZC4-3874), **60** (LC-USZ62-38554), **62** (top: LC-USZ62-52444, bottom: LC-USZ62-11478), **63** (top: LC-USZ62-37879, middle: LC-USZ62-64891, bottom: LC-USZ62-83590), **64** (LC-USZ62-59803), **65** (right: LC-USZ62-27798), **74** (LC-USZ62-2977), **75** (LC-USZ62-3435), **76** (LC-USZ62-37993), **79** (top: LC-USZ62-871, bottom: LC-USZ62-1659), **81** (LC-USZ62-59995), **83** (LC-USZ62-3108), **84** (LC-USZ62-63331), **92** (LC-USZ62-52130 [modified; see page 103 insert]), **93** (LC-USZ62-12821), **95** (LC-USZ62-3019), **96** (LC-USZ62-30892), **100** (bottom: LC-USZ62-64110), **102** (LC-USZ62-9926), **103** (larger photo: LC-USZ62-15933, insert: see page 92 LOC listing), **108** (LC-USZ62-17902), **111** (LC-USZ62-44963), **112** (LC-USZ62-11177), **114** (top left: Virginia Chamber of Commerce/LOC, middle left: LC-USZ62-5258, bottom left: LC-USZ62-53345, top right: LC-USA7-24315, middle right: LC-USZ62-890, bottom right: LC-USZ62-1495), **116** (top: LC-USZ62-12377, bottom left: LC-USZ62-33290, bottom right: LC-USZ62-17892), **117** (top left: LC-USZ62-8357, top right: LC-USZ62-15195), **118** (LC-USZ62-9095), **119** (left: LC-USZ62-15057, right: LC-USZ62-11976), **121** (LC-USZ62-51764), **122** (LC-USZ62-31953), **125** (LC-USZ62-16252), **126** (LC-USZ62-11822), **127** (LC-USZ62-2583), **128** (top: LC-USZ62-3282, bottom: LC-USZ62-55021), **129** (LC-USZ62-48951), **130** (LC-USZ62-1912), **136** (LC-USZC4-4290), **139** (LC-USZ62-1857), **140** (LC-USZ62-102852), **142** (top: LC-USZ61-193), **143** (top left: LC-USZ62-29029, top right: LC-USZ62-5809, bottom right: LC-USZ62-48963), **144** (LC-USZ62-48888), **147** (top: LC-USZ62-53483, middle: LC-USZ62-10293, bottom: LC-USZ62-44000), **150** (LC-USZ62-1800), **153** (right: LC-USZ62-42802), **154** (top right: LC-USZ62-51929, bottom right: LC-USZ62-44924), **155** (LC-USZ62-75545), **156** (LC-USZ62-51933), **162** (LC-USZ62-49546), **164** (top: LC-USZ62-33289, bottom: LC-USZ62-32093), **167** (LC-USZ62-50571), **168** (bottom: LC-USZ62-57648), **169** (LC-USZC4-4613), **174** (LC-USZ62-103), **181** (LC-USZ62-78235), **185** (top: LC-USZ62-42285, bottom left: LC-USZ61-539, bottom right: LC-USZ62-50288), **186** (top: LC-USZ62-9701, bottom: LC-USZ62-31958), **187** (LC-USZ62-9), **189** (top left: LC-USZ62-25563, top middle: LC-USZ62-15053, top right: LC-USZ62-115162, middle right: LC-USZC4-2542, bottom right: LC-USZ62-48402), **190** (top: LC-USZ62-5543, bottom: LC-USZC4-2737), **191** (LC-USZ62-96219), **192** (top: LC-USZ62-5012, bottom: LC-USZ62-19709), **193** (top: LC-USZ62-59597), **201** (LC-USA7-951), **205** (LC-USZ62-59464), **206** (LC-USZ6-279), **207** (top: LC-USZ62-33964, bottom: LC-USZ62-54402), **209** (left: LC-USZC4-5310, right: LC-USZ62-17704), **215** (left: LC-USZ62-46801), **222** (LOC # unknown), **224** (LC-USZ62-17479), **225** (top: LC-USZ62-1306, LC-USZ62-96380, bottom: LC-USZ62-102054, LC-USZ62-69452), **226** (left: LC-USZ62-112293), **227** (LC-USZ62-117116, LC-USZ62-13002), **229** (left: LC-USZ62-51136), **230** (LC-USZ62-8496), **231** (top left: LC-USZ62-117117, bottom: LC-USZ62-4940), **232** (LC-USZ62-33283), **233** (top right: LC-USZ62-50631, bottom: LC-USZ62-50630), **236** (top: LC-USZ62-13004, bottom: LC-USZC4-3616), **237** top left: LC-USZ62-15550, bottom: LC-USZ62-5314), **238** (LC-USZ62-1764), **244** (LC-USZ62-5412), **246** (LC-USZ62-117118), **250** (LC-USZ62-117119), **252** (top: LC-USZ62-117120, bottom: LC-USZ62-61531), **253** (LC-USZ62-38678), **254** (LC-USZ62-1292), **255** (bottom left: LC-USZ62-356, bottom right: LC-USZ62-86), **257** (LC-USZ62-13008), **258** (top left: LC-USZ62-5550, top right: LC-USZ62-13009, bottom: LC-USZ62-13010), **262** (LC-USZC4-1445), **265** (top: LC-USZ62-43346, bottom: LC-USZ62-1407), **266** (LC-USZ62-65469), **268** (left: LC-USZ62-1407), **269** (top left: LC-USZ62-77494, top right: LC-USZ62-28370, bottom: LC-USZ62-15549), **270** (top left: LC-USZ62-98456, top right: LC-USZ62-635, bottom: LC-USZ62-12900), **271** (left: LC-USZC4-3598, right: LC-USZC4-3672), **272** (LC-USZ62-8282), **273** (top left: LC-USZ62-802, top right: 9227-Z62-45990, bottom: 9522-Z62-8338), **274** (top left: LC-USZ62-16178, bottom: LC-USZ62-18093), **275** (left:

9522-Z62-8442, right: LC-USZ62-15398), **279** (top left: LC-USZ62-17896, top right: LC-USZ62-88421, bottom left: LC-USZ62-21, bottom right: LC-USZ62-44982), **280** (LC-USZC4-1837), **281** (LC-USZ62-78299), **282** (left: LC-USZ62-3898, middle: LC-USZ62-24161, right: LC-USZ62-59664), **283** (LC-USZ62-5818), **284** (LC-USZ62-38833), **289** (LC-USZ62-31010), **290** (LC-USZC4-2634), **292** (LC-USZ62-4220), **293** (bottom left: LC-USZ62-110029, bottom right: LC-USZ62-65432), **294** (LC-USZ62-13011), **295** (top: LC-USZ62-32678, bottom: LC-USZC4-4559), **296** (LC-USZ62-133), **297** (LC-USZ62-13012), **298** (LC-USZ62-17656), **299** (left: LC-USZ62-53324, right: LC-USZ62-49621), **300** (LC-USZ62-24396), **301** (top: LC-USZ62-17901, middle: LC-USZ62-51140, bottom: LC-USZ62-908), **302** (LC-USZ62-19259), **303** (LC-USZ62-31865), **304** (LC-USZ62-32272), **305** (left: LC-USZ62-858, top right: LC-USZ62-60770, bottom right: LC-USZ62-60771), **307** (LC-USZ62-19948), **311** (LC-USZ62-32283), **312** (LC-USZCN-149), **317** (left: LC-USZ62-13013, right: 2475), **318** (top left: LC-USZ62-2574, top right: LC-USZ62-39380, bottom left: LC-USZ62-28860, bottom right: LC-USZ62-15257, **320** (top: LC-USZ62-55713, bottom: LC-USZ62-13014), **322** (left: LC-USZ62-110141, middle: LC-USZ62-13015, right: LC-USZ62-5092), **323** (LC-USZ62-30970), **324** (left: LC-USZ62-5533, right: LC-USZ62-5803), **325** (left: LC-USZ62-38204, right: LC-USZ62-11191), **330** (LC-USZ62-5803), **333** (bottom: LC-USZ62-8376), **334** (LC-USZ62-8249), **335** (LC-USZ62-15623), **338** (top right: LC-B811-0602, bottom: LC-USZ62-2070), **339** (top: LC-USZC4-1976, bottom: LC-B8184-10612), **341** (LC-USZ62-35886), **342** (first: LC-USZ62-100855, second: LC-B8184-B-36, third: LC-B812-2881, fourth: LC-B8172-6454), **343** (LC-B8184-3611), **344** (left: LC-USZC4-602, right: LC-USZ62-2569), **345** (top: LC-USZ62-2480, bottom: LC-USZ62-984), **346** (left: LC-B817-7110, right: LC-8184-10064), **347** (LC-USZ62-17813), **348** (top: LC-USZ62-93555), **354** (LC-B8171-3448), **356** (left: LC-USZ62-680, right:LC-13809), **357** (LC-USZ62-37846), **358** (top: LC-USZ62-37848, bottom left: LC-USZ62-57937, bottom right: LC-USZ62-100845), **359** (left: LC-USZ62-86754, top right: LC-USZ62-37861, middle: LC-USZ62-37860, bottom: LC-USZ62-37852), **361** (top: LC-USZ62-5665, bottom: LC-USZ62-2814), **362** (left: LC-USZ62-38372, right: LC-USZ62-19234), **363** (top: LC-USZ62-40603, bottom left: LC-USZ62-2209, bottom right: LC-USZ62-9967), **364** (top left: LC-USZ62-12505, bottom left: LC-USZ62-22107, bottom right: LC-USZ62-13018), **367** (LC-USZ62-31166), **368** (LC-USZ62-17919), **369** (top: LC-USZ62-36288, bottom: LC-USZ62-114302), **370** (top: USZ62-100414, bottom left: LC-USZ62-64712, bottom right: LC-USZ62-57959), **390** (top: LC-USZ62-10517), **404** (LC-USZC4-768), **407** (top left: LC-USZ62-1481, top right: LC-USZ62-11055, bottom: LC-USZC4-2343), **409** (LC-USZ62-188), **410** (LC-USZ62-35453), **411** (top: LC-USZ62-43322, bottom: LC-USZ62-5443), **413** (LC-USZ62-2916), **414** (LC-USZ62-2169), **415** (top: LC-USZC2-783, bottom: LC-USZ62-24705), **416** (top: LC-USZ62-66542, bottom left: LC-USZ62-11715, bottom right: LC-USZ62-20212), **417** (top: LC-USZ62-2085, bottom: LOC # unknown), **418** (LC-USZ62-22971), **419** (top: LC-USZ62-51801, bottom: LC-USZ62-51802), **420** (left: LC-USZ62-71317, right: LC-USZ62-11568), **421** (left: LC-USZ62-2025, right: LC-USZ62-15909), **422** (top: LC-USZC4-4694, bottom: LC-USZ62-2669), **423** (LC-USZ62-37208), **424** (top: LC-USZ62-13398, bottom: LC-USZ62-2017), **426** (left: LC-USZ62-110999, right: LC-USZ62-31965), **432** (LC-USZC4-1584), **434** (LC-USZ62-50697), **435** (top: LC-USZ62-11166, bottom: LC-USZ62-2168), **436** (left: LC-USZ62-39892), **437** (top: LC-D401-96862, bottom left: LC-USZ62-61494, middle: LC-USZ62-8570, right: LC-D401-14756), **438** (top: LC-USZ62-87910, bottom: LC-USZ6-471), **439** (left: LC-USZ62-795, right: LC-USZ62-3526), **440** (top: LC-USZ62-2116, middle: LC-USZ62-39863, bottom: LC-USZ62-51204), **441** (LC-USZ62-3430), **442** (left: LC-USZ62-59596, right: LC-USZ62-41681), **444** (top left: LC-USZ62-11202, top right: LC-USZ62-2284, middle left: LC-USZ62-29337, bottom left: LC-USZ62-67910, bottom right: LC-USZ62-15539), **445** (LC-USZ62-31040), **446** (top left: LC-USZC4-4632, top right: LC-USZ62-3252, bottom left: LC-USZC2-2093, **447** (left: LC-USZ62-12318, right: LC-USZ62-16285), **448** (LC-USZ62-12902), **452** (top left: LC-USZ62-13019. top right: LC-USZ62-13020, bottom left: LC-USZ62-13021, bottom right: LC-USZ62-13024), **453** (left: LC-USZ61-480, right: LC-USZ62-13025), **454** (left: LC-USZ62-10760, right: LC-USZ62-8425), **458** (LC-USZ62-117340), **461** (LC-USZ62-25496), **462** (top: LC-USZ62-65484, middle: LC-USZ62-45727, bottom: LC-USZ62-55518), **463** (top: LC-USZ62-93331, bottom left: LC-USZ62-14440, right: LC-USZ62-7626), **464** (left: LC-USZ62-3920, right: LC-USZ62-37982), **467** (left: LC-USZ62-7222), **468** (LC-USZ62-30778), **469** (LC-USZ62-42262), **470** (left: LC-USZ62-33011, right: LC-USZ62-106238), **471** (LC-USZ62-63960), **472** (top: LC-USZ62-122792, middle: LC-USZ62-1733, bottom: LC-USZ62-117339), **473** (LC-USZ62-123622), **482** (LC-USZC4-4697), **483** (top: LC-USZ62-38564, bottom: LC-USZ62-22198), **484** (top left: LC-D401-12532, top right: LC-USZ62-45843, bottom left: LC-USZ62-93116), **487** (top left: LC-USZ62-113665, bottom right: LC-USZ62-32674), **488** (LC-USZ62-8672), **490** (LC-USZ62-7757), **491** (LC-USZ62-102210), **492** (LC-USZ62-13028), **493** (left: LC-USZ62-118173, right: LC-USZ62-22262), **497** (LC-USZ62-116257), **498** (LC- LOC # unknown), **500** (bottom: LC-USZ62-36566), **502** (LC-USZ62-31819), **503** (top: LC-USZ62-91464, bottom: LC-D4-34741), **504** (bottom: LC-USZ62-34576), **506** (left: LC-USZ62-107151, top right: LC-USZ62-54960), **507** (left: LC-USZ62-52429, middle right: LC-USZ62-36562), **508** (top: LC-USZ62-31069, bottom: LC-USZ62-36567), **509** (left: LC-USZ62-7483, right: LC-USZ62-47272), **510** (top: LC-USZ62-19656, bottom: LC-USZ62-37482), **511** (left: LC-USZ62-32600, right: LC-USZ62-55083), **524** (LC-USZC4-4840), **526** (left: LC-USZ62-13029, middle: LC-USZ62-13030, bottom: LC-USZ62-24155), **527** (LC-USZ62-51548), **528** (left: LC-USZ62-26766, right: LC-USZ62-54096), **529** (left: LC-USZ62-6166A, top right: LC-USZ62-93443, middle: LC-USZ62-97166, bottom: LC-USZ62-83653), **530** (left: LC-USZ62-15182, right: LC-USZ62-63118), **531** (LC-USZ62-15589), **532** (right: LC-USZ62-94999), **533** (right: LC-USZ62-100411), **536** (top right: LC-USZ62-95653, bottom left: LC-USZ62-73427), **537** (top: LC-USZ62-47353, bottom: LC-USZ62-94202), **538** (right: LC-USZ62-31111), **539** (LC-USZ62-26759), **541** (bottom: LC-USZ62-60009), **542** (bottom left: LC-USZ62-90003, bottom right: LC-USF34-016276), **550** (LC-USW33-19081-ZC), **551** (left: LC-USZ62-88713, top right: LC-USZ62-16265), **552** (LC-USZ62-10616), **553** (LC-USZ62-23570), **554** (right: LC-USZ62-64419), **555** (LC-USZ62-16555), **556** (LC-USZ62-15185), **557** (top right: LC-USZ62-78590, bottom left: LC-USZ62-43771, bottom right: LC-USZ62-96100), **558** (LC-USZ62-40291), **559** (top: LC-USZ62-25600, bottom: LC-USZ62-15187), **560** (top: LC-USZ62-33110, bottom right: LC-USZ62-43768), **561** (top left: LC-USZ62-107559, bottom right: LC-USZ62-64852), **562** (top: LC-USZ62-36452), **563** (LC-USZ62-25608), **564** (left: LC-USZ62-93707, top right: LC-USZ62-15192, bottom right: LC-USZ62-93709), **565** (top: LC-USZ62-44708, bottom (LC-USZ62-86679), **576** (LC-USZ62-117122), **580** (LC-USZ62-117772), **582** (LC-USZ62-117123), **583** (top: LC-USZ62-118471, bottom: LC-USZ62-111249), **594** (LC-U9-10360-5), **596** LC-USZ62-117124), **600** (right: USA7-25517), **601** (left: LC-USZ62-13036, right: LC-USZ62-95480), **604** (left: LC-U9-18868-5A), **614** (LC-USZC4-3612), **616** (LC-USZ62-13037), **618** (left: LC-U9-27678), **619** (top left: LC-USZ62-13038), **620** (top: LC-USZ62-13039), **622** (right: LC-USZ62-13040), **626** (top: LC-USZ62-98302), **628** (left: LC-USZ62-107700)

Mennonite Church USA Archives, 1700 S. Main Street, Goshen, IN USA 46526: *Photograph collections:* **513** (left: #1468-HM4-318), *Charles and Crissie (Yoder) Shank Collection:* **451** (#781-HM4-329), *Civil War Military Exemption Collection:* **348** (middle: #1463-HM5-11, bottom: #1464-HM5-11), **351** (#1465-HM4-57), *George R. Brunk Collection:* **532** (#260-HM4-361), *Indiana-Michigan Mennonite Conference Photograph Collection:* **449** (top right: #224o2-HM4-136), *John S. Coffman Collection:* **450** (left: #915-HM4-14), *John F. Funk Collection:* **449** (top left: #89-HM4-154 1/1, bottom: #606-HM4-154), *M. S. Steiner Collection:* **450** (right: #220-HM4-166), *Ontario Mennonite Churches Collection:* **382** (bottom: #1466-HM4-57), **383** (#1467o1-HM4-57), *Philemon Frey Collection:* **513** (#1469-HM4-318), **515** (#1470-HMI-825 1/56), *Mennonite Central Committee Collection:* **517** (left: #335o1-IX-13-2.1, top right: #324-IX-2.1 3/3, bottom right: #321o2-IX-13-2.1 3/5), **568** (top left: #129-IX13-2.2 1/8, top right: #39-IX-13-2.2 1/8, middle left: [Edgar Nafziger] #128-IX-13-2.2 2/17, bottom left: #9-IX-13-2.2 1/13), **569** (left: #15-IX-13-2.2 2/7), right: [Paul W. Hertzler, *Mennonite Community]* #12-IX-13-2.2 1/2), **570** (top left: [Heinz Wagener] #1471-IX-13-2.3 3/7, top right: [Deutscher Zentralausschuss fuer die Verteilung auslaendischer Liebesgaben beim Laenderrat] #1472-IX-13-2.3 3/7, middle left: #927-IX-13-2.3 5/7), **609** (top right: #1409-IX-13-2.4, bottom group of 5 photos: #[1473–1477] IX-13-2.5. Paul Gross took photos at top left and top right, and bottom right; photographer not listed for other two.)

Mennonite Historical Library, Goshen College, Indiana: 173 (top and bottom), **239, 242, 350** (middle and bottom:)

National Archives of Canada: 94 (Samuel de Champlain/NMC 15661), **98** (René Lochon/ detail of C-021404), **99** (Lawrence R. Batchelor/C-011925), **160** (Richard Short, Pierre Charles Canot/C-118259), **168** (top right: detail of C-027665, top left: William Hoare, Richard Houston/ detail of C-011235), **381** (top left: William Booth/C-010548), **382** (top left: James Peachey/C-002001), **386** (E. Hides, George Matthews/C-10721), **387** (retyped from MG24, B29, Vol. 13), **388** (Jules I. Livernois/ detail of C-006350), **389** (left: D. A. McLaughlin/ detail of C-003760, right: C-3207), **390** (bottom: detail of C-001229), **391** (retyped from C-125856), **392** (top: H. L. Hime/ detail of C-004572), **393** (left: Duffin and Co., C-052177), **394** (PA-202180), **395** (Frederick Dally/C-026181), **396** (O. B. Buell, PA-118760), **402** (David William Smith, William Fadden, NMC-098186), **403** (C-021873), **485** (#PA74737)

National Archives and Records Administration: 234 (W&C #75), **350** (top: W&C #238), **375** (#83-FA-6535), **467** (W&C #331), **480** (#102-LH440), **504** (W&C #694), **505** (W&C #433), **506** (bottom: W&C #490), **507** (W&C #586), **518** (W&C #562), **533** (left: #69-RH-4K-1), **538** (#79-AAB-4), **557** (top left: W&C #854), **561** (W&C #1103), **562** (bottom left: #342-FH-3A3545-60646a), **566** (#NWDNS-238-NT-592), **574** (#306-PS-59-13580), **578** (W&C #1433), **579** (top left: W&C #1433, top right: W&C #1477, bottom right: W&C #1503), **584** (#111-SC-515119), **587** (#NWDNS-311-D-15-1), **604** (right: #362-VS-3F-5999-13), **605** (#111-SC-651778), **606** (top left: W&C #405, middle left: W&C #406, bottom right: #111-CC-46331), **607** (#NWDNS-127-N-A900056), **608** (top right: #NWDNS-428-N-1175389), **617** (top right: #NLNP-WHPO-MPF-864901), **618** (right: #E3398-09), **619** (bottom right: #452-G-9-E38-30), *Records of Social Security:* **536** (#47-GA-90-497), *Tennessee Valley Authority:* **541** (top: #142-RS-25-2), *New York Times, Paris Bureau Collection:* **551** (bottom right: W&C #985), **554** (left: W&C #1003)

Nova Development Corporation: 20 (top left), **215** (right), **293** (top), **558** (bottom), **608** (middle right and bottom right)

Photri-Microstock: 18 (top left, #KAU.395.1231), **90** (#BA-35216X), **233** (top left, #hsx.600.6389), **247** (right: PT4-1867), **268** (right: #14793), **548** (#HIST 1114/125), **588** (left: #spx.550.3348, right: #2-45064), **599** (#2-08464)

Ronald Reagan Library (courtesy of): **622** (left #C3-15A), **624** (top: #C3241-20, bottom left: #C3015-7, bottom right: #C44071-15A)

U.S. Department of State, Courtesy Harry S. Truman Library: 579 (#72-810)

U.S. Senate Collection: 39 (right: #33.00009)

White House Historical Association: 577 (Abbe Rowe, National Park Service, #367)

White House Photo Office: 628 (right)

Woolaroc Museum, Bartlesville, Oklahoma: 255 (top)

Graph and Map Credits

The maps in the book are based on map images from:

Cartesia: front and back endsheets, 15, 17, 42, 111, 121, 124, 126, 163, 169, 192, 259, 340, 364, 384, 396, 507, 563, 597, 617

Hostetler, Bennie: 190, 472, 644, 645, 646, 647

Mountain High Maps ® Copyright © 1993 Digital Wisdom, Inc.: 1, back cover, 14, 15, 22 (both), 24, 38, 41, 45, 50, 53, 61, 77, 81, 84, 96, 104 (both), 107, 129, 152, 167, 193, 194, 205, 228, 229, 234 (both), 238, 248, 250, 254, 259, 268, 269, 270, 285, 294, 296, 297, 307, 303, 304, 317, 321, 325, 334, 344, 368, 381, 391, 396, 397, 412, 418, 423, 426, 461, 464, 466, 472 (insert), 474 (both), 489, 502, 511, 520, 537, 552, 553, 555, 567, 580, 582, 598, 608, 612, 633, 626

Beaufort Sea
Arctic Islands
Baffin Bay
Greenland
Great Bear Lake
Great Slave Lake
Hudson Bay
Canadian Shield
Bering Sea
Gulf of Alaska
Aleutian Islands
NORTH AMERICA
Coast Ranges
Rocky Mountains
Central Plains
Great Lakes
Appalachian Mts.
Coastal Plain
ATLANTIC
PACIFIC
Canary Islands
Gulf of Mexico
Hawaiian Islands
West Indies
Caribbean Sea
Cape Verde
Guiana Highlands
165°W
150°W
135°W
120°W
105°W
90°W
45°W
30°W
15°W
Galápagos Islands
SOUTH AMERICA
Amazon Basin
Andes Mountains
Polynesia
OCEAN
Brazilian Highlands
Gran Chaco
Pampas
Falkland Islands
Bellingshausen Sea
Ross Sea
Weddell Sea